Europe

Europe
The History of a Continent

JEAN-BAPTISTE DUROSELLE
TRANSLATED BY RICHARD MAYNE

An initiative by Frédéric Delouche

WITH AN AFTERWORD BY
ANTHONY TEASDALE

MICHAEL JOSEPH

UK | USA | Canada | Ireland | Australia
India | New Zealand | South Africa

Michael Joseph is part of the Penguin Random House group of companies whose addresses can be found at global.penguinrandomhouse.com.

First published by Viking as *Europe: A History of its Peoples* 1990
First published in this edition 2023
001

Copyright © Jean-Baptiste Duroselle, 1990
Afterword © Anthony Teasdale, 2023

The moral right of the author has been asserted

Set in 10.5/14pt Sabon LT Std
Typeset by Jouve (UK), Milton Keynes
Printed and bound in Great Britain by Clays Ltd, Elcograf S.p.A.

The authorized representative in the EEA is Penguin Random House Ireland, Morrison Chambers, 32 Nassau Street, Dublin D02 YH68

A CIP catalogue record for this book is available from the British Library

HARDBACK ISBN: 978-0-241-53408-3
TRADE PAPERBACK ISBN: 978-1-405-95029-9

www.greenpenguin.co.uk

Penguin Random House is committed to a sustainable future for our business, our readers and our planet. This book is made from Forest Stewardship Council® certified paper.

To the memory of Silvia and Jean Monnet

Contents

Foreword: From Fragmentation to Fellowship? by
Frédéric Delouche xiii

1 **What is Europe?** 1
   Strange design: unique geography 1
   Europe is neither an ethnic nor a linguistic unit 4
   The word 'Europe': no magic significance 7
   The development of Europe 9

2 **The Prehistory of Europe** 13
   Pre-European humanity 13
   The earliest Europeans: homo erectus 14
   The birth of art in Europe 17
   Art and religion 19
   Europe outstripped by the Neolithic revolution 20
   Megalithic civilization 21
   In search of metal: gold, copper, bronze 25

3 **The Celts** 29
   The great Indo-European family 29
   The Bronze Age and the first Celts 30
   The discovery of iron 31
   The Hallstatt Iron Age and the awakening of the West 32
   The brilliant civilization of the Tène Iron Age 36
   The Celtic world 38
   Conclusion 41

CONTENTS

4 Classical Antiquity: Greek Wisdom, Roman Grandeur — 42
- The Roman conquest — 42
- Roman law, the state, and the family — 49
- Civis Romanus sum: consolidation and assimilation — 55
- The Roman vision of Europe — 58
- Roman Europe: East and West — 60

5 The First Four Centuries AD in the West — 62
- Judaeo-Christian influence — 62
- The expansion of Christianity in the West — 66
- The Christian Empire — 71
- The influence of ecclesiastical geography — 75
- Conclusion — 78

6 The Germanic Age — 79
- The Germans reach Europe — 79
- Germanic migration by sea — 89
- Western monasticism — 92
- Germanic and Romance languages — 98
- Germanic traces — 102
- Invasion but not barbarism — 104

7 Charlemagne: King of Europe? — 105
- The arrival of the Carolingians — 105
- Charlemagne — 108
- The Empire — 111
- The 'Carolingian Renaissance' — 112
- The decay of the Empire and the growth of the kingdoms — 116
- The beginnings of Europe? — 119
- The true nature of the Carolingian epoch — 120
- Conclusion — 122

CONTENTS

8 Europe Under Siege — 123
- The Saracens — 123
- The Vikings — 129
- The Slavs — 138
- The Hungarian invasions — 144
- The break with Byzantium — 145
- The Empire and the Papacy: towards 'Western Christendom' — 151
- Conclusion — 159

9 The Heyday of Western Christianity: The Twelfth and Thirteenth Centuries — 162
- Temporal and spiritual power — 162
- St Bernard and the white monks — 167
- Europe and the Crusades — 173
- Mendicant orders and missionaries — 177
- University Europe — 180
- Pilgrimage — 186
- The Great Debate — 192
- Romanesque and Gothic Europe — 196
- A more humane civilization — 201
- Conclusion — 206

10 Towards a Europe of the States: The Fourteenth and Fifteenth Centuries — 208
- The birth of the modern state and the Hundred Years' War — 208
- The great European population crisis — 215
- The great crisis of Christianity — 220
- The advance of science in Europe — 230
- Europe masters navigation — 235
- The idea of Europe — 240
- Conclusion — 242

CONTENTS

11	Renaissance, Reformation, and Expansion: The Sixteenth Century	244
	Charles V and the European balance of power	244
	Europe and the rest of the world	249
	Europe confronts the Turks	255
	Four innovators: Machiavelli, Erasmus, Leonardo, and Luther	259
	Humanism as a factor for unity	268
	The Reformation and *Cujus regio, ejus religio*	271
	The third Renaissance	282
12	Absolutism, Liberties, and Cosmopolitanism	283
	From the divine right of kings to enlightened despotism	283
	The dawn of liberty: the Low Countries and Great Britain	286
	The seventeenth century: golden age or grim?	295
	The decline of deference and the growth of compassion	302
	'French Europe' and cosmopolitanism	310
	The dawn of nationalism	319
	Towards the Industrial Revolution	323
	Conclusion	325
13	Revolution and Disillusion	327
	The common roots of revolution in the West	327
	The 'Great Nation' and reactions in Europe	331
	The Revolution and the birth of nationalism	340
	Revolutionary expansionism and the disillusionment of the European 'patriots'	343
	The Second Coalition	350
	Conclusion	351
14	Napoleon: Europe by Force	353
	Napoleon's choice	353
	Napoleon's conquests	355

CONTENTS

The failure of a European economic community: the Continental System and the blockade	359
Did Napoleon seek European unity?	362
Napoleon's defeat	370
Conclusion	376

15 A European Phenomenon: The Industrial Revolution — 377

Inventive Europe	377
Europe at the centre of world production	384
A brief experiment in free trade	389
Europe and greater longevity	393
The other side of the coin: the proletariat	397
Conclusion	411

16 Europe, Romanticism, and the Nations — 413

The Congress of Vienna (1814–15)	413
The 'Concert of Europe'	421
Nationalism, 'Hydra of Revolution'	425
Romantic Europe	431
Disturbances and wars (1848–71)	438
Conclusion	441

17 The Road to European Disaster: 1871–1914 — 442

The escalation of nationalism	442
Bismarck, 'realism', and 'armed peace'	444
Europe continues her conquest of the world	451
The weakness of 'Europeanism'	454
Conclusions	460

18 Europe Destroys Itself: (1914–1945) — 463

'The Great War' and its wider effects	463
The Peace Treaties and their faults	470

CONTENTS

Aristide Briand and 'European Union'	472
The economic crisis and beggar-my-neighbour policies	477
Democracy, Bolshevism, and Fascism	487
The Age of Anxiety	490
Adolf Hitler's nightmare Europe	494
Conclusion	507

19 Europe's Recovery and Resurgent Hopes — 509

In the wake of disaster: the proposals of July 1948	509
Thirty years of European prosperity	517
Thirty years of decolonization	520
The makers of Europe	523
The building of Europe in the face of Gaullism	534
Change in Europe after de Gaulle	540
Envoi	548

Afterword: The Making and Breaking of Post-Wall Europe, 1985 to 2023 by Anthony Teasdale — 549

From sclerosis to relaunch: The new Europe of Jacques Delors, 1985–89	549
'Europe whole and free': The end of communism and reunification of Germany, 1989–90	554
Europe in the unipolar decade, 1990–2000	564
The fraying of Europe's political consensus, 2001–08	576
Age of anxiety: The economic crisis of 2008 and its after-shocks	589
Populism in Europe in the 2010s	594
Brexit: The dynamics of British exceptionalism	610
From poly-crisis to coronavirus	622
The end of post-Wall Europe: Ukraine and the future	641

Acknowledgements	651
The authors	653

Foreword

From Fragmentation to Fellowship?

Frédéric Delouche

The President of France, Emmanuel Macron, recently said that 'the history of Europe is not simply the sum of twenty-seven national histories. It has a coherence, a unity, that everyone senses but which cannot yet be fully seen.' His observation encapsulates the spirit in which Jean-Baptiste Duroselle (1917–94), a leading French historian in the second half of the twentieth century, wrote *Europe: A History of its Peoples*, first published by Viking in 1990. The concept of this book – which seeks in a single volume to chart a European journey across multiple centuries, showing how many threads are woven together in a surprisingly common experience – was first an idea in my mind, and then I had the great pleasure of working with Bertelsmann, the Penguin Group and others in bringing the idea to fruition.

For me personally, the concept of this book was a staging post in a longer journey. Born in England just before the Second World War, the son of a Norwegian mother and a French father, I have always been a European. But at school in England from the age of eight, I was imbued with the easy pride that post-war Britons had in their country and history, a feeling which contrasted with the dented morale of so many of my continental relatives. Britain seemed to have won every battle it had fought. Its empire was the greatest ever. Even if sweets were rationed, the British economy was the biggest and best in Europe.

Going up to Cambridge helped to alter my sense of England and my understanding of myself. I started to see in my contemporaries a degree of smugness and casualness towards other countries that concerned me – a frame of mind that continues, even if often unconsciously, more than sixty years on. During holidays with family and friends on the continent, I began to realize that I was *both* English and European, and that it was possible to be both at the same time. I started to see that there was a fundamental commonality of experience across Europe, including

Britain, that was bigger than anything that had divided European nations in the past. Whatever differences there might be in language or food, so much of what matters – our values, our cultures, our political systems, in sum our civilization – had evolved fundamentally in the same direction.

While living and working in Paris in the 1980s and 1990s, I had the privilege to meet Jean-Baptiste Duroselle, whose fascinating earlier book, *The Idea of Europe in History*, traced the development of Europe as a concept in Western thinking over time. Although published at the high point of Charles de Gaulle's 'Europe des patries' in 1965, this book pointed towards there being more of a genuine 'European community' of experience and attitudes than people generally appreciated. I convinced Duroselle that he should write a further volume to trace in greater detail the history of this common European experience and heritage, which seemed to have evolved in ways that were often very different to those of other continents or civilizations.

Instead of being a conventional history of Europe that was a series of separate histories centred on individual nations placed side by side, the new book would treat Europe as a whole, showing that different events and reactions in various countries, over the previous twenty-five centuries, were often facets of shared phenomena. To put our principles into practice, I suggested that we should aim, if possible, to publish the book in several different languages across Europe on the same day.

The result of this 'European initiative', as we called it, was *Europe: A History of its Peoples*, which was published simultaneously in eight languages in November 1990. Written in French, the English version was translated by my friend, the late Richard Mayne (1926–2009), a gifted journalist and historian in his own right, who had worked as an adviser to Jean Monnet in the 1950s and 1960s. The project also benefited from a small but distinguished panel of historical advisers: Karl Dietrich Erdmann, Sergio Romano, Keith Robbins and Juan Antonio Sánchez García-Sauco. The eight different (Western European) language versions of the book were launched at an event in the magnificent historic town hall in Brussels, with work on Polish and Hungarian editions starting just after the fall of the Berlin Wall in November 1989. At the time, it was considered a 'first' to have brought together so many European publishers under the leadership of Bertelsmann for such a multinational project.

The timing of the publication proved significant, even if this was largely fortuitous. Only a few weeks before the book came out, Germany was reunited, leading to the end of the post-war division of Europe and the Cold War, whilst later the same month (November 1990) Margaret Thatcher was ejected from power in Britain in events largely prompted by divisions over the country's future role in Europe. The optimism surrounding what the US President at the time, George H. W. Bush, called a 'Europe whole and free', together with the prospect of a borderless single market in 1992, generated a strong sense of momentum behind efforts to unite Europe, at exactly the moment the book was released.

Several people have asked whether Duroselle intended *Europe: A History of its Peoples* to be not only a work of history but also a plea for a more united Europe. The answer is that he (and indeed I) saw it as both. The book seeks to tell an evolving story and to see events from a distinctive, but hopefully dispassionate, *pan*-European perspective. At the same time, it works from the *pro*-European assumption that, by seeking to work together and accentuating common interests, European nations can avoid repeating the tragedies of the past and be stronger together in the future. In effect, awareness of the reality of a common history makes a common future more possible and perhaps more likely.

In his writing about Europe, Duroselle always looked to the bigger picture and took the longer view. For him, the notion of Europe as a 'shared experience' did not start with the 'founding fathers' of the 1940s and 1950s. Rather, it stretched back to what he called 'Greek wisdom' and 'Roman grandeur', and indeed before that. He saw European history not only as a mosaic of distinct events and narratives but as a confluence and intermingling of cultures and influences that formed an organic whole. Nationalism and the nation state were relatively recent developments in Europe's long history, and their sometimes destructive results tended to obscure the creative qualities that Europeans shared – born of diversity, but also with a strong instinct for individual liberty and an openness to new ideas and peoples. Conversely, whilst a united Europe would, in his view, be 'the culmination of a long historical evolution', rather than 'an artificial creation *ex nihilo*', that outcome was far from certain or preordained.

I am delighted that, a third of a century after the original project was realized, Penguin has chosen to re-publish and update Duroselle's book – now published in more compact form as *Europe: The History of a Continent*, so that it can be more easily available to a new generation of readers. The text, which originally tailed off in the late 1980s, just as historical events were accelerating, has been brought up to date by Anthony Teasdale, who has been closely involved in European policy-making for four decades, and whom it was my very good fortune to meet after reading his own book, *The Penguin Companion to European Union*. His elegant and broad-ranging Afterword, entitled 'The Making and Breaking of Post-Wall Europe, 1985 to 2023', charts an arc of events from the renewal of Europe in the mid-1980s and the collapse of Communism in 1989–90 through the multiple crises that buffeted Europe from September 11 to coronavirus, to the outbreak of the Russo-Ukraine war in February 2022.

Anthony shows how far Europe has come in recent decades in uniting in many policy areas and in building a putative continent-wide political system, but he also highlights the extent to which events have exposed Europe's weaknesses and divisions, and how we failed to take full advantage of the opportunities of peace and prosperity at their height. Sadly, the benign 'post-Wall' order that emerged in the 1990s – based on assumptions of American leadership, European integration and early globalization – was to prove short-lived, effectively ending with Vladimir Putin's recent aggression in Ukraine. So far, the twenty-first century has proved rather crueller to Europe than many of us expected or hoped.

As unwelcome challenges crowd in on an unsettled continent, Anthony argues that Europe is now facing a moment of decision in which its leaders will need to 'make a clear choice between alternative futures, to avoid seeing that choice made for it by others'. The central questions are about whether to pool greater resources and sovereignty to strengthen Europe's capacity for collective action – and on that basis, whether both to 'aspire to be a serious global actor' and to 'take the tough decisions necessary to become one'. The latter would mean 'stepping up to the responsibilities of power, with all the burdens, as well as opportunities, that this role would bring'. The United States chose both paths in the 1930s and 1940s, from the New Deal to the Cold War. Will Europe seek to do so too? Will it manage, as Anthony puts it, to 'turn events to its advantage and engage in a process or renewal' or will it be 'frustrated, perhaps overwhelmed, by forces it cannot guide or control'?

After a professional life living in and outside Europe and thinking about world affairs, I believe, now more than ever, that a strong, united Europe will have a greater say in the geo-politics and economics of the future than any individual nation can enjoy on its own. Such a Europe will best succeed if it is grounded in a more vibrant continent-wide democracy – democracy is after all a concept invented in Europe – and underpinned by a genuine sense of 'a destiny shared in common', as the founding fathers of today's European Union put it after the Second World War. The stakes are getting higher all the time – with China's trajectory sadly suggesting to the wider world that democracy and prosperity may no longer necessarily go hand in hand, just as the resilience of democratic institutions in the United States is visibly under threat, divisive national populisms are re-emerging in Europe, climate change risks destabilizing the global order, and artificial intelligence has the potential to change mankind both for better and for worse.

How Europe responds to these various challenges and choices will play a vital part in the future of our continent. Is it not conceivable that a better understanding of our shared history might contribute to the process of uniting Europeans and making our continent stronger and more resilient for the hazards that lie ahead? Can it not help us avoid the perils of fragmentation and build a greater feeling of fellowship among our peoples? Might it not be possible to pool some elements of our national sovereignties, which in any event are becoming increasingly irrelevant in an interdependent world, for the greater purpose of safeguarding our shared political and economic values? History at least teaches us that to understand one another is better than to coexist in ignorance and misunderstanding. In this spirit, Jean-Baptiste Duroselle's book and Anthony Teasdale's Afterword have been written with an eye to Europe's future, as well as to its past.

I am most grateful to Daniel Bunyard, Jillian Taylor, Agatha Russell, DeAndra Lupu and their colleagues at Penguin for steering this latest project so expertly to publication, and especially to my wife, Diana, for her unfailing encouragement, patience and support throughout.

Houlbec
August 2023

I
What is Europe?

STRANGE DESIGN:
UNIQUE GEOGRAPHY

Europe is the worst drawn continent in the world. The others at least are approximately geometrical. Australia is a vast rough-hewn rectangle; America, two huge triangles linked by a strip of land; Africa forms a massive crescent shape around the Gulf of Guinea. Asia is another giant rectangle, but with peculiarities of its own. Back-to-back with its neighbours, it mingles with the sea to the south and east. Its southern edge has three great peninsulas (Arabia, India, and Indochina), while on the east is a series of archipelagos, from the Kuril Islands to Japan, the Philippines, and Indonesia.

Fragmented and asymmetrical

Europe, by contrast, is a promontory of Asia – broad in the east, tapering towards the west. Conventionally, its eastern boundaries are the Ural Mountains and the Ural river which links them with the Caspian Sea; but its Atlantic coastline on the west is extraordinarily complicated.

Its southern frontier is an inland sea, the Mediterranean, linked to the Atlantic by the narrow Straits of Gibraltar. This southern edge of Europe comprises three peninsulas, each of them contrasting with the others: the square Iberian peninsula, the 'boot' shape of Italy, and the splayed fingers of the Greek Peloponnese.

To the north, aslant the map, lies a much smaller inland sea – the Baltic. Its south-western entrance is the winding passage through the Skagerrak and the straits which divide the Norwegian and Swedish peninsula from Denmark, its archipelago, and Jutland. Unlike the

Mediterranean, the Baltic is not a frontier but a 'lake' within Europe, surrounded by Sweden, Denmark, Germany, Poland, the USSR, and Finland.

On either side of a line from the Soviet–Norwegian frontier near the North Cape down to Cadiz in southern Spain, there are large islands and vast peninsulas, as well as a continental mass whose centre is Germany, until recently. Only the Iberian peninsula and the 'hexagon' – France – have anything like a geometrical shape. And all the regions of Europe are very different: there is no comparison between Scandinavia and Italy, or between the British Isles and the islands of the Mediterranean. Western Europe looks like the product of an eccentric fretsaw.

A temperate region

All of Western Europe except the far north of Norway, Sweden, and Finland lies in the north temperate zone. It roughly straddles the 45th parallel, which bisects the world's northern hemisphere. One third of France, most of Italy, and the whole of Spain and Portugal lie to the south of it, and all the other countries of Europe to the north.

A much more significant north–south divide in Europe is the 50th parallel. This really distinguishes northern Europeans from southerners. The lands to the north of it include the British Isles (except the Scillies and the Lizard), Flanders, the Netherlands, most of Germany, and the whole of Scandinavia – all essentially Germanic language areas.

Contrasting scenery

For 3,000 kilometres across the great plains of North America, through the forests of Russia, or over the expanse of Ukraine, the vista barely changes. The same is true of the Amazonian and African rainforests, the sub-tropical deserts, or the mountain ranges of Asia and the Andes.

In Western Europe, one can hardly travel 80 kilometres without seeing the landscape transformed. The continent is a mosaic – or a museum of geology and geography, with specimens of many kinds of terrain. There are ancient mountain ranges like the Caledonian foldings of Scotland and Scandinavia, or the Hercynian areas of Germany and France. There are more recent peaks like those of the Alps and the Pyrenees. There are the Rhône and Rhine valleys, the eroded uplands, the huge sedimentary basins, the high limestone plateaux, the mountain and coastal plains. There are volcanoes, some of them still active, as in southern Italy. There are forests of many different kinds. Europe, as Luis Diez del Corral said of the Iberian peninsula, is 'the very negation of monotony'.

Climates

Different latitudes produce very different vegetation. The northward-flowing 'Gulf Stream' or 'North Atlantic Drift', which affects Europe's western coasts as far north as northern Norway, only adds to the contrasts.

Despite its small size, in fact, Western Europe enjoys four distinct climates. That of the Atlantic coast is mild and rainy, with most rain in winter. The continental climate, further inland, is more severe, with heavy rainfall in summer. Near-polar conditions prevail in the tundras of the far north. In the Mediterranean, summers are very dry, while spring and autumn tend to be wet.

Being outside the sub-tropics, Western Europe grows no dates, coffee, tea, cocoa, or cotton. For animal husbandry, on the other hand, it is one of the most favoured regions in the world.

What unity it enjoys is that of a mosaic rather than a broad fresco with large areas of similar coloration.

Europe's unique geography has influenced its inhabitants

People adapt in a myriad different ways to natural circumstances, yet a few generalizations can be made:

1. A long, fretted coastline with many natural harbours has helped Europeans to become excellent sailors, explorers, and world traders. They include the Vikings, the Italians, the Portuguese, the Spaniards, the British, the Dutch, and many more.
2. Moderate climates, warmed in the west by the Gulf Stream, have encouraged European agriculture. The great glaciers, moreover, left moraines from which the winds spread a fine dust. Mixed with clay, this covered many rocky plateaux in Western Europe with rich, brown, fertile loam, ideal for

growing grain. The only non-temperate region in Western Europe is the far north of Norway and Sweden, peopled mainly by a few thousand Lapps and many thousand reindeer, but now rich in mines and hydroelectric power stations.
3. The multiplicity of different regions and resources seems likely to have stimulated European inventiveness. For centuries, dwellings, farm implements, and household objects in central and Western Europe have shown immensely varied ingenuity. Europe's diversity may well have contributed to this imaginative wealth.

Uncertain eastern borders

If Europe's western frontier is formed by the Atlantic Ocean, where is its frontier to the east? In the absence of any natural boundary between Europe and Asia, people have tended to set arbitrary limits. Nowadays, the eastern frontier is often drawn at the Ural Mountains, extending some 2,900 kilometres from north to south, then at the middle and lower reaches of the Ural river as far as the Caspian Sea. After that comes the Caucasus, followed by the Black Sea and the Turkish Straits. General de Gaulle used to speak of 'Europe from the Atlantic to the Urals', but he never explained what political meaning he attached to the phrase.

What is certain is that the post-war east–west division within Europe, which dated from 1945 and broadly coincided with the limits reached by the Red Army, was purely artificial. Only by examining European history as a whole will it be possible to attempt a more appropriate definition of Europe's eastern borders; and that in turn will of necessity be approximate.

EUROPE IS NEITHER AN ETHNIC NOR A LINGUISTIC UNIT

'Western Europe' not only shades imperceptibly into 'Central Europe', it also contains a multiplicity of peoples.

A racial melting-pot

Anthropology – still a science with very provisional findings – is not our present concern. Visible human features such as skin, hair, and eye colour, height, skull shape, and so on, are hard to determine except for periods from which there are portraits or written descriptions. For prehistory, we have to rely on scanty bone fragments which do not always include skulls.

We know very little, for example, of the people who lived in the Late Palaeolithic and Mesolithic periods (from 35,000 BC to about 6,000 BC). What we do know is that newcomers joined or perhaps replaced them. Was it the invaders or the invaded who were outnumbered and absorbed? Were the invasions a slow form of immigration, lasting for centuries – or sudden, brutal incursions? Invasion is a recurrent feature in Europe's history. Suffice it to say for the moment that megalithic tombs or 'dolmens' have been found to contain both long-headed and short-headed skulls, proving that by then Western Europe already had a mixed population.

The anthropologist Jean Poirier has distinguished three main groups, spread out broadly from north to south. In northern Europe, he believes, there was a comparatively long-headed, fair-haired group, the Nordic race; to the south of that, a central short-headed group comprising the east European race and four dark-haired races: Alpine, Dinaric, Anatolian, and Turanian; finally, a southern group, long-headed and dark-haired, made up of the Mediterranean, south-western, and Indo-Afghan races. To all these should be added a further race, the Aino, in the easternmost part of Asia.

Before the Indo-Europeans

Almost every native west European speaks as a mother tongue one of the languages in the 'Indo-European' family. The main exceptions are the Basques of northern Spain and part of the Basses-Pyrénées in France. Basque is the oldest language in Europe; but linguists and archaeologists have yet to agree on its origins. Further linguistic exceptions are Finno-Ugrian, spoken by 90 per cent of the Finns, Estonian, and Hungarian.

EUROPE

The Indo-Europeans

The Indo-Europeans probably came from the general area of present-day Iran. Only one branch of the family reached Western Europe. Of these the first were the Celts, followed or accompanied by the Italiots, to whom at first they were closely related.

Some of the Celts (the Goidels) went to Ireland; others (the Brythons) to Great Britain and the Channel coast. By then, they had also occupied almost all of present-day Germany. Some reached Spain: these were the Gauls, who mingled with the Iberians. Later, the Gauls conquered the Po Valley (Cisalpine Gaul), and some (the Galatians) even settled in Anatolia. To the east of the Rhine, the Gauls interbred with the Germans from the north.

The Italiots were the ancestors of the Latins, who founded Rome, and then of the Umbrians. In Gaul, southern Britain, Spain, and Portugal, the power of the Roman Empire ousted Celtic in favour of Latin, which in Western Europe gave rise to four great languages – Italian, Portuguese, Spanish, and French – as well as to Catalan, Provençal, Occitan, etc. The arrival of the Germans, mainly from the second century AD onwards, led the British Isles to lose both Latin and Celtic, although the latter still survives in Irish and Scottish Gaelic, in Manx, and in Welsh. Cornwall virtually lost its Celtic language in the eighteenth century.

Europe north and south

The linguistic map of present-day Western Europe, which largely dates from the ninth century AD, is very roughly divided by the 50th parallel. The northern countries, speaking mainly Germanic languages, are Norway (Norwegian); Sweden (Swedish); Denmark (Danish); Great Britain (English, a blend of Germanic and Romance); Ireland (seeking to revive Celtic but speaking English); the Netherlands (Dutch); Belgian Flanders (Flemish); Germany and Austria (German); German-speaking Switzerland (German and a spoken Germanic dialect); Luxembourg (Letzeburgesh, German, and French). The southern countries, speaking Romance languages, are Portugal (Portuguese); Spain (Spanish); France (French); Walloon Belgium (French); French-speaking Switzerland (French and Romansh); Italian-speaking Switzerland (Italian); Italy (Italian).

The 50th parallel also very roughly divides the mainly Protestant lands of the north from the mainly Catholic lands of the south. The most notable exceptions are the Republic of Ireland and Belgian Flanders, both Catholic, although in the north.

THE WORD 'EUROPE': NO MAGIC SIGNIFICANCE

What's in a name? Take the case of America. The whole huge continent owes its name to the explorer Amerigo Vespucci, born in Florence in 1441, the same year as Christopher Columbus. He claimed to have been the first to set foot on the American mainland, and was certainly the first to write about his voyage. His account, published in 1507, made him so famous that the New World was given his first name, Amerigo. Many, however, accused him of being an impostor.

So America owes its name to Vespucci's parents' choice of a first name for their son, and to that son's flair for publicity.

The origin of Europe's name is quite different, and older: but it too owes more to chance than to logic.

The demi-goddess Europa between Greece and Troy

The word 'Europe' first appears in Greek mythology. But it is not found in either of the two great epics attributed to Homer – the *Iliad* (on the Trojan War) and the *Odyssey* (on the return of Ulysses to Ithaca). According to Hesiod, in the late ninth or early eighth century BC, the demi-goddess Europa was either one of the ten thousand Daughters of the Ocean or – more probably – the daughter of Agenor, King of Phoenicia, and sister to his son Cadmus. Phoenicia covered the present-day coast of Syria, Lebanon, and Israel: so Europa was a Levantine, from the near east.

According to legend, Zeus, the king of the gods, fell in love with her, and to carry her off he assumed the shape of a bull. Bringing her to Europe, he fathered her three sons: Minos, who built the famous Cretan labyrinth, and Aeacus and Rhadamanthus, the judges of Hades. Her brother Cadmus is said to have set out for Greece in search of her, bringing with him the alphabet which the Phoenicians had just invented – a highly stylized form of Assyrian 'cuneiform' writing.

The Europa myth almost certainly expresses the rivalry between Greece and Troy. The latter – a city in fact as well as legend – lay in Asia, just south of the Dardanelles. Between Troy and Greece, successive abductions became a vendetta. The Phoenicians seized Io, the daughter of Argos. The capture of Europa was no doubt revenge on the part of the Greeks, who also made off with Medea. Then Paris, an Asian from Troy, asked by the three goddesses Hera, Aphrodite, and Athena to judge their beauty, chose Aphrodite, the Venus of the Romans. In gratitude, she helped him to abduct the beautiful Helen, wife of the Greek Menelaus, King of Sparta. That was enough. The Greeks laid siege to Troy. After ten years, with the help of Athena, angry at having been spurned by Paris, they conquered the city by a ruse and destroyed it.

Scraps of history entangled in legend: such are the dubious origins of Europe's name.

From legend to geography

As a geographical expression, the word 'Europe' was first used by a contemporary of Hesiod at the end of the eighth century BC. In his *Hymn to Apollo*, he spoke of 'those who live in the rich Peloponnese, those of Europe, and those of the islands bathed by the waves'.

Europe must therefore have then meant the northern part of continental Greece, excluding the islands and the Peloponnese peninsula. However, between the eighth and the fifth centuries BC, the word took on a much broader sense.

The first true historian, highly intelligent, much travelled, and full of curiosity, was the Greek Herodotus (484–406 BC). His compatriots, he wrote, 'divide the earth into three parts: Europe, Asia, and Libya' (Africa). For Herodotus, Europe stretched far away towards the north, well beyond the Danube, as far as the shores of the North Sea. In the north-east, it continued as far as the Don and the Sea of Azov. Even so, it was smaller than its definition today.

But why should the name 'Europe' be applied to this part of the world? Herodotus confessed his ignorance with a smile. 'I cannot conceive why the earth, which is one entity, should have three names ... I cannot discover who thus divided the world, nor where they found this terminology.' 'The most curious fact,' he added, 'is that the Tyrian Europa was born in Asia, and never came to this region which the

Greeks now call Europe, but merely went from Phoenicia and Crete to Lycia.' However, he concluded philosophically, 'we shall use the names established by common custom.'

Uncertain etymology

Nor does etymology shed much light on the subject. The explanation most frequently offered is that in Greek the adjective *eurus* means 'broad', while *opsis* or *optikos* indicates the eye, the face, or sight. Zeus *europa* means 'far-sighted Zeus'; while europa in the feminine would be a woman with large eyes, a beautiful face, or an attractive expression. All of which, however flattering, explains nothing at all.

Another hypothesis is that the words 'Asia' and 'Europe' derive from the Akkadian language of Mesopotamia, in which *asu* means 'rise' and *erebu* means 'enter'. The former would signify the east, where the sun rises; the latter the west, where it sets.

All that can be said for certain is that the word 'Europe' has emerged by a series of historical accidents no less random than that which led America to be named after Vespucci.

THE DEVELOPMENT OF EUROPE

Experiences shared

From the earliest times, western, northern, central, and southern Europe have passed through phases of shared experience. In Neolithic times, for example, many Western Europeans built dolmens – giant tombs which required not only immense labour and technical skill, to secure, transport, and erect the huge rocks, but also a shared religion or philosophy in the face of death.

A chronological list of such 'phases of shared experience' might look something like this:

1. the megalith phase (4,000 to 2,000 BC);
2. the Celtic phase (sixth to first centuries BC);
3. the Western Roman Empire (fourth century AD);
4. the Germanic centuries (sixth to eighth centuries);
5. the Carolingian Empire (eighth to ninth centuries);

6. Western Christianity and the schism with Greece (tenth and eleventh centuries);
7. the age of the Gothic cathedrals (twelfth to fifteenth centuries);
8. the Renaissance (sixteenth century), including the divisive effects of the Reformation and Counter-Reformation;
9. the Imperial Age: Europe's commercial, technical, scientific, industrial, and political colonization of much of the rest of the world (ending only in the twentieth century).

In each case, not all of Europe fully shared the collective experience. Ireland, Scandinavia, and Germany east of the Rhine were never subdued by Rome. Nor were the Scandinavians invaded by the Celts; while Ireland was only marginally affected by Germanic inroads.

Influences shared

Western Europe, in particular, has been a melting-pot in which a number of influences have intermingled. Examples of groups with prolific influence were the Celts, who were outstanding farmers, and the Romans, who brought with them writing, law, and administration, and who learned to develop city life and transport. Through the Romans, too, Greek art, literature, mathematics, astronomy, and philosophy spread into the West. The Germanic influence was felt chiefly in the exercise of power, in morality, and in the role of women, but also in metallurgy, strategy, and horsemanship.

Judaeo-Christian influence also played a cardinal role, notably through the Papacy. The schism between the Roman and Greek Orthodox Churches was profound.

At the same time, other groups that have influenced Europe have been absorbed into it, like the Vikings – some of whom became the Normans. Still others, like the Arabs of Spain, have remained influential but largely separate.

Internal contradictions

The present work in no way seeks to minimize those factors which have worked against the unity of Europe – the diversity of languages, or the schism between the churches of East and West.

Nor should one under-emphasize Europe's incessant wars. Many were at their height during Europe's own apogee, from the sixteenth to the twentieth centuries. And if the conquest of overseas empires may perhaps have increased Europe's wealth, it also contributed to the growth and aggravation of nationalism. War within Europe grew more and more destructive – to the point at which the First and Second World Wars put an end to Europe's predominance in the world. Then for several decades, war within Western Europe was not only unthinkable but impossible. Western Europe was divided from the East by the so-called 'Iron Curtain' until 1991, and European states' overseas empires had been wound up. All the nations of Western Europe had returned to democratic rule, accompanied by the growth of a 'European' awareness which was no longer unconscious and historical, but conscious and purposive. The determination to avoid a future world war seemed to be holding, despite the upheavals of the Bosnian War (1992–95) and the Kosovo War (1998–99).

That was to change in the new century, with a substantially more significant threat to peace and stability. Tensions had arisen in various parts of the former USSR, and Russia, under Vladimir Putin, had become militarily involved. The Russo-Georgian War in 2008 was followed by the Russian annexation of Crimea in 2014 and a full-scale invasion of Ukraine in 2022, triggering an escalation of responses from the rest of Europe and NATO. The unthinkable – a third world war – had ceased to be an impossibility.

Europe and the growth of compassion

Without making invidious or complacent comparisons with other parts of the world, it is nevertheless possible to discern in Europe's history a general if halting growth in compassion, humanity, and equality.

Examples include the abolishment of slavery and then of serfdom; the growing dignity accorded to women with the rise of 'courtly love'; the struggle against injustice, judicial error, and barbaric punishment; the development of human rights; the notions of national and popular sovereignty, of liberty and democracy; the achievement of universal suffrage; poor law reform; social security; the growth of philanthropic societies and political parties; and much more.

Such progress has by no means been uninterrupted. Western Europe has at times regressed into unspeakable horrors – inquisitions, tortures, witch-hunts, massacres, terrorism, exploitation, and genocide.

EUROPE

Leadership and lesions

Europe's achievements in art and literature are immense, but difficult to quantify in comparison with other parts of the world. But the creative wealth of European intelligence is undeniable. The first Industrial Revolution, which originated in Britain, soon spread to the rest of Europe, thanks to trade and the accumulation of capital. In fact, since the eleventh century, Western Europe has been very largely shielded from invasion. Eastern Europe has been less fortunate.

2

The Prehistory of Europe

PRE-EUROPEAN HUMANITY

The search for humanity's origins has made striking progress in recent years. Even as late as the 1930s, it was generally believed that men and women were descended from apes, and that their emergence had occurred, by genetic mutation, some three or four hundred thousand years ago, during the warm period between the last two ice ages, the third or Riss glaciation and the fourth or Würm.

In 1924, a fossil skull was found in Botswana and identified as belonging to Australopithecus africanus. This was followed by further discoveries of australopithecine remains, including those of the famous Lucy, a young female unearthed in 1974.

Palaeontologists also discovered, alongside the australopithecines, bones belonging to a different species, named first prae-canthropus (pre-human) and later homo habilis (skilled human). The oldest australopithecines have been dated at some eight or nine million years ago; the oldest hominids, first at two million eight hundred thousand, then at four or five million years ago.

Homo habilis

Physically, homo habilis differed somewhat from the two known varieties of australopithecine. He was 1.2 to 1.4 metres tall, he weighed between 30 and 50 kilograms, and his cranial capacity varied from 500 to 800 cubic centimetres. His forehead was much higher than that of the australopithecines. He was omnivorous, and was able to stand and walk on two legs.

Australopithecus africanus and homo habilis may well have shared a distant ancestor with the great primates such as the orang-utan, the gorilla, and the chimpanzee. But the lines of descent of the hominids and the primates are separate and parallel: each took its own course some thirty million years ago.

Some non-human animals use primitive tools; and all animals have intelligence as well as instinct. But human beings, even in so early a form as homo habilis, use more complex tools, have creative capacity, and can reason and reach conclusions.

In the words of Yves Coppens,

> the development of the brain and the enlargement of his diet led man to establish the broad outlines of a social structure: he formed small communities in places and dwellings organized for the purpose; he gathered and hunted; he shaped stones, bones, tusks, horns, and probably wood. The experience thus obtained he taught to his children, and so stored up, on top of their instinctive inheritance, the first elements of knowledge.

Intelligence is humanity's first line of defence.

THE EARLIEST EUROPEANS: HOMO ERECTUS

How did early man reach Europe from Africa? Homo habilis was superseded by a new subspecies, homo erectus, with a larger cranial capacity. It was homo erectus who invaded Mediterranean Europe, remaining in the south while the last ice age continued, but moving northwards as the glaciers receded. This expansion began rather more than one and a half million years ago.

It left its traces in a number of sites. The best known and most important are: Chilhac, Mauer, Tautavel, Terra Amata, Swanscombe, and Neanderthal.

Chilhac

The oldest human traces so far discovered in Europe were found at Chilhac in France, in the Brioude district in the Auvergne. They date back some 1,800,000 years. All they consist of is five tools – simple pebbles bearing traces of human workmanship adapting them for hunting. Those who fashioned them may seem primitive and clumsy:

but they and their forebears had already travelled a long road from Africa, leaving behind countless encampments or dwellings since destroyed or not yet discovered.

Mauer

Mauer is a village in Baden-Württemberg, not far from Heidelberg in Germany. There, alongside fossil remains of an 'ancient elephant', an 'Etruscan rhinoceros', and a sabre-toothed tiger, a human lower jaw was found in 1907. It dates from about 650,000 BC, and is thought to have belonged to a male adult about forty years old. So 1,150,000 years separate the so-called 'Mauer mandible' from the tools found at Chilhac – 575 times as long as the whole Christian era. Tens of thousands of generations of men and women are lost to sight in that gap in our knowledge – primitive, not very numerous, threatened by other predators and by the forces of nature, subject to famine, and too often dying young.

Tautavel

From 1964 onwards, excavations led by Henry de Lumley-Woodyear, of the Paris Natural History Museum, have unearthed the floors of more than twenty prehistoric dwelling-places at Tautavel, near Perpignan in the province of Roussillon, southern France. But the most notable find was made on 22 July 1971: the almost intact skull of a man aged about twenty, with a cranial capacity of 1,150 cubic centimetres. Since then, some fifty other human fragments have been discovered, all dating from between 650,000 and 450,000 BC.

Tautavel Man was a homo erectus, similar to those whose remains have been unearthed in Java, China, Africa, and in other countries in Europe – Hungary, Germany, Italy, and the United Kingdom.

Neither at Mauer and Tautavel, nor in any other site earlier than 400,000 BC, is there any sign of the use of fire.

Terra Amata, Vertesszöllös, Torre in Pietra

Mastering fire, in fact, was a key achievement for early man, and its traces are found in several later sites. One is Terra Amata, near Nice, on the slopes of Mont Boron, where archaeologists have discovered three successive levels of early human habitation, dating from 600,000 to 380,000 BC. In the topmost and latest of these, charred flints have been found. Further traces of fire exist at Vertesszöllös in Hungary, just over 56 kilometres from Budapest, at a site dating from 450,000 or 350,000 BC; and at Torre in Pietra and Castel di Guido, sites to the north of Rome which date from 430,000 BC.

From about 350,000 or 300,000 BC, specially prepared hearths seem to have been in general use.

One archaeologist has described human life at this time as having undergone 'a psychological revolution', accompanied by 'a rapid development of the social structure':

> Around the fire in the dwelling-place, during the long winter evenings, the hunters no doubt described their exploits, laid plans for the next day, and recalled the legendary feats of ancient hunting heroes, thereby strengthening the bonds that linked the family and the tribe ... From these early beginnings there gradually developed regional cultural traditions in all their diversity and wealth.

Swanscombe

Some 300,000 years ago, again in an interglacial interval, homo erectus reached Great Britain. His northernmost traces are found at Pontnewydd, in Wales, a site probably occupied only intermittently by small hunting groups. But the most important discoveries were made at Swanscombe, south of the Thames between Dartford and Gravesend. In 1935, 1936, and 1955 three bones were found, forming the back of a skull which had belonged to someone about twenty years old, probably a girl. It dates back to about 280,000 BC; and its cranial capacity of 1,325 cubic centimetres is greater than that of Tautavel Man.

Neanderthal Man: burial and religion

Unlike most of these discoveries, that of the Neanderthal skull was made more than a hundred years ago, in 1856. The Neanderthal is a deep valley or ravine on the Düssel river near Düsseldorf. There, in a small cave, were found some bones of limbs and a brain-pan. Other slightly later Neanderthal skulls have been found in Spain, Portugal,

Italy, Yugoslavia, France, Belgium, and Germany – all large, like that of modern man, but still with limited cranial capacity.

Before Neanderthal Man there is barely any surviving sign of burial. The few human remains discovered are often mingled with animal bones. From about 100,000 BC onwards, however, the sites begin to contain either heaps of burnt bones, apparently dealt with according to some ritual, or unmistakable graves with human skeletons either stretched out or slightly bent.

This new practice is of fundamental importance. Burial implies the beginnings of metaphysics. These early men, largely ignorant in the face of natural forces whose benign or terrible caprices they could not fathom, had to use their powers of reasoning to seek explanations: they found them in the unknown and the supernatural. Even today, humanity is still baffled by the same metaphysical hunger for a transcendent world and for survival after death.

It is well-nigh impossible to picture the immense stretches of prehistoric time – ten thousand, a hundred thousand, a million years, or the three hundred thousand which separate the people of Mauer from those of Swanscombe. It is equally difficult to imagine these families slowly progressing, meeting only rarely, gradually inventing and perfecting their primitive implements, and discovering fire at very roughly the same time in Europe as in China (where comparable hearths have been discovered at Chou Koutien).

Throughout all this time, small groups of people who may or may not have been the ancestors of present-day Europeans wandered across the face of Europe. They were too few, however, to form a true social fabric. As yet, there was still no 'Europe', even in a primitive sense.

THE BIRTH OF ART IN EUROPE

Cro-Magnon Man: homo sapiens sapiens

The age of homo habilis is numbered in millions of years, that of homo erectus in hundreds of thousands, that of Neanderthal Man in tens of thousands. Then, between 40,000 and 34,000 BC, came a decisive turning-point: the emergence of *homo sapiens sapiens* – or Cro-Magnon Man – or even 'modern man', for we are of that same mould. Now, time will be counted in only thousands of years.

In the words of Henry de Lumley-Woodyear:

> With the arrival of Cro-Magnon Man, that robust hunter with his proud bearing and his head held high, the great hunting civilizations of the Late Palaeolithic period began to spread across Europe, from the Atlantic to the Urals, from the Baltic to the Mediterranean, during more than 25,000 years ... New acquisitions enriched humanity's cultural legacy ... But the main cultural achievement of this modern man was Art: engravings, paintings, and sculptures which bear witness to the growth of symbolic thinking.

The earliest art

There is every indication that art first appeared with modern man. Its fruition took 26,000 years – thirteen times as long as the Christian era. But its practitioners were no longer the scattered, primitive, isolated families who wandered through a hostile world at the time of homo erectus. True, we know very little of the vast migrations and human changes that must have taken place during 26,000 years – only enough to cast doubt on any assertion that these peoples were our own direct ancestors. Nevertheless, and despite the fact that excavation has been more thorough and systematic in Western Europe than anywhere else, it is undeniable that art first appeared here and in the Sahara.

Lascaux and Altamira

The first wall drawing so far discovered is that of a horse at Pair-non-Pair, in the Bordeaux area of France. Twelve or fifteen thousand years later came the masterpieces of the Magdalenian culture in the Late Palaeolithic period, named after the Madeleine site in the Dordogne. Near there, at Lascaux, a cave was discovered in September 1940, nearly 150 metres long, with a fine-grained chalk ceiling and a whitish deposit of carbonate of lime on its walls. Both had helped to preserve the drawings, paintings, and engravings in the chambers of the cave: 150 paintings, mainly of animals, and some 800 engravings, many of these also coloured. Superimposed on each other over a long period, most of the pictures date back to the Aurignacian; but a number of them are of the Magdalenian, the heyday of cave art, around 15,000 BC. To prevent climatic deterioration and damage from the carbon dioxide exhaled by visitors, the Lascaux cave has had to be closed to tourists, who are directed instead to a modern facsimile, Lascaux 2.

Another masterpiece, the Altamira cave, has been called 'the Sistine Chapel of Palaeolithic art'. Discovered in 1879 by D. Marcellino de Santuola, this is situated in Santillana del Mar, not far from Santander in Spain. Its multicoloured painted ceiling, 18 by 9 metres, shows fifteen bison, a large horse, and three does, all dating from 13,000 BC.

The same period produced the cave paintings at Niaux in the Ariège *département* of southern France. Here, 2 kilometres from the entrance, are pictures of more than 100 animals – bison, horses, goats, and fish. Equally interesting are the bison in the Tuc d'Audoubert cave, which are modelled in clay. These were found shortly before 1914 by the three sons of Count Begouen, a celebrated Toulouse prehistorian.

In Britain, later Palaeolithic sites are unfortunately few, and restricted to a number of caves in Derbyshire, Somerset, and Devon. The same is true of Scandinavia and northern Germany: the obvious limiting factor was the fourth or Würm ice age.

ART AND RELIGION

These stone-age artists deserve respect. They not only invented the notions of an image and a symbol; they developed techniques for representing a three-dimensional world on a rough flat surface. They discovered ochre, and learned to change its colour with heat. They acquired the skills of drawing and engraving.

It seems likely that their motives were religious. Perhaps some of the animals they depicted were gods; perhaps some of their pictures represented prayers or incantations. Their symbolism was certainly related to hunting, which is shown in many of the paintings and drawings. No doubt these small bands of hunters invoked the protection of transcendent beings when they set out to seek food.

Two caveats are necessary here. First, we have no means of knowing whether or not we are the descendants of these distant hunters-turned-artists. Secondly, although around 12,000 or 13,000 BC Western Europe appears to have been in the fore-front of human progress, this is no longer the case in the ten thousand years that followed. The greatest change of all, the Neolithic revolution, took place in the Middle

East, and reached Western Europe only after some further thousands of years.

EUROPE OUTSTRIPPED BY THE NEOLITHIC REVOLUTION

The Neolithic revolution in the Middle East

Around 8,000 BC, the centre of advanced civilization seems to have shifted from France and Spain to the Middle East, where the Neolithic revolution took place.

'Neolithic' civilization derives its name from the new stone implements it used – polished and not merely cut. But it involved the biggest step forward in human history, including not only new tools but the invention of agriculture, stock-breeding, pottery and, later, weaving.

From gathering to growing

It is not easy, now, to imagine the extraordinary intellectual feat that was needed, first, to realize the relationship between seeds and plants, and then to discover that seeds once sown would multiply, producing many more seeds than the original sowing, and greatly increasing the amount available for food. The same principle was applied to animal husbandry, with goats, dogs, sheep, and eventually cows. So it was that humanity moved from hunting and gathering to food production.

Population growth and the earliest towns

More food meant more people. At the end of the Late Palaeolithic period, around 8,000 BC, the world's population probably numbered some 10 million. By the year 1,000 BC it may well have increased to 100 million.

The clearest indication of this tenfold growth is the beginning of community life in large villages or small towns. The first city known to historians is Jericho, dating from about 8,850 BC. It soon covered more than 12 acres of land, and was surrounded by towers some 9 metres high. A similar early town was Mallaha, in the upper Jordan valley. For reasons still unfathomed, the Neolithic revolution seems to have begun in Mesopotamia, Anatolia, and Cyprus, spreading slowly throughout the Middle East and Egypt, then not only towards Europe but also into eastern and south-east Asia as far as Indonesia.

Not until about 4,000 BC did Neolithic civilization reach the Atlantic coast, partly by way of the Danube, and partly through the Mediterranean, at this date already used by small numbers of seafarers.

That same period saw an astonishing efflorescence of civilization, centred in the Middle East. Around 3,500 to 3,300 BC appeared the world's first writing – the cuneiform of Sumer and Akkad in Mesopotamia, and hieroglyphics in Egypt. In about 2,600 BC the giant pyramid of Cheops was built. Murals, stone dressing, sculpture and bas-relief, symmetrical buildings and the use of the right angle: these are the most obvious signs of the scientific and technical progress being attained. Its culmination came in Egypt and Mesopotamia, in the second millennium BC, with the development of horsemanship and the invention of the wheel.

The West lags behind

What was happening in the West between 4,000 and 2,000 BC? With the exception of south-east Europe, which was marginally influenced by Middle Eastern civilization, Western Europe remained isolated. There is no trace here of the new weapons and art objects that were being made around the eastern Mediterranean. No doubt there was no trade because at this time Western Europe had so little to offer in exchange.

And yet, although backward and isolated, Western and Central Europe nevertheless developed, over the next millennium-and-a-half, a common culture of their own – the so-called megalith-builders' civilization.

MEGALITHIC CIVILIZATION

The megaliths made their appearance in the middle of the fourth millennium BC, around 3,600 BC. Rough-shaped and uncut, they were arranged in various ways: as single upright menhirs, in circles or double circles, in lines single or parallel, or in platforms. Some are bare and above ground; others are covered with smaller stones or with earth. In the latter case, the tumulus often has a passage leading from the entrance to a central dolmen. It may be – experts disagree on the subject – that stones which today are bare were all once covered. The only certain fact is that the dolmens, even when they were simply covered passageways, were collective graves for a limited number of individuals, probably chieftains or other important figures. They often contain objects of various kinds, such as have never yet been found at the foot of a standing stone. All these megaliths, whether menhirs or dolmens, must have required immense human effort – which implies that they could have had religious significance.

The megaliths and Western Europe

The majority of megaliths have been found in Western Europe. There are also many in Transcaucasia and Ethiopia, and a few in Iran, Pakistan, central India, and Indonesia; while in southern India, Manchuria, Korea, Japan, and Oceania there are quite a number which are 1,000 or 1,500 years younger than those in Western Europe. It may well be, therefore, that the megalithic cult or culture began in the Middle East around the fourth millennium BC and then spread into Western Europe. By land? Along the coast? We do not know.

What is certain is that the oldest dolmens, dating from about 3,600 BC, are found near the coasts of Portugal and Brittany: the Breton examples include the Barnenez 'cairn' in Finistère and the Kercado tumulus near Carnac.

In somewhat earlier graves, on the islands of Teviec and Moedic, six or seven people were buried together in a squatting position under piles of dry stones – perhaps an early form of dolmen grave. The same sites also show signs of primitive animal husbandry.

Towards the end of this period, around 2,000 BC, megalithic civilization came to full maturity at Stonehenge on Salisbury Plain in south-west England. Here, the vast standing stones seem to denote the boundaries of a sacred space.

The megaliths: technique and metaphysics

There are 2,000 dolmens in the British Isles, 3,000 in Denmark, 5,000 in France. All seem to point to two conclusions. First, when people build, with enormous effort, a huge heavy structure above ground for burying the dead whom they would previously have put in a simple earth grave, their motives can only have been religious. Some experts have called this motivation 'the megalithic idea'. It seems to indicate a cult of the dead, the hope of an after-life, and a belief in divine powers, represented perhaps by the menhirs. In other words, over a very large area, and for many hundreds of years, a philosophy and a religion were very broadly shared.

Secondly, to erect menhirs and dolmens, precise techniques were needed – at a time when the wheel was not yet invented and draught animals did not exist. Some blocks of stone weighing several tons were removed, we know, over many miles. The great menhir at Locmariaquer in Brittany, although now broken into five pieces, was 19.8 metres tall and weighed 360 tons. Others were some 9 metres tall and weighed 40–60 tons. Even the smaller menhirs were arranged in groups of hundreds, or even thousands, as at Carnac. To assemble and erect them, large numbers of people must have used ropes, billets of timber, and wedges; they must have cut pathways, using natural slopes where possible; many, as at Stonehenge, must have found ways to transport the stones by water.

Given the geographical extent of the menhir civilization, the various regions concerned must have communicated with each other and worked together. This tallies with the likelihood that they broadly shared religious beliefs. As a rough guide to the number of people involved, it takes 1,000 men to drag a slab weighing 50 tons 1 kilometre per day.

Curiously enough, there seems to have been little ordinary building at the time when the megaliths were erected. Polished stone axes appeared: specialized workshops were found, and trade evidently began. Between about 3,200 and 2,700 BC, pottery from Chassey in the Saône et Loire *département* of Burgundy spread into Brittany, Great Britain, and the south. So, later, did Lagozza pottery. Not long afterwards, the so-called Seine–Oise–Marne civilization was producing very sharp flint weapons; and around 2,000 BC bell-beakers appeared over a wide area of Western Europe.

The megalith builders lived in rectangular houses grouped in rectangular villages, except in Britain: here, most villages were circular. But even in Brittany, where so many megaliths were concentrated, experts estimate that there were no more than 100,000 inhabitants – in an area slightly bigger than Belgium, which has ten million inhabitants today.

Comparative backwardness

Strong religious convictions, powerful if rudimentary techniques for moving and erecting huge stones, and primitive art in which wall painting seems no longer to have figured: these were the marks of the megalith builders. Their Middle Eastern contemporaries were far more advanced. The Egyptians were handling even bigger stones, cutting them, assembling them, sculpting them; and they had rediscovered and refined the art of painting, in which they displayed, in Arpag Mekhitarian's words, 'balance', 'sobriety', 'purity', and 'power'. All that the West had to show was the megaliths themselves.

Urn burial

From about 2,000–1,850 BC onwards, the megalith builders' civilization quite suddenly disappeared. Its monumental, aristocratic collective graves gave place to small individual graves, which seem to have originated in the east. Later came urn burial-grounds, each urn containing the ashes of a human being.

During the second millennium BC and the beginning of the first, before the arrival of the Indo-Europeans, eastern influences began to mark western burial habits and, through the beginnings of trade, western art and technology. Metallurgy was on its way.

Had the megalithic population been driven out or replaced? Not necessarily. Many of today's specialists consider it possible that the megalith builders, who later may have become the pre-Celts, Ligurians, Iberians, and so on, may form our own ancestral stock. Subsequent invasions added to this stock, but without essentially changing it. It was not, however, racially homogeneous. Megalithic tombs have been found to contain both dolichocephalic (long and narrow) and brachycephalic (rounded) skulls, although the latter are more numerous in the Alps. The people in question were fairly short, but we have no indication of their eye, hair, or skin colour. Their numbers had grown: by clearing woodland, they had increased their food supplies. Over fifteen or twenty centuries, moreover, they had acquired the beginnings of a sense of community. As the German historian Karl-Ferdinand Werner put it:

It is hard to deny that there must have been some unifying 'megalithic idea'. The megalith builders were neither a people nor a civilization which was everywhere the same. But they shared an idea which was powerful enough to incite these people, five million years ago and scattered over thousands of miles, to honour their dead and some of their gods in very similar if not identical ways. We can only conjecture – and marvel – at what means of communication were involved, however slow their expansion remained.

IN SEARCH OF METAL: GOLD, COPPER, BRONZE

Palaeolithic people, as we have seen, fashioned remarkable implements from flint, quartz, and quartzite. Later, they made polished axes. For artistic purposes, they collected coloured stones which were more or less easy to break. Metal, however, was as valuable for war and hunting as it was for decoration.

It remains uncertain how mankind discovered metal. The first to be used was gold, which already existed in a pure state, then copper, found almost invariably in alloyed form. Next came bronze, and after that iron, which was probably first discovered in meteorites.

Palaeometallurgy

'Palaeometallurgy' is a modern science which seeks among other things to trace the earliest origins and growth of metalworking. It has already established that gold and copper were the first metals to be used: copperworking began in Anatolia in the second millennium BC. The techniques involved were identical: they called for a much more sophisticated use of fire for smelting, notably with the aid of charcoal and improved bellows. Chance, as well as experiment, no doubt contributed to the process, as it probably did to the discovery of bronze, an alloy of copper and tin. Bronze had the advantage of melting at a lower temperature than copper, and so could be more easily cast; it is also stronger. It seems to have been discovered between 4,000 and 3,000 BC, at about the same time as alloys of silver and gold.

These developments began in Egypt, from which Western Europe received both copper and then bronze. In the words of Professor Stuart Piggott:

> As with the beginnings of agriculture, the origins of non-ferrous metallurgy seem to lie within a restricted region of the Near East, but not in this instance because of the lack of sources of raw material outside this area, but by reason of the temper and tradition of the innovating societies of that part of the Old World – indeed Egypt, which quickly developed an elaborate copper-working industry from the late fourth millennium onwards, was always without resources of raw material nearer than the Eastern Desert and Sinai, and Mesopotamia too had to import its ore. So far as ready supplies of raw material were concerned, our Old World metallurgy could well have started in Ireland or Iberia, save for the fact that the stone-using peasantry of those parts lacked the precocity in technological innovation.

Bronze in central and Western Europe

Central Europe became pre-eminent in bronze metallurgy around 1,500 BC, owing largely to the co-existence of copper and tin mines in what is now Czechoslovakia.

Invasion also contributed. The so-called 'Battle-axe People', probably from southern Russia, entered Southern Europe, Spain, Portugal, Italy, Sardinia, Sicily, and the south of France around 1,800 BC, followed by the 'proto-Celts', the 'proto-Latins', and the 'proto-Germans'. Bronze metallurgy spread slowly, with the aid of tin mines in Cornwall and on the Atlantic coasts of France, from the Cherbourg peninsula to the Gironde.

There were five main centres of manufacture: the first on either side of the Channel; the second in Ireland; the third in Poland, southern Germany, Bavaria, Alsace, the Jura, southern Switzerland, and the Rhône Valley – all using copper ore from the Alps; the fourth in southern Scandinavia and northern Germany, whose inhabitants' trade in amber enabled them to acquire the ore they lacked; and the fifth in the Argde culture (the ancient name of Almeria), influenced by the eastern Mediterranean.

The Bronze Age: extensive trade

Bronze-Age Europe had a number of trade routes, many of them no doubt mere tracks. Along them travelled arms, implements, pottery, and art objects – for art, which in the form of painting had almost entirely vanished in the Neolithic period, now reappeared everywhere.

The earliest trade took the form of barter; but trade in the true sense gradually developed. So did primitive boats. One type, exemplified by the Pont d'Ancenis boat, was a canoe dug out of a single tree-trunk; another, as at North Ferriby in Yorkshire, was built from strips of wood; others, as in Wales and Scotland, had a wooden framework covered in leather. Most were used on rivers, but some were robust enough to face the Atlantic, and were equipped with sails. The heavy vessels used in the Gallic Wars were certainly derived from them. On land, transport was by chariot and pack-horse.

The metallurgists

For some idea of the scale of metallurgical production, take western Brittany. There alone, 23,700 bronze socket axes have been found. Assuming that these are only a third of the total, and that each weighed 200 grams, then the total amount of bronze worked in the region during one millennium was some 15 tons.

Little is known of the metallurgists' habitat. They no doubt lived near the tumuli, in stockaded circular camps, with large rectangular huts, probably built of logs and branches and covered with straw. Some such camps were fortified. Owing to their habit of urn burial, we know even less of these people's physical characteristics, since only their ashes remain.

Hunting and gathering

Hunting and gathering still provided much of the metallurgists' food. In the area of the Swiss lakes, large numbers of hunting implements have been found, including traps, snares, daggers and the points of lances, bows and arrows, and nets. The animals hunted were chiefly bison, deer, and wild boar. Bronze hooks were used to catch fish, while shellfish were gathered from the shallows and the rocks.

Agriculture

Our knowledge of prehistoric agriculture is derived chiefly from 'palynology', the study of pollens. But until the advent of the Celts, European agriculture was meagre in the extreme. Fire was used to make clearings; the main cereals sown were wheat and barley; mortars were used to mill the grain. Flax was grown, and the animals bred included small horses, half-wild pigs, sheep, and goats.

Handicrafts

The chief artisans were smelters, timber workers, carpenters, saddlers, and weavers. Towards the end of the Bronze Age, salters began to pan salt from the marshes and the sea.

Warriors and society

As always, warriors played an essential role, and held superior status to most other groups.

But in the middle and later Bronze Age, at least, their funerals were not marked by the building of large monuments. As one expert has put it: 'Society remained very communal in the Late Bronze Age. The soldier was of much the same value as the prospector, the smith, the herdsman or the labourer. In this world of trade and barter, only the merchant could accumulate wealth and emerge above the rest.'

3
The Celts

THE GREAT INDO-EUROPEAN FAMILY

From the eighth to the first century BC, much of Western Europe was occupied by peoples known collectively as the Celts.

From the first century to the fourth century AD, with the Roman conquest, their dominance was replaced by that of the Italiots. Rome brought to Western Europe not only its own civilization but also the great culture of the Greeks. Then, from the fourth century AD onwards the Goths invaded and divided the Roman Empire of the West.

Present-day Europeans are the product of successive civilizations: that of the megalith builders, that of the Celts, that of the Italiots, that of the Goths, and later that of the Slavs. They have also been influenced by factors from without. The influences in question are not so much racial as linguistic and cultural. We do not know even the name of our megalith-building ancestors: all we can say is that they coincided in time with the Ligurians, in the north, and the Iberians, in the south. The name of the Celts we know from history. The great fifth-century Greek historian and traveller Hecataeus of Miletus described a region which he called 'Celtic' alongside Liguria.

The Indo-European phenomenon

The Celtic expansion was a relatively late feature of a much more general phenomenon – the emergence of a great linguistic family, the Indo-Europeans or Aryans.

The theory most widely held today is that they came from southern central Asia or from what is now Iran, and that they originally shared a largely uniform language. As various groups of them separated and migrated to different regions, that language evolved into separate languages, with only certain roots in common, and even these not shared by all.

The evolution of these languages was extremely complex (because the Celts were divided into numerous and usually nomadic tribes), extremely slow (lasting from the fifteenth century BC to the eleventh century AD, which explains its diversity), and extremely overwhelming (since very often new arrivals in an area imposed their own language on the peoples they conquered).

Aryans, Hittites, and peoples of the sea

Outside Europe, the movements of peoples included those of the Aryans and, long before them, the Hittites, who had had the great advantage of writing, in hieroglyphics and cuneiform.

From about 1230 BC onwards, too, the Egyptian Empire, hitherto at the summit of civilization, began to be attacked by 'people from the sea'. Since the end of the third millennium BC, in fact, tribes of Aegeans, ancestors of the Greeks, in successive waves of Mycaenians, Dorians, Phrygians, Achaeans, etc., had begun to appear to the west of Asia Minor, in Greece, Crete, and southern Italy. And when in the sixth to the fourth centuries BC the Greeks became the most brilliant embodiment of world civilization, the Celts in the west reached similar if humbler heights. Greece is among our intellectual ancestors: but we are also descended from the Celts.

THE BRONZE AGE AND THE FIRST CELTS

New graves

Whereas at the beginning of the Bronze Age small individual graves had become common, tumuli reappeared with the first proto-Celts. Their mounds were generally smaller than those of the megalithic period, and the graves were buried underground.

Cremation and urn burial

At the end of the Bronze Age, human burial underwent a fundamental change. Around 1250 BC, cremation began to replace interment. It had already been the practice long before, in the area that is now Hungary: this was the urn burial civilization to which we have already referred in Chapter 2.

The urns were grouped in cemeteries on flat 'fields'. They have been found in Central Europe, southern Germany, and eastern, central, and southern France, especially in Burgundy and Champagne. This civilization, which appears to have been egalitarian – at least in respect of burial – has been described by Hatt as 'a peasant culture close to the soil and with little contact with the outside world'.

Urn burial of this sort reached northern Italy in the eleventh century BC, Gaul in the ninth century BC, the south of France in the eighth century BC, and Spain not long afterwards. By comparison with Great Britain, the change came relatively late: there, cremation had been practised as an alternative form of burial since the second millennium BC.

The proto-Celts continued with urn burial, except for their chieftains, until the fifth century BC. More widely accessible than the costly dolmens, it implied what might be called the democratization of death.

Meanwhile, whereas the megalith builders, despite their navigational skills, had known nothing of the brilliant civilizations of Egypt and Mesopotamia, with their advanced technology, now, in the second millennium BC, the door to the east began to open.

THE DISCOVERY OF IRON

Iron and the Hittites

Iron metallurgy is more complex than that of copper and bronze. Its great advantage, however, is that iron ore deposits are far more abundant.

It was probably in the fifteenth century BC that the Hittites began to produce appreciable quantities of iron. In the centuries that followed, production gradually spread westwards, reaching Greece and Crete in about the ninth century BC. In continental Europe and southern Italy, it made its appearance at the same time as urn burial, i.e. with the proto-Celts.

Not until the seventh century BC, however, did iron production develop on a large scale in Central Europe, where it was used to make long swords. During the Roman period, the technology changed very little, except in Scandinavia; and it was not until the Middle Ages that substantial progress was made, with techniques which were imported from India and Damascus where iron had begun to give place to steel.

The advantages of iron

Iron swords were stronger than bronze bucklers: but more important than that technical victory was the manufacture of implements which revolutionized agriculture and shipbuilding.

While in the Mediterranean area people continued to use swing-ploughs, merely scratching the soil with wooden ploughshares, in the broad rich plateaux and plains of the north they began to use wheeled ploughs with iron ploughshares. These not only dug deeper furrows, but tipped over less easily. This explains the shape of the long open fields that are typical of southern Britain, Belgium, much of Germany, and France north of the Loire – although some of these date from the eleventh century AD, when the double ploughshare was invented.

Archaeologists divide the Iron Age, which in Western Europe coincides with the period of Celtic ascendancy, into two main phases. The first phase, from the eighth century BC to about 500–450 BC, is called the Hallstatt Iron Age, after an Austrian village of the period.

The second phase, from 450 BC to the Roman conquest of Gaul in about 50 BC, is called the Tène Iron Age, after a village in Switzerland. Both Iron Ages are very important in the history of Western Europe.

THE HALLSTATT IRON AGE AND THE AWAKENING OF THE WEST

'If a name had to be found for the eighth to the fifth centuries BC, it might well be "The Awakening of the West".' This was a crucial period in the development of Gallic civilization. To quote Jean-Jacques Hatt again, it was then that 'the Celts not only entered history but also created their own civilization and art.' These took many forms in various regions, partly under a multiplicity of influences from outside.

The Celtic invasion

The Celts were driven westwards by an invasion of horsemen from the east. Under the latters' influence, they adopted new saddles and harness, and a light two-wheeled fighting chariot. Above all, the horsemen used iron, bringing with them long iron swords especially suitable for mounted combat.

Northern Italy

The Celtic invasion continued until the fifth century BC, spreading haphazardly in all directions. The Hallstatt civilization reached Czechoslovakia in the east and Germany in the north, and through France, via the Rhône Valley and Aquitaine, it covered the northern half of Spain. In about 500 BC, a wave of Celtic immigrants crossed the Alps from the west and settled in the Po Valley, the area that came to be known as Cisalpine Gaul. In 390 BC they captured Rome. Some of them entered Greece, sacking Delphi on the way; some went as far as Anatolia, where they were known as 'Galates', no doubt after the Gauls, one of the branches of the Celts.

The British Isles

Other branches spread north-westwards, in particular towards the British Isles. A first wave, the Goidels, went to Ireland, where they settled and interbred with the local population, imposing their own Celtic language. A second wave, the Brythons (whence 'British', 'Briton', 'Britain', and 'Brittany') invaded Great Britain, whose pre-Celtic name had been Albion, an Indo-European word related to the Latin *albus* (white). The Bretons, in Brittany, were using iron from about the middle of the sixth century BC.

The limits of Celtic expansion

Very few Celts settled in northern Scandinavia, north Germany, or present-day Denmark. In these regions another great Indo-European family, the Germans, slowly grew. South of the Po Valley, moreover, and beyond the Apennines, the Celts' relatively late incursions brought them up against the Etruscans, probably from the north-east, and the Italiots and Greeks in southern Italy and Sicily.

Chariot graves

Around 900 BC, most burial grounds still consisted of cinerary urns; but the beginning of the Hallstatt Iron Age, between 800 and 750 BC, saw a new custom take root: the use of tumuli and round trenches. The latter were for sacrificial purposes, in order to communicate with the subterranean powers which protected the dead and produced wealth from the soil. At first relatively empty of personal possessions, the graves began to contain more towards the end of the eighth century BC. By then, they could be called 'knights' graves': the dead were buried with items of harness, horses' bits, etc. The oldest examples of such burial have been found in Bavaria and Hungary; but other discoveries have been made at Court Saint-André in Belgium, Sesto Labule in northern Italy, Mailhac in the Languedoc, and Vix-les-Joyeuses in Burgundy. The contacts then established between Burgundy and Flanders foreshadowed – and may even explain – the emergence of Greater Burgundy in the fifteenth century AD.

With arms and harness, chariots appeared. At first they were large and heavy, with four wheels; but later, under Etruscan and Illyrian influence, the Celts developed light two-wheeled chariots like those which the Hittites and Egyptians had used a thousand years earlier. This suggests the existence, alongside the peasants and merchants, of a new class of knights.

In the Tène Iron Age, as we shall see, gold, silver, and bronze jewellery began to be buried with the other items interred earlier.

The birth of widespread trade

Recent discoveries have revealed that by the end of the eighth century BC, objects made in the Mediterranean area, mainly in Etruria, northern Italy, and Greece, had begun to appear much further inland. Archaeologists have patiently reconstructed the patterns of trade, which seem to have involved a network of roads or tracks and, for sea and coastal traffic, a large number of depots, warehouses, or by analogy with more modern times – 'trading stations'.

Land routes

On the mainland, there were several main trade routes. One led from Languedoc, then in the sixth century BC from Massalia (Marseille), up the valleys of the Rhône and the Saône, then divided in two – in one direction heading for Northern Europe and Great Britain, and in the other for Brittany. A second main trade route led into Switzerland, through the passes of the Alps, and to Alsace. A third, starting in the Balkans, climbed the valley of the Danube and met the other routes in the Rhône Valley.

Sea routes and the alphabet

The sea routes are more interesting still. Three seafaring peoples confronted or followed each other on the western coasts of the Mediterranean and even on the Atlantic seaboard: the Phoenicians (with their Carthaginian colony), the Greeks, and the Etruscans.

All three, in addition to their shipbuilding skill, had a further great asset: the alphabet, which had been invented by the Phoenicians. Its first surviving appearance is on a sarcophagus dating from the thirteenth century BC. The Greek, Etruscan, Latin, and later Cyrillic alphabets are all its direct descendants.

Highly educated as they were, these peoples were not the first to undertake long sea voyages. The megalith builders, as we have seen, had sailed between Great Britain and Brittany, and south as far as northern Spain. At the beginning of the Bronze Age, there had been a virtual explosion of sea trade, as witness the extraordinary spread of bell-beakers.

But with the Iron Age, shipping became still more important: the Phoenicians, the Greeks, and then the Etruscans (less extensively and only in the Mediterranean) established trading stations; from these, traders pushed into the interior and also, by sea, to the Atlantic.

What did they trade? West Europeans imported pottery, jewellery, arms, shields, and bucklers, but also salt and jars of wine. Wine and wine-growing later became one of the distinguishing marks of Western civilization. And it was the Celts who invented iron-bound wooden casks, so much more practical than the jars of the Mediterranean.

In return, the westerners exported copper, tin, and amber. This last, mostly from the Baltic area, was much prized for jewellery at the time.

THE BRILLIANT CIVILIZATION OF THE TÈNE IRON AGE

Between 500 and 450 BC there appeared in the Celtic world, in the north between the Meuse and the Main–Neckar area, what Jean-Jacques Hatt calls 'a very original, very novel, very personal civilization which, while maintaining links with the Euro-Asian east and with the Mediterranean world, nevertheless remained completely autonomous. This dominant civilization became that of the Tène.'

The originality of the Tène Iron Age

The relationship between the Hallstatt and Tène Iron Ages is very clear. Each had a landed aristocracy, chariot graves, well-to-do peasants, and skilful craftsmen. In the Tène, however, everything became richer and more brilliant. The aristocracy was more numerous. The graves contained not only two-wheeled chariots but also luxury objects, sometimes very fine. The peasants abandoned the swing-plough in favour of the plough with wheels. They cleared fields for pasture, using iron-bladed scythes. Stocks of hay, as Hatt has pointed out, made possible more efficient animal husbandry.

Greater wealth and a larger population were accompanied by more extensive clearing of the land. While Etruscan art objects became common, the Celts developed an equally impressive art of their own. It was at this time that they invaded northern Italy, and a whole area of the Celtic world, stretching from the Atlantic to the Rhine and the Alps, and from the Channel to the Mediterranean and the Pyrenees, acquired the name of Gaul – a term invented by the Romans. South of the Alps, as we have seen, it was known as Cisalpine Gaul.

From the fourth century BC onwards, towns began to develop.

Finally, whereas the Hallstatt Celts had been scattered in regional groups, 'Tène civilization was from the beginning homogeneous, united, and dominant.' What were the features it shared?

Town and country

Already, by this time, the Celts were living in small towns, of which there were broadly two kinds. Inland, they were fortresses of a type which was common throughout Europe from Bohemia to Brittany. Near the Mediterranean coast, they were true Greco-Roman towns, of which that of Glanum, near Saint-Rémy de Provence, is a fine example.

The houses, almost always made of wood, were generally rectangular. The only exception was in Great Britain, where the prevailing shape was still round.

A people of peasants

Most Celts were peasants. Farming had made great progress since the time of the megalith builders. The Celts used sickles, but they also invented an iron-bladed reaping machine of which Pliny the Elder has left us a first-century AD description. They developed the wheeled plough, which led to the open-field system. But there were also woodlands, with more isolated dwellings and smaller fields surrounded by dry-stone walls, hedges, or embankments topped with trees and shrubs. Ireland, Cornwall, Wales, western France, and in general all those places where cattle were preferred to arable farming, are the areas where enclosures predominated.

Traces of Celtic agriculture can even be found in the language of modern France. Words like *charrue* (plough), *soc* (plough-share), *morne* (head of a tilting lance), *glaise* (clay), *lande* (heath), *breuil* (copse), *bruyère* (heath or brier), *javelle* (sheaf), *glaner* (glean), *arpent* (acre), *chemin* (way), and *blé* (wheat) are all of Celtic origin. (The translations all derive from Old English, with the exception of 'glean', which is Celtic like the French, and 'copse' and 'brier', both from French.) All European languages contain words of Celtic origin, but in smaller numbers than French.

Although made up of different peoples, the Celts were all related, and appear to have shared a religion which formed one branch of the great Indo-European family of religions. They had a written language, but apparently no written literature. Socially, they seem to have been divided into a knightly class, with below it a warrior caste; a class of merchants with wider professional contacts; priests; healers; and perhaps also poets. The mass of the people were peasants.

The Gallic gods

Our only knowledge of the gods of Gaul comes from after the Roman conquest, when the Gallic pantheon was rapidly and artificially absorbed by the Roman. We know that there was a 'mother goddess', that there were gods of the after-life, and that there may also have been, beyond the triad of Esus, Teutates, and Taunus, a supreme Being who may have turned into a single God.

THE CELTIC WORLD

A vision of the world: no Celtic or Gallic nation

It would be totally anachronistic to believe that the many and various Celts felt anything remotely resembling Celtic solidarity. Nor did the Gauls, their main representatives in the Tène Iron Age, have any such early inklings of national awareness. What made the Auvergnat King Vercingetorix take up arms against Julius Caesar? Profound xenophobia, undoubtedly: a hatred of foreign domination. But there was no such thing as a Gallic 'fatherland'; there were only tribes, some of which – like the Arvernes or Auvergnats – sought to dominate the others.

The coalition formed by Vercingetorix included in fact all the peoples of central and Atlantic Gaul, between the Seine and the Garonne. After his victory at Gergovia (about 6.5 kilometres south of present-day Clermont-Ferrand), the coalition attracted new recruits; but the subsequent defeat of Vercingetorix, in 52 BC, put paid to the revolt.

Direct Greek influence

The Celts were surprisingly well-informed about the eastern world. From the sixth century BC onwards, Greek influence was so great that, even in the interior, Greek words were in use. They were mostly concerned with technology – meteorology, navigation, fishing, and grafting. So the powerful effect that Greece was later to have on Europe via the Roman Empire was nothing new. This may, as some historians believe, explain why Greco-Roman culture spread so easily into those parts of the Celtic world which the Romans conquered.

The emergence of the Teutons

The Teutons first appeared in the north and north-east of the Celtic world during the Tène Iron Age. The various tribes mentioned in this period, like the Suevi and the Marcomani, seem shadowy alongside the Celts. As for the Cimbri and other Teutonic tribes that invaded northern Italy in 113 BC, before being crushed by a Roman general ten years later, certain historians doubt whether they were Teutons at all, or in fact Germani of pure stock, since their leaders actually bore Celtic names.

Physically, the Teutons were certainly taller and fairer, on average, than the Celts in Gaul. But because the latter dyed their hair red for battle, the distinction was not always clear.

The Celts and the Teutons readily interbred with each other, especially after Caesar's Gallic victory and the Roman invasion which turned many of the vanquished into refugees, emigrating towards the east.

The remains of the Celtic languages

Unlike the Italiots and Romans, who later originated so many of the languages spoken in Europe, the Celts left few traces: a number of words that survive in modern speech, as we have seen; and the local languages still used in Brittany, Wales, Ireland, Scotland, and the Isle of Man, where they are now cherished and championed against the homogenizing tendencies that have eclipsed them elsewhere.

The deepest Celtic traces are perhaps to be found in place-names, especially in Britain, Ireland, and France – but not only there: the highest concentration of Celtic words in particular areas in fact occurs in west Germany, between the Danube and the Rhine.

All the eastern tributaries of the Rhine from the Neckar to the Lippe have Celtic names.

Châteaudun, Verdun, and Lyon (Lugdunum) all contain the syllable 'dun', which seems to signify a mound or fortress. So too does the suffix 'briga', as in Conim-briga, today known as Coimbra in Portugal. The ending 'magos', likewise, means a plain: it appears in Duromagus (Dormagen, near Düsseldorf), Novromagus (Neumagen, near Trier), Rigomagus (Remagen, near Coblenz), and in Nijmegen in the Netherlands.

The most interesting example is the Celtic name for water: *dubro* or *dubra*. This survives in many names of rivers or towns on or near them: the Douvre in the Calvados region; the Dobra, a tributary of the Sella in Spain; and the Vernoublan (from verno-dubra), a river near Freiburg. The Rhine, moreover, derives its name from the Celtic word for river, *renos* or *rinos*.

The impact of the Celts

Many historians, from classical antiquity to the present day, have seen the Celtic invasion as one of the greatest migrations in European history. Already in the fifth century BC, Herodotus described them as living along the banks of the Danube. Unfortunately, he located its source at the eastern end of the Pyrenees.

In the words of André Aymard, these vast migrations 'totally transformed the population of certain regions. They destroyed or at least weakened empires like that of the Etruscans. They sowed confusion and terror in long-settled societies and well-developed civilizations.'

There was, he says,

> a feeling of panic in Italy, and above all in the Hellenistic world. Civilized society became briefly and tragically aware of how frail it was against unbridled barbarism – just as it later felt when the Roman Empire suffered waves of invasion ... What seems to have happened most often is not the rout of a whole people or tribe, but the departure of one group after another in different directions ... Led by noble chieftains, accompanied by women and children in chariots, these bands roamed the countryside, ready to oust their predecessors and seize any chance of pillage, but above all seeking land to settle on, either by agreement or by force and massacre.

An unfinished civilization

As Aymard puts it, 'The Celts were the last of the western peoples to submit to the yoke of Rome ... But whereas the Etruscan and Punic civilizations had known a period of maturity before they perished, Gallic culture had not enough time to reach its apogee. Considered as a whole, it existed only in a state of promise.'

CONCLUSION

As the Bronze Age gave way to the Iron Ages, the whole of Western Europe was occupied by a Neolithic and then a Bronze-Age population, mingling perhaps with the Ligurians and Iberians described later by the writers of classical antiquity. But for some 2,000 years this area was repeatedly invaded. The invasions had three main phases: Celtic, Latin, and Teutonic.

'Invasion', however, is a complex and ambiguous word. It can mean a sudden attack by an army which pillages and then withdraws; an attack which involves massacre and enslavement, to establish the conquerors on the lands they have won; or, finally, slow immigration by a people which after several decades either outnumbers the existing population or remains in a minority. In these cases, either co-existence or assimilation can ensue.

Before looking in detail at these successive invasions, it is well to dismiss some of the distortions which narrow nationalism has imposed on history in the last 200 years.

One such myth is the belief that each of today's European peoples derives only from one or another of the three great invasions. In reality, we are almost all members of communities in which at least two of the three groups are mixed. The Irish in the west descended from the megalith builders and then the Celts, and influenced later by limited Teutonic invasions and finally by the English ascendancy. Likewise, the Scandinavians avoided invasion by the Celts, but nevertheless felt their cultural influence, and that of the Romans. In Portugal, similarly, the Celts joined their Neolithic predecessors, notably during the Hallstatt Iron Age; then came the Romans, who called the province 'Lusitania'. The Teutons – Alans and later Suevi – played only a minor role.

4
Classical Antiquity: Greek Wisdom, Roman Grandeur

THE ROMAN CONQUEST

Etruscans, Greeks, Gauls, and Carthaginians

After the invasion by the Celts, but before that by the Teutons, a small group of Italiot origin, from central Italy, took only three centuries to conquer the whole country, from the Alps to the heel and toe of Italy, including the islands.

This group had to reckon with four existing peoples: the Etruscans, in Tuscany and Umbria; the Greeks, in southern Italy and part of Sicily; the Gauls, in the Po Valley and the Alps; and the Carthaginians, in Sicily and Sardinia. Whereas in the fifth and fourth centuries BC the Gauls had briefly conquered Rome and in passing no doubt defeated the Etruscans, the third century BC saw the best part of the Romans' victory. By the year 200 BC, Rome and its Latin allies were in possession of all Italy, and had already sent a first expedition further afield.

Rome had achieved this dominant position partly by defeating Carthage in the Punic Wars. But Carthage remained both a military and a commercial rival. In the east, both the Greeks – linked by successive confederations – and their more primitive cousins the Macedonians were unwilling to see the defeated Greeks in Italy go unavenged.

The Macedonians

In the fourth century BC, Macedonia had produced two of the greatest conquerors in the history of the world: Philip II of Macedon (382–36 BC) and his son Alexander the Great (356–23 BC). Alexander's main conquests had been made in the east, whose empires were civilized, cultivated, and rich: western lands seemed less attractive. So it was natural for the Romans to look in the same direction, across the Adriatic, towards various parts of Alexander's empire, beginning with Macedonia and Greece. They first crossed the Adriatic in 229 BC; and as well as fighting the Punic Wars they engaged in the Illyrian and then the Macedonian Wars. It was during these wars, in 167 BC, that 1,000 Achaean Greeks, from the Peloponnese, were deported to Italy. Among them was one of the greatest historians of classical antiquity, Polybius.

Polybius

No history of Europe can ignore Polybius. Although he wrote in Greek, his *History* is the leading account of that irresistible Roman conquest of which he was both witness and victim, but also in a sense beneficiary. 'Vanquished Greece,' it is said, 'defeated its savage conqueror'; and Polybius is the example and the symbol of Greece's cultural influence on the Roman world. Before then, Greece had implanted coastal colonies in the west, as at Massalia (Marseille), but had never held extensive sway. Through its influence on Rome, however, it became one of the key ingredients in the development of European civilization.

Polybius was born between 210 and 208 BC. Like the majority of Greeks, he had opposed union between the city-states and been deeply hostile to the Macedonian conquest. His family was well-to-do and republican: his native town of Megalopolis had belonged to the Achaean Confederation, in which his father had played an important role. Polybius admired only the Achaeans: as well as the Macedonians, he detested the Boeotians, the Aitolians, the Athenians, and the Spartans. His education had been political and military rather than literary or philosophical.

Yet he was also thoughtful; and, reflecting upon events, he was able to explain why Rome alone, and none of its possible competitors, had succeeded in conquering so large a part of the known world.

Rome invades Greece

By 196 BC, the Achaean Confederation in the northern Peloponnese had formed an alliance with Rome against Philip V of Macedon. In 194 BC, after occupying Greece for several years, the Roman legions withdrew, laden with booty, and for a time made no attempt to annex the country. Soon, however, the process of Roman expansion became irresistible. The Romans also entered Asia in support of the King of Pergamums, the town which gave its name to pergamon or parchment, which came to replace papyrus.

Polybius may have taken part in that campaign, in an Achaean unit. In 170 BC he was certainly one of the leaders of the Confederation; but it was then that the Romans broke off the alliance and took as hostages 1,000 leading Achaeans, of whom Polybius was one. From 167 to 150 BC he lived in Italy as a deportee. It was there that he became acquainted with Roman affairs and was able to assess Rome's generals and statesmen, including Aemilius Paulus, the conqueror of Macedonia, Scipio Africanus, who conquered Carthage, and Cato 'the Censor'. He recognized and understood Rome's ascendancy over the Greek city-states; and in 147 BC he agreed to help Scipio Africanus in the third and last Punic War, which ended in the destruction of Carthage.

Subsequently, Polybius travelled along the Atlantic coast from Portugal to Morocco, then to Egypt, Syria, and Cilicia. He died in 126 BC, some years after his friend Scipio Africanus.

Polybius on the ascendancy of Rome

At the beginning of his *History*, Polybius wrote: 'Could anyone be so short-sighted or indifferent as not to ask how, and thanks to what government, the Roman state has been able to extend its dominion, unprecedentedly, over almost all the inhabited world, and that in no more than fifty-three years?' In fact, Rome had conquered not only Illyria, Macedonia, Greece, and part of Asia Minor, but also part of Spain, the whole of what is now Tunisia, and the coast of what is now Algeria. Polybius gave a complex explanation for this extraordinary historical fact.

It was not, he thought, because Rome enjoyed superiority in culture or industrial technology. The Latins, the Greeks, the Etruscans, and the Carthaginians all used the alphabet.

The Romans might be compared with the Persians: but they had always failed when they ventured out of Asia. The ascendancy of the Lacedemonians had been brief. The Macedonians had never tried to conquer Sicily, Sardinia, or Africa.

Polybius concluded: 'It was by very accurately assessing their chances that the Romans conceived and carried out their plan to dominate the world.' (I, Preface, 1–4). Polybius recognized and stressed the exceptional courage of the Roman soldiers, and the superiority of the Roman legion over the Greek phalanx and the often mercenary troops of Macedonia. 'The victories of the Carthaginians,' he wrote, 'were due not to better weapons or fighting units, but to the ability and clear-sightedness of Hannibal ... When the Romans had found as good a general, speedy victory was theirs.' (LXVIII, 1, 28).

But the fundamental reason for the ascendancy of Rome, Polybius declared, was the Roman constitution and political organization. The constitution, which was steadily being improved, was unique in being at once monarchical, aristocratic, and democratic.

The consuls were veritable monarchs. All judges, except the tribunes, were subordinate to them; and in time of war they enjoyed virtually sovereign authority. The Senate was aristocratic, with authority over the public treasury and all external affairs. The people had no less important a role. 'They alone have the right to bestow honours or inflict punishment.' They also elected the consuls and judges.

Polybius concluded:

> In any critical situation, there is perfect harmony among all three powers, so much so that no better system of government could be found. When there is an external threat which affects everyone and forces them to think and act together, the state is impelled by so great a momentum of concerted energy that nothing essential is overlooked ... Everyone plays his part ... This constitution is irresistibly efficient.

History III shows the complex process whereby Rome increased its power, thanks to a plan of campaign, political continuity, and a sense of its imperial mission.

Lasting conquest

The Greco-Roman and Judaeo-Christian influences on much of Europe have probably been greater than any so far mentioned – Iberian, Ligurian, Celtic – or, to be considered later – Viking, Saracen, Slav, or Byzantine. This is because the Roman conquest lasted so long. In effect, it was a patient series of military and diplomatic victories, interspersed with setbacks but pursued with admirable persistence. Even if Ireland, northern Scotland, Scandinavia, and all but the south-western area of

Germany, plus the Slav countries, escaped Roman domination, all were affected by Roman influence through trade and the movements of people.

Rome dominated not only Italy but also Gaul (for four centuries), Great Britain (two and a half centuries), much of Spain (five and a half centuries), and Portugal and the rest of Spain (three and a half centuries).

Roman script

Equally important was Roman script. Thanks to the Greeks and the Carthaginians, the Romans were able to evolve the simplest of all written alphabets. Used at first for archives and for funerary or other inscriptions, it became, under Greek influence, the vehicle for literature. True, the Gauls and the Scandinavians had various forms of primitive script. The Etruscans, too, had a fairly advanced system, used for accounting and for arcane religious rituals. None, however, produced any written literature until they adopted Roman script, which they used to write down legends previously transmitted by word of mouth. By then, Roman writing had become universal in the West.

Greek influence

The Greeks and the Romans stand in perfect contrast. For centuries, the Greeks were supreme in matters of the spirit and the intellect. At the very beginning of their history, they already possessed the *Iliad* and the *Odyssey*. In contrast to the East, where practical matters had been predominant, they had invented philosophical thought and pure science. They had created tragic theatre with Aeschylus, Sophocles, and Euripides; comic theatre with Aristophanes; learned history with Herodotus and Thucydides. Socrates and his disciples Plato and Xenophon, followed by Aristotle, had given brilliant demonstrations of logic in the original form of dialogues.

Yet despite these prodigies of taste and intelligence, the Greeks had never managed to unite. Their city-states had constantly fought against each other, and fallen easy prey to the Macedonians and the Romans. In a few centuries, the Romans conquered one territory after another: but at that time they had no vestiges of literature. The Greeks had a brilliant culture: the Romans had brilliant political efficiency.

But Rome could not conquer Greece without absorbing Greek civilization.

From the fourth century BC onwards, a century after the heyday of the great writers of Greece, Hellenism reached Rome. The Roman intelligentsia began to learn Greek, and Greek literature followed: Greek artists and writers came to Rome to seek their fortunes, and took the place previously held by the Etruscans.

Latin literature in its finest form, from the first century BC onwards, was largely based on Greek models. It reached extraordinary heights with such prose writers as Cicero and Tacitus, poets like Horace, Virgil, Lucretius, and Ovid. Seneca, the philosopher or moralist, and the poet Lucan, both of whom left a lasting mark on Latin literature, were actually of Spanish origin. But by then questions of origin made little sense. Latin had proved its power of assimilation.

Outside Italy, Greek influence took diverse forms. There was first that of the pre-Roman Greek colonies; then that transmitted through Rome. In the Middle Ages, from the fifth century AD onwards, westerners no longer learned Greek; and Greek authors – above all Aristotle, more than Plato, and philosophers and technical writers more than poets – were known only through partial and inaccurate Latin translations. From the twelfth and thirteenth centuries onwards, Arabic translations of Greek authors began to circulate, coming mainly from Spain, with among others its Toledo school of translators. It was not until the fifteenth and sixteenth centuries AD that increasingly accurate Greek scholarship was revived.

Marseille and Gaul

Even before the Romans, Greek navigators, especially from Massalia (Marseille), founded in 600 BC, had made their way through the western Mediterranean and also inland. Their influence can be traced in the Rhône Valley, eastern and southern Spain, and southern parts of the British Isles. In Marseille, the inhabitants spoke Greek, Latin, and Gallic: it was a centre of attraction for Gauls seeking more education. Elsewhere, the Western world absorbed Greek culture mainly through Latin.

It is from the Greeks, in fact, that all Western civilizations ultimately derive their sense of the abstract, their reliance on reason, their practice of pure science, and their use of dialectical logic.

Roman education: an influence on Europe today?

With their mastery of script and their gift for administration, the Romans sought not only to educate young aristocrats but to teach as many young people as possible to read and write. After the conquest of Greece, all teaching was based on Greek models. Some people taught their own children; others, often the more affluent, employed tutors. These might be Greeks, slaves, freedmen, or citizens. Some parents sent their children to Greece to complete their studies.

Rapidly, schools developed. They taught reading and writing; but they also instilled patriotism and prepared pupils for public life, demanding total allegiance to the state. In the early days, teaching was in Greek; later, Latin was more frequently used. There were even Latin–Greek schoolbooks.

Secondary education was reserved for the élite. It involved the study of grammar and logical analysis, but above all of literary texts. Analysing these, studying prosody and metre, and practising oratory were some of the pupils' main tasks. It is strange to think that a young middle-class European in the eighteenth century, if he studied the humanities, would be facing the same texts as a young Roman 1,800 years before.

'Everywhere,' wrote the Greek sophist and rhetorician of the second century AD Aelius Aristides, 'there are gymnasia, fountains, porticos, temples, workshops, and schools.' This was Rome in its prime. However, as André Aymard has pointed out, it was a time when the scientific spirit was declining; while Henri Marrou believes that 'philosophy and science were still essentially Greek'.

The Teutonic invasions destroyed this educational system, except in Italy, where the schools survived for a further century before succumbing to the Lombards. The disappearance of the Roman schools is one good reason for calling the invasions 'barbarian'. The new schools which were set up later by monasteries, bishoprics, and parishes had little in common with the old. Their location depended on the missionary activities of the fourth century AD, which concentrated on rural areas and rarely founded schools in the vicinity of the Gallo-Roman villas. They were of course Christian schools, needed for the recruiting of priests. It is from these religious institutions rather than the Roman schools that most modern schools derive.

The arts

In the arts there have been repeated attempts to return to classical antiquity in search of order and balance. The neo-classical style of architecture, spread by colonists throughout the world and even known in the United States as the 'colonial style', is European in origin and Greco-Roman in inspiration. The architects of the Renaissance abandoned Late Gothic and restored a number of pre-Gothic motifs. The so-called 'classical' style which followed imitated Greece and Rome more completely, as in Claude Perrault's colonnade at the Louvre in the seventeenth century. 'Baroque' architects in turn reacted against what seemed to them excessive symmetry; but then in the eighteenth and early nineteenth centuries neo-classicism produced a number of buildings inspired by classical antiquity: Marble Arch in London, the Brandenburg Gate in Berlin, the Arc de Triomphe at the Etoile in Paris, and the similar arch in the Place du Carrousel, not to mention the Panthéon, the Madeleine, and the Place de la Concorde.

The Renaissance also saw a revival of ancient Greek, studied most notably by the young Elizabeth Tudor, later Elizabeth I of England, and by Pierre de Ronsard, who read Homer's *Iliad* in two days.

ROMAN LAW, THE STATE, AND THE FAMILY

Res publica: the state

Beginning as a city governed by an oligarchy (for citizens formed only a minority of the inhabitants), Rome faced a problem when it acquired its immense possessions. The 'constitution' of the city-state was adequate for conquering but not for governing an empire. Would oligarchy have to be replaced by despotism? As their empire took shape, the Romans invented another solution – the *res publica* or state. The emperors – with, in principle, the blessing of the gods – ruled this 'legal person', composed of the Empire's possessions and its inhabitants; and when an emperor died, the res publica lived on.

When the Roman Empire finally broke up, in the fifth century AD, the Roman state, too, came to an end. But its example remained present in people's minds; and whenever attempts were made to consolidate an empire or a kingdom, the clergy in particular did their best to copy the Roman institutions they so admired.

Roman law

The Romans were much greater legislators than the Greeks. They believed above all in 'the law' – a coherent and rational system whose aim was to create a just society, in which every individual had full property rights, provided that he was male, a head of household, and a free citizen.

Around 450 BC, the Romans produced a written collection of laws, the Twelve Tables, now lost. It was only the first of many such compendia.

In his book *The Spirit of Roman Law*, the great German jurist R. von Ihering identified its two leading characteristics: first, clarity and precision, preventing arbitrary judgements; and secondly, the guarantee of liberty to heads of households and free citizens.

Under the Empire, legal treatises continued to be written; but Roman law was not systematically codified until very late in the day. The *Codex Theodosianus* was published in sixteen books in AD 438, during the war with the Persians and shortly before the attack by Attila the Hun. Justinian's *Codex* appeared in AD 529, followed soon after by the *Institutes*; then came the *Pandects* or *Digests* in 533, and finally the *Novellae*.

Politics

The late Sir Moses Finley, a British historian born in the United States, believed that the Greeks and Romans left a further legacy to the West. In his view they had invented politics. Indeed, elections and election campaigns, debates, eloquence, political parties (or at least factions), and propaganda (known as *captatio benevolentiae* or 'winning goodwill') all existed in the cities of ancient Greece and in the Roman Republic. So, if 'politics' means the electoral process, the West certainly modelled itself on Greece and Rome.

But if, on the other hand, 'politics' is the art of obtaining, sharing, or exercising power, it is as old as the earliest human communities, long before the Greeks and the Romans.

However, the Roman Empire undeniably set an example in three related fields: the army, the administration, and the levying of taxes.

A standing army

Clearly, only an efficient army could have conquered and defended so vast an area as the Roman Empire. The Empire was in fact a 'military monarchy', with a citizen army which gradually became professional. It was under Caesar that the Legion turned into a permanent body. Normally, its members served for sixteen years; but longer service was possible, and some soldiers stayed more than thirty years. Since they were unable to marry, they took concubines, who eventually acquired official status.

The soldiers' pay varied from unit to unit: they also received bonuses, decorations, and pensions in the form of money or land. A foreigner who served in the army became a Roman citizen. Training was tough: it included marches, races, jumping, swimming, target practice, fencing, riding, and gymnastics. In peacetime, soldiers built camps, aqueducts, temples, and bridges, drained marshes, or helped to build the famous Roman roads which, together with the sea routes, linked all parts of the Empire.

The army was divided into legions, roughly the size of small divisions. The legion was made up of ten cohorts, each of which contained three maniples; the maniple comprised two centuriae. There were also many auxiliaries and allied troops.

When the Empire was at its height, with a population 80 million strong, the army numbered only four hundred thousand men, and was therefore obliged to undertake difficult and dangerous forced marches to meet local emergencies. To avoid these constant moves, the Romans engaged local recruits. Gradually, regional armies emerged in Brittany, the Rhineland, the Danube, Spain, Africa, and the East, each increasingly unlike the others.

The whole army was strictly hierarchical, with officers, non-commissioned officers, and 'other ranks' or enlisted men. The Emperor had a large general staff of comites, a word from which are derived both 'companion' and 'count'.

In many respects, the army symbolized Rome. Its soldiers learned discipline, effort, fighting spirit, and mutual solidarity: they spent years together, and came to know each other as comrades-in-arms. But they also shared – at least until the beginning of the third century AD – the moral strength of a patriotic spirit which was common to all ranks.

Countless specimens of Latin literature attest to that fact. One can only guess what a deep effect they had on national armies in the nineteenth century, imbued with both Roman ideals and patriotic feelings.

The Roman army of the Empire was not intended to be a destructive force. Its task was to defend the *limes*, or fortified frontier – 9,000 kilometres in the Rhineland, 2,700 on the Danube, 2,000 in the East, 2,500 in Africa. Everywhere, except at Carthage and vis-à-vis the Jews, whose communities were broken up, the Romans proved themselves tolerant provided that the peace was kept. They respected national differences: some people they assimilated; others lived separately under Roman protection.

Permanent administration

In the first century AD, the various cities of the Empire retained their ancient liberties. Each had its own regime and system of government, part of the variegated urban network of which the Empire was composed. But in the fourth century AD these liberties were lost, and many towns were ruined – this despite the provincial assemblies which could tell the Emperor of complaints against the local governor.

There is no need to describe in detail how the Roman administration evolved. Suffice it to say that the vocabulary of Roman institutions has survived, with modifications, to this day, especially (but not exclusively) in European languages descended from Latin. Examples include magistrate, governor, prefect, legate, city, province, senate, censure, and tribune.

Permanent taxes

Roman fiscal arrangements were equally remarkable. Rome became a huge financial centre, a unique capital market, and an importer from the provinces, which found themselves ruthlessly exploited – at least until the Empire was established. At that point, the financial system had to be changed to make it less one-sided. So vast an empire, with a paid army and a powerful administration, in any case needed an organized fiscal system.

Both direct and indirect taxes were levied. The former began with a land tax. Then, under Gaius Octavius Augustus, a first population census was organized: it was this that caused the parents of Jesus to travel to Bethlehem. A complete land survey was not finally achieved until the time of Trajan (AD 98–117). In addition to land tax, the Romans also levied a poll tax, and a capital tax of 5 per cent on inherited wealth.

The main indirect taxes were customs duties, levied not so much on the external frontier, since the Empire was largely self-sufficient, but at appropriate points on the internal movement of goods. There was also a tax on commercial transactions.

In principle, there were two central treasuries. The first, the aerarium or public fund, drew its revenue from taxes in Italy and the Senatorial provinces. The second, the fiscus or Imperial treasury, gradually came to absorb all the Empire's fiscal revenue.

There eventually appeared a 'Vice-Chancellor of the Exchequer' with a large staff of freedmen and slaves. In each province, there was a tax-gatherer or procurator fiscal, replacing the old system of taxfarming.

The family and the law

Unlike Jewish and Christian law, Roman law codified inequality. One of the chapters in Justinian's *Digest* set out the distinctions between different categories of men.

Slaves, captured in war or born of a slave woman, had no legal status. Their masters could get rid of them, beat them, or kill them. Slaves could not own property or go to law.

Foreigners were divided into Latins, who were allowed to marry Romans, and Nomads, who except in privileged circumstances were not.

Except for fathers of families, free men and women also lacked legal status. Sons could acquire it by founding a family. Women could not: they passed from the authority of a father, an uncle, or a cousin to that of their husband when their previous guardian died.

The traditional Roman family, in other words, was far more rigid than that of the Celts or the Teutons. Somewhat greater flexibility was introduced at the end of the Republican period – for instance, enfranchisement, a new form of marriage, which enabled women to keep their own property.

Absolute property rights

Roman law also recognized absolute rights to real estate – the so-called dominium ex jure quiritum, or 'dominion under Roman Law'. (The word 'domain' comes from the same root.) The Napoleonic Code in France bears traces of the same idea. In Rome, however, as in modern times, various categories of land were not subject to this type of ownership. These included common land and 'public' land conquered in war.

Roman law over the centuries

The ascendancy of Roman law throughout so much of Europe was due less to its content, which was uneven, cruel, and violent, than to the admirable precision of its concepts.

At first, in the West, Roman law was displaced by the various 'laws' of the Germanic invaders. In some cases, as in Italy and Spain, the two systems co-existed. The minority, of Germanic origin, applied their own laws, while the Latins and the Hispano-Latins followed Roman law. The Franks, similarly, kept to the Salic Law, in which the family rather than the individual was the important unit.

Throughout the high Middle Ages, in the words of Jacques Ellul, 'law was almost entirely a matter of custom: sophisticated, systematic law had disappeared.' In England, Roman law was never re-established, and the common law prevails to this day.

Elsewhere, there was a strange dichotomy. Judges continued to apply the law of custom: agreements were drawn up and published under the title 'customary'. But the universities, and official doctrine, adopted Canon law – that of the Church – and Roman law.

The Renaissance, at the end of the fifteenth century, brought with it a more scientific study of Roman law. This was a typically European phenomenon: one of its leading representatives was Jacques Cujas, born in Toulouse in 1522, and a teacher at Valence and Bourges until his death in 1590.

In the eighteenth century, German and Dutch scholars produced notable work on Roman law. In the nineteenth century, one of the most brilliant contributions was made by the German Friedrich Karl von Savigny, a professor at Berlin from 1818 to 1842, and then a minister in the Prussian government. Like Montesquieu, he believed that law should be studied historically; and his *History of Roman Law in the Middle Ages*, published in 1815, is still the best general work on that subject.

CIVIS ROMANUS SUM: CONSOLIDATION AND ASSIMILATION

In 31 BC Gaius Octavius defeated Marcus Antonius at the naval Battle of Actium and became unchallenged leader of the Roman world. This is not the place to summarize the subsequent history of Rome until AD 476, when its last Emperor Romulus Augustus was deposed by Odoacer the Goth, but in the fourth century AD, the conversion to Christianity of the Emperor Constantine marked a new turning-point in the story.

Res publica, not royalty

Although given the title Augustus in 27 BC, Octavius did not seek to revive Roman kingship, which had earned itself a bad name. But like all monarchs he hoped to re-establish the hereditary principle. He could not openly proclaim it. Instead, he associated, while he was still in charge, with his hoped-for hereditary successor.

There thus succeeded a series of dynasties: the Julio-Claudian, founded by Octavius; the Flavian; and the Antonine – Trajan, Hadrian, Antoninus Pius, Marcus Aurelius, and Marcus Antoninus or Commodus. These dynasties held sway throughout the second century AD, when the Roman Empire was at its height.

Imperial Rome added a number of conquests to the territories already occupied by the Republic and by Caesar, including the eastern part of Brittany, and England from the Solway Firth to the outskirts of Newcastle – a new frontier marked by Hadrian's Wall, but later pushed further north into Scotland, roughly from Glasgow to the Firth of Forth. In Germany, the Empire conquered the area between the Danube and the river Lahn.

But it was Trajan who enlarged the Empire to its fullest extent. In Europe alone he conquered Dacia (present-day Romania) between AD 101 and 107; and the mark of the Roman conquest remains in both the name and the Romanian language, despite all subsequent invasions.

The historian Léon Homo has drawn up a chronology of Hadrian's travels in the Empire which gives some idea of its enormous extent:

> Hadrian believed that, to govern the Empire well, the Emperor should visit all its regions in turn. In his person he embodied imperial unity: he could strengthen it by appearing in flesh and blood before its many and varied inhabitants. He therefore travelled as a head of state, with his court acting as a peripatetic capital, taking with him his advisers and senior administrators. He made four great journeys across the Empire, of which the longest – the second and the fourth – took five years each. In the year 117, shortly after being proclaimed Emperor, he crossed Asia Minor, entered Europe, slowly inspected the Danube frontier, spent some time in Dacia, and after a year's travelling reached Rome in the summer of 118. Three years later, in 121, he set off again, towards Gaul. He visited the provinces of Rhaetia and Noricum on the upper Danube, and Germania on the Rhine; he went to Britain, crossed Gaul to reach Spain and Mauritania, then travelled by sea to Asia Minor. After spending the winter of 125–6 in Athens, he returned to Rome via Sicily. During the summer of 128 he visited Africa. Finally, in that same year, he left on his fourth and last grand tour. He spent the winter of 128–9 in Athens, then went on to Asia Minor, Syria, Palmyra, Palestine, Arabia, and Egypt, where he lingered for some time, visiting the country. Setting sail for Athens, he went north via central Greece, Macedonia, Moesia, and Dacia, returning to Athens for a third winter in 132–3. In 133 the revolt in Judaea brought him back to the east; and the following year he returned to Rome. Hadrian enjoyed his journeys as a tourist and used them as an Emperor. He visited such famous monuments as the tomb of Alcibiades at Melissa or the colossus of Memnon at Thebes. In 126, in appalling weather, he climbed Mount Etna, and in 129 Mount Masios in Cappadocia, to see the sunrise. In Libya he hunted lions: in Athens, he was initiated into the mysteries of Eleusinia. As head of state he fought in Palestine against a Jewish revolt. He inspected the army at Lambessa, in North Africa; he reviewed the 3rd Augusta Legion and gave it general orders, largely preserved in inscription. He renewed the frontier defences on the Rhine and the Danube and in Dacia; in Britain, he built the Wall that bears his name. He undertook administration and rendered justice; he summoned provincial assemblies like that of Tarragona in Spain; he founded cities like Hadrianapolis (Adrianople or Edreneh) or 'Aelia Capitolina', the name he gave to Jerusalem; he put up

buildings like the Maison Carrée at Nîmes in honour of Plotinus, or the Olympieion (Hadrian's Arch), completing work begun by Peisistratos, in Athens, where he also built a library and aqueducts and the new district of Illissus east of the Acropolis. At Pelusium in Egypt he rebuilt Pompey's tomb. In 134, after his final return to Italy, he began to build the sumptuous villa at Tibur (Tivoli) where he spent his last years reliving the great travels that had occupied so much of his life.

After an interregnum in AD 193, Lucius Septimius Severus and his successors inherited an empire whose defences, already weak, they allowed to run down even more. The Roman army became overmighty, and Septimius Severus curbed the power of the Senate, which could otherwise have been a useful counterweight to the military. Riots became frequent in Rome; some of the legions mutinied; and the Severus dynasty ended in a period of military anarchy which continued for fifty years, until AD 285. So-called 'barbarians' invaded the Empire from many directions. Emperors proclaimed by the army were assassinated one after the other: the only exception was Valerian, whose fate it was to be captured by the Persian Sapor I, and to be kept a prisoner until his death. One index of these unhappy times was the amount of wealth hidden by its owners and never reclaimed: no other period of Roman history has yielded such treasure troves to classical archaeologists.

The invasions and palace revolutions ended only with the succession of Diocletian in AD 285, and with his decision to divide the Empire into four areas, establishing the rule of the Tetrarchy.

Assimilation

Rome's great endeavour, which never finally succeeded, was to assimilate into the Empire all the peoples that it conquered. Citizenship was extended from Rome to Latium, then to the whole of Italy, and finally further still. The Jewish Saul of Tarsus, who became the Apostle Paul, was a Roman citizen. In AD 212, the Edict of Caracalla finally conferred Roman citizenship on all the free men in the Empire.

The unity of the Empire was also reflected in its architecture and building. Roman roads with broad paving-stones; porticos; rows of columns; imitation Greek temples; amphitheatres – all are to be found throughout the Empire, from Jerash in Jordan to Alba Iulia in

Romania, not forgetting Nîmes and Arles in France, and Volubilis in Morocco.

Roman art of varying quality, it now seems, remained the dominant model until the tenth century, when Romanesque and Gothic began to appear.

Naturally, assimilation was patchy. The Latin language survived, in ever-changing popular forms, only in Gaul, Italy, the Iberian Peninsula, and far-off Dacia (Romania). In Britain, it gave way to Saxon in the sixth century, although the Norman Conquest of 1066 later reintroduced a huge Gallo-Latin vocabulary. Ireland, Norway, Sweden, and Denmark never felt the impact of Latin. Church Latin we shall consider later on.

THE ROMAN VISION OF EUROPE

The Roman conquest shifted the political centre of gravity of the Mediterranean world in a westerly direction, bringing it to the European city of Rome. By this time, knowledge of the world had made considerable progress, as can be seen from the work of contemporary geographers.

Strabo's Europe

Strabo, a Greek who settled in Rome, wrote his *Geographica* in the last years of the pre-Christian era. He gave in it a more detailed and accurate account of Europe than any of his predecessors, including Polybius. Pointing out its numerous promontories and that in shape it was 'the most irregular of the three continents', Strabo had the ingenious idea of giving an overall view. 'I must begin with Europe,' he wrote, 'both because it is varied in shape and admirably suited to the development of excellence in men and in governments, and because its resources have enabled it to help improve other continents.' The whole of it was habitable, he added, except for a small cold area north of Lake Maeotis (the Sea of Azov) and in the region of the Tanais (the river Don).

The habitable regions consisted of mountains and plains. In the former, people were naturally poor, but if they were well governed they became civilized.

For Strabo, the plains with their temperate climate were more welcoming, and their inhabitants were peaceful. He saw them as complementing the courageous warriors from the mountains. The men of peace being in the majority, they were able to dominate the whole region, as the Greeks, the Macedonians, and the Romans had done. 'And for this reason Europe is independent of other countries in both peace and war. It is rich in metals and livestock, and imports nothing but spices and precious stones.'

Europe, in Strabo's definition, included Iberia, Celtica (between the Pyrenees and the Rhine), and Brittany. In the east, it was divided by the Danube. On the left bank were the Germans, the Getae, the Tyregetae, the Bastarnae, and the Sarmatians; on the right bank were Thracia, Illyria, and Greece. Interestingly, the Romans 'hold almost all of Europe, except the part beyond the Ister and those which border the Ocean between the Rhine and the Tanaïs [the Don].' Strabo had practically no knowledge of Scandinavia (since he confused the Baltic with the Ocean) or of the huge plain which stretches between the lower Baltic and the Don. At the time when he was writing, moreover, Rome had enlarged its Empire far more in Europe than in Africa (where it then held little more than present-day Tunisia) or Asia (where its possessions included the west and north of Asia Minor and a part of Syria).

The Europe of Pliny the Elder

Pliny the Elder wrote his *Naturalis Historia* less than a century after Strabo. Its Books III and IV are devoted to Europe.

Pliny divided the world into three parts: Europe, Asia, and Africa. He knew little of the north-east, where after the Borysthenes and a few other peoples he lists the 'Nomads', then the 'Anthropophagi', and finally the 'Hyperboreans' – a fortunate nation on the edge of the world, where fabulous miracles take place.

Not until Xenophon Lampsacenus were the northern frontiers of Europe better defined, and 'Baltia' and 'Scandinavia' mentioned. The greatest of all classical geographers, Ptolemy, in the second half of the second century AD, showed further knowledge of Europe: but even he thought that Scandinavia was an island.

Geography, however, was not what underpinned the Roman conquest. The centre of the Empire was the Mediterranean; and, from a geopolitical point of view, unity around a sea made just as much sense as unity based on a large land mass. In any event, geography is not the sole determinant of human affairs. Accidents of history often play a greater part in the creation or decline of empires.

For several centuries, as Aymard says, the Roman conquest 'shaped the destiny of the Mediterranean world . . . a world which Rome itself created by conquering it.' Was it on account of the need to trade? Or to counter the threat which Hellenistic kingdoms presented to the Roman Republic? What role was played by the fascination that Cleopatra exerted upon Caesar and then Antony? Whatever the explanation, Rome occupied the southern coast of the Mediterranean rather than Germania, and the Near East rather than the lands to the north of the Danube. The only exception was Dacia; and even that was not conquered until Trajan's time.

Europe ignored in literature

At that time, then, 'Europe' as a political entity did not exist. Indeed, it was little mentioned. Caesar never used the word. Virgil referred to it now and then, but merely in passing; and the same is true of Cicero, Horace, Statius, Sallust, Tacitus, Appianus, and St Augustine.

ROMAN EUROPE: EAST AND WEST

How real, then, were the unity and solidarity of the Roman Empire at its height? How great were the tensions within it? And were there already signs of cleavage between East and West?

The answers are complex, and they vary with time. Under Augustus, the East had just been conquered, and the Westerners were to boast their superiority. This was the case with Virgil, for whom Aeneas symbolized not only the union of East and West but also Western supremacy. It was no accident that he fled westwards from Troy. Where was there to go in the East? A storm drove him to Africa; but Dido's charms were powerless to retain him there. It was in Europe that he settled; and his choice foreshadowed the Battle of Actium in which the West, led by Octavius, defeated the East and Antony.

A century later, unity had eclipsed diversity. Easterners were flocking to Rome, bringing with them religions which spread throughout the Empire. Trade was on an Imperial scale, carried by the galleys and on the Roman roads. The legions were not yet composed of local recruits; and, even when they were, they were often moved from one side of the Empire to another. Roman citizenship was broadened: Roman law, worked out by jurists of genius, was the same for all citizens from Syria to Brittany; and from AD 212 onwards that included all free men.

Most important of all, perhaps, the Empire was a network of cities, each enjoying absolute control of the surrounding countryside. It was they, more than the legions, that held the Empire together. They formed the basis of a centralized administration; and only when they declined did the Empire begin to lose cohesion.

From Syria to Gaul, from Spain to Tunisia, there were the same temples, porticos, aqueducts, and arenas. The Empire was bilingual: Greek and Latin were superimposed on local languages which for the most part could not compete.

Despite the serious crisis of the third century, moreover, the Empire remained in being for 400 years. It was not just an ephemeral result of conquest, but a deep human reality, and historically unique. Even the Spanish and Portuguese Empires, which actually imparted their own languages to the colonial possessions, survived only 300 years at most. And how long-lasting were the Empires of Britain and France?

The Europe of classical antiquity, then, lay athwart the Danube which cut it in two, with Romanitas in the south and barbaria to the north. The political world of antiquity was centred on the Mediterranean, involving Europe in the north and Africa in the south. No one questioned this historical reality. No one could have foreseen a gradual shift of focus whereby, after six centuries of convulsion, a new entity more like modern Europe would emerge in the ninth century AD. This new entity resulted from a double schism – between east and west, and between north and south. Both might never have occurred without the Roman Empire's dramatic decline and fall.

5
The First Four Centuries AD in the West

JUDAEO-CHRISTIAN INFLUENCE

Classical history and sacred history were for a long time treated as distinct – so much so that nineteenth-century textual critics would sometimes deny the reality of events in sacred history which classical history had ignored, including the very existence of Jesus Christ. Twentieth-century scholarship – notably the Dead Sea Scrolls, discovered in pottery hidden in desert caves in Palestine – has produced plenty of evidence to link the sacred and the profane. It is now beyond dispute that Jesus really existed. *The Historical Jesus*, indeed, is the title of a remarkable work by Gaalyah Cornfeld published in 1982.

We now know that with Abraham, who left Ur in Chaldea around 1800 BC, in the Bronze Age, there began the history of a 'holy people' which later took the name of Abraham's grandson. He, originally known as Jacob, was renamed Israel after having a fight with an angel in a dream. The word 'Israel' in fact means 'he who has fought with God'.

The Old Testament

The historical record of the worshippers of the unique deity Yahweh – a passionate race of often victorious conquerors, sometimes defeated but never tamed – is the Bible, Biblos, 'the Book'. It remains the Holy Scripture of the Israelites, Hebrews, or Jews, whose name derives from Juda, one of Jacob's sons. For Christians, it is the Old Testament.

Dispersed throughout Europe and Africa, notably after Titus had conquered and sacked rebel Jerusalem in the year AD 70, the Jews of the diaspora, like the Christians, were frequently persecuted. Yet for the past 2,000 years their influence on Europe has been both direct and profound. Indirectly, moreover, through Christianity,

Jewish influence has helped to form a key element in the European heritage.

The New Testament

Christianity was founded in Palestine, as a development of the Judaic tradition, by a humble Nazareth carpenter named Jesus. Owing to an error of four years made in the sixth century by the Scythian monk Dionysius Exiguus, when calibrating the Christian and the Roman calendars, it seems likely that Jesus of Nazareth was actually born in the year AD 4. At Easter in the year AD 28 he was baptized in the River Jordan by his cousin John (the Baptist); and after three years spent preaching he was crucified, probably in April in the year AD 30, by order of the Roman procurator Pontius Pilate, under pressure from Jewish notabilities. Palestine had been part of the Roman Empire since its conquest and annexation by Pompey in 64 BC.

The four Gospels ('good news') which recount the life of Jesus, as well as the Epistles of St Paul, assert that on the third day after the Crucifixion he rose from the dead and appeared several times to the 'Apostles' and 'disciples' who had been his followers. Matthew, one of the four authors of the Gospels, declared that Jesus appeared to them on a mountain in Galilee and said: 'Go ye therefore, and teach all nations, baptizing them in the name of the Father, and of the Son, and of the Holy Ghost: Teaching them to observe all things whatsoever I have commanded you: and, lo, I am with you always, even unto the end of the world. Amen.' These words completed the teaching of the 'Christ', the anointed, a Greek translation of the Hebrew 'Messiah', saviour of the chosen people. They were in effect the founding charter of a society which has remained vigorous for 2,000 years: the Christian Church.

At first it was a modest sect, whose beginnings are described in the Acts of the Apostles, and whose first recruits were drawn only from the Jews. But a fundamental change occurred when an intellectual, a learned teacher of the Holy Scriptures, was converted on the road to Damascus. He was a Roman citizen, a devout Jew who until then had persecuted Christians. His name, of course, was Saul of Tarsus, and he took the name of Paul. A serious thinker and writer, he was the author of fourteen Epistles, and a tireless preacher and organizer. He believed that the Gospel message was addressed to all humankind, including the 'pagans', whom Latin translations of the Bible called 'Gentiles'.

Paul's central idea was to replace the meticulous rituals practised by certain Jews with the precepts taught by Jesus: to love one another, and to hope for eternal life.

Gradually, as we shall see, Christianity conquered the Roman Empire and spread further afield.

Dogma and mysteries

One essential feature of Christianity still deeply affects all westerners, whether they are believers or not. That is its distinction between dogma – the truth which Christians must accept by faith – and ethics – the precepts which they must follow in their works. At the heart of Christian dogma lie the mysteries of the Trinity, the Incarnation, and Redemption.

Western art and iconography – in sculpture, painting, stained glass, etc. – has drawn much of its inspiration from Christianity and from the Jewish Bible (the Old Testament) and the Christian New Testament. The Garden of Eden and the Serpent, Noah's Ark, Moses receiving the Tablets of the Law, the Annunciation, the Baptism of Christ, the Passion and the Resurrection – all are part of our daily surroundings, or at least of those to be found in hundreds of thousands of Western churches. We live in this world of myth and mystery – biblical, Christian, and also pagan, i.e. Greco-Roman: we are surrounded by Christian rites, ceremonies, emblems, robes, and symbols.

The deeply human nature of Christianity, and the ideals which it set up against the Roman worship of 'gods' whose weaknesses were all too close to those of mortals, gradually attracted multitudes of ardent followers. Its sexual ethics, formally strict but in practice forgiving, transformed not only society but also economic affairs. True, Christianity could not put a sudden end to slavery and war; but at least it sought to moderate their effects. Above all, piety or remorse led many of the rich to bestow part of their wealth on Christian churches, making them rich in their turn. Not all the recipients, however, used the proceeds in the interests of the faith or of the poor.

Heretical views of God the Son

The complexity of Christian dogma, notably as regards the Trinity and the Incarnation, gave rise to much debate and a number of 'heresies', to which the Eastern Church was far more prone than that in the West. Arianism, for example, held that Jesus was only a man: beginning in the fourth century AD, it persisted until the seventh. Nestorianism claimed that Jesus had not only two natures, but two persons – human and divine. It spread in Chaldea, Persia, and India, where traces of it still remain; and it was certainly present in China when Marco Polo travelled there in the thirteenth century. Equally, in the fifth century, the rival heresy of the monophysites maintained that Christ had but one nature – divine – and implicitly denied the humanity of Jesus. Monotheism, again, conceded that Jesus had two natures, but argued that he had but a single will.

All these Eastern heresies were remarkably subtle. There were fewer in the West, and those there were derived less often from questions of dogma than from ethics. So much intense debate may seem surprising today: but in ages when faith was intensely held and science had barely developed, intellectual effort was very largely concentrated on theology, the 'science of God', and great importance was attached to problems with which modern Christians are much less concerned.

The word 'heresy' is bound up with a principle which was rapidly accepted in the Latin Church but never so fully in the Greek: that is, the definition of dogmatic truth by the Communion of Churches, above all by the Church of Rome. Sacred texts, in other words, had to be interpreted according to a 'tradition' worked out by meetings of bishops, or Councils, of which the first was held in Nicea in AD 325, and in agreement with the Bishop of Rome.

St Peter and the Catholic Church

Bishops (epìscopi) were the successors of the Apostles, and the Bishop of Rome was the successor of St Peter, who (according to a tradition which archaeology has not challenged) died in Rome in AD 65 or 66. Jesus is said to have called this simple fisherman, whose name was Simon, 'Cephas' – an Aramaic word meaning 'rock' – and to have told him: 'You are Peter [πετρα], the rock, and on this rock I shall build my church.' Communion with Rome, accepted for some centuries by the East, was for the West the criterion of truth.

The word 'catholic' was also used, meaning in Greek 'universal'. St Ignatius the Martyr, who died in AD 107, wrote to the Church in Smyrna: 'Where Christ is, there is the Catholic Church.' Views that did not conform to those of the Roman Church were described as heretical.

The Church of Rome

St Irenaeus, who was born in Greece but became Bishop of Lyon at the end of the second century, wrote his book *Adversus haereses* ('Against heretics') between AD 175 and 189 to defend 'the tradition of the Apostles'. Every Church must be affiliated to them, and especially 'the greatest and most ancient, known to all, founded and established in Rome by the two great and glorious apostles Peter and Paul ... for it is with this Church, whose origins give it authority, that every Church must conform.'

As a long-term result of this claim, the Eastern Church – partly Greek and partly Slav – broke with Rome in the schism of the eleventh century, thereby limiting the sphere of influence of Roman Catholicism. In the sixteenth century, reacting against a series of moral and financial scandals, and against the intransigent authoritarianism of which the Church was accused, the 'Reformation' set up new Churches in which private conscience took the place of collective authority.

The schism of the eleventh century for a long time separated east and west. The Reformation, which barely touched the Greek Church, divided the Latin west into north and south.

THE EXPANSION OF CHRISTIANITY IN THE WEST

Why did the small groups that arose around the Apostles and disciples of Jesus spread throughout the Roman Empire and beyond, to the point at which, in the fourth century, the emperors themselves were converted?

Men and women do not pursue only their material interests. From the rich and prominent, Christianity demanded sacrifice. And history shows that it was as successful in the Imperial Palace and among the Emperor's own family as among the ragged crowds of Rome and other large towns.

It offered, essentially, a means of satisfying the aspiration to higher things. This was perhaps the central contribution made by Paul of Tarsus. But the Empire itself provided the means whereby small groups developed into larger communities and spread their influence far and wide, wherever Roman conquest and administration led. Having permeated first the eastern part of the Empire, Christianity was fortunate in that its two greatest Apostles, Peter, head of the 'Church', and Paul, the first missionary, both came to the Imperial capital and were martyred there.

What was more, the Empire possessed an admirable network of roads which linked its cities. Transport was organized and generally safe. Primitive Christianity followed these highways and won over the towns.

The first Christians in the West

The Crucifixion took place around AD 30. When did it begin to impinge on pagan literature? Suetonius makes it clear that in the year AD 49 the Emperor Claudius still identified the Christians with the Jews, whom he decided to expel because, he said, 'a certain Chrestos' was inciting them to stir up trouble. In the years that followed, the number of Christians greatly increased, but most Romans still confused them with various Eastern sects engrossed in bloody or orgiastic rituals. In the year AD 64, having probably been responsible for the burning of Rome, the Emperor Nero found it convenient to blame the Christians. Tacitus described very vividly, in his Annals, the tortures under which so many Christians met their death:

> Human effort, princely largesse, religious expiation – none of these succeeded in silencing the rumour that the fire had been started by deliberate order. To quell the rumour, Nero found scapegoats, and inflicted the most refined torture on these people commonly known as Christians, and detested for their abominations. Their name is derived from Christ, who under Tiberius was put to death by the procurator Pontius Pilate. Suppressed at that time, this hateful superstition was spreading again, not only in Judaea, where the evil had originated, but in Rome itself, where all that is infamous and horrible collects and finds adherents. A start was made by arresting those who confessed their faith, then, with the help of what they revealed, countless others, guilty less of incendiarism than of hatred for the human race. Their punishment was made a public spectacle. Some, covered in animal skins, were savaged and eaten by dogs. Many, crucified by day, were burned at the end of it to light up the night. Nero had opened his gardens to accommodate these entertainments, and he organized a circus, mingling with the people in a driver's uniform at the reins of a chariot. And so, although these men may have been guilty

and deserved their fate, people's hearts were filled with compassion at the thought that the victims had perished not for the public good but to satisfy one man's cruelty.

Persecutions

A legal point of some importance was that Nero seems to have put the Christians to death for the sole crime of being Christians. What most worked against them, in fact, was their refusal to take part in the religious cult of the Emperor, which was the Empire's unifying force. Hence the series of sporadic and shifting persecutions which they suffered from the days of Nero to those of Diocletian in 303–5.

Were there many 'martyrs'? Some Christian authors claim that there were, and even tend to exaggerate their number. Such, for instance, are Tertullian in his *Apologeticus* of AD 197, Lactantius in *De mortibus persecutorum* (fourth century), and Eusebius of Caesarea, author of the *History of the Church from the Time of its Founder to the Year 323*.

There was more persecution in the East than in the West. Yet, even in the West and even in the reign of the philosopher Emperor Marcus Aurelius, martyrdoms continued, including those of St Pothinus and St Blandina in Gaul in 177. Tertullian's dictum, according to which martyrdom was the seed of Christianity, led to much self-sacrifice, but volunteer martyrs were frowned upon by the religious authorities and regarded as sectarian fanatics or even heretics.

High-profile Christians

It is hard to trace the progress of Christianity during its first two centuries. Its missionaries and propagandists are unknown to us: they met in secret, in underground chambers or 'catacombs', where a new form of art developed.

From the first century AD onwards, Christianity was well established in Rome. It developed rapidly in the East, in Greece, in Egypt, and in north Africa; but not in the Western parts of the Empire, in Spain, Gaul, and Brittany, and still less in so-called 'barbarian' lands like Ireland or Germany. One reason for the relative delay was that at this time the only liturgical language was Greek, which unlettered people did not understand. Not until the end of the fourth century did St Jerome, born in about 331 in Pannonia (present-day Hungary), undertake the immense task of learning Hebrew so as to translate the Bible directly into Latin. Despite a few errors of detail, his text was so remarkable that once it had been adopted as 'canonical' by the Council of Trent in the sixteenth century, the Western Church continued to use it, as the 'Vulgate', into the twentieth century.

Italy

One of the characteristics of the Church in the second and early third centuries was the very small number of bishoprics.

In Italy, apart from Rome, there were at first only Milan and Ravenna. In about AD 25 Aquileia was added then, a little later, Verona and Brescia. Further south, a number of bishoprics were established near Rome, at Ostia, Albano, Tivoli, and elsewhere. At the beginning of the third century, Naples and Capua acquired their own bishops.

A letter from Pope Cornelius to Fabius of Antioch provides some revealing figures for the city of Rome in the middle of the third century. Apart from the Pope, there were forty-six priests, seven deacons and seven sub-deacons, forty-two acolytes, fifty-two exorcists, readers, and porters, as well as 1,800 widows and poor – suggesting that the Christian population numbered about 40,000 people, against a total population of nearly a million. (There were 300,000 seats at the Circus Maximus and 50,000 at the Colosseum.) The fact that Cornelius was able to hold a synod of sixty bishops in the year 251 also shows how the Christian population of the towns was growing.

Gaul

In Gaul in the second century there seems to have been only one bishopric, at Lyon; and its bishops, St Pothinus and St Irenaeus, both came from the East. Soon, however, Tournus and Autun became bishoprics. Between AD 200 and 250, the episcopacy developed further in southern Gaul, in the area around Narbonne. The sixth-century historian Gregory of Tours described in his *Historia francorum* how in the year AD 230 seven bishops left Rome to found bishoprics at Tours, Arles, Narbonne, Toulouse, Clermont, and Limoges. In the third century, in fact, Gaul was missionary territory. Other bishoprics were established at Rheims, Trier, Vienne, Paris, Rouen, Sens, Soissons, Châlons, Bourges, and Bordeaux.

By about AD 325 there were twenty-eight bishoprics in Gaul, and by AD 375, fifty-four. Most of the later establishments were in the north-west and north-east, notably in Basle, Strasbourg, Worms, Speyer, and Mainz.

Great Britain

According to Tertullian, Christianity had reached Great Britain by the beginning of the third century. In the fourth, under Diocletian, there were a number of British martyrs. A further sign of Christian penetration was the presence at the Congress of Arles, in 314, of three British bishops, from London, Lincoln, and York.

Spain

Shortly before his death, St Paul very probably went to Spain; but there is no information about the spread of Christianity there before the middle of the third century. By that time, however, it is clear that the Church was firmly settled in the Iberian peninsula. Seaports were the main entry points, and here as elsewhere Christianity began in the towns.

Diocletian's persecutions, it is clear, affected Christians in Spain. The first Spanish Council of which there is a historical record – in Illiberis-Elvira (Granada) at the beginning of the fourth century – included one bishop from Galicia, two from Tarragona, eight from the Cartagena area, twenty-one from the Betic mountain area in the south, and three from Lusitania (present-day Portugal).

Slower conversion in the countryside

The main proof that conversion to Christianity came later in rural areas is the rarity of Christian inscriptions there. Many country-dwellers remained unconverted at the beginning of the fourth century. The word *paganus*, peasant, also came to mean 'pagan'. Only in Gaul, it seems, did Christianity certainly spread to the countryside in the fourth century. A former officer, St Martin, supported by the Bishop of Poitiers, founded a monastery at Ligugé. In 373 he became Bishop of Tours, and founded the monastery of Marmoutier, where a number of missionary preachers gathered. For these reasons, St Martin, who died in 397, became known as the Apostle of the Gauls. However, similar tasks were being undertaken everywhere. By the end of the fifth century, there remained only a few small pagan 'islands' in the countryside of Western Europe.

THE CHRISTIAN EMPIRE

After three centuries of danger, persecution, and secrecy, the Christians were understandably jubilant when the Roman emperors rallied to their faith. This could only have happened once there were enough converts among the population to exert some pressure from below. The conversion of the emperors was also, however, a personal matter; and it lasted for the best part of a century, between 313 and 395.

Diocletian (285–305): from security to persecution

The Emperor Diocletian restored an empire which had been ravaged by invasion and civil strife. Realizing that its sheer extent required that power be decentralized, he divided it first into two and then into four. This Tetrarchy enabled the frontiers to be strengthened and the rebels put down. The Empire seemed to be safe.

When the Tetrarchy began, the Christians saw no reason to fear it. Their numbers were growing, and their acts of worship were no longer conducted in such secrecy. A number of them held important posts in the administration and in the municipal and provincial magistrature. At the same time, however, certain administrative procedures involved pagan rituals, which Christian officials naturally found repugnant. So it was that at the Council of Elvira (now Granada) the Spanish churches tried to lay down what precisely their religion sanctioned or forbade. Diocletian, under pressure from the majority of officials who were still 'pagan', saw this as potentially subversive, and he issued a series of edicts against the Christians which led on to their persecution. They were dismissed from the Roman army, and their congregations were banned. The Emperor next decided to destroy their churches and their sacred books; then he banished them from public service and public honours. Their priests were required to make pagan sacrifices: if they refused, they were punished by death.

Diocletian's persecutions were especially violent in the East. In the

West, the areas worst affected were Italy, Spain, and the Danube provinces. There were many executions and many recantations, except in Brittany and Gaul.

Constantine

Diocletian's abdication in AD 305 led to a lengthy civil war. In 306, the ruler of Gaul and Brittany under the Tetrarchy, Constantius Chlorus, died, and his son Constantine was proclaimed 'Augustus' (Emperor) by his soldiers. He soon defeated his rivals. Tradition has it that at the battle of the Milvian bridge on the Tiber, a few miles upstream from Rome, Constantine saw the vision that led to his conversion to Christianity: a standard bearing a cross and the inscription *In hoc signo vinces* – 'By this sign thou shalt conquer'. In fact, the story may well be apocryphal. Constantine was not baptized until he was dying, in 337; and the ceremony was performed by an Arian priest. Much more significant was the series of measures in favour of the Christians which Constantine undertook in conjunction with his brother-in-law Licinius, who was co-ruler with him until he was ousted and defeated in 323. Collectively, these measures became known as the 'Edict of Milan' (313). They gave back to the Christians the right to practise their religion, and restored any possessions that had been confiscated. Later, it was decided the priests should be exempt from taxes; subsequently, ever stricter conditions were imposed on pagans. The year 313 has been called 'the first year the Church was at peace'. Persecution had not stopped the spread of Christianity: its martyrs had inspired pity and respect. Now persecution had given way to privilege. The tables were turned.

Church buildings were exempted from property tax, and the churches were allowed to receive legacies. The Lateran Palace, which belonged to Constantine's wife, was given to the Bishop of Rome. The Emperor's mother had churches built in Palestine, where at Bethlehem and Jerusalem they became centres of pilgrimage. The Christian monogram appeared on Roman coins. A new procedure for liberating slaves was instituted – 'liberation in the presence of the bishop'. The Sabbath was declared a day of rest.

A further decision by Constantine had profound importance for the future of Europe. This was to transform the old Greek city of Byzantium into a 'second Rome', Constantinople, where Constantine put up many new buildings, and which he dedicated to God in the year 330. The establishment of an eastern replica of Rome, in a key strategic position, involved in effect the creation of a potential rival, not only within the Empire, but also within the Church. Where there was potential rivalry, schism could not be ruled out.

The Western Council of Arles

As protector of the Christians, Constantine saw himself as their leader, superior even to the Pope. It was the Emperor, in fact, who initiated the Council of Arles in 314, putting the Imperial mail service at the disposal of the bishops, and paying their travelling expenses as well as those of the priests and servants who went with them. Forty-six bishops, all from the West, attended the Council. The decisions or 'canons' on which they agreed followed the lines of those reached at the Council of Elvira (Granada). In particular, they now authorized Christians to become civil servants, and excommunicated soldiers who disobeyed orders. The service of the state, that is, was no longer considered impious, because, in effect, Christianity had become the state religion. So much so that Constantine had his own children brought up as Christians, under the care of the writer Lactantius, who in his book *De mortibus persecutorum* had presented the deaths of the persecutors as terrifying instances of divine retribution. Constantine also chose Christians to be among his advisers, of whom the most important was the Bishop of Cordoba.

Julian

When Constantine died in 337, Christianity was well established but not invulnerable. A pagan reaction remained possible; and this is indeed what happened in the reign of Julian, who ruled from Paris between 361 and 363.

Being of philosophical bent, Julian believed that paganism presented the advantage of synthesizing very divergent doctrines into one which served to unite the Empire.

Christianity, on the other hand, was universal and cosmopolitan: in principle, it was no respecter of frontiers. Yet, despite Julian and despite a brief renewal of persecution, Christianity continued to progress.

Arianism

Arianism was a further threat. Arius was a fourth-century priest in Alexandria who held that Christ was not consubstantial with God the Father. At the Council of Nicea (325) Arius was accused of heresy, with the Emperor Constantine presiding over the court. The council condemned Arius and banished him to Illyria. Ten years later, the Emperor recalled him. Constantine, as has been seen, was baptized by an Arian; his third son belonged to the Arian sect; and Julian's successor protected it.

Not until the reign of Theodosius I in the last decade of the fourth century was the Empire definitively converted to orthodox Christianity. Born at Coca in Segovia, Theodosius briefly re-established the unity of the Empire; but his lasting achievement was not this but his defeat of the Arians and his consolidation of Christianity as the official religion.

The bishops and Western unity

The intellectual unity of the Western Church was expressed and furthered by its use of Latin, in which all the Western bishops wrote. The fourth century saw a great deal of theological debate, in which the bishops argued against Eastern and African heresies, and in particular Arianism, which threatened not only the East but also the less speculative West. These bishops included Ossius, from Cordoba; Gregory, from Elvira; Maximinus, from Trier; Hilary, from Poitiers; and Ambrose, Bishop of Milan, who refused to allow the Emperor Theodosius to enter his church until he did penance for his sins.

Augustine

Of all these early 'Fathers of the Church', the greatest was an African, Aurelius Augustinus, better known as St Augustine. He was born in AD 354 in Tagaste, a town in the province of Numidia, to a pagan father and a Christian mother, St Monica. In his *Confessions*, Augustine described how as a young man he led an unsaintly life. Well educated, he taught rhetoric at Tagaste, Carthage, and Milan; and it was in Milan that he met St Ambrose, who with St Monica's support converted him to Christianity. He was baptized at the age of thirty-two. Relinquishing his teaching career, he returned to Tagaste, gave all his possessions to the poor, and embarked on a life of prayer, fasting, and penitence. Ordained as a priest by the bishop of Hippo in Bone,

Augustine became Bishop of Hippo himself in 395. Augustine's energy was prodigious. He founded monasteries, preached, taught, helped the poor, organized Church Councils, and fought against heresy. He wrote extensively and very well. In addition to his *Confessions*, Augustine wrote *De Civitate Dei* (The City of God), begun in 413 and finished in about 426, as well as *De Opere Monachorum* (Of the Works of Monks), *The Seven Books on Baptism* and his fierce attack on Manichaeism, *Contra Faustum Manichaeum*, against Faustus of Milan, his old friend and associate. Not believing in free will, he came close to espousing 'predestination', the doctrine that the salvation or damnation of human beings is predetermined by the omniscience of God.

How deeply Augustine marked the Church is shown by two paradoxical examples of religious leaders who disputed its authority. One is that of Luther, the so-called 'Founder of Protestantism': he was an Augustinian monk. The other, a century later, is that of Jansenius, Bishop of Ypres and founder of the extremist school of Jansenism: he entitled his posthumous work of theology the *Augustinus*.

The Church grows rich

The spread of the Christian faith had a further consequence: a great flow of wealth to the Church. Gifts and legacies helped to support priests, build churches, and succour the poor and the sick. They also gave the Church considerable economic power.

THE INFLUENCE OF ECCLESIASTICAL GEOGRAPHY

The geographical development of Christianity throughout Europe, first in the towns and then in rural areas, followed the broad lines of the Roman Empire.

Rome and the Papacy

First came Rome, capital of the Empire – and later of its western part. The Bishop of Rome soon became known as the Pope.

Even when Rome lost its political role as centre of the civilized world, after its conquest by the Visigoths in the year 410, the Papacy – far from declining – actually increased its power. The fact that St Peter and St Paul had come to Rome and been martyred there had given the Church and the West a fundamental advantage, a basis for authority which Rome now asserted with ever greater force. A letter from Pope Siricius in 385 declared: 'The Apostle Peter lives on in person in the Bishop of Rome. If the Pope bears the weight of all those who need his support, he never doubts that the blessed Apostle Peter bears it with and in him, and that he protects the heir of his administration, the Bishop of the Apostolic See, who is invested with rights and duties which the other bishops do not share.'

At the beginning of the fifth century, Pope Innocent I (Papacy 401–17) was dealing with ecclesiastical questions throughout the Church's realms: in the east, in Illyricum, in Africa, but also and above all in the west – in Italy, Spain, and Gaul.

Letters reached him from bishops everywhere, seeking guidance on problems of dogma, discipline, and ethics. 'Who can fail to realize,' he wrote to one of them, 'that what Peter, the Prince of the Apostles, taught the Roman Church, and what it still observes, must be observed universally? Moreover, in all Italy, in Gaul, Spain, Africa, Sicily, and the islands, no one has founded a church save those whom the venerable Apostle Peter or one of his successors has made bishops.'

Fourth-century organization: Imperial and ecclesiastical

The Roman Empire was divided into provinces. According to the fifth-century *Notitia dignitatum* (list of senior offices), the hierarchy was as follows: the Eastern and Western Empires each had two prefectures; under these came dioceses; under these, the provinces; and under these, the civitates or city-states.

The two prefectures of the Western Empire were those of the Gauls and of Italy. The prefecture of the Gauls, with its capital at Trier, was composed of three dioceses – Spain, Gaul, and Brittany. The prefecture of Italy, with its capital in Milan, had the dioceses of Italy, Rome, and Africa.

The Church based its geographical organization on that of the Empire. Each city had its bishop, assisted by suffragan bishops responsible for the surrounding rural areas. Each province had its 'metropolitan'. In Gaul, these were located in Mainz, Cologne, Trier, Rheims, Besançon,

Lyon, Rouen, Tours, Sens, Bourges, Bordeaux, Auch, Narbonne, Aix, Vienne, Embrun, and Moutiers. The word 'diocese' was not yet used to denote a bishop's territory.

The basic unit, then, was the civitas. Originally denoting an area, it gradually came to be applied to the main city. Thus Lutetia, the civitas of the Parisii, became Paris; the civitas of the Londoners became London; that of the Trevesi became Trôves or Trier.

In the East, meanwhile, there were four Patriarchs, in Antioch, Alexandria, Jerusalem, and Constantinople – whereas the Western Church had at its head only the Bishop of Rome.

Parishes

Still more important for Europe were its parishes. As well as those parts of the towns which were administered by priests, the countryside had in the sixth and seventh centuries a growing network of parishes where priests had the tasks of baptizing, preaching, and celebrating Mass. There were even urban and rural 'archpriests'. To begin with, there was often a church for every 'villa'; but many of these disappeared, to be replaced by villages, in which there was one church for every 'vicus' or borough. Their priests or presbyters were responsible to the bishops.

By the seventh century, the churches established by large landowners or potentes were regarded by their founders as personal property, adding value to their 'villas'.

In countries which had never been part of the Roman Empire, the bishops usually occupied cities with fortifications, such as Magdeburg or Hamburg. At that time, these were called civitates, while fortified cities without bishops were known as castri, or camps. Each episcopal city had a cathedral church, the names of whose patron saints have left lasting traces on the nomenclature of Western Europe.

In some countries, however, the influence of the Roman Empire's organization was less marked. One such instance is Spain, deeply affected by the Muslim conquest.

But the parish, throughout most of Europe, was the key unit – as, in many respects, it remains. By the ninth century, Gaul and Italy were covered with a close network of country churches. Still more were built in the tenth and eleventh centuries. In Germany, there were comparatively few in the ninth century, but forest-clearing and missionary activity greatly increased their number in the tenth. The eleventh century saw similar growth in Bohemia, Poland, and Hungary.

The influence of parish churches on Europe was immense. In particular, they formed the basis of the communes and local authorities of which our countries are made up. With their registers of baptism, marriage, and burial they were the origin of civic identity or citizenship, secularized as it has since become. Every parish, from Poland to Portugal, from Ireland to Sicily, from Norway to Czechoslovakia, has its church or its churches. We live in a social structure profoundly marked by the parish and the commune.

CONCLUSION

For two millennia, people of the Jewish faith championed a monotheistic religion. Judaism (from Juda, son of Joseph) has continued to exert a deep and direct influence, especially on Europeans.

After the death of one Jewish 'prophet', Jesus of Nazareth, crucified under the procurator Pontius Pilate in about AD 30, his Apostles and disciples believed that he had risen from the dead. Breaking with the Jewish Church, they formed what began as a small sect, whose main propagandist and theologian was Saul, later Paul, of Tarsus in Asia Minor, a Jew who was also a Roman citizen.

Within 300 years this small sect, the Christian Church, whose Latin name *ecclesia* meant 'assembly', had converted the Roman Empire, had reached out beyond its frontiers with the aim of becoming universal, i.e. 'catholic', and in the process had begun to transform Europe.

6

The Germanic Age

THE GERMANS REACH EUROPE

Germans and Celts

Just as the Celts had lived alongside the Romans before being conquered by them (except in Ireland and northern Scotland), so the Germans had already become a concern for the Romans in the age of Augustus. The very word 'German' made its appearance in the first century BC, in the writings of the Greek historian and Stoic philosopher Poseidonius.

Between 113 and 101 BC, the Cimbrians and Teutons left Jutland and the lower basin of the Elbe and invaded the Po Valley, only to be defeated by Marius at Aix-en-Provence and Vercelli. Very possibly, they were not Germans but Celts: their leaders certainly bore Celtic names. The uncertainty or confusion may well be due to Julius Caesar, who during the conquest of Gaul used the word Germani to describe the very Celtic-influenced tribes on the left and right banks of the Rhine. It also seems likely that certain Celtic and Germanic dialects were similar to each other, and after Caesar's conquest of Gaul, a number of Gauls settled in what is now Germany.

Germans and Romans

Not all those whom the Romans called Germani gave themselves any collective name. The word Alemanni (also 'Alamanni' or 'Alamans') from which the French *allemand* is derived, meant 'all men' in Old German, and probably referred to a grouping of several tribes.

Deutsch is a word which appeared only in the eighth century AD, denoting 'the people' on the European mainland as distinct from the

British Isles. Linguistically, the tribes in question may be classified as follows:

1. those using Nordic or Scandinavian dialects, from which today's Scandinavian languages are derived;
2. those speaking Estic dialects – the Goths, the Burgundians, and the Vandals;
3. those whose dialects were Westic – the Francs, the Alamans, the Bavarians, the Lombards, the Angles, the Saxons, and the Frisians; from these dialects came modern German, Dutch, and English.

These distinctions are perforce only approximate. Thus, in the Bronze Age, a pre-Germanic people from southern Scandinavia (where linguists have never been able to trace any 'pre-Germanic' substratum) settled between the Oder and the Weser Rivers, then in Pomerania, until in about 800 BC they reached as far as Westphalia in the west and the Vistula in the east. But the expansion of the Celts for a long time prevented their penetrating present-day south Germany and Central Europe.

The Roman frontier and the *limes*

The peoples whose advance Caesar halted on the Rhine in 58–1 BC in their turn barred the way to the Romans, and then invaded the Empire themselves. The Roman *limes* (cf. 'limit') was militarily effective as a fortified barrier; but it could not prevent the intermingling of peoples and the consequent infiltration of the Empire. In the first and second centuries AD, up to the time of Marcus Aurelius, the situation remained calm. But under Augustus, as has been seen, the Germans defeated the legions with which Varus had been sent to conquer the whole territory as far as the Elbe. The Romans were confined to a triangle stretching from the Lahn to the Danube and covering the Black Forest and the Swabian Jura.

Yet Roman influence continued in times of peace. Germans served as mercenaries in the Roman armies. The more prosperous among them acquired Latin culture and imitated Roman luxury. Even the Scandinavians were attracted by this new style of life, and trade routes went as far as Jutland to supply the Empire with amber.

In the second century AD, an alphabetic form of writing – runes – emerged in Denmark. It continued to be practised until the seventh century in Germany proper, until the ninth century in Britain, and until the fifteenth century in Scandinavia. Its literary role, however, remained modest.

Second- and third-century invasions in the Western Empire

Here there were two successive waves of invasion by land, and one by sea. The first land invasion began in AD 166, when the Marcomanni and the Quadi entered Venetia. In the third century, the Germans reached the left bank of the Rhine after breaching the *limes* in AD 254. They then invaded Gaul. In 260 and 270, the Alemanni entered Italy. The Goths attacked Greece and Asia Minor. At the end of the third century, Diocletian at last managed by brute force to put an end to these constant invasions and the suffering and disorder they had caused.

The fifth- and sixth-century invasions: the Huns

The second wave of invasion by land could not be stopped, but continued throughout the fourth and fifth centuries. It occurred under very heavy pressure from a non-Germanic people, the Huns, who were nomadic inhabitants of the steppes bordering the Black Sea.

They directed their attack against the Goths in the Ukraine. The Roman Empire, especially in the west, contemplated an alliance with them against the Germans at a time when Goths, Franks, and Burgundians were invading Italy and Gaul.

Who were the Huns? Were they Mongols? Probably not. At one time, they were identified with the white-skinned race whom the Chinese called Hioung-Nou, but this hypothesis has been refuted. Were the Huns 'pre-Turks'? Even that is by no means certain. Whatever their origin, they seemed to Westerners, both inside and outside the Empire, a race of appalling barbarians who lived in the saddle, ate raw meat, and slaughtered old people.

In about AD 425 the Huns settled in Pannonia (present-day Hungary). Their hereditary monarchs, of whom Attila is the most famous, were supported by a warlike aristocracy.

Born in 395, Attila attained power in 434. He negotiated with the Gaul Aetius, ruler of much of the West, and then in 451 suddenly ceased operations in the East and pressed towards the Rhine, crossing it near Metz. He ravaged Metz and Belgium before reaching Orléans.

Aetius, with an army composed of Franks, Burgundians, Gauls, and Visigoths, managed to defeat Attila in the Catalaunian Fields in Champagne. Then, in 452, Attila invaded northern Italy, and had an audience with Pope Leo I. After his death in 453, however, disputes over his succession weakened the Huns, and they disappeared from history after 474.

Brutal though they were, the invasions by the Huns were far less significant than those by the Germans in the fifth and sixth centuries. Some of these took the form of short-lived raids; others involved systematic conquest, slowly penetrating and occupying large areas wrested from the Romans or the Celts.

Vandals and Alans

The Alans crossed the Rhine in 406, and entered Spain in 409. In 414 they appeared in the Rhône Valley. But they were soon defeated by the Visigoths in Spain and by the Vandals in Spain and Africa. The King of the Vandals even bore the double title of rex Vandalorum et Alanorum.

The Goths

The Goths may have originated in Scandinavia, where two peoples bore similar names: the Gutar from the island of Gothard, and the Götar from Götaland in the southern part of ancient Sweden. Pliny and Tacitus knew of their existence, and they enjoyed great prestige among the Germans.

Driven out by the Huns, the Goths settled as refugees in Thracia, inside the Empire. The Ostrogoths or Goths from the East (also known as 'brilliant' Goths), and the Visigoths from the West (also known as 'wise' Goths) were converted to Christianity from 341 onwards by the Arian bishop Ulfila, who was proficient in their language.

The Visigoths, after threatening Constantinople in 378 and 395, made for northern Italy under their leader Alaric. Heading towards Rome, he succeeded in blockading Ravenna, despite its protective surrounding of marshes. On 24 August 410, Alaric entered Rome and sacked the city for three days.

Alaric died at the end of the same year. His successor Athaulf entered Gaul, settling in Bordeaux, Toulouse, and Narbonne (where the Goths remained for three centuries).

Athaulf married a captive, Galla Placidia, whose tomb at Ravenna is perhaps the greatest mosaic masterpiece in the world.

Having conquered Aquitaine, the Visigoths went on into Spain, but failed to cross the Straits of Gibraltar. From time to time they served Rome. The culminating period of their 'Kingdom of Toulouse' was the reign of Euric, from 466 to 484. His territory stretched as far as Auvergne in the north, and he strengthened his hold on Spain. He was much influenced by Latin literature.

After Euric's death, the Franks drove the Visigoths out of France, with the exception of Narbonne, and confined them to Spain.

The Visigoths in Spain

The Visigoths did not occupy the whole of the Iberian peninsula. The Vandals, another Germanic group, entered Africa in 418, and the Suevi (from which the name 'Swabia' is derived), who had crossed the Rhine in 406, entered Spain in 409, occupying part of the north-west, and making inroads to the south until they were finally defeated in 585.

The Visigoths had established their capital in Toledo. Their king, Atanagildoe, found himself fighting the troops of the eastern Emperor Justinian, who was trying to re-establish the Empire as a single whole. Justinian's attempt succeeded in Italy and Africa; but he was unable to overcome the Burgundians who were defending Gaul. In 551, however, his Byzantine troops landed in southern Spain and established footholds in the ancient provinces of Betica and Cartagena, between the mouths of the rivers Guadalquivir and Jucar, as well as at Cape St Vincent in southern Portugal.

Not until 628 were the Visigoths finally able to expel the Byzantines from Spain. This was the beginning of ninety years of Visigoth domination of the whole country, with the exception of the Basque area in the north.

The Visigoths, who numbered some three hundred thousand, were on reasonably good terms with the Hispano-Romans; and relations improved further at the Council of Toledo in 589, when the Visigoth King Recared abandoned Arianism for Roman Catholicism, and later when Bishop Isidore of Seville formally praised 'the nation of the

Goths'. Two thirds of the territory was held by the Visigoths, one third by the Hispano-Romans. A state was established, with a Royal Court, the *aula regia*, and its own provinces and *civitates*.

However, even before the Muslim conquest of 711, the kingdom fell into the hands of squabbling nobles, and its unity was lost.

The Ostrogoths in Italy

The exploits of the Ostrogoths were shorter-lived than those of the Visigoths but more brilliant. At the time of the Battle of Adrianople in 378, some of the Ostrogoths were living in Pannonia (Hungary) under the protection of the Huns. Others were in the Balkans; their allegiance was to the Empire in the East. When the power of the Huns began to weaken, the Goths in Pannonia drew closer to the Empire. A nephew of their King Theodoric, taken hostage in the East, spent nine years in Constantinople and then, in 473, became King of the Ostrogoths: he is known to history as Theodoric the Great. He seized the Balkans at the same time as the childless Romulus Augustulus, the last Western Roman Emperor, was deposed in 476 by Odoacer, king of a Germanic tribe, the Heruli. The Emperor in the East thereupon sought to use Theodoric against Odoacer. Starting from present-day Bulgaria with a mixed army, Theodoric entered Italy; and after four years he managed to have Odoacer and his family killed.

Theodoric thus became ruler of Italy, his exploits celebrated by his minister–writer Cassiodorus. He divided the administration of the country into two separate but interdependent parts, Gothic and Roman. He was accepted as ruler by the citizens of Rome, and had no hesitation in calling the Emperors of the past *majores nostri*, 'our ancestors'.

Theodoric the Great died in 526. His tomb is one of Ravenna's greatest historical monuments.

The Burgundians

The first traces of the Burgundians are found in the Baltic and around the Vistula; but their roots may well have been in Scandinavia, as is suggested by linguistic analogy with Borgund in Norway, on the Sognefjord, and with the Danish island of Bornholm, derived from 'Borgundarholm'.

In the third century AD they pressed westwards, entering the Empire sometime after the year 400. In 406, pressure from a number of Germanic tribes drove them across the Rhine, below Coblenz. They remained in the Rhineland for thirty years; then, forced back by the Alemanni, they obtained permission from Rome to settle around what is now Geneva, in 'Sapandia', from which the name 'Savoy' may be derived. Having helped the Romans to fight the Huns and the Suevi, they were rewarded by being allowed to spread from around Lyon to the Alpes Maritimes in the south of France. The Burgundian king was enthroned in Lyon, while his heir settled in Geneva. Their good relations with Rome enabled the Burgundians to live in comparative peace for many years. Eventually, however, they were attacked in the south by the Goths and in the north by the Franks, who finally occupied the whole of Burgundy.

The Alemanni

In the fourth century, the Alemanni made further efforts to drive westwards towards Alsace and southwards beyond Milan; and in the fifth, they played an important part in the Germanic incursion of 406. Their main enemies were the Franks, whose leader Clovis finally crushed them at the Battle of Tolbiac in 506. Tradition has it that Clovis gave thanks for this victory by becoming a Christian convert in Rheims. Nevertheless, the Alemanni survived in the Swiss plain and in the Jura around Besançon. They also remained pagan.

From 536 onwards, they fell under the sway of a Frankish duke from Austrasia, the eastern part of the Frankish kingdom; and in the eighth century they were gradually absorbed among the miscellaneous Germanic tribes to the east of the Rhine.

The Bavarians

The first mention of the Bavarians occurs in 551, by which date they were already settled in present-day Bavaria: they have never left it, except to cross the Alps and invade the Trentino–Alto Adige area on the borders of Austria and Italy. The Dukes of Bavaria remained independent until in 788 Charlemagne annexed Bavaria as part of the Frankish kingdom.

The Franks

The Franks, alone of all the Germanic tribes save the Visigoths, succeeded in establishing a kingdom which endured. They have been called the main beneficiaries of the barbarian migrations. Their earliest appearances in the written record are in 241 and 257. In 286, they were reported as arriving by sea. Although they later gave their name to the French, their language turned into Dutch, while many of them, to the east of the Rhine, were the ancestors of present-day Germans. In fact, they were made up of a number of small tribes from the lower Rhine area, originally living near the Roman frontier in the region of Cologne. The most important group were the Salian Franks, famous for their 'Salic Law', which in France came later to be cited as excluding succession through the female line.

Another important body of Franks occupied Francia rivensis, which in 475–80 stretched on both sides of the Rhine from Mainz to Nijmegen and on the Moselle from Toul to Coblenz.

Some of the Frankish kings are known to us through the uncertain medium of Gregory of Tours, writing in the seventh century. Childeric, the father of Clovis, appeared on the scene in 457; Merwig, Childeric's father and the 'founder' of the Merovingian dynasty, which lasted two and a half centuries, may be an apocryphal figure.

The Franks progressed both by 'colonizing' the Roman legions, which they joined in large numbers, and by settling peacefully on sparsely populated land. In the year 324, in the reign of Constantine, the first Frank became a senior officer in the Roman army. But although they fought alongside the Romans, the Franks did not take part in the great rout of 406. Instead, they occupied the Rhineland and Westphalia and other areas on the crumbling frontiers of the Empire.

Clovis and his conquests

Born in about the year 465, Clovis came to his modest 'throne' around 481 – and suddenly gave the Franks extraordinary notoriety and power.

At Clovis's accession, the southern limit of Frankish power was well to the north of the 49th parallel, not even reaching as far as a line drawn between Verdun and Worms. Clovis pushed south-westward, conquering a large area between the Seine and the Loire as far as Orléans, Tours, and Nantes, but also occupying the southern part of the Vosges. He then turned eastwards against the Thuringians and the Alemanni, and south against other Alemanni and the Burgundians.

When he was converted to Christianity, Clovis (unlike other Goths) did not adopt Arianism. This secured him support from the Roman Papacy, as well as the allegiance of his Gallo-Roman Christian subjects.

His great and decisive success came at the end of his life, when he crushed the Visigoths at Vouillé, south of Tours, with the aid of his cousin the King of Cologne. He thereupon occupied both Bordeaux and Toulouse. Nevertheless, two great areas of Western Europe still remained under domination by various Gothic tribes: Spain, and Italy (where Theodoric ruled until 526). They were linked by a narrow southern corridor over the Pyrenees to Narbonne (which long remained a great Visigothic centre), across to the Rhône and through Provence to the Alps.

Clovis retained in his kingdom the Germanic administrative structure. In the south of his realm there was close cooperation between the Germans and the Roman senatorial nobility. The latter comprised some 3,000 families, many of them refugees from northern towns. To judge from the names in the records, senior officials in northern Gaul, including bishops, were mostly Germans, while in the south they seem to have been Gallo-Romans who had accepted the new regime. Not until the eighth century were the two elements completely fused.

Frankish conquests after Clovis

The Franks continued their conquests after the death of Clovis in 511. In 533–4 they annexed the kingdom of Burgundy, and in 537 they overran Provence. Only the Narbonne coastal area remained in the hands of the Visigoths, while in the far west, lower Brittany also remained independent.

The Franks also made great inroads towards the east. In about 530, they conquered Thuringia, which became a ducal protectorate, although it remained pagan. Clovis had already taken the Rhineland from the Alemanni; and the rest of their territory was won by his grandson Theodebert, the King of Metz, in 539–55. Alsace and the Palatinate were then converted to Christianity, but not Germany beyond the Rhine. The Franks did however succeed from time to time in exacting tribute – from the Saxons in the north, from Bavaria in the south, and even from the Lombards.

Partial reconquest by Byzantium

Further turmoil was caused in the sixth century when the Eastern Emperor Justinian reconquered Africa, Italy, and south-eastern Spain. Italy in particular was laid waste. But around the year 560 the reconquest faltered, and Byzantium was driven on to the defensive. This gave an opportunity to another Germanic invading force, the Lombards, who in 568 left Pannonia, to be replaced by the Avars from the steppes to the north of the Black Sea.

The Lombards

The Lombard invasion was the last and most destructive of all.

The Lombards may well have originated in Scandinavia. In Italy, they owed their success to the ability of a number of their kings. One of them, who reigned from 510 to 540, married his daughters to Merovingian kings; another formed an alliance with the Emperor Justinian. Their greatest ruler was Alboin. It was he who in 568 took the original decision to leave Pannonia and invade Italy.

The subsequent occupation of Pannonia by the Avars cut communications between the Baltic and the Adriatic, assisting Slav incursions into the Baltic area, and isolating Scandinavia from the Mediterranean (and its gold) until the advent of the Vikings.

Alboin conquered the greater part of the Po Valley. Milan was reduced to ruins. He took three years to subdue Pavia, where he installed his capital after first establishing it in Verona. Then, encircling the Byzantine possessions, which in about 574 extended across the Appennines from Mantua to Ravenna, Rimini, and Rome, the Lombards invaded Tuscany and Latium. Their wars with the Byzantines continued for 100 years. The ensuing anarchy was appalling. For a time, Italy became 'Langobardia'. The province of Ravenna, which remained under Byzantine rule, took the name of 'Romagna' in the eighth century – and has kept it to this day. It was only in 770 that Charlemagne destroyed the Lombard kingdom.

GERMANIC MIGRATION BY SEA

Roman Britain acted as a pole of attraction for the far more savage tribes that lived to the west and north – the Picts and Scots – but it also drew to it invaders from the north-western corner of continental Europe – the Netherlands, north Germany, and southern Scandinavia, notably the coast of Jutland, southern Sweden, and the Norwegian coast.

These migrations began in the third century with the Heruli, little-known predecessors of the Vikings. Some went east; others attacked Gaul in 287 and 409. In about 456 they reached Spain and pillaged the north and north-western coasts, then the south in 459. After trying to ally themselves with the Visigoths against the Franks, they left no further trace.

They were followed by the Angles, Saxons, Frisians, and Jutes. The Angles or Anglii first appear in the records as part of a large group of tribes in the Baltic area of Germany, to the south of Jutland. The Saxons were mentioned by Ptolemy soon afterwards: they occupied north-west Germany, on the North Sea near the mouth of the Weser. The Frisians had been known since the first century; but the Jutes were much more obscure, and are not recorded until the end of the third century.

Why did these various people embark on maritime or amphibious expeditions, facing the double danger of the sea and of human enemies? One suggested explanation is a change in sea level as the retreat of the glaciers caused new parts of the land to emerge.

Another suggestion is progress in ship-building and navigation. The only boat of the period to have been discovered so far was excavated at Nydam in south Jutland between 1859 and 1863: it dates from AD 300–400, and can be seen in the Gottorp Museum. Twenty-three metres long, it is built of oak planks held together with iron nails, with a small keel and no mast; it was clearly propelled by oars, and was suitable only for coastal navigation or short passages on the open sea. The age of the Vikings still lay ahead.

Here again it seems likely that migration was the result of pressure from invaders who entered the emigrants' homelands.

Angles, Saxons, Jutes, and Frisians

While the Saxons laid waste the coasts and islands of the North Sea, the Channel, and the Atlantic as far south as the Gironde, a kind of coastal *limes*, the so-called *litus saxonicum* or 'Saxon littoral', was built in Britain at the end of the third century. Everywhere, the inhabitants took to the forests, leaving behind them a quantity of buried treasure. The Angles, the Frisians, and the Jutes invaded Britain from the east and the south. The Frisians, meanwhile, settled between the Ems and the Weser, and then in the ninth century between the Elbe and the Eider, replacing the Saxons. A few Frisians actually followed the Saxons to Britain: their respective languages were similar.

The Jutes remain more mysterious. In his *Ecclesiastical History*, the Venerable Bede (673–735) declared that the Jutes had colonized Kent, the Isle of Wight, and part of Hampshire. But there are no traces there of their language, as spoken in Jutland.

The Angles, who originated in eastern Denmark, had a language and a civilization similar to those of the Saxons. When they left, Denmark became the home of those Jutes who had not emigrated, of Danes, Swedes, and Frisians, and also of some non-Germanic Slavs. The town of Angelholm on the west coast of Sweden is a reminder of the Angles' presence.

Invasion from the east

The Anglo-Saxons invaded Britain from the east. They first arrived, no doubt, as mercenaries in the Roman armies fighting the Picts and Scots. But the real wave of immigration began between AD 430 and 440, and only became a mass movement from the year 500 onwards. The result was not only to remove Britain from the Roman Empire, but also, from about 420, to cut off trade with the continent. Most of the small towns and fortified *villae* of Roman times were gradually destroyed. From having been a dependency of Rome in the fourth century, despite various usurpations, Britain became in the fifth century an autonomous Celto-Roman country, before becoming purely Celtic in the west and Anglo-Saxon in the east. Meanwhile, on the far side of the Channel, in present-day Belgium and northern France, the Romans were likewise giving way before the Franks. And when the Romans remaining in Britain appealed for help to the Gallo-Roman general Aetius, he was too busy fighting the Huns to respond to the call.

The eclipse of the British Romans

In the sixth century, Anglo-Saxon kingships began to appear, obliterating the old Roman administration. Unlike French, English retained less than a score of words deriving from Celtic, plus a few proper nouns like Thomas, London, Lincoln, and York. Christianity, too, disappeared from the non-Celtic areas, and reappeared only after 597, when missionaries sent by Pope Gregory the Great arrived.

But this new world was in contact with other countries from the seventh century onwards – as witness the 'boat grave' discovered at Sutton Hoo, Suffolk, in 1939. Under a tumulus, excavators found a seagoing ship 27 metres long, 4.7 metres wide, and 1.5 metres from gunwale to keel. With it, however, there were no human remains. Instead, it contained jewels, Byzantine silver, weapons, Merovingian gold coins from the seventh century, and Scandinavian money, most of it Swedish.

By now, immigration by sea had virtually ceased. Latin had been abandoned and forgotten, replaced by 'Englix'. The small kingdoms that were beginning to establish themselves, such as Wessex, Mercia, and Northumbria, slowly extended their territories westwards, at the expense of the British – just as across the Channel in Brittany a similar westward advance took place between the fifth and seventh centuries. Many of the Celts who were thus displaced fled south by sea. Against those who remained in Wales, the Kings of Mercia built a huge earthwork, Offa's Dyke. Having themselves abandoned seafaring, the invaders settled in their newly conquered land. Except in Kent, where the population was dispersed, they lived in villages similar to those of Lower Saxony: rectangular wooden houses, long 'open fields' with a strip system of crop rotation. Not until the ninth century were their cultural links with the original homelands finally broken.

Unlike continental Europe, Great Britain was colonized by repopulation. Whereas in France a relatively small number of invading Franks was absorbed into a vast mass of Gallo-Roman Celts, in Britain – save in the Celtic north and west – the Anglo-Saxons became a dominant majority. The result was that the Roman influence, profound as it may have been, was much less obvious in Britain than on the other side of the Channel.

EUROPE

Ireland

Despite continual raids on the west of Britain, in Wales, Devon, and Cornwall, the Irish Sea sheltered Ireland from the Anglo-Saxon invaders. Populated by the Picts and, later, the Scots, the island retained its own civilization, and its inhabitants went on speaking Gaelic. Its monastic life was vigorous and austere. Irish monks, with crescent-shaped tonsures, were brave and tireless missionaries whose Latin remained purer than elsewhere because Gaelic was so dissimilar as not to corrupt it. Their links with Western civilization were strengthened also by the fact that Pope Gregory the Great sent to Ireland a number of monks from the new Benedictine order.

WESTERN MONASTICISM

Hermits and cenobites

In a world politically fragmented into small local power-centres, where trade had largely given way to self-sufficiency, civic authority had been replaced by seignorial hierarchy, and the organization of the Church had in places fallen under lay domination, Western monasticism emerged as an extraordinary and Europe-wide phenomenon. In the East, the hermit life predominated: men and women seeking sanctity became anchorites, withdrawing from the world to lonely refuges where they lived in solitude on the charity of pious donors. In the West, their counterparts became cenobites, choosing the 'life in common' that the word (from the Greek) implies.

In the fifth century there were a number of different monastic 'rules', many of them extremely strict. But from the sixth century onwards, two great orders of monks extended their respective 'rules' throughout the West. These were the Rule of St Benedict of Nursia, in Italy, and that of St Columbanus, from Ireland. Both Rules involved three essential activities: prayer, intellectual effort, and manual labour.

1. Prayer, under a Rule which required hundreds of monasteries and millions of monks to follow the same procedure and liturgy in countries far and wide, helped to spread a single form of religious thought or spirituality irrespective of political boundaries.

2. Intellectual effort made the monasteries, in these difficult times, the only flourishing centres of culture, with large numbers of literate people piously copying manuscripts, composing chronicles, and writing the history of various ethnic groups. Examples of such histories include *Historia Francorum*, written by Gregory of Tours in about 538; *Historia ecclesiastica gentis Angliorum*, written by the Venerable Bede between 673 and 730; and *Historia de regibus Gothorum, Vandalorum, Sueborum*, written by Isidore of Seville from 590 to 636.
3. Manual labour included clearing land for cultivation, draining and rehabilitating marshes, building (rarely in stone before the ninth century), and artisan work, in which craftsmanship gradually improved. With the aid of 'brother servants' and peasants who were sometimes serfs, the monks played an important part in the farming economy.

Although the monastic Rules were similar, monasticism was by no means uniform. At one extreme, its precepts could be mild, as in the case of St Benedict or, later, Cluny – or, as in the case of the Jesuit order founded by St Ignatius Loyola, could encourage an adequate diet because those defending the faith needed physical strength. At the other extreme, austerity was regarded as the source of sanctity: such was the case with the Rule of St Columbanus, with the later Cistercians, and later still with the Trappists.

St Benedict

St Benedict of Nursia in central Italy is known to us through his biographer Gregory of Tours, who in 599 wrote *Of the Life and Miracles of the Italian Fathers*. Born into a well-to-do family, Benedict lived the life of an anchorite in a cave at Subiaco, then gradually came to favour a community life. Founding a monastery at Monte Cassino, he there wrote his famous *Rule*, which synthesized a number of existing Italian orders. Eventually, Popes and Councils actually prescribed the Rule of St Benedict as the monastic norm. The Roman Catholic Church still in fact uses Latin prayers and chants which are of Benedictine origin. The Benedictines were also responsible not only for making land available to cultivation but also for setting up farming villages. They developed hostelries to lodge and protect pilgrims and other travellers, including merchants, thereby encouraging trade. They also built up important libraries and copied ancient manuscripts, including the works of pagan authors – although these were all too often erased to make room for sacred texts.

St Benedict wrote his monastic *Rule* at Monte Cassino in about AD 530. It prescribed regular work, physical and spiritual. The Benedictine Rule, both substantial and full of wisdom, was adopted all over Europe. One of its best-known provisions was that meals should be taken together in silence, while one monk reads aloud an edifying religious text, adding spiritual to earthly nourishment.

In general, monasticism appealed to people who could find no foothold in the society of the time; it offered them a humble life but a secure one. Pope Gregory the Great, who ruled from 590 to 604, may have been educated in a Benedictine monastery. The *Rule* soon spread throughout Western Christendom: it came to Britain with St Augustine of Canterbury; it penetrated Gaul and Germany; and it had a great influence on Spain through Isidore of Seville.

St Columbanus

St Columbanus was born in Leinster, Ireland, in about 540. A monk in the celebrated Bangor monastery, he was seized at the age of fifty with the desire to become a missionary, and he left for Gaul with a dozen other Irish monks. The King of Burgundy offered him land in the Vosges, where he set up a number of monasteries, including that of Luxeuil, which became his headquarters. He then wrote an extremely strict and ascetic Rule, based on penances, flagellation, fasting, cold water, and other austerities.

Columbanus continued to found monasteries, some of which have remained very well known: they include Coutances in Normandy, Jouarre to the east of Paris, Bregenz in Austria, St Gall in Switzerland (named after an Irish fellow-monk), and Bobbio in Italy, where St Columbanus died in 615. After his death, disciples continued to join the order in large numbers, and new monasteries were set up. Many were offshoots of Luxeuil: these included St Wandrille in Normandy, Corbie in Picardy, and Remiremont in the Vosges.

As time went on, St Columbanus's stringent *Rule* was gradually eclipsed by the milder, wiser precepts of St Benedict, which in various forms have survived the centuries and are still followed to this day.

According to the Venerable Bede, Pope Gregory the Great asked a companion who were the good-looking young slaves he saw in a Roman market. They were Angles – *angli*. '*Non angli, sed angeli*' – 'not Angles, but angels', he is said to have replied.

Whether this old story be true or not, Gregory certainly decided to convert the British by training native British priests. He sent a mission under Augustine, prior of a monastery in Rome. It landed in Kent near the mouth of the Thames, at Easter 592, and found Ethelbert, the Kentish king, prepared to become a Christian. After he was baptized in 597, thousands of his subjects followed suit, thereby forming the Church in England, with Augustine at its head as Archbishop of Canterbury, and two subordinate archbishops in London and York. Canterbury thus became the first Benedictine foundation in Britain, followed by Westminster, Peterborough, Ripon, Malmesbury, Hexham, Wearmouth, Jarrow (home of the Venerable Bede), and Exeter (whence Wynfrith, or Boniface, set out to convert Germany).

Alongside this new Anglo-Saxon Church, however, there remained the British Celts in the north and west of the country. Augustine would have liked their clergy to work with his own: but so great was the hatred between the Celts and their conquerors that collaboration was out of the question. What was more, their respective liturgies and robes were mutually incompatible.

The other Anglo-Saxon kingdoms nevertheless soon followed the lead given by Kent and then Essex. This was the case with Northumbria, East Anglia, Wessex, Mercia, and finally Sussex.

The Venerable Bede

The infant Church in England, for all its difficult beginnings, gave to Western Christendom one of its greatest scholars, the Venerable Bede (673–735). Bede was a monk at Jarrow, and became a priest in 702. The monastery at Wearmouth, in whose territory he had been born, and where he spent much of his time, had received from Rome and from Gaul a magnificent collection of manuscripts; and with their help Bede became one of the great writers of the seventh and eighth centuries – not unlike Pope Gregory the Great at the end of the sixth and the beginning of the seventh. Gregory left a large number of works and some 850 letters. Bede produced a mass of writings on rhetoric, philosophy, theology, and history, of which the best known are his *Ecclesiastical History*, already mentioned, and a *Manual of Dialectic*. (See also chapter 7, page 113.)

Celtic Christianity

Driven back to the far west of Europe, the Celts lived for a long time in total isolation, especially in the sixth century, until the missions sent by Gregory the Great. It was natural, therefore, that they developed a number of unique institutions and customs. One such was the ascetic Rule of St Columba, the founder of the great monastery of Iona, who devoted his life to Ireland, to the Picts of Scotland, and to Brittany. Columba also established monastery–bishoprics – unheard of anywhere else in Christendom. As has been seen, the Irish monks' tonsures were crescent-shaped as compared with the round tonsures of Rome. They also celebrated Easter at a different date. It was no wonder that when Gregory the Great's missionaries arrived there were fierce and sometimes physically violent disputes.

Finally, the Irish monks were great travellers, like St Columba himself and the still more legendary St Brendan.

The conversion of the Low Countries and Germany

The seventh and eighth centuries saw the end of missionary work by the Eastern Church. The fragmentation of Byzantine Christianity, the rapid expansion of Islam, the outbreak of civil wars and a wave of invasions all put a sudden stop to what in Justinian's time had been very successful missions. Now, it was only in the West that Christianity made new conquests.

Western missionaries indeed helped to knit Europe together in a very profound sense. While preaching the Christian faith and obedience to Rome, they did not destroy local customs or languages: but they brought with them a philosophy and a language of their own – Latin. This became the *lingua franca* of the intellectual élite (mainly the clergy); and that élite came to share the same attitude towards the life of the illiterate masses. A major feature of Christianity was the strictness of its ethics. Human beings continued to sin; but they now feared Hell and the Devil, and this led them to repent, to make donations to the Church and, on occasion, to perform remarkable acts of piety.

One typical Western missionary was St Amand of Maastricht. Born in Lower Poitou in about 584, he lived as a hermit for fifteen years, then in his mid-forties went on a pilgrimage to Rome. Having been made a bishop with no fixed see, he preached the Gospel in what is now Flanders, probably also in Gascony, and among the Danubian Slavs. When he was nearly ninety, he retired to the abbey of Elnone, where he died in 679.

St Columbanus, leaving his monastery of Bobbio in Italy, also sought to convert the Slavs – in his case the Wends around the Vistula. His disciple St Gall preached the Gospel in what is now Switzerland, between Zurich and Lake Constance. Between Basle and Constance, the Alemanni were converted by a Scottish missionary, St Fridolin, a former Abbot of St Hilaire in Poitiers who later founded monasteries in the Rhineland. St Firmin founded several in Alsace; St Rupert, an Irish missionary who died in 715, helped to convert Bavaria; and another Irishman, St Kilian, had marked success in Thuringia.

Willibrord and Boniface

Two Anglo-Saxon saints deserve especial mention: St Willibrord and St Boniface. Willibrord, educated at the monastery of Ripon, Northumbria, under St Wilfred, went to Ireland in 678 and was ordained as a priest ten years later. In 690, with eleven companions who became martyrs, he began to preach the Gospel in Friesland; five years later he was consecrated bishop at Utrecht. In about 700 he established a second missionary centre at Echternach in Luxembourg, where he died in 739.

Boniface, originally christened Wyn-frith, was born at or near Crediton in Wessex, now Devon, and was a monk at Exeter and later Nursling, near Southampton, until about the age of forty. In 718 he left Britain to preach in Friesland, then went to Rome, where in 719 Pope Gregory II renamed him Boniface and sent him on an ambitious evangelizing mission. He spent three years with Willibrord in Thuringia, then converted several thousand inhabitants of Hesse, as a result of which he was made bishop in 722, eventually establishing his see at Mainz. Pope Gregory III made him Archbishop of Germany, where he was most notably successful in Bavaria, and founded the famous abbey of Fulda. He was over seventy when he decided to return to Friesland. There, at Dokkum, he was set upon and killed by pagans while quietly reading in his tent. His body was taken to Fulda to be buried. Archbishop

Cuthbert of Canterbury wrote: 'We in England lovingly reckon Boniface among the best and greatest teachers of the faith.'

GERMANIC AND ROMANCE LANGUAGES

The three great waves of invasion – Celtic, Latin, and German – left deep and lasting imprints on the languages of Europe.

The Celts came first, conquering the original inhabitants (perhaps Neolithic) of a vast area stretching from present-day Germany to the far west of Ireland, and including much of the Iberian peninsula as well as the plain of Lombardy in northern Italy. They did not, however, reach Scandinavia except by trade (see chapter 8).

The linguistic legacy of Rome was immense. In the West, four national languages, each with a long and distinguished literature, derive from Latin: French, Italian, Spanish, and Portuguese. Latin is also the ancestor of Romanian, of Catalan, and of various dialects deriving from the old *langue d'oc*.

All the rest of Western Europe, except for a few Celtic areas, adopted Germanic languages – German, English, Dutch, Danish, Norwegian, and Swedish; plus Icelandic, Faroese, and a few others.

Celtic, in other words, was barely able to hold its own against Latin and German, different though they were.

Latins, Greeks, and Celts

The Latin alphabet was said to be the simplest in the world. It dates from the sixth century BC, before which the Latins had imitated Etruscan and then Greek writing. As a language, Latin was spoken by the rulers of all the western part of the Empire. Greek became more and more the norm in the east, and eventually the frontier between them was made official.

The use of a language by foreign conquerors does not, of course, mean that the population is likely to give up its own maternal dialects, unwritten, badly written, or rarely written as they may be. In Gaul, for instance, there are numerous inscriptions in Celtic. From the third century BC onwards, 'Gallo-Greek' inscriptions reflect the influence of the wealthy Greek colony of Massalia (Marseille). Then came 'Gallo-Latin' inscriptions. But *none* of the Gallo-Greek or Gallo-Latin linguistic remains is a literary text. There must however have been oral literature in Gaul. We have no trace of it, and can base speculation only on the oral traditions of Ireland, transcribed by the monks much later, in the fourth century AD.

The absence of literature and the near-absence of any written remains imply that the conquerors imposed their own language on those they taught – who, it has to be added, were quite quickly absorbed.

Assimilation by Rome

The conquerors' language, in fact, had to be used for any and every official purpose: laws, contracts, accounts, letters, notices, messages, and – when Christianity appeared – religious texts.

Prior to Christian conversion, Celtic and Latin deities had tended to co-exist. The Romans were not religious missionaries. And because in Gaul and Spain, for example, they brought greater comfort, better buildings, good roads, sanctuaries, theatres, games, circuses, why not accept them? The legions supplied engineers who built canals and aqueducts to enrich the country. So, at the very time when the Germans were invading Gaul, Spain, Italy, and Britain, many of the conquered peoples were being assimilated by Rome. In the fifth and sixth centuries, even the Britons were still deeply Romanized.

Latin in Britain: limited success

Great Britain was not defeated by the Emperor Claudius until AD 43, a hundred years after the Roman conquest of Gaul. North Britain, inhabited by the pre-Celtic Picts and by the Scots, Celts who for the most part had come from Ireland, was separated from the Roman-occupied area by a *limes* which was easy to defend. For this reason, when the Roman Empire in Britain began to crumble, it was in the south and east rather than the north. Between AD 410 and 420, owing to internal disorders, local disputes, and the weakness of an army ever more thin on the ground, Britain ceased to be a Roman dependency. The Germans settled in what is now Belgium; the Saxons invaded Britain and drove the Britons towards the west. For a time, England itself was divided along a line running from north to south. But what is noteworthy is that the main areas of resistance to the Saxons – Scotland in the north, Wales (an Irish kingdom until the tenth century) in the centre, and Cornwall in the south-west – continued for a long time to speak Celtic languages rather than Latin. They were not Roman but Celtic strongholds; and indeed, Romanization in Britain had been less pronounced than in Gaul. Only later, in the eleventh century, when the Romanized Normans invaded Britain, were so many Latin words brought in, giving the English language its huge and varied vocabulary.

Germanic lands beyond the Roman Empire: the linguistic frontier

The Germanic peoples gave their languages to all the countries of Northern Europe, but in various ways. In Scandinavia, and in the eastern Germanic lands, as has been seen, there was no Roman conquest. What Roman influence did reach these regions through mutual trade was too diffuse to involve the adoption of the Latin language. In Britain and in the Low Countries, Roman domination was insufficient to prevent wholesale invasions which transformed the linguistic map.

Yet the Germans also invaded the rest of Europe, whose present-day languages derive from Latin. The explanation must be that here they were too few. In general, the predominance of Romance or Germanic languages seems to depend on the relative density of the populations concerned. At the same time, various specific factors also determined the exact course of the Germanic/Romance dividing-line. According to Lucien Musset:

> It began at that time at Boulogne-sur-Mer: Latin later reached Dunkirk. It ran eastwards towards Lille, leaving Saint-Omer Germanic, then to the north of Tournai. After that it was in parallel with the Sambre and the Meuse, about 30 kilometres to the north, and crossed the Meuse between Liège and Maastricht, going as far east as Aix-la-Chapelle. From there it turned sharply south, across the Ardennes as far as the southwest of Arlon (Germanic).
>
> Then, turning again, it went round to the north-east of Metz, evidently a Romance stronghold, to reach the Donon. Further on, in the Vosges, where its winding course left a number of the upper Alsatian valleys to the Romance side, and on the edge of Burgundy, the contact was no longer with Frankish dialects, but with Alemannic.

While Romance strongholds are thought to have persisted for some time to the north-west of Brussels and around Tongres, Maastricht, Aix-la-Chapelle in the Eifel and in the land around Trier, some authors believe that Germanic languages penetrated as far as the Loire, with bilingualism prevailing from the sixth to the ninth century, followed by a total victory for Romance languages. For instance, to the north of a line running from Abbeville through Versailles to Nancy, there are place-names ending in '-bais', which corresponds to Bach in German and comes from the Frankish word baki, for 'brook' or 'beck'. Examples include Marbais in the Hainaut province of Belgium, Gambais to the east of Paris, and Rebais in Brie. Above all, Frankish influence can be detected in the changing of village names, affecting half the communes in France, and in the almost total alteration of personal names.

The linguistic frontier between Romance and Alemannic is well defined from Donon in the Vosges as far as the Great St Bernard pass. From the high Valais onwards it becomes much less clear and gives more ground to the Germanic side. The ancient provinces of Rhaetia and Noricum completely lost their Romance characteristics; yet to the east what used to be Dacia and is now Romania, one of Trajan's late conquests, has kept its Romance language despite being surrounded by Bulgars and Slavs.

There was a further Romance reconquest at the end of the Carolingian period, when Brittany became French. We now know that the dividing-line between the Breton-speaking areas, with five separate dialects, and the so-called 'gallos' area, cuts the peninsula in two along an axis south-south-east to north-north-west, from a point 5 kilometres east of Vannes as far as Saint-Brieuc. We also know that place-names there beginning in 'Tre-' (hamlet), 'Lan-' (hermitage), and 'Plou-' (parish), all date from the period between the fifth and the eighth century. Large numbers of such Breton place-names occur in an area more than 100 kilometres wide to the east of the present dividing-line: a clear indication of how it was driven back. From the tenth century onwards, the pockets of Romance language virtually disappeared into the Germanic-speaking areas surrounding the South Tyrol, and the Romans were absorbed into Bavaria. But the Ladins in the Tyrol have retained their Romance-based dialect until the present day.

GERMANIC TRACES

Throughout the Romance area of Europe, often subject to Germanic incursions and finally dominated by 'barbarian' kingdoms, Germanic traces remain: but they differ markedly from country to country.

Portugal

In Portugal, there remains virtually no trace of the Suevi – so much so that Lucien Musset claims: 'There would have been no notable historical difference if the Suevi of Spain had never existed.' Only five or six words of Suevi origin have survived in Portuguese.

Spain

In Spain, the Vandals who passed through on their way to Africa left almost as little trace. The Vandal state in Spain, at the beginning of the fifth century, seems to have amounted to little more than a military occupation accompanied by pillage.

The Visigoths, on the other hand, had a deep and lasting effect. Like their cousins the Ostrogoths, they were almost unique in seeking to promote intellectual life and culture.

From the Goths came the European practice of consecrating and anointing royalty. At the time of the Reconquista, or reconquest of Spain from the Moors, the Goths were praised as the great founders and ancestors of 'Spanishness'. A number of personal names, such as Aldefonsus, Alvarus, Fredenardus, or Rodericus, are of Gothic origin: so are some place-names near Burgos and Segovia. Gothic Spain was very much attached to the classical Roman authors; but it seems to have been too isolated to be aware of contemporary writers such as Cassiodorus or Boethius in Italy, or any of the Franks. The monumental *History of the Goths* by Isidore of Seville, who was Bishop there from 601 to 635, shows both the strength and the limits of Gothic culture in Spain.

France

Among the legacies of the Franks, particularly in Gaul, was first of all the name that Gaul acquired – Francia, later restricted to the slightly smaller area of France. But this was only one of their many and fundamental contributions.

The case of the Franks is indeed unique. They were the only people whose achievements lasted throughout the high Middle Ages. The Goths in Spain were crushed by the Arabs; the Ostrogothic kingdom of Theodoric in Italy was conquered by the Byzantines and Lombards; the Lombard kingdom was defeated by the Franks and Byzantines. The Franks, by contrast, managed gradually to unify a large part of Gaul, first under the Merovingians, then under the Carolingians. The two 'races' were fused into one – despite the racist myths of the eighteenth century, according to which the nobility had been Franks and the populace Gallo-Romans.

France, which as a nation did not emerge until many centuries later, was at that time somewhat more extensive, including the Walloon area of what is now Belgium, and the French-speaking part of what is now Switzerland, *la Suisse romande*. It was in fact an ethnic and cultural melting-pot, whose basic ingredient was perhaps Neolithic, but which was also composed of Celts (Gauls), Romans, and Germanic Franks.

Italy

Geography tended to hinder political unity in Italy, which it did not attain, after the fifth century, until the Risorgimento in the nineteenth. It has been estimated that some seventy words of Gothic origin are still in ordinary use in the Italian language; while Gothic influence can be seen in place-names in Lombardy which end in '-engo', such as Marengo, Gottolengo, or Offanengo. Traces of the Lombards themselves are still rarer: but their treatment of the indigenous population was far more savage. They confiscated land, massacring its owners or reducing them to the status of meagre share-croppers. From the seventh to the tenth century, as has been seen, Italy was actually called Langobardia, while that part of the Exarchate of Ravenna which resisted the Lombards was known as Romania (today Romagna). In the ninth century, the name Italy reappeared.

INVASION BUT NOT BARBARISM

The first century BC can be regarded as symbolic. It was the time when the Celts, largely defeated by the Romans, relinquished the political role they had had since the eighth century BC. It was also the time when the 'Germans' first came on the European scene. In the third century AD they emerged more fully; in the fifth they conquered the West, reaching their apogee from the fifth century to the ninth.

Germani or 'Germans' was the name given in the first century BC to certain tribes in Central Europe: but many of them, at that time, were still speaking Celtic languages. The true Germans were those who spoke Germanic languages – a fact which became evident from the fourth century AD onwards.

It was then, in fact, after many invasions and much recruitment into the Roman legions, that the Germans, in seventy years, from 404 to 474, destroyed the Roman Empire in the West. In the continental part of the Empire, the Franks, the Burgundians, the Visigoths, the Vandals, and the Suevi made their new home; in the British Isles, the Angles, the Saxons, the Frisians, and the Jutes.

Scandinavia would seem to have been the original source of the Germanic tribes. In that harsh region, any great increase in the population was bound to force people to emigrate; and it was towards the south and the west that they went.

Even if they did not transform the languages and customs of all the places where they settled, the Germans dominated at least as much of Europe as the Celts had done, and even more than the Romans.

In broad terms, Europe underwent two great invasions by at first rather primitive peoples who were nevertheless able, influential, and adaptable. These were the Celts and the Germans. Between these two invasions there was a period of brilliant, vigorous, intellectual, and literary civilization, that of the Romans. The less polished nature of the Germanic invaders has long led people to see the fall of the Western Roman Empire as a return to 'barbarism'. The aim of this chapter has been to show how simplistic that notion is, and how great a contribution the Germanic peoples made to the development of Europe.

7

Charlemagne: King of Europe?

THE ARRIVAL OF THE CAROLINGIANS

The successors of Merwig and Clovis, known as the Merovingians, ruled a regnum francorum or Kingdom of the Franks, which was sometimes united under a single monarch and sometimes shared: but it was regarded as one entity, subdivided into three parts. In the west was Neustria or Francia; in the east, stretching well into what is now Germany, was Austrasia; in the centre and to the south was Burgundy, now dominated by the Franks rather than the Burgundians. Spain was then called the patria gothorum, or land of the Visigoths. Italy, meanwhile, was bitterly fought over by the Germanic Lombards and the Byzantines, who reached the height of their power in the sixth century when the Emperor Justinian recaptured parts of Africa and Spain. From 711 onwards, moreover, the Spanish Kingdom of the Visigoths, for all its brilliance, fell victim to invasion by the Islamic Moors (see chapter 8).

Elsewhere, other peoples were stirring. Scandinavia, the original homeland of the Germans, was soon to produce the Vikings with their newly improved longships. In what is now Germany, outside the area occupied by the Austrasian Franks, there were Saxons and Frisians to the north, Bavarians and Alemanni to the south, and to the east the Slavs.

Finally, there were the British Isles, with Ireland entirely Celtic, and Britain split into small principalities – Scottish and Celtic to the north and west, Angle and Saxon to the east. The major losers, in Britain, were the Roman Britons. Unlike the Gallo-Romans, whose language survived all invasions, the Roman Britons disappeared – although Latin, the only written language and that used by intellectuals and by the Church, nevertheless persisted at a time when Greek was virtually forgotten in the West.

Yet despite this fragmentation on the outskirts of Europe – soon to be complicated further by fresh waves of invasion – the heartland of Western Europe was being drawn together by the growing power of the Kingdom of the Franks, which covered a large part of what today are France and Germany.

The Kingdom of the Merovingian Franks

The growth of that kingdom and the emergence of the Carolingians was a long and complex process, with two contrasting tendencies at work. One was the quest for unity, associated with the 'mayors of the palace' (see below); the other was the rise of 'regional nationalities'. In the words of K. F. Werner:

> The Merovingian dynasty ruled for 263 years, but only for 72 of them was there a single king at the head of the regnum francorum. Discounting the 52 years at the end of the dynasty during which the nominal rulers were rois fainéants or kings without power, this leaves only 20 years of unitary kingship. In complete contrast, Austrasia had its own kings for 138 years, Neustria for 119, and Burgundy for 49 and a further 69 in union with Neustria. This continuity explains the coherence of the communities which emerged again later: Burgundy, Lorraine, and northern France.

The major domus or mayor of the palace

From the seventh century onwards, the power of the king was gradually eroded by that of the major domus. Since the year 700 there had been a single king, from Neustria, in charge of the whole realm. He was assisted by a major domus for Austrasia and another for Neustria; but their posts became hereditary and they formed a single dynasty. While the king or *rex* 'reigned' with mystical *auctoritas* (authority), the mayor of the palace or *princeps* ruled and wielded *potestas* (power).

It was Pepin II, Mayor of the Palace of Austrasia, who at the very end of the seventh century seized power after fighting the Frisians and Saxons in the north. His son was named Charles (Cearl in Anglo-Saxon, Charal in Old High German, Kerl in New High German, and Karl in modern German): the name meant 'brave soldier'. He was later nicknamed 'Martel' or 'hammer'. In 719, Charles Martel defeated the Neustrians, secured Austrasia, drove the Saxons as far as the Weser, and recaptured Utrecht from the Frisians.

He also devised a system which, although it antagonized the Church, enabled him to raise a very substantial army: he gave to a number of nobles and freemen the profits from Church lands. In exchange for this privilege, known as a 'benefice', the 'vassal' was not required to pay a tax, but was obliged instead to supply a warrior complete with his weapons and his horse. Charles and his successors thereby acquired a truly professional army. Charles's son Pepin the Short and his grandson Charlemagne later refined this system by having its beneficiaries compensate the Church with a form of tithes.

Until his death in 741, Charles Martel continued to extend the theoretical rule of the fainéant Merovingian kings – which from 737 onwards became even more his own, since he now governed alone, without a king. He built fortifications, crisscrossed Germany with Roman-type roads, and set up staging-posts of horses supplied by the 'colonists' whom he settled in conquered territory. This included Hesse, Franconia, Thuringia, Alemannia, and the 'Nordgau' of Bavaria, where Charles backed the missionary efforts of St Boniface. He also laid waste Aquitaine and defeated the Muslims at Poitiers. In 734 he savagely crushed a Frisian revolt; and in 739, with the help of the Lombards, he conquered Provence.

Charles's son Pepin the Short, after gradually wresting power from his brother Carloman, pursued the same policy, but made sure to secure the blessing of the Church, in particular by protecting the Pope against the Lombards. By the 'Donation of Pepin' he forced the Lombard King Aistulf to cede Ravenna to the Pope, thereby founding the Papacy's temporal power. He thus achieved two outstanding aims:

1. he once more united Austrasia and Neustria, this time more firmly;
2. he deposed the last Merovingian king in 751. The Pope confirmed his succession to the throne; an assembly of the nobles elected him; St Boniface anointed him; in 754 the Pope came to France and crowned him; he was also made a 'patrician of Rome'. In exchange, that same year, he 'donated' to the Pope the city of Rome and, in principle, the whole of Italy.

Pepin was buried in 768 in the Basilica of St Denis, leaving to his sons Charles and Carloman II the task of building a larger and more magnificent church.

CHARLEMAGNE

Charles and Carloman came to the throne jointly in 768; Carloman died three years later leaving Charles as the sole king. His achievements won him the title 'Charles the Great', Carolus magnus – Charlemagne in French and English, Carlomagno in Italian, and in German Karl der Grosse.

In many respects he was indeed a great man. As a leader in war he was skilful and indefatigable; as a diplomat he was imaginative and wise. Although prone to vengeance and to the temptations of the flesh, he was a man of great piety who, like his father, enjoyed the constant support of the Pope. He was not the bearded Emperor of legend: he wore only a large moustache. But his fame was legendary – as 'champion of the Faith' for the French, as 'founder of institutions' for the Germans. Some even thought him a saint. That would have surprised him greatly.

The conqueror

As K. F. Werner said, 'Not until Napoleon was another European military leader so constantly on the move.'

In the case of Italy, having protected the Pope from the Duke of the Lombards, who had been attacking Ravenna and was making for Rome, Charlemagne seized Lombardy. The Duke capitulated in 774. Charlemagne had himself crowned King of the Lombards, and left central Italy largely, if not entirely, to the Pope.

Charlemagne's subsequent conquests were to the north and south of Frankish Austrasia, in what is now Germany. In the north was Saxony, then a largely pagan area between the Ems and the Elbe. In the south, Charlemagne pressed as far as Hesse. The struggle continued for thirty cruel years. Louis Halphen has pointed out that 'one capitulary decree left the inhabitants no choice but between the baptismal font and the executioner's sword'.

Not until 804 did Charlemagne call a halt. By then, his troops had reached Denmark.

As for the Eastern Marches, Bavaria, by contrast, was already a Christian country. Its duke abdicated in 794, and Charlemagne had him tonsured and confined to the monastery of Jumièges, while compelling his wife and two daughters to become nuns and his two sons to become monks.

To protect his newly acquired territory, Charlemagne peopled the frontier regions with Franks. In the south-east, he crushed the Avars, driving them back to the Danube. Invading what is now Hungary, he forced the Avar leader or 'Khagan' to become his vassal and to embrace Christianity. He also made the Slavs to the east of the Elbe his allies and payers of tribute.

Charlemagne had hoped to annex Spain, but an expedition which set out for Pamplona and Saragossa in 778 was a total failure. It was on the return journey that his rearguard, commanded by Roland or Hroland, prefect of the Breton Marches, whom legend claims to have been Charlemagne's nephew, was defeated and killed by the Gascons at Roncevaux. South of the Pyrenees, in fact, Charlemagne was able only to establish an outpost in Catalonia, to occupy Barcelona and Tortosa, and to influence the affairs of the peninsula by diplomatic means. He supported the Christian King of Galicia and the Asturias, who in 798 seized Lisbon; and a Muslim claimant to the crown of Cordoba actually travelled to Aix-la-Chapelle to seek Charlemagne's aid.

The Carolingian hierarchy

Once a year, the counts (who came from all parts of the Empire) had to visit Charlemagne. Also once a year, a large number of subjects, considered to represent the whole kingdom, met in a *placitum generalis* or general assembly. Itinerant inspectors, the *missi dominici* or lord's envoys, travelled through the regions to give orders in Charlemagne's name. The Church hierarchy, organized under bishops who were in theory elected by the people and clergy, was also used as an auxiliary network of official control.

The realm was divided into ecclesiastical districts: archbishoprics, bishoprics, and abbeys with local military leaders or 'counts'. Orders were disseminated rapidly from above. Once they were received, the count would mobilize his vassals and their *milites* or mounted troops. The bishop or the abbot supplied horses and rations, as well as wagons, rather larger than their Roman predecessors and somewhat similar to the Conestoga wagons of the American West, with waterproof coverings of hide. Altogether, there were some five hundred counts, each with twenty or thirty men; there were also rather more direct vassals of the king, each of them commanding ten or a dozen soldiers. On this reckoning, the army must have numbered about 50,000 horsemen and many more infantrymen. It was divided into a number of different units, notably in the Marches designed to ward off the Arabs, the Bretons, the Saxons, the Vikings, and the Slavs.

Discipline was ferocious because Charlemagne believed it his duty to command obedience. After one Saxon rebellion, for example, which in about 778 destroyed a Frankish contingent, he had 4,000 Saxons put to death.

Charlemagne's army was well equipped for attack and conquest, which promised land and riches to its aristocratic leaders and even to the clergy. But it was far less effective as a defensive force.

For an offensive, the whole of the Frankish kingdom – western Francia, eastern Neustria or Austrasia, Burgundy, and Germany beyond the Rhine – all would rally to the cause. They were acting in the name of the *populus Christianus*, the Christian people, and no longer on behalf of the ancient kingdoms. But if there was no more land to be won, their unity faltered and the old antagonisms reappeared.

Lucien Musset puts it in a nutshell: the Empire 'had neither a standing army nor a fleet; it had no solid fortifications, no finances worthy of the name, and perhaps even no genuine popular support.'

The absence of any overall defensive system, and the failure of the Marches, led to the illegal building of private castles. In Italy, which was fairly well defended, the inhabitants lived in fortified enclosures. An alliance with Byzantium might have made it possible to resist later invasions more effectively; but mutual antagonism was still too strong. Musset concludes: 'The Carolingian world therefore fought alone and died alone, largely owing to its own faults.'

THE EMPIRE

Charlemagne became Emperor in the year 800, at the age of fifty-eight and after reigning as king for thirty-two years. The idea of re-establishing the Empire was popular among the potentes of the West, and Charlemagne's own chief adviser was its fervent advocate. But it was Pope Leo III who seems to have played the decisive role. In 792, Charlemagne had taken the title 'King of the Gauls, of Germany, of Italy and of the Neighbouring Provinces'. In Constantinople, however, the 'Basileus' reigned – the Byzantine Emperor. For Pope Leo III, to give Charlemagne the Imperial Crown would be to give himself a protector, and one not only superior to others but also far enough away to cause him no trouble. His aim was to make Charlemagne Emperor of the whole Christian world, including Byzantium, and thereby re-establish Papal authority in the east, where it was much contested.

Charlemagne's own ambition, it seems, was simply to be the equal of the Basileus.

The coronation

In April 799, a scandal erupted in Rome – an uprising in which, the Roman nobles alleged, Pope Leo III had been involved. He was attacked and wounded, and narrowly escaped being blinded. Once he had recovered, he went to Charlemagne, who was then at Paderborn in Saxony, and begged him to come to Rome.

Charlemagne prepared his visit with care. He knelt in prayer at the tomb of St Martin in Tours; he sent to Rome an advance-guard of *missi dominici* to organize a form of tribunal before which Pope Leo III was to affirm his innocence. Charlemagne followed shortly before Christmas in the year 800. The Pope duly pleaded his innocence, thereby implicitly recognizing Charlemagne's superior authority; and on Christmas Day he crowned him Emperor.

Charlemagne wanted above all to be the Christian Emperor – 'the new Constantine, chosen by God to rule the people'. He had himself portrayed on his coins wearing a laurel wreath and a Roman general's cloak, the *paludamentum*, buckled at the shoulder. At the same time, he once more recognized the false 'Donation of Constantine' and confirmed the Pope's authority in Rome.

Recognition by the Byzantines

The Byzantines, however, had not accepted Charlemagne's imperial title: so he went to war with them in the northern Adriatic. They had a much stronger fleet, but Charlemagne overpowered them on land, seizing Friuli, Carniola, Istria, and Venice, which sought to remain neutral to safeguard its growing trade.

A settlement was not reached until 814. The Byzantines agreed to recognize Charlemagne as Emperor; Charlemagne agreed to give up Venice, while retaining Friuli and the other north Adriatic lands. However, when the Byzantine delegation arrived to formalize the settlement later that year, Charlemagne had just died. It was his son and successor Louis the Pious who received the title 'Emperor and Augustus', and not 'Roman Emperor', which the Byzantines kept for themselves.

THE 'CAROLINGIAN RENAISSANCE'

As has been seen, the so-called 'Dark Ages', especially the sixth and seventh centuries, were less dark than they have sometimes been painted. But it is in contrast to them that historians came to speak of a 'Carolingian Renaissance'. Broadly speaking, Ireland and Spain had by now become the main if not the only centres of culture; and Spain was soon cut off from the rest of Christian Europe by the Arab invasion. It was an opportunity for the Frankish Empire to fill the gap.

Education

Charlemagne is traditionally regarded as the father of scholasticism. In fact, in this respect as in many others, his advisers followed the precepts of Isidore of Seville, and thereby the precedents of Rome. Teaching was divided into eight subjects: the trivium comprised grammar, rhetoric, and dialectic (i.e. logic); the quadrivium covered arithmetic, astronomy, music, and geometry; while the discipline dominating all the others was theology.

The Venerable Bede

Already in the second half of the seventh century, there were monasteries in Britain whose schools taught along these lines. Many had libraries which for the time were very extensive; they contained several hundred volumes. The most remarkable of these centres was Jarrow, in Northumberland, largely on account of the exceptionally learned monk, the Venerable Bede (673–735) (see also chapter 6, page 95). He was well versed in pagan Latin literature, but also in Christian culture, and especially in the Fathers of the Church. A great collector of manuscripts, he was also an indefatigable author: he wrote in Latin, although his native language was probably Celtic. He tackled every kind of subject – grammar, Latin verse, ecclesiastical history, the exegesis of Scripture, natural sciences, astronomy, and computation, i.e. the complex calculation of the date of Easter.

Bede left us not only the eighth-century *Ecclesiastical History of the English People*, mentioned already, but also many other historical works, grammatical studies, a treatise on physical science, *De natura rerum*, manuals of physics and mathematics, many scriptural commentaries, a poem on the Last Judgement, and sermons on the Gospels.

Of particular interest is the fact that twice in his *Ecclesiastical History* Bede used the word 'Europe'. In the first chapter, describing the British Isles, he wrote: 'Britain, an ocean island formerly called Albion, is situated in the north-west, exactly opposite Germany, Gaul, and Spain, the three largest countries in Europe, but divided from them by a broad stretch of sea.' Later, in chapter 13, Bede declared that Attila 'remained so fearful an enemy of the community that he devastated almost all of Europe, attacking and destroying castles and cities'.

Bede seems to have seen himself more as an Anglo-Saxon than as a European, but his ideal was evidently a Catholic Church on a universal scale.

From the British Isles, this Anglo-Saxon 'pre-Renaissance' spread to the Frankish kingdom through St Boniface, who reformed the Frankish Church with the aid of the first Carolingians. He, indeed, played an essential role in the intellectual reform which was the most attractive aspect of the 'Carolingian Renaissance'.

Moral reform

The gradual decay of discipline and morality in the Frankish Church has already been noted. Charles Martel had exacerbated the situation by expropriating for his soldiers a large part of the immense wealth of the Church, mainly in the form of land originally donated by pious kings and congregations. Charles Martel's two sons – Pepin in Gaul and Carloman in the Rhineland – undertook the long-term task of reform. Both invoked the aid of St Boniface, and the Council of Soissons in 774 based itself on his directives.

At the very time when Charlemagne was extending his territory by conquest, Western Christendom was shrinking under the assaults of Islam. Eventually, except for the British Isles, Christendom was confined within the Empire; and from the Marches of Spain to Carinthia, Bavaria, Thuringia, and Saxony as far as the Elbe, from the North Sea to the Roman Campagna, Charlemagne was in effect the temporal head of the Church.

'Our role,' he told the Pope in the *Caroline Books*, a theological work attributed to him,

> is with the help of divine mercy to defend the Church of Christ everywhere against the attacks of the pagans and the ravages of the heathen; to strengthen it within and without by conversions to the Catholic faith. Your role is to raise your hands to Heaven with Moses and to help our struggle, so that with your prayers and under the leadership and grace of God, the Christian people will be victorious everywhere.

Charlemagne certainly intended to take an effective part in the internal affairs of the Church. In his mind, there was no clear-cut distinction between spiritual and temporal power. His 'capitularies' or laws are steeped in moral and religious preoccupations. He was seeking to establish, within the society of the high Middle Ages, the perfect 'Christian city'.

But Charlemagne's 'European' endeavour was most marked in his efforts for intellectual reform.

The quest for scholars

Unlike the Anglo-Saxons whose example he otherwise followed, Charlemagne intended from the first that intellectual reform should involve the laity as well as the clergy. He sought, moreover, to bring together many different representatives of the intellectual life of his time. This is clear from the diverse origins and achievements of his main advisers.

From Italy, Charlemagne brought the grammarians Peter of Pisa and Paulinus of Aquileia, and the historian Paulus Diaconus; from England came the Anglo-Saxon Alcuin, who had been taught by several pupils of the Venerable Bede. Alcuin had visited Rome and headed the school of York. By 773 he had become Charlemagne's trusted adviser and received from him the wealthy abbeys of St Martin of Tours, Ferrières, and St Loup of Troyes. Like Bede, although less original, Alcuin was a good theologian and a scholar of encyclopaedic breadth. He originated the palace school for children of the aristocracy and others of more humble birth. He was no doubt also responsible for a capitulary decreeing the organization of episcopal and monastic schools to extend learning among the population in general.

Other leading figures in the Carolingian Renaissance included: Rhabanus Maurus, a further indirect disciple of the Venerable Bede; Germanus of Mainz, a monk at Fulda who later became bishop at his birthplace and was nicknamed 'the teacher of German'; and the Visigoth Theodulf from Spain, who collaborated on the Caroline Books and became both a missus dominicus and the Bishop of Orléans.

The arts

The Carolingian Renaissance, with its strong Byzantine influence, had its limitations, but it left its mark on the arts. Charlemagne built many churches and cathedrals; and although almost all of them were later replaced, as in Cologne, Paderborn, and Saint-Denis, enough examples remain to show what was achieved – the magnificent dome of Aix-la-Chapelle, for instance, or the church at Germigny-des-Prés near Orléans. All over Europe, moreover, Carolingian miniatures attest to the skill and taste of their makers.

Still more important, in a broader European context, was Charlemagne's reform of handwriting. In the words of Robert Lopez, 'The handwriting reform was his greatest success. Evolved in the scriptoria or copying centres of France, the Caroline minuscule ousted one after another of the "national" scripts that had been the withered fruit of degenerating Roman hands ... In the end, it triumphed long after the

Carolingian dynasty had ended, as far away as Spain, England, and southern Italy.' It gave us our present lower-case printed letters, the upper-case or capitals being derived from Roman inscriptions.

The Caroline minuscule, Robert Lopez concluded, 'was one of the first examples in the series of cross-frontier standardizations that simplify international life, ranging from the Gregorian calendar through the metric system to the universal postal union'.

THE DECAY OF THE EMPIRE AND THE GROWTH OF THE KINGDOMS

In 814, when Charlemagne died, all appeared to be well with his Empire. But it took a mere thirty years for the whole gigantic edifice to crumble.

Louis the Pious

Louis, who had already been crowned Emperor, was near Saumur when he learned of the death of his father. He proceeded to Aix-la-Chapelle; and there, not unexpectedly, installed his own servants and advisers in the place of Charlemagne's. Chief among these was St Benedict of Anianec. Charlemagne, it has been said, had the piety of a layman, whereas Louis had that of a priest or a monk. He was later known as Louis the Mild – an adjective which today might be read as 'weak'.

Emile Amann described him thus: 'A man of average intelligence, average personality, average goodwill – to carry further an enormous task! That was the origin of the final disaster.'

The seignorial system

This period saw the universal spread of the seignorial system, which when organized and codified became the feudal system. At the highest level, the proceres, whether lay grandees or princes of the Church, were tending to see themselves as more and more independent. Charlemagne had been able to compel their obedience. Louis was not.

The three sons of Louis the Pious

In 817, at Aix-la-Chapelle, the Empire was formally divided. This *divisio imperii* associated Louis's eldest son Lothaire with the government of the Empire, and gave the title of king to each of his two younger sons – Pepin, King of Aquitaine, and Louis (Lewis the German), who was given Bavaria and its eastern dependencies of Austria, Pannonia, and Carinthia. Great precautions were taken to safeguard 'the unity of the Empire', which was identified with that of Christendom: but, as the years went by, unity gave way to fragmentation. The sharing of power was further complicated when Louis the Pious remarried: his second wife, a Bavarian princess, gave him another son, Charles, for whom a portion had to be found. To make matters worse, the Empire was under threat from outside. There was fighting on the frontiers of Denmark in the north; in the east, Pannonia was invaded by the Bulgarians; on the Spanish Marches, uprisings had given the Saracens fresh opportunities. All this was naturally blamed on the sins of the Emperor and his entourage. Church dignitaries claimed that the remedy was to subordinate the Emperor to the Pope and the nobles to the bishops. It was the beginning of a conflict that lasted 400 years.

When in 829 the seven-year-old Charles was promised that he would inherit Alemannia, Alsace, Rhaetia, and part of Burgundy, his three elder half-brothers were incensed, and began to plot against their father. At first Louis defeated the rebels, but not for long. Making for Colmar with a large army to fight his sons, Louis began a negotiation. In the course of it, the rebels persuaded many of Louis's soldiers to desert him – hence the name 'the Field of Lies' which was given to the site of these events. Lothaire imprisoned both Louis the Pious and his young son Charles, and in 833 the Emperor was formally deposed.

The deaths of Pepin and Louis the Pious

The three elder sons of Louis thus became direct rivals for the succession. The deaths of Pepin in 838 and of Louis the Pious in 840 left Lothaire, Lewis the German, and the young Charles as the sole claimants to the Imperial Crown. Lothaire proclaimed himself Emperor, and was backed by the bishops; but Lewis and Charles remained hostile, as did much of the nobility.

The Strasbourg oath

On 14 February 842, in Strasbourg, Charles and Lewis the German swore allegiance to each other by an oath whose text, drawn up both in German and in the Romance language of the Franks, was the first linguistic token of the two separate nations of the future, Germany and France, as compared with Latin, which still symbolized the universality of European Christendom.

The two half-brothers defeated Lothaire, and in August 843 concluded with him a partition agreement, the Treaty of Verdun. The map shows how Western Francia, to the west of the Saône and the Rhône, was allocated to Charles, while Eastern Francia, essentially to the east of the Rhine, with Saxony, Alemannia, Bavaria and the former Austrasia, went to Lewis the German. Between the two, stretching from Friesland to Provence and Lombardy, was the area left to Lothaire – Lotharingia or Lorraine. Although seemingly the richest territory, it lacked natural defences. Lothaire also received northern Italy, the Lombard kingdom, which was now coming to be known as the Kingdom of Italy. Central Italy, from Ravenna to Rome, belonged to the Pope; while southern Italy, at this time still dominated by the Byzantines, later fell prey to the Arabs and the Normans. Italy was thus divided. Robert Lopez wrote of the Lombard kingdom: 'One hundred years after the Treaty of Verdun, it became a dependency of Germany, in a broken Empire which no longer included France.'

The dividing-line between the Romance languages (French, Provençal, and Italian) and the Germanic crossed Lotharingia from Aix-la-Chapelle to Switzerland. It was the scene and the cause of innumerable and age-long disputes between the two Frankish realms.

The end of the 'kingdom of Europe'

This was the end of what the poet had called 'the kingdom of Europe', and the beginning of political anarchy. But intellectual culture lived on, to produce in the ninth century one of the greatest writers of the Middle Ages, John Scotus Erigena (c.810–c.877), from Ireland, a philologian, theologian, and neo-Platonist philosopher who became head of the palace school in Paris.

When Lothaire died in 855, his estate was divided among his three sons. One of them, Louis II, became Emperor; but the King of France,

Charles the Bald (the son of Louis the Pious and his Bavarian princess) and Lewis the German made common cause against him. When Louis II, the son of Lothaire I, died in 875 without a male heir, Pope John VIII had Charles the Bald proclaimed Emperor. But Lewis the German, of course, rejected the claim and fought him. To all intents and purposes, it was the end of the Empire of Europe.

THE BEGINNINGS OF EUROPE?

Did the Carolingian adventure, with its apogee in the year 800 and the Imperial Crown, really involve a clear awareness of Europe as an entity, mainly in the west?

Historians differ on the significance of Carolingian unity

Unsurprisingly, historians have hotly debated whether or not the Carolingian Empire marked 'the beginnings of Europe'. For the Italian Carlo Curcio, if 'Europe' means political or cultural unity, then this can indeed be traced back to the Carolingian era. If, on the other hand, 'Europe' implies a harmonious diversity of peoples who nevertheless share a common awareness – a 'league of nations', so to speak – then no such thing can be discerned before the thirteenth or the fourteenth century, if not later. 'The most important question,' Curcio adds, 'is whether there was "a certain idea of Europe" and whether it had a name. It certainly did for Charlemagne.' From his reign onwards, therefore, Curcio believes it legitimate to speak of Europe. Against this, the French historian Edouard Perroy, in his *Histoire générale des civilisations*, while certainly stressing the profound unity of the Carolingian world, entitled his chapter on the eighth and ninth centuries 'the effacement of Europe'.

There could be endless discussion about the 'birth of Europe'. The Italo-American Robert Lopez declared: 'The word "Europe", today, does not so much imply a unitary faith or a universal state, but rather a set of political institutions, of secular knowledge, of artistic and literary traditions, of economic and social interests, which are shared or closely related. In this light, the Carolingian Empire appears to have been a remarkable but finally abortive effort.'

The word 'Europe'

The word 'Europe' was rarely used in classical antiquity, and still less from the sixth to the eighth century. It reappears in a very clear sense, to denote Western Christian unity (and, to tell the truth, not including the British Isles).

In 769, a Christian living in the Muslim Caliphate of Cordoba, Isidore the Younger, described the Battle of Poitiers (otherwise known as the Battle of Tours). He described the army that Charles Martel led against the Saracens as the *Europeenses* – 'Europeans' – no doubt because it included non-Christians, since otherwise it would probably have been called *Christiani*. 'Leaving their houses in the morning,' wrote Isidore, 'the Europeans espied the well-aligned tents of the Arabs.'

Again, shortly before Charlemagne's coronation in the year 800, he was described by the poet Angilbert as 'the venerable head of Europe', 'the king, the father of Europe', 'the summit of Europe', 'Europe's venerable leading light'. For others in the ninth century, the Empire was *tota occidentalis Europe* – 'all of western Europe'.

Nithard (790–858), Charlemagne's grandson from his daughter Bertha, wrote: 'Charles, called by all nations the great Emperor, left all Europe satisfied by his bounty.' Some years later, in about 884, the Monk of St Gall, the rather dull author of the *Acts of the Emperor Charles (De gestis karoli imperatoris)*, dedicated to Charles the Bald, wrote that the work of Charlemagne had affected 'all of Europe'. And Widukind, who died after 973, wrote in his *Rex gestae saxonicae* that 'the Emperor is by right the master of all Europe'.

THE TRUE NATURE OF THE CAROLINGIAN EPOCH

Charlemagne (Karolus magnus) was not a 'king of France'; nor was he, under his German name of Karl der Grosse, a 'king of Germany'. Such titles are wholly anachronistic.

Charlemagne was 'King of the Franks'; and they were divided mainly into Neustrians in the west (in what is now France) and Austrasians in the east (spanning the Rhine). The Pepin dynasty, to which he belonged, was Austrasian; but he was probably born in Neustria, where he spent his youth. He was bilingual at a time when pure Neustrians had to go to Prüm or Fulda Abbey to learn Germanic languages.

The 'Carolingian Renaissance' was not inspired by German values, but by the Latin past. So much so that, centuries later, Hitler, obsessed by the myth of race, believed that Charlemagne was not 'a true German'. Charlemagne, indeed, was no precursor of future Franco-German conflicts.

The Partition of 843

Similarly, it would be anachronistic to conclude that because Charlemagne had been both 'king of France' and 'king of Germany', the Partition of 843 made the French and the Germans hereditary enemies, bound to dispute the kingdom of the centre – Lotharingia or Lorraine – for a further thousand years or more. The German historian Heinz-Otto Sieburg has demonstrated that the idea of hereditary Franco-German enmity did not appear until 1840 in Germany and 1866 in France.

The Empire remained 'Roman'

The idea of a new Empire, separate and distinct from the Roman Empire, and alien from the Byzantine Empire in the East, is equally false. The ideal that was shared by Charlemagne, by the Popes, by the intellectual élite, and by very many bishops, counts, and military leaders, was to re-establish the Roman Empire. That Empire had covered both East and West. And one of the arguments used in the year 800 to justify Charlemagne's coronation was that the Byzantines, led by a woman, Irene, had no real Emperor: hence Charlemagne could legitimately take over the Empire.

Charlemagne's dream, then, and one which was briefly realized, was to re-establish the Roman Empire on the solid basis of the Catholic Church and the religious authority of the Pope – who in reality was under the Emperor's protection. Ideally, the Empire should be united, as it had been under Constantine or Theodosius the Great. If not, the most that could be accepted was its division, into two great sections, East and West, as under Diocletian or Theodosius's two sons.

CONCLUSION

We have sought to identify any signs of a sense of community in the geographical area of Western Europe during the Carolingian era. Clearly, it was constantly rent by internal conflicts based on rival sovereignties and ambitions. When on rare occasions Europe appears to be united under a single political ruler, the meaning and the duration of such unity need to be examined with care. We have already seen how ephemeral were attempts to build the Roman Empire of the West. Did Charlemagne's conquests amount to the revival of such an Empire? They certainly created an entity covering much of what is now the European Community, the main exceptions being Greece, Denmark, the British Isles, Portugal, most of Spain, and the south of Italy. The size of Charlemagne's Empire, indeed, was astonishing, at a time when communications were so difficult. Was it a provisional and incomplete form of what came to be known as Europe? It was certainly ephemeral, since the Empire was divided in 843. Even so, as an example of a community with cultural and civilizing ambitions, it remained a fascinating object-lesson.

8

Europe Under Siege

THE SARACENS

When the Prophet Mohammed founded Islam, the West took little notice of what seemed a distant, Oriental phenomenon. Those most likely to be affected directly were the Byzantine Christians; but they were generally unpopular in the West. Yet on the death of Mohammed in 632, as André Miquel put it, 'the great history of Islam was on the march'.

This revealed religion, monotheistic and intransigent, involving total submission to Allah or God (as the word 'Islam' implies), created a system in which theology and politics were merged. Like Christianity, Islam later divided into different sects; but it first appeared as the inspiration for gigantic conquests by the nomadic Bedouins of the desert, mostly on horseback. Their seizure of Jerusalem in 636 was the first blow of an attack that was felt by all of Christendom.

The Arab conquest

From Syria and Arabia, the Muslims – then often known as 'Saracens' (from the Arabic word *sharkin*, 'oriental') – advanced not only towards the east but also into north Africa, conquering Egypt, Libya, and the Maghreb by the end of the seventh century. In the process they defeated and converted the Berbers. Seven thousand Berbers, profiting from the weakness of the Visigoth monarchy, crossed the Straits of Gibraltar and pushed into Spain. Certain Visigoth princes actually welcomed them. Within a few months they had occupied Cadiz, Seville, Cordoba, and Toledo. In 713, the last Christian Visigoth king of Spain was defeated and killed; and in the same year the Caliph of Damascus proclaimed that Spain had been annexed to Islam. Aragon fell in 714, followed in 719–20 by Catalonia, Roussillon, and Bas-Languedoc, including Narbonne.

The Saracens in Gaul: Poitiers

Muslim horsemen made their way up the Rhône Valley in 725 without meeting any real resistance, and they sacked Autun. Carcassonne and Toulouse were defended by Eudes, Duke of Aquitaine. A second group of Muslim cavalry, setting out from Pamplona in 732, came through the pass at Roncevaux, reaching Dax and crossing the Garonne near Bordeaux, and heading for Poitiers and Tours.

This time, however, they met organized resistance. The mayor of the palace Charles Martel now held sway over a large part of Frankish Gaul. In October 732 the Franks attacked the Saracens between Tours and Poitiers, with cold weather as an additional ally against the invaders from the south. The Saracen leader was killed, and his army retreated. Charles Martel pursued them and defeated them south of Narbonne in 737. From 759 onwards, they withdrew beyond the Pyrenees. Meanwhile, in 750, the Umayyad dynasty in Damascus, which had inspired this Saracen conquest, found itself unable to maintain unity in its vast empire. It was replaced by the Abbassid dynasty, founded by an Iranian, Abu Abbas, who settled in Baghdad as 'Imam' or spokesman of God and Commander of the Faithful. It was the end of Arab hegemony.

The Emirate of Cordoba

In the Iberian peninsula, real power was now in the hands of the Abbassids. In 756, the grandson of the last Umayyad Caliph landed near Malaga, went up the Guadalquivir valley and defeated the Governor of Cordoba, to be acclaimed 'Emir of Spain'. He soon gave orders that prayers were to be said in his name: but he did not dare take the title of Caliph or Prince of the Faithful. That had to wait until 932. Around Cordoba, the capital, a powerful and prosperous state developed in the tenth century, reaching a level of culture worthy of that then prevailing in Baghdad.

The conquest of Sicily

In 788, Idris ben Abdallah, a descendant of the Prophet, founded in Meknes and Fez another dynasty, that of the Idrissids. It was followed in the year 800, around Kairouan in Tunisia, by a further Emirate under Ibrahim ben Aghlab, founder of the Aghlabid dynasty.

The Aghlabids were the more important in the history of Europe. They set out from Tunisia on the conquest of Sicily. They began by taking Mazara in the west in 827, then Palermo in 831 and Messina in 843. From here they attacked southern Italy, in Apulia, Calabria, and Campagna, and then even central Italy. In 846, landing at Ostia, they advanced on Rome and sacked St Peter's. In the south-east they held Brindisi, Taranto, Bari, and Benevento; and although they soon lost Bari and Taranto they nevertheless continued their progress, making their way up the Adriatic to sack Comacchio, north of Ravenna.

In 870 they seized Malta, thus gaining control of the seaway between the eastern and western Mediterranean. The Emir of Cordoba, meanwhile, continually mounted raids on the coast of Languedoc, sometimes sending expeditions up the Rhône Valley. In Provence, his soldiers set up a permanent base in La Garde-Freinet.

Arab influence

Many European Christians naturally hoped for what the Spaniards called a Reconquista to recover the lands lost to the Saracens. But other Christians had to live with the invaders of Spain and southern Italy. In the ninth and tenth centuries, the Muslims dominated Europe's trade by sea, and controlled that of the Italian merchant fleets. They flooded the western Mediterranean with goods from central Asia and even China. Their coinage – the golden dinar and the silver dirhem – replaced the Byzantine golden solidus. Their boats were small, and had triangular sails; they took to caravan routes rather than the Roman roads; they carried their boats overland. Between cities they built caravanserais, often on a large scale. The native peasants, oppressed by their soldiers and landowners, scratched a meagre living from the soil.

In the year 800, the Caliphate of Cordoba had some three and a half million inhabitants; by the year 1000, their number had grown to seven million. As well as the ruling Muslims, both Arab and Berber, there were Spaniards converted to Islam (the Muwallahs), unconverted Christians (the Mozarabs), Jews (mainly in the towns), and slaves (black Africans and Slavs).

In the end, Spain achieved stability in all this diversity. Arabic was the sacred language, and also that of literature, poetry and philology. For trade in the Mediterranean there was a lingua franca much influenced by Arabic; while the Christians retained their own

Romance language derived from Latin, in which they held Councils and communicated with the Christian kingdoms to the north. Via Spain and southern Italy, a number of Arabic words entered European languages, including English: alcohol, algebra, apricot, artichoke, chess, cipher, cotton, crimson, elixir, tariff, zenith, and zero are only a few of them. For their part, some Muslim poets chose to write in a mixture of Romance and Arabic languages known as *muwachchah*.

Even so, the history of Spain until the fifteenth century is not essentially a story of mutual assimilation, like that of the Vikings in Normandy or Britain. Instead, it was a long struggle with repeated advances and retreats. The latter included in particular counter-offensives by the Almoravides, from 1080 onwards, and the Almohades in the twelfth century.

The Christians in the north

The north-west of the Iberian peninsula – Galicia and Asturia – was never fully conquered by the Muslims. Charlemagne, moreover, buoyed up by his predecessors' victories and his own successes in Italy and Saxony, dreamed of reconquering Spain. As well as enlarging the Empire, it would be a holy war of Christians against Muslims. In 778, therefore, Charlemagne marched on Saragossa via Pamplona. He failed completely.

Retreating to counter a new danger in Saxony, he lost the rearguard of his army, massacred at Roncevaux by the Gascons (or perhaps the Basques). A little later, he managed to capture Gerona and then, in 801, Barcelona, giving him some hold on Catalonia. The King of Galicia and Asturia, Alfonso II, secured Charlemagne's help in capturing Lisbon from the Muslims in 798; but it was soon lost again, and was not recovered until 1135.

However, part of what is now Portugal remained free. At the same time, Charlemagne did not scruple to receive a number of Muslim princes at his court in Aix-la-Chapelle.

Between 950 and 1100, the only part of Spain recaptured from the Muslims was Castile, plus Salamanca. The King of Castile, Alfonso VI, entered Toledo in 1085, and the Muslims never reconquered it.

What most obstructed these first attempts at a Reconquista was the arrival in Spain of two successive African dynasties.

The Almoravids and Almohads

In the words of André Miquel:

> Islam's salvation dawned in the western Sahara, in the Senegal–Niger region, where groups of Berber warriors, under the command of Ibn Yasin, trained for a holy war in their fortified monasteries. These were the ribâts, marabouts, the almurabitûn or Almoravides. Their first skirmishes were with the surrounding Berbers, whom they defeated and recruited into their fighting units, and with the black people. They conquered the kingdom of Ghana in about 1076.

Then they moved north, making Marrakesh their capital, and conquering half of Algeria: they took Algiers in 1082. In response to appeals from the Islamic princes in Spain, they crossed the Straits of Gibraltar and reunified Muslim Spain from the Tagus to the Ebro, except for the Christian outpost of Toledo.

This period of armoured knights is famous for the exploits of a noble Castilian, Rodrigo Diaz, from Viva near Burgos, known as 'el Cid' (from sidi, lord) and as the 'Campeador' or conqueror. He captured Valencia in 1094.

Twenty years after the Almoravids' first conquests, their hold on Spain was becoming precarious as the Christians attacked them ferociously, especially in Portugal and Catalonia. Eventually the attacks succeeded and Portugal was completely freed in 1189. Thus, in the twelfth century, the Christians repulsed the Almoravids with irresistible force.

The Almohads were not Moors from Mauretania, but Moroccans – non-nomadic Berbers from the mountains. Their leader was Ibn Tumart, 'the redresser of wrongs': a fundamentalist, he preached the absolute unity of God (Al Murvahhid – whence the Europeanized word *Almohad*). Ibn Tumart proclaimed himself the Mahdi or new prophet, sole interpreter of law and tradition. His successor seized Marrakesh, Algeria, and what is now Tunisia.

In 1145, he undertook the conquest of Spain. Almohad Spain became a new Empire, whose leader Abd al Mu'min was proclaimed Caliph, counterpart to those of Baghdad and Cairo. The Almohads lasted longer than the Almoravids; but in 1212 the Christians of Aragon, Navarre, Castile, and Leon inflicted a crushing defeat on them at Las Navas de Tolosa. In 1236, the Muslims lost, and for good, their famous capital of Cordoba, where they left many monuments, including a magnificent mosque. All that remained to them was the small Islamic kingdom of Granada in the south-east.

Saracen influence

A later chapter will discuss the extraordinary intellectual influence that Islam exerted on Europe after 1100. But its material influence was considerable too.

The fact that Islam came from the East determined the nature of many of the contributions that it made to Western Europe: animals are among the examples. The Romans had already imported horses from central Asia. With the Saracens came the barb, or Barbary horse, from Numidia, which produced the Spanish jennet and, by breeding the barb with the Iranian horse, the famous 'Arab' steed. Similarly, Maghreb sheep produced the merinos of Spain and led indirectly to the 'Mesta', the powerful organization of shepherds which greatly influenced Spanish society.

Among the new fruits and vegetables which, to quote 'Le Roman de la Rose', 'came straight from the land of the Saracens', were apricots, artichokes, lettuces, cauliflowers, parsley, beetroot, fennel, celery, melons, marrows, lemons, and aubergines. Islam extended in Spain the cultivation of olive groves and vineyards; it introduced hard wheat to Spain and southern Italy, as well as rice from India, which began to be grown along the Guadalquivir; and it brought the date palm to Spain. The gardens of rich Muslims greatly encouraged the development of horticulture, symbolized by the white damask (Damascus) rose.

Other innovations included silk and cotton, which were brought to Sicily and Spain, and paper. Of Chinese origin, this was first made of linen and hemp. It reached Baghdad in about 800, then Andalusia and later Rome. It came into use in south-west France in the fourteenth century. Its success spelt the end of papyrus and parchment, especially since it was better suited for the widespread use that printing eventually made possible.

The great East–West trade routes of the high Middle Ages were almost all of Muslim origin, although the Arabs established only one port – Almeria – in Spain.

Part of the trade they plied was in slaves from central Asia, Africa, and the Slav areas of Europe.

THE VIKINGS

The word 'Viking' derives from *vik* or *vic*, as in Brunswick, Schleswig, or Lundenwic (London). In Western Europe there are 870 place-names ending in vic. Vik or vic is derived in turn from *weichen*, a place of retreat but also the borderline between land and water, but their origins were German.

In the first six centuries AD, what is now Denmark – Jutland and the Danish islands, as well as much of southern Scandinavia – was somewhat isolated from the rest of Europe. Its Germanic inhabitants, who travelled the sea in boats propelled by oars, did extensive trade with the Roman world. They sold furs and amber in exchange for amphorae and various objects of bronze, silver, and glass, many of which have been found in Danish burial-grounds. Some Scandinavian warriors enlisted in the Roman legions, and took back to their homelands gold coins and other souvenirs.

Later, the westward thrust of the Slavs temporarily isolated this Nordic world by blocking the Oder and even the Elbe. For a hundred years, only the Frisians and a number of Jewish merchants from the south maintained some trading links.

It was between AD 650 and 800 that the Vikings came on the scene. The first to appear were the Svear or Sver, the founders of what came to be Sweden, near to old Uppsala and Lake Mälar. Then came a number of small Danish and Norwegian kingdoms. Their great innovation was to build boats of oak, with strong bulwarks and a pronounced keel, which made it possible to supplement the oars with a sizeable sail. These vessels enabled the Vikings first to make many more voyages to Britain, and later to travel much further. The objects unearthed by archaeologists in Sweden include many whose decoration is clearly of English origin.

The first westward invasion: Lindisfarne

These seafaring peoples, based on the rivers rather than the shores of the Baltic, rapidly came to dominate the Straits of Denmark. While Charlemagne battled against the Saxons, the Vikings began the series of raids that made them widely feared. On 8 June 793, the monks of Lindisfarne, a rich monastery on the borders of England and Scotland, saw dragon-prowed ships approaching. Their occupants leapt ashore, massacred the monks, overthrew the Cross, seized treasure, killed cattle and loaded their boats with the carcasses, then set fire to all that remained, and made off. As pagans, they had no reason to respect the monks; and unless they met firm resistance they were encouraged to make further raids, which they did for 200 years, somewhat refining their technique. These raids earned the Vikings an appalling reputation, since all accounts of them were written by their enemies. In fact, more and more trade came to alternate with pillage. What the Vikings wanted was to enlarge their land and sea domain. They were in effect at once merchants, seamen, and warriors.

The Svear or Swedes

Sailing east, the Svear landed on the eastern and southern coasts of the Baltic, where they set up trading posts. From there they went up the Russian and Baltic rivers. Carrying their longships overland, they came to the rivers that flow into the Black Sea, and reached Byzantium and the Muslim states of the Near East. Along the way, they never ceased to trade. The diplomat Ahmad Ibn Fadlan, sent by the Caliph of Baghdad to the town of Bolgar on the Volga in 922, gave a good description of the Vikings, there known as Rus:

> Never have I seen men of more magnificent bearing. They are as tall as palm trees, with reddish-blond hair and pale skin. They wear neither shirts nor sleeved coats. The men wear coats which they toss on their shoulders so as to have a hand free. Every man bears an axe, a dagger, and a sword: they are never seen without them.

The women wore chains – one for every 10,000 dirhem possessed by their husbands. The main trade was in furs (sable, squirrel, ermine, marten, fox, and beaver), as well as amber, wax, honey, swords and breast-plates, and finally slaves for the Muslims. The Svears brought back to Sweden bronzes, fine glass vases, silver cups, and, above all, silk, which they bought in Byzantium. Arab coinage played a very important role: in the island of Gotland alone, in the Baltic, 40,000 Arab silver coins have been found, and 17,000 in the rest of Sweden and Denmark. At that time there were highly productive silver mines in Afghanistan, and gold was only a secondary, supplementary precious metal.

Very soon, however, Arab coinage was displaced by coins of German origin; and in westward-facing Norway, only 400 Arab coins have been found.

The Norwegians and the Atlantic

Naturally enough, it was the Norwegians who ventured westwards, eventually a very long way.

To the north, they sailed towards Narvik, which the Gulf Stream protected from ice. 'There they met the Lapps, who face snow even in summer, eat raw meat, wear animal skins, and breed reindeer.' But the Lapps barely traded with the rest of the world before the twelfth and thirteenth centuries. At the end of the ninth century, Ottar, a farmer from Tromso in the far north, sailed up the coast to the North Cape; going further than the whalers, he finally reached the mouth of the Dvina, where the land was inhabited by a large number of Finns.

The great Norwegian expeditions were in the west. They went first to the Shetland Islands, which they used as bases, and where they established farms. From there they continued to the Faroes or 'islands of sheep', so-called after the flocks installed there earlier by Irish hermits. In the ninth century, this was the furthest Viking outpost.

From Iceland to America

But the greatest achievement of the Viking explorers was to have discovered the American continent. At the end of the eighth century, Gardar Svarvarsson, a Swede living in Denmark and married to a Norwegian, was blown off course by storms until he reached a large island. A number of Norwegians followed him there: they called it Thule and later Iceland. In about 874, the first Norwegians settled there and founded the town of Reykjavik. It was at this time that King Harald Harfagr ('the beautiful-haired') was uniting Norway, and the settlers in Iceland had left the kingdom to escape his authority. By 930, they numbered 16,000–20,000. The Icelandic national hero, Egil Skallagrimsson, was born there in 904. It was in Iceland that the 'Thingvellir' – the first parliament in Europe – made its appearance.

At the end of the ninth century another Icelandic explorer, Eric the Red, reached Greenland (it was he who named it) and explored all its fjords. In 896, twenty-five ships with 500 men, women, and children aboard, as well as cattle, horses, tools, and wood, set out to colonize the south-west coast. Eventually, its population numbered 3,000. From October to May every year they were cut off from the rest of the world.

Sailing alone towards Greenland, a young man named Bjarne Herjulfsson set a course too far south and found himself approaching a coastline of wooded hills. It was America, near Labrador.

Later, Leif Eriksson, the son of Eric the Red, explored part of this new continent, starting from Greenland and following the Labrador coast. He claimed to have reached 'Vinland', a land of vines, forests, and salmon. But since he added that the dew there was as sweet as honey, he may have been stretching the truth. In fact, the Vikings seem to have gone as far south as about the 41st parallel, near present-day New Haven. In 1004, Leif's brother Thorwald undertook a similar voyage, but in 1020, an attempt at colonization was foiled by the natives. The Vikings were unable to settle in large numbers in the New World; in Greenland, however, they prospered for a time: there was a bishop, as well as sixteen churches and two monasteries. Eventually, an Inuit invasion brought the Viking occupation to an end.

The Vikings in north-west Europe

The Norwegians first made for Ireland, then north and west Scotland. The Danes preferred the coasts of Friesland, Holland, Zeeland, and southern England, where there were no fighting ships to resist them. The shallow-keeled longships drew only a metre of water, and so could sail up the rivers. Reaching the mouth of the Loire in 819–20 and that of the Seine in 820, they sailed upstream and up the Scheldt and the Rhine. While the Norwegians occupied most of Ireland between 830 and 840, the Danes dealt heavy blows to the Empire of Louis the Pious, from whom they tried to capture Friesland and the Netherlands. They settled at Duurstide, where they remained until 885. In 840–1 they conquered Essex, Kent, Hampshire, and Dorset, as well as Rouen and Picardy. In 843 they sacked Nantes. In 844 they sailed up the Garonne, and along the Spanish and Portuguese coasts, going up the Guadalquivir as far as Seville. On 29 March 845 they sacked Paris. In 848 they laid waste Bordeaux, and in 849 Périgueux.

The Mediterranean

From 850 onwards, the Vikings began to settle in the region to which they later gave their name – Normandy. The King of France paid them to leave, and between 859 and 861 they moved south. They crossed the Strait of Gibraltar, sailed along the coast of Roussillon to winter in the Camargue, then sacked Avignon, Arles, and Nîmes. Reaching Italy, they sacked Pisa and ravaged Tuscany. They then returned to the Atlantic. Using the same tactics, but now accompanied by mounted troops, they went up the river valleys and attacked Poitiers, Limoges, Clermont-Ferrand, Angers and other towns in 872–3.

The Danes in Britain

In two separate periods, the Danes played a leading role in the history of Britain. First, throughout the second half of the ninth century, they profited from the fact that the country was split into small Anglo-Saxon and Celtic kingdoms to make temporary but damaging inroads. Only the famous Alfred the Great, King of Wessex (871–900), was able to stem their advance. Baulked by him in the south, they made their way up the Trent and Humber estuaries to conquer the Kingdom of Mercia in 874. Meanwhile, they went on fighting Alfred. An intelligent and cultivated man, he set the seal on a number of indecisive battles by finally concluding with Guthrun, the Danish leader, the Peace of Wedmore (878).

Guthrun accepted Christian baptism, and England, together with some western tribes, was divided between the Anglo-Saxon zone in the south and south-east and a Danish zone in the north-east. Alfred was then enthroned in London.

During the tenth century, Alfred's successors continued his efforts and drove the Danes back. In 980, however, they counter-attacked in force. By then, Denmark had been practically united under Harald Blaatand ('Blue-tooth'), himself a Christian convert. His grandson Canute II ('the Great') reconquered south-east England, then the rest of the country, including London. In 1028 he conquered Norway, establishing thereby a vast Danish Empire which also included Iceland and Greenland. Canute made a point of winning over the clergy: he built churches and monasteries throughout the Empire, and even went on pilgrimage to Rome. He also arranged dynastic marriages between English and Danish noble families. He died in 1035. His son, Canute III, was a far less impressive ruler. He managed to retain his hold on England, but when he died in 1041, the brief Danish reign there died with him.

William the Conqueror: 1066

Yet even this was not the end of Viking influence on Britain. In 1066, William the Conqueror, Duke of Normandy, crossed the Channel and defeated the last Saxon king of England, Harold II, at the Battle of Hastings. It was the beginning of the Norman dynasty; and the Normans were of Viking stock.

From their base in what is now the Netherlands, the Norse invaders had taken advantage of a dynastic dispute in the Frankish kingdom between Charles the Simple, a descendant of Charlemagne, and an elected king, Odo, ancestor of Hugh Capet, who later, in 987, founded the new Capetian dynasty. Charles the Simple, finding that the Norsemen were arriving in ever greater numbers along the Channel coast, made his peace with them by the Treaty of Saint-Clair-sur-Epte, ceding Normandy to the Norse chieftain Rollo or Rolf. Thus the Duchy of Normandy was born. Rollo, a giant of a man whom no horse was strong enough to carry, accepted baptism and married Gisèle, the daughter of his overlord, the King of France. William the Conqueror, also known as 'the Bastard', was one of Rollo's descendants.

Viking traces

Several hundred place-names in Normandy are of Viking origin, including Caudebec, Honfleur, and Cap de la Hague. At the same time, many historians believe like Louis Halphen that 'the native population of Calvados and the Seine valley themselves contributed greatly to French Norman stock'.

In England, there are countless Norse place-names in Northumberland, Yorkshire, Norfolk, Suffolk, and elsewhere. The Isle of Man and the Hebrides remained Norwegian until the end of the thirteenth century. The Orkneys and the Shetlands were Norwegian, and then Danish, until 1468; and Scandinavian languages were still being spoken there in the late eighteenth century.

The Normans in Sicily

The Normans who ruled the Kingdom of Sicily between 1058 and 1090 came from France. Tancred of Hauteville sent eight of his twelve sons there: they included Robert Guiscard and Roger, the founders of the dynasty. The island, which in its time had been Carthaginian, Greek, Roman, Vandal, Byzantine, and Arab, was further greatly influenced by these men from the north. In the thirteenth century, Sicily even provided a powerful Emperor, Frederick II of Hohenstaufen.

The Viking contribution

The legacy of the Vikings included shipbuilding and navigation, iron swords and other weapons, and domestic objects such as furniture, which were sometimes of outstanding workmanship. Their decorative skill was remarkable, as can be seen from the prows of their ships. But neither their architecture nor the graves that mark their wanderings in Europe bear comparison with those of the countries they invaded. They had a rich literary heritage in the Norse sagas, but only from the ninth century onwards; and their own writing, the so-called 'runes', was used only in a few inscriptions, for instance in the Isle of Man.

The Vikings' most significant contribution may well have been political or moral. They applied the principle of equality, and they elected their leaders. When Charles the Simple sought to negotiate with them, he asked to see their chieftain. 'We have no master,' came the instant reply: 'We are all equal.' However, they did send Rollo, who was indeed their chief. Their slow and gradual conversion to Christianity only strengthened their spirit of freedom, which became a key strand in Europe's common heritage.

From the Vikings to the Hanseatic League

As time went on, however, the Vikings themselves lost ground. Their northern trade suffered from a lack of manpower, owing to their incessant wars. At the very moment when they were firmly settling in Normandy, in England, and in Sicily, Wendish pirates of Slav origin were pillaging the coasts of Denmark and Sweden, usurping their trade and (in the thirteenth century) taking thousands of slaves. Above all, in 1143 the town of Lübeck was founded, and around it the 'Hanseatic

League'. This began building large merchant ships or 'cogs'. They had no fighting capacity, but they could carry large cargoes economically, and their draught and stability made them much better than the Vikings' longships at sailing across the wind. Among their innovations were the jib and the bowsprit, which was less dramatic than the longships' dragon, but more effective. The Vikings, who could carry only small cargoes, found themselves crowded out.

Unlike other peoples, including the Slavs, the Vikings influenced Europe long before their conversion to Christianity. But it was only after being converted that they took a full part in the European élite. There were three main stages in their gradual adoption of the Christian faith, headed by Anskar, by Harald Blue-tooth, and by St Olaf and Canute.

Anskar

Denmark was the most accessible of the Scandinavian territories; and the court of Louis the Pious hoped to introduce Christianity there by supporting rival claimants to political power. In 822, the Emperor and the Pope together sent Ebbo, Archbishop of Rheims, to Denmark as a missionary. The only result was a few baptisms, notably that of a pretender to the throne named Harald. Ebbo therefore proposed to send a permanent legate, and the choice fell on Anskar, a former monk of Corbie in Picardy who was then teaching at 'New Corbie' or Corvey in Westphalia. Anskar accepted his mission enthusiastically. His first visit was brief; but on returning to the Imperial Court in Worms, he met envoys sent there by the King of Sweden, Björn, and he agreed to go to Sweden to preach the Gospel. It took him several months to reach the town of Björkö (Birca), a trading centre on Lake Målar. There, too, he was able to secure a number of conversions.

Finally, it was decided to establish for Anskar the Archbishopric of Hamburg. He received in Rome itself his Archbishop's cope or pallium. But although he was now entitled to establish several dioceses, there were too few Christians to fill them, and the results were disappointing.

As the Frankish Empire's influence declined, the Vikings redoubled their raids on the northern coasts. Hamburg itself was pillaged and burned. When Anskar died, in 865 in Bremen, Christianity was still an alien religion in Denmark and Sweden. The joint archbishopric of Hamburg–Bremen had no suffragan bishopric. Rather than being the spearhead of a missionary movement aimed at all of Scandinavia, it was in effect a beleaguered outpost of the faith.

Harald Blue-tooth

Unni, Archbishop of Hamburg–Bremen (917–936), took the risk of going to the court of the King of Denmark, Gorm, who was a great enemy and persecutor of Christians. He preached the Gospel in Schleswig, then obtained from Gorm's son Harald Blaatand, or 'Blue-tooth', and from his Christian queen their authorization to extend his mission to Denmark. Harald Blue-tooth, who succeeded his father Gorm in 950, had himself baptized with his wife and his son Svend. The then Archbishop of Hamburg–Bremen, Adallag, who was there for fifty years before his death in 988, took the opportunity to establish new dioceses not only in Denmark itself, but also in the islands and in Norway, where King Haakon contemplated holding a plebiscite on whether or not to adopt Christianity. Harald finally died in 986.

St Olaf and Canute

Harald's successor was his son Svend Gabelbart ('Fork-beard'). Although Svend had been baptized, he saw Christianity as essentially Germanic, and hence in his view a sworn enemy of the old Scandinavian Viking spirit of which he made himself the champion, complete with raids, pillage, conquests, and distant expeditions. During his reign, which lasted until 1014, persecution became general throughout the vast domain that he sought to establish over all the Scandinavian countries – though with many difficulties in Sweden – and even over England. Svend entered London in 1013, but died – after a tardy return to the Christian faith – in the following year.

It was time for Christianity to prevail. In Norway, which for a while had become independent again, the reigning prince was Olaf, nicknamed 'Olaf the Saint'. From his court in the north at Trondjheim he waged a constant campaign against the pagan sorcerers and other magicians who had so much influenced Scandinavian culture. Olaf himself also worshipped at Hamburg–Bremen.

But the key figure in the process of conversion was Svend's son, the famous Canute. His great empire, comprising Denmark, Sweden, Norway, and Great Britain, was converted to Christianity. Like Charlemagne,

Canute did not always adhere to Christian ethics: but his faith was undeniable. In 1026–8, he went on pilgrimage to Rome. 'I tell you,' he wrote, 'I came to Rome to pray for the forgiveness of my sins and for the salvation of the kingdoms and peoples that are subject to my Empire.' He gave careful attention to establishing the Catholic hierarchy and restoring the Christian ideal. His reign saw the end of paganism in this part of the world, except for some popular superstitions.

This third wave of conversion, of which Canute was the triumphant architect, was marked by a further change: a quasi-break with the Archbishopric of Hamburg–Bremen. From now on, it was no longer the German Church that exerted influence on Scandinavia, but the English Church. English, Irish, and Scottish clerics, monks, and bishops flocked to Scandinavia in response to appeals from local or royal authorities. For a time, Hamburg–Bremen tried to reassert its influence. There was talk of establishing a 'Nordic patriarchate' – which would have been against the traditions of the Roman Church. It was simpler to incorporate the Scandinavian churches into the English system – particularly when, a generation after Canute's death in 1035, the descendants of the Vikings, the Normans from Normandy, settled firmly on the English throne.

THE SLAVS

The Slavs played a considerable role in the history and civilization of Europe. Even today, as well as Russian, Byelorussian, and Ukrainian, Slav languages spoken by tens of millions of people include Polish, Czech, and Slovak in the north, and Bulgarian, Slovene, and Serbo-Croat in the south. Romanian, which is basically a Latin language, has also undergone very strong Slav influence.

The arrival of the Slavs

In about the fourth century AD, the 'inchoate mass' of the Slavs was to be found around the sources of the Niemen, Dnieper, and Pripet rivers. They had probably been there for centuries. Urn burial, as seen in the Bronze Age, was characteristic of their graves. In the west, they had trading links with the Germans and the Celts.

There followed a series of westward invasions. Mongols and Turks in Asia began to expand into Slav areas, driving the Slavs towards Western Europe, sometimes in mixed invading hordes. The Avars (of Mongolian origin), the proto-Bulgarians or Bulgarians (of Turkish origin), the Khazars, the Pechenegs, the Cumans, then the Mongols, and in the sixteenth century the Kalmucks – all eventually came to grief, one after another. Only one group, the Magyars, managed to settle, in the eighth to twelfth centuries, in Pannonia, alongside the Slavs and not far from the Germans. The Slavs, however, remained.

The Avars were first reported in Europe in 558. In 561 they reached the Danube. In 567, in alliance with the Germanic Lombards, they crushed the Byzantines. The town of Salona in Dalmatia, where Diocletian had once lived, was besieged by the Slavs in 600, then destroyed by the Avars in 614. The town of Sirmium, capital of Pannonia, where Marcus Aurelius had died, also fell to the Avars. After a long and chequered history, no more was heard of them after 822.

The Bulgars are mentioned for the first time in 482, when they were living in Ukraine. They were thought to be related to the Turks. Their Slav troops brought them into the southern Slav ambience, with a Slavic language of their own. In 680, they crossed the Danube and occupied Moesia, or what is now northern Bulgaria. The centre of this first domain was Pliska.

The Khazars remained in the region of the Ural, the Volga, and the Don; but they disappeared in the tenth century.

The Slavs: north, centre, and south

Among those who stayed on were the Slavs in the north, the centre, and the south. They were fine infantrymen; and the Avars and others from the steppes made excellent cavalry troops. Their combined prowess explains their success against Byzantium, and also against the Germanic lands. The age-long conflict between Slavs and Germans was most evident in the eighth to tenth centuries.

At the time of Charlemagne and his earliest successors, the Slavs could conveniently be classified in four main groups:

1. The eastern Slavs need not detain us here. Their sole contacts with the West were via the Swedes and the Byzantines. They lived in the steppes and forests amid the turmoil of invasions from Asia: but their courage and their numbers enabled them

to put up a superb resistance. It was the beginning of a tradition that would last.

2. The northern Slavs included the Obodrites and the Wilzes, on the eastern bank of the lower Elbe, facing their fierce Saxon and Frankish enemies on the opposite shore. A little further upstream on the Elbe were the Serbs and the Wends.
3. The central Slavs were essentially the Moravians, in eastern Bavaria, and the Czechs and Slovaks in northern Pannonia.
4. The southern Slavs travelled up the Danube towards the Drava and Sava valleys; they also settled to the south of the Danube in what is now Yugoslavia. Meanwhile, the Venetians, having freed themselves from Byzantine rule in 1008, were establishing small ports along the Dalmatian coast.

The Slav Marches

There are few perceptible traces of Slav influence on Western Europe at this time. Not until the Slavs were converted to Christianity were they integrated into either the Roman or the Byzantine community. Charlemagne tended to impose conversion on the peoples he conquered, such as the Saxons. He did so with the northern Slavs and the Moravians in Pannonia, establishing 'Marches' under his rule. They were not easy to control; but Charlemagne's son Louis the Pious and his grandson Lewis the German managed to reconquer them, at least temporarily, after sporadic revolts. Unlike Charlemagne, Louis the Pious disapproved of conversion by force. Instead of soldiers, it was courageous missionaries, often Germans, who led pioneering missions into these 'barbarian' countries, as they were then called.

The southern Slavs

The first Slavs to be converted, however, were those in the south, beginning in the eighth century with the Slovenes. Threatened by the Avars in the north, they sought the protection of Pepin the Short, King of the Franks and ruler of Bavaria. Two Slav princes from Carinthia, held hostage in Bavaria, were brought up in the Christian faith at the monastery of Chiemsee. When in turn they came to the Carinthian throne, they asked the Irish Bishop Virgil of Salzburg to help them convert their subjects. Churches were built and monasteries were founded – at Imichen in Trentino and Kreuzmünster in Upper Austria. There was a pagan revolt, but Tassilo, the Duke of Bavaria, reconquered Carinthia. Then Charlemagne seized both countries. He completed the process of conversion, peacefully, among the Slavs but not the Avars. In this way, the Latin Church established its authority over a minority of the Slav peoples. Anskar, who was so active in converting the Danes, lacked the resources to extend his efforts to the northern Slavs, although the Pope had authorized him to do so.

The Moravians

The great event of the ninth century in this respect was the conversion of the Moravians, in the central Slav area. A pagan prince, Moimir, was establishing a Moravian Empire, and although not a convert, he allowed a church to be built shortly before 850; this owed allegiance to the German Church in Salzburg and Passau. The Emperor Lewis the German deposed Moimir and replaced him with his nephew Ratislav, an extremely able man who soon realized that the Roman and Byzantine Churches were competing for converts. To offset the mounting influence of the Germans, Ratislav sent a Moravian delegation to Constantinople in 862 to see the Patriarch Photius.

Cyril and Methodius

Photius saw his chance to steal a march on the Roman Church. He sent to Moravia two remarkable missionaries, Methodius and his younger brother Constantine, who on his deathbed took the name of Cyril. Cyril and Methodius, as they are now universally called, had been born in Salonica, where there were many Slavs. They were educated in Constantinople, at what was virtually the Imperial university, itself distinguished by the eminent scholar known as Leo the Mathematician. Cyril himself taught there for a time. Both, however, were imbued with missionary zeal. Cyril first preached to the Khazars, many of whom at that time had been converted to Judaism. On his return he was sent with his brother to Moravia. Their great idea was that since the Slavs understood neither Greek nor Latin, the sacred texts should be translated into their own language, and a Slav liturgy should be produced. To this end, they added half a dozen characters to the Greek alphabet, inventing what was probably the alphabet now known as Glagolitic. The 'Cyrillic' alphabet may have been a derivative of this invented by Cyril's successors in Bulgaria; he may actually have originated it himself. Cyril and Methodius converted a number of Moravians; meanwhile, in 864 Ratislav vowed allegiance to Lewis the German, who had defeated him in battle.

The presence of the two Byzantine missionaries alongside the German Christians led to serious friction. Cyril and Methodius decided to take the case to Rome. They arrived in the middle of a public quarrel between Photius and Pope Nicholas I. They had brought with them what they believed to be the relics of the third successor of St Peter, Pope Clement I. For the time, this was 'an incomparable treasure'. Nicholas I having died, his successor Adrian II welcomed them 'as if they were envoys from God.' They convinced the Papacy that God could be worshipped in a language other than the three sacred tongues (Hebrew, Greek, and Latin).

Cyril was about to be made Bishop of Moravia when he died in 869. So Methodius set out again alone. At the request of Moravian nobles, the old archbishopric of Sirmium (Mitrovitza) was re-established for him. This displeased the Byzantine Church, which in theory held sway over Illyricum in the Dalmatian area of the Adriatic coast; and Methodius soon found himself in difficulties. His powerful protector Ratislav was attacked, defeated, and killed by the sons of Lewis the German. Suddenly vulnerable, Methodius was put on trial by the German bishops and imprisoned in a tower. He nevertheless managed to inform Rome of his plight, and the Pope condemned the German bishops. Methodius later returned to Rome, and resumed his Moravian mission with the full support of the Roman Church.

For the first time in eighteen years he revisited Constantinople. He was very well received there by Photius and by the Emperor. His Moravian troubles, however, continued, and had still not been settled when he died in 885.

On the death of Methodius, the German bishops reasserted their authority in Moravia and forbade the conduct of the liturgy in Slav. They expelled Methodius's disciples, most of whom took refuge with King Boris of Bulgaria. He and his successors adopted the Slav liturgy.

So it was that while the Moravians were absorbed into western Latin Christianity, the Bulgarians opted for the Byzantine Church. The reconciliation sought by Cyril and Methodius had failed.

The conversion of the northern Slavs

The conversion of the northern Slavs took place still later. From about the middle of the tenth century, the Piast dynasty of Poles, originating in the east, began to make its mark in Central Europe. The Polish Empire stretched from the Baltic in the north to the Carpathians in the south and to the Vistula in the east. Under Micislas I (962–92) and his son Boleslas I ('the Great', 992–1025), the Poles began to press westwards. In a successful campaign against the Emperor Henry II, Boleslas seized Silesia and, for a time, Moravia and Bohemia. Before he died, he took the title of King.

The Wends

During the tenth century the northern Slavs (principally the Wends) had been conquered and colonized by Germanic kings. 'From 940–950 onwards, it was no longer the Elbe, but the lower reaches of the Oder, which marked the easternmost limit of the Germanic lands. But the merging of Wends and Germans was possible only if the former adopted the religion of the latter.' Their conversion was achieved – not without a struggle – under the auspices of an archbishopric established in Magdeburg. Its first incumbent was Adalbert, the former abbot of the powerful Weissenburg Abbey in Alsace. But Wendish resistance continued; and it was not until the end of the eleventh century that the Wends and all the northern Slavs adopted Christianity.

The Poles

Further east, the conversion of the Poles appears to have been much easier. In 966, Micislas had married Dobrawa, daughter of Boleslas, the King of Bohemia. She, with the help of the Czech clergy, managed to convert her husband. F. Dvornik, the great historian of the Slavs, used to regret that the Poles and the Czechs, whose languages are so similar, failed to remain united. The main reason for this failure was that the Czech Church was very closely linked with the Church in Germany. But the Duke (and later King) of Poland, Boleslas – the son of Micislas and Dobrawa, named after his Czech grandfather – decided to establish a Polish hierarchy outside German influence. To this end, he secured the foundation of an archbishopric at Gniezno, to which the Polish bishops now owed allegiance, rather than to Magdeburg.

THE HUNGARIAN INVASIONS

Although the Hungarians were not Slavs but 'Finno-Ugrians', they too have a place in the story, and an extraordinary one. Between AD 900 and 950, they succeeded in invading all of continental Western Europe, and then in turning themselves from nomads into settlers, while retaining their own language. The only other European languages which belong to the same family as Hungarian are Finnish and Estonian; and even they are very different.

The Hungarians appeared in the mid-ninth century, probably from Central Asia.

Brilliant horsemen, they employed tactics which help to explain their fifty years of success in long-distance invasion. Once within range of the enemy, they demoralized him with an avalanche of arrows: then they charged on horseback. They pillaged and burnt everything, especially churches. The fine Romanesque church at Tournus, on the river Sâone north of Mâcon, only exists because the Hungarians burned down the Carolingian church that preceded it. In Pavia, in 924, they set fire to no fewer than forty-four churches.

The Hungarians were divided into seven 'hordes', which sometimes joined forces. Spreading into Pannonia, where they made their base in the valley of the Tisza river, separating the northern from the southern Slavs, they attacked everywhere, and made deep inroads into neighbouring territory. Their main victim was Germany. Their invasion began in 862 and ended only in 955 when the German King Otto, using all his troops, including Bohemian Slavs, crushed them outside Augsburg on the banks of the river Lech. In the north-west, the Hungarians went as far as Flanders, via Bavaria, Alsace, Lorraine, and Champagne. In the west, they reached Basle and Burgundy; in the south-west, the Alps, the Isoré valley, Languedoc, and Aquitaine. In the south, they invaded Venetia, Lombardy, Tuscany, Apulia, and Abruzzi; in the east, the Kingdom of Bulgaria and Thracia almost as far as the Bosphorus; and in the north, Westphalia and the Weser valley as far as Bremen.

Gradually, as Europe strengthened its defences, the Hungarian onslaughts died down. Their conversion to Christianity slowly followed.

With it, as in the case of the Poles, came tension between the German Church and the idea of a national Church with its own hierarchy. At the end of the tenth century, German missionaries began preaching the Gospel among the Hungarian people, under the authority of Pilgrim, Archbishop of Passau. The Hungarian Duke Geza, for all his pagan ancestry, realized the need to come to terms with this potential political threat, as did his son Vaik, who at the age of ten, in 985, took the name of Stephen. A remarkable statesman, whose piety earned him canonization as a saint, Stephen ruled from 997 to 1038. He founded the 'Crown of St Stephen', with a wholly autonomous Church, and had himself crowned with a diadem blessed by Pope Sylvester II.

THE BREAK WITH BYZANTIUM

Byzantine isolation

In the eighth and ninth centuries, the West maintained rather distant relations with the Byzantine Empire. Byzantium was in fact cut off: from the north by the Slavs, the Avars, the Bulgarians, and the Hungarians; from the south by the fact that Syria and the 'fertile crescent', Egypt and the Maghreb, had converted to Islam. With its merchant fleet increasingly outnumbered by that of its Arab rivals, the Byzantine Empire might have continued to claim that it represented the whole Roman Empire; but all it had in the west were a few trading posts along the Adriatic. The Emperor Leo III compelled the Pope, the Patriarch of Rome, to cede Illyria to the Patriarch of Constantinople; and Charlemagne agreed to return Venetia and Istria so as to reach an agreement. But the Exarchate of Ravenna foundered in 754–6 when Pepin the Short, the Frankish King, recaptured it from the Lombards and passed it not to the Byzantines but to the Pope. By the year 812, all that Byzantium still possessed in Italy was Venice, Naples, Calabria, and Sicily: and the Arabs were on their way.

What was more, the Latin and Greek parts of Christendom were no longer able to present a united front.

The divergence had begun with what Paul Lemerle has called 'the interruption of Greek culture in the West'. By the year 600, this was almost complete. Pope Gregory the Great (590–604), a rich Roman and former Nuncio in Constantinople, knew no Greek: nor did Isidore of Seville, Gregory of Tours, or the Venerable Bede. This, in Paul Lemerle's words, amounted to 'a shipwreck'.

The iconoclasts

The enthronement in 717 of the Emperor Leo III, the Isaurian, and in 740 of his son Constantine Copronymus – a good general but a fanatical despot – did nothing to heal the growing breach. Both, and especially Constantine, were 'iconoclasts' or 'image-breakers'. The exaggerated cult of images or icons seemed to them a return to paganism – as for instance when priests added to the chalice, at Mass, a vestige of paint scraped off some hallowed portrait. Despite such abuses, however, the Roman Papacy never endorsed the iconoclasts' breaking of images.

Charlemagne: universal Empire or Empire of the West?

When Charlemagne became Emperor in the year 800, the Byzantine sovereign was the Empress Irene, who in 769 had married Emperor Leo IV, the son of Constantine Copronymus. Although intelligent and beautiful, she was an unscrupulous woman: she even had her own son's eyes put out. Western theologians believed that Charlemagne could be anointed Emperor at St Peter's in Rome, as the Byzantines were in Santa Sophia: but by 'Emperor' they meant ruler of the Empire as a whole. A Byzantine chronicler reports that Irene sent ambassadors to Charlemagne with an offer of marriage (Leo IV having died in 780), but she died in 803. For Charlemagne, always devoted to the unity of the Empire, the only remaining alternative was to reach an agreement with the Byzantines to establish, as under Diocletian and the sons of Theodosius, a single Empire but with two Emperors, one ruling in the East, the other in the West. This was achieved in 812–14. But it was no more than an ephemeral solution.

The breach between Rome and Constantinople was in no way sudden. It took a long time, involving many incidents, rapprochements, and disputes.

What gradually happened was that a lasting frontier came to divide Western, Latin or Roman Christianity, which called itself 'Catholic' or universal, from Greek Christianity and its Slav offshoots.

Briefly, there were five main reasons for the breach.

Asian luxury in contrast with the West

This atmospheric difference was particularly marked. The Byzantine Empire, with its wealth and ostentation and its intellectual subtlety, despised the crude Westerners and their apparent theological naïveté. The Greek language, the Eastern liturgy, the Byzantine ecclesiastical robes – all seemed more brilliant in the 'second Rome' than in the first.

The 'Apostolic' role of Constantinople

Constantinople was indeed a 'second' Rome, not established until about 330 by the Emperor Constantine. This implied inferiority, because the great Church centres were held to have been founded by the Apostles – so much so that in many places, notably in Spain and Gaul, local Churches were given fictitious but tenaciously cherished 'apostolic' pedigrees. Constantinople maintained that there were five 'patriarchates': the so-called 'Pentarchy' of Rome (the bishopric founded by St Peter), Jerusalem, Antioch, Alexandria, founded by other Apostles, and . . . Constantinople. Hence the legend later devised by Photius, according to which St Andrew, on a mission in the Black Sea, had implanted Christianity in Byzantium. St Andrew was none other than the elder brother of St Peter. In Rome, by contrast, there was no belief in a Pentarchy, but only in the superiority of the Church of Rome and St Peter over all the rest.

The Filioque dispute

There was also a dispute about dogma. In their Creed – a summary of the faith – the Latins had added a word, *filioque*, to the effect that 'The Holy Spirit proceeds from the Father and from the Son.' The Orientals, on the other hand, believed that in the mystery of the Holy Trinity, the Holy Spirit only 'proceeded' from the Son via the Father. This dispute shows the extent to which both sides were concerned with unfathomable theological minutiae.

Canon or ecclesiastical law

They disagreed also about discipline, settled in the East by the so-called 'Quinisext' Council of 692, which sought to complete the work done by the fifth and sixth Ecumenical Councils. For the West, priestly celibacy was the rule, however often it might be broken. In the East, marriage was permitted to priests before their ordination. There were also different rules for fasting and more complicated marriage rules. The Asians took Communion in both kinds – bread and wine; the West took only 'azyme' or unleavened bread. The very spirit of the Mass was different, too: in the Greek liturgy, there was no place for the Western practice of preaching a sermon. It is not surprising, perhaps, that in the Ecumenical movement of the twentieth century, rapprochement proved easier to achieve between the Greek Orthodox and the Lutheran Churches than between the Greek Orthodox and the Roman Catholics.

Rival missions

Finally, and perhaps most seriously, East and West disagreed about missionary work, particularly among the Bulgarians. Were they to be Latin Christians subject to Rome, or Greek Christians under the Patriarchate of Constantinople? There was also rivalry in Illyria, and in what is now Yugoslavia.

Photius and Ignatius

The first serious crisis was associated with Photius, an outstanding and prolific writer. Born in Constantinople in about 810, he had been a brilliant pupil, perhaps under the great Leo the Mathematician, and had quickly become a civil servant, ending up as a Chief Secretary. As a young man, he was sent on an embassy to the Arabs. He wrote on grammar (a *Lexicon*), on literature (*The Library*), and on theology; he also worked in logic, metaphysics, exegesis, and other areas. His authority was great. He despised Rome, and was ready to act accordingly.

In 858, the Patriarch Ignatius, although backed by the monasteries, was dismissed and interned by the Emperor, and Photius, although still a mere layman, was elected Patriarch in Ignatius's stead.

The brief Photian Schism

According to custom, Photius wrote to Rome and to the other patriarchates to secure their recognition. Antioch, Jerusalem, and Alexandria had been conquered by the Muslims and were in a parlous state. Pope Nicholas I hesitated, and sent two legates to Constantinople. They favoured Photius, but were disavowed on their return to Rome. In 863, a Roman Council declared that Photius should be deposed and replaced by Ignatius. It was the Bulgarian question that had exacerbated the dispute. King Boris of Bulgaria, first converted by the Byzantines, had had the Byzantine Emperor as godfather at his baptism, but for political reasons he was also in negotiation with Rome. In the year 866, a Roman mission went to Bulgaria in an effort to undo the work of the Byzantines. The result was that in 867 the breach between Rome and Constantinople became public and dramatic. A Council held in Constantinople decided to depose the Pope.

The Emperor Basil the Macedonian

This 'schism' was cut short by a political coup d'état in Byzantium. A general of peasant origin, Basil the Macedonian had the Emperor assassinated, and took his place. One of his first acts was to depose Photius and restore Ignatius, in September 867. The Macedonian dynasty, which ruled until the eleventh century, also restored the greatness of Byzantium. It recovered the valleys of the Tigris and the Euphrates, reconquered Cilicia and Aleppo, and crushed the Bulgarians in 1014 at Strumica, where the victor Basil II earned the nickname 'Bulgarochton' or 'killer of Bulgars'. Basil favoured union with Rome and with the Western Emperor Lewis II, who proposed that his daughter Irmgard should marry Basil's son Constantine. Although the marriage did not take place, both parties nevertheless proclaimed union between the two parts of Christendom.

This did not stop King Boris once more turning towards the Greeks. On the death of Ignatius, he made his peace with Photius, who once more became Patriarch – only to be deposed for the second time in 886.

Brief as the 'Photian Schism' had been, however, nothing fundamental had changed. Disputes continued for another 150 years until there was a new breach which turned out to be definitive. Photius, meanwhile, remained the great hero of the Byzantine Church.

Michael Cerularius

A further breach resulted from the success of the Macedonian dynasty. It took place during the Patriarchate of Michael Cerularius (born 1000, Patriarch 1043–58), a man of more ability than piety. By this time, the union of the two Churches had worn thin, and the poor state of the Roman Church, before the Gregorian Reform, could not but increase the Orientals' sense of superiority.

Cerularius was anxious to prevent the Byzantine Emperor coming to an agreement with Rome. He therefore began a campaign against those Latins who were settled in Constantinople, and told the Pope that reconciliation with Rome was acceptable only if the West adopted the ecclesiastical law of the East – an obviously impossible condition.

The solemn breach

On 16 July 1054, delegates from Rome, led by Cardinal Humbert, realizing that there was no hope of agreement, decided on a dramatic step. They went to Santa Sophia in the middle of a service, and placed on the high altar a Papal Bull excommunicating Cerularius. Then they left the cathedral, shaking the dust from their feet. They paid their respects to the Emperor, and returned to Rome. On 24 July Cerularius replied with a 'Synodal Edict', formalizing the breach. Both Latins and Greeks considered that they had won.

The consequences for Europe

This was no mere quarrel between rival sects, based only on religious disagreements. It involved real hatred. In Constantinople, a new literary form proliferated: innumerable tracts against the Latins. The Greeks and the Latins who met in Italy and Constantinople reviled each other as heretics and schismatics. There was also a military conflict. By the Treaty of Melfi in 1059, the Popes formed an alliance with the Normans in Sicily, who were doing their best to conquer the Byzantine outposts there and on the Italian mainland. In 1081, they attacked Epirus. 'One may say that for the average Byzantine,' wrote Hélène Ahrweiler, 'Norman aggression seemed on the one hand a result of the Church schism and of Papal perfidy, and on the other a prelude to the Crusades, which were soon seen as the most fearful form of western aggression.' Mme Ahrweiler concluded:

> It is no exaggeration to say that the notion of the West, in the sense of a human community inspired by the same values, was born in Byzantium at the end of the eleventh century. It was justified above all by the spiritual unity of the Western world, and in some measure by its relationship

with the Western Roman Empire. It is significant that the term 'Latin' was used by the Byzantines to denote the peoples of the West, irrespective of their ethnic or political connexions. Latinity, that is, was henceforth a kind of counterpart to Greekness. These terms now referred to two worlds with different cultural traditions and intellectual aspirations; once their common feature, Christianity, was weakened, these two terms would end up referring to two opposing worlds.

THE EMPIRE AND THE PAPACY: TOWARDS 'WESTERN CHRISTENDOM'

For three turbulent centuries, as we have seen, non-Christian peoples attacked all parts of what we call 'Europe' – a word which barely reappeared before the fourteenth century. But what was happening within the Western world? The break-up of Charlemagne's Empire became permanent in 843 with the 'Partition of Verdun'. Emperors remained in Germany, and the 'Holy Roman Empire of the German Nation' lasted until it was dissolved by Napoleon in 1806. The successive dynasties of Saxony (the Ottos) from 919 to 1024, Franconia from 1024 to 1125, Swabia, c.1125–c.1268 (the Hohenstaufen), and finally in 1273 Rudolph of Habsburg and his descendants, occupied the Imperial throne with varying degrees of success. Their Empire was now limited to Germany, part of Italy, sometimes the Low Countries, and sometimes as far as the 'Kingdom of Arles'. They were no longer able, moreover, to make other sovereigns respect their supposed superiority. This was notably true of the Kings of England and France.

Christianity and lay power

Was this the end of Western unity? As regards political sovereignty, it was. As regards society, however, there remained one potential spiritual leader of the 'Catholic' and 'Latin' west. This was the Church. It was slow to establish itself, however, and the painfully acquired unity of Christendom disappeared in the fifteenth century.

Westerners were less concerned than the Byzantines with matters of heresy and theological subtlety: but they succumbed more easily to material temptations. These can be summed up in two words: simony and nicolaitism.

Simony

Simony, named after Simon Magus, who is supposed to have asked St Peter to sell him his power to perform miracles, is the granting of ecclesiastical benefices (bishoprics, abbeys, parishes, etc.) in return for money, accepting not the best candidate but the best offer. This practice was encouraged by the fact that the patrimony of each bishopric had become an honor, a fief which a suzerain 'gave' to the new incumbent. The bishop, normally elected by the clergy and the faithful, canonically 'instituted' or given religious authority by his fellow archbishops, had also to be invested with his fief by a lay lord. The latter could thus profit by selling it, or impose his own candidate – a good and economical way to reward his friends.

Nicolaitism

Still more frequent, although difficult to quantify, was the practice of nicolaitism – the marriage or concubinage of priests. This lowered both the moral tone of the clergy and its prestige with the faithful. According to Atto, Bishop of Verceil, writing to his clergy in the middle of the tenth century:

> A number of you are so enslaved by passion that they allow obscene courtesans to live in their dwellings, to share their food, and to appear with them in public. At the mercy of their charms, they allow them to run the household, and they appoint their bastards as their heirs ...

The most serious result of these failings was that dioceses were fragmented into small units which were more political than religious, and sometimes at war with one another.

Nicholas I (pope from 858–67), who dealt with Photius, was the first outstanding Pope for some time. Firm with lay rulers (he unequivocally condemned the divorce of Lothair II), he also extended the Papacy's control of the Church. When Hincmar of Rheims, the most powerful Bishop in Frankish Gaul, deposed his suffragan Rothad, Bishop of Soissons, without allowing him to appeal to the jurisdiction of Rome, Nicholas I protested, called Rothad to Rome, and insisted on his being reinstated. Rothad brought with him to Rome, incidentally, a very curious document drawn up in Francia, the False Decretals. This apocryphal collection of ancient Papal decisions, actually forged in about 830, affirmed very precisely the universal primacy of Rome.

Accepted in good faith as authentic, the False Decretals continued to be used in support of Papal power throughout the Middle Ages, until in the sixteenth century their pious deceit was finally exposed.

The decline of the Papacy

After the death of Nicholas I, the energetic John VIII (872–82) was murdered by members of his entourage. In the tenth century, the Papacy reached its lowest ebb. It fell into the hands of factions – one siding with the Emperor, others representing various groups of the Roman aristocracy; and Papal elections were continually subject to scandal.

Marozia, the daughter of the senator Theophylactus and wife of the Marquess Alberic of Spoleto, had Pope John X suffocated with a pillow. She then appointed his successors – including John XI (931–6), the illegitimate son she had had with Pope Sergius III (904–11).

The culminating point of this indignity was the enthronement of John XII (955–63). Not yet twenty years old, he scandalized Rome by holding banquets instead of matins, going hunting instead of doing good works, and leading a life of debauchery. On occasion, there were two Popes at once.

At the end of the tenth century, the situation improved. A German, Bruno, son of the Duke of Carinthia and Chaplain to the King, became Pope at the age of twenty-three under the name of Gregory V (996–9). He was followed by a Frenchman, Gerbert, previously a teacher who had later been Archbishop of Rheims, and who had helped to secure the succession of Hugh Capet to the throne of France: he became Pope as Sylvester II (999–1003). Both Gregory and Sylvester were staunch defenders of Papal independence. But the real reform of the Church came in the eleventh century.

Our concern here is not so much ecclesiastical history as the reappearance of a Western community under the aegis of the Papacy, and its thoroughgoing reform. In this respect, the figure of Hildebrand, who became the great reforming Pope Gregory VII, is more important than the precise detail of his achievements.

Gregory VII

Hildebrand was born in Tuscany, at Soano, between 1015 and 1020. His family was modest. Brought up in a Roman monastery where one

of his uncles was the abbot, he soon became an adviser to successive
popes. On missions in Germany and Gaul, he showed himself to be an
exceptional administrator and diplomat. In 1073, by popular acclam-
ation and with the backing of the cardinals, he became Pope, taking
the name of Gregory VII. A saintly man, he was also a prolific writer.
No fewer than 848 of his letters have survived: their recipients
included his penitent, Countess Matilda of Tours, Abbot Hugh of
Cluny, and a number of European kings. Humble and charitable,
Gregory believed that he owed his authority to Christ. He intended to
use it to cleanse the Church of simony and nicolaitism, to unify it, and
to safeguard its rights in the face of lay rulers.

Gregory VII and the kings

Gregory's relations with lay princes varied from perfect agreement –
with William the Conqueror and the rulers of northern Italy – to the
most extreme controversy – with the Emperor and the King of
France. He had little difficulty in reasserting Papal suzerainty over
the principalities of Benevento and Capua, which the Normans had
recaptured from Byzantium; but his relations with the German
Emperor Henry IV were difficult in the extreme. The problem was
to secure acceptance for the reforming decree issued by a great
Council held in Rome in 1074. In France, Gregory faced the ill-will
of King Philip I, 'a hardened simoniac'; in Germany, he was opposed
by most of the bishops.

Gregory VII and the outskirts of Europe

Gregory sought to establish Papal influence in the most distant lands.
He played an active role in Denmark, where King Svend II (died
1077) eliminated the last vestiges of paganism and sought the 'patronage of the Blessed Peter'. He had the Gospel preached in Norway, and
wrote to King Olaf III. He had much influence on King Boleslas II of
Poland – until Boleslas murdered the Bishop of Cracow. He corresponded with Duke Wratislas II of Bohemia, and sent Papal legates to
his court. He had some contacts with Hungary. Duke Zvonimir of
Croatia sought to become subject to his authority.

In the south, Gregory used the Abbey of St Victor in Marseille as a
base for work in Provence, and from there he extended his influence
into Spain. He corresponded with the Kings of Aragon, Leon, and
Navarre. His aim was not only to 'snatch Spain from the hands of the

pagans', but also to place reconquered lands under the suzerainty of the Roman Church. He had partial success in Catalonia and Castile, where he sent Cardinal Richard, Abbot of St Victor.

The Dictatus Papae

It was not enough, however, to organize a number of Councils: there had to be a programme of reform. In 1075 Gregory drew up an extremely audacious document, which came to be known as the Dictatus papae – the 'Orders of the Pope'. These are some of them:

2 Only the Roman Pontiff may be called universal.
9 The Pope is the only man whose feet all princes kiss.
12 It is his right to depose Emperors.
17 No canonical text exists outside his authority.
20 No one may condemn a decision of the Apostolic See.
22 The Roman Church has never erred and, as Scripture attests, never can err.
26 Those who are not with the Roman Church cannot be considered Catholic.
27 The Pope may release subjects from oaths of loyalty sworn to the unjust.

The Dictatus papae were a maximalist programme, aiming to give the Pope absolute power not only over the Church, but also over lay Christendom: 'Priestly dignity is superior to royal dignity.'

It goes without saying that sovereigns and even bishops put up a fierce and often effective resistance to these decrees. But for the twelve years of his pontificate, Gregory went on imposing his reforms, aided by the legates whom he sent everywhere and who were extremely unpopular.

The struggle between Empire and Papacy

Gregory's pontificate was dominated by the struggle between the Empire and the Papacy, which continued into the following century. The Dictatus papae, after all, were a challenge to the old tradition whereby Emperors had played a part in appointing the Popes and had been able to depose them. The Emperors, and especially Henry IV, favoured such 'Caesaropapism'.

Henry IV (1056-1106) had greatly strengthened his hold on Germany. His first reaction to the Dictatus papae was to have Gregory deposed by the German bishops at the synod of Worms in 1076, accusing him of having ignored the doctrine of the 'two swords' prescribed in Luke 22:38. Imperial power, he held, was given by God and could not depend upon a man, even if that man were Pope.

Gregory riposted by deposing Henry — which led to consternation in Germany, where a number of princes seized the opportunity to rise up against the Emperor. They were followed by a large number of bishops, ashamed at having been party to deposing the Pope. Henry thus found himself isolated. The Pope was invited to Germany to pronounce a definitive sentence: but Henry decided to forestall him. Shortly before Christmas 1076, he left Germany and travelled through Besançon, Geneva, the Mont-Cenis Pass, and Turin, to arrive with a small escort at the fortress of Canossa, south-west of Reggio Emilia. The castle belonged to the Countess Matilda, and she was present; so was Abbot Hugh of Cluny. The Emperor, dressed as a penitent, with bare feet and no royal insignia, spent three days imploring the Pope to pardon him. At first, Gregory refused; but then he relented in exchange for an oath of loyalty.

The celebrated capitulation at Canossa nevertheless left the problem itself unsolved; it was followed by further mutual condemnations and depositions. Henry IV had an 'Anti-Pope', Clement III, elected, a dim client of his own; then he went to Rome and had himself crowned as Emperor on 31 March 1084, expelling Gregory VII. Rome was freed by the Norman Robert Guiscard; but Gregory himself, defiant though defeated, went into exile in Salerno, where he died on 25 May 1085.

Gregorian Reform and Cluny

Insofar as the so-called Gregorian Reform of the Church was possible, it was largely due to the monastery of Cluny. For centuries, Europe had had a large number of monasteries, to which had been added 'chapters' of canons, who lived and prayed together but were dispensed from the vow of poverty. Like most ecclesiastical 'benefices', the majority of the monasteries at this time had become extremely decadent. Pillage by Normans and Saracens was not their only affliction. 'Secular abbots' kept monastic wealth for themselves, leaving almost nothing for the life of the monks, who were obliged to wander afield and work as artisans. Many had practically abandoned the Rule of St Benedict. The abbots of the greatest abbeys were appointed by the king, as at Fulda in Germany, Hereford in England, or Saint-Germain-des-Prés in France. Elsewhere, the appointments were made by dukes and local lords.

This monastic decadence alarmed pious opinion. The Cluniac Reform was an attempt to put things right.

Two men decided to found a new, purified monastic order which would return to the genuine Rule of St Benedict. One was a monk from Burgundy named Berno; the other was a layman, William the Pious, Count of Auvergne and Duke of Aquitaine. William gave Berno the villa of Cluny, where in September 910, he established a monastery independent of all temporal power. Cluny owed allegiance only to the Pope. Berno was its abbot from 910 until 926, and from the beginning it had extraordinary success. Berno's successors were also outstanding. A number of princes, also anxious to secure reforms, asked for Cluny's help, and some persuaded it to found further monasteries on its own model and under its authority. In this way, Cluny became the head of a growing order of monasteries, many of them reformed by its own monks: 'priories' and 'cells' dependent upon it were founded in many different places.

Berno's successor St Odo (926–40) extended the Cluniac order throughout Europe. A tireless traveller, he and his black-robed monks visited the monasteries in need of reform, recruited and trained their better representatives, and left Cluniacs in place. Odo went to Italy, since he owed allegiance only to the Pope; there, among other things, he was put in charge of all the monasteries in Rome.

Odo's successor, St Maieul, a nobleman from Avignon, ruled Cluny for forty years. He too travelled widely, in France, Burgundy, and Italy. In Germany, however, his activities were resisted by the Germanic Emperors, and almost all the monasteries remained royal.

St Odilo of Mercoeur succeeded Maieul in 994 and governed Cluny until 1049. Thanks to the Emperor Henry II, he was able to spread Cluniac influence into Germany. Altogether, he increased the number of large monasteries controlled by Cluny from thirty-seven to sixty-five, while the 'priories' and 'cells' were numbered in hundreds.

Thus Cluny established not only a tight network of preaching and piety, but also a formidable political pressure group, a centralized power with its headquarters in France, where there were 300 monks and very many more lay brothers, with some 10,000 monks under their control elsewhere.

Cluny reached the height of its power in the eleventh century, when Odilo, who had ruled for fifty-five years, was succeeded by St Hugh. Aged twenty-five when he became abbot in 1049, Hugh remained until 1109 – a full sixty years. In 200 years, in fact, Cluny had only five different abbots; and it gained greatly from that continuity.

Centralization was now complete. A single abbey – Cluny – had full power over the whole order, whose abbots and priors it appointed. Hugh, a Burgundian, the son of a Count of Semur, soon became a figure on a European scale. Godfather to Henry IV of Germany, and a friend of Popes Gregory VII and Urban II, he maintained close relations with other kings.

Yet Cluny itself was a French rather than a strictly European order. By the end of the eleventh century, it had 815 houses in France, 105 in Germany, 23 in Spain, 52 in Italy, and 43 in Great Britain. There were also a few Cluniac outposts in Poland and even in the Holy Land.

In Germany, Cluny faced stubborn resistance. It finally broke through with the help of a remarkable Bavarian monk, William, the Abbot of Hirschau. He, however, was not content simply to extend the Cluniac rule to a large number of German and Swiss monasteries: he also took an eager part, on the Papal side, in the struggle against the Empire. St Hugh, by contrast, had tried to act as mediator between Gregory VII and the Emperor Henry IV.

In Britain, it was William the Conqueror and his ecclesiastical adviser Lanfranc who really established the influence of Cluny. Here – as in Spain – there was great resistance to Cluniac centralization. As we shall see in the next chapter, the Cistercian order which appeared in 1098, with its white-robed monks and its very independent monasteries, was much more egalitarian and much more European. Nevertheless, in the intellectual field as in agriculture (with the help of servants and oblates), and especially in art, the influence of Cluny spread throughout Latin Christendom.

CONCLUSION

By the end of the eleventh century, the reform of the Church had brought it two advantages: it had recovered its independence from lay power, and Latin Christendom was spiritually more united than ever before. At the same time, the Church had not acquired – and perhaps not sought – complete supremacy. The West had in fact escaped the twin dangers of Caesaropapism (with the civil Emperor as supreme religious leader, as in ancient Rome) and theocracy (with the religious leader as political leader, as in present-day Iran).

Nevertheless, as always in Europe, individual reactions – in this case, the life of the spirit – remained distinct from politics. Flagrant and widespread as were the evils of a partly unreformed Church, some exceptional individuals led a very intense religious life. While many people, great or otherwise, were indifferent to the Christian doctrine of love and renunciation and, moved only by the fear of Hell, 'combined an irregular life with the most punctilious religious observances', others embodied exemplary piety. Such, for instance, were Robert the Pious, King of France, and above all the Emperor Henry II, crowned in 1146.

Religion in general was still tinged with superstition and magic. Some even sought the intervention of Satan to counterbalance too strict a rule by Providence. Scarcely anyone feared the end of the world, and it is wildly exaggerated to speak of 'the terrors of the year 1000'. What people did expect was constant and miraculous intervention by God in their daily lives. This was the basic rationale of 'trial by ordeal'. To prove the guilt or innocence of the accused, they were tested by a duel, by red-hot iron, or by boiling water: God was thereby called upon, as it were, to perform a miracle which would prove the prisoner innocent.

Yet religion had a civilizing influence on this violent society, despite the failings of certain priests. It did its best to make feudal society more ethical, to awaken kings and nobles to their duties and responsibilities, and to discourage homicide and war. By modern times, slavery on the ancient model had almost completely disappeared. Was the Church responsible? It had never explicitly condemned it; but it had encouraged emancipation and humanized relations between masters and slaves, on the principle that Catholicism seeks not social revolution but the gradual transformation of the existing social structure from within. The end of slavery and the establishment of serfdom were certainly due in part to technical, demographic, economic, and social changes. But the Church, by spreading a new spirit, helped to create greater humanity in social relations generally.

Peace programmes

The Church's most important contribution was its opposition to war. Insecurity at that time was not limited to frontier zones: it prevailed everywhere. The Norman invasions, coupled with internal feudal warfare, had led to Europe being dotted with castles – Castra, Roccae, Firmitates, Oppida, Castella, Turres, etc. 'Medieval life,' wrote Philippe Contamine, 'was riddled with insecurity... No region was immune... The frontier was everywhere and nowhere, if only because the land was so divided and political power was so diffused.'

A movement for peace seems to have taken shape at the end of the tenth century. A number of Church Councils, notably that in Narbonne in 1054, laid down principles establishing:

1. the Peace of God (respect for non-combatants and for Church and peasant possessions); and
2. the Truce of God, which forbade fighting during certain parts of the Church calendar, including Christmas, Easter, Ascension, and the Feasts of the Virgin Mary, St John the Baptist, and the Apostles, as well as from Friday to Monday.

This movement spread to Spain, at the Council of Gerona in 1068; to the Anglo-Norman kingdom, thanks to William the Conqueror; to Germany, with the help of the Bishop of Liège and the Council of Mainz in 1085; and to southern Italy, at the Council of Melfi in 1089.

The Papacy itself remained hesitant, until Nicholas II held the Council of Rome in 1059, which forbade attacks on travellers, priests, monks, and the poor. It was finally Urban II, at the Council of Clermont in 1095, who extended the peace movement to the whole of the Church. Paradoxically, however, while he championed peace among Christians, he also preached the Crusade or Holy War against the infidel.

After the Partition of Verdun in 843, political power in Europe became fragmented, and within each kingdom the 'seignorial' system grew up. The kingdoms themselves were very frequently contested by rivals. The Western Empire, under the last Carolingians, was in a state of advanced decay. In Germany, Saxony in the north was practically independent, as were Bavaria in the south and the Alemanni of the Upper Danube and the Upper Rhineland. It was from Saxony that the Empire was rebuilt, by Duke Henry, who became King, and died in 936, and above all by his grandson Otto, crowned King at Aix-la-Chapelle (Aachen) and then, in 962, becoming Emperor.

More important for Europe, in the period from the eighth to the eleventh century, were the Saracens (Muslims who in principle were Arabs, but whose troops were essentially Berbers). They crossed the Straits of Gibraltar (named Jebel-el-Tarik after their leader) in 711. In the north came the Vikings: Scandinavians who were increasingly known as 'men of the North', 'Norsemen', or 'Normans'. Their first appearance was at the Anglo-Scottish monastery of Lindisfarne in 793. Finally, in the east, though less distinctly, there was strong pressure from the Slavs, themselves driven on by the 'steppe peoples', Avars, Bulgars, and Hungarians. Their incursions reached as far as the Po basin and the valley of the Rhône.

Of these three invading groups, only the second and third finally settled in Europe. The influence of the Saracens was certainly far-reaching; but, no doubt because of their Islamic religion, they lived alongside the people they conquered (especially in Spain) without trying to convert them by force. Only at the end of this period did the Europeans launch the 'Crusades' to recover the 'Holy Land' or to effect the Reconquista, the reconquest of Spain.

In the midst of these troubled three centuries, the intellectual and spiritual unity of Europe was marked by the appearance and development of the new monastic orders.

9

The Heyday of Western Christianity: The Twelfth and Thirteenth Centuries

TEMPORAL AND SPIRITUAL POWER

Pope Urban II

At the beginning of the twelfth century, the Pope seemed to have the upper hand in the bitter contest between Empire and Papacy.

The great Pope from Châtillon, Urban II (1088–99) had succeeded in reducing and finally destroying the power of the Anti-Pope Clement III (Guibert, Archbishop of Ravenna, who had been elected in 1080 and who died in 1100). The 'schism' between the two was healed by incessant and energetic action on Urban's part – appointments, investitures, moral and legal reforms – with the local help of legates or other leading churchmen. These included Lanfranc, Archbishop of Canterbury; Hugh of Lyon in France; Gebhart of Constance for Germany; and Odo, Bishop of Toledo, in Spain. The greatest difficulties were in Rome itself, where Pope and Anti-Pope each had his own 'no go area'. As for the Emperor Henry IV, after Canossa he had been defeated and deposed; he died in poverty in Liège in 1106.

Urban II was 'theocratic' by nature. Understandably, he wanted a unified Church. 'Work,' he wrote to Lanfranc, 'to help the Roman Church bring into Catholic unity our very different local churches.' But he also saw unity as a basis for claiming authority over kings. He made this clear in writing to Alfonso VI, the King of Castile who had just recaptured Toledo from the Saracens: 'There are two powers, O King, which mainly rule the world: priestly dignity and royal authority. But priestly dignity, my very dear son, so much surpasses royal authority that we have to account to the sovereign of the universe for the acts of kings themselves.'

The investiture dispute

The contest continued, with varying intensity, until the year 1250. The form it took was a debate about the 'investiture' of bishops.

In feudal or seignorial society, vassals were 'invested' by their suzerains with their benefices or fiefs. Bishops, whose duty was to teach and defend faith and morality, were also in charge of the vast temporal wealth of their dioceses; and temporal rulers naturally tended to choose and invest the bishops on their domains. Inadmissible, declared the Popes: a layman cannot 'invest' a priest. But a new thesis appeared at the end of the eleventh century. This was the doctrine of 'the two swords', spiritual and temporal, which also invoked the Gospels, as quoting Matthew 22:21: 'Render therefore unto Caesar the things which are Caesar's; and unto God the things that are God's.' On this theory, investiture with a temporal benefice could be distinguished from investiture with spiritual power.

Very soon, in 1107, the Kings of England and France agreed to recognize the Pope's right to accord investiture 'with ring and staff'. The Emperor Henry V, however, long wanted to keep this right to himself, and to preserve it he sent military expeditions into Italy and appointed Anti-Popes favourable to himself. Not until the Concordat of Worms between Henry V and Pope Calixtus II, in 1122, did the dispute come to an end. The Concordat distinguished between the priestly or spiritual functions of the bishop, in which he was invested by the Pope with ring and staff, and his feudal obligations, symbolized by the sceptre, in which he was invested by the king.

This solution was sensible: it proved that compromise is often the best way out. But it involved more than just a concession by the Emperor and the kings. The Popes, imbued with the theocratic doctrines of Gregory VII and Urban II, felt that they had been forced to acquiesce in what was barely tolerable. They accordingly kept pressing the claims of Rome. In 1139, for instance, Pope Innocent II convoked an ecumenical or 'universal' Lateran Council, attended by more than 500 bishops. At its opening session, Innocent declared: 'You know that Rome is the head of the world.' Not long afterwards, a monk from Bologna, Gratian, published his *Decretum*, an enormous compilation of 3,458 texts relating to canon law. This made clearer than ever:

1. that the Pope dominated the Church;
2. that the Church was totally independent of lay power; and
3. that on very many matters temporal princes should obey the priests.

The Emperor Frederick Barbarossa

The dispute was revived during the Papacy's long conflict with Frederick Barbarossa, Duke of Swabia, who was born in about 1123, was crowned Emperor in Rome in 1155, and died in 1190. His Papal opponent was Orlando Bandinelli, who became Pope Alexander III (1159–81) after a brilliant career teaching canon law at Bologna. In this case, too, the process remained the same. The Emperor had an effective sanction – to invade Italy; the Pope's weapon was excommunication, to which Barbarossa responded by electing three successive Anti-Popes. Once again, the Pope came off best. Alexander obliged Barbarossa to accept the Pact of Venice in 1177. It was a second Canossa. In 1179, he held a further ecumenical Lateran Council and once more consolidated his power.

It was during this period that the Emperor's partisans became known as 'Ghibellines' and the Pope's supporters as 'Guelphs'. The names derived from two rival dynasties: that of Conrad III of Hohenstaufen, known as Weibling, from Weiblingen Castle, and that of Duke Henry of Bavaria, from the Welf family. Frederick Barbarossa was in fact descended from both.

The age of Pope Innocent III. Was Europe becoming theocratic?

It seemed possible when in 1198 the greatest of all the medieval Popes took office under the name of Innocent III. As Lotario de Conti, a scion of the old Roman nobility, he had undergone extensive studies in Rome, Paris, and Bologna, where he had specialized in canon law. He had become a cardinal-deacon, but he was not ordained as a priest until after his unanimous election to the Papal throne.

A scholar, a lawyer, a writer, and a man of deep faith, Innocent has nevertheless been seen by some historians as ambitious, disingenuous, authoritarian, and inflexible. Others attribute his inflexibility to the fact that he devoted his whole life to the service of God. 'Two things

I have set my heart on,' he wrote in 1213, three years before his death: 'the deliverance of the Holy Land and the reform of the universal Church.'

He strove with apparent success to restore Papal authority over the Greek Church. The German historian Hauck called this 'Papal imperialism' (*Weltherrschaft*). It certainly involved demanding from the Patriarch of Constantinople that he recognize the Pope's *plenitudo potestatis* or 'plenitude of power'.

Papal 'plenitude of power' was primarily exercised over the Church, since the Pope was the Vicar of Christ. But it also extended, in Innocent's view, to the states, whose sovereigns owed the Pope the same allegiance as did the bishops. In practice, however, Innocent modified his theory. He was often content simply to remind lay sovereigns of their duties, and call them to order if they infringed the moral code. He acted thus with Philip Augustus, the King of France, with several Spanish princes, with the Duke of Austria, and with the young Frederick of Sicily, the future Emperor Frederick II. He went so far as to call on sovereigns to make peace. But his doctrine was explicitly that 'priesthood is necessarily superior to kingship'.

Was his ambition to exert temporal sovereignty, and thereby unite Europe under his own rule?

He undoubtedly claimed temporal power over much of Italy, so as to defend himself against fresh incursions by the Emperors. And King Peter of Aragon offered his realm in fief to the Papacy: he had to promise that he 'would always be loyal and obedient to his lord Pope Innocent and his Catholic successors, as well as to the Roman Church'.

But if in theory Innocent III professed the Papal vocation to govern 'not only the Church but the world', he realized that in practice this was not feasible. He contented himself – and it was no minor role – with acting as the supreme tribunal in cases of sin, oath-breaking, or breach of the peace.

He reached the height of his power at the fourth ecumenical Lateran Council in 1215. There were 412 bishops present, including the Patriarchs of Constantinople and Jerusalem.

A further 800 abbots and priors took part in the meetings, as did ambassadors from the Latin Emperor of Constantinople, the Kings of Germany (including Frederick II of Sicily), of France, of England, of Jerusalem, of Aragon, of Portugal, and of Hungary, as well as numerous lords from the south of France and some Polish and Dalmatian prelates. Most of the Greek bishops, however, refused to attend.

The Council took innumerable decisions on matters political, doctrinal, and juridical. It discussed new religious orders. It dealt with the Albigensian heresy. It prepared for a Crusade.

Innocent III died soon after the end of the Council, in 1216.

The defeat of Emperor Frederick II

A final phase of the conflict between the Popes and the Emperor Frederick II developed over the years until the latter's death in 1250. Born near Ancona, of a Sicilian mother, and brought up in Sicily, Frederick had been much influenced by Islam.

In Sicily, the watchword was tolerance. Roman Catholic churches, Greek churches, synagogues, and mosques all existed side by side. We shall examine in the next chapter Frederick's role in promoting science and philosophical speculation. What concerns us here is his determination to revive the policy of the Emperors and destroy the power of the Popes.

He wanted the Emperor, in fact, to have universal power. He believed himself to be Emperor by divine right, as he had been taught by his jurist masters at Bologna. The Church should be part of the Empire and under its control. The Emperor should be like the Roman Emperor, Caesar Augustus, *felix, victor et triumphator* – happy, victorious, and triumphant. He should also dominate the other sovereigns. If diplomacy could not attain these ends, he should use war.

Innocent III's successor, Cencius Savelli, who became Pope as Honorius III, was a peaceful, conciliatory old man, who had been Frederick's tutor, and was happy to do his bidding. He agreed that the Emperor be crowned in Rome in 1220.

The next two Popes, Gregory IX (1227–41) and Innocent IV (1243–54), reacted vigorously against the Emperor's encroachments on their power. It soon became clear that he would be unable to fulfil his ambitions. Several times excommunicated and accused of heresy, he found his influence declining. An ecumenical Council held at Lyon by Innocent IV put him on trial. He was excommunicated and deposed, 'stripped by God of all his honours and dignities'.

Frederick held out for five years, protesting, and thinking perhaps of going to found a new Empire in Syria. Then he tried to march on

Lyon; but the King of France, Louis IX (St Louis), prevented him. He died in 1250 in his kingdom of Sicily, the only territory he still retained.

The 'Great Interregnum'

The Papacy had won – all the more convincingly because the Imperial throne was now vacant, and remained so until 1273, when the election of Rudolph of Habsburg ended the so-called 'Great Interregnum'. Yet the Papacy scarcely profited from the vacancy. When Gregory IX and then Innocent IV tried to impose their authority on the Western sovereigns, they were rebuffed, even by the saintly King of France. On one particular point the lay rulers were adamant: this was the competition between royal and Papal taxation. 'The King,' wrote one of St Louis's councillors, 'cannot tolerate that the churches in his kingdom be thus despoiled; he intends to reserve their treasures for the needs of this kingdom and is at liberty to treat them as his own.'

So, just when Christian unity briefly seemed about to triumph, the power of the states reasserted itself. The influence of Roman law led to the principle that 'the king is emperor in his kingdom'. This may seem an unfortunate foreshadowing of nationalism. But the true gain, for Europe and its future liberties, was to have escaped from that confusion between secular and religious power which is undoubtedly one of the sources of fanaticism and totalitarianism. It goes without saying that when that confusion reappeared, so did its attendant evils.

And yet the idea of unity was not dead. The Italian poet Dante, a supporter of the Ghibellines, proposed in his *De monarchia* the union of Christendom under the Emperor.

ST BERNARD AND THE WHITE MONKS

Cluny in the twelfth century

It is very difficult for religious orders to avoid decadence, especially if they enjoy great prestige. In a period of intense piety, that is, they become rich from the gifts and legacies of the godly and of repentant sinners, terrified by the prospect of eternal suffering in Hell. At Cluny, the signs of decadence were modest indeed – rather better food, bedrooms for the monks, habits of finer cloth. Even so, this was not exactly asceticism.

The great Rule of St Benedict, moreover, which had inspired Cluny, laid down that the day should be divided among manual work, intellectual work, and prayer. At Cluny, there was little insistence on manual labour. By the beginning of the twelfth century, therefore, the Cluniac order had lost much of its lustre.

Peter the Venerable, the Abbot elected in 1122, tried to re-establish discipline and to curb the taste for luxury and good food. He had some success, and he continued to support the Roman Papacy as best he could. But from this time onwards, the real driving force of Europe's spiritual community began to be in Cîteaux and Clairvaux rather than Cluny.

Further orders, in fact, were following in Cluny's wake.

Carthusians and Premonstratensians

It was a German priest, St Bruno from Cologne, who with six companions founded a monastery on the present Franco-Italian frontier at what is now known as Chartreuse. This was the beginning of the Carthusian order. Purely meditative, and based on silence, isolation, and meatless meals, it soon acquired a great reputation. Bruno was called to Rome to be an adviser to Pope Urban II, but he refused an archbishopric and went on to found a further Carthusian house at Squillace in Calabria.

Another German, from Cleves, set about reforming the Canons of St Augustine. This was Norbert, a friend of St Bruno's and former chaplain to the Emperor Henry V. He founded a house at Prémontré, near Laon, in 1120, based largely on the Augustinian Rule but with more emphasis on manual labour. This was the Premonstratensian order. Norbert later became Archbishop of Magdeburg and subsequently Primate of the two Saxonies. There were also, as we shall see, orders of chivalry established for the Crusades.

But above all the twelfth century was dominated by the Cistercian order, from Cîteaux, and its great European representative St Bernard.

Cîteaux

Cîteaux lies some 22 kilometres north-east of Beaune. In 1099, a saintly man named Robert of Molesme came there with some companions to occupy a Benedictine monastery which was in a parlous state. His intention was rigorously to apply the Rule of St Benedict – sleeping rough, eating only a pound of bread and two dishes of vegetables a day, with no meat, fish, or dairy products, putting up modest, unadorned buildings, wearing simple white robes of coarse weave, and maintaining silence.

This fierce asceticism, far from discouraging recruits, attracted them from far and wide. In 1113, a 23-year-old, Bernard, from Fontaines near Dijon, the third of seven sons of a nobleman, came to Cîteaux with some companions, soon to be followed by several of his brothers, uncles, and cousins.

St Bernard

From Cîteaux, a number of missionary monks set out to found other monasteries, the first four of which were at Pontigny, La Ferié, Morimond, and Clairvaux.

On 25 June 1115, thirteen monks, with Bernard appointed as their abbot by the Abbot of Cîteaux, arrived in the wild, inhospitable 'absinthe valley' near Langres. Jesting, they nicknamed it Claire-vallée ('Bright Valley') or Clairvaux, and set about building a monastery in which God enjoyed little more luxury than the monks.

Clairvaux in turn founded further abbeys – Trois-Fontaines, Fontenay, and Foigny. Each was independent, and free to make further foundations; but such was the reputation of St Bernard that, with no formal power at all, he not only dominated the Cistercian order for some forty years, but also had an extraordinary influence on the Church, the Popes, the Emperors, the Kings of France and of England, on Aragon and Castile, on the Italians, the Danes and the Poles.

Bernard's asceticism had gravely damaged his stomach. He was badly injured when he travelled the roads of Europe with his escort of monks and wrote his hundreds of letters on doctrine and religious policy – often in an authoritarian tone which he justified as being in the service of God, but always with great personal modesty – as well as sermons, theological treatises, and so on.

Looking at Cluny's less ascetic regime, Bernard was hesitant. He admired the fine Cluniac order, but he refused to recruit Cistercians from it, and was greatly saddened when one of his own monks left

Clairvaux for Cluny. He not only advised the Abbots of Cluny, but did the same in order to hasten the reform of the famous royal Abbey of Saint-Denis, whose Abbot Suger (1082–1152) was the influential adviser to Kings Louis VI and VII of France.

Two episodes in St Bernard's life are worth recounting here. One was his struggle against the Anti-Pope Anacletus. The other was his role in the Second Crusade.

Pope and Anti-Pope

In February 1130, on the same day, two rival groups of cardinals elected two Popes: at dawn Innocent II; at noon Anacletus, with powerful feudal support, which obliged Innocent to flee.

In August 1130, the King of France, Louis VI, organized an assembly at Etampes to choose between the two Popes. St Bernard's authority tipped the scale decisively in Innocent's favour. Innocent came to Cluny and met Abbot Suger, who announced that he had won; but the rest of Christendom had yet to be heard. After having seen Louis VI at Etampes, Bernard met King Henry I of England at Chartres and convinced him that he must persuade the English clergy to abandon Anacletus. At the same time, in liaison with Bernard, Norbert (the founder of the Premonstratensians) induced Lothaire, the Emperor-designate, to recognize Innocent and even to go to Rome to install him. In March 1131, Innocent met Lothaire, and found him hesitant: but Bernard, who was also present, argued so forcefully that Lothaire could not resist. Bernard then returned to Clairvaux. From there he sent out two further groups of missionary monks, one to the Vaud canton in Switzerland, one to Hesse. Monasteries were now springing up everywhere. As Georges Goyau has remarked, 'Thanks to Bernard, the Cistercian order had begun to spread throughout Europe.'

When the Pope passed through Clairvaux, he found that little exception to the ascetic rule would be made in his honour. He had to accept a modest lodging; his only privilege was to be served a fish at table. Bernard and Innocent then proceeded to Rheims, where Innocent received the formal allegiance of Aragon and Castile. Only Aquitaine and southern and central Italy now remained loyal to Anacletus. Bernard's first concern was with Aquitaine, where he had only partial success. Then, in 1133, Lothaire invaded Italy in order to march on Rome. Bernard joined him at Pisa. Since the Duke of Sicily was backing Anacletus, Bernard decided to immobilize him – which could be done if the Genoese and Pisan fleets were to join forces. But they were at war with each other; so Bernard set about engineering a reconciliation. He succeeded. His achievement showed the extraordinary authority then wielded by this man of forty-three.

Innocent, Lothaire, and Bernard entered Rome on 30 April 1133, and Lothaire was crowned Emperor at the Lateran. But Anacletus was still in control of the Vatican area, and Bernard was unable to fulfil his dream of seeing St Peter's tomb. Moreover, when Bernard returned to Clairvaux, Lothaire withdrew to Germany; and Anacletus drove Innocent out of Rome, forcing him to take refuge in Pisa.

In 1135 it was Lothaire's turn to be threatened.

Bernard, that tireless traveller, went to Germany, where at Bamberg he reconciled Lothaire with Frederick of Hohenstaufen, the future Frederick Barbarossa. Then he made for Pisa, where he acted as arbiter in a number of disputes. He also took the opportunity to found the Cistercian monastery of 'Chiaravalle' near Milan – an Italian Clairvaux. Finally, he returned to Clairvaux – but then left a third time for Italy, travelling first to Bari and then to Monte Cassino.

The death of Anacletus in 1138 at last put an end to the battle of the Popes.

Nor was the rest of Europe forgotten. A great Irish prelate, St Malachy, came to see Bernard at Clairvaux. The situation in Ireland was far from satisfactory. Malachy left with four Cistercians who founded the order's first Irish monastery.

Bernard also played a part in the story of Peter Abelard (see page 194), who he decided was indeed a heretic. After all his misadventures, Abelard ended his days at Cluny, where Abbot Peter the Venerable, on Abelard's death in 1142, had the delicacy to send his old friend Heloïse an account of her former lover's last moments. 'Once linked by the bonds of the flesh, they were now united by the stronger and more sacred power of divine love.'

St Bernard and the Second Crusade

The other major action by St Bernard which is relevant here was his attempt to rally Western Christendom behind a Second Crusade, to recapture from the Muslims the domain of Edessa which the Emir of Aleppo had recently conquered.

In 1145, a year after the loss of Edessa, a Cistercian by the name of

Paganelli, who had been the sovereign of Pisa, and whom Bernard had persuaded to enter Clairvaux, was elected Pope as Eugenius III. The moment seemed propitious; and set off Bernard on his travels once more.

The King of France, Louis VII (whose wife Eleanor of Aquitaine later married Henry II of England), agreed to go on the Crusade. At Vézelay on 31 March 1146, in the presence of the king, Bernard read out to a huge open-air meeting the Papal Bull announcing the expedition. The next step was to convince the Emperor. 'As Caesar,' wrote Bernard, 'you have two duties: your duty as a king, which is to protect your crown, and your duty as advocate of the Faith, which is to defend the Church.'

On his way to meet the new Emperor Conrad in Germany, Bernard put paid to a movement which claimed to want to expand the Crusade by considering Jews as much enemies as Muslims. 'They are the flesh and bones of the Messiah,' he declared. He went through Breisgau, German Switzerland, and Constance, then sailed in triumph down the Rhine as far as Cologne. By Christmas 1146 he had reached Speier, where he talked with Conrad and persuaded him to join the Crusade. Returning to Clairvaux, he sent letters in all directions to mobilize the rest of Europe: to the English, who in agreement with the Flemings were preparing to make war in the Mediterranean; to certain Italian bishops; to the Bohemians; and to the Bavarians. Then, hearing that the Saxons and Moravians on the Elbe in the east, and the Danes in the north, were thinking of joining the expedition, he persuaded them that fighting the pagan Slavs was just as much a Crusade as fighting the Saracens, and that they should not leave Europe's eastern flank exposed to further Slav invasions. The Spaniards, likewise, had their own Crusade to fight at home.

St Bernard: a European

It was not Bernard's task to command troops.

On the field of battle, the Second Crusade was marred by disputes and strategic errors, and was not a success. Later, Bernard actually considered taking personal command of a further Crusade; but his roots were in Europe and in the peace of Clairvaux, and his health by then had seriously declined.

It nevertheless remains extraordinary to see how in this age of intense piety one ascetic man, who sacrificed everything to God, could at times provide the impetus to unite Western Europe, not only in matters of faith, but politically too.

Although a Frenchman, Bernard by no means concentrated on the defence of France. The monk Guibert of Nogent, who entitled his history of the First Crusade *Gesta Dei per francos* ('The exploits of God performed by the Franks'), clearly thought in 'French' terms: so did the monk and minister Suger. But 'Bernard, born to feudalism, became a European,' as Georges Goyau points out. 'The very idea of the nation had less place in his mind than it had in that of Guibert.'

It may seem strange that this ascetic man, who sought to pacify the Church under the authority of the Pope, should have taken so aggressive a stand against the Muslims. His conviction, fanatical as it may appear, was that Christendom, by conquering Jerusalem, had recovered its legitimate possession; but that it now found itself threatened by 'intolerable irruptions'. Of the warrior–monk Knights Templar he declared: 'The soldiers of Christ can fight the good fight without a care. They have nothing to fear – neither sin if they kill the enemy, nor perdition if they are slain: for to take life on behalf of Christ is in no way criminal, and to lose one's life for Christ is to merit an abundance of glory.'

Worn out by his exertions, Bernard died in August 1153, one month after the death of Pope Eugenius III.

EUROPE AND THE CRUSADES

The idea of a Crusade

The First Crusade was launched by Pope Urban II. At a Council which he held at Piacenza in 1095, with 4,000 priests and 30,000 laymen assembled in the town, he received a delegation from the Byzantine Emperor Alexis Comnenus, seeking the help of all Christians against 'the infidel' – the Muslims – who had conquered a large part of his Empire.

Urban II, who was leaving for a visit to his native France, at first considered simply organizing the help the Byzantines had requested. Then his thoughts turned to a much more ambitious idea – that of repeating in the east the resounding success of the Spanish and

Portuguese Reconquista, which had freed Toledo in 1085, Valencia in 1092, and Lisbon in 1093.

On his way through central France, Urban visited Puy, whose Bishop Adhémar of Monteil was later made religious leader of the Crusade. Urban then went on to Cluny, where he had been a monk, and convoked a Council at Clermont. There, on 27 November 1095, outside the church where the Council was meeting, he put to the crowd his proposal to send an expedition to Jerusalem. The response was enthusiastic. Adhémar of Monteil and the knights who were present 'took the Cross' – represented by a cross sewn on the shoulder. Those taking part in the expedition were guaranteed by the Council that their possessions at home would be protected.

This First Crusade reflected Urban's concern for Papal supremacy. He wanted to be its commander-in-chief; but since he was not accompanying the expedition himself, he decided to put Adhémar of Monteil in charge of it. Traditionally, the Emperor Henry IV should have led the forces of Christendom: but he had been excommunicated. So had Philip I, the King of France; while William Rufus, King of England, had not formally committed himself between Pope Urban II and the Anti-Pope Clement III. Raymond of Saint Gilles, Count of Toulouse, therefore accompanied Adhémar as his lay adjutant.

While the Crusade thus represented a bid for unity, it also embodied the not unknown but rarely practised principle of a 'Holy War' – in this way abandoning the peaceful traditions of the Church. Nothing could be more dangerous: for even if the objective be to rescue oppressed fellow-Christians, fanaticism can easily lead to appalling atrocities.

The First Crusade

The Pope had envisaged a single crusading army. In the event, three others went with it: 'Frenchmen from the Royal Domain', led by the King's brother, with the Counts of Normandy and Flanders; 'Frenchmen from the North', with Lorrainers and Germans, led by Godfrey of Bouillon, Duke of Lower Lorraine, who became the first Christian ruler of Jerusalem; and finally an army of Normans from southern Italy.

The feudal world had responded amply to the Pope's appeal. Motives were mixed: profound faith, the quest for adventure, and – for landless younger sons, especially among the Normans in Normandy and Sicily, with their high birth-rate – the hope of carving out a fief and sharing in the fabled riches of the Orient. As well as the knights, moreover, there was a band of hungry peasants, recruited by Peter the Hermit, a rabble-rousing monk from Picardy, and encumbered with their carts and their families. Many were undoubtedly true Christians; but many resorted to mob violence, especially in Germany, where they massacred a number of Jews.

The knights' expedition left in ships chartered from Genoa, and converged on Constantinople. There, the Emperor Alexis was annoyed to discover that the Crusaders were intent on their own affairs rather than his. They crossed the Bosphorus and marched through Asia Minor and Syria towards Jerusalem.

On the way, Adhémar of Monteil died of the plague. Without his restraining hand, the military leaders were more inclined to quarrel; and some turned aside from the main objective to capture Edessa and Antioch. The remainder took Jerusalem on 7 June 1099 – and tarnished their achievement by a fearful massacre. The chroniclers reported 'rivers of blood'.

Pope Urban died too soon to hear the news. A Latin Patriarch was soon installed in Jerusalem; but political power there was wielded by Godfrey of Bouillon and, after his death, by his brother Baldwin of Boulogne, who took the title of King.

One result of the Crusade was to deepen still further the split between Latin and Greek Christendom. The gradual elimination of the Greek hierarchy in areas of the Levant reconquered by the Latins caused great resentment among the Byzantines. Even in the face of Islam, Greeks and Latins were unable to unite.

The later Crusades were mounted mainly to come to the rescue of the Kingdom of Jerusalem and the other Christian principalities in the Levant. Never again did the whole of Western Christendom unite, as it more or less had in the First Crusade, in one vast international enterprise. Whenever a number of sovereigns formed a coalition, it always ended in dissension.

The Second and later Crusades

The aim of the Second Crusade, preached by St Bernard (1147–9) was to take Damascus and reconquer Edessa (see p. 171). Its leaders were

King Louis VII of France and Conrad, Emperor of Germany. Disputes between the French and the German knights led to its failure and withdrawal to Europe. Some forty years later, after Saladin, the Muslim sovereign of Egypt, had recaptured Jerusalem in 1187, a Third Crusade (1189–92) was led by Philip Augustus, King of France, Richard the Lionheart, King of England, and Frederick Barbarossa, the Emperor, who was defeated and killed in Cilicia in 1190. When Richard and Philip Augustus reached Acre, they quarrelled. On his own, Richard was unable to take Jerusalem.

A further outcome of the Crusades was the creation of a number of military religious orders. The Order of the Knights Templar, founded in 1118, spread from Acre and Cyprus all over Europe, where the Templars had as many as 6,000 houses and immense riches. They were dissolved in 1312 by Pope Clement V and King Philip Augustus. The Order of St John of Jerusalem, commonly called the 'Knights Hospitallers', formed at the beginning of the eleventh century, made its headquarters on the island of Rhodes, but also founded many houses in Europe. When the Hospitallers were expelled from Rhodes at the time of Charles V, they established the small sovereign state of Malta, and took the name 'Knights of Malta'. The 'Teutonic Knights', an order which originated at Acre in about 1190, were financed by the burghers of Bremen and Lübeck. They established themselves in Italy, Hungary, and Transylvania, but above all in Germany, where Frederick II made their Grand Master a Prince of the Empire. Summoned to Prussia, they converted the still pagan inhabitants and imposed their political will. In 1237 they merged with the 'Sword-bearing Knights' and spread into Estonia, Livonia, and Kurland. Later came their decline. In the first half of the sixteenth century, their Grand Master Albert of Brandenburg was converted to Lutheranism, took a wife, and seized power for himself and his descendants.

MENDICANT ORDERS AND MISSIONARIES

The Dominicans

In a period when religious faith is very fervent, its adherents make such large gifts to churches and monasteries that these acquire great wealth. This in turn attracts those whom money tempts, and abuses follow. Others then feel their piety affronted. Hence the emergence of sometimes heretical sects which preach and practise poverty. The Waldenses and the Cathars in the south of France were the best known. Should they be crushed by force? This was the course adopted by Simon de Montfort's 'Albigensian Crusade' of 1208–15. Or could their communities be brought back into the Church? Some of them were recognized by the Papacy, as were the 'Humble Poor' of Lombardy, the 'Poor of Lyon', and the 'Catholic Paupers'.

Dominic, a Spanish priest born in 1170 at Calaruega in the province of Burgos, apparently a member of the illustrious Guzman family, initiated another approach. With Bishop Diego of Osma, of which cathedral he was a canon regular, Dominic at first wanted to preach the Gospel among the Cumans, a people living between the Carpathians and the Black Sea. They both went to Rome to seek the blessing of Pope Innocent III: but he told them to go and preach not to the Cumans but to the Cathars.

That was in the summer of 1205. From the discussion in Rome there arose the idea of establishing an 'order of preachers', which like the Cathars would practise the strictest poverty, accumulating no possessions and living from day to day on pure charity. They would proceed 'with humility, acting and preaching according to Christ's example, on foot and with neither gold nor silver, in all respects copying the Apostles'. Innocent III issued a Bull on 17 November 1206, confirming the creation of this new model order, and its first forty members set out to accomplish their task. Diego died in 1207, and Dominic in 1221.

The Inquisition

Dominic was associated, however, with a new Church institution which later gave rise to serious abuses. This was the Inquisition. Its first representatives were Cistercian monks; and Dominic received the title of Inquisitor General from the Pope in 1215. Essentially, the Inquisition was a tribunal whose task was to seek out heresy and punish it. It had a short-lived career in France; it reached Italy in 1221; later, it operated in Germany. But it was in Spain that its influence was greatest, after being introduced into Catalonia in 1232. In 1481 the 'Catholic monarchs' Ferdinand and Isabella reorganized it under the name of the 'Holy Office'. Torquemada, a Dominican cardinal from Valladolid, became 'Grand Inquisitor General'. The repression to which he resorted has remained sadly notorious: it was very different from the aims of St Dominic.

The Dominican Rule

The Dominican Rule, inspired by that of the Augustinian Canons, was not definitively established until 1217, with the support of the great Archbishop Fulk of Toulouse. From the beginning, the order of 'preaching friars' or Dominicans was a great success. St Dominic also set up a version of the order for women.

In 1217, Dominic sent friars from Toulouse to Spain and Paris. His own headquarters were in Rome. As time went by, Dominican foundations multiplied: in about 1221, they spread into the Rhineland, and they had quickly appeared in Italy, Britain, Poland, and Hungary. By 1221, there were some 500 male and 100 female members of the order, divided into eight provinces in Spain, France, Provence, Lombardy, Rome, Germany, Britain, and Hungary. By 1228, four more had been established, in the Holy Land, Greece, Poland, and Dacia. They produced a large number of Popes and other great men, who in this period included Albertus Magnus and St Thomas Aquinas. The secret of the Dominicans' strength was their outstanding intellectual education, which enabled them to become extremely effective preachers.

The Franciscans

The other great 'mendicant order' was founded by someone very different from St Dominic. This was Francis of Assisi, in Umbria, whose father Bernardone was a rich linen merchant. Born in 1182, Francis at first led the comfortable life of a rich middle-class youth, avoiding debauchery but far from embracing poverty.

In 1202, fighting in a war between Assisi and Perugia, he was taken prisoner. Once set free, he set his heart on becoming a great warrior prince; but at the age of twenty-three, after seeing a vision, he shut himself away in a cave near Assisi, did penance, responded to the appeal of 'Lady Poverty', and in 1206 made a pilgrimage to Rome, dressed in rags and begging his bread – to the scandal of his family. In 1209, at Mass, he heard an order from God: 'Take no gold, silver, or money in your belt, nor a bag for the road, nor two habits, nor shoes nor staff; but, if you enter a house, say in greeting "May peace be in this house".'

A disciple of earlier ascetic Italians, and in particular of St Peter Damian, Francis differed from them in two respects: in wanting to recruit a number of others, and in regarding preaching as an essential duty. He tried, without success, to reach Syria and then Morocco; later, he went to Damietta in Egypt, courted martyrdom, and made a pilgrimage to Jerusalem. But he succeeded in attracting to asceticism many young people, including the daughter of a rich Assisi family, Clare de Favorino, who under his guidance established the order of 'Poor Ladies' or 'Poor Clares'.

Missions

The itinerant preachers were not at first well received. But when Francis met Pope Innocent III in Rome in 1210, he won him over as Dominic had done four years earlier. An order of 'Friars Minor' or Franciscans was set up, and its Rule was established in 1223.

Until then, individualism had prevailed, leading to disorder, which Francis had deplored. Once organized, the Friars Minor had an immense success. There were thousands of them, spreading from Italy to France, Spain, Germany, and Hungary. Francis died in 1226, after having written his 'Canticle of the Sun' and received the stigmata of the Passion.

Popes Gregory IX (1227–41) and Innocent IV (1243–54) realized the use they could make of these many and devoted militants, eager to preach the Gospel not only in Europe, but also in distant lands. Although the Papacy still favoured crusading, it slowly moved towards espousing missionary activity. 'We believe,' wrote Gregory IX to the Franciscans in 1238, 'that in the eyes of our Saviour it is as good to persuade infidels to acknowledge the word of God as it is to crush the Saracens' perfidy by force of arms.'

Francis had gone to Egypt and Dominic had preached to the Danes in 1203. Their successors followed their example.

Those who followed Dominic at the head of his Order – Jordan of Saxony (a German), Raymond of Peñafort in Catalonia, John the Teuton (another German), and Humbert of Romans (a Frenchman) sent their friars in all directions. So did the Franciscans. The Holy Land, Constantinople, Cyprus, Antioch, Baghdad, and Egypt saw the establishment of numerous friaries. Others appeared in Tunisia and Morocco; and the Dominican chapter in Toledo instructed eight friars to learn Arabic.

Dominican missions to the Cumans, where St Dominic himself had wanted to go, were crushed by the Mongols: many missionary friars were killed. The Pope even sent further missionaries among the Mongols, both to increase the Christian strength and, if possible, to make converts.

In Northern Europe, the Franciscans supported the activities of the Teutonic Knights. Starting from Danzig, they preached the Gospel in Prussia, Pomerania, Livonia, Estonia, Kurland, and Finland. In 1245, an 'Archbishop of Prussia' was appointed. The bishoprics were divided among the Dominicans, the Franciscans, and the Teutonic Knights. Some Dominicans even went as far as Kiev.

UNIVERSITY EUROPE

Monastic and episcopal schools

After the fall of the Western Empire, it was in the monastic schools that classical learning was maintained. In the sixth century, as we have seen, Ireland played a major role in thus conserving culture. By now, however, these schools were in decline, since the Cluniacs and especially the Cistercians had little interest in the subject. A certain number of 'episcopal' schools filled the gap: they included Rheims, Chartres, Paris, Laon, Angers, Bourges, Orléans, and Montpellier in France; Canterbury and Durham in Britain; Toledo, Salamanca, and Palencia in Spain, where science and Arabic philosophy were taught; Bologna and Ravenna in Italy, centres of Roman law; Salerno, specializing in medicine; Naples, and so on.

The establishment of universities

Nevertheless, the growing number of students, the quest for greater independence from the bishops and the lay authorities, and the community spirit which was developing everywhere in the twelfth and thirteenth centuries, all encouraged the establishment of universities.

These were corporations of a new kind, bringing together the totality (universitas) of the masters and pupils. At a time when workers and craftsmen, following the example of the municipalities, were uniting in guilds to defend their interests, masters and 'scholars' were virtually doing the same. They maintained a link between education and civic life; but the major universities received students from all over Europe, and, thanks to the Papacy, they had the right to teach anywhere, the so-called *licentia ubique docendi*. In the thirteenth century, the universities were truly European institutions. In the fourteenth and fifteenth centuries, they became more and more national.

In Paris, the 'Faculty of Arts', headed by a 'Rector', gave the initial teaching course for pupils aged fourteen to twenty, leading to the baccalaureate after two years. This was followed by one or other of the three 'High Faculties': canon law, medicine, and theology, each headed by a Dean.

The study of law or medicine took twenty to twenty-five years. Theology required fifteen years of study, and doctorates thirty-five years.

Such, with minor differences, was the organization of all the universities. Papal protection gave them the exclusive right to confer degrees. They also enjoyed legal and fiscal privileges and exemptions.

The degrees they offered were practically the same throughout Europe: the baccalaureate, the licence (licentia docendi), and the doctorate. The licence enabled its holder to become a master or magister.

Rich students lived in town, with servants and even private tutors. The less well-off lived in 'colleges' established by patrons or benefactors, where they had relatively modest board and lodging. The *pauperes*, the really poor, were sometimes spared any expenditure at all.

Teaching was by lecture (*lectio*), discussion (*disputatio*), and questions (*questiones*). The lectures were sometimes 'published'. The masters, who were often eminent, vied with each other to recruit students. All the members of the university, masters and students alike, were known as 'clerks'. Latin, of course, remained the common language. Altogether, this university world, highly mobile and given to bold speculation, had a propensity for freedom which over the centuries came to be a characteristic European trait. There was, indeed, a veritable 'intellectuals' International'.

The universities were always short of room. The masters themselves often hired the overcrowded halls. Students sat on benches or even on bales of straw; they had rudimentary writing-boards. Gradually, parchment became finer and whiter, and wooden stylets were replaced by goose quills. Books began to be produced in a number of copies (with a sheepskin, the *pecia*, folded into sections of four folios). Forty or so scribes could thus produce a small edition. Paper, which was fifteen times less expensive than the equivalent surface in parchment, had long been known to the Chinese, but reached Europe only after the foundation of the great universities. Paper mills made their first appearance in Europe at Sativa in Spain in 1238, under Arab influence, then at Fabiano in Italy in 1268, at Troyes in France in 1338, and at Nuremberg in Germany in 1390.

The status of a university involved considerable independence from the power of the bishops. The 'privileges' guaranteeing this independence were granted by the kings and the Popes.

The first three universities were those of Bologna, Paris, and Oxford. How did they come into being? They certainly grew out of episcopal schools, and their development was sometimes slow.

The University of Bologna

Bologna, the outstanding centre for the study of Roman and canon law, received its first Statute from Frederick Barbarossa in 1158. But there were also rival centres in Padua, Vercelli, and above all Naples, which was supported by the Emperor Frederick II. To prevent the emigration of students towards these centres, the Popes improved Bologna's Statute, with the help of its teachers, the *antiqui doctores* or 'Masters Regent', who formed a new association from 1179 onwards. These teachers had the support of the Commune of Bologna – whereas the students, seeking to defend their rights against their masters, relied on backing from the Holy See, whose aim was political domination.

Courses and degrees were in principle free of charge; but the teachers expected to receive donations. In the thirteenth century, the Popes reacted against this custom, and fixed salaries took its place. Before long, the community of students took charge of running the university, every student taking an oath of obedience.

Bologna was already famous in the twelfth century. Before 1150, its teacher of canon law was Orlando Bandinelli, the future Pope Alexander III (1159–81) and resolute opponent of Frederick Barbarossa. A Bolognese law student, Lotario Segni, soon afterwards became Pope as Innocent III (1198–1216), the most powerful of all medieval pontiffs. Innocent's nephew Gregory IX (1227–41) was also a brilliant product of the Bologna law school. He it was who finally made the Statute of the universities general by a Papal Bull of 1231, Parens scientiarum, 'Father of the sciences'.

The University of Paris

Paris was the second of the universities. Evolving out of the cathedral chapter school, it soon acquired European standing and influence. At the end of the twelfth century, growing numbers of students settled in a new district which was being built on the left bank of the Seine, the Montagne Ste Geneviève. They were a lively lot, many of them wandering scholars, enjoying life to the full: amorous, anti-clerical, and fond of coarse Bacchic poetry. They were known as 'Goliards', and they left their traces in Goliardic literature: the *Carmina Burana* in France, the *Cambridge Songbook* in England, and the *Manuscript* of the Abbey of Benedictenbeuern in Germany. This perennial characteristic of Europe's students seems not to have interfered unduly with the universities' serious work.

In 1179, Pope Alexander III laid down that teaching at the University of Paris should be both free of restriction and free of charge. In 1200, Philip Augustus exempted the students from royal jurisdiction. In 1208, the *universitas magistrorum* or University of Masters made its appearance. In 1215, Robert de Courçon, the legate of Pope Innocent III, established a Statute for 'all Parisian masters and scholars' (*universis magistris et scolaribus parisiensibus*). In 1222, the University obtained its full rights.

The University of Oxford

Oxford's university was partly an offshoot of Paris, or so it would seem. Schools had certainly existed there before 1167; but in that year, it is thought, a group of mainly English scholars migrated from Paris to Oxford, possibly as a result of Thomas Becket's quarrel with Henry II, who recalled to England clerks who possessed 'revenues' in England. At all events, a charter from the Papal legate in 1214 strengthened Oxford's legal position, and in 1219 the word 'university' was applied to it for the first time. By 1221 at the latest, Oxford had a 'Chancellor' chosen from among the masters and possibly elected by them, but under the authority of the Church. One early well-known incumbent was the learned Bishop of Lincoln, Robert Grosseteste, the translator of Aristotle's *Nicomachean Ethics*; while eminent Oxford teachers included Edmund of Abingdon (Edmund Rich, c.1170–1240) and Roger Bacon (c.1214–92).

Other universities

Many other universities followed these first three. In Italy, Padua was founded in 1222, Siena in 1246; then came Vercelli, Arezzo, Rome, and Naples; later, after 1300, there were Perugia, Pisa, and Florence. In France, in 1229, came Orléans, a great law centre, followed in 1231 by Angers and in 1220–40 by Montpellier, already famous for its school of medicine. In 1229, Count Raymond of Toulouse founded a university in that city to combat the Cathar or 'Albigensian' heretics. In the fourteenth century, further universities were established in Cahors, Grenoble, and Avignon.

The University of Cambridge began as an offshoot of Oxford. In 1209, an Oxford scholar reputedly killed a townswoman, whereupon the mayor and burgesses raided the offender's hostel. King John agreed to the execution of two or possibly three of the imprisoned students. The remainder, with the masters, fled – some to Reading, the nearest sizeable town, some to Paris, and others to Cambridge. 'What attracted them to that distant marsh town we know not,' wrote Hastings Rashdall, the Oxford historian of medieval universities. It certainly became Oxford's great rival – as his words suggest.

In Portugal, the school which had existed in Coimbra since the twelfth century became a university in the thirteenth, and moved to Lisbon.

In Spain, the first universities were Salamanca, Palencia, Lerida, and (Roussillon having been annexed to the Crown of Aragon) Perpignan. Valladolid, where a school had existed since the mid-thirteenth century, acquired university status early in the fourteenth.

In Central Europe, Germany had no true universities before 1300. In Prague, capital of the Kingdom of Bohemia, a flourishing university, set up by Charles IV of the Luxembourg dynasty, nevertheless attracted students from Germany, Italy, and France.

Further universities were established, as will be seen, in the second half of the fourteenth century: by the year 1400 there were no fewer than fifty-five.

The mobility of scholarship

University members were extremely mobile; but as well as dividing into different disciplines they naturally tended also to congregate in national groups, known at the time as 'Nations'. In Paris, each 'Nation' was headed by a Procurator. There were four of them: English, Norman, Picardy, and French (which included central France, Italy, Spain, and the East). In Oxford there were two such 'Nations'; in Bologna, four 'Communities' – Lombards, Romans, Campania, and 'Ultramontane'.

The masters were as mobile as their pupils: indeed, when there was trouble in a university, the teachers often followed their pupils in moving elsewhere. Thus, in 1229, when several students were killed in disturbances in Paris, the whole university moved out of the city. Only the Bull Parens scientiarum of 1231 made it possible to collect most of the exiles and re-open the university.

A few examples will show how readily university teachers moved from place to place. The great Dominican scholar Albertus Magnus (1193–1280) was born in Swabia, then studied in Bologna, Padua, and Paris; he taught there from 1242 to 1248, and went on to found a *studium generale*, an embryonic university, in his native Germany, at Cologne.

Roger Bacon, the Oxford scholar, was a Master of Arts in Paris, and taught there from 1245 to 1247. Thomas Aquinas (1225–74), a descendant of the Counts of Aquino in southern Italy, studied at Naples, then in Cologne under Albertus Magnus, and then in Paris. He taught there, then in the Roman Curia, then in Paris again, and finally in Naples. His main philosophical opponent, Siger of Brabant

(1240–c.1284), was a Fleming, but a Master of Arts in Paris – though his unorthodox philosophical views obliged him to leave in 1277.

PILGRIMAGE

Pilgrimage is, among other things, a remarkable opportunity for different peoples to meet and know a little more about each other. Obviously, it was not invented by Christianity. It forms part of the Jewish Old Testament tradition, and exists in most religions.

These are revelations whereby a transcendent, supernatural, or metaphysical world impinges on human time and space. There are thus places and dates at which God or His Prophets, or their disciples, have become manifest to human beings. Naturally, such places are revered. Equally naturally, people see virtue in visiting them. And since in periods of very fervent faith a belief in miracles tends to make them seem part of everyday life, it becomes easy to imagine that spectacular miracles are most likely to occur in places where the great saints have lived, and where their 'relics' can be found.

Thus people went on pilgrimages not only to improve their worthiness for eternal life, or to seek forgiveness for grave sins, but also to thank their God(s) and saints for some benefit or, more often, to plead for a cure, a success, or the acquisition of some longed-for possession.

Pilgrimage in Europe

Despite incessant feudal wars, despite the Mongol and Turkish threats from the East, and despite very difficult communications now that the Roman roads were in decay and unreplaced, the eleventh, twelfth, and thirteenth centuries probably saw more pilgrimages than any other time. Hundreds of thousands of people, perhaps more, the poor on foot, the rich and lordly on horseback or in carriages, set out on various well-trodden routes, often in groups which sometimes comprised several hundred pilgrims.

The development of pilgrimage can be explained in various ways. The general expansion of the West was one. This included the Reconquista in Spain and Portugal, virtually completed in the thirteenth century; the reconquest of Sicily; the Crusades; the growth of safer maritime transport; the expansion of industry and trade; and the conversion of the Scandinavians, Hungarians, and Slavs. From now on, large numbers of pilgrims came from Scandinavia, Britain and the East. The temporary conquest of Palestine, moreover, made possible the discovery of large numbers of relics, many of dubious authenticity although supposedly guaranteed by miracles.

There was in fact a roaring trade in relics, which the Fifth Lateran Council condemned in 1215. There were also thefts and sometimes bloody conflicts among different monasteries seeking to lay their hands on the sacred spoils.

What were the geographical centres of attraction for pilgrims?

The Holy Land

The most important, in point of merit, were the Holy Places where Christ had lived. It was partly the need to come and pray there that had spurred the idea of the Crusades – an idea current throughout the eleventh century, long before the conquest of Jerusalem in 1099. Its recapture by Saladin in 1187, and its final loss in 1244, in no way put a stop to pilgrimage: it was simply that in the thirteenth century the Papacy no longer encouraged it. The Muslim authorities were in general prepared to allow Christians into the Holy Land, but they naturally demanded a high price. The Popes, who dreamed only of fresh Crusades, preferred to see the money spent on preparing military operations.

The Holy Land was reached by sea, although a land route opened up after Stephen I of Hungary was converted to Christianity. In the eleventh century the Mediterranean had been relatively unsafe, but conditions improved in the twelfth. The largest number of pilgrims to the Holy Land came from Germany, Italy, and France, with rather fewer from Britain and Spain.

Rome

Pilgrimage to Rome, where the relics of St Peter and St Paul were revered, was in decline until the year 1300, the date of the first Roman 'Jubilee'. The conflict between the Empire and the Papacy, in fact, had led to continual violence. In 1083, Rome was occupied by the Emperor Henry IV; in 1084 it was sacked by the Norman Robert Guiscard.

Pilgrimage continued, however, thanks to so-called *ad limina* visits by bishops, and to the practice of 'indulgences'. These were connected with the belief in Purgatory, where sinners who did not deserve Hell were sent to be purified by suffering before they could enter Paradise.

An indulgence could shorten one's time in Purgatory. It could be obtained by prayer or pilgrimage – but also by giving alms. This later led to many abuses, and was one of the causes of the Reformation.

Marian Pilgrimages

As well as journeys to Jerusalem and Rome, there were also 'Marian' pilgrimages made to honour the Virgin Mary, mother of Jesus. In this case, there was no question of relics, since the Assumption had raised Mary to Paradise. But the cult of the Virgin developed, and some admirable sanctuaries were built, generally containing miraculous statues. There was a Notre-Dame in Chartres, in Paris, and in Le Puy; there was Our Lady of Walsingham in England; there was Mariazell in Austria; there were similar shrines at Montserrat in Catalonia, and all over Europe. The most popular of all, in the thirteenth century, was Notre-Dame of Rocamadour, named after Amadour, the legendary servant of Mary, who was said to have come to Gaul after the Assumption. Many high-ranking pilgrims went there; they included several Dukes of Lorraine, King Henry II of England (twice, in 1159 and 1170), Louis IX of France with his mother Blanche of Castile and his three brothers in 1244, and Philip of Alsace, the Count of Flanders. A *Book of Miracles* from Notre-Dame of Rocamadour, written in 1172, describes the pilgrim routes there from England, Germany, and Italy.

Saint Michael

Two other leading places of pilgrimage were sacred to St Michael the archangel. One was at Monte Sant'Angelo on the Gargano peninsula in southern Italy. The Church of St Michael there, initially under Byzantine influence, became a dependency of Monte Cassino. The second sanctuary, whose importance grew immeasurably, was founded on 'Mont Dol', where there had been an eighth-century Temple of Mithra. This was the famous Mont-Saint-Michel, which benefited in particular from the increasing power of the Dukes of Normandy. Duke William the Bastard (William the Conqueror) went there with the Saxon King Harold in 1065, the year before his successful invasion of England. Numerous Kings of France also made their pilgrimage there.

Canterbury

The murder of Archbishop Thomas Becket on 29 December 1170, by knights from the court of King Henry II, very soon made Canterbury

Cathedral a place of pilgrimage. Three years after his death, in fact, Thomas was canonized as a saint and martyr by Pope Alexander III. Pilgrims came to his shrine not only from the north of England, Wales, and Cornwall, but also from Flanders and northern and central France. They included the Archbishops of Cologne and Lyon, the future Pope Innocent III (while he was a student in Paris), and the King of France, Louis VII.

St James of Compostela

But of all the great places of pilgrimage, the most important was St James of Compostela, in north-western Galicia in Spain. In about AD 800, the relics of St James the Apostle were thought to have been found there, in a marble tomb. Indeed, there was a whole Christian necropolis or compositum, whence the name 'Compostela' may be derived.

In the tenth century, the sanctuary began to exert an influence well beyond that region of Spain. But the Muslims were still close at hand. They captured the town, destroyed the basilica, and herded the inhabitants into slavery. Only the Reconquista saved Compostela.

In the eleventh century, pilgrims flocked there from all parts of Western Europe: there were French, Belgian Walloons, Flemings, Germans, English, and Italians. Compostela, whose Bishop became an Archbishop in 1120, was now a centre of attraction for such notabilities as the widow of Henry V, the Duke of Aquitaine, King Louis VII of France, the Bishop of Winchester, the Archbishop of Mainz, the Archbishop of Liège, the Duke of Austria, St Francis of Assisi, the King of Portugal, Dutch and German Crusaders, and Nestorian monks from the court of the Great Khan of the Mongols, as well as a Swedish princess and assorted Hungarians.

For the Spaniards, St James was the great champion of the Reconquista. He was believed to have appeared during battles against the Muslims, notably that of Las Naves de Tolosa in 1212. For others, he was the intermediary and healer, whose influence with God was greater than that of any other saint. As a result, Compostela was for a time as famous throughout Europe as Rome itself.

A pilgrimage

Let us follow a pilgrim – from Britain, from Scandinavia, from Hungary, from Italy, or wherever it may be. To begin with, there is a choice to be made among innumerable local places of pilgrimage established by monks, often on the sites of ancient pagan shrines.

Their sheer number explains their obscurity, for competition between them was keen. According to Chelini and Branthomme, 'Local patriotism was very much alive among those in charge of these places of pilgrimage, and the hagiographers who celebrated the miracles performed by "their" saint seldom failed to point out that the saint at the neighbouring church had been unable to help those whom his rival at their church had successfully cured.' Beginning with a local pilgrimage, one could then range further afield. Here, all European pilgrims were alike.

First, they all wore the same costume, which can be seen almost everywhere in Gothic statues of St James. It consisted of a tunic, long for women and shorter for men, with a cape which in the fourteenth century became a huge draped mantle, aptly known in French as a *pèlerine*, from *pelerine* or 'pilgrim'. If they were going to St James of Compostela, they wore on their hat or hood the famous scallop emblem – the *coquille Saint-Jacques* – which denoted their purpose. They walked with a pilgrim's staff or *bourdon*, and over their shoulders they carried a double bag, closed at both ends with an opening in the centre, their pilgrim's scrip. All these were blessed before they set out.

But how did pilgrims decide to set out? And how, in a world without good roads and without maps, could they find their way?

It was the monks whose sermons and advice encouraged pilgrims. For Compostela, which was the principal destination, the highly centralized Cluniac order organized the journey. There were guidebooks which showed the routes to follow and the holy places to be visited when setting out. For Rome, for example, there were the *Einsiedeln Itinerary* in the ninth century, the *Mirabilia urbis romae* or 'Marvels of the City of Rome' in the twelfth century, and the *Descriptio plenaria totius urbis* or 'Complete Description of the Whole City' in the thirteenth century. For Mont-Saint-Michel, a late twelfth-century troubadour, William of Saint Pair, wrote the *Roman de Mont-Saint-Michel*, its 'romance'. And the 1172 *Book of Miracles* describes among many other things the itinerary between Notre-Dame of Le

Puy and Notre-Dame of Rocamadour, showing all the churches on the way that were dedicated to the Virgin. Naturally, however, the largest number of guides were devoted to Compostela, culminating in the *Book of St James* in 1139.

Four great itineraries in France, worked out by the monks of Cluny, show the starting-points (Tours, Vézelay, Le Puy, and Arles), the sanctuaries to visit on the way, the passes over the Pyrenees (via Roncevaux for the first three routes and by the Col du Somport for the 'Toulouse Way' or *via tolosana* coming from Arles). All the routes met in Spain at Puente-la-Reina, continuing via Burgos, Leon, and Villafranca.

Generally, the pilgrims travelled on foot, and sometimes, as a penance, barefoot. But they also used horses, and above all asses and mules, especially for crossing the mountains.

Those who fell ill would be carried in a wagon or on the back of a relative. The risks were appalling. There were highwaymen disguised as pilgrims and known as 'shell men' on account of their false insignia. Ferrymen exploited pilgrims at river-crossings, and sometimes carried so many passengers that they capsized, and some were drowned. Some guides held the travellers to ransom. By sea, there was a risk from Muslim pirates. And even without such dangers, conditions in the ships which sailed for the Holy Land from Marseille or Venice with as many as 500 pilgrims on board can hardly have been comfortable.

Along the way, lodging had to be found. True, one could sleep in churches. But what about food? It was here that the system established by the monks came into play. Every monastery had a reception service, the *porta*. From the ninth century onwards, this was divided into two sections: the hostelry, for those with financial resources, who mostly arrived on horseback, and the almonry, for the poor. Kings and nobility gave donations to finance this network of hospices, which were at the same time hospitals.

Other orders, as well as Cluny, helped to serve the pilgrim routes: the order of Aubrac in the twelfth century, in the Rouergue district of France; the order of Roncevaux; the famous order of the Knights Hospitallers of St John of Jerusalem; and the order of the Holy Sepulchre in the Holy Land. There were also private inns charging a commercial rate.

It is hard to picture the polyglot crowds from all over Europe, meeting on the road and flocking towards the sanctuary in ever greater numbers. Any educated clerks in the throng could communicate in

Latin. And once arrived at the sanctuary, everyone shared the same experience, praying together, touching the relics, making votive offerings. Then they returned to tell the story of their journey, their chance meetings, and the secondary pilgrimages they had made along the way. Some joined associations such as the Fellowship of St James, or of Rocamadour.

Pilgrims ran great risks; but once they had taken their vows, which were binding and could be rescinded only by the bishop, they nevertheless enjoyed very special protection.

There was indeed, in the thirteenth century, a veritable system of international European law. Canon and civil law protected pilgrims from arbitrary arrest, from violence, and from financial exploitation. Anyone breaking these rules was excommunicated. The murder of a pilgrim was more severely punished than that of anyone else. Various rules safeguarded pilgrims' property during their absence. In other words, nowhere was a pilgrim treated as a foreigner.

In this way, during the so-called 'ages of faith', pilgrimage helped Europeans to mingle and gradually to evolve something of a sense of what they shared.

THE GREAT DEBATE

The new intellectual 'public'

The 'Great Debate' in question, of course, was that between faith and reason, which had begun in the early days of Christianity and which continues even in the present time.

In the twelfth and thirteenth centuries, this debate became more general, for several reasons. The first was the growing number of what today might be called 'intellectuals' – not only clerks or clerics in the full sense, but also university students, wandering poets or minstrels (the so-called 'troubadours'), and some lords and ladies of the manor. From now on, writers had a 'public'.

Greek texts passed on by Arab scholars

But this new 'Renaissance', the precursor of that which ended the Middle Ages, also arose from the fact that Europeans were now discovering lost Greek texts, and above all further fragments from Aristotle. These came to Europe not from the Byzantines, but from the Arabs. In the past, the few Greek passages known in Latin translation had been for the most part quotations collected by such authors as Boethius in the late Roman Empire. These writers and their successors had been in the habit of inserting 'glosses' or commentaries into the text, without specifying whether or not they were part of the original. However, at those times when Arab civilization was flourishing, a number of Muslim scholars had translated Greek texts; and now these Arabic versions were being rendered into Latin. The process was as yet unscientific: not until the sixteenth century did scholars begin to study what after the Renaissance became known as philology, papyrology, and epigraphy.

Apart from Aristotle, the main Greek authors in question were the mathematician Pythagoras, the physicians Hippocrates and Galen, the geographer Ptolemy, and the 'neo-Platonists' Plotinus, Proclus, and Porphyry. Strangely, there were very few texts from Plato himself, or from the geographer Strabo; and despite the number of philosophical and scientific writings thus recovered, there were very few literary works. The emphasis on Aristotle – used by the Muslims in an attempt to bolster faith in the Koran – was due chiefly to Ibn Sina, known in the West as Avicenna. (Please see also p.232.) Born in Persia, he died in 1037; he was nicknamed 'the Aristotle and Hippocrates of the Arab world'.

The Arab transmission of Greek texts took place in three main areas. The first was that of Syria and Palestine, scene of the Crusades. The second was the Norman court in Sicily, where after the Normans had taken over from the Byzantines and the Arabs there nevertheless remained many traces of Muslim life. The Muslims had in fact lived alongside Jews, Orthodox believers, and Catholics: they had even helped to build and decorate Christian churches. But the third and most important scene of culture-contact was Spain, where Islam had made an especially brilliant showing.

Two men among many others may be said to epitomize the way in which Greek learning was passed on to Europe. One was Ibn Rushd – Averroës to the Europeans. Born at Cordoba in about 1126, he died in Morocco in 1198, and was known as 'the Commentator' for having published among other things a *Commentary* on all the works of Aristotle. The other was a Jew, Moses Ben Maimon, or Maimonides, born at Cordoba in 1135; he died in the East in 1206 after spending thirty years in Egypt and the Maghreb. A theologian, philosopher, and physician, he was best known for his *Moreh Nevochim* or *Guide of the Perplexed*, originally written in Arabic, then translated into Hebrew and later into Latin, and his *Yad Hazakah* or *The Strong Hand*, which contained a complete digest of the Hebrew laws.

Greek, at that time, was known only by a few European scholars like Robert Grosseteste, the first Chancellor of Oxford University. But new translations from Greek were made between 1260 and 1285 by the Flemish Dominican William of Moerbeke. These at last revealed to Latin readers an Aristotle unadulterated by glosses, whether late Roman or Arabic.

Faith and reason

The thirteenth century had more right than its predecessors to be called 'the age of philosophy'. Metaphysics and logic were so dominant as to eclipse somewhat the pursuit of pure literature, as in the great eleventh- and twelfth-century 'romances'.

Everyone, certainly, adhered to the Christian faith – if only to a form of it condemned by the Church as heretical. But the problem was to determine what role reason should play in human understanding. In this respect, several main lines of thought could be discerned.

The Pure Rationalists

The most purely rationalist tradition led from John Scotus Erigena, the great ninth-century Irish metaphysician, down to Siger of Brabant in the thirteenth century. One of its best-known representatives was Peter Abelard (1079–1142). Please see p. 171.

Born in Nantes, the son of a Breton nobleman, Abelard studied in Paris under William of Champeaux, and soon became his rival, attracting audiences of 3,000 students. Giving private lessons to Héloïse, the niece of Canon Fulbert, he became her lover, and she bore him a child. She wrote him passionate letters; and their idyll gave him lasting fame. So, brutally, did its outcome. Fulbert had him seized in his bed and castrated. Abelard then became a monk. His intellectual achievement was immense.

A century later, Siger of Brabant went still further than Abelard in championing reason, even when it contradicted faith. Reason made it clear that the universe was eternal and had not been created; that man was an animal; and that there was no individual immortality.

Small wonder that Siger was condemned as a heretic and an 'Averroist' – although Dante consigned him to Paradise.

The Anti-Rationalist Mystics

At the other extreme stood St Anselm (1033–1110), a Piedmontese from Aosta and a disciple of the great St Augustine and of the neo-Platonists. He was a monk at the Abbey of Bec, in Normandy; and it was there that he wrote his *Monologion* or 'Example of Meditation on the Rationality of the Faith', and his *Proslogion* or 'The Faith in Search of Intelligence'. He later became Archbishop of Canterbury.

In the thirteenth century, St Bonaventure (1221–74), a Franciscan from Tuscany who became a teacher at Paris, was cast in the same mould. For him, the influence of Aristotle was secondary to that of St Augustine and the neo-Platonists. God had to be discovered in the natural world, and contemplated: such contemplation would lead to revelation.

Bonaventure's main work was *The Soul's Journey towards God*. He became known as 'the Seraphic Doctor'.

Reason supports faith: Thomas Aquinas

Between Siger of Brabant's rationalism and the mysticism of St Bonaventure, the most influential school, which more and more came to be seen as founding a true Christian philosophy, was that of the Dominican Thomas Aquinas. His nickname was 'Universal Doctor'. He wrote extensively: his best-known works were his *Commentaries on Aristotle* and, above all, his *Summa Theologica*, in which all of Aristotle was incorporated. For Aquinas, reason and faith were perfectly compatible. Reason was the basis of faith, supplying supplementary proof for all of its tenets.

Thomas Aquinas was not without enemies. The Bishop of Paris accused him of 'Averroism'; the Archbishop of Canterbury and the University of Oxford condemned him; and in England, although it was the home of empiricists like Robert Grosseteste and Roger Bacon, he was long considered a dangerous rationalist. It was the Franciscan Duns Scotus (1275–1308) who opposed Aquinas most fiercely: known as 'the Subtle Doctor', he taught first at Paris, then at Cologne. The 'Scotists', unlike the 'Thomists', believed that reason was wholly separate from faith, rather than one of the ways towards it.

This great debate continued for centuries in different forms. It already transcended frontiers, leaving Europeans with an accumulation of thoughts and ideas which led some to prefer mysticism and others to cease believing altogether, because in their eyes reason was all-powerful and incompatible with faith. There were fanatical believers, for whom all sacred writings had to be taken literally: there were others who sought to distinguish essential truths from written allegories like the biblical text of Genesis. There were rationalists and empiricists, 'nominalists' and 'realists'. There were also those who distinguished the domain of reason from that of faith.

In the thirteenth century this new humanism, which sharply differentiated Latin Christianity from both Byzantium and Islam, was applied above all to theology. When it was applied to science, and began to replace reliance on authority by the use of reason, Europe was on the threshold of a Renaissance which later enabled it to outstrip all the rest of the world.

ROMANESQUE AND GOTHIC EUROPE

'A white mantle of churches'

With the onset of the third year following the year 1000, churches began to be rebuilt and embellished almost everywhere, but especially in Italy and Gaul. Although most of them were already very well constructed, and had no need of improvement, mutual emulation led each Christian community to seek to outdo the splendour of its neighbours. It was as if the world itself were shaking off its old rags and putting on, everywhere, a white mantle of churches.

These often-quoted words were written by an eleventh-century French monastic chronicler, Raoul Glaber. That he was telling the truth can still be seen today. Of the Greeks and the Romans, there remain only ruins, sometimes magnificent ruins, all round the Mediterranean. Of the Carolingian or Germanic epoch, very few monuments have survived. Many were made of wood: many fell victim to the weather, to invasion and pillage, or to the rebuilding that Raoul Glaber described.

In complete contrast, Europe still boasts thousands of buildings from the tenth to the twelfth centuries, in the Norman or 'Saxon' style which since 1819 has also been called 'Romanesque'. From the twelfth to the fifteenth centuries, this style was replaced by 'Gothic'.

Religious building stemmed both from fervent belief and from material changes: a growing population, larger towns, more skilled workmen, and technological progress which included new forms of harness for draught animals, new methods of working wood, stone, and metal, new tools, and ever more precise calculations by architects. But there were also social needs. Monks maintained hostels for pilgrims; hospitals were built; the movement of merchants and pilgrims led to the building of bridges; towns built defensive walls. Feudal castles appeared at strategic points: some of them were enormous, using a huge mass of stone. It was as if a new Europe was springing up from the soil.

A creative spirit, indeed, characterized this phase of Europe's history. The underlying unity of Christendom was expressed by 'reciprocal exchanges in which every country constantly showed its own original characteristics'.

European art is marked by constant inventiveness and new techniques.

First came the great Romanesque churches, from Cluny and Vézelay to St James of Compostela; then, in sober reaction, the great Cistercian abbeys: Pontigny and Royaumont in northern France, Senanque in Provence, Fountains in England, Maulbronn in Germany, Poblet in Spain, and Alcobaça in Portugal. There were the great medieval fortresses, of which the most imposing example was the Crusaders' castle at Crac des Chevaliers in the Holy Land. Finally, there were the huge Gothic cathedrals, with their soaring windows and magnificent stained glass. It was a formidable achievement.

Romanesque art and monasticism

The basic feature of Romanesque architecture was the semi-circular arch of the vaulting and over doors and windows, supported by massive walls and buttresses. The ground plan of the typical church was a cross formed by the nave, choir, and transept. Behind the choir there would be an ambulatory, and on either side of the nave, aisles. The windows were small, and the church was dark, with decoration imitated from antiquity or from Byzantine, Armenian, or Muslim motifs. The spandrels above the doorways, and the capitals of the pillars, were finely sculpted, sometimes with hieratic designs but often full of movement. The cupola, of Byzantine origin, would usually be above the crossing of the transept. But Romanesque art took many forms and varied immensely from one region to another.

The multiplicity of the Romanesque 'schools'

The origin of Romanesque art is very difficult to pin down. In the eleventh century, architects began to find their way towards solving the problem of the vault; and from then onwards their progress was rapid. In Germany, Romanesque showed some continuity with Carolingian styles; but there were also Byzantine influences, especially in Italy, and in Spain there were similarities with Arab or Muslim and Mozarabic (Christian in Muslim territory) buildings.

The Germanic school seems to have been the most prolific. It affected not only Germany, but also Sweden and Denmark, and in the south, as a result of the Germanic Holy Roman Empire, it blended with the Lombard school in northern Italy.

In the west, it spread along the valleys of the Meuse, the Moselle, and the Scheldt; in the south-west it followed the Rhône Valley; and in the south-east it was evident in Austria and on the Dalmatian coast. It also reached Switzerland, Poland, and the Netherlands.

The French school was much more varied, embracing the northern style (in the Île-de-France, Picardy, Flanders, and Champagne), and the Norman, Burgundian, Auvergnat, Poitou, and Provençal schools. The oldest of all these was the Norman.

Normandy rather than Germany was the source of the English school: 'Norman', after all, is the usual term for English Romanesque. Durham Cathedral, which some consider the most beautiful in the country, was begun in 1093 and finished in 1133. In Ireland, the Carolingian style remained very influential — as witness the superb porch of Clonfert Cathedral.

In Norway there was an indigenous Romanesque style of churches built in wood, some of which have survived, like that of Gol, later removed to Oslo.

In Spain, Romanesque architecture was confined to those regions reconquered by the Christians before the thirteenth century, i.e. Castile, Leon, Navarre, and Catalonia. This was also the case in Portugal, where one fine example is the Cathedral of Evora. The Iberian peninsula saw a confluence of the art of Languedoc, Gascony, and Burgundy, with the influence of Cluny on the roads to

Compostela, plus a contribution from Mozarabic art. The greatest example of Spanish Romanesque, St James of Compostela, was begun in 1078 but not completed until between 1168 and 1188, at the beginning of the Gothic period.

All this shows how much exchange of ideas and practices took place among the architects of the time, almost all of them anonymous, and many of them monks. Cluny, Cîteaux, and the Crusades were all in their different ways the forcing-houses of the Romanesque style: but each school was in its way unique. In building as in sculpture, it was a period of extraordinary brilliance.

The emergence of Gothic

'Gothic' is a misnomer: the term was invented in the sixteenth century, when the revival of classical taste made the art of the high Middle Ages seem 'barbaric'. Still, the label remains.

The general ground-plan of Gothic churches was the same as that of Romanesque: but the differences between them were striking. Solidity gave way to lightness. Now, it was no longer the walls and buttresses which supported the vaulting, but pillars with *flying* buttresses. The walls, already much thinner, could be pierced to make ever larger windows. Romanesque gloom was banished by Gothic sunlight, tinted by stained glass. Pointed arches replaced the semi-circles of Romanesque. Finally, the vaulting changed. Groined vaults, crossing each other, were not strictly a novelty: they had appeared in a number of Romanesque buildings. What was new was their being strengthened by prominent ribbing, to produce the so-called 'feathered arch' with its three-dimensional appearance. At the same time, Gothic sculpture flourished. By contrast with Romanesque it was supple, graceful, radiant, and natural.

National versions of Gothic

According to the British historian Kingsley Porter and his Italian colleague Paolo Verzone, the earliest examples of the crossed ogive are to be found in Italy in the region of Novara and Vercelli. The British historian John Bilson has shown that the system was adopted in 1100 at Durham Cathedral; while Elie Lambert from France and Gomez Moreno from Spain have detected it in the Great Mosque at Cordoba and in Mozarabic art. But in the second quarter of the twelfth century it began to be used more and more in northern France – first in such small churches as Morienval and Bellefontaine in the Île-de-France, then in larger buildings like the basilica of Saint-Denis, the last resting-place of a number of Kings of France. Before long, it was adopted for the great cathedrals of Sens, Noyon, Senlis, and Laon, later by Paris and Chartres, and at the beginning of the thirteenth century by Rheims and Amiens.

These magnificent buildings were admired and imitated throughout the Christian world. German Gothic emerged somewhat later, brought in mainly by the Cistercians. Germany, in fact, has kept more of her Romanesque cathedrals than France: fine examples include those of Worms and Speier. The Gothic cathedral in Bamberg was inspired by Laon and Tours; and Cologne Cathedral, which although partly modern is still the greatest in Germany, was modelled on Amiens. Perhaps the most beautiful is Strasbourg Cathedral, built in pink limestone.

Gothic also reached Scandinavia, where one of its best-known examples is the cathedral of Uppsala in Sweden, designed by the French architect and sculptor Etienne de Bonneuil.

Spanish Gothic differed more markedly from French Gothic on account of the Arab influence, especially on Spanish sculpture. Arabic motifs can be found in the cathedrals of Toledo, Burgos, Leon, Barcelona, Palma and elsewhere. The masterpieces of Spanish Gothic include the Christ in Majesty and the Assembly of the Apostles, both in Toledo.

English Gothic was greatly influenced in the twelfth century by Normandy and the Île-de-France – notably in Canterbury Cathedral, completed in 1192 by an architect from Sens. But very soon English Gothic or 'Early English' took on a character of its own, favouring a rectangular apse with no ambulatory, and sometimes including a double transept. Salisbury Cathedral, built at the same time as Amiens, had a spire 123 metres tall – only a little less than Strasbourg's 147. Lincoln, York, Worcester, Exeter, and Ely Cathedrals are all of the same type. Their lines are more complex; their vaults are fragmented; their windows are ever more elaborate. This is the 'Decorated' style, marked by what has been called 'exuberant ornamentation'. Westminster Abbey, however, remained much closer to the style of the French cathedrals.

Gothic architecture entered Bohemia after the year 1230 under the influence of German colonists. Its masterpiece was begun during the reign of the Czech Emperor Charles IV (1346–78): this was the cathedral of St Vitus in Prague, designed by the French architect Mattieu d'Arras. Above all, however, it was his successor Peter Parler, of Swabian origin, who filled Bohemia with churches and extended his influence to Vienna, Bavaria, Swabia, Strasbourg, Breslau, Cracow, and even Milan.

Poland reached the summit of its artistic development only in the sixteenth century. Until then, Polish art imitated that of Germany. The religious orders did, however, put up a number of buildings: the Cistercians in the Romanesque style, the Franciscans and Dominicans in the Gothic. The Teutonic Knights were also extensive builders.

Art, architecture, sculpture, and painting thus added their contribution to the cross-fertilization of European Christendom.

A MORE HUMANE CIVILIZATION

Chivalry

The two centuries that were the apogee of Western Christendom, despite continued violence, were also marked by the growth of certain values making for an improvement to human life.

War, as has been seen, was somewhat tamed by the 'Truce of God', the 'Peace of God', and the protection of pilgrims against violence, on pain of excommunication. Warriors themselves were also subjected to restraints.

The title of 'knight' first appeared at the end of the tenth century – associated, save for landless warriors, with the castle. By the end of the eleventh century, the order of chivalry had become an hereditary caste, and the feudal system began. In effect, a new nobility had replaced the old.

'Greek philosophy, Roman Law, and the Christian religion did much to fashion the conscience of Europe,' wrote the Italo-American historian Robert Lopez. 'Feudalism also made an important contribution, by stressing the principle that the ties of dependency are made up of reciprocal obligations, and that every right implies a duty.'

Thus there developed the ritual ceremonies attending the dubbing of knights: a purifying bath, a night of prayer, and the laying of weapons on the altar. The duties of a knight were especially well described in the *Liber de vita christiana* (*Book of the Christian Life*) by Bonizo of Sutri. He must be faithful to his lord, unless the latter leads him into an unjust war. He must protect his lord. He must fight for the state, for the poor, for widows, and for orphans. He must abstain from pillage and plunder. He must hunt down heretics and schismatics. He must respect his vows. He was in fact a servant of both Church and state; and the order of chivalry was thus an upholder of the peace.

The 'chivalric ideal' developed throughout Christendom. *The Song of Roland*, written between 1120 and 1128, was in Old French. Bonizo of Sutri was an Italian. The Spanish knight described in the *Cantar de mio Cid* was like a knight of France.

Alongside the orders of chivalry inspired by the Crusades and recruited from all nationalities, like the Templars and the Hospitallers, there was one which was purely German: the Teutonic Knights. Their influence was so great on the southern and eastern shores of the Baltic that they virtually established a state there. In Spain, likewise, purely Spanish orders of chivalry were established between 1158 and 1176 at Calatrava, Evora, Santiago, and Alcantara.

The great German epic poem known as the *Nibelungenlied*, from the beginning of the thirteenth century, combines both violence and the spirit of chivalry. The 'Breton Lays' of the twelfth and thirteenth centuries (*Tristan and Isolde* and *The Knights of the Round Table*) combine Celtic traditions with the gentler influence of English chivalry. Welsh chivalry appears in the *Mabinogion*, a collection of tales influenced by French writing. There was even a Czech religious order, the Knights of the Cross, set up by the Princess Agnes, daughter of the great King of Bohemia Premysil Ottokar I (1197–1230).

Courtly love and the condition of women

The status of women has evolved very slowly through the centuries.

Roman law gave to the *paterfamilias* complete power over his wife and children, including the right to kill at birth any children that displeased him – either because they were daughters or, if they were sons, because they were ill, handicapped, or weak. True, in the upper classes, women were not always mere objects of pleasure, and some played a preponderant role. But Roman women did not enjoy the full rights of male citizens: the father, the father-in-law, and the husband were all-powerful.

Christianity could not accept that. In about 390, the Church had a law passed to remove the father's right of life or death over his children. And if a Merovingian Church Council solemnly debated whether women had souls, its conclusion was that, yes, they did, just like men.

From the tenth to the thirteenth century, the conjugal couple became the normal centre of the family, of life in the community, and of the seigneurial system. Within that framework, the woman had the central place. She was mistress of the house, in charge of its furniture and equipment, its linen and its kitchen.

The essential novelty at this time was what has been called 'courtly love'. 'Love,' said Régine Pernoud in her book *La femme au temps des cathédrales* (*Women in the Age of the Cathedrals*), was 'a twelfth-century invention.'

André le Chapelain wrote his twelfth-century *Treatise on Love* for the Countess Marie of Champagne, daughter of Louis VII and Eleanor of Aquitaine. It had nothing in common with Ovid's *Art of Love*. 'It is clear,' wrote the author, 'that everyone must try to serve the ladies so that he may be illumined with their grace . . . Nothing that is great in life can be achieved without love.' He called for the creation of 'courts of love', where poets, troubadours, lords, and ladies might discuss, courteously and chivalrously, that infinite and ever-absorbing subject, the relationship between the sexes. The subtlety and 'casuistry' of this approach recall the seventeenth-century *Précieuses*.

'Courtly poetry' became a favourite form of literature, and one that was characteristic of feudal society. As the vassal rendered homage to his lord, so the knight rendered homage to his lady, the true ruler of his heart. The same period saw many 'Romances of Chivalry', in which love and bravura occupied centre stage.

In this feudal world, moreover, in which knights were so often at war, their ladies were in many cases more cultivated and better read than men, with the exception of the clergy.

This phenomenon was general throughout Europe. The court of Castile, at the beginning of the thirteenth century, was famous as one of the centres of courtly chivalry. Eleanor of Aquitaine had married one of her daughters in Saxony, one in Sicily, and a third, Eleanor the Younger, to Alfonso VIII of Castile. In their castles at Burgos and

Palencia they attracted many troubadours. One of Eleanor the Younger's daughters, Blanca ('Blanche of Castile'), became wife of the King of France and mother of St Louis; while Berengar married the King of Leon. The courts of England and Sicily often played similar roles.

The communes

Another form of progress was the slow advance of local freedom. From the eleventh century onwards, this was general throughout Europe, although with many different variations.

It seems to have begun in northern Italy. Local townsmen (burgesses or 'bourgeois'), including knights and poor freemen, would seize power in the town. The case of the Lombard towns was the most remarkable: they became city-states. Often they fought against each other, or united against the most powerful of them, Milan. Frederick Barbarossa sometimes used the support of middle-sized cities against the Pope and against Milan. But they all became truly independent when they defeated him at the Battle of Legnano in 1176.

Besides the city-states, there were cities whose liberty had been acquired, after a long struggle, by means of a 'franchise charter', which limited or abolished seigneurial rights. The feudal lord, all-powerful in the countryside, thus lost his authority over the towns. But to obtain such a charter, it was often necessary to rely on the power of the monarch, and to pay him taxes. This was the case with many French communes, which were weaker than their Lombard counterparts.

King Philip Augustus of France was the first to seek the support of the communes against the feudal lords. It was they who helped him to win an important victory over the Emperor, the King of England, and the Count of Flanders at Bouvines in 1214. This also strengthened his centralizing resolve and helped him to escape from the aegis of the Church.

England – or rather the Anglo-Norman monarchy, which became Anglo-Angevin and Aquitaine through the conquests of the Plantagenet Henry II in 1154 – was the first really organized state in medieval Europe. Here, the towns were more firmly under royal control than anywhere else: but this was counterbalanced by the strong British tradition of decentralized and autonomous 'local government', partly associated with the knights of the shire, and also with Saxon and, later, Norman influence.

What was more, after the inept King John's defeat at Bouvines and his difficulties with the Church, the Barons, the citizens of London, and some of the clergy forced him to sign Magna Carta, the 'Great Charter of Liberties', at Runnymede in 1215. Complex and confused as this document may seem, it is nevertheless the remote ancestor of the parliamentary regime.

In the Scandinavian countries, less involved in international affairs because less densely populated, the king could do nothing without the approval of a local popular assembly inherited from the Vikings, the *Thing* or *Ting*. Iceland and Greenland were each governed by a general Assembly, the *Althing*. This is still the name of the Icelandic parliament; while Denmark has its *Folketing* ('People's Thing') and Norway its *Storting* ('Big Thing').

Spain, preoccupied by the struggle against the Muslims, was a country of castles, each like a fortified village. The very names Catalonia and Castile mean 'land of castles'. The autonomous municipalities were dependencies of the crown. But there too, several decades before Britain, there were the beginnings of parliament, the Cortes, comprising nobles, bishops, and representatives of the municipalities. The Cortes of Leon made their first appearance in 1188.

Townsmen against nobles, incessant feuding, rival factions like the Guelphs and Ghibellines or the Montagues and Capulets – these were regular features of the towns' turbulent civilization in the thirteenth century. The cathedrals reflected and redeemed them, built with the wealth of the rich and the unpaid labour of the poor.

In Germany, the decay of the Empire gave full reign to the feudal lords, and communal liberty was more under threat than elsewhere. Hence the tendency for towns to league together, as in the Hanseatic League, the Swiss cantons, and so on.

In the rich land of Flanders, the communes flourished economically. Politically, however, they never obtained the total independence enjoyed by the Italian city-states.

Communal institutions varied considerably. Like the states, each had an assembly comprising all free citizens, often meeting in the town square; they had councils, comprising the most important citizens – or revolutionary factions; and each had an executive, originally collective and later individual. This was the mayor or burgomaster or (from Byzantium) the duke or (in Venice) the doge.

The towns and communes, in fact, introduced the principle of a number of citizens taking part in the conduct of public affairs. The assembly 'offered a platform to any citizen with the lungs and the courage'. It was a step forward, and one typical of Europe, towards the ideal of freedom.

CONCLUSION

Thousands upon thousands of Romanesque churches, monasteries, and cloisters, followed by Gothic churches and cathedrals, bear witness to the spiritual, intellectual, artistic, and philosophical wealth of these two centuries, and to the underlying unity of Europe at that time, although the word 'Europe' was still little used.

True, the growing feudal system was totally hierarchical; true, feudal lords were constantly at war. True, the power of the Popes, then at its zenith, was constantly at odds with that of the Emperors. True, believing Christians – and at that time it was almost impossible not to believe – thought that they must use violence against the 'infidel' – usually the Muslims.

But the unity of Europe prevailed. Its basis was a principle which proved to lie at the heart of liberty: the separation of powers between the 'two swords', spiritual and temporal – religious authority and political rule. The twentieth century has taught us that the fusion of these two forms of power and their concentration in a single pair of hands is the main source of fanaticism and totalitarian dictatorship.

But Europe's unity at this time took other forms too. There was the expansion of the great religious orders: the black monks of Cluny, who continued to prosper and in particular to oversee the Compostela pilgrims' route; the white Cistercians, who were far more 'international', and in the eleventh century were dominated by St Bernard, a truly European figure. In the thirteenth century there were the 'mendicant orders' from Italy, who replaced the notion of the Crusade with that of the 'mission', and played a major part in establishing a new and typically European institution, the university.

This was the Europe of pilgrimages, of a more humane life, of chivalry and courtly love, of the growth of civil liberties. It was the Europe of the great debate about faith and reason.

Finally, it was the Europe of stone – of castles and monasteries, but also of towns, with their walls and churches and cathedrals.

The next chapter will examine the Europe of merchants and scholars.

The scene of all these events was Europe both west and east. Western Europe was from now onwards shielded from invasion: but Eastern Europe, in the thirteenth century, was subject to the huge wave of Mongol conquest which struck at Poland, Hungary, and Bohemia.

10

Towards a Europe of the States: The Fourteenth and Fifteenth Centuries

THE BIRTH OF THE MODERN STATE AND THE HUNDRED YEARS' WAR

General evolution

The barbarian kingdoms of the ninth and tenth centuries, the feudal authorities of the eleventh century, the huge 'community' of Christendom in the twelfth and thirteenth centuries – none of them corresponded to what we mean by the term 'state'. For anything like the modern state to emerge – and it could only be a gradual process – a number of conditions had to be fulfilled.

First, the personal link between the king and his vassals had to be replaced by 'sovereignty' or royal power over the different estates of the realm, whether great feudal lords, free cities, or even the clergy in their temporal role. This presupposed the regular levying of taxes and hence, at least to begin with, the consent of those concerned, transmitted by delegates with representative powers, in assemblies or 'estates', usually temporary.

The sovereign had likewise to possess greater military power than that of his subordinates – the nucleus of a standing army.

Finally, instead of a group of vassals looking after the sovereign's affairs, there had to be a genuine 'administration'.

The growth of these various attributes of the state was slow and complex: they bore fruit only at the end of the fifteenth century. But the general evolution in this direction was irresistible, although in some places it was contested and delayed.

Europe could have been organized quite differently, for example across the seas. An Anglo-Danish empire was held together for a time by Canute, spanning the North Sea; and three times, with the Normans, the Angevins, and the Hundred Years' War, a Franco-British kingdom seemed possible, spanning the Channel. In reality, these groupings proved temporary, and Europe's states were established in contiguous land masses. England, from the eleventh century onwards, was a united kingdom at a time when the Kings of France were having great difficulty in extending their small 'royal domain'. But in the thirteenth century, under Philip Augustus, St Louis, and Philip the Fair, the French monarchy became the most powerful in Europe.

Unlike France, Germany and Italy could not achieve unity: their sovereigns were not strong enough to resist their feudal vassals and, above all in Italy, the power of the towns. Only the Kingdom of the Two Sicilies (Sicily and Naples), recaptured from the Muslims by the Normans, and entrusted to a French dynasty by the eleventh-century Papacy, managed to survive until 1860. The Scandinavian kingdoms, Poland, Hungary, and even Spain remained in this sense midway between total success as in France and Britain, and failure as in Germany and Italy.

The king: an emperor in his kingdom

Many texts of the period insisted that 'the king is emperor in his kingdom' and that the Emperor was a sovereign equal but not superior to others. Such assertions were often made to contest 'imperialist' or 'theocratic' works. Take for instance the *Disputatio inter clericum et militem* (*Dispute between a Cleric and a Knight*), which dates from 1296 or 1297, and in which the knight has the last word. *The Rex Pacificus* of 1302 declares:

> The Pope is not the supreme ruler in temporal matters for those kingdoms which are not subject to the Roman Empire. France is not subject to the Roman Empire: on the contrary, there are and have been since time immemorial definite frontiers between this kingdom and the Empire. Hence the Pope is not ruler of the kingdom of France, nor is his the supreme authority in temporal affairs, but only in spiritual matters, as everywhere on earth. For more than 100 years the Kings of France have peacefully enjoyed the right to acknowledge only God as their superior in temporal matters, recognizing therefore no other superior, whether Emperor or Pope. Thus it is established that by long and uninterrupted possession they have acquired the right of absolute supremacy in their kingdom.

Similar arguments can be found in *De potestate regio* (*Of Royal Power*) by Jean de Paris (1302). 'It is not necessary,' he wrote, 'for all the faithful to be united in a single community. Since climates, languages, and human conditions vary, there can be different types of life and different constitutions. What is good for one people may not be good for another.'

The main champion of this thesis was an Italian, familiar with the life of the city-states. He was Marsilius of Padua (c.1280–c.1343). His *Defensor pacis* (*Defender of Peace*) – in which Pope Clement VI found 240 errors to be condemned – was both secular and republican. It defended the independence of states and described at length their constitutions. Its title, incidentally, was deceptive. Marsilius, a fierce opponent of the Papacy, did not believe in perpetual peace. His notion of independent and if necessary rival states already has a modern air.

The Hundred Years' War: an overview

There is no need here to recapitulate the events of the Hundred Years' War, which lasted, with interruptions, from 1337 to 1453, and can be seen as having two phases.

During the reigns of Philip VI and John II of France, the French suffered defeat after defeat. John was captured, and the Treaty of Bretigny in 1360 gave a quarter of his kingdom to King Edward III of England (1327–77). Then Charles V, known as Charles the Wise (1364–80), won back the occupied territories, including even Guyenne, leaving only Bordeaux, Cherbourg, Calais, and various fortresses still in the hands of the English. Charles also marched into Castile, where he dethroned Peter the Cruel and helped to power Henry II, founder of the new Trastamare dynasty.

The second phase of the Hundred Years' War is associated with the madness of Charles VI of France (1384–1422), which came upon him in 1392. Power was then disputed by his uncles, notably John the Fearless, Duke of Burgundy, and his brother the Duke of Orléans, son-in-law of the Duke of Armagnac. This led to an appalling civil war between the two factions known as the Armagnacs and the Burgundians. King Henry V of England (1413–22) thereupon seized his chance. Crushing the French at Agincourt in 1415, he formed an alliance with Isabel of Bavaria and with the Burgundians, who by the Treaty of Troyes made him Regent of France and potential successor to the throne should the Dauphin Charles (later Charles VII) die. The Dauphin, who had taken refuge in Bourges, doubted whether he was indeed the son of Charles V, since his mother had been notoriously unfaithful. But a shepherd's daughter, Joan of Arc, inspired by the 'voices' of a number of saints, assured him that he was indeed the legitimate heir. Such mystic 'proof' was then seen as wholly valid.

Joan's brief, dramatic, and tragic intervention (1429–31) led to Charles's coronation at Rheims, while the young English King Henry VI, son of Henry V and Princess Catherine of France, was crowned at Notre-Dame in Paris. Joan of Arc won a number of victories, which continued after her death, burned at the stake as a witch at Rouen. It was when Henry VI quarrelled with the Burgundians that a French counteroffensive enabled Charles VII to reconquer almost all of France. A peace treaty was signed in 1445, and Henry VI married a French princess, Margaret of Anjou. Soon afterwards, England was divided by the civil wars known as 'the Wars of the Roses' between the King, a Lancastrian, and the family of York. The roses in question were the rival emblems, a red rose for Lancaster and a white rose for York.

The problem of homage

What concerns us here is the link between these wars and the establishment of the modern state. England was the first country to acquire firmly based institutions. Understandably, King Edward III found it less and less tolerable that he should render homage to the King of France for the province of Guyenne, which England had held since Eleanor of Aquitaine, repudiated by the King of France, had taken as second husband the English King Henry II, in 1152. The homage in question was 'liege homage', with priority over other ties. So it was that, wanting to hold his continental territory *in allodium*, i.e. as full owner, as in England itself, King Edward III took the opportunity of a change of dynasty in France to lay claim to the French crown.

The change of dynasty resulted from the death of King Charles IV at the age of thirty-four, without a son. His successor was Philip of Valois, the son of a younger brother of King Philip the Fair (1285–1314). This was because French custom forbade succession through the female line: but such succession was normal in England, where King Edward III was the son of Isabel of France, who in turn was the daughter of Philip the Fair. In English eyes, therefore, Edward's claim to the French throne was valid, and better than that of Philip of Valois.

Edward's real aim, no doubt, was to capture a number of French provinces and hold them *in allodium* as rightful owner. His great victories at the naval Battle of Sluys in 1340 and at Crécy (1346) and Poitiers (1356) gave him what he wanted: in 1360, the French waived the question of homage. The significance of this was that full sovereignty was beginning to replace feudal law. The Kings of France, too, were moving in the same direction: their 'officers' were gradually asserting royal authority in the fiefs. Centralization was on its way.

The first prerequisite of centralization was a *permanent administration*. The king's personal servants and vassals would gradually be replaced by genuine civil servants, retaining their posts from one reign to the next.

Permanent administration

It was with Philip the Fair that royal administration began to develop in France. Its nucleus was the *curia regis*, made up of able and devoted men whose aim was to establish everywhere the exclusive authority of the king.

By the fourteenth and fifteenth centuries, supreme justice was dispensed by the Parlement and the Chamber of Accounts. The French administration was based in Paris; the English – the future Civil Service – in London.

Much more easily, owing to their small size, the Italian city-states also established permanent administration. The Italian historian Alberto Tenenti described the situation in Florence at the time of the Medici:

> As regards the Italian peninsula, it can be said that Florence, like the Papal States, followed more closely than its fellows the general process that was taking place in the west. At this time, in fact, the Kingdom of Naples was falling under Spanish domination, and Venice was much more set in its medieval ways than Florence; while Savoy was only very slowly moving in the direction of statehood, and Milan, although further advanced, was soon to lose its independence and thereby any hope of autonomous development.

After England, France, and the Italian cities, it was the turn of Spain to take on the structure of a modern state when it achieved unity. In

1465, King Henry IV of Castile was deposed by turbulent vassals and replaced by his heir, his sister Isabella. In 1469, she married the heir to Aragon, Ferdinand, who died in 1516. By this time, Aragon had expanded to include Catalonia, the Balearic Islands, Sardinia, Sicily (1409), and the Kingdom of Naples (1435). Ferdinand was indeed a remarkable ruler: in 1492, when he took Granada, he finally drove the Muslims out of Spain. That same year, it was in his name that Christopher Columbus reached the New World. In 1512, four years before his death, Ferdinand also annexed Spanish Navarre.

A standing army

As well as a permanent administration, the state required a standing army. Until the fourteenth century, when kings went to war they raised troops for a limited period. This was the so-called 'host', a large and undisciplined body of knights, with their equally rowdy gaggle of servants and hangers-on.

On occasion, the reserves or *arrière-ban* would be mobilized, involving almost all vassals. The large numbers recruited in this way in France at the beginning of the fourteenth century were frequently defeated: by the burghers of Flanders at Courtrai in 1302, and by the English, who were far fewer but also far better organized. The Black Prince, son of Edward II of England, won many battles at the head of a mixed English and Gascon army which never numbered more than 7,000. So in 1369 Charles V decided to maintain a standing army of some 5,200 troops and pay them regular wages. The practice took on. In the fifteenth century, many of the 'French' soldiers were foreign mercenaries – Spanish and Italian infantry and crossbowmen, Scottish archers and men-at-arms, as well as Aragonese, Castilians, Piedmontese, and Lombards. In 1424, even the French High Constable or commander-in-chief was a Scotsman, John Stuart.

Regular taxation

At this time, regular taxation posed a problem. Under feudal law, the king could levy taxes only in his own domains, and even there only where he was Lord High Justiciar. But from the end of the twelfth century, France and Britain began to need very large sums for distant expeditions. So it came about that in 1198 King Philip Augustus of

France levied a tax throughout his kingdom for a Crusade against Saladin, who had captured Jerusalem. This was known as the 'Saladin tithe'. Little by little, royal taxation began to take the place of feudal dues.

Nor was it only that large sums were needed: they were needed on a regular basis. To begin with, in 1302 King Philip the Fair of France called together for the first time an assembly of nobles, senior Church dignitaries, and burgesses from a number of chosen towns. The aim was not only to canvass moral support for the King, but above all to persuade those present to grant him subsidies. From the end of the fifteenth century, these 'States-General' became elective and representative.

The great turning-point came in the 1430s, at the meetings of the States-General of Tours in 1435 and of Orléans in 1439. These assemblies in fact voted for permanent aid (indirect taxation) and for the toll or *taille*, intended to pay Charles VII's standing army. The *taille* was a form of income tax imposed almost exclusively on the rural population. With the help of his lawyers, in other words, the King was able to levy taxes on his own authority.

The British system was rather different from the French. Since Magna Carta, Parliament had met very frequently, and had acquired much more power than the States-General. This became very evident during the long reign of Edward III (1327-77). He made many concessions to Parliament, notably on laws affecting persons; but when it came to levying taxes, he often forgot the clause in Magna Carta under which Parliament's consent was required. His great victories against France made him popular enough to ignore the energetic protests of the House of Commons. And the expenses of war were such that taxation became annual and permanent. Edward III's practice cut across established law; but in 1367, when the Pope sought to summon him to Rome for failing to pay an ancient tribute, Parliament unanimously backed his refusal to go. The King, it declared, could in no way submit to a foreign power, even a spiritual power.

Eastern Europe

The wars in the East, against Tamerlane or Timur Beg and then against the Ottoman Turks, did not have the same effect as the Hundred Years' War. The Slavs played a defensive role. The Poles and the Czechs threw off the Mongol yoke much more quickly than Russia. Then, in the fourteenth century, the national dynasties of Bohemia, Poland, and Hungary died out, leaving these countries to be governed by foreign princes. It was against German invasions that they next had to defend themselves – in particular the Czechs, who were attacked from every direction. Poland, however, had its hour of glory in the face of the Teutonic Knights. In 1389, its queen married Jagello, the King of Lithuania. This powerful and savage man dominated a vast area between the Baltic and the Ukraine; and in 1410 he crushed the Teutonic Knights at Tannenberg. Then, while the Scandinavians were putting an end to the Hanseatic League's monopoly of the Baltic trade, Jagello's successor seized Danzig. He also supported the Hussites in Bohemia, and added Hungary to his domains.

It was at this time that the Ottoman Turks invaded Europe. They occupied the Balkans, crossed the Danube and the Carpathians, and ravaged Hungary. For a century, Poland played the leading role in this eastern part of Europe. But the feeble remnants of the Byzantine Empire were in no condition to resist the Turks; and in 1453 Mohammed II, 'the Conqueror' (1451–81) took Constantinople and put an end to the eastern Empire's thousand years of history.

THE GREAT EUROPEAN POPULATION CRISIS

The demographic peak in the thirteenth century

There is every reason to believe that from the year 1000 to the end of the thirteenth century Europe's population greatly increased, and that there was marked economic progress, with all the gains and losses that this implies. Historians have studied the available data with immense care, and they continue to do so – for there are of course no comprehensive statistics. True, from about 1250 onwards, a number of great lords and princes began to draw up lists of households, for taxation purposes. But how numerous was an average household? In England, the Domesday Book of 1086 gave more precise data: it reckoned that the population was then 1.1 million. By 1348, the estimate was 3,757,000. For France, a survey of parishes and households in 1328 suggests that the total population was somewhere between 12.5 and 15.5 million.

By collating the work of the British historians Julius K. Beloch and J. C. Russell with that of the French historian Pierre Chaunu, it is possible to arrive at some global estimates. The Roman Empire may have had some 54 million inhabitants, 23 million of them in Europe. Latin Christendom, at the beginning of the fourteenth century, probably had between 50 and 55 million. Around the year 1400 there were no more than 40 million; a century later, some 50 million.

On the eve of the Black Death, France had approximately 16 million inhabitants, the Iberian Peninsula 8.3 million, Italy 8.5 million, the Low Countries 1.1 million, England 3.3 million, Scotland and Ireland together 1.5 million, Switzerland 600,000, Scandinavia 600,000, Germany between 6 and 8 million, Poland 1.3 million, and Hungary 2 million.

All Christendom was becoming over-populated, save for the regions east of the Elbe and for Spain and Portugal, recently recaptured by the Christians.

The rural economy

The growth of Europe's population helped the economy by supplying an abundant labour force, but economic progress was also favoured by new inventions. They included a new form of harness for draught horses, using the shoulder collar; new means of yoking oxen; and a new form of plough with a double steel ploughshare. This, unlike the swing-plough, was used on all good farming land, from Scandinavia to the Loire. Marc Bloch has explained in a celebrated study how this led to the elongated form of the open field, which required the minimum number of turns when ploughing. There was similar progress in crop rotation, and in the land clearance which continued on a large scale until the thirteenth century.

The rural economy, in this mainly peasant world, remained very closed and often near to subsistence level, with huge local differences: in status, between serfs and freemen; in farming methods; and in the size and extent of the settlements, some scattered, some tightly knit.

Trade and money

With trade, the towns developed. Primitive capitalism emerged, involving lords and abbeys, but also burgesses. All aspects of commerce as it later developed began in embryo then. Metal coins, which for centuries had been scarce, began to accumulate: the West's trade surplus brought in Arab and Byzantine money, through Venice, Genoa, and Pisa. The Crusades brought back plundered treasure. But above all, new deposits of copper and silver were discovered, mainly in the Harz Mountains in Germany, but also in the Vosges, the Jura, and the eastern Alps. The biggest discovery, made in about 1170, was of the rich silver mines at Freiberg in Saxony. Then, in the thirteenth century, the West began minting gold coins again. Bimetallism, using both gold and silver, had been the practice under the Roman Empire and at the beginning of the barbarian invasions; but since then monometallism, using only silver, had prevailed. Now, beginning in Italy, gold began to circulate alongside silver once more. At the same time, handicrafts and cloth manufacture flourished, as did trade in spices, wine, and salt.

Trading methods also developed: travelling salesmen, fairs, and especially the use of credit. Christians as well as Jews became lenders, notably to princes going to war. It was in Italy in the twelfth century, and beginning in Genoa, that the banking profession first appeared: its members were at first known as money-changers, but the word 'bank' soon came into current use: *banco*, in Italian, in fact meant 'counter'. Deposit banks and merchant banks appeared; so did new types of trading firm, made up of groups of merchants. Here again, Italy led the way. In the wealthy Belgian city of Bruges, banks developed only in the fourteenth century.

The thirteenth century marked the zenith of medieval activity. 'The population is growing every day and the town is expanding with new buildings ... The fertility of the soil and the abundance of consumer goods are obvious to everyone ... No able-bodied man, unless he is a good-for-nothing, can fail to earn his living with the dignity that his social position entails.' Those words, which date from 1288, applied to Milan, a city of some 200,000 inhabitants. They were written by Fra Bonvesin de la Riva. What he said was true of much of Europe, whose growing population led in the west to new hamlets, villages, and parishes. To the east lay the 'frontier' – in the American sense of the term, i.e. the border between relative civilization and the wild. Western colonists crossed the Elbe, making variously for Mecklenburg, Pomerania, northern Prussia, Upper Saxony, Bohemia, Moravia, Silesia, Austria, and the Danube basin as far as the Carpathians. The *Reconquista* in Spain involved similar expansion. Yet the growth of the population greatly increased both the price of land and the crowding of the towns.

Famine and the Black Death

The situation changed at the end of the thirteenth century. Demographic expansion was halted, and the population sharply fell. Farming declined in Normandy, in England, in Italy, and in Spain. The reasons were famine, war, and – above all – plague.

The first famine, in 1315–17, was widespread, stretching from England to Russia, and from the Low Countries to Italy. Many people died. Then, from 1335 to 1345, came a financial crisis. But these were as nothing compared to the 'Black Death' or 'black plague' – bubonic plague. It first appeared in China; then, along the caravan routes, it reached Constantinople in 1347. From there, or from the Crimea, it came to Italy. In 1348, it covered north Africa, Spain, France, and southern Austria. Northern Austria, Hungary, Switzerland, the Rhône and Rhine valleys, the Low Countries, northern Germany, and England were afflicted by it in 1349. In 1350 came the turn of Scandinavia, the Baltic lands, Prussia, and Poland.

There are scarcely any precise statistics of deaths from the plague. Only for England are there even approximate population figures. In 1348, as we have seen, the country had some 3,757,000 inhabitants. By 1350, there were only 3,127,000, and by 1377 only some 2,073,000 – a fall of 40 per cent in twenty-nine years. By 1430, the population was only 2,100,000; and the 1348 figure was not attained again until about the year 1600 (J. C. Russell, quoted by Fourquin).

For other parts of Europe, studies of particular towns and regions confirm the extent of the catastrophe. In Sicily, the population fell from 600,000 in 1277 to 500,000 in 1374. A number of Italian towns lost 30–60 per cent of their inhabitants. The population of Florence was more than halved, from 110,000 to 50,000, between 1338 and 1351. In Vienna, 500 to 1,200 people died every day. In three months, there were 60,000 deaths in the Avignon region. The County of Nice and that of Upper Provence lost two thirds of their inhabitants between 1320 and 1400. In 1348, the population of Toulouse numbered 30,000, but in 1405 only 22,500, despite some immigration. The population of Zurich was 12,375 in 1350, but only 4,713 in 1458. Brabant and Holland suffered less: Ghent maintained its population of some 50,000. But Hainaut and Artois were greatly affected: the population of Ypres fell from 30,000 to 18,000, and that of Arras from 20,000 to fewer than 10,000. In the countryside, many villages disappeared, some of them for ever. In Germany, these were known as *Wüstungen*, in Britain as 'lost villages'. Out of 170,000 German villages and hamlets, 40,000 are believed to have disappeared. The proportion of such disappearances in England was 20 per cent, in Tuscany 10 per cent, in the Roman Campagna 25 per cent, and in Sicily and Sardinia 50 per cent.

The horrors of war

Those who survived the plague still had to face the horrors of war, which were now more fearful than in the thirteenth century. First, in the east, came the last and fiercest Mongol invasion, led by the violent Tamerlane. In effect, Europe was saved by the resistance of the Mamluks, who had founded a powerful state in Egypt. Then came the Ottoman Turks.

In the west, the devastation was mainly caused by the Hundred Years' War, with its further effect on Britain, and by the civil war in France between Armagnacs and Burgundians. As well as the depredations committed by regular soldiers, badly paid and obliged to live off the land, there were also professional bandits, soldiers of fortune, and peasants driven to desperation. There were the sinister 'Great Companies' of vagabonds, tramps, thieves, beggars, and false pilgrims or *coquillards*, wearing the emblem of the pilgrim's shell. In Germany they were known as *Raubritter* or 'thieving knights'; in England as 'outlaws', living in the forests as successors of the famous Robin Hood of Richard I's day, but without his legendary prestige. They thrived on the wars between the Scots and the English, as on the Wars of the Roses between Lancaster and York. Often, as in Catalonia, starving peasants attacked the towns. In Castile there was civil war; in Flanders and southern Germany, there were riots and disorders. In Italy, the *condottieri* or captains of mercenary bands continually disturbed the peace.

Small wonder that economic life was deeply affected by all these events. Prices fell almost everywhere, and the huge reduction in manpower led to a rise in the level of wages. As Guy Fourquin has written, 'The significance of the trend has to be understood – i.e. the effect of economic change on social conditions. Falling prices do not necessarily mean a worsening of human welfare. F. Lütge, discussing

Germany, and M. M. Postan, writing about England, have affirmed that this relative economic decline in the late Middle Ages may actually have improved social conditions.' Historians disagree, however, about the date when the depression ended. Some place it at the beginning of the fifteenth century; others believe that the recession continued until two thirds of that century had passed.

THE GREAT CRISIS OF CHRISTIANITY

Unlike the later secularization of society, the fourteenth- and fifteenth-century crisis of Christianity was a crisis within the Church, and one that occurred essentially at the summit. It was political, a bitter dispute for power. It was theological, in that some of those involved professed extreme doctrines which the Church condemned. And it was a moral crisis, provoked once again by the corrupting effect of wealth amassed from the pious donations of the faithful.

Despite the crisis, the great majority of Christians remained as deeply religious as in the preceding centuries. True, popular piety was still primitive, simple, and superstitious. As E. Delaruelle put it, 'Christianity in the fifteenth century, far from seeming weary and devoid of spirituality, was rather in a state of religious hypertension and sometimes morbid sensitivity.'

Confraternities

One truly European example was the development of confraternities, associations of laymen, including a minority of priests, aimed at bringing Christians together and deepening their faith. Usually, they included women as well as men. At a time when the Papacy was distant and divided, and the excesses of the Inquisition gave rise to fear, it was natural to seek safety in numbers. The confraternities also sought to be of practical service – helping prisoners or those ill in hospital, administering the catechism, mounting spectacles such as mystery plays or, when linked to one of the craft guilds, improving relations within it. As well as saying prayers, sometimes in a specially built chapel, the confraternity would hold banquets, celebrate feast-days, and organize public merrymaking.

There were large numbers of confraternities in France, Britain, the

Low Countries, Poland, Dalmatia, Germany, and elsewhere. In England, Chaucer made several allusions to them; in Germany, some of those in the Hanseatic towns acted as travel agencies for pilgrims and others. They flourished most in Italy. Florence, for example, had fifteen in the thirteenth century, twenty-seven in the fourteenth century, and thirty-six in the fifteenth century. One confraternity, that of the Holy Spirit in Rome, had more than 1,000 members. Some had branches abroad: there were Catalan confraternities in Bruges, Flemish in Florence, and Breton in Paris. Their significance was not solely religious. They exemplified the growing tendency to form associations, along the lines of the old German *Genossenschaften*. At times, governments viewed them with suspicion, since at times of crisis they could form a cover for dangerous plots.

'Flamboyant Gothic' and religious art

Another proof that piety was general was the development of art. Gothic architecture continued to evolve, growing ever more light and graceful. Huge windows with delicate tracery soared upwards like leaping flames, giving the new style the title of 'flamboyant Gothic' – in Spain, *flamigero*. Vaulting became still more complex, especially in England, with new forms of lierne and tierceron. It was from England, indeed, that the flamboyant style came to France. But the great artistic glory of this period was its religious painting, culminating in the Italian *quattrocento*, the fifteenth century, but already reaching the heights in the fourteenth with Giotto, who died in 1336, and continuing with Fra Angelico, who died in 1455.

The Avignon Popes

The first serious sign of crisis in the Church was Pope Clement V's decision to leave Rome in 1309, to avoid the incessant faction fights there, and to settle in Avignon. He intended the arrangement to be temporary. Avignon was in the Vaucluse County, which belonged to the Papacy; and in 1348 it bought the town itself from the Queen of Naples, who was also Countess of Provence. The whole area remained a Papal enclave within French territory until 1791.

The Popes remained in Avignon until 1377, and built two successive palaces there. But the important fact was that in Avignon even the

Italian cardinals were subject to pressure from the King of France rather than from the Romans – to whose great annoyance only French Popes were elected until 1379. The most important of these was Pope Clement VI (1342–52), originally Pierre Roger, a monk from Chaise-Dieu in Auvergne, who had been Bishop of Arras, Archbishop of Rouen, and then Chancellor to King Philip VI of France. It was during his pontificate that two cataclysmic events occurred: the beginning of the Hundred Years' War and, in 1348, the onset of the Black Death. Clement further annoyed the Romans by the costly luxury of his Papal court. Rumour was rife in Europe that the plague was divine punishment for the 'Babylonish Captivity', as the Avignon Papacy was called.

Pope Urban V, former Abbot of St Victor in Marseille, returned to Rome in 1367; but part of the Papal administration remained in Avignon. Urban's successor Gregory XI, another Frenchman, decided to transfer the Papacy back to Rome in its entirety in 1376, perhaps under the influence of a mystical Dominican sister, St Catherine of Siena. He died in 1378.

The origins of the Great Schism

It was then that the Church's troubles grew worse. The conclave summoned to elect a new Pope consisted of the sixteen cardinals who were then in Rome; and they split into three groups: southern French, northern French, and Italian. The Roman crowd besieged them, calling for the new Pope to be a Roman, or at the very least an Italian. By fifteen votes out of sixteen, Bartolonico Prignano, the Archbishop of Bari, was elected, and he took the name of Urban VI. Immediately, King Charles V of France protested; and thirteen French cardinals, a number of whom arrived after the election, denied that it had been valid. Meeting at Fondi, they elected the most energetic of their number, Robert of Geneva. He took the name of Clement VII. It was the beginning of the Great Schism in the west.

The Schism lasted until the election of Pope Martin IV in 1417, with further quarrels until 1449 – a total of seventy-one years. Christendom was thus divided into two camps, the 'Urbanists' and the 'Clementists'. The Urbanists dominated the Empire, Flanders, England, and much of Italy, including Rome – except for the Castel Sant'Angelo, which was held by Clementist cardinals. The main Clementists were the King of

France and his vassals, especially in Languedoc, where it was hoped that the Papal court would return to Avignon.

Ranged with France were the County of Savoy, Scotland (often allied with France), some German princes, including the Dukes of Luxembourg, Juliers, and Lorraine, and Duke Leopold III of Austria. Switzerland, Bohemia, and Moravia were divided.

Clearly, feudal allegiances complicated the taking of sides. The Spaniards at first remained neutral; but Aragon, Castile, and Portugal soon rallied to Clement. Legates and counter-legates conducted intense propaganda campaigns; and there were frequent outbreaks of violence, because pious 'anti-schismatic' action on the part of the princes was often a mere veil for purely temporal ambitions, as when the French invaded Italy and the English invaded Flanders. Christendom was divided, and there seemed no way out.

The Pope and the Council

Since neither violence nor negotiation could solve the problem, any more than what was called 'withdrawal of obedience' from either Pope, the idea arose of holding a General Council. In the universities, a number of people began to argue that the Council's authority was superior to that of the Pope. Three successive Councils were held in the fifteenth century: at Pisa in 1409, at Constance from 1413 to 1418, and at Basle from 1431 to 1443.

The Council of Pisa deposed the two existing Popes and elected a third; but since the others failed to obey its edicts, the Church was split in three.

This triple breach was finally healed towards the end of the Council of Constance, when in 1417 a single Pope was elected and took the name of Martin V.

A further significant feature of the Council of Constance was its organization by nations. These were:

1. The Italian, with Crete and Cyprus;
2. The English, with Wales, Ireland, and Scotland;
3. The German, comprising the Empire, the Low Countries, Switzerland, Dalmatia, Croatia, Hungary, Bohemia, Poland, and Scandinavia;
4. The French, limited to the Kingdom of France.

This clearly left out the Spaniards and the Portuguese, who came to Constance only in 1415, when they formed a fifth 'nation'. Christendom, indeed, seemed to be becoming more and more an assembly of 'nations'.

With a single Pope elected, there remained on the agenda the reform of the Church, which the Schism had so far prevented.

The third important Council in the fifteenth century met in Basle from 1431 to 1443. As well as Church reform, it aimed at reconciliation with Greek Orthodox Christians and defensive measures against the Turks. But in fact, far more boldly than the Council of Constance, it tried to establish a system whereby the Church would no longer be governed by the Pope, but by the Council itself. This led to immediate conflict, not only between the two putative authorities, but also between the bishops and the lower clergy – bachelors or other graduates in law or theology – who sought to challenge episcopal authority. Was the Council to become a sovereign assembly, whose decisions would be 'inspired by the Holy Spirit'? At Basle, it may be noted, the 'nations' were not recognized: in their place, a 'popular party', backed by France and Germany against England, succeeded in securing individual suffrage.

Voting thus, the Council elected another Pope, Felix V, in opposition to Eugenius IV; but the latter's successor, Nicholas V, finally won the day. His supporters included the future Pope Pius II (1458–64), a theologian, historian, geographer, orator, diplomatist, canon lawyer, and poet. It was the end of a very long crisis, and it coincided, more or less, with the close of the Hundred Years' War. But the wounds it had inflicted had by no means healed. What was more, these long years of dispute had helped strengthen the states, whose rulers had seized the opportunity to develop national churches, to the detriment of the universal or European spirit of the 'Christian republic'. Three examples may illustrate this tendency: the universities, heresies, and liberties *vis-à-vis* the Pope.

The universities

With the Great Schism, the number of universities grew, and their vocation began to become less theological and more scientific. At the same time, the intermingling of Europe's intelligentsia, through the exchange of pupils and teachers, gave way in practice to an ever closer surveillance by the temporal power.

In England, the only universities at that time were those of Oxford and Cambridge, but these acquired 'colleges' and fine libraries. In Scotland, there was only St Andrews. It was now that English became the national language. And Britain was less affected by the crisis in learning and the decay of teaching which were general in the rest of Europe.

In Flanders, in 1425, a Papal Bull established the University of Louvain. Attracted by high 'salaries' – a word which was already used – were teachers from Paris, Bologna, Vienna, Cologne, and Pavia.

Germany saw the establishment of universities at Vienna (1384), Heidelberg (1385), Cologne (1388), and Erfurt (1379), as well as Würzburg, Leipzig, and Rostock, which welcomed a number of Parisian masters and pupils with 'Urbanist' leanings.

In Spain, where there were several monarchies, each tended to found its own universities, such as Salamanca and Valladolid in Castile, or Lerida and Perpignan in Aragon.

In Portugal, it was King Ferdinand (1367–83) who transferred the University of Coimbra to Lisbon.

In France, the University of Paris remained the most famous – and its pretensions swelled. It claimed to be the arbiter of theological orthodoxy; and it became more and more the University of the King of France. It even intervened in the case of Joan of Arc. But the price of this was the loss of many of its liberties. What was more, the Schism benefited other universities; and so did political conflicts. The University of Caen was founded by the English in 1420; Bordeaux was in English-occupied Guyenne; Dole belonged to the Burgundian State; Poitiers was for a time the University of Charles VII and the Kingdom of Bourges (since he had lost control of Paris); Aix was the University of Provence; and Toulouse, founded in 1368, was the scene of much political disturbance. The 'nation' of Guyenne was pro-English, and in 1418 it went on strike. The old University of Orléans declined under the influence of Paris, while that of Montpellier, thanks to its 1380 statutes, became a celebrated medical centre. Angers was less important; Avignon benefited from the presence of the Popes. Grenoble was founded in 1430.

Italy was similarly compartmentalized. Around the year 1400 it had some fifteen universities – more than France. But then the Italian states and city-states were totally independent. In Bologna there were numerous foreigners, from Spain, Germany, and England. Other important Italian universities included those of Padua, Pavia, Turin, Siena, Naples, Catania, and Florence, which later played an important part in the development of humanism. The two universities in Rome, however, were mediocre, since Bologna (within the Papal States) attracted many of the best Roman scholars.

In the Kingdom of Bohemia, the University of Prague, already very venerable, comprised four 'nations': the Saxons (Saxony, Brandenburg, Brunswick, the Low Countries, and Westphalia); the Bavarians (Bavaria, Austria, France, Switzerland, the Rhineland, and Holland); the Poles; and the Czechs. The first three 'nations' remained loyal to the Pope of Rome. Bohemia itself, however, was Clementist; and in 1409 King Wenceslas – a somewhat dubious character who had been ousted from the Imperial throne – rigged the electoral system by giving three votes to the Czech 'nation' and only one to be shared by all the other three. The result was that the Germans left Prague and declared that the Czechs were heretics.

In Poland, a university was founded at Cracow, and in Hungary at Budapest.

Heresies

As well as the Great Schism and the Conciliar crisis, a further divisive factor now troubled the Church. This was the spread of heresy. The crises had delayed ecclesiastical reform; so a number of idealists took it upon themselves. The phenomenon has been called 'the Pre-Reformation', since the Reformation proper came a century later.

The two main 'Pre-Reformers', John Wyclif in England and his disciple John Huss in Bohemia, both helped to consolidate their countries' national consciousness.

Wyclif (c.1320–84) was a mystic and a contemporary of those other great mystics Johannes Ruysbroek, from Flanders, and St Catherine of Siena. But he was also an eminent Oxford teacher and theologian, the theorist of 'royal prerogative'. *Vis-à-vis* the Papacy, he was protected for a long time by the Duke of Lancaster, John of Gaunt (from Ghent). The novelty of his teaching was that he gave Holy Scripture priority over the Church, and drew the conclusion that there was no need for either Papacy or clergy. The truth, he held, would be found by 'free inquiry' on the part of the individual, not through the official teachings of the Church. The sacraments themselves were not all-important, and the Eucharist was merely symbolic. Expounded in sometimes violent popular sermons, Wyclif's doctrines led to his condemnation by the University of Oxford and by the Pope: he was even suspected of having organized, with the help of his 'poor priest' followers, the Peasants' Revolt of 1381. Wyclif died three years later, in 1384; but despite his final failure, he remained very popular in England, where among other things he had had the Bible translated into English. His followers were known as 'Lollards', from the Dutch *lollaerd*, a mutterer.

John Huss (c.1369–1415) was more than a generation younger than Wyclif. He too was a university teacher, practising at the University of Prague. More of a moralist than a mystic, he was a very talented polemicist and popular preacher. He too wanted to reform the Church, and admired Wyclif more for his reform proposals than for his theological doctrines. Like Wyclif, he thought that the Pope did the Church more harm than good.

Unsurprisingly, although Huss was very popular in his own country, he was detested in Rome. The targets of his invective included the cardinals, who had become opulent and lordly, and their traffic in indulgences and their 'arithmetic piety', adding up the number of days in Purgatory that the purchase of an indulgence could spare the sinner.

Huss sought to expound his ideas to the Council of Constance; but it was an ill-judged move. He was put on trial and faced the hostility of the University of Paris and its great teacher Jean Charlier de Gerson. Condemned, he was handed over to the secular authorities, stripped of his priesthood, and executed in 1415. But his numerous disciples were very influential in developing a sense of nationality and statehood in Bohemia.

The 'Liberties' of national Churches

At all levels, from cardinals to humble priests, the clergy lived on church 'benefices'. And secular rulers were more and more anxious to control these funds by deciding who should receive them. If they could choose the incumbents, here was a fine way to recompense their friends and partisans without contributing a penny themselves. In the fifteenth century, this was well recognized. In about 1410, the great Paris master Gerson wrote: 'When Papal authority is weak, it is nevertheless essential to maintain the cohesion of the national Churches and preserve their apostolic strength. This is the task of the Christian prince.'

Rather than allow secular rulers to distribute ecclesiastical benefices by purely unilateral decision, the policy of the Popes, from Martin V onwards, was to seek bilateral agreements or *concordats*. These differed from country to country.

Gallicanism

In France, the 'liberties' of the national Church took the name of Gallicanism. Its origin may be a celebrated work, *The Dream of the Verger*, written in 1372, shortly before the Great Schism. The doctrine itself had taken shape by the beginning of the fifteenth century, and was defined at the Council of Paris in 1406. It held that the King was fully entitled to allocate benefices. Royal officials, no longer fearing excommunication, abolished clerical privileges one after another: special courts, exemption from taxes, and so on. 'All churchmen must pay dues, since these are for the defence of the realm.' This and similar rulings culminated in a series of Gallican 'ordinances' – and in sharp hostility between the partisans of the Pope (such as the University of Toulouse and the Burgundians) and the Gallican party (including Gerson, the theologian Pierre d'Ailly, and the Armagnacs). In 1438, King Charles VII of France adopted the so-called 'Pragmatic Sanction' of Bourges, the real charter of the Gallican Church, which made the King 'the leading ecclesiastical personage in the realm'. In principle, bishops and abbots were elected: so there was what may be called 'episcopal Gallicanism', extremely hostile to the Pope. The Duchy of Brittany, however, renounced Gallicanism by the Redon Concordat of 1441.

Anglicanism

In England, opposition to the Avignon Papacy was total: it came from Parliament as well as from the King. In 1398, a concordat was signed with the Pope of Rome, simply sharing out the allocation of benefices between the Pope and the King. The Lancastrian dynasty denounced the concordat and practised an 'Anglican' policy, but this was not as extremist as Gallicanism.

When the English occupied part of France, they brought Anglicanism with them. One example of how the French clergy fell under English authority was the position taken by the Bishop of Beauvais, Pierre Cauchon, whose court tried Joan of Arc. It has been said that in France the defence of 'liberties' meant resistance to the Pope, whereas in England it meant obedience to the King.

The Irish, incidentally, did their best to prevent the King's interference in Church affairs.

German 'Liberties'

In Germany, the Empire was now coming to seem more of a *regnum teutonicum* or Teutonic kingdom, and no longer a universal monarchy. Nor, in the fifteenth century, did the very diverse German nation coincide with the Empire's boundaries. Popular piety was still very intense; and the Church, divided among a large number of princes, was very attached to 'Germanic liberties' and often very hostile to the Pope. This was especially true of the bishop-electors of Mainz, Trier, and Cologne, although those in the east, more vulnerable to invasion, shared greater mutual need for links with the Holy See.

The poverty of the country, the disorganization of the Church hierarchy, and the rapacity of a number of bishops not only intensified the call for reform in Germany, but also encouraged anti-clericalism. Sects proliferated; Hussite influence was felt. Mysticism was rife: one of its great exponents was Nicholas of Cusa. Born in the year 1400, he has been described both as 'the herald of a new age' and 'the man who broke with medievalism'.

At Frankfurt, in 1446, a huge meeting was held, bringing together dukes, counts, bishops, knights, delegates from the towns, Papal legates, representatives from the Council of Basle, the Grand Master of the Teutonic Order, and the King of Denmark. The outcome of their proceedings was the *Fürstenkonkordat* or 'Princes' Concordat', which proclaimed the 'eminence' of the Council – not its supremacy. In 1448, the Concordat of Vienna gave the Pope far more power in Germany than the Pragmatic Sanction had left him in France.

Poland

In Poland, the Pope kept the lion's share of the distribution of benefices.

Scandinavia

In Scandinavia, after the Union of Kalmar in 1397, which brought together the three monarchies of Sweden, Norway, and Denmark, each state kept its own institutions. The Danish Church remained under German influence; the Norwegian distanced itself from that of Scotland; the Swedish kept its links with Rome. Many of the Scandinavian bishops were foreigners; while the lower ranks of the clergy were ill-educated and disinclined to celibacy.

In Iceland, the Church was isolated and insular.

Hungary

In Hungary, the bishops were appointed by the King or by the nobility, whose sympathies were not with Rome.

Spain

The Spanish nation was very united, but very loyal to the Pope and disinclined to accord supremacy to the Council.

The Church in Spain produced some remarkable people, in particular the great Dominican preacher St Vincent Ferrer, who died at Vannes in 1419.

Portugal

Portugal, influenced more by England than by France, remained largely aloof from the Church's quarrels. Like Aragon, it undertook conquests which were readily called 'crusades'. In 1415 the Portuguese captured Ceuta, the only town 'in Africa, the third part of the world, which upheld the name of Christ'.

THE ADVANCE OF SCIENCE IN EUROPE

In the twelfth and thirteenth centuries, Latin Christendom – i.e. almost the whole of present-day Europe – seems to have been backward by comparison with the other great peoples of the world: the Chinese, the Arabs, and in some measure the Byzantines. But for the next four centuries, Europe forged ahead – in pure science, applied science, and technology. At the end of the eighteenth century, it applied its discoveries on a large scale to the manufacture of goods which contributed greatly to human comfort.

In earlier times, however, Europe was much influenced from outside, notably by China and the Arabs.

Distant influences: China

With China, contact was obviously difficult. Many discoveries had been made there long before they were made in Europe: they included silk, gunpowder, the grenade, and the cannon, already used by the Chinese as early as the thirteenth century. The West first used it at the Battle of Crécy in 1316; and its use became general mainly in the fifteenth century. Other Chinese inventions included the compass, paper, ink, the sedan chair, and the artesian well.

Chinese technology reached Europe via the Arabs. Direct contacts between China and the West were very rare; and in 1368, the arrival of the traditionalist Ming dynasty, coupled with the expulsion of the Mongols and the emergence of Tamerlane, meant that the frontiers of China were closed to Europeans for a very long time.

Closer influences: the Arabs

Arab influence faced fewer obstacles, despite religious difference and wars. Western and Arab civilization met at common frontiers and in the Mediterranean. Starting from Baghdad, the influence came more and more through Spain and, from the thirteenth century onwards, through Sicily.

R. Arnaldez has compiled a telling list of medieval scholars who were either Arabs or, if Jewish or Christian, Arab-educated. Numerically, the results can be summarized as follows. In the second half of the eighth century, there were eight, all Asian; in the ninth century, thirty-nine, again all Asian; in the tenth century, out of thirty-four, thirty-one were Asian and three Spanish Arabs; and in the eleventh century, out of thirty, twenty-one were Asian and nine Spanish Arabs.

The best-known Arab – and Indian – innovations include 'Arabic' numerals, the abacus, and the astrolabe.

Medicine

In medicine, this same period saw the growth of a unique institution: the School of Salerno, a virtual symbol of the cultural maelstrom in southern Italy, so hotly disputed by Byzantines, Arabs and, later, the Normans. Great progress was made there as a result of dissection, practised mainly on pigs. Trepanning was developed, and studies were made of cancerous tumours and stomach wounds. The Salerno doctors are thought to have been the first to distill wine and condense alcohol vapour, with important results for pharmacy, perfume manufacture – and alcoholism.

Avicenna and Averroës (See also p. 193)

Avicenna (Ibn Sina), born in Persia in 980, was one of the greatest representatives of Arab science and philosophy: he was himself a doctor as well as a philosopher. He was one of the major translators of Aristotle, and was invited to the courts of several oriental princes to serve as vizier and physician. He died in 1037.

After Avicenna, the great translator of Aristotle was Averroës (Abou Ibn Rushd). Born in Cordoba in about 1120, he was the pupil of an Arabic-speaking Jewish doctor, Avenzoar, born in about 1070 at Penaflor. His commentaries on Aristotle were published in Latin. He died in Morocco between 1198 and 1206.

One of Averroës' pupils was his contemporary, the Jewish Maimonides (1135–1204). A theologian and astronomer, he published among other things a *Treatise on Poisons* and a *Book Explaining Medicinal Drugs*. Since the days of Charlemagne, trade in drugs and spices had mainly been conducted by Jews, and there were Jewish pharmacists all over Europe, the profession being handed down from father to son.

These great teachers had disciples throughout the Christian world: all Europe was affected by the currents of thought that spread from Arabic centres or from the border in places like Salerno, Cordoba, and Sicily. Toledo, when it was recaptured, also became a remarkable centre of intellectual influence.

The Arabs, in particular, had preserved and translated Greek and Latin writings. For all those in which the content was more important than the style, their transmission by this means was a blessing. And, as R. Arnaldez adds:

> We may conclude that the Arabs did more than transmit knowledge: they aroused and developed the taste for it. They used their critical faculties, and began to test Greek concepts against experience. They

were greatly helped by their decidedly modern tendency to pursue technology and apply their knowledge in practice. We are in their debt for instruments used in astronomy, mechanics, and chemistry; and, in medicine, for the first great hospitals, the *maristans*, where the care of the sick was combined with scientific research and the training of young doctors.

Two 'enlightened' thirteenth-century rulers stood out among their contemporaries: the Emperor Frederick II (1194–1250) and Alfonso the Wise, King of Castile (1252–84), known outside his kingdom as 'the Astronomer'.

The Emperor Frederick II

Frederick II spent most of his life in Sicily. Impious, continually excommunicated, and a cruel debauchee, he was nevertheless highly intelligent. As a patron, he protected his astrologer Michael Scot and the greatest mathematician of the whole Middle Ages, Leonard of Pisa. He wrote an extraordinary *Treatise on Falconry*, largely based on practical experience; and he introduced into Christendom its first giraffe.

Alfonso X

Alfonso X (the Wise) is known to us as a poet, a musician, a jurist, and an astronomer. In 1280 he published the *Libros del Saber Astronomia*, about the stars and astronomical instruments, and he caused to be published, also in Spanish, the *Alfonsine Tables*, dealing with the problems of the calendar.

How can the development of science be explained? From the fourteenth century onwards, it was certainly perceptible. The 'Carolingian Renaissance' had been the work of a handful of intellectuals for whom sacred matters were at the heart of all scholarship. The thirteenth-century university scholars were far more numerous; and they by no means despised the *quadrivium*, the contemporary counterpart of the Science Faculty. In itself, religion was no obstacle to inquiry, save where it intruded into 'secular' affairs. Yet many of the clergy were convinced that no branch of learning was outside the scope of theology.

Take one example: dissection, which was essential to the progress of medical science. No dissection of human bodies had taken place since the third century BC; and the practice was resumed only at the end of the thirteenth century. A Council held in Venice in 1368 authorized one dissection a year.

While religious restrictions were thus being eased, however slowly, there was also a growing tendency to be critical of time-honoured authority, and to trust, like the Arabs, to observation and empiricism as the surest guides to truth.

Technology

Generally speaking, applied science or technology progressed faster than pure science. As always, people were constantly seeking to improve the material conditions of life.

More effective use of energy, first of all, may help to explain the decline of slavery. The shoulder-collar for draught animals and the curb-bit with cheek and chain made their appearance; roads began to be paved; windmills reached Spain in the tenth century; water-mills spread throughout Latin Christendom; the crank-handle was used in Germany at the beginning of the fifteenth century. Other medieval innovations included the breeding of silk-worms, falconry, the smoking and salting of herrings, the making of sparkling white wine, the spinning-wheel, the blast-furnace, and metal-casting. Important progress was made in glass-blowing, notably at Murano near Venice. The principle of the magnifying glass was discovered by an Arab in the eleventh century and by an expert from Oxford.

Paper, ink, and printing

The twelfth century saw the introduction of rag paper, invented by the Chinese in the third century AD, and of ink. Paper was manufactured mainly in Italy, which became a great exporter, and later in France around Paris and Troyes.

With Roman capital letters, the Carolingian minuscule (see p. 115), ink, and paper, the time was becoming ripe for the still more crucial invention of printing, made by Johann Genfleisch Gutenberg, who was born in Mainz in about 1400 and died around 1468. His and Fust's *Biblia latina* was printed in 130 copies in 1450: three years later,

Constantinople fell to the Turks. A new epoch had begun. By 1480 or thereabouts, there were ten printing works in France and Geneva, four in England, thirteen in the Low Countries, nineteen in western Germany and German-speaking Switzerland, five in eastern Germany, one in Prague, one in Cracow, one in Budapest, one in Breslau, six in Spain, forty in northern Italy, and three in southern Italy – making a European total of 104.

Thanks to paper – which cost eight times less than an equal area of parchment – and to printing, which made possible repeated new editions, intellectual life could develop on a new scale. Between 1450 and 1500, some 15 to 20 million copies of books were produced. In the sixteenth century, there were between 150 and 200 million copies of 150 to 200,000 editions. About a quarter of them appeared in France, a quarter in Germany, and a quarter in Italy; an eighth of the total was in the Low Countries, and the remaining eighth was divided among Spain, England, and the rest of Europe, including the countries of the east. Private citizens formed libraries, but it was rare for any individual to have more than 200 books. However, the French philosopher Montaigne, at the end of the sixteenth century, was said to have had a thousand volumes in his famous 'Tower of Books'. Printing also encouraged the emergence of professional writers. From now on, indeed, a powerful intellectual movement developed outside the universities. It was the germ of the humanism which transformed the sixteenth century.

EUROPE MASTERS NAVIGATION

From the thirteenth century onwards, the champion navigators were no longer the Vikings or the Byzantines, but the Italians and the Germans of the Hanseatic League – soon to be followed by the Spaniards and the Portuguese.

Old and new types of craft

The descendants of the Vikings used narrow, shallow-draught boats propelled by sails and oars. The sailing ships of Western Europe, with more rounded hulls, were more stable but slower. The Byzantine navy followed the tradition of the very long single-decked galley, with a ram on the stern: the longest were known as *dromons* or 'runners'. Merchantmen, however, used sails instead of oars.

In 1161, after peace had been restored between the north Germans of Hamburg and Lübeck and the Swedish inhabitants of the island of Gottland, the German merchants who traded with the island formed an association known as the Hansa, from the Old German *hansen*, to band together. Other ports, including Bremen, joined in; but Hamburg and Lübeck remained the leaders. The great success of the Hanseatic towns was to invent the cog, a roomy, deep-draught vessel (3 metres below the waterline), drawn by a single sail. From 1220 onwards, its steering oar began to be replaced by a stern-rudder.

In Italy, the essential development was the growing ascendancy of Venice, followed by Genoa and Pisa. The Venetian merchant galley, the *galea de mercato*, was like a broader version of the Byzantine ship. There were few of them, however, and a multiplicity of smaller boats.

Large-scale commerce

The big northern and southern maritime trade routes were at first linked by land – which explains the great success of the fairs of Champagne, between prosperous Flanders and wealthy Italy. But land transport was expensive; and the Hundred Years' War discouraged trade routes through France. In the fourteenth century, the land link was replaced by a sea route. The Hansa, with heavy goods to carry, invented a vessel which superseded the cog: this was the *hooker*. The Genoese and Venetians had doubled the tonnage of their galleys; and in the mid-fifteenth century the *carrack* became general, which had no fewer than three masts. At about the same time, the *caravel* appeared, perhaps of Italian origin, but certainly used for Atlantic voyages. This was a fast vessel, and could carry a cargo of 400 metric tons.

Navigational instruments and methods

The compass, which had originated in China, first reached Europe in about 1200, after which date a number of writers described its use. In early models, the magnetized needle floated on water; but in versions devised by Guyot de Provins in France, Alexander Neckham in England, and Petrus Peregrinus in Italy, it rotated on a pivot. Magnetic variation, however, suspected in the fifteenth century, was not fully confirmed until 1492, when Christopher Columbus noticed that the further west he sailed the more magnetic north differed from true north.

Already at the beginning of the thirteenth century, the stern-rudder had replaced the steering oar. The same period saw the development of charts and pilot guides, *portolani* or 'portolans' to help mariners reach port. As Denys Hay has written, 'The new maps were less continent-conscious than the old literary diagrams designed to show a symmetrical world pivoted on Jerusalem ... but they often revealed more sharply than ever before the virtual identity of Christendom and Europe.' In some maps, 'the areas of Muslim domination were marked by the Crescent of Islam.' These charts were at first rare and very inaccurate. The so-called 'Anglo-Saxon' Cotton chart, created in the second quarter of the eleventh century, very roughly showed the three continents of the Old World. The Hereford and Ebsdorf *Mappae Mundi* (1284) followed this same tradition of ignorance and mediocrity. But even before those maps were drawn, true geography was being revived. The Arabs brought to the West the work of Ptolemy, the greatest geographer of classical antiquity. From the twelfth century onwards, more and more maps were produced, sailing instructions were compiled, leading as far as China, and the notion that Scandinavia was an island was shown to be false. Practical experience, indeed, proved the need for accuracy and precision.

The first mention of a marine chart dates from the year 1270, when St Louis travelled to Tunis in a Genoese ship. The main centres of maritime cartography were Catalonia and Mallorca. As trigonometry was being developed at the University of Oxford, and astronomic observation grew more precise, the first halting steps towards celestial navigation became possible. Unknown in the Mediterranean, it was first practised in the Atlantic, off the coast of Africa.

The earliest discoveries

According to the great Sicilian Arab geographer Al Idrisi, it was Arab explorers who discovered Madeira and the Azores in 1124. Attempts were made to find a sea route to India. The north-east trade winds drove ships towards the 'Fortunate Isles' or Canaries; while some sailed north to find the west winds that would take the caravels towards the Iberian peninsula. Between 1341 and 1393 Madeira, the

Canaries, and the Azores were visited more and more often by Portuguese, Italians, Mallorcans, Catalans, and Andalusians. In 1402, there was a French expedition, led by Jean de Béthencourt: but the master mariners were the Genoese and the Catalans. Portugal often hired the services of the Genoese; and the Catalans led a certain number of Spanish expeditions, as in 1346, when Jaime-Ferrer explored the African coast beyond Cape Bojador on the 26th parallel. The Infante John of Aragon encouraged such African expeditions.

In the fifteenth century, Portugal became for a time the leading naval power. The young Henry the Navigator methodically directed the exploration of Africa from 1415 to 1460 without ever leaving Portugal. He collected charts, books, and navigational instruments, and assembled experts, especially from Mallorca. Soon after his death, the noon sun-sight was used to establish latitude. More and more, the taking of bearings replaced the medieval method of dead reckoning. But establishing longitude remained difficult until really accurate timepieces could give the difference between local and Greenwich time.

Old and new trading powers

In the second half of the fifteenth century, the two great European traders – Italy and the Hansa – were still very active. So was Flanders: the port of Bruges was not yet silted up, and the Italians came in large numbers to sell their goods there. In Antwerp, there were streets named after Hamburg and Lübeck. In Italy, rivalling Venice and Genoa, Milan and Lombardy were in full expansion, and Naples was becoming a major port of call.

New powers were beginning to challenge the existing leaders. In Spain, the great centres were Seville and Cadiz; in Portugal, Lisbon. Southern Germany was in the ascendant, mainly owing to its silver, tin, copper, and zinc mines. German merchants were setting up in all the main trading towns – as witness the 'Fondaco dei Tedeschi' in Venice. England, with its companies of 'merchant adventurers', was trying to impose a monopoly on its trade: the merchant adventurers succeeded in having Hanseatic privileges abolished, and led a violent campaign against the Hansa until the Peace of Utrecht in 1474. A further challenger of the status quo was Holland, where Amsterdam and Rotterdam were rapidly developing their trade.

France, on the other hand, ruined by war and depopulation, took little part in this commercial rivalry. The great French trade fairs declined: first Champagne, then the 'Lendit Fair' at Saint-Denis. Their place was taken by the fair of Frankfurt.

The Popes try to share out the world

What has been called 'the expansion of Europe' was just beginning. Overseas exploration and exploitation changed the world, enlarged the horizons of Europeans and gave a new scale to their thinking and their activities. But even in Europe there was another side to the story: rivalry among the explorers and colonists, and a grave blow to the power of the Church.

As 'Vicars of God', the Popes claimed universal sovereignty over newly conquered lands, and the right to share them out among the secular powers. The Papacy accordingly followed with keen interest the rivalry between Portugal and Castile. In 1443 the King of Portugal had affirmed his absolute control of Africa and its trade beyond Cape Bojador.

When Castile contested this monopoly, the King asked the Holy See to confirm it, which Pope Nicholas V did: his Bull *Romanus pontifex* of 1455 forbade any but the Portuguese to trade there. In 1479, at Alcaçovas, King Alfonso V of Portugal signed a partition agreement – the first in a series which continued until 1914 – with Ferdinand and Isabella of Spain. Portugal gave up the Canaries in exchange for Spain's abandoning all claims on the coast of Africa. The agreement indicated that the Spaniards were anxious to push westwards towards the unknown, while the Portuguese wanted to continue south along the African coastline. Both were looking for new routes to India; Spain via the west, Portugal via the east. The Pope confirmed the share-out, which excluded all other nations.

Matters became more serious after Christopher Columbus's famous expedition of 1492. Approached by his friend and compatriot King Ferdinand of Aragon, Pope Alexander VI published the Bull *Inter coetera* of 1493, giving the Catholic Kings the exclusive right to acquire any island or other territory beyond a north–south line 100 leagues west of the Azores and Cape Verde. No one would have the right to explore this area without the agreement of the Spaniards – who were determined not to give it. The King of Portugal, John II, rejected this ruling: but Spain and Portugal continued to negotiate. Finally, on 7 June 1494, by the Treaty of Tordesillas, the partition was agreed, but the north–south dividing-line was pushed 260 leagues further west, to some 1,500 kilometres west of Cape Verde. This enabled Portugal to colonize Brazil.

The Treaty of Tordesillas was in effect a serious blow to Papal authority. It was not, however, contested by the other European powers. France and England were both exhausted by the Hundred Years' War; while the great navigators of the past, the German Hansa and the Italian city-states, were little attracted by distant, uncertain adventures. Spain and Portugal had no other rivals – as yet.

THE IDEA OF EUROPE

The word 'Europe' virtually disappears

From the eleventh century onwards, the word 'Europe' rarely appears in medieval texts. Europe, with its precise geographical connotations, was hard to fit into the vocabulary of universalists. What was more, Christianity took the offensive beyond Europe's borders. From 1099 to 1187, Christendom held Jerusalem. For a further century, there was a Frankish kingdom at Acre. In 1204, Frankish barons seized the Byzantine Empire. Thus, for a time, Christendom overflowed its European boundaries. Only when the Turks were advancing, and approaching Constantinople, did a priest at the Council of Constance declare: 'Now, only Europe is Christian.'

Denys Hay, Carlo Curcio, Robert Lopez and others have assembled the few texts in which Europe is mentioned by name. Neither Du Cange nor Godefroi includes the word in their Latin and French dictionaries.

The term was used, first of all, by geographers, who knew that there were three continents: but until the thirteenth century geographers were rare. Nor did they incorporate in their amateurish maps the results of contemporary exploration. They ignored the Scandinavian discovery of Greenland and America; they even ignored the Crusades.

By a curious tradition, Europe was linked to the Bible by way of Japhet, the son of Noah; Sem was attached to Asia, and Cham to Africa.

This legend first appeared in the fourth century, in St Jerome's book *In Genesim*. It continued to flourish in the Middle Ages.

In the thirteenth century, the monk and encyclopaedist Bartholomew the Englishman wrote: 'Just as in former times the city of Athens was the mother of liberal arts and letters, the nursemaid of philosophers and of all the sciences, so is Paris in our day, not only for France, but for the whole of Europe.' This recalls the somewhat later proposal by Alexandre de Roes that France should be made the pole of science in Europe. But the use of the word 'Europe' here is significant. It shows that a scholar interested in antiquity could use the word to signify the West. Perhaps, in the usage of the time, this was a learned pretension. But it was certainly not esoteric. Frederick II spoke of *Europa imperialis*. Dante (1265–1321) used the word a dozen times in all his works. However, although he was a Guelph, Dante defended the Empire against the Church and denied that the latter had temporal power. 'Who could imagine,' he wrote in *De monarchia* (III, 14), 'that the Church had received such power by the consent of all or of a majority, when not only everyone in Africa and Asia, but the majority in Europe, would be revolted by such a suggestion?'

At a time when, as we have seen, the first modern states were beginning to emerge, intellectuals of every kind pursued their dreams of unity. Unity through the Empire – not the Papacy – was championed not only by Dante but also by a scholarly German monk of noble family, Engelbert of Admont. In his book *On the Origin and the End of the Roman Empire*, written between 1307 and 1310, he called for 'a single Empire with a single head', and noted that 'the Kingdoms of Spain, France, England, and Hungary, with those of the Slavs, Bulgaria, and Greece, which were once provinces or realms of the Roman Empire, are now no longer under its law; while in Africa and Asia, beyond the sea, the Empire no longer owns anything.' This situation, he thought, must be remedied, if only in case there were a war 'between all Christendom and the pagan world'. It would also be a way of keeping the peace between the various communities which were part of the Empire. It seems, in fact, as if Engelbert wished to maintain the kingdoms in being, and regarded the Emperor as a supreme arbiter for the maintenance of peace. He was very open to the idea that while 'natural law' was common to all peoples, 'positive law varies according to the diversity of countries, customs, and traditions, so that different peoples have different kings.' This, he held, was not incompatible with the existence of the Empire.

The idea of unification for peace can be found in other prominent authors, including the Englishman William of Ockham (writing between 1338 and 1341) and the Frenchman Pierre Dubois (in 1308). The same idea recurred in the fifteenth century. It can be found, for instance, in *The Origin of the Authority of the Roman Empire* (1445) by Aeneas Silvius Piccolomini, the future Pope Pius II, for whom 'all temporal powers are subject to the Roman Prince' – i.e. the Emperor. Compare also the curious proposal made in 1464 by the King of Bohemia, George Podiebrad, and inspired by the French adventurer Antoine Marini. This, rather like Dubois' work, proposed a *Congregatio concordiae* – an assembly of Christian princes brought together to ensure peace. Arbitration was envisaged and planned for, with armed sanctions against anyone who refused it. It was hardly surprising that when Podiebrad put this revolutionary plan to Louis XI, it was politely rejected. Its interest is that for the first time it proposed the idea of a 'League of Princes' – or nations.

CONCLUSION

The unification of Europe by Christianity – or at least by Latin Christianity – could have taken place under the authority of either the Pope or the Emperor. The 200-year conflict between theocracy and Caesaropapism ended in a victory for the kingdoms, and in particular those of England and France, followed by Castile, Aragon, and Portugal. Their kings regarded themselves as 'emperors within their kingdoms'. Permanent administration, regular taxes, and standing armies took the place of that infinitely complex network of personal allegiance which was the feudal system. The arrival of the Mongols, followed by the Turks, prevented Eastern Europe from following this model: it also culminated in the fall of the Roman Empire in the east. This period saw the fragmentation of sovereignty confirmed. The Hundred Years' War between England and France both exemplified and symbolized that fact.

But the ill effects of war were only part of the 'great crisis' of the fourteenth and fifteenth centuries. It was a demographic and economic crisis, caused by famine and the Black Death. But it was also a spiritual and religious crisis, marked by the Great Schism and by the growth of movements which Rome called 'heretical', some of them the precursors of the sixteenth-century Reformation.

And yet, amid all these troubles, and perhaps because freedom of thought was increasing, Europe was experiencing what today might be called a 'take-off', which in science and technology gave it a growing lead over other great civilizations, whether Chinese, Indian, or Muslim. Finally, this movement, by means of progress in marine navigation, opened the way for Europe's future conquests. The whole scale of the world, in fact, was about to change.

11

Renaissance, Reformation, and Expansion: The Sixteenth Century

CHARLES V AND THE EUROPEAN BALANCE OF POWER

It was in the sixteenth century that the increasing disunity of Christendom gave rise to the notion of a European balance of power. This was no legal concept, universally recognized, but a practical arrangement, imposed by events. It eventually set limits on national power which were dangerous to exceed. In fact, in any international system based on a number of sovereign states, the ambitions of any one of them can be curbed in one of two ways: by the existence of a larger community in which the states have their recognized place, as at certain times in the history of medieval Christendom, or by the interplay of weight and counterweight, strength balancing strength. Charles V of Spain was the last monarch who sought to become Emperor of the West. His European rivals collectively thwarted his ambition.

The inheritance of Charles V

Just when Christendom was losing its last vestiges of supranational authority, European states were developing, consolidating, and expanding. In some cases they became what Fernand Braudel has called 'broader and more monstrous groupings, conglomerations, federations, coalitions, and even empires – if this convenient expression may be used without anachronism, for how else can such monsters be described?' The 'monsters' included the Ottoman Empire, France with its warlike ambitions in Italy and above all Charles V's Spain. Braudel saw its ascendancy as more than the accidental outcome of inheritance. It was, he thought, the result of 'circumstances which inexorably favoured large and even very large States' – at least until 1550. This may be so: but the accidents of history certainly played their part in giving a young man still not twenty years old the richest imaginable heritage. Born in Ghent in 1500, the son of Philip the Fair of Burgundy and Joanna, daughter of Ferdinand and Isabella, Charles received a series of fabulous legacies between 1516 and 1519. They were due in part to astute matrimonial policy; but they also involved extraordinary good fortune.

From his father's side of the family, Charles inherited his Austrian and Burgundian possessions. From his mother's side came Spain, with its expanding colonial empire and its Italian territories (mainly Milan and the Kingdom of Naples). There remained the Empire. Francis I, the King of France, was its rival claimant. Both he and Charles repeatedly showered the Electors with money, much of it gold and silver from Mexico. In the end, the Electors bowed to the overwhelming wishes of the German population, who would not accept a French Emperor at any price.

Charles proclaimed himself King of Spain in 1516, on the death of his grandfather Ferdinand: his own father Philip had died in 1506. His younger brother Ferdinand had been their grandfather's favourite, so Charles had been brought up in Flanders under the care of his aunt, Margaret of Austria. As a young man, he felt more Flemish than Spanish, and he surrounded himself with advisers from the Low Countries. He waited eighteen months before setting foot in Spain; and when he did so he was not well received by the Cortes of Valladolid and Saragossa. In 1520, when he left Spain to visit his new Empire, workers' and peasants' revolts broke out in Valencia, New Castile, and the Balearic Islands. Spain's only hope, in her impoverished condition, was the gold and silver from the New World.

Charles was a melancholy man. He made grandiose plans, and achieved great successes. The period from 1540 to 1545 saw the end of the *conquista* and the beginning of Spain's colonial Empire. But in many respects he was unlucky. Above all, the vast extent of his possessions united his neighbours against him.

France encircled

Most significant for the history of Europe was the fact that Charles's Empire surrounded France on three sides – north, south, and east. It may be more than a matter of chance that this situation persisted for 200 years. Even after Charles's abdication in 1555, and the subsequent partition of his lands between the two branches of the Habsburgs – his brother Ferdinand and his son Philip II – France continued to be encircled. It was a fate against which she struggled, almost by instinct, until 1714.

Despite all its difficulties, internal and external, the French monarchy concerned itself more and more with religious affairs. In this respect, the ideas espoused by Martin Luther echoed the 'Gallicanism' practised by the King. Nor were theorists lacking who could find justification for his absolute power. It was Jean Bodin who, in his *Six livres de la République*, published in 1576, gave the first rigorous definition of sovereignty. This, declared Bodin, belonged to the Prince; and 'it is essential that those who are sovereign should in no way be subject to the orders of others, and that they should break or revoke laws that are useless and have them replaced. This is why the law dictates that the prince is absolved from the power of laws.' Absolution in this sense led to absolute power.

The balance of power in Italy and in Europe

It may have been Niccolò Machiavelli who first consciously formulated the notion of 'the balance of power'. Unable to pursue in the short term the vision of Italian unity, he thought of establishing a certain equilibrium among the five main Italian states – the Papal States, Naples, Florence, Milan, and Venice – until Italy was 'delivered from the barbarians'.

Who first envisaged transposing this 'equilibrium' to Europe as a whole? Was it Cardinal Wolsey, Henry VIII's adviser, who allied England first with Spain and then with France, according to circumstances – and to the financial inducements offered by Charles V and Francis I? Or was it the Italians, who realized that to resist the French invasion they would have to form large 'confederacies'? Such was the opinion expressed by the Scottish historian William Robertson in his *History of the Reign of Charles V*, first published in 1770. 'The sudden and decisive effects of this confederacy,' he wrote,

> seem to have instructed the Princes and statesmen of Italy as much as the irruption of the French had disconcerted and alarmed them. They had extended, on this occasion, to the affairs of Europe, the maxims of that political science which had hitherto been applied only to regulate

the operations of the petty states in their own country. They had discovered the method of preventing any monarch from rising to such a degree of power, as was inconsistent with the general liberty, and had manifested the importance of attending to that great secret in modern policy, the preservation of a proper distribution of power among all the members of the system into which the states of Europe are formed ... Nor was the idea confined to them. Self-preservation taught other powers to adopt it. It grew to be fashionable and universal. From this æra we can trace the progress of that relationship between nations which has linked the powers of Europe so closely together.

The alliances made by Francis I

The lesson was certainly not lost on Francis I. Defeated at the Battle of Pavia in 1525, he had been taken captive to Madrid. No sooner was he freed, in 1526, than he undertook to form a 'league' against Charles V. The complex history of his successive alliances need not be retold here. The essential point is that the need for success – or reasons of state – led the French king to deal a serious blow against Christendom, allying himself not only with the German Protestants but, of all things, with Suleiman the Magnificent, the Sultan of Turkey. In 1531, Francis put out feelers to the Protestant princes of the Schmalkald League. But by that time, he was at peace with Charles V, and he contented himself with giving them money and arms. Only later did he conclude alliances with them; and these were often made difficult by the fact that he was simultaneously persecuting Protestants in France. His first alliance with the Turks, formed in 1536, aroused widespread horror and condemnation in Europe. There was still more consternation in August 1543, when Nice, which belonged to the Duke of Savoy, was besieged by an army of both French and Berber troops. On one side stood the cross of the House of Savoy; on the other floated standards bearing the *fleurs de lys* of France alongside others which bore the dreaded crescent of Islam.

The rules of the balance of power

Henceforward, the balance of power became one of the essentials of Europe's political system. It was accepted that coalitions would be formed against any state with overweening ambitions. Despite disagreements, this created a new kind of solidarity, well described by William Robertson: 'No prince was so much superior in power that his efforts were irresistible and his conquests easy ... The advantages of one State were counterbalanced by circumstances favourable to others, and this prevented any of them from attaining such superiority as would have been fatal to all. The nations of Europe, then as now, were like a great family.' A disunited and quarrelsome family: but a family nevertheless. A new Europe was emerging, composed of states that were ever more vigorous and coherent.

Theory was not slow to follow practice. Trajano Boccalini (1556–1613) wrote commentaries on Tacitus which were posthumously published in 1678 under the title *Bilancia politica*. They analysed very precisely the European balance of power, taking as one example the Flemish insurrection against Spain in 1578, in which a number of Italian princes also played a role. Boccalini likewise praised the balance-of-power tactics used by King Henry IV of France. Another Italian author, Tommaso Campanella (1568–1639), who spent twenty-seven years in Spanish prisons and who in 1602 wrote a famous utopian fantasy, *Civitas Solis* (*The City of the Sun*), passionately longed to see Christendom reunited under a universal monarchy. Even so, in his *Discorsi politici ai principi d'Italia* (*Political Discourses to the Princes of Italy*) he recognized the value of the balance of power. Europe was then living under the double strain of the Habsburg–Turkish and the Habsburg–French conflicts. The Italian princes sought to counter Spanish power by means of France; but if Spain declined and France became over-mighty, they would do exactly the opposite and side with Spain.

Thus Europe adopted both the balance of power and the concept of 'reasons of state' or *raison d'état*. Machiavelli had described both of them; and their interconnection was brilliantly demonstrated by Friedrich Meinecke in his 1924 classic, *The Doctrine of Raison d'Etat and its Place in Modern History*.

EUROPE AND THE REST OF THE WORLD

Maritime Europe

The word 'overseas' was now about to take on a new meaning. The 'seas' in question were no longer inland seas like the Baltic or the Mediterranean, nor coastal areas like the North Sea, the Irish Sea, or the Channel. In the space of a few years, all Western Europe launched a seaborne exploration and eventual conquest of the world. Those same peoples who three centuries later separated Africa and South-East Asia now discovered America – or rediscovered it, in view of what the Vikings had achieved. In Africa and Asia at this time, they merely established coastal outposts and trading stations, or captured a few islands to facilitate trade. Europe, indeed, became a maritime entity; whereas in the East, although the Russians certainly conquered vast areas, they did so only in waves of invasion by land.

All Western European countries were involved in Europe's overseas expansion, including those like Germany and Italy which made no immediate conquests. Christopher Columbus, from Italy, was in the service of the King and Queen of Spain. The astronomical tables he used for navigation had been drawn up in Nüremberg, where the astronomer Regiomontanus (Johann Müller, 1436–76) had invented a new form of astrolabe. In 1505, moreover, three German ships sailed for the Indies as part of a Portuguese fleet.

Portugal's leading role

This is not the place to describe in detail the expeditions and battles undertaken by the Portuguese. In 1486, Bartholomew Díaz de Novaes discovered the 'Cape of Storms', later renamed the Cape of Good Hope, either by Diaz or by King John II of Portugal. In 1498, Vasco da Gama rounded it, entered the Indian Ocean, and in May reached Calicut on the Malabar Coast. In this way the Portuguese discovered a new route to India. Within fifteen years they controlled the Indian Ocean and dominated the trade in spices, for which Lisbon became the international market.

The Asian bases of the Portuguese Empire were founded by Francisco de Almeida in 1504–9 and Alfonso de Albuquerque in 1509–15. They were Goa, Malacca, Ormuz, Socotora, the Moluccas or Spice Islands, and Macao in China. One of the greatest poets of all time, Luis Vaz de Camoens (1524–80), celebrated Portugal's achievements in *Os Lusiadas* (*The Lusiads* – from *Lusi* or *Lusitani*, the Latin term for the Portuguese).

Portuguese conquests in the East, however, did not prevent Portugal from maintaining a presence in the Americas, where under the Treaty of Tordesillas in 1494 it occupied Brazil.

The leading role of Spain

Christopher Columbus's expeditions were a decisive stage in the great Renaissance voyages of discovery.

Like most other educated Europeans at the time, Columbus was convinced that the world was round. But he was misled by the false calculations of distance handed down by the second-century geographer Ptolemy. He thought that Cipangu (Japan) and Cathay (China) were closer to Europe than in fact they are. In the course of his four voyages, he discovered the Lesser Antilles, Jamaica, Puerto Rico, and the coast of Central America. Less important voyages by other navigators, such as Alonso de Ojeda, Juan de la Cosa, Amerigo Vespucci, and Vicente Yañez Pinzón, made it possible to trace the outlines of the Gulf of Darien, the Antilles, and the coasts of Venezuela and Brazil, as well as the extent of the Caribbean Sea.

In 1500, only eight years after Columbus's discovery of America, Juan de la Cosa produced a map which already gave the broad outline of its eastern seaboard. The Spaniards rapidly settled there. In 1508 Juan Ponce de Léon conquered Puerto Rico; in 1509 Juan de Esquivel took Jamaica; in 1510 Diego Velasquez began the conquest of Cuba. In 1513 Vasco Nuñez de Balboa discovered what he called the South Sea: it was the Pacific Ocean. Realizing that these newly discovered lands were in fact a continent, explorers began to seek a passage from the Atlantic to the Pacific as a route to Asia. This was the essential purpose of the expedition undertaken in 1519–22 by Ferdinand Magellan and Juan Sebastian del Cano.

From 1517 onwards, the Spaniards began to invade the American mainlands, where the climate was temperate and the native population more numerous. The two most important phases of this invasion were, first, the conquest of Mexico by Hernando Cortés between 1519 and 1521, in which the central Mexican plain became the basis of the vice-kingdom of new Spain; and, secondly, the conquest of the Inca Empire in the central Andes by Francisco Pizarro between 1527 and 1533. By the middle of the sixteenth century, a handful of Spaniards had wrested the bulk of Spanish America from its millions of indigenous inhabitants, opening the way for Western Europe as a whole. The Spaniards did not regard this new world as a group of colonies, but as a subsidiary of the Castilian kingdom: its natives were therefore seen as legal subjects of the Crown.

The central administration, based in Spain, comprised two main institutions: *La Casa de Contratación*, a kind of 'Trading House', set up in Seville in 1503, and the Council of the Indies, formed by Charles V in 1524 along the lines of the Councils of the Monarchy. The Spaniards also, however, founded institutions in the 'New World', creating two vice-kingdoms, which in the eighteenth century became four. They introduced European culture by means of universities and religious colleges. The University of Mexico, founded in 1553, received the same privileges as that of Salamanca.

One great evil of the Spanish occupation in the New World was administrative malpractice, which proved impossible to stamp out despite the so-called 'residency visits', tours of inspection intended to keep an eye on senior officials. There were also ethical problems. In an attempt to remedy them, the Burgos Laws of 1512 codified the system of tutelage (*encomienda*) exercised by the colonists over the Indians. The latter supplied free labour, and in exchange received a Christian education. The Spanish missionary Bartolomé de Las Casas (1474–1566) criticized this tutelage system, and under the New Laws of 1542 was able for a time to have it suppressed.

While Spain was conquering much of the New World, wielding immense power in Europe, and leading the struggle against the Turks, Spanish literature was developing apace. The fifteenth century was the age of the *romanceros* or short poems celebrating the age-old fight against the Moors. In the sixteenth century, Spanish poetry attained new heights with Luis de Góngora y Argote, born in Cordova in 1561. His subtle, precious, rather euphuistic style, known as 'Gongorism' or *stilo culto*, influenced writers throughout Europe. Spain likewise invented the pastoral romance, of which one example was the unfinished *Diana enamorada* written in 1558 by Jorge de Montemayor. This inspired, among other things, Honoré d'Urfé's *L'Astrée* (1610–18). Spain was also the birthplace of the picaresque novel – *un pícaro* meaning a 'rogue', whose scapegrace adventures the novel gleefully described.

More germane to the present purpose, however, is the historical and mystical writing that Spain produced. The historical works were mainly devoted to the New World. As well as the letters and dispatches of Hernando Cortés, there were the *Historia general de los Indios*, by Gonzalo Fernandez de Oviedo; the *Historia verdadera de la conquista de la Nueva España*, by Bernal Diaz del Castillo; and the *Brevissima relacion de la destruccion de los Indios*, by Bartolomé de Las Casas, which in 1552 revealed the brutality inherent in all colonial adventures.

Spanish mystical writing, in this 'golden age', reached a level rarely attained elsewhere. Suffice it to mention Teresa Sánchez de Cepeda y Ahumada (Santa Teresa de Jesús), the Carmelite nun and founder of numerous convents, whose *El camino de la perfeccion* (1565) deeply influenced European Catholics.

English, Dutch, and French explorers

On the heels of the Spaniards and Portuguese, and above all at the end of the sixteenth century, English, Dutch, and French explorers appeared. Since there undoubtedly was a 'New World', they founded 'New France', 'New England', 'Nova Scotia', 'New Brunswick', 'New Amsterdam' (later New York), and 'New Grenada' alongside the more substantial New Spain. The French expeditions included that led in 1524 by the Florentine Giovanni da Verrazano on behalf of Francis I, and those of Jacques Cartier, who in 1536 discovered the St Lawrence river.

New resources

Gold, of course, was the main focus of human greed. It was not the only motive for exploration: there was also intense curiosity, backed by a taste for risk and adventure, as well as missionary zeal. But gold, and silver from Peru, played a fundamental role in the story. Growing production of these two precious metals led to a fall in their price – and a consequent rise in the relative price of everything else. Between 1501 and 1525, for instance, prices in Spain rose by 50 per cent – a phenomenon which contemporaries found both alarming and incomprehensible. The result was quasi-paralysis in the Spanish economy.

Between 1493 and 1520, 5,800 kg of gold and 47,000 kg of silver were produced. The years 1521–44 produced 7,660 kg of gold and 90,000 kg of silver, and by 1545–60 production had risen to 8,510 kg and 311,600 kg respectively.

The New World supplied Europe with other products which in some cases formed habits hitherto unknown. A few of them remained for many years mere curiosities in European eyes; but turkeys, tomatoes, kidney or bush beans, pineapples, vanilla, and quinine became very important. Tobacco began to be grown in Castile from 1519 onwards. Potatoes, from Peru and Chile, were brought to Spain in 1535 and to Britain in 1585; they were known as 'car-touffles' (little truffles) – hence their German name, *Kartoffeln*. Chocolate became popular in Europe, as did sweetcorn, in the seventeenth century; in the eighteenth, the cultivated strawberry was produced from two transatlantic strains. Conversely, Europe introduced into the New World sheep and cattle, and draught animals such as the horse, the donkey, and the mule. Europe also infected the Americas with diseases previously unknown there and brought back a number of parasites. There thus appeared in Europe phylloxera, mildew, oidium, and the notorious Colorado beetle.

Humanity and relativity

Europeans also discovered that the New World was quite densely populated – that it possessed two highly developed civilizations, each remote and quite cut off from the other. In sixteenth-century Mexico there were the Aztecs and the Mayas; in Peru, the Incas.

Elsewhere, the inhabitants were more primitive. Yet, as Charles-André Julien has pointed out, Europeans were neither totally surprised nor wholly fascinated by what they found. A number of medieval legends, including that of St Brendan, had prepared them for the shock of discovery and muted their excitement in advance. The earliest Spanish navigators had been discreet about what they had seen; but later stories distorted the picture – as did hasty judgements. This makes still more remarkable the ideas about Europe and the New World expressed by Michel de Montaigne (1533–92). What is striking about this cool, inquisitive, dispassionate observer of humanity is his sense of relativity.

People being what they were, and climate and society acting upon them, Montaigne wrote that 'The diversity of manners from one nation to another affects me only with the pleasure of variety.' In the same essay, he trounced the French 'tourist': 'I am ashamed to see our people besotted by such foolish ill-humour as to be aghast at ways which are foreign to them: they seem to be out of their element as soon as they are outside their village. Wherever they go, they cleave to their own habits and abominate those of others.' Then came a further sentence, eloquent and chilling: 'So many towns destroyed, so many nations exterminated, so many millions of people put to the sword, and the richest, most beautiful part of the world laid waste – for the sake of trade in pearls and pepper!' (*Essays*, Book III, Chapter 9).

There yet remained one fundamental purpose: to convert these alien peoples. The Spanish missionary St Francis Xavier (1506–52), a friend of Ignatius de Loyola, founder of the Society of Jesus, went to Goa, Malacca, the Moluccas, and Japan, but was forbidden to enter China. In the Americas, missionary activity was more widespread and successful.

Bishoprics were created; religious orders established themselves and vied for converts.

Rivalry, indeed, was a feature of colonization for four centuries, setting European states against each other, and leading to so many wars and so much violence that Europe's colonial legacy became one of the greatest obstacles to its unity. Furthermore, the massacres described so poignantly by Bartolomé de Las Casas, the slave trade, slavery, and pillage all weigh very heavily on the negative side of the scales.

Yet, all the same, the colonial exploration did open Europeans' eyes – not only to peoples and products hitherto unknown, but also to a new world, or a better sense of the whole world's geography.

Geography

Only very gradually were the explorers' discoveries collated to form a new map of the world. It was a long time before people realized that the 'Cathay' described by Marco Polo in the thirteenth century was none other than the China now reached by the Portuguese. Was Aristotle still a reliable guide? He had divided the world into two parts: the West, or Europe, and the East, or Asia, with Greece enjoying the advantages of both. This distinction was maintained throughout the Middle Ages. Now, however, with the development of climatic theories, emphasis began to be placed on the contrast between North and South. Jean Bodin's *Six livres de la République* included the most advanced study of climatic influence to be undertaken until Montesquieu in the eighteenth century. Bodin distinguished between three climatic zones: the North, the South, and the Temperate zone between them. Each, he believed, produced a characteristic type of people.

EUROPE CONFRONTS THE TURKS

The Ottoman Conquest

The Osmanlis or Ottomans, who took their name from their first leader Osman or Othoman I (1259–1326), originated in Asia Minor, near the borders of what was left of Byzantium. In religion, they were Sunni Muslims.

Before capturing Constantinople (later Istanbul) in 1453, they had already overrun Bulgaria, Serbia, Bosnia, Thrace (including Adrianople, later Edreneh), and part of Greece. At the same time they also seized Anatolia. By the sixteenth century, their pressure was felt all round the Mediterranean. Their greatest Sultans, like Selim I (who reigned from 1512 to 1520) and Suleiman II (called by Europeans 'The Magnificent'), increased their conquests by both force of arms and diplomacy. As well as Syria and Egypt, and North Africa as far as the Eastern borders of Morocco, they captured a number of islands: Lesbos (from the Genoese), Euboea (from the Venetians), Rhodes (from the Knights of St John) in 1522, and, in 1570–71, Cyprus. For a short time, the Turkish fleet occupied Otranto. On the mainland, the Turkish army with its elite 'Janissaries' defeated and killed the last Hungarian king, Lewis II, at the Battle of Mohacs in 1526. In 1529 the Turks besieged Vienna. Their 'Sipahi' cavalry ravaged Bavaria and Moravia. Was Vienna to suffer the fate of Constantinople? In René Grousset's words, 'What was at stake was Europe, body and soul.'

Vienna survived the siege. But in 1541 Suleiman recaptured the Hungarian capital Buda, and in 1543 Gran, turning their cathedrals into mosques. At that time, he was in alliance with Francis I against Charles V and the Duke of Savoy – enabling him to pillage Nice, while the port of Toulon was made available to his corsairs. One of the latter, Khair-ed-din Barbarossa (who was by birth a Greek from Lesbos) captured Tunis and established a pirate state in Algiers. Both cities remained in Turkish hands despite the efforts of Charles V and, earlier, Cardinal Francisco Ximines de Cisneros.

Not until the great naval victory of Lepanto (in the Gulf of Corinth some 160 kilometres west of Athens) when, on 7 October 1571, the combined strength of Venice, Spain, and the Pope defeated the fleet of Selim II, Suleiman's successor, did the Ottomans begin slowly to be repulsed. And they never lost Istanbul.

'Europe' as a factor against the Turks

There were several possible reactions to the Turkish threat. They ranged from all-out resistance, united in a crusade, through forms of compromise, to the actual use of Turkish forces in conflicts between European states. And what were the Turks themselves?

Heathen barbarians? Or a model Empire, whose powerful organization Europe would do well to copy? Should they be resisted at all costs? Or should Europeans flee before them to those new worlds now opening up to the colonists? 'Poor Europe,' wrote Pierre de Ronsard (1524–85) in his poem '*Les îles fortunées*' (1553). Should it be abandoned to its fate? Aeneas Silvius Piccolomini, later Pope Pius II, called for a crusade by 'Europe' against the Turks, both before and during his pontificate. That the Turks were in Constantinople meant, for him, that they were 'in Europe, in our country, in our own house, in our domain'. These mournful words expressed the conviction – repeated here and there since the time of Charlemagne – that Christendom, which Aeneas Silvius called 'the Christian Community', *Christiana communitas*, was Europe. '*Christianus orbis Europam omnem tenet*' – 'the Christian world comprises all of Europe': so wrote Cardinal John Bessarion (1395–1472), an indirect victim of the Turks. A Greek cleric, Bishop of Nicea, he was commissioned by the last Byzantine Emperors to negotiate reconciliation between the two Christian Churches; but when the Pope made him a Cardinal, the Greek clergy rejected him. The Turkish capture of Constantinople forced him to remain in the West, where he played an important part in the development of Platonism.

The Italian poet Ludovico Ariosto (1474–1533) cursed the fact that 'the filthy Turk is occupying Constantinople, the finest part of the world'. Tasso saw the struggle against the Turks as that of Europe against Asia

(Canto 11, 24). The great Portuguese poet Luis de Camoens wrote in the *Lusiads* of 'poor Europe' at war with 'the ferocious Ottoman'. Against the Turks, declared the poet Battista da Mantua (Giambattista Spagnoli), 'we are all one nation, that of Christ,' and he called for a union of 'all the peoples of Europe', of 'magnanimous Europe'. Erasmus himself called for a crusade, both in his *Praise of Folly* and in *De bello Turcis inferendo* (*Of the war to be fought against the Turks*), a work in which he unequivocally identified Europe with Christendom. The Spanish scholar and educationist Juan Luis Vives (Ludoricus Vives) did the same in his *De conditione vitae Christianorum sub Turca* (*Of the condition of life of Christians under Turkish rule*), and in other works where he referred to the 'nations of Europe'. He even wrote a book whose title included the word 'Europe' – a novelty at the time. This was *De Europae statu ac tumultibus* (*Of Europe's situation and disorders*).

Vives, who was born in Valencia in 1492, became a professor at Louvain, then at Oxford, and finally settled in Bruges. He died in 1540. Erasmus was one of his close friends. In another of his works, Vives wrote:

> We occupy, from Gades to the Ister [i.e. from Cadiz to the Danube], a region which stretches between the two seas: powerful and valiant Europe. There, if we were united, we should not only be equal to Turkey, but stronger than all Asia. This is shown by the genius and the courage of the nations, and taught by the effect of their exploits. Never, in fact, has Asia been able to resist even the moderate strength of Europe.

But the proposed crusade did not take place; and the sultan scorned the appeal of Pius II that he should become a Christian convert. What was more, Francis I formed his unprecedented and much deplored alliance with the Turks against a Christian sovereign, his great enemy Charles V. It was a proof that the concept of Christendom was in irremediable decline.

During the second half of the sixteenth century, many fervent Christians saw Charles V and his two successors – Ferdinand, the Austrian Habsburg and Philip II, the Spanish Habsburg – as the great hopes for Christendom. One of them, wrote Briezio in his *Mappamundi Historica* (1558), 'will without doubt be the master of all Europe'. It was they, at all events, who were fighting to the death on the Danube and its tributary the Save, as well as in the Mediterranean.

Since a crusade was out of the question, who could withstand the

Turks except Germany, the valiant survivor of the catastrophe, and heir to what was left of the Empire? 'From such immensity we have been reduced to one unique constituent part of Europe – Germany,' wrote the German historian and diplomatist Johannes Sleidanus (Johann Phillipson) in 1556. In the eyes of Martin Luther, the decadence of Europe was due to Papal idolatry – a Mediterranean weakness. For another prophet of doom, Peucer, there was only one possible saviour: the Emperor, defender of the West.

In the event, it was not the Emperor but his Spanish cousin who put a stop to the Turkish advance. In 1559, indeed, when the Emperor negotiated a truce, Philip II of Spain rejected it in the name of 'Christendom'. The Holy League formed by Pius V in 1590, the *foedus perpetuum*, was only a pale reflection of the great crusade proposed by Pius II a century earlier. Even the victory at Lepanto in 1571 was followed by further Ottoman successes.

But as Fernand Braudel wrote in his celebrated study, *La Mediterranée et le monde méditerranéen à l'époque de Philippe II*, 'the magic spell of Turkish power was broken'; and, at least on the sea, a turning-point had been reached. From now on, the Turks were on the defensive.

The impression left by these years of sad confusion is that the 'Turkish terror' failed to enhance the idea of Europe. Proud visions of *Europa nostra* had faded: *misera Europa* was an apter slogan now. At odds with each other, incapable of forming a united front, a *concordia* or *congregatio* against the Turks, Europeans only just escaped the worst of dangers; and not all of them did so escape. As James Brown Scott, the editor of Hugo Grotius, put it, 'Europe' in Grotius's definition had shrunk to a small area bordered on the south-east by the Ottoman frontier and on the north by the Western frontier of Poland – which, like Muscovy, was on the outside. Indeed, although writing at the beginning of the seventeenth century, Grotius mentioned Europe only once in his great treatise on international law, *De Jure Belli et Pacis*.

The Turkish model

That Europe, divided and fearful, made a pitiful contrast with Turkey. True, the Turks were regarded by Europeans as 'the beast of the Orient'; but a whole branch of European literature now began to celebrate their virtues and their successes, and to hold them up as an example to be followed. A typical writer in this tradition was Trajano Boccalini (1556–1613), whose main work was the satirical *Ragguagli di Parnaso* (*News of Parnassus*).

Boccalini was disenchanted, if not thoroughly despairing: he saw the world as 'corrupt' and its sovereigns as 'scoundrels' – which, among other things, led him to prefer a republican regime. What was more, he could not believe that the situation would improve. 'Mankind's true mother country,' he wrote, 'is a free city' – such as Venice, where he retired. But European sovereigns did their best to prevent the triumph of freedom: they would even league together against it. Failing liberty, there should at least be a measure of efficiency afforded by 'reasons of state'. In all the world, only Turkey had managed to achieve this. This 'Turkophilia' or even 'Turkomania' grew even stronger in the seventeenth century, thanks in part to travellers' tales. Of these, the most famous was Sir John Chardin's *Travels in Persia and the East Indies*, published in three volumes between 1686 and 1711.

Was Turkey, then, gradually being assimilated into Europe? The decline of Christianity might have made it possible, from the eighteenth century onwards. But the birth of nationalism among the Christian countries of the Balkans delayed such assimilation, and encouraged resistance against it, on both sides. Not until the nationalist revolution of Kemal Ataturk in 1919 did Turkey really aspire to European status.

FOUR INNOVATORS: MACHIAVELLI, ERASMUS, LEONARDO, AND LUTHER

Four men may perhaps be singled out as representatives of the different facets of a century both extraordinarily rich and infinitely complex. One was a 'positivist' student of political science and the father of modern Realpolitik: Niccolò Machiavelli. The second, Erasmus of Rotterdam, was the best known intellectual of his time, a man of culture and tolerance who in some respects prefigured Voltaire two centuries later. The third, Leonardo da Vinci, was an artist of genius who was also a great scholar and technician. The fourth, Martin Luther, the great reformer of the Church, was a man of passion and torment, the very opposite of Erasmus.

Niccolò Machiavelli

Niccolò Machiavelli is one of the best known and least understood figures in Italian history.

In common parlance, the word 'Machiavellian' implies deceitful ruses, dishonest or cruel means held to be justified by the ends, cynical realism for the benefit of the Prince. *Il Principe* (*The Prince*), was indeed Machiavelli's most important book. But its realism was the foundation of modern political science, based not on theology but on its author's experience as a senior official. Politically, he remained extremely hostile to both the clergy and the Pope.

Machiavelli was born in Florence into an ancient bourgeois family that was probably a member of the corporation of notaries: it was rich and cultivated, but unpopular among the debtors and the poor. Niccolò's father, a lawyer and financial specialist, and his mother, who also came of an old Florentine family, gave the boy a thorough education. His special subject was law. This was the period of Lorenzo de' Medici, whom Niccolò's father served, but without great enthusiasm.

After Lorenzo's death in 1492, his successor Pietro de' Medici was unable to withstand the invading army of King Charles VIII of France, and was deposed by a popular revolt in 1494. For four years, Florence was ruled by a Dominican friar, Girolamo Savonarola (1452–98), who established a fanatically puritan populist republic; condemned as a heretic by the Pope, he was hanged and burnt in 1498. It was then, in the more moderate republic which followed Savonarola's regime, that Machiavelli became secretary of the chancellery. He was twenty-nine years old, and deeply versed in Latin and Greek historians such as Livy and Polybius, as well as in Petrarch, Dante, and others.

His work gave him valuable practical experience. He was involved above all in foreign affairs – in the war between Florence and Pisa, and in the attacks on Italy by the kings of France, Charles VIII, and Louis XII who in 1499–1500 seized Milan and captured its ruler, Duke Lodovico Sforza ('il Moro'). Machiavelli came to know Pope Alexander VI and his son Cesare Borgia, who tried by wholly cynical means to secure a principality in the Romagna. His other acquaintances included the King of France, Louis XII, Ferdinand of Aragon, Pope Julius II, Cardinal della Rovere, and the Emperor Maximilian. He visited all the Italian republics, went as Ambassador to Southern

Germany, travelled to France, and was appointed in 1512 as Ambassador to Ferdinand of Aragon and Castile.

In 1512, the Papal coalition defeated the Florentine militia that Machiavelli had organized. The supporters of the Medici seized power, and Machiavelli, with no job and scant resources, retired to his small property at San Casciano near Florence, where his only occupation was writing. It was there that he composed *The Prince and his Discourses on the First Decade of Titus Livius*. Later, however, he took paid work again, this time for his former enemies the Medici. For Cardinal Giulio de' Medici he wrote a *Discourse on the Reform of the State of Florence*, followed in 1520–5 by the eight books of his *Florentine History*.

Only after the Battle of Pavia in 1525, when Charles V crushed Francis I's armies and made the French king prisoner, was Machiavelli once more called upon to exert his diplomatic skill. He conducted negotiations in Rome, and the Pope, France, Venice, Milan, and Florence formed a league against the Emperor under an agreement reached in Cognac in 1526. This, however, was a failure: in May 1527, the Imperial forces seized Rome and sacked the city, whereupon the popular party in Florence overthrew the Medici and established a republic. Machiavelli, who was absent at the time, returned in the hope of securing office; but he was soon taken ill, and died on 22 June 1527, at the age of fifty-eight.

Machiavelli's originality lay not in his career, which was by no means unusual for that turbulent period, but in the quality of his thought. He totally separated politics from metaphysics. In this respect he was the precursor of positivist political science and of the so-called 'secular idea'. He was not anti-religious, but strongly anti-clerical, detesting Papal power, which he saw as the main source of Italy's suffering. He was also a precursor of Italian patriotism: he advocated a unified or federal Italy, not a kingdom like France or England, but a republic with the possibility of establishing, at times of extreme danger, a temporary dictatorship like that of republican Rome. He had few illusions; but in the face of invasion by France, Aragon, and then Germany, he condemned the Italian city-states' use of mercenaries, who were always ready to change sides if offered enough inducement.

Machiavelli thought in terms of Italy, not Europe. But the methods he proposed could be applied to Europe, and they had the advantage of not asking the impossible. Unlike his English contemporary Sir Thomas

More (1478–1535), author of *Utopia* or *Of the Beste State of a Publique Weal, and of the New Yle, called Utopia* (1516), he based his work on his experience of real life. As another great English writer, Francis Bacon, remarked: 'We are much beholden to Machiavel and others, that write what men do, and not what they ought to do.'

Desiderius Erasmus

Desiderius Erasmus, the most international, the most European of the men of his time, was born in Rotterdam in about 1466, the illegitimate son of a priest. His parents died young, and at the age of nine he was sent to Dutch schools, first at Deventer, then at Hertogenbosch. In 1487–8 he spent some time in an Augustinian house, St Gregory's at Steyn, and in 1492 was ordained a priest. He was no zealot: he preferred reading to preaching, and had extensive knowledge of the classics. He was highly independent, thoroughly capable, and deeply averse to quarrels and dramatic gestures. His pleasures were culinary, literary, and conversational: he enjoyed the company of sharp minds.

Appointed 'Latin' secretary to the Archbishop of Cambrai, Erasmus lived in Brussels for a time, then had himself sent to the University of Paris to take a doctorate in theology.

Enjoying only a small allowance from the Archbishop – whom he nicknamed an 'anti-patron' – he lived in the College of Montaigu in the University of Paris, but came to dislike it and eventually left. To eke out a living he then began to give lessons to German and English pupils; and in 1499 one of the latter, William Blount, Lord Mountjoy, invited him to England, which was just then recovering from the Wars of the Roses.

Erasmus's brilliance – and his Latin, far superior to that of the universities – won him friends in cultivated society. At Oxford he met scholars who spoke Greek, a language he had never studied. The Prince of Wales, the future Henry VIII, summoned him to Court. He made the acquaintance of Sir Thomas More; of John Colet, founder of St Paul's School and then a teacher at Magdalen, Oxford, and a great opponent of scholasticism; and of John Fisher, Chancellor of the University of Cambridge. England, it has been said, was then 'convalescing from the Middle Ages'; and Erasmus sang its praises.

He travelled elsewhere, in Italy and France and again in England, conversing in Latin but forming very few permanent ties. Neither music nor painting was among his interests: he knew nothing of Raphael, Michelangelo, or Leonardo da Vinci. He was essentially a bibliophile, and spent long hours in the Aldine Press in Venice and in Johannes Frobenius's printing office in Basle.

Erasmus knew all the great men of his age, and his own reputation was universal. In 1519, Martin Luther (who at that time had not quarrelled with him) wrote in a letter: 'Is there a corner of the world where the name of Erasmus is not renowned?' Francis I proposed that he should become director of the Collège de France, which the King had founded as a rival to the University. Jealous of his freedom, Erasmus refused. Perhaps his favourite places in Europe were Italy (he took his doctorate in theology at Bologna in 1506, and spent some time in Venice) and Basle, where he settled in 1521 and died in 1536.

His immense literary output included satires like *The Praise of Folly* or the *Colloquia* (modelled on the silver-age Greek dialogues of Lucian), translations from the Bible and the Fathers of the Church, philosophical and theological works such as his *Diatribe on Free Will*, in which he sought to refute Luther, and also a large number of letters, rich in the humanism of the time. By the end of his life he had some 3,000 correspondents. There are six portraits of him by Hans Holbein, two by Albrecht Dürer, and one by the Flemish painter Quentin Massys.

Leonardo da Vinci

Leonardo da Vinci (1452–1519) was more than a very great painter. A number of his contemporaries achieved the same heights, and many produced far more. There was Sandro Botticelli, eight years his senior; there were younger artists like Michelangelo and Raphael in Italy, or Albrecht Dürer and Hans Holbein in Germany. Earlier, in the Netherlands, there had been the brothers Van Eyck, who, according to Giorgio Vasari, the sixteenth-century art historian, had invented oil painting. And, at the end of the century, there were major schools of Flemish, Dutch, French, and Spanish painting.

What made Leonardo outstanding was that, in André Michel's words, 'he belonged less to the history of art than to the history of human intelligence'. An architect and sculptor, he was also a musician and a poet. Nor was that all. He was a mathematician, an astronomer, a physician, a chemist (for the study of colours), an anatomist who performed dissections, a botanist, a geographer, a geologist, an optician, and finally an engineer who (among many other inventions) envisaged flight in a 'heavier-than-air' machine.

Leonardo was born in 1452 in the village of Vinci, near Florence. The natural son of a notary and a peasant girl, he was given by his father the chance of a thorough education. In 1472, he joined the studio of Andrea del Verrocchio. At first he worked in Florence – not always finishing what he began, because his lively curiosity readily tempted him in other directions. In about 1483, he left Florence for Milan, whose ruler Lodovico Sforza, though a tyrant and ostentatious, was a man of taste and a patron of the arts. Lodovico commissioned from Leonardo an equestrian statue of his father Francesco Sforza.

Accepting the task (though he never completed it), Leonardo also proposed a number of mechanical inventions: war machines, new types of cannon, fireproof ships, roads, bridges, tunnels, aqueducts, etc. It was in Milan, too, in the convent church of Santa Maria delle Grazie, that he completed his famous wall painting of the Last Supper.

The French invasion of Lombardy and the fall of his patron caused Leonardo to leave Milan in 1499, first for Mantua, then for Venice, and finally for Florence again. It was here, between about 1500 and about 1504, that he painted the celebrated portrait of the wife of a Florentine official, known as the 'Mona Lisa' or 'La Gioconda'. Meanwhile, however, his passion for chemical experiments let him down badly when, imitating an antique technique to produce a huge wall painting in the Council Chamber of the Signoria, only the central part was completed, because the colours ran. Discouraged by this setback, Leonardo left Florence in 1505. He spent some time in Milan, which the French had now left; he travelled to Rome to the court of Pope Leo X; then, after Francis I recaptured the city in 1515, Leonardo accepted the French king's invitation to live in France, in the Château of Choux, near Amboise. He spent his last years mainly in scientific pursuits, and he died there in 1519.

More than other encyclopedic Renaissance scholars, and more even than his own compatriot from Modena, Pico della Mirandola (1463–93), who had ventured to write *De omni re scibili* (*On all there is to be known*), Leonardo was the representative of secularized science, freed from scholasticism and based on experiment and calculation. He left more than 5,000 pages of very varied notes in almost indecipherable handwriting, with thousands of sketches of every imaginable kind.

In mathematics, he was above all interested in geometry, and had what Alexandre Koyré has called 'an extraordinary talent for spatial vision'. 'Science for Leonardo,' Koyré continued, 'as for many of his contemporaries, was not for contemplation but for action.' In astronomy, however, contrary to popular belief, Leonardo did not invent the telescope. A disciple of the famous German scholar and philosopher Nicholas of Cusa (1401–64), he nevertheless recognized that the Earth was not the centre of the universe; and he realized that the Moon was made of the same elements as the Earth. 'The moon has no light of itself,' he wrote, 'but so much of it as the sun sees it illuminates.' He very probably believed in the rotation of the Earth: he certainly wrote, on one page of mathematical notes, and in large letters: 'The sun does not move.' Yet on these subjects Leonardo played a far lesser role than an astronomer twenty years his junior, Nicolaus Copernicus (1473–1543). Copernicus knew the work of Nicholas of Cusa, but not that of Leonardo.

It was in physics, in fact, that Leonardo's contribution was the most striking and original. He was, to quote Koyré once more, 'an unparalleled technological genius'. His drawings show how he derived from technical experimentation a real 'science of mechanics'. He had an extraordinary understanding of simple machinery, and under the influence of Nicholas of Cusa he studied dynamics. He did not discover the law of falling objects or the principle of inertia: but he did formulate, more or less precisely, the principle that 'action and reaction are equal and opposite'. In chemistry, quite naturally, he concerned himself mainly with the composition of pigments for painting.

But his wide-ranging intellect went still further afield. He studied physical geography, investigating erosion and alluvial deposits in lakes and seas. He was deeply versed in anatomy, and demonstrated the similarities between human and animal bone structure. He rediscovered what the Greeks had known, but had since been forgotten, about the true origin of fossils. He made countless meticulous drawings of animals and plants. He took a keen interest in botany and in meteorology. He epitomized, in fact, the passion for discovery which marked sixteenth-century Europe, and he contributed to that flowering of human intelligence which made the Renaissance so different from earlier periods and other civilizations.

Martin Luther

Of all these great innovators, the most outstanding – for his achievements, his fiery nature, his wide-ranging intellect, and his overwhelming faith – was surely Martin Luther. That great tortured soul succeeded where John Wyclif and John Huss had both failed in varying degrees: he brought about, in the Reformation, the reform of the Church which for three centuries had been debated but never achieved. He was not, of course, alone. John Calvin and Ulrich Zwingli played their part; the Church of England reformed itself. And there was a reaction – the so-called Counter-Reformation, which might be better termed the Catholic Reform.

Martin Luther's was an extraordinary career. He was born, probably in 1483, in the small town of Eisleben in Saxony. His childhood was poverty-stricken and sad. His father was a slate miner, his mother a superstitious housewife. At the age of fourteen, he was sent to school at Magdeburg and then to Eisenach: he was so poor that he was forced to beg and sing in the streets. In 1501, aged eighteen, he enrolled at the University of Erfurt, receiving his first degree in 1503 and his doctorate two years later. In that year, 1505, he entered an Augustinian monastic house at Erfurt, where he strictly and piously observed the rule. But he was continually tormented by fear of Hell. Could he hope for salvation by pious works, by daily Masses, by ascetic self-denial? He remained deeply unsure.

The Vicar-General of the German Augustinians, Staupitz, singled Luther out and persuaded him to study theology at the new University of Wittenberg, established in 1502 by the Elector of Saxony, Frederick the Wise. Staupitz himself was a teacher there. In 1512, Luther received his doctorate in theology.

Two years earlier, however, he had undergone a new and demoralizing crisis. He had been sent to Rome, where he had hoped to find 'the living centre of Christendom'. But what did he see? 'The Rome of the Borgias, recently become the Rome of Pope Julius II.' The Borgia Pope Alexander VI had led a life of debauchery and crime. His successor Julius II was less concerned with Christianity than with politics and war. Luther was appalled to see him, booted and helmeted, at the head of his troops.

As Lucien Febvre wrote: 'When in desperation Luther fled this accursed Babylon with its courtesans, its bravi, its ruffians, its simoniac clergy and its cardinals without morality or faith, he returned to his native Germany with his heart full of inexorable hatred for the Great Whore.'

It was after that visit, probably in 1512, that Luther made his 'great discovery'. While going round his Wittenberg monastery, he had what seemed to him to be a divine revelation. At first in silence, and then in public from 1517 onwards, he began to consider himself a genuine new apostle. In brief, he seized upon a sentence in St Paul's Epistle to the Romans (III.28): 'Therefore we conclude that a man is justified by faith without the deeds of the law.'

'The deeds of the law' were generally thought to be the formal and external practices of the Jews, which St Paul held were not for Christians. This definition, declared Luther, was a mistake. Mankind was so wretched and God so all-powerful that all human actions, however good they might be, remained tainted by sin. God alone could 'justify' people – that is, lead them to salvation. The sign that one had been chosen to be 'justified' was *faith*, implicit faith, which consisted in being with God. Hence Luther's paradoxical precept, schematizing the notion of justification by faith alone: *Pecca fortiter sed crede fortius*, 'Sin mightily, but believe more mightily still.' Nothing could be further from rationalism – even from that of St Thomas Aquinas, who sought to establish, in one vast synthesis, perfect harmony between reason and faith. It seems, incidentally, that Luther had never studied Aquinas, the 'angelic doctor'.

Together with his hatred for the corruption of Rome, this 'discovery' led to Luther's expulsion from the Catholic Church. He was denounced as a heretic and a schismatic. The break began on 31 October 1517, when Luther nailed to the door of the castle chapel in Wittenberg his famous Ninety-five Propositions. They were directed against a particular scandalous abuse, the sale of 'indulgences' by the Princes of the Church to shorten their purchasers' time in Purgatory. With this, Luther rapidly became famous – and subject to threats. He took the risk of going to justify his position before the Emperor Charles V and the Papal Legate at the imperial Diet in Worms in 1521. He refused to give way on any point: he stood his ground and went even further, advocating the free study of the Bible instead of its interpretation along compulsory lines, arbitrarily fixed by the Church. Too popular to be imprisoned, Luther was placed under a form of house arrest in the castle of Wartburg in the Thüringer Wald mountains. It was there that he set about translating the Bible into German – an action of the first importance for the history of Germany, since this was the first great literary text in modern German.

Luther was never a man of politics. Convinced that his ideas were the truth, he expounded them orally and in writing, often with an excessive polemical bluntness in total contrast to Erasmus, and not at all to his delicate taste. In 1525, indeed, Erasmus criticized Luther's views in a treatise, *De Libero Arbitrio* (*Of Free Will*), to which Luther heatedly replied with *De Servo Arbitrio* (*Of Will Enslaved*).

That same year saw the outbreak in Germany of a widespread peasants' revolt. It was provoked by the fact that the peasantry, unlike the townspeople, who enjoyed wealth and often freedom, were still very poor and still dominated by the Princes. But instead of leading this social rebellion, whose activists he admired, Luther condemned it. Also in 1525, he married Catherine von Bora, a young Cistercian nun who with eight companions had fled the cloister under the influence of his teaching. He died in 1546, at his birthplace of Eisleben, aged sixty-three, just when the Catholic Church was convening the Council of Trent.

HUMANISM AS A FACTOR FOR UNITY

The universities, which in the thirteenth and fourteenth centuries had flourished, began in the fifteenth century to decline, turning more and more to scholasticism. This tended to replace creative thought by a set of pre-ordained formulae, ever more subtle but ever less original. Scholasticism, in fact, was traditional thinking fossilized.

There were two strains to such thinking: 'realist' and 'nominalist'. The 'realists', in the tradition of Aristotle and St Thomas Aquinas, believed that concepts, categories, and generalizations had an objective existence. For them, all human beings belonged to the category 'humanity', and therefore resembled each other very much more than any resembled members of another category – animals, for instance. By contrast, 'nominalists' such as the Scottish Duns Scotus (c.1266–1308) or the English William of Ockham (c.1285–1347) believed that such 'archetypes' did not exist: they were simply names that were given, for convenience's sake, to a large number of beings. Only each individual being was real.

The later disciples of both schools of thought turned their theses into fixed doctrine; and the human spirit usually rejects such fossilization. Neither 'realism' nor 'nominalism' could explain the objective world. There therefore arose a powerful reaction against scholasticism. This was known as humanism.

Humanism was not a doctrine, but an attitude of mind. It did not reject doctrine as such, but it made humanity, not abstract ideas, the main focus of reflection. What was the nature of humanity? What was its place in the universe? What was its origin? What was its destiny? Instead of giving ready-made dogmatic answers to such questions, the humanists studied the problems they raised.

Humanism was not necessarily un-Christian. Erasmus, its finest sixteenth-century exemplar, was a Christian himself. But some forms of humanism might well be anti-religious, while others could be simply secular – drawing a distinction, that is, between religious thought and human reason. Whereas scholasticism had been a closed *system*, commenting on itself in 'glosses', and essentially going round in circles, humanism was an open *method*, constantly subject to improvement. Scholasticism believed that in some respects perfection had been attained. Humanism introduced the idea of indefinite progress. It was a break with a long-established tradition in human thought.

What is significant, moreover, is that sixteenth-century humanism was a purely European phenomenon, and pan-European at that.

The birthplace of the movement, which set a new 'intelligentsia' against the university scholastics, was Italy. One of its precursors was the great poet Petrarch, or Francesco Petrarca (1304–74). Born in Arezzo, he went with his parents to Avignon at the age of eight, studied at Montpellier, was ordained but lived a secular life, travelled in Germany, France, Flanders, and Italy, was a friend of Dante, and nursed a hopeless love for the Laura of his sonnets, who died of the plague in 1348. Ernest Renan and Jacob Burckhardt both regarded him, in Burckhardt's words, as 'one of the first truly modern men'. One aspect of that modernity, paradoxically, was a return to classical Latin and to the purity of Cicero or Horace. Research into Latin antiquity was indeed a critical element in Renaissance humanism, which added to well-known texts, already encumbered with 'glosses', newly recovered originals, including inscriptions now deciphered by the growing study of epigraphy.

Following Petrarch, another Italian, Lorenzo Valla (c.1407–57), continued the 'recovery' of classical Latin. Erasmus both admired and edited his work. But Greek, too, was enjoying a revival, partly owing to attempts at reconciliation between Rome and the Byzantines, which in the religious sphere came to nothing.

Florentine humanism continued to develop with Marsilio Ficino (1433–99), the translator of Plato, and Pico della Mirandola (1463–93), one of whose works sought to combine the teachings of Plato and Aristotle. From Italy, moreover, humanism spread in all directions, including the Rhine Valley and England.

In England, whose universities had not suffered the decadence of their Continental counterparts, Oxford in particular welcomed humanistic teaching. King Henry VIII (1509–47) was at once a Latinist, a theologian, and a musician; and his children wrote in both Latin and French. It was thanks to Henry that Greek and Hebrew were taught at Cambridge. The king's chancellor, Thomas More, and his daughter, the future Queen Elizabeth, both spoke classical languages. In Spain, apart from the so-called 'Alcala group', humanism progressed only slowly at the beginning of the sixteenth century. But the 'Alcala Bible', published by the Alcala de Henares University set up by Cardinal Ximenes in 1510, evinced careful study of Greek and Hebrew.

In France, Italian humanism was introduced mainly by a native of Savoy, Guillaume Fichet (1433–82). A Northern Frenchman, Lefèvre d'Etaples (c.1450–1536), also played an important role: although no theologian, he did much to restore ancient Greek and the true texts of Aristotle. And it was a Parisian, Guillaume Budé (1467–1540), who persuaded Francis I to found what became the Collège de France. In 1503, Lefèvre d'Etaples wrote of French students: 'They are giving up philosophy and dialectic in droves, and – put off by the barbarity of the philosophers – are hurrying to read grammarians and poets.'

In 1517, a 'College of the Three Languages' (Latin, Greek, and Hebrew) was set up in Louvain. University chairs of Greek and Hebrew were founded in Heidelberg, Mainz, Tübingen, and Colmar; and in Rome Pope Leo X (1513–21) founded a 'College of Wisdom' where Hellenists were trained. Nevertheless, according to Pierre Chaunu, 40 per cent of Europe's humanists were living in Italy at the beginning of the sixteenth century. As Roland Mousnier wrote, 'Italy set the fashion for the whole of Europe.'

The curiosity, energy, and enthusiasm of classical and humanist scholars were evident in every field. In art, Gothic was replaced by Renaissance styles based on 'classical' models.

Literature imitated the poems and other forms used in classical antiquity. Science adopted empirical observation in medicine and astronomy; and the social sciences developed. All this caused tremors in a world which until about 1500 had seemed unchanging and stable.

THE REFORMATION AND *CUJUS REGIO, EJUS RELIGIO*

The reform of the Church, so long awaited and desired, finally took place in the sixteenth century. We know it as 'the Reformation'; but 'the Reformations' would be a more appropriate term, since the 'Protestants' formed many Churches with many contrasting views. There was also, in response to these dissident movements, a Catholic Counter-Reformation which was a great reform movement itself. Altogether, the century saw an intense and creative spiritual adventure. What concerns us here is the way in which the reform movements served to consolidate Europe's nation-states. In fact, on the Protestant as on the Catholic side, in a world where tolerance – despite Erasmus – was virtually unknown, the final result was to apply the principle that nations should normally follow the religion professed by their sovereigns: *Cujus regio, ejus religio*. It nevertheless began to be accepted that individuals might have the right to emigrate to a country which practised the religion of their choice.

The Lutheran Church

Having rejected the Roman Church and advocated the free study of the Bible, Martin Luther conceded that princes who had been converted to his reformed Church could extend their civil power to authority over Church possessions, 'secularized' for this purpose, and that they could enjoy the supreme right to govern these Churches, of which they were the leading members. Between 1526 and 1538, Luther in fact organized a new Church of Saxony, on which all Lutheran churches later modelled themselves. In it, the princes appointed the pastors and 'superintendents' who were in charge of the various congregations; and these churchmen were allowed to marry. The cult of the Virgin and of the saints was abolished, as was their representation in painting and sculpture. Only two sacraments were maintained: Baptism and the Eucharist, the only services instituted by Christ Himself. Mass was celebrated on Sundays, in the language of the country, but with a simplified liturgy.

Often out of conviction, but sometimes for selfish or political reasons, a large number of princes embraced the new Lutheran Church. Its adherents came, as Roland Mousnier pointed out, from all social classes. In addition to the Elector of Saxony, they included the Landgrave of Hesse and the Grand Master of the Teutonic Order. They were followed by the Swedes, in revolt against Denmark (1523-9), and then, after its defeat, by the Danes themselves (1530-5). There were also many Lutherans in the Low Countries.

The Emperor Charles V, the 'Catholic King' of Spain, did his best to re-establish Catholic bishops in Germany, and to restore their 'secularized' possessions. The Protestant princes joined together in the 1531 Schmalkald League, named after the town in Prussia where it was founded; and they further formed an alliance with King Francis I of France. In 1539, the princes of Württemberg and Brandenburg also became Protestant. In the end, Charles V had to grant Lutheranism official recognition. This he did at the Peace of Augsburg in 1555, where the principle of *Cujus regio, ejus religio* was effectively applied. Two thirds of Germany remained Lutheran, including part of Westphalia and the Rhineland. Charles V, weary of his immense power and responsibilities, then abdicated, leaving Austria and the Empire to his brother Ferdinand, and his possessions in Spain, the Low Countries, Italy, and the New World to his son, Philip II.

Zwingli

Many people, however, regarded Luther as too moderate. The very continuation of an organized Church seemed to them to contradict the principle of free study of the Bible. One such dissident was Ulrich Zwingli (1484-1531), a Swiss priest officiating in Zürich. After having followed Luther for a time, he at length rejected all the sacraments, and gave each Church a democratic structure of its own. Zürich, Basle, and Berne adopted his teaching. But freedom to interpret texts individually led to a proliferation of opinions, sects, and quarrels.

John Calvin

It was against this background that John Calvin appeared. Born in 1509 at Noyon in Picardy, he came of a middle-class family and studied at the universities of Paris, Orléans, and Bourges, learning among other things Greek and Hebrew. In 1534 he was converted to Lutheranism, and fled from France: King Francis I, after some hesitation owing to his sister, Marguérite of Navarre, who protected the Protestants, had finally issued an edict ordering heretics to be exterminated. Calvin's escape took him through Strasbourg to Basle, where he published the *Christianae Religionis Institutio*, with a preface exhorting Francis I to support the Reform movement. Like Luther, Calvin believed that 'tradition' – the authoritarian interpretation of the Bible by the Roman Church – should be rejected.

Scripture alone should be the guide. Only Divine Grace, which was all-powerful, could save mankind. Calvin preached 'justification by faith', condemned certain sacraments, advocated marriage for priests, and called for services to be conducted in the vernacular.

In 1541, his *Institutio* was published in a French translation as *L'Institution chrétienne*, and became one of the classics of French literature.

Calvin differed from Luther in rejecting the doctrine of Christ's 'real presence' in the bread and wine of the Eucharist. More than Luther, above all, he believed in predestination. God was so powerful that He could not be bound by prescience. 'For Calvin,' wrote Roland Mousnier, 'God is free. What He foresees is not identical with what He wishes for all eternity. He chooses those to whom He will give eternal life, or condemns them, as He desires. His will is irresistible: no one can stand against it.' In Calvin's view, the Church must not tolerate error. But it was not subject to the state.

From 1541 until his death in 1564, Calvin lived in Geneva – which became, it has been said, 'a Calvinist Rome'. He established there a College for the training of pastors, headed by the Burgundian Theodore de Bèze. After passing their examination, its pupils had to be elected by the people. A consistory of pastors elected by their colleagues superintended the citizens and could if necessary punish them. This was the fate of the physician Michael Servetus, a heretic accused of denying the Trinity: he was burned in 1553. Despite its severity,

Calvinism was strongly imbued with social and democratic elements. But Calvin in no way condemned capitalism.

Calvinism spread in Scotland (with the Presbyterian movement), in the Low Countries, in Bohemia, Hungary, and Poland. It even found support in France, from several members of the nobility.

France and the 'Wars of Religion'

From 1559 to 1598, France was the scene of the Wars of Religion – a bitter and ferocious conflict marked by some atrocious episodes, of which the most notorious was the 'Massacre of St Bartholomew' ordered by King Charles IX and his mother Catherine de' Medici. On that occasion, on 24 August 1572, on St Bartholomew's Eve, most of the Protestants who were in Paris for the wedding of Henry of Navarre and Marguérite de Valois were done to death.

The last French kings of the Valois dynasty died without leaving male heirs. Their nearest relative was Henry of Bourbon, a descendant of the sixth son of St Louis, their common ancestor, who had died in 1270. Henry was the son of Anthony of Bourbon, who had supported both the reformers and their persecutors, according to his interests at the times. But Henry's mother, Jeanne de Navarre, was a convinced Calvinist; and Henry was the head of the 'Huguenot' party (whose title almost certainly derived from the German *Eidgenossen*, 'bound by oath', and adopted by the Calvinists in Geneva and later in France). In 1589, Henry was proclaimed King by part of the French army. Against him there arose the 'Catholic League' or 'Holy League', led by the nobility and backed by the prosperous middle classes of lawyers, doctors, and merchants. Henry finally won, and became King as Henry IV – at the cost of conversion to Catholicism: hence his dictum that Paris was worth a Mass.

In 1598, he issued the Edict of Nantes, allowing Protestants to practise their religion unhindered and, as a guarantee, to maintain 'places of safety' – fortresses defended by their own militia. These they lost in 1629; and the Edict itself, too tolerant to be tolerated by an absolute monarch, was revoked by Louis XIV in 1685. Some French Protestants remained to face their persecutors: others emigrated. These French 'Huguenots' settled all over Reformation Europe.

Anglicanism

The Reformation in England took a form of its own, far less 'doctrinal' than that of Luther, Zwingli, or Calvin. A simple 'schism' vis-à-vis Rome, establishing a national 'Anglican' Church which maintained the title 'Catholic', it was in effect straight opposition to 'Papism': hence the slogan 'No Popery'.

King Henry VIII, who came to the throne in 1509, at first supported the Oxford humanists, disciples of Erasmus like Thomas More and John Colet, who gave hospitality to the great Continental humanist when he was staying in England. But two very mundane factors soon came into play. On the one hand, Henry sought to divorce his wife Catherine of Aragon and marry Anne Boleyn. When the Pope refused his consent, Henry had the marriage dissolved by a Church tribunal. Later, of course, Anne Boleyn was executed on a charge of adultery, and Henry VIII had four further legitimate wives. But the essential drama took place between 1533 and 1537.

First, Henry published the Act of Supremacy, declaring that the sole authority over the Church in England was no longer the Pope, but the King – and that he would therefore enjoy not only spiritual leadership but also, much more to his taste, disposal of Church property. Parliament gave him its full backing. Those who remained loyal to Rome and refused to accept royal supremacy were executed – among them the unhappy Sir Thomas More. By 1537, the break with the Pope was complete. The Chancellor of the Exchequer, Thomas Cromwell, organized the new Anglican Church. The monasteries were closed, their property confiscated; then they were sold off cheaply by the King, with rather unfavourable economic results. The hierarchy of bishops and clergy was maintained. Both Catholics and Calvinists were persecuted.

The Catholic countries and Cardinal Ximenes de Cisneros

A number of countries remained almost totally Catholic. These were Italy, Spain, Portugal, Bavaria, Habsburg Austria, and Poland, as well as the Archbishoprics of Trier, Mainz, Cologne, and a few other cities, and the southern part of the Low Countries. France, Bohemia, and Hungary retained a majority of Catholics.

In Italy, the Papacy – which had now become exclusively Italian – was able to bypass the Reformation. In Spain, the Church underwent a Catholic Reform. This was due to the outstanding Cardinal Francisco Ximenes de Cisneros (1436–1517). A Castilian who had taught law at the University of Salamanca, Ximenes became a Franciscan, confessor to Queen Isabella, Archbishop of Toledo, and Regent of Castile until the time of Charles V. In 1498 he had founded the University of Alcala de Henares, which under his direction produced the six-volume Polyglot Alcala Bible in Greek, Latin, and Hebrew. The reform undertaken by Ximenes was a major enterprise, at once disciplinary, intellectual, and spiritual. It was a reform of the religious orders, re-establishing the rule of poverty and obliging them to distribute their wealth to poor churches or use it to build hospitals. It was a reform of the clergy, forced to accept greater discipline. It involved the publication of an elementary catechism, the distribution of religious literature, and encouragement for the production of spiritual texts in the vernacular.

In Portugal, it was the religious orders themselves which ensured effective reform – in particular the Franciscans, one of whose branches, notably austere, took the name of 'Capuchins'. Here, some have called the Counter-Reformation an 'ultrareform'.

The Bologna Concordat

In France, anti-Papist reforms were restrained by the fact that the King had less incentive than Henry VIII of England to seize the possessions of the Church. The so-called 'Pragmatic Sanction' of Bourges, in 1438, had been simply a unilateral decision by the King providing for election to confer a number of Church benefices, but reserving to himself the role of 'counsellor'. The Popes had never accepted this situation, which was a potential source of severe disputes. Hence the great importance of the meeting between King Francis I of France and Pope Leo X in Bologna on 11–15 December 1515. There they decided to agree on a Concordat. This, the Bologna Concordat of 1516, revoked the Pragmatic Sanction of Bourges: but the Pope gave the King the right to make appointments to metropolitan churches (archbishoprics), cathedrals (bishoprics), monasteries and priories, in France, the Dauphiné, and the County of Vienne, as well as in Brittany and Provence. The Pope was to accord 'canonical institution' to those appointed, who would have to meet criteria of age, aptitude, etc.

Despite the opposition of the French Parliament and the University of Paris, which found the Bologna Concordat insufficiently 'Gallican', the King enforced it. Since he now had disposal of the benefices, there was no need to confiscate them.

The Council of Trent

It was not enough for the Catholic Church to resist the Protestant Reformation as best it could in the various countries concerned. It also needed to reform itself. This was the task that faced the Council of Trent, in the far north of Italy, in lands belonging to the Habsburgs.

Pope Paul III (Alessandro Farnese) differed from many of his predecessors; not in asceticism – he came of a noble family, and lived like a prince – but in energy. He reigned from 1534 to 1549. His struggle against the Turks, his excommunication of Henry VIII of England, his mediation between Charles V and Francis I, and his commissioning of Michelangelo to build St Peter's in Rome: all these would have sufficed to make his Papacy historic. But he was also the prime mover in the Counter-Reformation or Catholic Reform, in that he approved the foundation of the Society of Jesus in 1540 and convened an ecumenical Council precisely in order to reform the Church. The Council of Trent began in 1545 and continued, with a number of interim suspensions, until 1563. Its aim was to define Catholic doctrine in the face of all those – including some whole countries – who were now contesting it. The Council fulfilled its task. First, it reaffirmed free will: salvation and damnation were not wholly predestined by God, and people could be justified by their works, not only their faith. In this way the Council recommended a traditional, Christian form of humanism which was faithful to classical antiquity and optimistic in the manner of St Augustine, St Bernard, and St Thomas Aquinas. For Catholics, the essential point was that humanity had been created in the image of God, able despite human weakness to be creative too, in science, art, music, poetry, technology, and so on. God was not only pure power. He did not preordain those who would be accorded Grace. He was also pure goodness, and gave it liberally to all. What was essential was love.

The Church was the emanation of God on earth, and its aim was to guide Christians towards salvation. Holy Scripture was certainly the source of truth, but the Holy Spirit made its interpretation possible. Tradition, the Church's official interpretation, must therefore be followed, not the practice of free study. So the faithful should read the Bible in books which provided these official explanations.

As for the forms of worship, the seven sacraments were all created by Christ and must be maintained: Baptism, Penitence (including confession), Confirmation (receiving the Holy Spirit), the Eucharist (communion in which the bread and wine were actually transformed into the body and blood of Christ by a change of substance or 'transubstantiation'), Holy Matrimony, Ordination, and Extreme Unction.

By contrast with the Protestants, the Council encouraged, after the adoration of God, veneration of those who could intercede with Him, i.e. the Virgin and the saints. Images, statues, relics, and so on all had great spiritual and educative value, once they were freed from superstition. Worship was regulated by the 'liturgy' which prescribed the order of services. Discipline was to be restored to the clergy: plurality of benefices was banned. To acquire a benefice, one must be at least fourteen years old; to become a priest, twenty-five. Future priests would be trained in 'seminaries', one in each diocese.

So the Council of Trent did an immense amount. Some of its members – in particular the Papal Legate, the Augustinian Alessandro Seripando – made sure that the door of the Catholic Church was not wholly closed to the Protestants. The Jesuits, on the contrary, would have preferred more intransigence. What is now clear, however, is that two profoundly different forms of spirituality were emerging, to mark those who belonged to the Protestant Reformation, mainly in Northern Europe (with the great exception of Ireland) and those who belonged to the Roman Catholic Church, mainly in the South.

Roland Mousnier defined the contrast as 'the Catholic spirit of community versus Protestant individualism'.

The militant force in what became the Catholic Reform or Counter-Reformation was the Society of Jesus, established by the Spaniard Inigo Lopez de Ricalde, better known as Ignatius de Loyola.

Ignatius de Loyola and the Society of Jesus

He was born in about 1491, the thirteenth and youngest son of an old family of minor nobles, in the Spanish Basque province of Guipúzcoa.

After serving as a page to the Grand Treasurer at the court of Ferdinand and Isabella, he became an army officer; but in 1521, defending Pamplona against the besieging French armies, he was seriously wounded by a cannon-ball which broke his right leg. His convalescence was long and painful, and he was lame for life. He was tormented by the choice between a worldly career and a life of piety; then a vision led him to renounce worldly things, and he entered a monastery at Montserrat in Catalonia, and cared for the sick in a hospital at Manresa, some 10 kilometres away. He lived in poverty, begging for his bread. As a result, he fell ill, and was assailed by doubts. The experience taught him that to serve God actively required good health, and hence a limit to mortification of the flesh.

It was at this time that he wrote his *Exercitia Spiritualia*, or *Spiritual Exercises*, although they were not published until 1548. Their avowed aim was 'to guide people to victory over themselves and to the ordering of their lives, without hindrance by any harmful emotion'. The voice of the former soldier was clear. Henceforth, Ignatius de Loyola became a 'Knight of Christ'.

But he had no wish to remain alone. One day, unbelievers would have to be converted. This entailed lengthy preparation. As a start, in 1523, he made a pilgrimage to Jerusalem; then he decided to undertake the studies that were essential to a vocation in the Church. He went to the University of Alcala; but there he became suspect to the Inquisition, and was imprisoned. On his release he moved to the University of Salamanca, but was no happier there.

Finally, in 1528, he went to Paris. He was now thirty-seven years old. He entered the College of Montaigu, which Calvin, eighteen years younger, had just left. Despite great material difficulties, including the continued need to live on alms, he resumed his studies at the beginning again, with Latin grammar. He was helped by his room-mates, Paul Le Fèvre from Savoy, and a fellow-Spaniard, Francis Xavier, both of whom later, under Loyola's powerful influence, became founder-members of the Society of Jesus. He obtained his master's degree in 1533. Then, with his two friends, he recruited a small band of colleagues eager to devote their lives to the service of the Pope and the Church. There were three fellow-Spaniards: Jaime Lainez, Loyola's future successor; Alfonso Salmeron, an excellent linguist; and Nicholas Alfonso, known as Bobadilla. There was also a Portuguese nobleman, Simon Rodriguez d'Azevedo – making up the so-called

'Group of Seven' who formed the first nucleus of the Society of Jesus. Together, they took a solemn oath in a chapel in Montmartre.

While Loyola absented himself to settle some problems at home, the group continued to live in Paris, and acquired three new members, from France and Savoy. In 1538, Loyola, Le Fèvre, and Lainez travelled to Rome. They had decided to establish the Society of Jesus, whose distinguishing feature would be a special oath of obedience to the Pope.

In 1540, a Papal Bull approved the creation of this 'spiritual militia' in the service of the Church and under the orders of the Pope. Its Constitution was not completed until 1550. It provided for a 'General' to lead the Order, under Papal authority: he was to be elected for life by a 'General Congregation'. Seventeen years of study were needed to become a full member of the Society.

Its aim was not only to edify its members, but to play a missionary role, bringing Protestants back to the Catholic fold (as happened in some German towns), and going overseas to convert the heathen. It spread like wildfire. Skilfully trained, given special duties which fitted their individual aptitudes, the Jesuits became the champions of the Catholic Reform or Counter-Reformation. In the hands of popes more religious than the likes of Alexander VI or Julius II, they were a formidable weapon of influence and authority – which later earned them much hostility from worldly rulers, much persecution, many expulsions, and many prohibitions. When Ignatius de Loyola died in 1556, the Society had 101 houses (many of them secondary colleges) organized in twelve provinces, with about 1,000 members in Europe, Brazil, India, Japan, the Congo, and Abyssinia. By 1616, it had 436 houses, 37 provinces, and 13,112 members.

The Gregorian Calendar

Among the divisions caused by the Reformation in Europe, one had a very direct effect on daily life. This was the question of the calendar.

For more than fifteen centuries of the Christian era, the whole of Europe, including the area in which the Greek Orthodox Church was dominant, lived by the Julian Calendar, adopted by Julius Caesar in the year 46 BC. This divided the year into 365 days and one quarter, the latter being made up by having a 'Leap Year' with an extra day in it, every fourth year. But, a century before Caesar, the Greek astronomer

Hipparchus had discovered that the true length of the year was not 365 days and six hours, but 365 days, five hours, forty-eight minutes, and forty-seven seconds – a difference of eleven minutes and thirteen seconds. The effect of the disparity was cumulative. By the middle of the thirteenth century, the official equinox was already seven days later than the real one. The problem was discussed at Court (see the *Alphonsine Tables* compiled in 1252 by Alfonso X of Castile), as well as in the universities, where scholars like Robert Grosseteste and Roger Bacon debated what, if anything, could or should be done. Several popes pondered the question. But despite wide-ranging inquiries among the ablest astronomers, the Councils of Constance (1417) and Basle (1437–9), and the Lateran Council of 1514, came to no conclusion. The Council of Trent, during its last session in 1563, entrusted the task to the Holy See; and it was Pope Gregory XIII who in 1581 established what became known as the Gregorian Calendar. Gregory decided to cut ten days from the year of the reform, so that 5 October became 15 October; and to drop three Leap Years every 400 years, so that the year 1600 would be a Leap Year, but not 1700, 1800, or 1900. The year 2000, on the other hand, would.

In 1581, however, a decision by the Pope was no longer automatically accepted throughout Europe. Italy, Spain, and Portugal adopted the reformed calendar immediately. They were soon followed by Denmark, France, Lorraine, and the Catholic states of Germany and the Low Countries (present-day Belgium and Luxembourg). In 1582, they were joined by Savoy, Holland (Rotterdam, Amsterdam, Leyden, Delft, and The Hague), and Zeeland.

But these Protestant countries regarded the Edict of a Spanish king as null and void, and in 1594 they reintroduced the Julian Calendar. A number of Swiss cantons adopted the Gregorian Calendar in 1583, as did Poland in 1583, Austria in 1584, and Hungary in 1587.

The Protestant countries took much longer to apply the Gregorian Calendar. France introduced it into Alsace in 1648 and Strasbourg in 1682. Sweden, to avoid trading difficulties, dropped eleven Leap Years between 1696 and 1784. The Protestant states in Germany altered their calendar in 1699, the Protestant Low Countries in 1700, and the remainder of the Swiss cantons, including Geneva, in 1700–1. The last to change were England and Ireland, from 1752 onwards. By this time, the disparity was eleven days, and the passage of the Calendar (New Style) Act was accompanied by an outcry from the mob: 'Give us back our eleven days!' The countries of the Greek Orthodox rite, including Russia, retained the Julian Calendar until the twentieth century.

THE THIRD RENAISSANCE

The third Renaissance, following the Carolingian Renaissance and that of the twelfth century, was especially brilliant in Quattrocento (fifteenth-century) Italy. From there it spread throughout Europe, leading people to think differently and have a new conception of the world. Greater freedom to criticize, and a growing taste for free study of the Bible, together with disgust at Roman corruption, spurred the break-up of Western Christendom as a result of the Reformation. But these fundamental changes of outlook were accompanied by major political upheavals, which transformed the map of the world. In 1453 the Turks captured Constantinople; in 1492 Spain recovered Granada and completed the *Reconquista* from the Muslims, while in the same year Columbus landed in America. In 1498–9, Vasco da Gama took the Cape route to India. At the beginning of the sixteenth century, the East India trade was in the hands of the Portuguese. The Spaniards and others were beginning to explore and colonize the New World, soon to be called America. Europe discovered the rest of the world, and used her strength to conquer it. At home, meanwhile, Europeans discovered humanism, which was cosmopolitan, and brought about the Reformation, which in some countries strengthened the modern state but at the same time strengthened in Europe as a whole the spirit of freedom.

Meanwhile, in science, technology, literature, philosophy, and the publication of printed books, Europeans were taking a lead which they kept for four centuries to come.

12

Absolutism, Liberties, and Cosmopolitanism

FROM THE DIVINE RIGHT OF KINGS TO ENLIGHTENED DESPOTISM

In the eyes of political historians, the seventeenth and eighteenth centuries are the apogee of absolute monarchy, with a variant in eighteenth-century enlightened despotism, and a marked exception in the British regime after 1688.

For historians of strategy, this is a period of division and discord, scarred by fearful conflicts. Some, like the Franco-Spanish wars of 1515 to 1713, arose from the European balance of power. Others, like the four Anglo-Dutch wars between 1641 and 1674, or the eight Franco-British wars between 1689 and 1815, were the result of colonial and commercial rivalry – to say nothing of Swedish ambition. The 'Thirty Years' War' from 1619 to 1648, prolonged until 1659 between France and Spain, was in part a residue of the wars of religion between Catholics and Protestants, but in part also an expression of the rivalry between France and the Austrian and Spanish Habsburgs. The period also saw the successive rise to power of two Northern countries – first, and fleetingly, Sweden; then, more permanently, Russia.

The 'Estates of the Realm' and absolute monarchy

The absolute ruler, 'absolved from all laws', as Jean Bodin wrote in *Six livres de la République*, was not the same as the despot, whose power was arbitrary. The monarchs of Europe being Christian, they saw their sovereignty as derived from God. Therefore, as Charles Loyseau maintained in his 1611 *Traité des Seigneuries*, the Christian absolute monarch must respect the commandments of God, the rules of natural justice, and the fundamental laws of the state.

With a few exceptions, absolute monarchy did not prevail in the sixteenth century. Earlier, Western Europe had shakily recovered from the chaos and fragmentation caused by the great invasions. With the beginnings of feudalism, it had gradually formed a great variety of political entities: small states, rural or urban, privileged bodies organized at length into 'orders' with their own authorities, or political organizations created by the kings themselves to strengthen their power. All this had culminated, throughout Europe, in what have been called the 'Estates of the Realm', or *Standestaat*. In this typical situation, the king or prince with his court and his administration (later, his bureaucracy) faced the Assembly of the Estates. The latter, by the sixteenth century, was known in France as the Estates-General, in England as the Parliament, and in the Germanic Holy Roman Empire as the Diet. In the Diet, however, each member was in fact sovereign; and the Treaties of Westphalia which in 1648 ended the Thirty Years' War consolidated this fragmentation of Germany. It was, declared the German jurist Samuel von Pufendorf in 1667, an 'irregular and monster-like body'.

For the Austrian House of Habsburg, of which the German Emperor was a member, but whose possessions were not all included in the Empire, the 'Estates of the Realm' were very heterogeneous. There were three State Assemblies – one for the hereditary German-speaking countries, one for Bohemia, and one for the Kingdom of Hungary. These Assemblies comprised the Order of the Prelates, the Order of the Lords, the Order of the Knights (which was declining), and the Order of the Towns.

In Spain, after destroying the Cortes, Philip II employed a series of Councils: the Council of State; the Council of Castile or Royal Council; the Council of Finance; the Council of the Orders of Chivalry; the Council of Aragon (Aragon, Catalonia, Valencia); the Council of Navarre; the Council of Italy (Sicily, Sardinia, Naples, Milan); the Council of Flanders and Burgundy; the Council of Portugal (1580–1665); the Council of the Indies.

Similar 'Estates of the Realm' were found in Sweden and in Brandenburg–Prussia before the establishment of the monarchy in 1700.

The quest for efficiency

If 'Estates of the Realm' were characteristic European phenomena, so too was their general replacement, during the sixteenth century, by absolute monarchy. The Holy Roman Empire remained fragmented, but within its two main constituent parts, the Habsburg monarchy and Prussia, absolute power prevailed. The only country where it crumbled was Poland, which ended by disappearing from the map of Europe for 120 years. The Low Countries and Great Britain, however, were notable exceptions.

The general trend was due largely to the weakness of the Estates of the Realm. Given an Assembly whose members were continually squabbling over power and privilege, arbitration by the monarch, whose sacred power had never been disputed, might well seem essential. The 'Orders', 'Corps', and 'Estates' remained in existence, but the monarch could easily ignore them: the 'Estates-General' in France were not convened between 1614 and 1789. When in 1789 the King summoned them to solve the problems of the realm, it was too late: they put an end to royal absolutism and, in so doing, to the fundamental laws of monarchy.

It was under Louis XIII and Richelieu, and then Louis XIV and Mazarin, that the Protestants and the nobles in France lost their power. The monarch set up a Council of the King, divided into several subgroups; one of them, the 'Upper Council', was composed of four or five 'Ministers' appointed by the King alone and subject to dismissal at any time. This placed a considerable work-load on the monarch: but rulers like Louis XIV in France (1643–1715), Philip II of Spain (1556–98), and the Emperor Joseph II (1765–90) accepted and discharged their duties without stint. In this way, absolutism involved personal power.

In Sweden, absolute monarchy developed relatively late, after the coup d'état of 19 August 1772, when a new constitution gave the essentials of power to King Gustavus III.

In the exercise of absolute power, a number of the monarch's first or prime ministers became very well known. They included Lerma under Philip III of Spain, and Olivarez under Philip IV; George Villiers, Duke of Buckingham, under James I and Charles I in England; Concini, the Marquis d'Ancre, during the regency of Marie de' Medici following the assassination of Henry IV of

France; Richelieu under Louis XIII, and Mazarin at the beginning of the reign of Louis XIV.

'Enlightened despotism'

In the second half of the eighteenth century, there was much talk of 'enlightened despots'. These included Frederick II of Prussia (1740–86), Joseph II of Austria (1765–90), Catherine II of Russia (1762–96), and Charles III of Spain (1759–88). These rulers were, or claimed to be, disciples of Reason, admirers of the philosophers, and representatives of the Enlightenment. They presented themselves as the leading servants of their subjects: calling themselves 'virtuous', 'generous', and 'sensitive', they adopted what Roland Mousnier termed 'republican rhetoric'. Some of them professed to have drawn their reforming ideas from the *Encyclopédie* of Denis Diderot and Jean le Rond d'Alembert, of which more later. They established, developed, and protected academies and learned societies, supported writers and artists, and undertook economic reforms. In practical politics, however, they were just as absolutist and unyielding as anyone else.

The enlightened despots, in fact, were monarchs who had understood the importance of 'opinion leaders' in public affairs, and notably of the intellectuals they sought to charm and enlist as propagandists. Typical examples were Voltaire's reception at the court of Frederick II, and the assistance given to Diderot by Catherine the Great of Russia.

THE DAWN OF LIBERTY: THE LOW COUNTRIES AND GREAT BRITAIN

While most European political units appeared to be moving towards the efficiency of absolutism, the system of 'Estates of the Realm' continued and even developed – with some violent vicissitudes – in two countries of Northern Europe; the Low Countries and Great Britain.

Merchants, middle classes, and religious zealots

The Low Countries and Great Britain were both great trading powers, with Britain in second place. 'Who commands the sea commands trade; who commands the trade of the world commands its riches, and so commands the world itself.' This was the view of Sir Walter Raleigh; and it was borne out by events. The rapid expansion of trade by sea greatly enriched not only certain enterprising members of the traditional gentry, but also middle-class citizens who were now numerous enough to play a political role and defend their own interests, which were not necessarily identical with those of the monarch. For the most part they called for royal authority to be limited, and demanded 'guaranteed liberties' for themselves.

Was there, as the German sociologist Max Weber and the English historian R. H. Tawney both believed, a link between the Protestant Reformation and this capitalist free-trading movement? There was certainly a link between free study of the Bible and freedom of thought. In Weber's view, moreover, the Catholic Church's suspicion of usury – lending money for interest – was contradicted by the Protestant conviction that wealth was a reward bestowed by God upon the diligent and frugal.

At the same time, Protestant support for free study of the Bible encouraged the emergence of extremist sects. In the north of the Low Countries, for example, the Anabaptists proclaimed the coming of the 'Thousand-year Kingdom'. Protestant zealotry took countless other forms, and was sometimes markedly democratic. Examples in England included Oliver Cromwell's Roundheads and, still more extreme, the tiny group of 'Levellers', some of whom were communists before their time. Ideas such as these never completely disappeared from the European scene; but in practical politics they were gradually eclipsed by another anti-absolutist movement, representing a moderate and relatively liberal form of oligarchy.

The Spanish Low Countries

The Low Countries, which had been in the possession of Spain under Charles V, remained Spanish under his son Philip II (1556–98). Of their seventeen provinces, only those in the north had become Protestant; but they fought for forty years to seek independence. When a league of the nobility demanded that the Estates-General be convened and the Inquisition abolished, Philip II's half-sister Marguerite of Parma called its members *'gueux'*, or beggars – a name that remained a proud symbol of Dutch resistance.

The United Provinces

The 'United Provinces' of the Northern Low Countries – roughly, the present-day Netherlands – were formed between 1576 and 1586. In 1576, the 'Pacification of Ghent' confirmed the authority of Philip II but also freedom for Calvinism in the north. Three years later, in January 1579, the main provinces of the south met at Arras and affirmed that they would maintain Roman Catholicism. A few days after that, the seven provinces of Holland, Zeeland, Utrecht, Gelderland, Overyssel, Friesland, and Groningen formed the 'Union of Utrecht', which soon took the name of the 'United Provinces'. Their possessions also included Northern Flanders and Northern Brabant, which southern zone was known as 'the country of the Estates-General'.

The Union of Utrecht, led by the Calvinists, continued the struggle against Philip II, sometimes with the support of England, sometimes with that of France. In 1588, the 'Estates-General' seized power and officially founded the Dutch Republic, a federation of its seven constituent republics.

The 'New Republic' was a relatively liberal regime. In each province, legislative power was entrusted to the Provincial Estates. Each of these appointed, first, a Pensionary Counsellor, who was a jurist in charge of the administration, and, secondly, a *Stathouder*, who in the past had been the King's representative but was now in effect the President of the provincial republic.

Federal power was in the hands of the Estates-General, consisting of some forty delegates elected by the Provincial Estates. A twelve-member Council of State controlled the Army and the Exchequer. Two further federal offices were soon created: that of Grand Pensionary and that of the *Stathouder*, who was at once a leader, a General, and an Admiral, and who in practice was always the Prince of Orange. These two dignitaries were not slow to become rivals. The Grand Pensionary was supported by the leading merchants, seeking autonomy for the rich province of Holland; the *Stathouder* had the backing of the peasants and sailors, all convinced Calvinists, who wanted firm government of a highly centralized state.

The Kingdom of England

Already in the sixteenth century, widespread opinion in England held that the King was subject to the law, and that he could neither levy new taxes nor pass new legislation without the consent of Parliament, made up of the House of Lords and the House of Commons. But the kings and queens of sixteenth-century England actually behaved like absolute monarchs – especially Henry VIII (1509–47), Mary Tudor (1553–8) and, above all, Elizabeth (1558–1603).

Conflict between King and Parliament broke out with the Stuart dynasty of James I (1603–25) and his successor, Charles I (executed in 1649). In that conflict, an important factor was the alliance between the aristocracy and the prosperous middle classes, explained in part by the fact that noble families enjoyed few privileges, and in particular did not lose caste if they worked for a living. 'At the village school or the grammar school in the nearby market town,' wrote Roland Mousnier, 'children from the leading county families sat alongside the children of farmers, merchants, and artisans. The sons of needy squires would often espouse the dowries of yeomen's daughters.' Henri Hauser noted too that 'Support for the strictest Calvinism was growing, among the middle classes and the artisans, among merchants in the seaports, for whom the struggle against Catholic Spain had seemed the fruitful embodiment of the Protestant faith, among the gentry, enriched under the Tudors, and hence among a majority of the House of Commons.'

When Elizabeth died in 1603, the Stuart James VI of Scotland came from that less prosperous kingdom to reign in England as James I. But he took little interest in his new subjects or in the Commons, which never ceased to protest.

The fate of Charles I

James's son Charles I succeeded his father as ruler of the Kingdom of Great Britain, formed by the gradual unification of England and Scotland. Although a firm absolutist, he had to appeal to the House of Commons for finance. As a result, he was forced to accept a 'Petition of Right' under which no tax could be levied without Parliament's consent. In the field of law, an equally notable step forward was the adoption of habeas corpus, the principle by which no one could be imprisoned without first appearing before a judge.

Charles retaliated by staging a coup d'état. He sent nine members of the House of Commons to prison, and ruled for eleven years with no Parliament at all.

The upshot was revolution. It began in Scotland; but in 1640 the election of the House of Commons spread it throughout Great Britain. By 1642, there were clearly two authorities in the land. One was the Parliament in London; the other was the King, who had taken refuge first in York, then in Oxford. Despite appeals for help, he found support neither in Holland nor in France. Parliament raised troops, but Charles was so poor that he could barely pay his army. Soon, the country was divided in two: in the West, in Wales and Cornwall, the majority was Royalist, while the East supported Parliament. Its troops were headed by the squires and the middle classes, many of them Puritans who believed that God was on their side. Some called this 'the army of the saints': but its members were better known as 'Roundheads', because they wore their hair short, in contrast to the prevailing fashion. The Parliamentary army crushed the King's Cavaliers at the Battle of Naseby in 1645. In April 1646 Charles fled to Scotland; but his Presbyterian subjects there, who detested the Anglican episcopacy and would have liked to abolish it, arrested him and, in February 1647, handed him over to the representatives of the Westminster Parliament.

By now, indeed, there was only one authority in the land – that of the Roundhead army under its commander Oliver Cromwell. Cromwell came of a well-to-do family in the county of Huntingdon, north-west of Cambridge: he was a Puritan with firm views. In 1640 he was elected a Member of Parliament for Cambridge University; and it was he who organized the army's cavalry, mainly manned by yeomen. The army occupied London and 'purged' Parliament of Royalists, so that it became known as the 'Rump Parliament'. With the ultra- Puritans who remained in it, Cromwell arranged the convening of a High Court of Justice; and Charles I was executed on 9 February 1649 – or 30 January in the Julian Calendar, which was then still in force in Britain.

Cromwell and the 'Commonwealth'

The Rump Parliament proclaimed the abolition of the monarchy and the House of Lords, and the establishment of a republic, the 'free Commonwealth'. It lasted eleven years, and was continually under threat. But Oliver Cromwell's energy triumphed over all obstacles.

The truncated Parliament proving useless, he dissolved it and was made 'Lord Protector'.

He carried out Puritan reforms, but showed relative tolerance to Catholics, episcopalian Anglicans, and even Jews. He was very severe, however, with the Irish and with partisans of the Stuarts. In foreign policy, he fought alongside France against Philip IV of Spain. He strengthened the fleet under the command of Admiral Robert Blake, who among other things seized rich Spanish convoys in both the Atlantic and the Mediterranean. Blake also fought successfully against the Dutch, and captured Dunkirk from the Spaniards. Louis XIV bought it back from Britain in 1662.

Nevertheless, this first English revolution ended in failure. Cromwell died in September 1658. His son Richard, who succeeded him, was no match for either the Royalists or the Republicans; and in 1660 General George Monck, commander of the army in Scotland, marched on London and declared Charles Stuart II King of England.

The first English revolution, like the events in the Low Countries, showed that it was not impossible to form a republic even in the seventeenth century, when absolutism was in the ascendant. But England's second revolution – the 'Glorious Revolution' of 1688–9 – was more interesting, because it had lasting results.

Charles II and James II

Charles II, who reigned from 1660 to 1685, tried to restore absolute rule. When Parliament refused him financial aid, he resorted – both for war and for festivities – to subsidies from King Louis XIV of France. Unpopular as this was with his subjects, the King's prestige remained unblemished, and his brother James was able to succeed him in 1685, despite the fact that he was Catholic. Not the most tactful of men, he pressed for the removal of restrictions on his fellow-Catholics, and organized Catholic services in the royal palace. The English expected his sister Mary, wife of William III of Orange, to succeed James; but at the beginning of 1688 James's second wife, Mary of Modena, found that she was pregnant, and on 10 June she gave birth to a son, James Edward. Meanwhile, on 27 April, James II had published a second 'Declaration of Indulgence' in favour of Catholics and Dissenters, and ordered it to be read in churches. When the Archbishop of Canterbury and six other bishops refused, they were arrested and tried – but acquitted. This led seven statesmen – Admiral

Edward Russell, Henry Sidney, the Earl of Shrewsbury, Lord Lumley, Sir Thomas Danby, the Earl of Devonshire, and Henry Compton, Bishop of London – to sign a petition to William of Orange, asking him to land armed forces to defend the liberties of England against his Stuart father-in-law.

The 'Glorious Revolution' of 1688

On 10 October 1688, supported by the Estates-General of the United Provinces, William completed a Declaration to the English and the Scots, part of the preparation for an expeditionary force of 600 ships, including fifty men-of-war. He landed in Torbay on 15 November. The British army, which was largely favourable to William, put up little resistance; and the people, especially in London, rallied to his cause with cries of 'No Popery!' On 22 December, James II fled, reaching France on 2 January. Despite help from Louis XIV, he never regained the throne. William meanwhile waited until Parliament was re-elected. On 7–8 February 1689, it declared that James II was deposed, and then decided that England should be ruled, not by William alone, but by William and his wife Mary, born a Stuart. The new reign's coinage bore the pictures of both William and Mary.

The Bill of Rights

This decision was accompanied by a Bill of Rights, to which William listened in the very Banqueting Hall in Whitehall in which, forty years earlier, his grandfather Charles I had been beheaded. It was not an abstract philosophical document like the French 'Declaration of Human Rights' of 1789, but rather a compilation of concrete points. There were complaints against James II; there was the nomination of William and Mary, and the question of the succession. The principles it embodied made it seem radical and a presage of times to come. The power of the laws, it declared, was superior to that of the King. Taxes could not be levied without the consent of Parliament, and then only for a year. There could be no standing army in time of peace. Every citizen must have the right of petition. The King could not suspend the application of any law passed by Parliament. Judgements in criminal cases must be made by a jury. Excessive fines and vindictive punishments were banned.

Great Britain was more fortunate than the United Provinces, in that when William died in 1701, it was Parliament that decided on his successor. Its choice was Anne, Mary's younger sister. When she died in 1714 without issue, it was decided that the Crown should go to the Electress Sophia of Hanover, granddaughter of James I, or to the eldest of her children, provided that the heir was Protestant. The first two Hanoverian Kings of England, George I and George II, were both much more interested in their Hanoverian possessions than in Great Britain. Only when George III (1760–1820) came to the throne did the monarchy make a last attempt to re-establish, if not absolute rule, at least the 'royal prerogative'. A landmark in the struggle was the 'Wilkes affair', which broke out in 1763 when John Wilkes was arrested for a libel published in his periodical, *The North Briton*. When found guilty, he pleaded privilege as a Member of Parliament. In 1764 he was expelled from Westminster, but four years later was re-elected – and again expelled. Three times he was re-elected; he was also elected Lord Mayor of London. In 1790, he was at last allowed to take his seat. It was a victory for the freedom of the press.

The 1689 Bill of Rights influenced both the American Declaration of Independence of 1776 and the French Declaration of Human Rights in 1789.

Developments in political thought

It was no accident that the United Provinces and Great Britain, both more liberal than other countries at the time, produced some of the greatest political thinkers of the seventeenth century: Grotius, Hobbes, and Locke.

Grotius

The Dutch jurist Hugo van Groot, better known as Grotius, was born at Delft in 1583 and died in 1645. As a child, he was already a prodigy, composing Latin verses at the age of eight. After studying at Leyden, he was eighteen when he was appointed 'Historian of the Estates of Holland' in 1601. A friend and ally of the Grand Pensionary Jan van Olden Barneveldt, he opposed the *Stathouder* Maurice of Nassau, and was arrested and condemned to prison for life. He escaped in a box of books, and took refuge first in France, then in Sweden. His written output was huge: it included theology, philology, literature, history, and law. Two of his works are of particular interest here: *Mare liberum* (*The Freedom of the Sea*) and *De Jure Belli et*

Pacis (*The Law of War and Peace*), which for the first time set out the customary and contractual obligations among fully sovereign states with no judge or arbitrator to settle their disputes.

Hobbes

Thomas Hobbes (1588–1679) was also a prodigy, as was his friend the French philosopher and mathematician Pierre Gassendi, the critic of Descartes and teacher of Cyrano de Bergerac. Gassendi became a professor of rhetoric when he was sixteen, and of philosophy and theology at twenty-one; Hobbes, the son of an Anglican clergyman, translated Euripides's *Medea* from Greek into Latin verse when he was still a schoolboy. A fervent Royalist, Hobbes took refuge in France in 1640, and was one of the tutors to the Prince of Wales, the future Charles II. It was in France that he made the acquaintance of Gassendi, Galileo, and Descartes. He returned to England in 1651. Essentially, he was a pessimist who believed that humanity was naturally filled with 'a perpetuall and restlesse desire of Power after power, that ceaseth onely in Death'. In a time, therefore, 'wherein men live without other security, than what their own strength, and their own invention shall furnish' – i.e. without organized society – 'the life of man,' in Hobbes's famous phrase, would be 'solitary, poor, nasty, brutish, and short'. In such a state, might would be right, and war perpetual. To ensure peace, an authority must be established, and it must be despotic. The clergy, too, must be subject to this royal authority. These views Hobbes expounded in his best-known work, *Leviathan, Or the Matter, Forme, and Power of A Commonwealth Ecclesiasticall and Civil* (1651).

Locke

John Locke (1632–1704) came of a younger generation. His father was a country attorney who had been an officer in the Roundhead army; but Locke himself remained a moderate. After taking his MA at Oxford in 1658, he became a tutor at Christ Church in philosophy and Greek. In 1666 he met Anthony Ashley Cooper, later 1st Earl of Shaftesbury and founder of the Whig party: he became his personal physician and secretary at the Board or Council of Trade. After Shaftesbury's fall from power, Locke sought refuge abroad, living for five years in Holland and returning to England with William of Orange. He was at the same time a philosopher, much respected for his *Essay*

Concerning Human Understanding (1690), and an expert and theorist on politics. His *Two Treatises of Civil Government*, also published in 1690, condemned absolute monarchy, championed civil liberties, and confirmed the principles underlying the 'Glorious Revolution' and the Bill of Rights. Like Hobbes, Locke posited a 'state of nature' in which people lived as equal and separate units; but, unlike Hobbes, he believed that each unit would recognize limitations, notably the right of property and the punishment of wrongdoers. These rudimentary social conditions would be improved when the individuals decided to unite to establish a 'civil society' and a government, to which they would delegate certain of their sovereign powers. But the government must not be absolute: it should be limited to exercising those powers which people possessed in the state of nature. If it became tyrannical, citizens had the right to rebel; and the tyranny of a Parliament would be just as culpable as that of a king. Locke also believed in freedom of speech and freedom of the press.

His influence ran deep. It affected not only the founders of the future Republic of the United States of America, but also, in France, Voltaire and Montesquieu, and in Geneva, Jean-Jacques Rousseau. But whereas Locke's philosophy implied freedom, that of Rousseau attributed a kind of infallibility to what he called the 'general will', if openly and directly expressed. This foreshadowed a much more authoritarian system, that of the Jacobin Republic.

THE SEVENTEENTH CENTURY: GOLDEN AGE OR GRIM?

Between the Renaissance in the sixteenth century and the Enlightenment in the eighteenth, the seventeenth century, known in France as '*le grand siècle*', seems at first sight a period in which the human spirit shone brightly, at least in the fields of literature and art.

In France, 1636 saw the triumphant first production, in Paris, of Pierre Corneille's *Le Cid* and the first contract, in Holland, for the publication of René Descartes's *Discours de la Méthode*. Blaise Pascal died in 1662, aged thirty-nine; Jean-Baptiste Molière, aged fifty-one, in 1673. With Jacques Bénigne Bossuet, Jean Racine, Jean de la Fontaine, Jean de la Bruyère, and many others, they formed a dazzling galaxy in the age of Louis XIV.

In England, after the so-called 'Elizabethan springtime', William Shakespeare began to write in or about 1591, and died in 1616. But he was followed by a wealth of writers: playwrights like Thomas Dekker, Ben Jonson, John Webster, and the Restoration dramatist William Congreve; poets like John Donne, Lord Herbert of Cherbury, John Milton, George Herbert, Thomas Carew, Robert Herrick, Henry Vaughan, Andrew Marvell, John Dryden, and Samuel Butler; miscellaneous writers like Francis Bacon, John Selden, Robert Burton, George Sandys, Sir Thomas Browne, Izaak Walton, John Bunyan, and Gilbert Burnet – not to mention the anonymous collective translators of the Authorized Version of the Bible in 1611 and those who produced the virtually definitive 1662 version of the *Book of Common Prayer*.

Germany at this time was suffering greatly from continued warfare, and hence undergoing a decline. But it too produced some very notable works, in particular Johann Jakob Christoffel von Grimmelshausen's *Der Abenteuerliche Simplicissimus Teutsch*, or *The Adventurous Simplicissimus* (1669), which not inappropriately included a vivid portrayal of the horrors of war.

Italy remained in many respects a focal point for Europe; but its political weakness had led to apparently irremediable decline. Its luminaries included Galileo – without whom it remains hard to imagine either Descartes or Isaac Newton – as well as Cardinal Borromeo, founder of the Ambrosian Library in Milan, the composers Claudio Monteverdi and Alessandro Scarlatti, and such artists as Giovanni Lorenzo Bernini and Michelangelo da Caravaggio. It was the heyday of the Baroque and the *Commedia dell'Arte*.

In Spain, by contrast, this was the golden age *par excellence*. The great Miguel de Cervantes y Saavedra, the contemporary of Shakespeare, was born in 1547 at Alcalá de Henares. As a soldier, he fought in the Battle of Lepanto, mutilating his left hand; later, he was captured by the Turks and ransomed after four daring but unsuccessful attempts to escape. He was over fifty when he published, between 1605 and 1615, his epoch-making picaresque tragicomic *Don Quixote*, or *El ingenioso Hidalgo Don Quijote de la Mancha* which, it has been said, 'contains all the major elements of the modern novel'. At the same time, Spain could boast two painters of genius, El Greco and Diego Rodriguez de Silva y Velasquez, as well as outstanding writers, notably for the theatre, who influenced all of Europe: Lope de Vega, Tirso de Molina, and Pedro Calderón de la Barca. The death of Calderón in 1681 is often held to signal the end of Spain's 'Golden Century'.

The United Provinces, too, enjoyed a golden age, especially after the truce with Spain in 1609. As Paul Rodenko has written:

> The 17th century, and especially its early years, became for the Northern Low Countries the most glorious period of their history. In politics, when the war with Spain was resumed after the 12-year truce, the Republic quickly attained the status of a great power ... In the field of science, as in those of painting and music, it produced people of international renown: Zacharias Janssen, Peter Paul Rubens, Sir Anthony Van Dyck, Frans Hals, Rembrandt van Ryn, Jan Pieterszoon Sweelinck ... And literature too made great strides.

The poet and historian Pieter Cornelis-zoon Hooft (1581–1647) was one of its finest representatives. His *Nederlandsche Historiën* or *Dutch Chronicles* tell the story of the Wars of Independence from 1555 to 1587 in twenty-seven books. In the later part of the seventeenth century, the United Provinces had a less brilliant history: invaded by the French in 1672, they were later obliged by William III to follow in the wake of Britain. But the relative freedom prevailing among the Dutch made their country a centre for publications forbidden elsewhere, a refuge for philosophers like Descartes and Spinoza and for French Huguenots after the revocation of the Edict of Nantes in 1685, as well as a focus of brilliant universities like those of Leyden, Utrecht, Groningen, and Rotterdam. Three key publications in French were first printed in the United Provinces: Pierre Bayle's *Nouvelles de la République des Lettres* (1683–7), Jean Le Clerc's *Bibliothèque Universelle et Historique* (1686–93), and Basuage de Beauval's *Histoire des ouvrages et des savants* (1687). Bayle worked in the United Provinces on his great *Dictionnaire historique et critique* (1697), which became a symbol of the contemporary 'crisis of European consciousness', marked by growing scepticism and doubt.

Painting in Europe was flourishing no less than literature. Italy, although no longer so pre-eminent, remained influential on account of the studios in Bologna where the pupils of Caravaggio and the three Carracci were working: Guido Reni, Francesco Albani, and Giovanni Francesco Barbieri, better known by his nickname Guercino ('squint-eyed'). They greatly influenced such French artists as Charles Lebrun and Pierre Mignard; while Nicolas Poussin spent most of his life in Rome. In Spain, meanwhile, it was the heyday of Jusepe de Ribera, Bartolomé Estebán Murillo, Francisco Herrera, Francisco de Zurbarán, and above all of the great Diego Rodriguez de Silva y Velasquez. From Antwerp came Rubens and Van Dyck; from Leyden, Rembrandt. Britain, meanwhile, seemed for a long time to be content to 'borrow' great painters from the Low Countries, such as Van Dyck, the painter of Charles I, and Rubens, who was both a painter and a diplomat. In architecture, however, the country could boast both Inigo Jones and Sir Christopher Wren. Meanwhile, despite these artistic glories, life for the mass of Europe's inhabitants remained very hard. Pierre Corneille was well aware of it. In the Prologue to his little-known play *La Toison d'Or (The Golden Fleece)* in 1660, France addresses the young Louis XIV, who had just signed the Pyrenees Treaty and married the Spanish Infanta Maria Teresa:

> The State may flourish but the People groan; Their fleshless limbs are bent to my great deeds, And royal Glory crushes those it rules ... I weep to see my Towns reduced to shame, My People pillaged, and my Fields aflame.

On his death-bed, fifty-five years later, Louis XIV confessed: 'I have been too fond of battles and of buildings.'

The demographic crisis of the seventeenth century

The surest sign of the prevailing poverty can be found in demographic history. 'The growth of population which had marked the 16th century slowed down in its last years throughout most of Europe, to be followed by a standstill, if not a decline, which continued until the mid-18th century.' This is the view of Marcel Reinhard, André Armengaud, and Jacques Dupaquier in their remarkable *Histoire générale de la population mondiale*. They entitle their chapter on this period 'The European Crisis, 1600 to 1740'. There was indeed a crisis. It was less catastrophic than that caused by the Black Death in the fourteenth century; but it was marked by a number of scourges which increased the mortality rate. These included famine, pestilence, and war. Nor was this all. There is some connection, obscure and complex but none the less certain, between these scourges and the birthrate. In hard times, while direct methods of birth control might be unknown, others were available. For example, as Pierre Chaunu points out, 'The marriageable age of daughters was Europe's classical method of contraception... In bad times, marriage was postponed. In good times, it was hastened.'

Europe's poverty may have been influenced by climate. There seems to have been a cold period lasting some 250 years, which on the one hand produced the cruel winters of 1709 and 1740, and on the other devastated the harvests, especially in the spring, leading to very high wheat prices in 1606–9, 1639–44, 1663–4, 1672–7, 1691–1703, and 1703–16. 'The food crisis,' in the words of Reinhard, Armengaud, and Dupaquier, 'was accompanied by higher mortality, followed by a lower birthrate, and countered by the postponement of marriage.'

Disease, notably the plague, did not always coincide with famine. The plague, indeed, 'was ceasing to be the main scourge', although it recurred in many places from time to time. Leprosy was finally disappearing from Europe. But since immunization was still unheard of, the defeat of the plague was no doubt due to more effective sanitation. 'As regards the plague,' declared Pierre Chaunu, 'the Middle Ages stopped in 1685.' There was, however, a further major outbreak in Marseille in 1720.

Civil, religious, and foreign wars added to Europe's misfortunes. 'On the field of battle, the slaughter increased; but indirect losses, in the countries at war, seem to have diminished.' There was nevertheless an obvious connection between the movement of troops and the spread of epidemics. Germany suffered especially from the effects of the Thirty Years' War. The population of the Palatinate fell by 70 per cent; that of Württemberg fell from 450,000 to 100,000; that of Mecklenburg by 80 per cent. By the year 1700, the German population was smaller than it had been in 1600. Not until 1750 did it reach its former level.

The brutality of the seventeenth century's wars would seem astonishing if our own time had not known the horrors of the Second World War. In 1576, for example, Spanish troops broke into Antwerp, which supposedly was on their own side. They sacked it, as was the frequent custom, and killed some 6,000 people. In Ireland in 1649, 'appointed Commander-in-Chief and Governor for three years, Cromwell landed at Dublin and captured Drogheda'. As Henri Hauser's account cotinued: 'Haunted, like all the English, by the memory of the 1641 massacres [when the Irish rebels had killed thousands of Protestants], he showed no mercy, either at Drogheda or at Wexford, killing their defenders out of hand, putting all priests to the sword, and not sparing even women and children. This appalling campaign, of which Cromwell actually boasted, followed by the resumption of wholesale colonial repression for eight years, finally sowed in that unhappy island the seeds of ineradicable hatred.' In Germany the Palatinate, which had suffered so badly in the Thirty Years' War, was twice laid waste by French troops, in 1674 and 1688, so cruelly that this was still remembered in Germany as late as the twentieth century.

Europe's population in the seventeenth century: an estimate

It is difficult to estimate precisely the size of Europe's past population. The first census in France, set in motion by Jean-Baptiste Colbert, took place in 1663. It was soon followed by censuses in Britain, in the Spanish Netherlands, and in the United Provinces; but there was no census in Prussia until 1740, or in Spain until 1787. What estimates can be made show a marked contrast between the eighteenth century and the seventeenth, when there was certainly a decline between 1630 and 1650.

According to Fernand Braudel, a 'reasonable hypothesis' for the world's population would be about 470 million in 1650 and between 660 and 694 million in 1750 – a growth of 41–47 per cent. The corresponding figures for Europe, including Russia, show a probable rise from 100–105 million to 140–144 million – an increase of some 37.1 per cent. There was a 'marked dip' in the mid-eighteenth century, when the population of Spain is thought by some authors to have dropped from 8 to 6 million – although this is contested by the Spanish expert Vincent Unes.

Demographically, as has been suggested, the eighteenth century showed a great contrast with the sixteenth. Real poverty remained widespread; but large-scale famine occurred no longer, and disease abated. The series of revolutions that took place from 1770 onwards showed that people still found the situation more and more intolerable; but population growth continued apace. In England and Wales, numbers increased from 5,826,000 in 1700 to 6,140,000 in 1750 and 9,156,000 in 1801. In Sweden, the figure rose from 1,450,000 in 1720 to 2,347,000 in 1800. In Norway, there were 616,000 inhabitants in 1735, and 883,000 in 1801. The Italian states had a population of some 13 million at the beginning of the eighteenth century and some 18 million at the end.

In Germany, so seriously affected in the seventeenth century, the eighteenth century saw rapid population growth: by 94 per cent in Württemberg between 1700 and 1800, by 132.5 per cent in East Prussia, and by 138 per cent in Pomerania. In the Habsburg Empire the total was 8,100,000 in 1725 and 22,496,000 in 1789.

In the Low Countries, there were even signs of over-population. In the United Provinces, the total rose from 1,900,000 in about 1750 to 2,078,000 in 1795–6. In Belgium, it rose from 1,750,000 in 1714 to 2,800,000 in 1784 and 3,300,000 in 1813.

For France, at the beginning of the eighteenth century, the figures are hard to ascertain; but by 1791 there were 26,300,000 inhabitants, a probable increase of some 7 million in a hundred years – without, incidentally, the major economic transformation which had taken place in Britain.

Finally, Spain and Portugal seem also to have had an increase in population of some 3 million between 1723 and 1797. The 1797 census gave a figure of 10.5 million for Spain.

To sum up, Reinhard, Armengaud, and Dupaquier estimate that in 1750 Europe including Russia had a population of 140 million, or 19.2 per cent of the world total of 728 million. By 1800, they believe, Europe's population was 167 million, or 20.6 per cent of the world total of 906 million. In other words, it was with one fifth of the world's population that Europe increased its existing preponderance, making it for nearly two centuries the world's dominant power.

The same period saw a notable growth of towns. In Eastern Europe, these were few and far between. Poland, in 1772, had only five towns with more than 20,000 inhabitants. There were barely more in Russia: 4 per cent of its population lived in towns in 1794, against 13 per cent in 1897. There was no city in the East as populous as London, Paris, or Naples. In 1700, Europe had ten cities with more than 100,000 inhabitants; in 1800 the number had risen to seventeen, five of which contained more than 200,000 people.

Berlin, in 1783, had 140,000 inhabitants, 33,000 of them soldiers. London, in 1580, already had 123,000; and this figure rose to at least 550,000 in 1700, and between 745,000 and 900,000 in 1801. By then, London was the biggest city in the world. Paris in 1789 had between 450,000 and 600,000 inhabitants. Naples had 337,000 in

1776, and 417,000 in 1796. Vienna had 175,000 in 1754, and 235,000 in 1793. Moscow's population reached 230,000 in 1800.

One of the most notable features of seventeenth-century poverty was the fact that peasants' revolts became a European phenomenon. They were usually reactions to some form of tax; but one of their root causes may well have been the increase in population, which meant more mouths for the family to feed. These 'peasant furies' (to borrow the title, *Fureurs paysannes*, of a book by Roland Mousnier comparing outbreaks in France, Russia, and China) were especially numerous in France from 1629 to 1639 and from 1675 to 1680. Taxation, increased to meet the costs of the military, 'placed an extra burden on the peasantry just when they could least afford it'. There may also have been a link with the slowing-down of the century-long rise in prices. From 1630 to 1640, prices were stable; from 1640 to 1675 they fell; and from 1675 to 1685 they remained stable at a very low level – all of which reflected the slowdown in imports of precious metals from the New World. Some of the peasant revolts, too, were the result of disastrous weather, including such calamities as a hailstorm which destroyed a whole crop in a matter of minutes. But few of the uprisings were wholly spontaneous reactions by peasants. Most of them were organized by the squires or the middle classes, and were aimed against the fisc or the 'tyranny' of the state.

THE DECLINE OF DEFERENCE AND THE GROWTH OF COMPASSION

It is not easy to expound in a few pages the revolution which over two centuries transformed European thinking – and, it must be stressed, that of Europe alone. The seventeenth century saw the beginnings of an attack on the principle of authority; the eighteenth saw that attack succeeding everywhere. As the English historian Norman Hampson put it in his book *The Enlightenment*:

> The cultural horizon of most educated men in Western Europe in the early seventeenth century was dominated by two almost unchallenged sources of authority: scripture and the classics.
>
> Each in its own way perpetuated the idea that civilisation had degenerated from a former Golden Age. The most rational preoccupation for

contemporary man was, therefore, by the study of the more fortunate ancients to move back towards the kind of society which the latter had known. Recent European movements, the Renaissance and the Reformation, had reinforced this attitude and enhanced the authority of the sacred texts. The Renaissance and humanistic educational movement had been largely based on a revival of Greek and Latin learning.

And Hampson went on to speak of the 'eager veneration' then felt for the classics.

In the seventeenth century, then, the principle of authority began to be questioned more and more. That principle was firmly entrenched. However vigorous and critical the human mind may be, it always seeks assistance in the face of the unknown. And if the civilization of classical antiquity was thought to have been perfect, its writings must have contained the truth. Aristotle was the guide for philosophy, as St Thomas Aquinas, the Dominicans, and many theologians believed; Hippocrates and Galen for medicine; Vitruvius for architecture; and so on. Even the theatre claimed to have inherited from antiquity the rule of the 'three unities' – of space, time, and action – which it was thought that any good play must respect.

Growing resistance to the cult of antiquity may have seemed fairly anodyne in matters of art and literature. In science, on the contrary, it had momentous results.

Architecture

While it was true that the ancients, and especially the Greeks, had produced unsurpassable masterpieces in sculpture and architecture, it still might be possible to equal them by following other paths. Gradually, this realization began to grow in people's minds.

Thus, while the Renaissance had turned away from the lingering influence of late Gothic and sought to copy classical models, the seventeenth century saw the emergence of a new style of sculpture and architecture, the baroque. This had its origins in Rome. The architect Francesco Borromini (1599–1667) and the sculptor Giovanni Lorenzo Bernini (1598–1680) were the main founders of an art which, in the words of Victor L. Tapie, 'liberated lines and volumes, gave detail its own value, seemingly independent of the overall conception, and expressed a freedom and inventiveness which could lead to extravagance'.

The baroque style spread mainly in Italy and Spain (and in Spanish and Portuguese America), as well as in Central Europe, especially Germany – as at Weingarten Abbey, the Abbey Church of Weltenburg, or St John Nepomuk in Munich. There was baroque building in France and Britain; but in both countries it had to compete with a classical style, much less luxuriant, much more measured and orderly, which was taken up by Louis XIV and by 'the Court and the Town'. When Bernini was invited to Paris in 1665 to design the eastern colonnade of the Louvre, he proposed a grandiose and costly plan. On grounds of taste, or economy, or perhaps nationality, a design by a French artist, Claude Perrault, was preferred to Bernini's. This has often been hailed as the triumph, in France, of the classical over the baroque. Yet the latter was very popular with the mass of the people, who saw in baroque church monuments the embodiment of the beliefs reaffirmed by the Catholic Counter-Reformation and the Council of Trent. And while France possessed relatively few baroque buildings, there was a very great deal of baroque decoration, including in particular thousands of altar-pieces.

In England, the baroque had some success before 1666, the year of the Great Fire of London. Sir Christopher Wren (1632–1723) was given the task of supervising the reconstruction, and notably of building St Paul's Cathedral. A mathematician and philosopher, a connoisseur of French *châteaux* and a critic of Bernini, Wren was the greatest English architect of his time. For St Paul's, in 1675, he adopted the classical style. The dome and its colonnade are famous throughout the world.

In the eighteenth century, while the taste for curves increased, especially in furniture and decoration, two contrasting styles developed. One was 'rococo', full of small curves, prettiness, and gaiety; the other was neo-classicism, more faithful to its original models than the classicism of the seventeenth century, and exemplified in Paris by Jacques-Germain Soufflot's Panthéon, begun in 1755.

Literature

Here, too, there was stylistic rivalry between 'ancient' and 'modern' throughout the eighteenth century. Partisans of the former maintained that nothing written was valid unless it was modelled on Greek or Latin; but this school was finally overwhelmed by an immense urge for novelty. At the same time, the idea of imitating the classics remained widespread, though less so than in the sixteenth century, when Pierre Ronsard had written, for example, an 'Ode to the Bellerie fountain' directly copying Horace's ode, 'O fons Bandusiae'.

Science

How dangerous reliance on authority could be in scientific matters can be seen from two examples. The first concerned the circulation of the blood. The second-century physician Galen knew nothing of it. It was discovered by William Harvey (1578–1657), a fellow and lecturer at the College of Physicians in London, and doctor to James I. Harvey published an account of his demonstration of it in 1628 under the title *De motu cordis* (*On the Movement of the Heart*). Yet for many years the medical disciples of Aristotle and Galen continued to deny the phenomenon. One such was Gui Patin in the Faculty of Paris, whose opposition to Harvey's 'alleged discovery' Molière satirized in 1673 in *Le Malade Imaginaire*.

The second example of misplaced faith in authority concerned the rotation of the Earth. In 1543 Nicolaus Copernicus (1473–1543) published his *De Revolutionibus Orbium Coelestium Libri VI* (*Six Books on the Revolutions of Heavenly Bodies*) in which he demonstrated that they revolved round the Sun. The Danish astronomer Tycho Brahe (1546–1601) sought to reconcile the Copernican system with the old Ptolemaic model, and made observations which enabled his German colleague and coworker Johannes Kepler (1571–1630) to produce the three Laws of planetary motion which bear his name: they were later confirmed by Sir Isaac Newton (1642–1727) in his 1687 *Principia Mathematica*. Meanwhile the Italian scientist Galileo Galilei (1564–1642) had perfected the refracting telescope, and in 1632 published his *Dialogue on the Ptolemaic and Copernican Systems*, further demolishing the Aristotelian theory which held that the Earth was the immobile centre of the universe around which all the other heavenly bodies revolved in circles every twenty-four hours. Now it should have been clear that the Earth, far from being central, was only a small element in a universe more and more of which was coming under observation.

That in itself, however, may explain the simplistic reaction of the Church authorities, who were accustomed to derive all their theories from authority, as embodied in the Book of Genesis and supplemented by Aristotle. Already in 1616 the Roman Tribunal of the Inquisition had condemned 'the view that the sun is immobile at the centre of the universe' as 'mad, philosophically false, and altogether heretical, because contrary to Holy Scripture'. It continued: 'The view that the earth is not at the centre of the universe and that it even rotates daily is philosophically false and, at the very least, an erroneous belief.'

After the publication of his *Dialogue*, Galileo was summoned to Rome by the Inquisition, and arrested there in February 1633. Threatened with torture, he retracted his views and was condemned to prison. Legend has it that after his retraction he could not help adding: '*Eppur si muove*' ('And yet it moves'). Galilean physics, based on observation and experiment, had in fact shown that the Earth's movement obeyed mathematical laws.

Empiricism and reason

An Englishman and a Frenchman may be said to have symbolized this intellectual revolution. The first was Francis Bacon (1561–1626), who criticized the authority of Plato and Aristotle, who had failed to study the world about which they theorized: it could only be known, he declared, by empirical *experimentation*, several of whose principles he defined. Even so, empiricism alone was not enough.

René Descartes (1596–1650) sought to replace the teachings of Aristotle by a new universal doctrine based on evidence and reason: 'Never take on trust anything for which there is no evidence.' Of gentle birth, Descartes served for a time as a soldier in 1618–19, but spent the rest of his life in philosophical pursuits, settling in 1628 in Holland, where the atmosphere was more liberal than in France. His *Discours de la Méthode*, or *Discourse on Method*, was first printed at Leyden in 1637, although the first edition of his *Philosophic Meditations*, completed in 1640, was published in Paris in 1641. His aim was to base both geometry and physics on pure reason. Without adequate experimentation, however, reason alone could also lead to error.

By the end of the seventeenth century, Britain led the rest of Europe as a centre of intellectual life: by 1712, it was producing more books than France. And it was in Britain that Isaac Newton, Professor of Mathematics at Trinity College, Cambridge, really achieved a synthesis between reason and empiricism. Following the principles of the great French philosopher and mathematician Blaise Pascal (1623–62), Newton went further. On the basis of both analysis and experiment, he devised a mathematical instrument of his own, differential and integral calculus – a method worked out almost simultaneously by the German philosopher and mathematician Gottfried Wilhelm von Leibniz (1646–1716).

Newton also evolved the theory of 'universal gravitation' as a general explanation of movement in the world. His compatriot Alexander Pope wrote of Isaac Newton:

> Nature and Nature's laws lay hid in night: God said 'Let Newton be!' and all was light.

Religion

Growing intellectual freedom clearly posed serious problems for the Church. Christianity is a 'revealed religion': its basic tenet is that God was made manifest in historical time to teach humanity the truth. Pure reason, therefore, could not by itself lead to faith, which the Council of Trent defined as 'a supernatural virtue whereby, forewarned and aided by the Grace of God, we hold as true what God has revealed to us, not because we have exposed essential truth to the light of reason, but because it is the truth itself and can neither err nor lead us astray'.

If the essential truth about non-religious matters like the origin of the world or the laws of nature was enshrined in some sacred text, then the Church would dominate human understanding. The Protestant Reformation allowed 'free study', but this was free study of the Old and New Testaments of the Bible, whose divine character was beyond dispute. If part of the Bible's contents was now to be contradicted by science (for example, the creation of the world in six days only 6,000 years ago), this raised the question of how much of Scripture remained valid.

Descartes held that the 'methodical doubt' which he thought necessary for science should not be applied to religion. But was this not, on his part, a mere precaution? Newton, rather than believing in constant divine intervention, thought that God had set up a system of general laws whose perfection was to be admired. Believers in every age have no doubt preferred to base their faith either on a higher form of awareness – as in the case of Pascal – or on the absolute dictates of ethics – like the 'categorical imperative' invoked by the German philosopher Immanuel Kant (1724–1804) in his *Critique of Pure Reason* (1781). But the new critical spirit spread into biblical criticism or exegesis, study of the life of Christ, and all areas of the spiritual and the ideal.

This encouraged freedom of thought, despite all the brutality of the Inquisition and all the tortures inflicted on those who rejected the teachings of the Church or the state. The new ideal was what the French philosopher Hugues Félicité Robert de Lamennais (1782–1854) called 'the free combat of truth against error'. Unfortunately, the battle still continues, and there are still a number of countries where 'crimes of opinion' are punished by the loss of liberty or of life.

Tolerance and pity

The decline of the principle of authority, and increased respect for reason, should logically encourage a quality rarely exercised – *tolerance*. This did gain ground in the eighteenth century, mainly in matters of religion. Already in 1598, it is true, King Henry IV of France had issued the Edict of Nantes, proclaiming tolerance for French Protestants. But it had been a political act; and when Louis XIV, as a pious Catholic, revoked the Edict in 1685 and persecuted Protestants, this was considered normal. In 1689, again, the Elector of Brandenburg issued the Edict of Potsdam, opening his country to French Huguenots; but at the same time Catholics were excluded from public office there until 1829.

In the eighteenth century, however, important practical progress was made. The French 'Edict of Tolerance' issued on 19 November 1787 gave back to the Protestants and their clergy the same rights to office and employment as those enjoyed by their Catholic counterparts. In France, it has been said, tolerance was 'won', whereas in the Germanic-language countries, such as Britain and especially Prussia and Austria, it was rather 'accorded' by government.

A symbol of this struggle for toleration, which in France was achieved by the Protestants and elsewhere by the Catholics or by some other church or sect, is the arresting figure of Voltaire (1694–1778). His real name was François-Marie Arouet, and he was the son of a notary at the Chambres des Comptes or Audit Office; he took the pen-name Voltaire when he was twenty-one. It rapidly became famous all over Europe, and was much feared by those in power, who felt themselves greatly threatened by Voltaire's ferocious pen, his critical spirit, the clarity of his style, and the breadth of his interests and connections. He made his headquarters at Ferney, near to Geneva and the Swiss border in case he had to flee from France. Some rulers cultivated and flattered him. What was significant, however, was that he used the authority of his wit and his intellect to serve the cause of tolerance and compassion. In some respects, he was what is known today as a 'committed' writer. In 1762, for example, when a Protestant merchant in Toulouse, Jean Calas, was broken on the wheel for the alleged murder of his son (who had probably committed suicide), Voltaire's efforts had the sentence posthumously annulled and the stigma removed from the family. A similar case, where he was able to intervene in time, was that of another Protestant, Pierre Paul Sirven. One of his daughters had been kidnapped, so as to be converted by force to Catholicism: she went mad and was released, but on 4 January 1762 was found dead in a well. Her father and mother were condemned to death for murder. Fleeing across the Alps to Geneva in winter, Sirven lost his elder daughter, who was with child: but after nine years of effort, Voltaire secured his acquittal in 1771. Nor did he defend only Protestants. What he sought to demonstrate was the enormity of judicial error, above all when fired by fanaticism.

Another writer, the Milanese Cesare Bonesana, Marquess of Beccaria (1738–94) published in 1764 a small volume called *Crimes and Punishments* which created a stir throughout Europe. It argued that the right to punish should be limited, and that the punishment should fit the crime – whereas people were still being hanged for theft or even for poaching. Beccaria also called for an end to barbaric forms of execution such as burning to death or breaking on the wheel. A Parisian doctor, also born in 1738, agreed with him. Since the death penalty was widely used, he argued, at least it should be rapid. He was Joseph Ignace Guillotin; and although he did not invent the guillotine, his name became inseparable from it when it was adapted in 1789 by the French Academy of Surgery.

Fearsome as it was, the machine was at least an improvement on what had gone before. Despite the cruelty in which so many Europeans took part in, including slavery and the slave-trade, there were thus a few points of light in Europe. Justice, tolerance, and liberty were gaining ground. Habeas corpus and the jury system, the efforts of the '*philosophes*' in France, and the influence of Beccaria and his disciples: all these were small but vital steps towards a more compassionate society.

'FRENCH EUROPE' AND COSMOPOLITANISM

At first sight, Europe seemed to be growing cosmopolitan. The intelligentsia, who tended to set the intellectual fashion, often regarded the idea of a 'mother country' as a survival from barbarism. This attitude seemed justified by the fact that enlightened rulers spoke as if they shared it, apologizing like Frederick II ('Frederick the Great') of Prussia for the terrestrial duties they were obliged to perform. 'I hope,' wrote Frederick in his *Memoirs* (1743), 'that posterity, for whom I am writing, will distinguish in me between the philosopher and the prince, between the gentleman and the politician. I have to confess that it is very difficult to maintain decency and probity when one is thrown into Europe's great political whirlwind.' Writing in French and corresponding with Voltaire, this faithful disciple was outdone in skill and cunning only by Catherine II ('Catherine the Great') of Russia. She took advantage of the fact that her letters were widely distributed to extol her Empire's victories, minimize its defeats, conceal revolts, and tell shameless lies, letting it be thought, for example, that all Russian peasants ate chicken as often as they pleased.

French Europe in the Enlightenment

Its fashionable *salons* made Paris seem like the centre of Europe. But it had a rival in Ferney, near Geneva, where Voltaire spent the last part of his life. And Europe's cosmopolitanism was first expressed in the general use of French as the language of cultivated society and the aristocracy. *French Europe in the Enlightenment – L'Europe française au Siècle des Lumières –* is the title of a brilliant book by Louis Réau. Yet already in the eighteenth century it was foreshadowed by another: *Paris, the model for foreign nations or French Europe – Paris, le modèle des nations étrangères, ou L'Europe française* (published by the Italian Francesco Caraccioli in 1776).

Why was French the *lingua franca*? Was its adoption regarded as permanent? This was a question that was asked. As early as 1685, a certain Bougle declared: 'The French language is henceforth the point of contact for all the peoples of Europe.' Guy Miège, a Genevese who published in London an English–French and French–English dictionary, thought that 'the French language is in a certain sense becoming universal'. Gregorio Leti, who translated his own *Life of Cromwell* into French, added that 'the French language has become, in this century, that which is most generally known by all Europe'. By 1714, when French was used to prepare the Treaty of Rastadt between France and Austria at the end of the War of Spanish Succession, the language had effectively become that of European diplomacy.

How did it fare in the second half of the eighteenth century? English became its rival, encouraged by growing fashion and by the brilliance of English literature and science. Even Jean-Jacques Rousseau was critical of the prevailing Gallicization. In his *Considerations on the Government of Poland*, he expressed the hope that Poland would retain 'its civil and domestic usages'. 'A great nation which has never been too much involved with its neighbours must have many habits and customs which are peculiar to itself, but which are perhaps becoming tainted every day by the general tendency in Europe to adopt French tastes and manners. These ancient ways must be maintained and re-established.'

The best analysis of the situation was made by Jean le Rond d'Alembert (1717–83) in the *Discours préliminaire* he wrote in 1751 for the *Encyclopédie* which until 1759 he helped Denis Diderot to edit. 'Since our language,' he wrote,

> has spread throughout Europe, we thought that the time had come to substitute it for Latin, which since the renaissance of learning had been the language of scholarship. I admit that there is more excuse for a philosopher to write in French than for a Frenchman to compose Latin verses. I would even agree that the use of French has helped to make Enlightenment more general ... But it has a disadvantage which we ought to have foreseen. The scholars of other nations, to whom we have set an example, have rightly decided that they express themselves better in their own language than in ours. England has thus copied us in abandoning Latin, but in favour of English; Germany, where Latin seemed to have taken refuge, is beginning gradually to desert it: I doubt not that this precedent will soon be followed by the Swedes, the Danes,

and the Russians. In this way, before the end of the 18th century, a philosopher who wishes to study in depth the discoveries of his predecessors will be obliged to burden his memory with seven or eight different languages; and having devoted the best years of his life to learning them, he will die before beginning his true studies.

The hegemony of the French language and its literature was compounded by the influence of art. A single example will suffice: the *château* and park of Versailles were imitated all over Europe. As Louis Réau has put it: 'The satellites of the Château of Versailles are as numerous as the imitations of St Peter's or the Gesù Church in Rome.'

The Spanish Bourbons built the Real de la Granja; the Bourbons of Naples, La Reggia in Caserta; the Bourbons of Parma, the Ducal Villa of Colarno. In England there was Hampton Court; in Holland, Het Loo. But the largest number of imitations were in Germany: their sites included Bonn, Koblenz, Mannheim, Stuttgart, Schleissheim and Nymphenburg in Bavaria, Würzburg, and Potsdam, as well as Schönbrunn in Austria.

In Sweden there was Drottningholm and the Royal Palace of Stockholm; in Russia there were Peterhof, Tsarskoye Selo, and Pavlovsk. In the Belgian Hainaut there was Beloeil, and in Vienna the Belvedere (both residences of Prince Eugène of Savoy); in Hungary there was Esterhaza, and in Galicia there was Lancut. There were many more.

Nor was it only Versailles that inspired emulation: it was also Marly, the Trianons, Mme de Pompadour's Hermitage, as well as parks and gardens. At least at the beginning of the eighteenth century, Court art showed a family resemblance.

The Europe of music

There was also one characteristic art in which Europe gave the world a rich source of beauty: music. Not, of course, that other parts of the world were lacking it. But, to take one point, Europeans over the centuries invented a variety of musical instruments that was unique in its growing sophistication and in the immense range of the sounds it could produce. The organ, mentioned by Tertullian as early as the third century AD; the early key-action clavichord in the ninth century; Bartolomeo Cristofori's *Florentine gravicembalo col piano e forte* in 1709; and hundreds of different instruments – woodwind, brass, with strings plucked or bowed, percussion, keyboard: almost all were invented and developed by Europeans. The German Gottfried Silbermann, for instance, adopted Cristofori's final double-action design in 1745 after several failures of his own; and in about 1770 Johan Andreas Stein devised a different, lighter action which became known as the 'Viennese'. In London, John Broadwood (1732–1812) built a double-action piano; in France, Sebastien Érard (1752–1831) developed his double escapement or 'repetition' action, and took the final step towards creating the modern harp, competing with the 'chromatic harp' devised by his Austrian-born contemporary in Paris, Ignaz Joseph Pleyel (1757–1831), also a rival producer of pianofortes. After the lyres, citharas, and harps of antiquity, the six-string viola appeared in the ninth century, followed in the seventeenth century, at Lyon, by the four-string violin. The best known violin-maker was of course Antonio Stradivari, who was born in Cremona in 1644 and died in 1737. Nor was it only in devising musical instruments and musical notation that Europeans excelled. They also developed a multiplicity of musical forms. Until the twelfth century, unison singing was the normal practice; but then polyphony developed, mainly in two urban centres. In Belgium, it was associated with Roland de Lassus (1530–94), a native of Mons who became choirmaster at St John Lateran in Rome, worked in Antwerp, and finally served at the royal Court of Bavaria. In Italy, his close contemporary was Giovanni Pierluigi da Palestrina (1525–94), described on his coffin as 'Prince of Music', who was choirmaster of the Julian Chapel at St Peter's in Rome, and later at Santa Maria Maggiore. There also arose a German school into which Heinrich Schütz introduced Italian ideas, and a Spanish group whose leading representative was Tomás Luis de Victoria – sometimes spelt 'Vittoria' in the Italian style, since he worked in Rome for twenty years.

The combination of instruments and voices gave rise to a great Italian invention – opera. Its greatest early practitioner was Claudio Monteverdi (1567–1643), born, like Stradivari later, in Cremona. In the seventeenth century, all the Courts in Europe employed Italian musicians and set up Academies of Music on the Italian model. The best-known Italian court musician was the naturalized Frenchman Jean-Baptiste Lully (1632–87), born Giovanni Battista Lulli in Florence and taken as a boy to France where he worked as a scullion before becoming a violinist and eventually head of music to Louis XIV.

In the eighteenth century, however, it was Germany that produced the most outstanding musicians. They included Georg Friederich Händel (1685–1759), who became a naturalized Englishman as George Frideric Handel and director of the Academy of Music in London; and Johann Sebastian Bach (1685–1750), who during his lifetime was less well known than Handel. It was German composers, again, who in the second half of the eighteenth century developed a new and epoch-making musical form: the symphony. Unlike opera, this no longer blended theatre with sounds, voices, and instruments: it was pure music. The symphony reached the heights with Joseph Haydn (1732–1809), who died in despair when the French recaptured Vienna; with his Austrian compatriot Wolfgang Amadeus Mozart (1756–91); with Ludwig van Beethoven (1770–1827) from Germany; and with Franz Schubert (1797–1828) from Austria.

Philosophical cosmopolitanism: Voltaire

The archetype of the cosmopolitan writer was Voltaire. In his *Philosophical Dictionary*, however, there is no article on 'Europe', but only on 'Mother country'. Voltaire announced at the outset of it that he would not supply definitions but simply ask questions. These had a precise purpose: to demonstrate that only a small number of fortunate men, owners of property, believe that they have a mother country. Did the Jews have one? Did the generals who offered their services indiscriminately to one side or another? Did Abraham, who left Ur? Did the nomadic Attila? Did the monks, who renounced the world?

The mother country, for Voltaire, was 'a composition of many families'. He went on: 'The greater a country becomes, the less we love it; for love is weakened by diffusion.'

Finally, even for those who feel they belong to a country, 'It is lamentable, that to be a good patriot we must become the enemy of the rest of mankind ... To wish the greatness of our own country, is often to wish evil to our neighbours. He who could bring himself to wish that his country should always remain as it is, neither bigger nor smaller, neither richer nor poorer, would be a citizen of the universe.'

A fine phrase: but it hardly stands out in the article, because Voltaire cannot refrain from irony. 'Can one exclaim,' he asks, 'like Horatius in Corneille: So worthy he who for his country dies, Men should contend to win the glorious prize? ... He might as well exclaim

"Fiddlesticks!"' The couplet is, indeed, a touch overblown. Voltaire's cosmopolitanism was avowedly European. Why? Because:

> the peoples of Europe are closely linked with each other; they have similar laws; all their royal families are related; their citizens are continually travelling and forming mutual ties.
>
> Christian Europeans are as the ancient Greeks used to be: they may go to war with each other, but despite these conflicts they so observe the proprieties ... that a Frenchman, and Englishman, and a German, when they meet, often seem as if they were born in the same town.

Rousseau, Montesquieu, Diderot

Jean-Jacques Rousseau went further still. In his *Considerations on the Government of Poland*, published posthumously in 1782 but written a decade earlier, he declared: 'Today, whatever may be said, there are no longer French, Germans, Spaniards, or even English: there are only Europeans. They all have the same tastes, the same passions, and the same customs, because none has been led into national ways by any particular institution.' But whereas Voltaire delighted in this 'Europeanization', Rousseau bitterly scorned it. 'What does it matter which master they obey, which State whose laws they observe? So long as they find money to steal and women to corrupt, they are at home in any country.'

Montesquieu, for his part, never ceased to be cosmopolitan. He would refuse, he said, to propose to his ruler anything beneficial to his own nation but ruinous to another. 'I am a human being first and a Frenchman second,' he declared. Something beneficial to the mother country but ruinous to others would be a crime; so would something beneficial to Europe but harmful to humanity. Diderot, likewise, spoke of:

> narrow minds and ill-bred souls who care not what happens to the human race, and are so obsessed by their own little group – their nation – that they see nothing beyond its self-interest. These people want to be called good citizens; and I will concede that, so long as they allow me to call them bad specimens of humanity.

So it seemed quite natural to the *philosophes* of the eighteenth century to see themselves first as human beings and then as Europeans. 'Our

Europe' was the phrase used by Voltaire in his *Essay on Manners and Morals*. Belonging to a 'country' or a 'nation' rankled with them.

True, the phenomenon was complex. Rousseau, for example, with some reservations regarding the nation's size, felt his 'nationalism' stronger than his cosmopolitanism. The opposite was true of Voltaire. And in other countries, including Britain, cosmopolitanism could turn into patriotism. A typical example was Henry St John, first Viscount Bolingbroke. As leader of the Jacobite Tories, he lived in exile in France for many years, and was a spokesman for philosophic deism and rational behaviour: the poet Alexander Pope based his *Essay on Man* partly on his suggestions. But Bolingbroke's *On the Idea of a Patriot King* was later used by the future George III's tutor, the Earl of Bute, to try to teach his charge the elements of kingship.

Universal peace and the organization of Europe

In the eighteenth century there was much talk of peace. Clearly, there was a link between European cosmopolitanism and a certain form of pacifist utopianism. An excellent study of the subject is Sylvester John Hemleben's *Plans for World Peace through Six Centuries*.

William Penn

In 1693 the English Quaker William Penn wrote his *Essay towards the Present and Future Peace of Europe*. What he proposed was an agreement among Europe's rulers to convene an assembly – a 'sovereign or imperial Diet, Parliament or State of Europe'. This assembly would play the role of arbitrator, and any power which refused to accept its decisions would have to face the armed forces of all the others. Except in case of conflict, national rulers would enjoy complete sovereignty. Disarmament, if it could be achieved, would help to make possible the development of agriculture, commerce, science, and education. The reputation of 'Christendom' would be preserved and, as Pierre Dubois had argued nearly four centuries earlier, it would be able to unite against the threat from the Turks.

A Quaker disciple of William Penn's, John Bellers, actually put to the British Parliament a plan which he entitled 'Some Reasons for a European State, 1710, Proposed to the Powers of Europe by an Universal Guarantee and an Annual Congress, Senate, Dyet or Parliament. To

Settle any Disputes about the Bounds and Rights of the Princes ...'
Unlike Penn, Bellers thought that this organization should be primarily directed against France, which was then at war with most of Europe. Once peace had been won, however, France could be brought into the fold. The status quo established by the system would be immutable: all its members would give up any further territorial demands; and Europe would be divided into a hundred equal provinces. Each of these would supply the League with 1,000 soldiers, or with ships or money. The states would remain in being, and would be represented in the Diet. The compulsory arbitration procedure would be very much the same as that proposed by William Penn.

The Abbé de Saint-Pierre

These proposals created little stir. It was quite otherwise with the three volumes published between 1713 and 1717 by the Abbé Charles-Irénée Castel de Saint-Pierre, who had been secretary to the Cardinal de Polignac, one of the three French plenipotentiaries at the Congress of Utrecht which ended the War of Spanish Succession. The first two volumes were entitled *Project to Render Peace Perpetual in Europe*, the third was a *Project to Render Peace Perpetual among Christian Sovereigns*. The Abbé de Saint-Pierre seemed to be hesitating between the idea of Europe and the idea of Christendom.

What he proposed was a Confederation limited to Europe and designed to preserve peace against the rivalry between France and Austria. To this end, the sovereigns should establish a 'European Society' and send 'permanent representatives' to a 'perpetual Congress or Senate'. Here, too, the sovereigns would be pledged to maintain the status quo. All wars would be forbidden, unless they were decided upon as a form of military sanction. 'Chambers for the Maintenance of Commerce' would settle trade disputes. Religion, finally, the Abbé regarded from an ecumenical point of view.

As Leibniz told its author in 1715, this was a utopian plan. 'Every great prince,' declared Frederick II of Prussia in his last will and testament, 'is wedded to the idea of extending his power.' Yet if the influence of the Abbé de Saint-Pierre in the short term remained purely intellectual, in the longer term he provided inspiration for a number of statesmen, including the banker and finance official Jacques Necker, Napoleon Bonaparte, Prince Metternich, and those responsible for the League of Nations – especially as regards compulsory sanctions, controlled disarmament, and the bringing together of sovereign states rather than peoples.

Jean-Jacques Rousseau

Rousseau read the Abbé's work with great interest. In 1761 he published a shorter version of it, and in 1782 added his own *Judgement on Perpetual Peace*. His basic idea was to prevent war by forming a federation of princes, since they were the makers of war. He also adopted the idea of a permanent Diet.

The princes, he thought, would accept such a project only if it seemed to serve their interests. What was in their interest was peace. Rousseau was therefore at pains to provide a clear and logical proof of his thesis – something rather neglected by the Abbé de Saint-Pierre. In fact, Rousseau mistrusted princes, and would have preferred their replacement by states based on the principle of the general will.

Jeremy Bentham

Between 1786 and 1789, the English writer on law and political economy Jeremy Bentham composed an essay – not published until 1843, eleven years after his death – entitled *A Plan for an Universal and Perpetual Peace*. His use of the word 'universal' had a limited application: he proposed that any warmaker should be 'banished from Europe'. His plan was also limited – and utopian, since he believed that public opinion would be powerful enough both to ensure that the decisions of the 'World Court' were respected, and to impose disarmament.

Immanuel Kant

The last great eighteenth-century plan of this kind was published at Königsberg in 1795 by Immanuel Kant. Its title was *Zum ewigen Frieden* (*For Perpetual Peace*). Like his predecessors, Kant proposed a general confederation of European states. Also like them, he was opposed to secret treaties, standing armies, and the pursuit of national advantage by force. Influenced by the rising tide of nationalism, and by the third partition of Poland in that same year, he added the thought that no independent state could be subordinate to another. But his system was based on the highly novel idea that, to ensure perpetual peace, the states should have republican regimes, because in a republic the consent of the citizens was needed if the state was to go to war. Although much vaguer as to the workings of the confederation, Kant's proposal was less utopian than the others, and it certainly exerted great influence on the twentieth-century US President Woodrow Wilson. Kant was indeed one of the early advocates of collective security.

The Francophobe reaction

Seductive as it may have seemed, Europe's cosmopolitanism was based on a false premise. In his masterly *La Pensée européenne au XVIIIe siècle*, Paul Hazard makes a telling distinction between 'Europe' and 'the false Europe'. The temporary predominance of the French language and the success of French fashion very quickly led to a 'Francophobe' reaction, partly expressing the wounded pride of national self-esteem. The upshot was a series of campaigns against not only French ways, but also the French language, which by the end of the century was losing ground in Germany, the Low Countries, Denmark, and Russia. As the 'Romantic Movement' dawned, French literature – rationalist and often anti-religious – began to be despised by the new German writers. French art went out of fashion too. From the rococo style, taste moved towards antiquity. Landscape planners designed gardens in the English style, imitating untamed nature – a tendency that Jean-Jacques Rousseau strongly supported. It was 'Julie's Garden' in Rousseau's novel *La Nouvelle Héloïse* which launched the fashion to which the Queen of France, Marie-Antoinette of Austria, paid tribute when she had the architect Richard Mique devise the 'rustic village' at the Petit Trianon, complete with water mill, Alpine sheep, and beribboned cows.

THE DAWN OF NATIONALISM

The origins of nationalism in Europe

According to Jacques Godechot, the word 'nationalism' was first used by the Abbé Augustin Barruel in 1789. But the reality preceded the word. Its portents had been gathering for centuries. 'Patriotism', local or provincial, and dislike of strangers or foreigners, had long begun to be overlaid by a more positive notion: that of belonging to a larger living community, its members interdependent with one another, and sharing a mission in life.

Was Europe the community in question? No: it was too big. But within its constituent kingdoms, the double quest for internal political freedom and for independence from outside interference led to a phenomenon that Hans Kohn analysed very effectively in his book *The Idea of Nationalism*. The notion of the state developed into that of the nation-state, and with it there arose the passionate conviction that one's own nation was the finest, greatest, noblest, most cultivated, and most valuable to mankind, and hence that its rights must prevail over those of others.

But European nationalism was not homogeneous. In countries still divided, like Germany and Italy, it could not be the same as in countries like France, Britain, the United Provinces, Spain, or even Switzerland, which in their different ways already had highly developed organs of state. The French Revolution soon threw the growth of nationalism into sharp relief. In the meantime, its blurred outlines in the eighteenth century may be summarized as follows.

British nationalism

In Britain, nationalism had a longer history, perhaps, than anywhere else. The British were the first to contest 'French Europe'. British intellectuals refused to be 'Gallicized' – a refusal which coincided with deep-seated religious trends, the so-called 'Protestant awakening'. Britain felt superior to continental Europe, in wealth, cohesion, culture, and a political system that was the envy of foreign observers, including Montesquieu and Voltaire. Eighteenth-century Britain was conscious of becoming a nation.

It was in the name of British principles – of individual freedom and independence (later known as 'the right of self-determination') – that Britain's thirteen American colonies rebelled in 1776. Two years later, without success, the Irish followed their example. The American nation, founded on the Declaration of Independence, was the first example of 'decolonization', and one to which many eyes were turned.

Dutch nationalism

In the Low Countries, too, there was a reaction against French cultural hegemony and the French language. The Prince and the bourgeois aristocracy found themselves opposed by a party of 'Democratic Patriots', whose leader, Joan Derk van de Capellen, published in 1781 a pamphlet, *To the People of the Netherlands*, clearly inspired by nationalist fervour.

France and Switzerland: nationalism, Rousseau-style

In France and Switzerland, too, nationalism grew from the double urge for freedom at home and independence in foreign affairs.

The influence of Jean-Jacques Rousseau, however, gave it a more rational and political coloration. Rousseau's ideal was that 'small mother country', Geneva. Because the general will could be effective only if it was expressed freely and *directly*, large-scale republics were impossible. None, in fact, should be bigger than Corsica. Rousseau compromised, however, in his *Considerations on the Government of Poland*, in which – as in his *Social Contract* – he most clearly affirmed his love for the nation. This, for him, had absolute value; and his influence in France was all the greater because his theories corresponded to the basic aspirations of the 'patriots'.

The same was true, on a smaller scale, in the Swiss cantons. Here, the growing nationalism of the 'patriots' was expressed in the *Swiss Library of Johann Jakob Bodmer and the Schweizerlieder* or *Swiss Songs*, a book of poems published by Johann Kaspar Lavater in 1767. Rousseau's didactic manual *Emile*, moreover, greatly influenced the Swiss educational reformer Johann Heinrich Pestalozzi, who tried to bring up his own child on the principles it prescribed.

Germany

German nationalism took a different form, and appeared later. In a country largely separated cosmopolitanism faced less challenge. Even the Prussian monarchy, which Frederick II developed with a success which earned him his title of 'Frederick the Great', remained a state rather than a nation. Neither Immanuel Kant nor Friedrich Schiller thought in terms of a German Fatherland. Johann Wolfgang von

Goethe actually refused to harbour patriotic enmity for France, which he described as 'one of the most cultivated nations on earth'. For him, one of the Germans' virtues was their individualism.

Even so, nationalism did arise in Germany. Its literary spokesmen included the poet Friedrich Gottlieb Klopstock, the historian Justus Möser, and above all Johann Gottfried Herder (1744–1803), the great theoretician of the *Sturm und Drang* or '*Storm and Stress*' school of literature.

Whereas the British and the French, Rousseau included, saw the nation in intellectual and practical terms, Herder's idea of it was thoroughly Romantic. From his time onward, 'German nationalism' was seen as the inevitable expression of Germany's language and culture, as distinct from what the German historian Gerhard Ritter has called the 'classic nationalism' of France.

Herder's patriotism was not exclusive: he admired and embraced foreign culture as well as his own. But he remained a nationalist at heart, wedded to his concept of the *Volk*, the people – that national community whose limits were set by the mother tongue, the only language involuntarily learned. Always evolving, the nation had its part to play in the future evolution of humanity. Herder also looked backwards, however: he was always seeking the origins of things. Hence his frequent use of the German prefix 'Ur-', meaning 'age-old' or 'original', in quest of the *Ursprache* or 'first language' and the *Urvolk*, or 'ancestral people', whose primitive virtues must be regained. It was a dangerous doctrine, for it implied that all those who spoke the same language must belong to the same nation – the germ of many violent conflicts to come.

Italian nationalism

The Italian example was perhaps the most complex of all. Already in the sixteenth century, despite their political divisions, all Italians called themselves 'Italians'. But by the eighteenth century Italy had lost the pre-eminence it had enjoyed at the Renaissance – so much so that it only gradually felt its way towards real national awareness, and then only in reaction against French cosmopolitanism. The poet and dramatist Vittorio Alfieri (1749–1803) is the best exemplar of this evolution. His pamphlet *Il Misogallo* (*The Hater of the French*) (1793–9) was a violent diatribe against France, intended to use hatred as a stimulus to Italian national pride.

Spanish nationalism

In Spain, nationalism remained for a long time latent, restrained by the Church and by a series of absolute monarchs, the most remarkable of whom was the 'enlightened despot' Charles III (1759–88). It erupted, however, in the uprising against Napoleon in the years between 1807 and 1814. And while it produced no really outstanding writers, the poet, dramatist, and statesman Gaspar Melchior de Jovellanos (1744–1811), who held a legal post in Seville, was also a member of the Junta in charge of the rebellion against the French.

TOWARDS THE INDUSTRIAL REVOLUTION

The Industrial Revolution will be dealt with later, in chapter 15. But like most historical phenomena it had deep roots. Not least, it was a further proof that human beings are essentially creative.

The technological creativeness of Europeans assisted their further exploration and conquest of the world.

The Dutch in the seventeenth century

In the seventeenth century, the Dutch were Europe's greatest shipbuilders. They dominated trade in the Baltic, owned mines in Sweden, and delivered to its King Gustavus Adolphus a whole fleet, including the famous 64-gun warship *Vasa* – or *Wasa* – which sank on its maiden voyage in 1628 and was not salvaged until 1961. The British Navigation Acts drove the Dutch out of ports in Britain; but they pushed on into the Mediterranean and then into South-East Asia, where there was fierce competition between the Dutch and British East India Companies. The Dutch ousted the Portuguese from Ceylon and Indonesia; they sailed as far as Japan, seized Malacca on the Western coast of the Malay Peninsula, and discovered Tasmania. In America, admittedly, they were obliged in 1665 to cede New Amsterdam to the British, who renamed it New York; but they continued to occupy a number of West Indian islands as well as the coast of Guyana; and they also had outposts in Guinea and at the Cape.

EUROPE

Pacific exploration in the eighteenth century

In the Far East, the Russians pushed as far as the Kamchatka Peninsula, between the Bering Sea and the Sea of Okhotsk, in Siberia. In North America, the British explored the St Lawrence river, the Great Lakes, and the Mississippi. But the eighteenth century was above all the period of discoveries in the Pacific, made by such British commanders as George Anson (1697–1762) in the early 1740s, James Cook (1728–79) some thirty years later, and George Vancouver (1757–98) in the 1790s. Among their French counterparts were the Comte Louis Antoine de Bougainville (1729–1811), after whom the flamboyant *Bougainvillaea* is named, and Jean-François Galoup, Comte de La Pérouse (1741–c.1788).

These expeditions were greatly helped by the development of the sextant in 1757 and by the use of increasingly accurate chronometers.

France's colonial setbacks

French attempts to build a vast colonial empire in India and in Canada were foiled by the more systematic efforts of the British. In 1713 France lost Newfoundland, and in 1763 both Canada and India, except for five fortified Indian towns. All that remained to the French were some West Indian sugar islands, Mauritius and La Réunion in the Indian Ocean, and the Senegal river.

Broadly speaking, colonial conquests were a source of conflict among European countries, and a major obstacle to European unity. The war between France and Britain, for example, which broke out in 1755, was almost entirely caused by colonial rivalry.

European roads

Intra-European trade might perhaps have been expected to palliate the rivalry between Europeans overseas. At the beginning of the eighteenth century, however, Europe's roads were still in a deplorable state. Not for some decades did anything resembling a road network begin to be built by such central bodies as the French *Ecole des Ponts et Chaussées*, the School of Bridges and Highways, set up in 1747. Even then, the aim was essentially strategic – the rapid deployment of troops towards the frontiers. The French road system radiated mainly out of Paris; and Piedmont, the other Italian states, the Netherlands, Prussia, Spain,

Belgium, and Russia largely followed this model when building road networks of their own. In Britain, the practice was different: the roads were built by private companies made up of landowners, farmers, merchants, and manufacturers who recovered their costs by imposing tolls. It was in Britain, in the early years of the nineteenth century, that the Scottish inventor John Loudon Macadam perfected the road-surfacing method which bears his name.

Canals

If France may be credited with having initiated a modern road system, credit for canals must go to the Dutch. For many years their *Waterstaat*, which trained the best hydraulic engineers in Europe, had made it possible gradually to reclaim the polders from the North Sea. Their system of canals spread into France and was copied in Britain and Spain. Even so, journeys remained long and uncomfortable. In 1660 it had taken ten days to travel from Paris to Lyon; but in 1770 the same journey still took five. The system of 'post-horses' was also badly organized.

Wholesale trade

Wholesale trade was marked by permanent competition between the trading companies, many of them 'chartered' and allowed to raise troops and conquer fresh territory, and the private firms.

All the countries engaged in sea trade possessed trading companies. Frederick II founded one in Prussia; Russia established one for the Black Sea trade as soon as she reached it in 1774. Gradually, however, the monopolies enjoyed by the trading companies were eroded by competition from private firms which were much more adaptable.

Here, too, rivalry was the dominant theme. In economic matters as in politics, Europe's predominance was tarnished by the conflicts between European states, which seemed unable to settle their commercial and colonial differences without resort to war.

CONCLUSION

Yet, despite these conflicts, the seventeenth and eighteenth centuries were both marked, if not by moves towards European unity, at least by a certain 'cosmopolitanism'. The seventeenth century was an 'age of iron' in which repeated armed conflict, beginning with the Thirty Years' War, harassed a population already scarred by famine, pestilence, poverty, and peasant revolts. While the masses suffered, however, European philosophers were beginning gradually and effectively to question the principle of authority. The 'ancients' were slowly supplanted by the 'moderns': Galileo in Italy, Francis Bacon and Isaac Newton in Britain, and René Descartes in France helped lay the foundations of experimental science.

In the eighteenth century, large-scale poverty greatly decreased, and *philosophes* almost everywhere spread the light of reason. Meanwhile, paradoxically, absolute monarchy prevailed throughout Europe save for Great Britain; wars, and especially colonial wars, continued unabated; and national sentiment grew. Yet universalist and especially European plans for perpetual peace abounded. One author after another argued that with a few more revolutions of a 'liberal' variety, like Britain's 'Glorious Revolution' of 1688 or – still more – the American Declaration of Independence of 1776, Europe, already a beacon of progress in the world, would be able to unite.

The 'Western Revolution' which is the subject of the next chapter, and which included the shocks and counter-shocks of the French Revolution, replaced monarchical rivalry with something deeper and far more dangerous: conflicts between armed nations.

13
Revolution and Disillusion

Most of the states, large and small, which were ruled by the more or less authoritarian monarchies of the *ancien régime* knew little of the calm that more peaceful periods enjoyed. Riots, popular uprisings, 'peasant fury', and rebellions made the seventeenth century, in particular, an 'age of iron'. Yet although that century saw two revolutions in England which had profound economic and political effects, the first – the Civil War – was too remote, and the second – the 'Glorious Revolution' – was too moderate, for either to spark off any general European crisis.

This was not the case with the 1776 American Declaration of Independence and the French Revolution of 1789. Both had deep and lasting repercussions on the history of the West.

THE COMMON ROOTS OF REVOLUTION IN THE WEST

Complex causes

The reasons for any revolution are inevitably diverse: they involve vast numbers and a great confusion of forces. But the American historians R. R. Palmer and Louis Gottschalk agree with their French colleagues Georges Lefebvre and Jacques Godechot in stressing the interrelatedness of the revolutions that marked eighteenth-century Europe – its 'revolutionary climate', so to speak. As Jacques Godechot remarks:

> One can hardly fail to be struck by the series of revolutions that broke out between 1763 and 1848. There was the American Revolution between 1763 and 1783; there were revolutions in Genoa in 1768 and 1781. From 1782 to 1784 there was revolution in Ireland; from 1783 to 1787, in the United Provinces; from 1787 to 1790, in Belgium and

Liège. From 1787 onwards, the French Revolution gathered momentum: gradually, it spread through most of Western Europe, first affecting Belgium and the United Provinces, where the unrest of 1787 and 1790 had scarcely been quelled before it broke out again. It next spread to Germany, Italy, and Switzerland, finally reaching Malta, Poland, and even Egypt. A certain stability appeared in about 1800 with the emergence of Napoleon Bonaparte in France and the election of Thomas Jefferson in the United States. But the Revolution was not yet over.

The agrarian structure in Europe

In fact, several types of revolution coincided, each varying in importance from one country to another.

To understand the nature and scale of these revolutions, one has to realize the infinite diversity of Europe's institutions, territorial divisions, tax systems, feudal obligations, and local privileges. European countries could, however, be classified in three broad groups.

The first included countries to the east of the Elbe, as well as southern Italy and Spain. These were the lands of the great estates. The peasants who worked them were either slaves or what in southern Italy were known as *cafoni*, landless and desperately poor. The Prussian Junker, the Russian nobleman, the Polish or Hungarian grandee each wielded enormous power. Trade was dominated by the Jews; industry was rudimentary; there was little or no sign of a prosperous middle class.

The second group of countries covered the whole of continental Europe to the west of the Elbe and to the north of the Pyrenees and the Apennines, with the exception of the United Provinces. Here, aristocratic and Church property co-existed with a substantial proportion of land owned by the peasantry – which, however, owed feudal dues to the lord of the manor. He did no work: if he worked the land himself he would lose his title to nobility.

Serfdom, by this time, had virtually disappeared.

Britain and the United Provinces, thirdly, enjoyed a more prosperous and advanced type of economy. Here, as has been seen, the nobility could work without losing caste, and was little different from the prosperous middle classes. Both took part in government. Only the eldest son of a lord could sit in the House of Lords; the younger sons, like the gentry and the middle classes, were 'commoners' and could be elected to the House of Commons, which as a result became a further point of contact between the aristocracy and the bourgeoisie. Peasants and artisans, however, were not necessarily better off in Britain and the Netherlands than anywhere else. The larger landowners continually sought to extend their property by appropriating, with the aid of Enclosure Acts, part of the common land on which the peasants relied. Thus impoverished, a number of country-dwellers drifted into the towns, forming an underclass of poorly paid labourers who were later known as the 'industrial proletariat'.

The peasant revolution

There were no more famines in France after 1715; and the same was true of Western Europe as a whole. But the peasant population was too big to live off the land available, and many suffered great hardship. The more prosperous peasants, the tillage farmers, admittedly enlarged their holdings; and there were now very few actual serfs to the west of the Elbe. But 'land hunger' was widespread, and it affected every kind of smallholder. He might be a 'farmer', paying a fixed rent to his landlord; he might be a 'share-cropper', owing the landlord a proportion, usually half, of all he produced; he might be the owner of his land. But full freeholders were rare. Most owners – who could sell, buy, and bequeath their property – were still subject to feudal dues, justified in theory by the role of the lord of the manor as 'head landlord'. The dues might take the form of annual taxes, in cash or kind; forced labour; 'occasional' taxes levied on sales or inheritance; or a monopoly enjoyed by the lord of the manor over the wine-press, the mill, the bread oven, the oil-store, the rabbit-run, or some other key element of rural life. Such feudal privileges weighed very heavily on large families with meagre resources, living in primitive squalor. But on top of all this, the peasants had to pay a number of 'common' taxes, such as *tallage* (in France *la taille*, in Spain *la talla*), from which, unlike priests and nobles, they were never exempt. Finally, they also owed 'tithes' to the Church.

Nor does this description do justice to the gross inequalities created by urban or provincial privileges and by local customs. One example is the salt tax in France. It is hard now to realize how much this levy on an essential commodity – a vital preservative if nothing else – haunted the poor and contributed to their distress. Those appointed to police the tax could turn violent; and those who evaded it or dealt in contraband were arrested and condemned to the galleys.

There was also a general price rise, caused indirectly by the discovery of gold mines in the state of Minas Geraes in Brazil, as well as by an increase in the production of silver. The growing amount of precious metal in circulation led to a fall in its value, and thereby to a rise in the money cost of other goods: but wages rose only slowly to match the new inflation. When a bad harvest lessened the supply of food, as it did in France in 1770, 1774, 1784, and above all in 1788, food prices rose still more sharply. The result was greater hardship and discontent among peasants and urban artisans alike. The peasants, seeing that their landlords were using old documents to justify heavier feudal dues, began in some areas to pillage and burn the archives – which sometimes led them to burn the manor houses too.

The middle-class revolution

The importance of the peasants' and artisans' revolution was that it supplied reserve troops for what has been called the middle-class or bourgeois revolution. This arose out of the growing prosperity of middle-class town-dwellers, the *'bourgeois'* (literally, *burgesses*), who had made their fortunes in banking, commerce, handicrafts, industry, or the professions. In France, only the legal profession could lead to a peerage, on condition that one bought the appropriate office. What then did the bourgeois demand? First and foremost, the abolition of the privileges enjoyed by the nobility and the clergy, which enabled these 'orders' to pay less tax. At the same time, the bourgeoisie sought a share of political power. This implied replacing absolute monarchy with constitutional monarchy, with powers limited by a written constitution, together with a Bill of Rights modelled on the United States example, which was famous throughout Western Europe: the US Constitution dated from 1787.

The aristocratic revolution

It was in that year that the 'aristocratic revolution' began in France, as a first move against absolute monarchy. It had an apparent precedent in Britain's 'Glorious Revolution' of 1688. Only Parliament, in Britain, could raise taxes; it therefore controlled the executive, and all the efforts of King George III (1760–1820) failed to restore the Royal prerogative.

There were 'Parliaments' in France: but these were in fact high courts of justice. Their members or 'officers' had not been elected, but had bought their posts and thereby acquired peerages. To propose that these Parliaments or *parlements*, notably that in Paris, should be empowered to impose or refuse laws and taxes meant seeking to give part of the nobility, known as 'the nobility of the robe', unprecedented power. Since 'the nobility of the robe' was still close to the bourgeoisie, the latter began by backing its demands. Then, however, the bourgeoisie discovered that the first concern of members of the *parlement* was to entrench their privileges, and in particular the privilege of paying less tax. With that, they lost all widespread support. In general, in fact, the aristocracy, like the clergy, turned out to be the main victim of the Revolution. Not only did it fail to take over the power of the monarchy: it also lost its privileges; and many of its members paid with their lives for their real or supposed resistance to the Revolution.

THE 'GREAT NATION' AND REACTIONS IN EUROPE

The French Revolution, clearly, could not fail to affect the rest of the world. In the first place, it had more or less enthusiastic supporters in most of the countries in Europe: as in France, oddly enough, they were known as *'patriots'*. Their growth was encouraged by a number of things: the widespread use of French in eighteenth-century Europe, the international influence of the philosophes; and the arrival of observers from other countries. These included Arthur Young from England, author of *Travels in France* (1792) and other publications on the state of the country after the Revolution, and Thomas Paine, born British but naturalized American, who in *The Rights of Man* (1790–2) compared the French Constitution of 1791 with that of Britain. Paine's works were widely distributed by two British radical societies: the Society for Constitutional Information, originally founded in 1780 and revived ten years later with Horne Tooke, Thomas Holcroft, Thomas Erskine, and William Godwin among its members and supporters; and the London Corresponding Society, founded in 1792, whose Secretary, Thomas Hardy, together with Horne Tooke and John

Thelwall, was arrested for High Treason in 1794. Tooke and Thelwall were acquitted, and the prosecution of Hardy was dropped.

In Ireland, hostility to England led to the establishment of the 'United Irishmen' league, headed by Theobald Wolfe Tone, in 1791. In 1795 Tone went to the United States, and in 1796 to Paris, where he worked closely with the National Convention and helped to promote the abortive invasion of Ireland.

In the United Provinces, 'French patriots' were recruited mainly from among the lower middle classes, artisans, and peasants, while 'Dutch patriots' came from the upper middle class. Both called for 'freedom'; but the former sought union with France whereas the latter, who were more numerous, wanted a Dutch Republic.

In Belgium, where the struggle was against Austrian domination, the leader of the democrats, François Vonck, made contact with the French, while the conservatives or 'statists', led by Henri Van der Noot, were less favourable to France and essentially sought to return to the old system which Joseph II of Austria had swept away.

In 1790 Van der Noot's faction broke with the 'Vonckists' and set up a Republic of the United States of Belgium. Its Act of Union, proclaimed on 10 January 1790, was based not on the French model but on that of the United States. Within a few weeks, the Belgian Republic was overthrown by a small Austrian army.

In Germany, a number of intellectuals followed the French Revolution with keen interest. In 1790, to celebrate the anniversary of the fall of the Bastille, the traveller and writer Georg Heinrich Sieveking organized a banquet in Hamburg for eighty people, all wearing the tricolour cockade. Among them was the celebrated poet Friedrich Gottlieb Klopstock. The best-known German philosopher, Immanuel Kant, who by now was sixty-five and a professor at the University of Königsberg, remained loyal to the Prussian monarchy, and opposed to violence; but he willingly declared himself a 'Jacobin' or radical supporter of the French Revolution. So did the philosopher Johann Gottlieb Fichte. Johann Wolfgang von Goethe actually witnessed the Battle of Valmy, where the French Revolutionary forces defeated the Prussians on 20 September 1792; but he preferred not to take sides, and it was only much later that he published his *French Campaign* and described how he had told his companions on the battlefield that evening: 'This place and this day mark a new epoch in the history of the world, and you will be able to say: "I was there".'

In Poland, where there were eight or nine million illiterate serfs, 100,000 nobles (often poor, but still sovereign), a few magnates with enormous estates, and very few middle-class town-dwellers, King Stanislas Poniatowski professed to support the Enlightenment. But he feared reform. On 3 May 1791, under the influence of 'patriot' leaders and in an effort to resist the Russians and the Prussians, the Poles adopted a Constitution inspired by French Revolutionary laws. A year later, however, at the request of the magnates, the Russians and the Prussians invaded Poland. They abolished the Constitution and on 25 January 1793 partitioned the country between them. This was the 'Second Partition of Poland'.

Hungary sought increased autonomy against the Austrian Emperor Leopold II, by means of a *Hungarian Declaration of the Rights of Man and of the Citizen* and a *Constitutional Act*. Francis II, who succeeded Leopold in 1790, firmly opposed any such thing.

In Switzerland, made up of thirteen cantons and of dependent joint *'bailliages'*, many people favoured the French Revolution. This was partly because the country had a large and well-educated middle class which opposed any form of 'vassalage', and partly because the larger cantons were in fact aristocratic republics, which the 'patriots' hoped to make more democratic. In the old mountain cantons, where 'direct democracy' was the rule, French Revolutionary influence remained much less strong.

In Italy, agitation on behalf of the French 'patriots' was more lively than elsewhere. A number of revolutionary clubs were formed, notably in Piedmont and Bologna, but also in other parts of the peninsula.

In Spain, by contrast, the Government quickly stifled any pro-French demonstrations, which were also denounced by the clergy.

In Russia and the Scandinavian countries, any repercussions from the French Revolution were very much attenuated.

On 24 August 1792, pro-French and pro-Revolutionary foreign 'patriots' were accorded an unusual honour: on the proposal of the poet Marie-Joseph Chénier, the title of 'French citizen' was conferred on writers who had 'undermined the foundations of tyranny and prepared the way to freedom'. Those thus rewarded in England included the scientist Joseph Priestley, the political economist Jeremy Bentham, the anti-slavery reformers William Wilberforce and Thomas Clarkson, and the political philosopher James Mackintosh, who attacked Edmund Burke's *Reflections on the Revolution in France*. In Germany, those chosen included Jean Baptiste du Val; Baron von Cloots, self-styled 'orator of the human race', who took the name 'Anacharsis Cloots'; the idealistic teacher Joachim Heinrich Campe; the epic poet Friedrich Gottlieb Klopstock; and Friedrich Schiller, who was not in fact wholly sympathetic to the cause. In Switzerland there was the educationist Johann Heinrich Pestalozzi; in Poland, the soldier and patriot Tadeusz Kosciuszko; in Holland, Cornelius de Pauw, author of a well-known book on America; and in the United States, George Washington, James Madison, Alexander Hamilton, Thomas Paine, and the poet Joel Barlow. Cloots and Paine, incidentally, were also elected to the French National Convention.

Peaceful beginnings

This haphazard sprinkling of supporters, with a few clubs, a few periodicals, and a few pamphlets, cannot of course account for the conquests which from 1792 onwards made France for a time the proud and dominant 'Great Nation', poised at the turn of the century to found the Napoleonic Empire.

At first, everything seemed to favour a very peaceful policy. French officers, all of them nobles if above the rank of captain, sided with the King against the Assembly, and often refused to wear the tricolour cockade (red, white, and blue for Paris as against white for the King). One result was a series of quarrels between officers and other ranks, sometimes amounting to outright mutiny. Many officers went abroad. In 1792, 6,000 officers were absent out of a total of 9,000. The National Guard, set up in July 1789 on the American model, and headed by the Marquis de Lafayette, who had fought in the American War of Independence and so was known as 'the hero of two worlds', could only be used within France. On 14 July 1789, of course, the Paris crowd had stormed the Bastille: but although this was later interpreted as a symbolic blow for liberty, its original purpose had been to secure arms.

Undermanned and inadequately armed, the French army was not in a strong position. This may explain why, on 22 May 1790, the Constituent Assembly voted a 'Declaration of Peace to the World', renouncing 'any war of conquest' and promising 'never to use its forces against the liberty of another people'.

And yet this same Assembly, after long hesitation and in response to a local insurrection, decided on 13 September 1791 to annex the enclave of Avignon and its environs, which belonged to the Pope.

France declares war

On 20 April 1792, moreover, with the approval of the Jacobin Club (including Jacques-Pierre Brissot's faction but not that of Maximilien de Robespierre), King Louis XVI declared war on 'the King of Bohemia and Hungary' – i.e. the Emperor Francis II, brother of Queen Marie-Antoinette – on the pretext that he was refusing to disperse meetings of refugee émigrés, deemed to be a threat to France.

The early defeats suffered by small French units on the frontier of the Austrian Low Countries – present-day Belgium – were taken by foreigners as a proof that France no longer possessed an army. So it was that when Prussia entered the war, in July 1792, its military commander the Duke of Brunswick felt able to announce that he would wipe Paris off the map of Europe.

As well as the remnants of the Royal Army – professional soldiers enrolled for twenty years – France had 'national volunteers'. The proclamation of 'the motherland in danger' had produced a large number of recruits, many of them artisans, smallholders, and bourgeois from the National Guard. The Jacobins believed, in fact, that the war would reveal a secret agreement between the King and foreign monarchs, in particular his brother-in-law Francis II. After the failure of the 'flight to Varennes' in June 1791, Louis XVI and Marie-Antoinette were certainly counting on the defeat of the disorganized French army.

As it happened, France's initial setbacks, and Brunswick's invasion of the country, which by September 1792 had reached Verdun, greatly speeded up the Revolution. The King's rule was suspended on 10 August 1792; the American-inspired 'National Convention' was summoned; and a first wave of the Terror began with the 'massacres of September 1792'. The discovery in November of the *armoire de fer*, the iron safe in the Tuileries Palace where the King concealed his correspondence, led to his trial before the National Convention and finally to his condemnation and execution on 21 January 1793.

Valmy

Meanwhile, on 20 September 1792 – the eve of the National Convention's proclamation of the Republic – the French had faced the Prussian army at the Battle of Valmy. It was a relatively minor engagement, but its historic importance was immense. The French occupied the Valmy plateau, dominated by a windmill. The Prussian troops, all highly trained professional soldiers, had in the previous few days had to assuage their hunger by eating excessive quantities of the local white grapes. When the mist dispersed, they were surprised to see that, far from having retreated, as they had imagined, the French were still in position and looking remarkably calm. King Friedrich-Wilhelm of Prussia, and Brunswick, gave the order to attack. 'Nothing could have been finer or more imposing,' wrote the Prussian General, the Prince of Nassau-Siegen. 'It looked like a well-drilled Potsdam exercise. Never had I so firmly believed in victory, for this sight would have exalted the stoniest of souls.' But when the French stood their ground and shouted, '*Vive la Nation!*' the Prussians faltered and stopped. Then, despite the King, who courageously exposed his great height to enemy fire, Brunswick ordered the retreat. A storm broke out, and the troops withdrew in chilly disorder. 'Old Fritz' – Frederick the Great – 'would not have behaved like that,' wrote one eyewitness. And Goethe declared: 'In the morning, there was no doubt that all the French would be skewered into a single mouthful. In the evening, the Prussians avoided each other's eyes.' The significance of Valmy was that it introduced into warfare, alongside the professional army, a new army made up of citizens.

One of the victorious French Generals was François Christophe de Kellermann, from Alsace. He wrote: 'I offered battle to the Prussians, and they never dared attack me: the most hardened enemy cannot defeat those who are dedicated to the defence of liberty.'

From 1792 to 1795, Revolutionary France successfully confronted almost all of Europe. Success against the Prussians at Valmy was followed by victory over the Austrians at Jemappes in November 1792. France now seized the whole of present-day Belgium; and while the Prussians retreated towards the Rhineland, the French pressed forward to Frankfurt and Mainz.

The First Coalition: revolutionary expansionism

Why did the so-called 'First Coalition' emerge at the beginning of 1793? One by one, Britain, Portugal, the United Provinces, Spain, several Italian states (the Kingdom of Piedmont and Sardinia, Tuscany, and the Papal States), and a number of German principalities, all went to war. It would be a mistake to see this as a monarchical reaction to the execution of Louis XVI. Only the Bourbon King of Spain, Charles IV, was perhaps deeply moved. The real reason was determination to resist a growing phenomenon still familiar in the twentieth century – 'revolutionary expansionism'. Because the Revolution, in the eyes of its most fanatical partisans, represented Truth, it should obviously be implanted in neighbouring countries. If the latter – as was often the case – contained a certain number of 'patriot' sympathizers, then annexation was in order. It might be preceded, as in Avignon, by a form of plebiscite, sometimes rigged.

Rigged or not, the principle of spreading the Revolution was endorsed by the French National Convention on 19 November 1792, when it promised to 'bring fraternity and assistance to all peoples desirous of regaining their liberty'. It was a commitment both to endless warfare and to the responsibility of deciding which peoples needed 'assistance'. Before long, such decisions were taken without the recipients' consent.

Britain had a reason of her own for entering the war against France. As the new rulers of Belgium, the French National Convention decided to do what the Spaniards had given up since 1609 – reopen the port of Antwerp. Its closure, the British thought, was what had enabled London to become the trading metropolis of Europe and the world. If the strongest power in Europe was now to use Antwerp as a major seaport, this would be an economic disaster for Great Britain.

The Committee of Public Safety and the Terror

In March 1793, the allies managed to drive the French out of Belgium and the Rhineland, and to invade France via the Alps and the Pyrenees. They were helped by the fact that the French General Charles-François Dumouriez, the victor of Valmy and Jemappes, had been charged with plotting against the National Convention: he was charged with treason for attempting to restore the monarchy, and took refuge with the

Austrians before finally settling in England, where he died at Great Marlow in 1823. France's setbacks led to the establishment of a strong 'Revolutionary Government', based on a 'Committee of Public Safety', directly dependent on the National Convention and practising dictatorship by terror. Its leading lights, for internal policy, included Maximilien de Robespierre, Georges Couthon, and the 25-year-old Louis Antoine Léon Florelle de Saint-Just, whose motto put his creed in a nutshell: 'No liberty for the enemies of liberty'. 'The despotism of liberty' was another way of putting it.

The positive result of this governmental system and of the new strength acquired by the French Revolution – and well noted by Goethe – was the reconquest of Belgium and the Rhineland. On 27 July 1795 (known in the Revolutionary calendar as the 9th of Thermidor in Year II), Robespierre, Couthon, and Saint-Just were overthrown, to be executed on the following day: but their fall coincided with the French recapture of Antwerp and Brussels. In 1795 France occupied the Netherlands; and in the same year the Treaties of Basle and The Hague saw the break-up of the 'First Coalition'. One by one, its members made peace with France: Tuscany (whose Grand Duke Ferdinand III was the Emperor's brother-in-law), Prussia, Hesse-Cassel, the United Provinces (occupied and renamed 'the Batavian Republic', in forced alliance with France), and finally Spain. Only Britain, Austria, Portugal, some Italian states, and Southern Germany now remained at war with that 'Great Nation', France.

The success of the Revolution

How had France managed to achieve so much? The size of population was clearly a factor in success. In the year 1800, France's inhabitants numbered 28.2 million – the second largest population in Europe, behind Russia with 40 million. The next in size was Austria, with 28 million, followed by the rest of Germany (23 million), Italy (18 million), and the British Isles (16 million). The total population of Europe was 153.2 million.

Apart from Russia and the British Isles, protected by the North Sea and the Channel, no European country alone was therefore a match for France. But how did she manage to resist the First Coalition?

Basically, there are two ways to overcome an enemy: to be better armed or to deploy more troops. Neither the Revolution nor, later,

Napoleon, substantially improved French weapons. The army was still using the 1777 Charleville flintlock musket, which weighed 4.4 kilograms or 9.5 lb, with a steel cleaning-rod. When the bayonet was fixed, it was 1.8 metres long, taller than many men. The bronze muzzle-loaded cannons used as field artillery were still variants of the *Gribeauval* model devised under Louis XVI, although Napoleon made them more manoeuvrable.

The big change was in the troops themselves. Valmy had shown the effectiveness of French volunteers. In February 1793, at the suggestion of Edmond Dubois-Crance, a member of the Committee of Public Safety, it was agreed to merge the old white-trousered regular army (colloquially known as '*culs-blancs*' or 'white-bums') with the volunteers, who wore blue like the National Guard (and were known as '*bleuets*', which also meant 'kingfishers').

In the same year, 1793, a law was passed to 'requisition' men. Later, in 1798, this became the system of conscription, or equal military service for all.

It was the plan decreed by the National Convention on 24 February 1793 to levy 300,000 men that sparked off the great rising in the Vendée which began on 11 March. The Vendée, in western France, was a region of Royalists and in particular of fervent Catholics who resented being mobilized for a cause which they detested. The rebellion was bloody, and for a time successful: so, later, was its punishment. In August 1793 came the famous *levée en masse*, or mass levy, the creation of a conscript army, and prelude to the general mobilizations which took place in the nineteenth century. The decree of 23 August 1793, which established it, saw it as a necessary response to any invasion of France:

> From that moment on, until all enemies have been driven from the territory of the Republic, all French people are requisitioned for army service. Young men will fight; married men will forge weapons and carry supplies; women will make tents and uniforms and serve in hospitals; children will shred old linen; old people will be brought to the public squares that they may encourage the soldiers and preach hatred against Kings and unity for the Republic.

The *levée en masse* made possible something unheard-of at that time – an army of 1,200,000 men. In practice, it produced only 750,000: but that was already exceptional. To raise such numbers required efficient administration; and, quite apart from open resistance as in the Vendée, the army was constantly depleted by desertions, sometimes also *en masse*, and by failures to report to the colours: *'recalcitrants'* took refuge in remote areas, as did those in the Second World War who sought the maquis to escape conscription by the occupying Nazis for forced labour in Germany. 'Conscription' into the Revolutionary army became more and more of a burden: after twenty years of war, it made Napoleon especially unpopular in country areas of France. Meanwhile, by nationalizing Church property in November 1789, and then by voting for a 'Civil Constitution of the Clergy' which made priests mere civil servants and no longer recognized their true vocation, the Revolutionaries had permanently antagonized European Catholics.

THE REVOLUTION AND THE BIRTH OF NATIONALISM

Patriotic feelings are no doubt as old as humanity itself. The patria is the land of one's parents, the 'motherland' or 'fatherland'. The great majority of human beings feel some warmth for their own part of the world, whatever its boundaries or size. This basic feeling can give rise to others, such as xenophobia or dislike of strangers, and nostalgia on the part of those exiled from home. World literature expresses these feelings with an infinite variety of nuances.

The nationality principle

The nationality principle, as developed in nationalism, is no longer a mere feeling, but an intellectual concept. Everyone belongs to a well-defined human community, extending over a certain area and possessing a certain number of common characteristics. This community is the nation. If in addition the nation is not divided or subject to foreign domination, but governs itself by means of its own institutions, then it is a nation-state. In the twentieth century, the aim of every political community was to become a nation-state.

Compared with patriotism, which is as old as the hills, nationalism is very recent. It emerged in the eighteenth century in Western Europe and in Britain's North American colonies; then, during the first half of the nineteenth century, it spread to Central Europe and the Balkans, as well as to Latin America. In the second half of the nineteenth century it reached the Arab world, India, South-East Asia, and the Far East. In the twentieth century it permeated Africa.

Generally, as it develops, nationalism makes any form of foreign domination intolerable, and gives those who are dominated the firm determination to win their independence, if necessary by violent rebellion and war.

Political theorists normally distinguish between two kinds of nationalism. The first used to be thought of as 'nationalism of the German variety', but Professor Gerhard Ritter prefers to call it 'romantic'. The second, the Anglo-American or French variety, may be described as 'classic'.

Romantic nationalism

Romantic nationalism is based on the idea that belonging to a particular nation is not a matter of choice. Everyone inherits a mother tongue, national customs, literature, art, and folklore. All these amount to what the main founder of this doctrine, Johann Gottfried Herder, called the *Volksgeist* or 'national spirit'.

Herder, born in Prussia in 1744, studied at Königsberg under the philosopher Immanuel Kant. A teacher and Protestant pastor, he travelled in France, met Goethe in Strasbourg, and eventually became general superintendent of the Lutheran Church in Weimar, where he was reunited with Goethe. Two of Herder's most important works were *Another Philosophy of History* (*Auch eine Philosophie der Geschichte*), published in 1774, and the four-volume *Outline of a Philosophy of Human History* (*Ideen zur Philosophie der Geschichte der Menschheit*), which appeared between 1784 and 1791. Herder was opposed to rationalism, which in his opinion implied that all individuals were alike, so that all nations were identical and had the same rights, as the French Revolutionaries seemed to advocate. On the contrary, each *Volksgeist* was 'unique, prodigious, inexplicable, inexpressible'. It gave the nation a character all its own. Germany, therefore, must avoid being influenced by the French Revolution. Perhaps surprisingly, Herder showed no interest in the idea of a single political authority for Germany, which was divided at that time into more than 350 political units, some of them very small. It was his disciples in the Napoleonic era, such as Johann Gottlieb Fichte, Friedrich Ludwig Jahn, and Ernst Moritz

Arndt, who preached what might be termed political patriotism. Even for Herder, however, the inhabitants of Alsace were Germans because they spoke Germanic dialect.

Classic nationalism

The French Revolutionaries – or at least the moderates among them – were essentially universalists: what was true for one human being, they thought, was true for all. Had not Descartes declared that 'Good sense [i.e. the ability to reason] is the one thing in the world which is most fairly distributed'? For this reason, the members of the Constituent Assembly, and then those of the National Convention (which also drew up a Constitution, but this time on Republican lines), saw themselves as legislating for humanity as a whole. The first group were disciples of Montesquieu, calling for the separation of powers and for a constitutional monarchy; the second followed Rousseau in his doctrine of popular sovereignty. *The Declaration of the Rights of Man and of the Citizen*, which dated from 26 August 1789, and was used to introduce the Constitution of 1791, spoke of 'the natural, inalienable, and sacred Rights of Man'. In other words, what applied to the French applied to all other peoples too. Article 3 of the Declaration significantly stated: 'The principle of all sovereignty essentially resides in the Nation.'

For the national community, the conclusion to be drawn from this Declaration – and from its more 'revolutionary' successor in 1793 – was that all peoples had the right to self-determination. In contrast to Herder, who gave pride of place to a *Volksgeist* which was not chosen but inherited, the French Revolutionaries believed that the Nation embodied its citizens' free will. To express this will, the idea of the plebiscite took root: it had already been used in June 1790 by the Avignon rebels against the Pope. Needless to say, in accordance with this 'classic' nationalist doctrine, based on free will, the inhabitants of Alsace were French, if that was their preference, irrespective of their mother tongue.

On 14 July 1790, to mark the first anniversary of the storming of the Bastille, a Festival of Federation was staged on the Champ de Mars in Paris, with delegates from National Guard units all over France. In the presence of the King, they swore to live and die together. The ceremony echoed what had been said by a speaker at Pontivy a few months earlier, in February 1790: 'There are no longer Bretons or Angevins, but citizens of the same Empire ... who swear on the altar of the Motherland ... to live as heroes or to die.' Bretons, Angevins, Alsatians, people of Languedoc, Provence, or the Dauphine: all that was swept aside. Henceforth, everyone was French.

REVOLUTIONARY EXPANSIONISM AND THE DISILLUSIONMENT OF THE EUROPEAN 'PATRIOTS'

The French Revolutionary regime might perhaps, as it had originally promised, have ensured 'peace in the world'. A powerful France might have helped other peoples to overthrow their 'tyrants', and then have left them to order their affairs as they chose and live in harmony with other regimes that shared the same ideals. This, indeed, was the hope of the 'patriots' – the Revolution's sympathizers – almost everywhere: all of them called for liberty, the rights of man, and a constitution (a word made popular by the American Revolution and, nearer home, by that in the Netherlands in 1783).

But the Revolution did no such thing. Although its natural enemies were the supporters of the *ancien régime* and all those who opposed the ideas of the 'patriots', it eventually antagonized the 'patriots' themselves. To their deep disappointment, they saw the Revolution turn into a conquering, dominating, hegemonial force.

The counter-revolutionaries

The Revolution's opponents of course included those who had fought it from the start. There were the aristocratic émigrés and those who sheltered them in their countries of refuge; there was the Catholic Church, which resented the 'Civil Constitution of the Clergy'. Die-hard defenders of privilege gave the counter-revolution a solid base both in France and abroad.

Edmund Burke

But the counter-revolutionary case also had intellectual backing. Its best spokesman was the Anglo-Irish writer and orator Edmund Burke. Born in Dublin in 1729, the second son of an Irish Protestant lawyer and his Catholic wife, he was educated at the Quaker school in Ballitore and at Trinity College, Dublin, before being admitted to the Middle Temple to study law. He disliked the narrowness of legal education, however, and was never called to the bar. A great reader of the eighteenth-century *philosophes*, a traveller in France, the editor of a new political publication, *The Annual Register*, and a very effective Member of Parliament, Burke hardly seemed a typical 'reactionary'. He championed justice for Irish Catholics and for the native inhabitants of British India, and independence for the American colonies, even after the War had begun. But like Herder, whom he may have read, Burke was an avowed opponent of universalism and rationalism. Everything, he believed, was a product of history in all its diversity. 'Man' in general was an unreal concept: he spoke of 'the false doctrine of the supposed Rights of Man'. For Burke, there was a British people, adapted to liberal practices, a French people, a German people, and so on.

It was in 1790, long before the outbreak of war between France and Britain, that Burke published his *Reflections on the Revolution in France*. In it he expressed his anger at British partisans of the French Revolution, and especially at the 'Revolution Society' some of them had formed. For him, the Revolution of 1789 was quite unlike the 'Glorious Revolution' of 1688. He was scathing about the institutions which the Constituent Assembly was setting up in France, because in the name of universal reason the Revolutionaries were sweeping away the past and trying to establish a secular state: they believed in abstract Liberty, whereas only liberties existed, patiently established through the vicissitudes of history. Burke had no belief in Rousseau's 'state of nature', in which humanity had supposedly been virtuous, until corrupted by society. In his view, society itself produced, from time to time and in various places, during the course of history, beneficial effects. Britain's unwritten constitution, for instance, was excellent because it had grown up over centuries. Burke pointed to the contrast between English gardens, with their rambling curved paths, their clumps of trees, their naturally flowing streams, and French gardens at that time, geometrically designed, with piped water, fountains, ornamental lakes, and severely pruned trees.

Burke's book had immense success throughout Europe, and even in France. In Germany it was translated by Friedrich von Gentz, the future adviser to Prince Metternich; it also influenced Baron de Stein in Prussia and the Geneva counter-revolutionary Jacques Mallet du Pan. It received limited acclaim in Italy, however, and in Spain it was banned by the Inquisition.

Jacques Mallet du Pan

Unlike Burke, Mallet du Pan was not an anti-rationalist: he was actually a Liberal. In the 'Republic of Geneva', alongside the 'Representatives' who ran the government and the 'Burgesses', who were less wealthy and did not sit in the Councils, but enjoyed the rights of citizenship, there was a third group, also outside the Councils, known as the 'Natives', although they were in fact recent immigrants. Mallet du Pan had defended them when they rebelled in 1766, and had had to leave Geneva. He travelled widely in Europe, and from 1789 to 1792 was editor of the *Mercure de France*. Here, when a new revolution broke out in Geneva in 1782, he called for compromise; and he expressed similarly moderate views in 1793 in his *Considérations sur la France*. Revolution, he thought, was simply a 'shift of power'; and if revolution had erupted it was because the old regime had foundered. He believed that 'The shifting of power leads inevitably to the transfer of property, which will pass to the *sans-culottes*. They in turn will cease to be the poorest of the poor, and will become property owners, using power for their own ends.' There was, however, the unknown factor of war, which could lead to military dictatorship.

Mallet du Pan opposed both the Declaration of the Rights of Man and the revolutionary Constitution. His *Considérations sur la France* made him famous throughout Europe. From Berne, he kept up a political correspondence with Berlin, London, Turin, and above all with Vienna, where the brothers of King Louis XVI, the Counts of Provence and of Artois, had taken refuge. He also influenced Gentz and Kant.

Although the most prominent, Burke and Mallet du Pan were not the only counter-revolutionary writers who were well known at the time. In France there was Louis de Bonald; in Savoy, Joseph de Maistre; in Germany, Herder, Gentz, Brandès, Rehberg, and Moser. Their thoughts and actions, however, had almost certainly less influence on events than those of the former 'patriots' who were disillusioned by the self-assertiveness of 'la Grande Nation', Revolutionary France.

French war aims

On several occasions, under the National Convention and at the beginning of the Directory in 1795, the question of France's war aims arose. The first and most simple aim was to survive and resist the anti-French coalitions. Lazare Carnot, who helped lead the winning faction in the Committee of Public Safety and, at the outset of the Directory, wanted France to be content with her 1792 frontiers – those of the old regime plus Avignon and its surrounding Venaissin County. Similarly, Robespierre – on 17 November 1793, at a time of great difficulties for France – called for a moderate foreign policy based on friendship with 'free' countries (the United States and Switzerland), loyalty to traditional alliances (with Turkey, Genoa, Venice, and Denmark), and the renunciation of further conquest, propaganda, or wars of liberation.

This cautious approach clashed with two other ambitions.

The first was the idea of 'natural frontiers', propounded mainly by 'patriots' in the Rhineland, such as Anacharsis Cloots or Georg Forster, from Mainz. Georges Jacques Danton put this policy to the Convention on 31 January 1793: 'The frontiers of France are defined by Nature: we shall find them, from whatever starting-point, at the Rhine, the Ocean, and the Alps. Here the limits of our Republic must be.' For some members of the Convention at the time of the Gironde, up to 1793, this formula justified the annexation of Savoy, Belgium, the Southern Rhineland, the Porrentruy region near Basle, and the County of Nice – as well as Montbéliard twelve months later, in February 1794. The same idea was vigorously pursued at the beginning of the Directory in the following year, notably by Jean-François Reubell, from Alsace, and largely for strategic reasons. Already, by this time, many inhabitants of the Rhineland were bitterly opposed to being annexed by France.

The second ambition was more dangerous still. This was revolutionary expansionism, voiced by many of the 'patriots' who had emigrated to Paris from Switzerland, Italy, Germany, and the United Provinces. It was the doctrine of the 'Sister Republics'.

Its most active promoters were the Dutch or 'Batavians', who in October 1792 formed the 'Batavian Revolutionary Committee' of Paris. They hoped to overthrow the Stathouder William of Orange and to set up a 'Batavian Republic'. Their only dilemma was whether

Belgium – the Austrian Low Countries and the Archbishopric of Liège – would join their Republic or be added to France.

The idea of 'Sister Republics' was passionately championed by Louis-Marie de La Révellière-Lépeaux, a member of the Convention and then of the Directory, well known as patron of the deistic 'theophilanthropy' cult. The attraction of beginning with the 'Batavian Republic' was the wealth for which Holland was famous at the time.

The Batavian Republic

The Republic became a real prospect after France reconquered Belgium in 1794, and French troops pressed on into the Netherlands owing to an exceptionally cold spell which froze the canals. They occupied Amsterdam and The Hague; the Stathouder fled; and the 'Batavian Republic' began to be formed. Under the Peace of The Hague on 16 May 1795, France annexed only Dutch Flanders – the Lower Scheldt, Maastricht, and Venlo. At the same time, it gave the new Republic official recognition. It was a compromise peace.

Inspired by this example, Italian and Swiss 'patriots' asked for 'Sister Republics' on their own soil. They failed to realize that France had established the Batavian Republic only in order to exploit it and reduce it to satellite status for its own strategic ends.

At the beginning of 1796, the Directory proposed a major attack on Germany, using the 'Army of the Sambre and the Meuse' between Düsseldorf and Mainz and the 'Army of the Rhine and the Moselle' between Mainz and Basle.

Bonaparte in Italy

In the south-east, the small 'Army of the Alps', with some thirty to forty thousand men, badly equipped but ardent revolutionaries and mountain-dwellers accustomed to difficult terrain, was supposed to play an auxiliary role. The Directory put in charge of it, in March 1796, General Napoleon Bonaparte, who had recently won fame for quelling a Royalist uprising in Paris. His appointment soon ensured that the policy of revolutionary expansionism would prevail, and with it a sharp increase in the discrimination and domination already apparent in the case of the Batavian Republic. What was more,

Bonaparte was undisciplined: he often acted without consulting the Directory, and sometimes against its orders.

What was left of the revolutionary ardour, the humanitarian idealism, and the universal yearnings of a de La Révellière-Lépeaux? Very soon, they were lost in an ocean of practically limitless personal ambition.

Napoleon's first Italian campaign (April 1796 to February 1797) was a series of bold and unexpected manoeuvres which isolated the Austrian army from its Italian allies – Piedmont-Sardinia, the Duke of Modena, the King of Naples, and the Pope – all of whom were persuaded to sign an armistice. In every case, they had to hand over exorbitant indemnities, including carefully chosen works of art, such as the famous bronze horses of St Mark's Basilica in Venice. These and other masterpieces were taken to Paris, where it was explained that the aim was to enlighten people, make them happier, and to give the nation superiority in the arts and sciences, matching the preponderance it had won by force of arms. 'It is certain,' wrote the historian Jacques Godechot, 'that the removal of these works of art, like other requisitions and forced reparations, effaced all memory of France's immense contribution in the realm of political ideas, and turned against her a large proportion of those who had initially acclaimed her emancipating mission.'

The 'Sister Republics'

'Sister Republics' were then established, with the support of only the local 'patriots'. These included Filippo Michele Buonarotti in Italy, Frédéric-César de La Harpe in Switzerland, former tutor to the Russian Grand Dukes, and Pierre Ochs from Basle, the son-in-law of Frédéric Dietrich, the Mayor of Strasbourg at whose house Claude Joseph Rouget de Lisle composed La Marseillaise. In this way, between 1796 and 1798 a handful of Republics was set up: the Cispadane, later Cisalpine; the Ligurian, centred on Genoa; the Helvetic; the Roman; and the Parthenopean (centred on Naples).

Except for the Cisalpine Republic, which Napoleon considered his own, these artificial creations proved inefficient and ephemeral. Annexation (as in Belgium and the Rhineland) produced the same effect as the establishment of satellite states: ceaseless attempts to rebel against France. These revolts were especially active during Napoleon's Egyptian expedition in 1798-9. For thirteen months Austria occupied the whole of Italy, and the Russian armies for the first time fought the French in Switzerland. Generally, the anti-French revolts were led by counter-revolutionaries. But they clearly gained impetus from the disillusion felt by the 'patriots'.

Disillusion in Italy

In Italy, where Vittorio Alfieri produced his fiercely anti-French poem 'Il Misogallo' in 1793-9, the peasants of the north and the centre, although generally free from serfdom, had remained very much subject to the Church. Whereas in France the peasants and the bourgeoisie were in sympathy and often in alliance with each other, in Italy the peasants disliked the bourgeoisie even more than the nobility, since the bourgeois was the *gabellotto* or taxman, the collector of seigneurial dues. Furthermore, almost all of Italy had fought the French between 1793 and 1795. Despite the peace imposed by Napoleon, anti-French insurrections broke out on all sides. On 28 December 1797, General Duphot was assassinated in Rome, where he had come to get married. His death led to a punitive expedition by General Berthier, the expulsion of the Pope, and the establishment of the Roman Republic. But unrest continued, especially after Napoleon had left for Egypt.

Revolt in Germany

In Germany, the year 1796 saw a general uprising by the peasants on the east bank of the Rhine, backed with supplies from the Austrians; but this failed to spread across the river to the west.

Problems in Switzerland

In Switzerland, the 'patriots' de La Harpe in Lausanne and Pierre Ochs in Basle had asked the French to intervene to put an end to the oppression of 'subject lands' by the powerful cantons, like the Canton of Berne which ruled the Vaud. In 1797 this appeal suited the interests of the Directory and of Napoleon, who wanted to open a direct route to Milan. As it happened, the 'patriots' were more numerous in large cantons like Berne or Zurich than in the four old mountain cantons. These, known as the 'primitive' cantons, put up a fierce resistance against the French in 1798 and 1799, as did the inhabitants of the Valais, which was not yet a full canton, but only an 'ally'.

Peasant revolt in Belgium

After the annexation of Belgium, it was the extension of conscription, under the Jourdan–Delbrel law, which lit the fuse of rebellion. The French had taken no precautions against it because they believed that Belgium's incorporation into France was widely and definitively accepted. The 'peasant revolt', now famous in the annals of Belgium, broke out on the west bank of the Scheldt between Antwerp and Ghent. Conscripts cut down the 'liberty trees' which the revolutionaries had planted or erected, and replaced them with crosses; they burned registers of births and deaths, and rifled the public treasuries. A state of siege was declared, and the National Guards were called in (sometimes from towns such as Antwerp). Within two weeks, the whole area to the west of the Scheldt had been beaten into submission. But then the revolt spread to Luxembourg (the so-called 'forest Department'). Its methods were well adapted to guerrilla warfare: mass riots, then dispersal and return to work. If the insurgents had received weapons from Britain or Germany, they could have held out for a long time. But they never reached the sea, and the Rhineland stood between them and the most Francophobe regions of Germany.

THE SECOND COALITION

In 1799, while Napoleon was in Egypt, a Second Coalition arose against him. It comprised Britain, Russia, Austria, Turkey, and Naples; and it seemed capable of obliterating France's conquests. Britain put up the funds to finance a general insurrection, but it was badly co-ordinated. Revolts broke out in Calabria, Switzerland, and Holland. The 'Parthenopean Republic' was soon overthrown, to cries of 'If we still have to pay, we don't want the Republic! Long live the King and down with the Republic!'

These outbreaks were to have been accompanied by an extensive insurrection in France. Napoleon's return and the *coup d'état* of 18 Brumaire, Year 7 in the Revolutionary calendar (9 November 1799) abruptly altered the whole situation.

CONCLUSION

After ten years of a revolution in France which overshadowed the whole revolutionary era in the West, the greatest initial hopes had been disappointed. As often happens, early enthusiasm had included naïve illusions. Time was bound to erode it: hard facts could not be ignored. They included human egotism and the resistance of those who enjoyed positions of privilege; but no less important was the ambition of those who successfully sought to replace these holders of power. At first, attempts were made at reform by general consent. Then force was used, and finally Terror. The Revolution 'devoured its children'.

When opportunity arose, power was seized by false revolutionaries, cynics, and profiteers. First came Thermidor and the fall of Robespierre, then the Directory; then military dictatorship to combat corruption and poverty.

True, the Revolution achieved great reforms – political, social, administrative, fiscal, and constitutional. The abolition of 'orders' and privileges, whether local or personal, and the establishment of equality before the law are undoubtedly those that French people still prize the most. They also benefited some of France's neighbours and temporary conquests.

But in Europe disenchantment with the Revolution ran deep. Revolutionary France had not been able to impose 'peace in the world'. Once embarked on war, France had succumbed to the thrill of conquest, made possible by the mass levies and conscription that had revolutionized the Army and provided its 'big battalions'.

Whether by annexation, on the specious pretext of reasserting 'natural frontiers', always illusory, or by setting up satellites, the so-called 'Sister Republics', France treated foreigners badly. They not only had to pay large indemnities; they were also increasingly conscripted to fight for an alien cause.

These injustices were wholly inconsistent with 'classic' or 'French' nationalism, which was based on 'peoples' right to self-determination'. France could not be at one and the same time the model nation, champion of a Europe of equal states, free from tyranny, and la Grande Nation, Europe's conqueror. Nationalism, as the next chapter will show, arose in Europe from two main sources: the direct influence of revolutionary ideas (coupled, in Germany, with those of Herder), and a passionate and violent reaction against France's abuse of power. It never quite recovered from this initial contradiction.

Many of the people of 1789, imbued with Latin culture and the doctrines of the *philosophes*, found it easy to believe that the overthrow of the 'tyrants' would lead to the unification of Europe. The 'patriots' in every country felt part of a brotherhood of equals. But a great European Coalition arose against the National Convention, which was not only republican but also regicidal, and not only triumphant but also prone to revolutionary expansionism. The Coalition in turn inflamed French national ardour and led to the concept of la Grande Nation, which other countries understandably found threatening. Whether preaching 'natural frontiers' or establishing 'Sister Republics', France seemed bent on hegemony. Its people's army, recruited by mass levies and conscription, was both bigger and more unbridled than those of other countries. Under Napoleon's command, it could wreak havoc in Europe.

Europe's revolutionary era thus put an end to a century which had been both European and cosmopolitan; and in doing so it quelled both tendencies for a very long time. La Grande Nation, France, brought nationalism to Europe in two ways, each complementing the other. One was its propaganda; the other was the hatred it aroused.

14

Napoleon: Europe by Force

NAPOLEON'S CHOICE

Pragmatism: the guiding principle 'plan'. In one sense his intelligence was indeed that of a theoretician, incredibly adept at making comparisons and syntheses. But against that he had a great propensity to change his plans. He was above all a pragmatist. At different times – and even at the same time – he could be many different people. He was an ambitious egotist, indifferent to the interests of France: but he was a great French patriot. He believed in natural frontiers – but also in the universal Empire. He dreamed of the Orient and, once Europe was at peace, of following in the footsteps of Alexander: but he was a pure European, and cared little for problems overseas. At home on the continent, he had no interest in the sea – yet was determined that France should rule the waves. He pursued hegemony, but also confederation. He was a soldier, but also a man of peace incessantly obliged to react to aggression by foreign powers.

Napoleon's early career

Napoleon Bonaparte was born in Ajaccio, Corsica, on 15 August 1769, a few months after the Republic of Genoa ceded the island to France. After studying at the Military Academy of Brienne in the Champagne countryside, he was assigned to the artillery. He professed French rather than Corsican patriotism. Then came the Revolution: Napoleon was twenty years old, an obscure lieutenant. Faced with the choice between the King and the 'patriots', he opted for the Revolution. He distinguished himself at the siege of Toulon in 1793, and in December of that year was promoted to Brigadier-General. He became for a time a disciple of Robespierre.

When the Convention was nearing dissolution, Napoleon was appointed second-in-command to Paul de Barras, who had helped contrive the fall of Robespierre and who had been made commander of the Army of the Interior in Paris. Together they crushed the Royalist insurrection of 12–13 Vendémiaire Year 4 (4–5 October 1795). It was a further turning-point in Napoleon's career. At twenty-six, he was made a full General and succeeded Barras at the head of the Army of the Interior. The Italian campaign in the following year revealed his qualities to the world.

After the Italian campaign, Napoleon decided to invade Egypt – a choice that has led to much speculation about his motives. The explanation would seem to be sheer ambition. One can apply to him, in fact, the definition that Hannah Arendt gave of Imperialism: a desire for expansion, not for a limited end, but in all possible directions. Napoleon was hungry for power. Whether in the East or the West was a matter of indifference.

The force of circumstances led him to choose the East. Then, on 9 October 1799, he returned to France, and a month later, on 9–10 November, staged the coup d'état of 18–19 Brumaire which made him First Consul and ruler of France.

First Consul

It was now that Napoleon faced his most decisive choice of all. Like all his educated contemporaries, he was steeped in Latin culture. He knew that the Roman Empire had followed the Roman Republic, and he no doubt had in his mind the examples of Sulla, Caesar, and Augustus. He also knew that after the English Civil War, the monarchy had been re-established by a General, George Monck, the Duke of Albemarle. Furthermore, Louis XVI's younger brother, Louis XVIII, wrote to Napoleon as early as 20 February 1800, to sound him out about his attitude towards restoring the monarchy.

Emperor

Having been made First Consul, and in 1802 First Consul for life, Napoleon no longer hesitated: he chose to become a Caesar. There was no turning back after 21 March 1804, when on Napoleon's orders the Duc d'Enghien, one of the most prominent of the Bourbon princes, was shot on a false charge of conspiracy. On 2 December 1804, Napoleon became what the Romans had called 'Augustus': he was crowned 'Emperor of the French'. As such, he sought to establish a new dynasty: but although he found places for most members of his family, there was one exception. This was his brother Lucien, who had helped bring about the 18 Brumaire coup d'état, but who in October 1800 had published a pamphlet entitled *Parallel between Caesar, Cromwell, Monck, and Bonaparte.*

Meanwhile, Napoleon had had to choose between two forms of government. Already in 1801 he had signed a Concordat with Rome in an effort to reconcile Revolutionaries and Catholic Royalists. His relationship with the Pope showed that he always had in mind, as a possible alternative, some form of populist Empire.

NAPOLEON'S CONQUESTS

The 'Great Nation' had become the 'Great Empire'. Could there be a 'Universal Empire'? Or, as a compromise, a united Europe?

Early conquests and the Peace of Amiens

When Napoleon seized power in the 18 Brumaire coup d'état, he faced a difficult situation. Except for Genoa, Italy was lost to France, and Austria was advancing towards the Rhine and the Var. The war ended with the 'Second Italian Campaign' and victory at Marengo on 14 June 1800, followed by the German campaign and victory at Hohenlinden on 2 December. The Treaty of Lunéville, on 9 February 1801, restored peace with Austria, leaving only two major enemies still at war with France – Britain and Russia. Tsar Alexander I strengthened his alliance with Britain: but her position was growing weaker, while Napoleon was consolidating his links with Spain, with the Bourbon King of Naples (who ceded to France the island of Elba), with the United States, and with the beys and deys of Algiers, Tunis, and Tripoli. In August 1801, however, the French had to capitulate to Turkish and British forces in Egypt; and after lengthy negotiations a compromise was reached, whereby Britain kept Trinidad and Ceylon, while France remained in Antwerp and in Italy. This Peace of Amiens, signed on 29 March 1802, was widely welcomed. In France, the Concordat had helped to quieten the Chouan rising of Breton Royalists whose main inspiration was religious; and the economic crisis of 1801 had been overcome. The First Consul was now immensely popular.

Internal problems

Napoleon faced, however, two major choices. In internal affairs, could the First Consul remain the symbol of revolutionary liberty and become, as he later said, 'a crowned George Washington'? He was too fond of power to be content with such a solution. On 2 August 1802, after holding a plebiscite, he had himself proclaimed First Consul for life – scarcely a democratic innovation. But at the same time Napoleon consolidated the achievements of the bourgeois revolution by issuing the Code Civil on 21 March 1804. Significantly, the coins bearing his portrait, at the beginning of the Empire, were inscribed 'French Republic – Emperor Napoleon'. There was a curious resemblance between the State and the Res publica established by Augustus (see chapter 4), and between the Civil Code and Roman law.

External problems

There remained foreign affairs. And for once in history, they were the determining factor. The peace was broken after thirteen months, on 17 May 1803. Who was responsible – Britain or France? It is often difficult fairly to apportion 'war guilt', as for instance in 1914. But in this case, the Peace of Amiens was for Britain the absolute limit of tolerable concessions, while Napoleon, dizzy with success, saw it as a point of departure for further triumphs.

It was Britain that resumed hostilities. The main pretext was Napoleon's refusal, under pressure from French manufacturers, to sign a commercial treaty, as stipulated by the Peace of Amiens. His aim, in fact, was to give French goods a monopoly of the continental market – soon to be protected by a blockade.

The Empire, at this time, had three different types of territory. There was France and its *départements*; there were the subject countries; and there were the allies.

When the 18 Brumaire coup d'état took place, France had ninety-eight *départements*, including Savoy, Nice, Avignon, and those of Belgium and Switzerland (Basle and Geneva). At the end of the year

1800, four further *départements* on the west bank of the Rhine were added to the total. These 102 *départements* broadly occupied the 'natural frontiers' proposed by Danton in February 1793. Psychologically, they involved great dangers, since at a time when nationalism was growing they included minorities whose language was not French. But the frontiers in question were really based on strategic arguments, as was confirmed by later French demands in 1918–19 and even in 1945. By 1812, the number of *départements* had grown to 130, forty-four of them outside France.

Geographically, this was absurd. What sense did it make to go from the 'Bouches de l'Elbe' (the Mouths of the Elbe) to 'the Tiber', passing through the *départements* of 'the Forests' (Luxembourg) and 'Mont Terrible' (Basle)? The main reason for annexations, from 1806 onwards, was the 'Continental System' – the blockade intended to close continental Europe to British goods. Measures against smuggling were easier to impose if the whole of the coast was under direct French rule, with its préfets, its gendarmes, and its customs officers.

The significance of this for the history of Europe was that the non-French *départements* were subject, for however short a time, to all the Napoleonic institutions, which in France are still more or less intact: the Civil Code; the *préfet* system, with subprefectures, cantons, and communes; the fiscal system, involving mainly indirect taxes; the system of law and order, with gendarmes dependent on the army and police under the Ministry of the Interior; the religious organization set up by the Concordat, whereby bishops were nominated by the civil authorities and given spiritual investiture by Rome; and the university and school system. In certain cases, as for instance with the Civil Code, Napoleonic influence outside France was long-lasting. It was also widespread, since the Civil Code was adopted in Italy, part of Poland, some of the German states, such as the Kingdom of Westphalia and the Grand Duchy of Baden, and the so-called 'Illyrian provinces' on the eastern coast of the Adriatic.

The subject countries

These were not invented by the Empire. The 'Sister Republics' of the Directory period were their direct precursors. And they continued to multiply, except at the end of Napoleon's reign, when some of them were absorbed into the Empire. The main subject countries were: the

Kingdom of Italy, ruled from Milan; the Kingdom of Naples; the Swiss Confederation, which had been a satellite since 1803; and Germany, a more complex and interesting case.

On 12 July 1806 Napoleon established the Confederation of the Rhine, bringing together the rulers of Baden, Württemberg, Bavaria, and thirteen other states, all in the south of present-day Germany. Very soon, he added part of Northern Germany, notably Hanover, which had become the Kingdom of Westphalia after the Treaty of Tilsit between Napoleon and Alexander I of Russia in 1807, and which was ruled by Jérôme Bonaparte, Napoleon's youngest brother. The Batavian Republic became the Kingdom of Holland, and was entrusted to Louis Bonaparte, Napoleon's third brother – although he was later deposed for laxity in maintaining the blockage.

In the Eastern part of Europe, after the Fourth Coalition and further French successes, including the battles of Jena and Auerstedt, the occupation of Berlin, and the victories at Eylau and Friedland, Napoleon and his troops held the whole of Central Europe as far as the river Niemen in Lithuania. He established a new satellite state, the Grand Duchy of Warsaw, in 1807, and in 1812 turned it into 'the Kingdom of Poland'. The end of the year 1812, however, saw the retreat from Moscow, and the advance of the Tsar's armies, which occupied the Polish Grand Duchy.

At its most extensive, the French Empire – France plus the non-French *départements* – had 44 million inhabitants, and the subject states had 38 million. Altogether, Napoleon ruled 82 million out of the 167 million people in Europe, including Russia.

He had subjects and satellites, but few allies. Even when an ally supplied troops, it was under duress. This explains why Russia, Prussia, and Austria changed sides, and why so many problems arose with Spain.

When Spain left the First Coalition, she concluded two treaties with France – one in August 1796, and a second in 1800 whereby she ceded Louisiana to the French, who then sold it to the United States. The Spanish and French fleets were both destroyed by Nelson at the Battle of Trafalgar in 1805. In October 1807, France and Spain signed the Treaty of Fontainebleau with a view to dividing Portugal between them. But the weakness of King Charles IV of Spain and his Prime Minister Manuel Godoy led to an uprising, and Ferdinand, Charles's eldest son, was proclaimed King in his stead. Napoleon seized this opportunity to have his brother-in-law Joachim Murat march on Madrid, on 2 May

1808. It was a date long remembered in Spanish history as the *Dos de Mayo*: Murat was ruthless in repressing the Madrid rebels. Napoleon then placed on the Spanish throne his elder brother Joseph. But, as will be seen, the Spanish reaction was defiant and fierce.

The colonel and the corporals

In the satellite countries, disobedience to the Emperor was unthinkable; and the same applied to his brothers and sisters. 'I can no longer tolerate mediocrities among my relations. Those who do not rise with me can no longer be of my family. I am making a family of kings – *or rather, viceroys*' (emphasis added).

True, a certain number of high-ranking outsiders benefited; but a witness remarked in 1809: 'All these sovereigns wait for his orders like a corporal attending a captain.'

The ills of occupation

The presence of any army, even when friendly, has always been a burden for the civilian population, above all at a time when the soldiers were billeted 'on the locals'. Spain in particular suffered from this: it was one of the reasons for the popular revolt. Even more of a burden was the financing of military campaigns, based on the principle that 'war feeds on war'. The contributions demanded of the vanquished were very large. The Prussian and Polish campaigns cost the French taxpayer nothing: but they were a huge liability for Prussia.

THE FAILURE OF A EUROPEAN ECONOMIC COMMUNITY: THE CONTINENTAL SYSTEM AND THE BLOCKADE

Napoleon's French chauvinism

Failing a Europe of political equals, there might at least have been scope for a European economic community. This was the dream of several economists, generally disciples of the great Adam Smith, whose main French follower was Jean-Baptiste Say (1767–1832). His *Traité* d'*Economie Politique*, or *Treatise on Political Economy*, appeared in 1803, when the brief Peace of Amiens was coming to an end. In 1806, in a work entitled *Du commerce français dans l'état actuel de l'Europe* (*On French Trade in the Present State of Europe*), Jean-Baptiste Dubois proposed that the 'continental federal system' should be extended to the economy. Napoleon, as is generally agreed, knew little of economics. But he was not prepared to allow others to deal with economic policy. He interfered incessantly, and grew angry when, as often happened, economic phenomena disobeyed his orders. 'He suffered the mortification,' wrote André Fugier, 'of being unable to make the economy march in step.' Furthermore, he was a 'mercantilist', a disciple of the seventeenth-century statesman Jean-Baptiste Colbert. He believed in accumulating as much gold as possible in French coffers, public or private, by means of customs duties and their attendant quotas, prohibitions, etc. In particular, Napoleon always sought to ensure that economic progress should benefit France alone, if necessary at the expense of agriculture and industry in the subject states. Their inhabitants therefore felt more and more acutely that they were working for the benefit of France rather than for themselves. This – especially in economic crises, as in 1805 or 1810–12 – became a powerful stimulus to anti-French nationalism.

Even the roads bore the mark of 'Franco-centrism', radiating as they did from Paris towards Germany, the Simplon and Mont-Cenis passes, and elsewhere.

The blockade

After Nelson's naval victory at Trafalgar on 21 October 1805, Britain was in command of the seas; and she went on adding to her sea power by building more warships. This enabled her to overrun all the French and Dutch colonies, and to establish a monopoly in colonial produce. Britain's economic chauvinism matched only that of Napoleon.

In the complex cat's-cradle of international rules and regulations, the British and Napoleon applied ever more stringent measures of commercial policy. On 16 May 1806, the British imposed a blockade on the mouths of all German rivers and then on all French ports, from the Elbe to Brest. On 21 November 1806, after his victory over the Fourth Coalition, Napoleon issued the Berlin Decree which imposed the 'Continental Blockade'.

The idea was simple. All trade with Britain was now banned. One after another, the subject states were obliged to comply. The British retaliated; Napoleon countered with two Milan Decrees in November and December 1807.

The neutral countries, and especially the United States, were badly affected by these measures; but in the early days so was Britain. Then contraband trade began. The British needed continental wheat, wines, and silks; the United States needed cotton. British smuggling was well organized, with trading-posts and warehouses in poorly guarded places: Salonica, the Black Sea, the Danube, Malta, the Balearic Islands, Gibraltar, the coast of Spain, Holland, Heligoland, the North Sea, and the straits of Denmark.

In 1810 and 1811 France – and especially the subject states – suffered a severe economic crisis. French trade dwindled. Unemployment spread.

Napoleon thereupon decided to raise money from contraband by diverting smugglers' profits into the French *fisc*. This, he thought, would be a way of financing the expedition against Russia which he planned. So, on 3 July 1810, the Saint-Cloud Decree authorized the sale of licences to trade with British ports (where, for instance, wheat might be sold).

Meanwhile, colonial produce entering France would be subject to very heavy customs duties. In practice, this scheme worked badly. A number of French ships, once offshore, failed to return: they went on trading outside the blockade, i.e. on behalf of Britain. She in turn underwent a serious crisis in 1811–12. Having sold so many contraband goods, she found that she had swamped the market, causing a sharp drop in British sales.

In France, the Empire was becoming less and less popular with both peasants and bourgeois capitalists. In 1812, the economic crisis admittedly ended: but that was also the year of Napoleon's disaster in Russia and the retreat from Moscow which ensued.

The Continental System

The restrictions on trade already mentioned – the 'Continental Blockade' – were wartime measures. But there was also what was known as the 'Continental System', an attempt to organize Europe's economy in ways which some have called a 'Continental commercial confederation'.

But that [in André Fugier's words] was by no means Napoleon's objective. To a mind like his, which found the co-operation of equals so alien an idea, only one relationship was conceivable: that of dominance and subordination. There would have to be one dominant economy – the French – and subordinate economies – those of the subject States. The former would manufacture, process, and sell its finished products: the others would supply raw materials and buy the resultant goods. In this way, political domination would be strengthened by economic dominance, and the victories of the Imperial years would bring in the gold which, for mercantilists, was the only form of wealth. (emphasis added)

All that is in stark contradiction to the unification of Europe. But was unification part of Napoleon's vision? The question demands examination.

DID NAPOLEON SEEK EUROPEAN UNITY?

Before considering some of Napoleon's ideas and visions, it may be as well to summarize what he did.

The Europe of Amiens

A reasonable starting-point is the Europe created by the Peace of Amiens in 1802. Britain thereby had to accept the 'natural frontiers' of France. What was more, she accepted the 'Sister Republics', already greatly changed – but without officially recognizing them. The result was that France retained her sphere of influence, notably in Italy (despite a promise to the Tsar to evacuate Naples some time in the future). Altogether, Napoleon's idea at that time was la Grande Nation, with its neighbours as satellites and in practice without the right of self-determination. When a plebiscite on a new constitution in Holland produced 16,000 'yes' votes against 25,000 'no', Napoleon declared the constitution approved, because he counted as 'yes' votes the 347,000 abstentions.

The Europe of family kingdoms

From 1805–6 onwards, after Austerlitz and Jena, the Emperor established a second Europe. This time it was a 'Confederation' under his personal guidance: but it was based on the novel substructure of family ties – not so much 'Sister Republics' as 'Brotherly Kingdoms'. At their collective head, however, was the Emperor, who brooked no sign of independence and had no hesitation in humiliating members of his family.

Outside the family kingdoms there were Napoleon's allies. His great achievement in this field was the Confederation of the Rhine, which established in Germany, between Prussia and Austria, a third force entirely subject to the Emperor, and one that was continually expanding. The 'Holy Roman Empire of the Germanic Nation', which Edmund Burke saw as essential to the balance of power in Europe – because it was weak but could not be partitioned by Prussia and Austria – had evaporated. Firmly based in Italy and the whole of Germany, Napoleon acquired subject states as far as the Slav countries, including the Grand Duchy of Warsaw in Poland and the Illyrian Provinces among the Slavs of the south.

The Continental System

After 1809–10, a third conception of Europe began to emerge. This was that of the Continental System. The Continental Blockade required more direct French control: hence the Empire's annexation of a series of mainly coastal areas. Outside the Empire and its subject states, Napoleon imposed compulsory alliances – on Prussia, crushed, weakened, and (in Metternich's words) 'no longer anything'; and on Austria, forced by defeat into the 'family alliance' of Napoleon's marriage to the Archduchess Marie-Louise. Even Russia, which had been his ally since 1807, Napoleon looked upon as a possible prey; and at all events, he insisted, she must be a faithful and obedient ally. Already in 1809, Metternich gave his colleague Count Philip Stadion his own horrified view of how a future Europe might look:

> Europe will undergo a total reform. A monstrous central Government will bear down upon its weak dependencies, each able only to drag out a miserable existence riveting its own chains. Spain will be subjugated;

the Ottoman Porte will be driven beyond the Bosporus. The frontiers of the great Empire will stretch from the Baltic to the Black Sea; Russia, in a few months, will be confined to Asia. Napoleon's longstanding plan will have succeeded. He will be the ruler of Europe.

For this to become a reality, Russia would have to be defeated. The great army which in 1812 crossed the Niemen river en route for Moscow was itself a symbol of Napoleon's near-success. Its 611,000 men included Frenchmen and citizens of the annexed territories, Germans, Austrians, Prussians, Swiss, Poles, Lithuanians, Italians, Illyrians, Spaniards, and Portuguese. But the extent of these motley forces could not disguise their fragility. How many of Napoleon's soldiers relished serving their foreign master? How many secretly hoped that the Tsar would win?

Napoleon's disastrous defeat in Russia was the signal for breaking ranks. But if he had triumphed, it seems likely that the Continental System would have ended as a kind of Empire on the Roman model, unified at least by common institutions and the Napoleonic Code, and under the Emperor's domination.

Such, then, with constant minor changes, were the three successive Europes created by Napoleon. How did he see them in retrospect, in his various reflections and writings in exile on St Helena, and particularly in the *Memorial of St Helena* by Emmanuel, Marquis de Las Cases?

A European or a universal Empire?

The idea of a 'universal Empire' appears frequently. For Napoleon, who had some classical education, especially in Latin, it evoked the Roman Empire: 'The Emperor believed in Roman history, if not in all its details, at least in its results.' It also evoked the Carolingian Empire. Napoleon, said Metternich, hoped for success in the Russian campaign 'as the keystone of the edifice he saw in his dreams ... a sort of Charlemagne's Empire under a Bonapartist dynasty'.

> Myself, said Napoleon, I could be no more than a crowned George Washington. And that I could become only if surrounded by kings I had convinced or mastered. Then, and then only, could I fruitfully show Washington's moderation, his detachment, and his wisdom; and I could reach that position, realistically, only by achieving universal

dictatorship. I tried ... What motive could I have had for stopping, since all I could have reaped were benefits?'

What, in his eyes, did a universal Empire involve? Much more than Europe. First, 'I had to win at Moscow.' Why at Moscow? Because Russia was the cornerstone of the system.

'Russia still has an immense advantage over the rest of Europe: she has the good fortune to have a well-established Government.' And beyond Russia lay the Orient. Talking with the Comte de Ségur, before his exile on St Helena, Napoleon described what he would have done if he had captured Acre: 'Instead of a battle in Moravia, I should have won a battle of Issus [where Alexander the Great had defeated 500,000 Persians]: I should have made myself Emperor of the East, and returned to Paris via Constantinople!' He said the same to Las Cases: 'I should have reached Constantinople and India. I should have changed the face of the world.' Nor did he have any scruples in this respect:

> Paris is certainly worth a Mass. Does anyone imagine that the Empire of the East, and perhaps rule over all of Asia, is not worth a turban? ... But look at the results it would have had! I should have taken Europe from behind: the old European civilisation would have been surrounded, and who then would have dared to interfere with the destiny of France and the regeneration of the century?

From the East and from Asia, the dream of universal rule turned towards Africa. If Napoleon had stayed longer in Egypt, 'he would have pushed much further our geographical researches in Northern Africa.'

Even America was not beyond his dreams. After Waterloo, he imagined settling in the northern part of the state of New York. It would have been to the advantage of the United States, for such refuges 'would soon become a natural pole of attraction for the people of Canada, who are already French, and thereby form a powerful barrier or even a centre of resistance to the English'.

So all Napoleon's reflections on Europe have to be seen in the context of his universalist ambition. To regard him as a great 'European' before his time is to forget that he was above all greatly ambitious, and an imperialist in the full sense of the word.

Europe seen from St Helena

There is some point, however, in examining how he saw the ideal Europe which he claims he sought to create. If the British had not resumed the war after the Peace of Amiens, 'I should have lost nothing by way of glory, and gained a great deal by way of influence; I should have won Europe in a moral victory, as I was on the point of doing by force of arms.' So begins a famous statement in which the Emperor describes a sort of European confederation of rehabilitated nation-states.

> One of my greatest ideas was to bring back together peoples who were geographically similar but who had been dispersed and fragmented by politics and revolution. In Europe, although they are scattered, there are more than 30 million French people, 15 million Spaniards, 15 million Italians, and 30 million Germans. I should have liked to make each of these peoples a single, solid nation . . .

After this summary simplification, it would have been possible to embrace the chimera of an ideal civilization: for it would have been the best opportunity to achieve unity in matters of law, principle, opinion, feelings, views, and interests. Then, perhaps, universal enlightenment would allow one to dream of giving the great European family something like the American Congress or the Amphictyons of Greece. What a prospect of strength, greatness, wellbeing, and prosperity!

These words, which might well be echoed by present-day partisans of a federated, integrated Europe, should nevertheless be treated with the utmost suspicion. First, Napoleon's further remarks make clear that he saw this 'confederation' as subservient to his own authority. On the Spaniards, for example:

> In the crisis facing France, in the battle for new ideas, and in the great campaign of the century against the rest of Europe, we could not leave Spain behind, a prey to our enemies. We had to lock it into our system, if necessary by force.

The annexation by France of a number of Italian regions 'had in my mind been only temporary, and intended only to supervise, guarantee, and promote the national education of the Italians'. These regions, incidentally, 'remained among those most attached to us'.

Italian and German nationhood

In Italy – although the case is unique – Napoleon did demonstrably try to create a unified nation. When he received the crown of Italy in 1805, he told Count Melzi, former President of the Cisalpine Republic: 'I have always intended to build a free and independent Italian nation. I accept the crown, and I will keep it, but only so long as my interests demand.' The same idea was taken up by Napoleon's brother-in-law, Joachim Murat. On 10 November 1813, he proposed to Napoleon to unify Italy under his own rule, and to declare the country independent. This ambition led him to declare war against Napoleon – although later, after the ex-Emperor had landed from Elba at Golfe Juan on 1 March 1815, Murat once more volunteered his services to Napoleon, without, however, consulting him. On 30 March Murat addressed a famous proclamation to the Italian people: 'Italians! The hour is come when Italy's great destiny must triumph. Providence calls you at last to become an independent nation. From the Alps to the Straits of Sicily, a single cry rings out: "The Independence of Italy!"' But Murat, checked by Napoleon's troops at Ferrara, was routed at Tolentino, and finally captured and shot at Pizzo in Calabria. His ambition had led him to disaster.

In Germany, Napoleon thought unification inevitable. Once elected by its inhabitants, he told Las Cases, 'I should have governed, without fail, 30 million united Germans.' Over Russia he thought he could have been victorious. But since he was defeated and exiled, would Russia not unify Europe? 'If there were a Tsar of Russia who was valiant, impetuous, and capable, Europe would be his.'

Altogether, if Las Cases is to be relied on, Napoleon had a singular view of Europe. How could he expect 'compact', unified nations to accept being dominated by France – or rather, by himself? How could he fail to realize that nationalism was exacerbated above all by France's wars of conquest?

It would be wrong to make too much of Napoleon's ideas on a united Europe. It would be a mistake, too, to confuse his real thoughts with the seductive embroiderings of the Napoleonic legend. The only certainty is that he clearly saw Europe as a whole, and one which included Russia but excluded Britain. The continent seemed to him to have a great deal in common, especially in intellectual and legal matters. 'He would have liked the whole of Europe to have a single currency, uniform weights and measures, and uniform legislation. "Why," he used to ask, "could my Napoleonic Code not have formed the basis of a European Code? In that way, we in Europe should really have formed a single family."' 'He had had the idea, he said, of having all the histories of Europe since Louis XIV collated and combined; and he greatly regretted being unable to carry this out.' Metternich, in his *Memoirs*, gave a curious confirmation of this historical ambition:

> At that time, one of his favourite projects was to assemble in Paris all the archives of Europe. He told me that he would put up a grandiose building for them between the Ecole Militaire and the Dome of Les Invalides; only stone and iron would be used in its construction, to prevent any danger of fire.

Metternich wondered whether other states would accept this plan. '"Well!" answered Napoleon, "That's typical of the narrow ideas that statesmen in Europe can't get rid of. I'll carry out my project."'

Rather than 'European', Napoleon was inordinately ambitious. His fertile mind toyed with a thousand different and even contradictory ideas: a united Europe was only one of them. He certainly underestimated the reactions that his conquests and his domination were bound to arouse. In that way, probably without realizing it, he greatly helped to kindle the nationalism that was already smouldering in Europe and soon became a raging fire.

The Italians

Italian national feeling grew during the French occupation, but less vigorously than in Germany: it was strongest at state level, and involved no popular uprisings. Apart from the area annexed to France, along the north-west coast and south as far as Rome, Italy was in fact divided into the Kingdom of Italy, with Napoleon as its ruler, and the Kingdom of Naples, where Murat was King. From 1813 onwards, the British and the Austrians also intervened to support the Bourbons who had taken refuge in Sicily.

Napoleon's stepson Eugène de Beau-harnais, who was Viceroy of the Kingdom of Italy, capitulated in 1814 at the same time as the Emperor himself. In Milan, one group of aristocrats formed the 'Austrian Party', and a larger group the 'Italian Liberal Party', which called for independence for the Kingdom of Italy, or at least for Lombardy and Venetia.

Austria opposed the latter group.

Murat was backed by the radical and republican Carbonari and by the revolutionary 'patriots', middle-class intellectuals who sought independence for Italy but also wished to preserve the civil liberties and liberal reforms introduced by France. As previously mentioned, Murat proposed to Napoleon that he should proclaim the independence of the Italians and unite them in a single kingdom with himself as King. When Napoleon refused, Murat declared war on him, on 3 February 1814, and occupied Rome, Ancona, and Bologna. But he was opposed by the allies and by Metternich, who wanted to maintain the Pope in Rome and, rather than Italian unity, sought to create an 'Italian Confederation' based on the 'Lombardy–Venetia Kingdom' and under Austrian sovereignty.

The 'Hundred Days' of Napoleon's return from Elba until his final defeat and exile on St Helena turned everything upside-down. Murat rallied to Napoleon and occupied the Roman Campagna. On 30 March 1815, at Rimini, he issued the famous proclamation, already quoted, which earned him the title of one of the fathers of Italian nationalism. 'Eighty thousand Italians,' it declared, 'are advancing under the orders of their King. They swear to take no rest until Italy is free.'

Murat then visited Bologna and Modena. But enthusiasm for him was limited to intellectual circles, young people, a few nobles, and a small number of officers. Pellegrino Rossi, the economist and legal expert who later became Professor of Political Economy at the Collège de France, was put in charge of administration in the province. Gioacchino Antonio Rossini composed a 'Hymn to Independence'. But the venture was short-lived. Murat had to abdicate; not long afterwards, he met a violent death. And for many years Italy remained divided, back in the hands of its 'legitimate' princes, dominated by Austria and, in Metternich's phrase, a mere 'geographical expression'.

NAPOLEON'S DEFEAT

The Prussian military theorist Karl von Clausewitz wrote in his book *Vom Krieg* (*On War*) that a great power was one which could maintain its security against any other single state. France was by this definition a great power: to defeat her required coalitions of as many countries as possible. Only the Sixth and the Seventh Coalitions included all the great European powers. The Sixth, formed in 1813, comprised Britain, Russia, and Prussia, whom Austria joined when it declared war on 11 August 1813. The Seventh Coalition, with the same members, put an end to Napoleon's 'Hundred Days' at the Battle of Waterloo.

It was thus the states and their armies which defeated Napoleon. But in a broader European context it is also worth examining popular resistance to the 'Great Empire'. In places, this was intense.

The Spaniards

As has been seen, the abdication of Charles IV and his son, followed by the appointment of Joseph Bonaparte as King of Spain in June 1808, sparked off a powerful revolt. The tragic events of 2 May 1808, when the crowd in Madrid attacked French troops and was shot and sabred down, are commemorated in a magnificent painting entitled *1808* or *The Charge of the Marmelukes*, by Francisco Goya. There were indeed some pro-French Spaniards; but, as Jean Tulard has stressed, the main resistance came from the peasantry and the Church, and 'was less the result of patriotism than a reaction to economic hardship'. The Continental Blockade had interfered with trade between Spain and the colonies. All the same, Tulard adds, 'National pride also played a decisive part.' Within a few weeks, 100,000 men had joined the revolt. The Portuguese rebelled too; and the French General Andoche Junot, Duc d'Abrantes, Governor of Portugal, was defeated at Vimiero in August by a British General soon to be celebrated – Arthur Wellesley, later Duke of Wellington. Already, in July, an entire French army corps of 18,000 men under General Pierre Dupont had had to surrender at Bailen in Andalusia. Napoleon's 'Great Army' was no longer invincible.

Nor could the Emperor save the situation, for no sooner had he reached Madrid than he learned that Austria was preparing for war; so he had to return to Paris and make for Central Europe.

The Spanish insurrection continued; the civil war in the French Vendée and the Chouans' rebellion in Brittany spread. The idea of 'subversion' as a strategic weapon began to take shape, although the military and its theorists were not convinced of it until the twentieth century. Warfare of this kind needs mass support and implacable severity against those who 'collaborate' with the occupying power. But, with time and experience, it can be effective.

The Russians

The Russian campaign of 1812 ended in disaster. There were a number of reasons: the vast size of Russia, the hard Russian winter, and the fact that the Russian army was not destroyed at the great battle of Borodino on 7 September. But there was also an uprising by the Russian people in the areas crossed by the French. Field-Marshal Mikhail Kutuzov, the Russian commander, admirably exploited these advantages; and the retreat from Moscow became a legendary ordeal. One Soviet historian, Tarlé, has claimed that the guerrilla warfare mounted by Russian 'partisans' was mainly responsible for Napoleon's defeat. Jean Tulard has certainly shown that Napoleon invented the 'People's War', in which 'a whole Nation is mobilized against the invader ... and any tactic is permissible, irrespective of the rules'.

The Germans: an intellectual change

In Germany, the intellectual turning point came with Johann Gottlieb Fichte's fourteen *Addresses to the German Nation* (*Reden an die deutsche Nation*), given between 13 December 1807 and 20 March 1808, at the Berlin Academy. At that time, the city was actually occupied by a French garrison.

As a philosopher, Fichte was deeply influenced by Herder, who saw the German nation as defined by its language and its folklore. But, unlike Herder, Fichte wanted there to be a German state. Popular culture, he thought, must be based on the original German language, the *Ursprache*; there was such a thing as a German 'national self'; and the German people had a mission, as the only regenerative force in the contemporary world. Fichte did not believe, however, in 'national character' or a German 'racial identity'. He simply thought that the Germans had a special aptitude for liberty and progress.

These theories soon replaced those of the 'patriots', the partisans of Revolutionary France, and the 'Carolingians', who called for an amalgamation of the Germanic and Latin worlds. Fichte attracted many disciples, including in 1815 the statesman Heinrich Friedrich Karl Stein, who four years later founded an historical research society which published the outstanding document collection known as the *Monumenta Germaniae Historica*. This was characteristic of the immense efforts made at that time to rediscover German history, legends, and ancient literary texts. They involved such eminent figures as the theologian and philosopher Friedrich Ernst Schleiermacher, the biblical critic Johann Jahn, and the poet and patriot Ernst Moritz Arndt.

The beginnings of revolt in Germany

On 12 October 1809, after the capture of Vienna, there was an attempt on Napoleon's life at Schönbrunn Castle. In the same year there were mutinies in the army, with indecisive results. Between April and October, an innkeeper in Bavaria, Andreas Hofer, with the help of a Capuchin friar, fomented a revolt in part of the Tyrol. His movement had more popular support than the military rebellions; but Hofer was an Austrian, and the uprising was hardly an expression of pure German patriotism. In Prussia, the Freemasons formed the 'League of Virtue' or *Tugenbund* to denounce collaboration with the French. The Prussian government was suspicious of it, and dissolved it in 1810.

It was after Russia's defeat that the real revolt in Germany began.

The Prussian revolt

East Prussia was the first area to revolt, when the French were retreating from the Niemen to the Vistula in December 1812. In January 1813, the former Prussian Minister, Heinrich Stein, gave the rebellion his backing and set up a form of government, with an assembly representing the provincial states. It was a real *coup d'état*. The assembled states raised a 'territorial army', the *Landwehr*; and the insurrection spread to Brandenburg. Prussian patriotism and German nationalism especially attracted young students. Soon, the Prussian and Brandenburg example was followed by Silesia, Bohemia, Westphalia, the Tyrol, North Germany, Hamburg, and the Hanseatic towns.

The rest of Germany

Stein, who saw himself as more German than Prussian, tried to stir up a general insurrection of German 'national war'. Together with the Russian statesman Karl Robert Nesselrode (who was of German descent), he launched an 'Appeal to Germany' on 19 March 1813. It proposed that Germany should be liberated from the French; that the Confederation of the Rhine should be replaced by a provisional commission; and that there should be a Council of Delegates with Stein at its head. Any prince who failed to respond to this appeal should lose his possessions. A few days later, the Russian commander, Field-Marshal Mikhail Kutuzov, issued a similar proclamation.

There ensued a wave of highly charged emotional patriotism, best exemplified by the collection of poems, *The Lyre and the Sword*, by Theodor Körner, who at the age of twenty-two was killed at the battle of Leipzig or 'Battle of the Nations' of 16–19 October 1813. The German princes were a little more cautious, although only Saxony remained for long in alliance with Napoleon.

Was the German revolt a popular insurrection? Yes, in so far as recruits flocked to join the *Landwehr*; no, by comparison with the Spanish case, which was a virtual civil war. Moreover, the German Rhineland remained aloof. Jacques Beugnot, the administrator of the Grand Duchy of Berg, noted that the upper classes in the Rhineland were delighted by Napoleon's defeat in Russia, but that the mass of the population was dismayed.

Broadly speaking, however, Germany was swept by a great wave of patriotic animus against the French. Its ambitions, based on Romantic nationalism, included greatly broadening Germany's frontiers. Stein called for them to be extended to the Meuse, Luxembourg, the Moselle, and the Vosges. The German writer Jakob Joseph von Görres, in his paper *Der Merkur*, denounced Germany's 1792 frontiers. During the 'Hundred Days' he wrote an article, 'France Partitioned or France in Chains', in which he called for Germany's frontiers to be set in the Vosges and the Ardennes. France, he claimed, had to be crushed. 'There will be no security against that nation unless it is powerless and our superiority is clearly overwhelming. The French are incapable of ethical behaviour.'

The Dutch

In the Netherlands, too, popular insurrection played a major role. This was partly because of General Jean-Baptiste Bernadotte. Although French, he had incurred Napoleon's displeasure for congratulating the Saxons on their courage at Wagram; and in 1810 he had been offered succession to the throne of Sweden. He was therefore now fighting on behalf of the allies against Napoleon and commanding the right flank. Instead of marching against Holland, however, he went north to invade Denmark and force the Danish king, who held Norway as his personal possession, to cede It to the king of Sweden – in which he was successful. This meant that the Dutch, for want of allied troops, had to liberate themselves. Since 1811, the Netherlands had been turned into a *département* of France: but, faced with the prospect of popular revolt, Napoleon's chief representative there, Charles François Lebrun, fled on 16 November 1813. Next day, The Hague and Amsterdam were in the hands of the rebels, who set up a triumvirate headed by Van Hogendorp. This provisional government at once appealed to Prince William of Orange, the son of the last *Stathouder*, William V, who had died in 1806. The prince, who had served in the allied armies and was now in England, arrived at Scheveningen on 30 November, to be met by cheering crowds. At the beginning of December, Prussian troops under Count Friedrich Wilhelm Bülow entered the Netherlands. On 21 July 1814, William secured allied agreement to a union of the Northern Low Countries with the former Austrian Low Countries and the Bishopric of Liège (present-day Belgium), the whole to be known as 'the Kingdom of the Netherlands', with himself as King William I. This well suited the policy of the British, who were anxious to see the port of Antwerp removed from control by a great power, and France surrounded by a *cordon sanitaire* of medium-sized countries.

The Belgians

Belgium, by contrast, had no popular insurrection. The country was bilingual, as it still is, and had been possessed in turn by the Dukes of Burgundy, by Spain, by Austria and then by France. Nationality, for the Belgians, was therefore a complex problem. They had seemed satisfied in the early days of French rule, especially after the Concordat of 1801. But discontent grew – first in the form of mounting opposition to Napoleon's religious policy and his persecution of Pope Pius VII. Resistance was led by the bishops and clergy, who several times tried to foment a peasant revolt. The Belgians also suffered grievously from the economic depression caused by the Continental Blockade. In 1813, the cotton industry had to dismiss thousands of workers; the ports of Antwerp and Ostend were virtually closed; prices rose accordingly, and bankruptcies multiplied. Added to which, taxes were heavy, and conscription was draconian: from Belgium's modest population it took 110,000 men in 1811, 120,000 in 1812, and 160,000 in 1813. The local authorities and local police assisted with deserters, thereby clashing with the inquisitorial and highly unpopular 'High Police'. Even the Mayor of Antwerp was arrested on suspicion of encouraging smugglers to break the blockade.

The news of Napoleon's defeats in 1812 and 1813 had a mixed reception in Belgium. Some were delighted, others afraid; but the bulk of the population remained passive. The idea of Belgian independence was mooted; but not until 1830 was independence achieved.

The Swiss

There were some 9,000 Swiss soldiers in Napoleon's armies. But the Swiss themselves were weary of French rule. After Napoleon's defeat in Russia, the Diet (set up in 1803 by the 'Act of Mediation') decided that Russia should remain neutral and simply occupy the frontier area. Metternich, secretly encouraged by a certain number of Swiss aristocrats, intended to use Swiss territory as a corridor into France. When 150,000 Austrian troops came across the frontier with a view to crossing the Rhine between Basle and Schaffhausen, there were too few Swiss troops to put up an effective resistance, and Geneva was occupied. The presence of the Austrians made it possible to repeal the 'Act of Mediation' on 29 December 1813, clearing the way for the later 'Federal Pact'.

Switzerland (including Geneva) was represented at the Congress of Vienna in 1814–15. During the 'Hundred Days', although Swiss neutrality had been recognized by the Vienna Declaration of 20 March 1815, Switzerland decided to fight Napoleon alongside the allies, and Swiss troops actually crossed the frontier to take part in the siege of Huningen, near Basle.

CONCLUSION

Not since Charlemagne had a politically united Europe seemed so close as under Napoleon Bonaparte. Yet that Europe aroused universal hatred. The French themselves, who were in a sense the heroes of the story, came out of it infinitely weary. Most of the French people were country-dwellers. They, and the artisans from the towns, made up the bulk of the army's conscripts. This was reason enough for widespread discontent; and with the economic hardships caused by the blockade, it could only grow. That was why Louis Bonaparte, Napoleon's brother and briefly King of Holland, opposed his policy and tried to break the blockade. As a result, Napoleon deposed him and annexed the Netherlands, making them into a *département* of France – to most of the Dutch an odious situation.

At the same time, the Empire had its adherents. In the Rhineland, for example, Jeanbon Saint-André was a very successful *préfet* of Mainz. In Switzerland, Italy, and Poland, too, there were many partisans of the Napoleonic regime.

Yet, finally, the experience showed that Europe cannot be united by force. The Revolution, and Napoleon himself, were both far bolder than Louis XIV had been. His limited efforts to defy the 'balance of power' in Europe were nothing compared to Napoleon's attempt to destroy it. Napoleon, in fact, sought to unite Europe by armed might, to the advantage of France. A century and a quarter after his defeat, Adolf Hitler tried to unite Europe under German hegemony, using not only military power but also, unforgivably, systematic genocide. As conquerors, Hitler and Napoleon were detested throughout Europe. Against the Europe of dictatorship, Europeans banded together – in alliances made by governments, and resistance movements formed by the people themselves.

15
A European Phenomenon: The Industrial Revolution

INVENTIVE EUROPE

From the eighteenth century onwards, Western Europe began to abound in inventions. Some involved pure science, whose results were not immediately exploitable. Others came in applied science, and were aimed at practical production. New technology was the most concrete form of applied science.

Why did so much research take place in Europe?

> The eighteenth century [wrote Charles Morazé] awoke first in England and France. But what of the rest of the world? China, India, Africa, and what survived the ruin of Indian America – none showed the slightest sign of belonging to that century.
>
> Only European America kept pace with Europe, and especially with England. Beyond Europe (and the Europeans), a science-based civilization was not yet born. It was not even suspected.

One powerful motive was the growth of curiosity. It was linked with the increasing number of intellectuals trained in mathematics rather than theology, and the willingness of the rich to use their leisure to build laboratories and conduct experiments (as did Voltaire, Madame de Châtelet, and the Tax-Farmer-General Antoine Laurent Lavoisier, who discovered 'elements' – but was guillotined during the Terror).

There were also families of scientists like the Bernoullis – Jacques, Jean, Nicolas, Daniel, two more Jeans and another Jacques – originally from Antwerp, but driven out by Spanish persecution to find refuge first in Frankfurt and later in Basle. And there were many isolated figures: Leonhard Euler (1707–83), a mathematician from Basle; Count Joseph Louis Lagrange (1736–1813), a mathematician born in Turin of French parents; Gaspard Monge (1746–1818), a mathematician and physicist from Beaune; Pierre Simon, Marquis de Laplace (1749–1827), a mathematician and astronomer from Normandy; and all the English disciples of Sir Isaac Newton, who were especially drawn towards geometry and astronomy.

These are only examples among many: the number of potential researchers capable of making discoveries never ceased to grow; and every new revelation led to greater curiosity.

Charles Morazé has well described this European thirst for novelty:

> Europe developed a civilization which carried within it the seeds of progress. Nor was the progress it sought purely intellectual: it involved a quest for comfort and luxury as much as a search for Reason and the truth. This perpetual interplay between the material and spiritual desires of humanity was the driving-force for further social progress, whose essential instrument was education.

In the key field of applied sciences, the following chronology (drawn mainly from J. A. Lesourd's and Claude Gérard's authoritative *Nouvelle histoire économique*, Vol. I, *Le XIXe siècle*, Paris 1976) gives some idea of the main discoveries.

Energy production in Europe

Human ingenuity has invented not only machines for producing energy, but also machines for using it to manufacture ten, a hundred, or a thousand times as much as artisans working by hand with simple tools or rudimentary machinery.

The interaction of these two types of invention can be seen in the case of the steam engine on the one hand, and spinning and weaving on the other, as well as smelting and the production of iron.

Many of these inventions were made in Britain. Some came from France, but the Revolutionary and Napoleonic Wars slowed down French progress; and very soon Belgium, northern Italy, and western Germany began to catch up with their predecessors, and even overtake them. It was a general European phenomenon, unmatched by anything really comparable in China, the Arab countries, India, or Africa.

It was a French Huguenot who first applied steam to produce motion by raising a piston, and even used it to work a small boat. This was Denis Papin (1647–1714): a refugee in England, he became a member of the Royal Society in 1681 before going to Germany as Professor of

Mathematics at the University of Marburg in 1687. He was also a Correspondent of the French Academy of Sciences. In 1698, Thomas Savery devised a pumping engine which used steam, to drain water from mines; then came Thomas Newcomen's 'fire-engine' (1705), Nicholas Cugnot's three-wheeled *chariot routier* or steam carriage (1769), and the Marquis de Jouffroy d'Abbans's steamboat (1776). But it was James Watt in 1792 who took the decisive step by using a condenser separate from the cylinder to save heat, and a double-action cylinder and valve gear to save power, thereby producing a really effective machine. With the help of Matthew Boulton, a generous and intelligent industrialist, Watt began to manufacture and market his steam engines. By 1800, 500 of them were powering looms, forge-hammers, etc.

Textile machinery

At the beginning of the eighteenth century, a cotton weaving-loom needed four hand-spinners to supply it with yarn, while a wool weaving-loom needed ten spinners. In 1733 a Lancashire clock-maker, John Kay, devised a 'flying shuttle' which enabled one weaver to make cloth of a width that had previously required two. The weavers, already often out of work for want of spun yarn, were so angry that Kay had to flee to France.

Clearly, there was a need to spin more yarn. Sometime between 1764 and 1767, James Hargreaves, a weaver and carpenter from Blackburn, invented a 'spinning jenny' which at first enabled one person to spin six or seven threads at once, and later as many as eighty.

Jenny-spun yarn, however, was soft and suitable only for the weft: the warp still had to be hand-spun. Then Richard Arkwright, a successful barber and businessman from Preston, designed with the help of John Kay an improved spinning-frame or 'water frame', using hydraulic power to produce a thread strong enough for the warp.

In 1779, combining the spinning jenny and the water frame, a Bolton weaver, Samuel Crompton, invented a machine known as the 'mule' which was able to produce a strong, fine, and even yarn suitable for both warp and weft, and especially for fine muslins, which had previously been imported from the East.

In France, in 1804, Joseph Marie Jacquard invented a silk-weaving loom which could produce patterns.

Between 1779 and 1812, the cost of cotton yarn fell by 90 per cent. As A. P. Usher has pointed out, this enabled the great majority of the population to obtain better cloth than the rich had enjoyed in the past. It also gave Britain a valuable product for export.

These are only examples of an accelerating and cumulative process, whereby mechanical energy and new inventions were applied in many related fields. Alfred Sauvy estimated that as a result of such technological progress, Europeans living in the late twentieth century had at their disposal several hundred times as many ordinary articles for use or pleasure as were available to their eighteenth-century ancestors.

Iron and other minerals

Smelting and ironworking inventions played a vital role in the development of machinery; and in this field Britain had a very clear lead. In the words of Lesourd and Gérard:

> In 1709, the ironmaster Abraham Darby, of Coalbrookdale in Shropshire, tried using coke instead of charcoal to produce pig-iron. The process was not perfected until 1830. Until 1753, Darby and his family were alone in producing pig-iron smelted with coke: they recovered the hot gases it gave off and used them to heat the air blown in at the base of the furnace, thereby cutting coke consumption by half. Their output was some 20 tons a week. Later, the process was more widely used; by 1806, 97 per cent of all English pig-iron was coke-smelted. There were sixty coke furnaces in Britain in 1788, 227 in 1806, and 305 in 1826. In France, François de Wendel conducted similar experiments at Hayange, in Lorraine, in 1769. By 1784 he had coke-fired blast-furnaces in operation at Homburg; in the following year, with the British engineer John Wilkinson, he inaugurated four more at Le Creusot. But in 1805, 98 per cent of French pig-iron was still being produced with charcoal, and 50 per cent in 1850. Not until about 1870 did the proportion fall to 9 per cent.

In Germany, as well as the Ruhr, Upper Silesia developed into an important zone. The town of Königshütte (now Chorzów) developed from a metallurgical works founded there in 1798.

The Industrial Revolution was slow in coming to Spain; but from 1850 onwards the Spaniards discovered rich mineral resources. They led the world in mercury production, and in lead production until about 1900. They produced zinc, and for a time were the second biggest producers of copper. Top-quality iron pyrite, from north-western Spain, was exported mainly to Britain. In bauxite and oil, however, Spain was poor.

Railways

In 1803, a steam carriage built by the Cornish engineer Richard Trevithick made several journeys through the streets of London; and in the following year he and the American inventor Oliver Evans ran the first locomotives on rails. Rails had long been used to carry mining wagons: originally in wood, they were later made of pig-iron and eventually of steel.

In 1814, the colliery engineer George Stephenson built a locomotive, forerunner of the *Rocket*, to run on iron rails: the design was later improved upon by the French engineer Séguin with his 'multi-tubular boiler' (1817). On 27 September 1825, passenger coaches, pulled by Stephenson's locomotive, made the journey from Stockton to Darlington.

France, in 1832, completed the Lyon–Saint-Etienne line and in 1835 that between Paris and Saint-Germain. In 1851, however, France still had only 3,500 kilometres of track, carrying only a fifth of the country's total goods traffic, whereas the British rail network by that time covered 10,500 kilometres.

Between 1850 and 1914, Britain's rail network expanded from 10,000 to 38,500 kilometres. During the same period, Germany's 6,000 kilometres grew to 63,000, Belgium's 800 kilometres grew to 8,800, France's 3,500 kilometres grew to 39,500, and Italy's 120 kilometres grew to 18,000. Spain's network increased from 102 kilometres in 1852 to 5,706 in 1866 and 10,800 in 1914. But the choice of a different gauge (1.67 metres) somewhat isolated the system. All other European countries, except Russia, followed the British gauge of 4 feet 8 inches or 1.435 metres; so travellers could now go with ease from one city in Europe to another – and with a great saving of time.

In the seventeenth century, when Madame de Sévigné went from Paris to Vitre in what is now the Ille-et-Vilaine *département*, where she had her estate of Les Rochers, she first had to travel to Orléans by coach. This was then shipped aboard a 'water-stagecoach' or *coche d'eau* down the Loire as far as Nantes. From there the coach had to take the primitive road to Vitre – a total journey of 172 hours. The building of the 'Royal roads' had cut this journey time to ninety hours by 1782, and fifty-six hours by 1814. In 1854, by rail, it was seven hours and twenty-three minutes. In 1971, the journey took three hours and eighteen minutes.

In the United States, where distances were vast, land was cheap, and rough conditions were accepted, the rail network grew from

14,500 kilometres in 1850 to 386,000 kilometres in 1916. A quarter of the capital for its development came from Europe.

Meanwhile, improvements to steam locomotives greatly reduced their consumption of coal, and the price of tickets fell dramatically. After 1870, iron rails were replaced by the much more durable steel.

Another feature of railways in Europe was the construction of great international tunnels. They included the Mont-Cenis (1857–71), 12.8 kilometres long, linking Modane in France with Bardonecchia in Italy; the Saint-Gotthard (1870–80), 15 kilometres long; the Simplon (completed in 1921), 19.8 kilometres long, linking Brig in Switzerland with Domodossola in Italy; and the Loetschberg (1900–5), 14.6 kilometres long. Merchandise, and especially heavy goods, continued to travel by the networks of rivers and canals so extensively developed in Belgium, the Netherlands, and Germany.

Unlike Britain, Germany still relies on her canals. In 1903, she had 14,500 kilometres of canals and canalized rivers, of which the Rhine was the most important. Like the Danube, it remains a great European highway.

Ending as it does in 1914, this chapter can note only the beginnings of the new means of transport which later rivalled the railways. It was now, for instance, that oil began to be used instead of coal as fuel for steamships. Alongside the steamers, there also appeared motor vessels, using the heavy-oil engine designed by the German engineer Rudolf Diesel in 1897.

Still more promising was the ordinary internal combustion engine. At the beginning of the 1860s, Nikolaus-August Otto from Germany and Joseph-Etienne Lenoir from France invented a motor which used the gases produced by the burning of petrol. Scientists, engineers, and technicians from all over Europe worked to adapt this engine – which was both lighter and cleaner than the steam engine – for travel on the roads. They included in particular three celebrated Germans: Siegfried Marcus, Gottlieb Daimler, and Karl Benz.

Creative freedom

Every nation likes to pride itself on having invented everything: but it is now generally agreed that the first inventions in the Industrial Revolution came from Britain (plus America), followed by France, until about 1850. Then, in growing numbers, they came from Switzerland,

Belgium, Germany, the Netherlands, Sweden, Denmark, Italy, and later Spain and Portugal. Why should this have been so?

It has been suggested already that *creativity, other things being equal, proves most vigorous where there is freedom of thought.* Although not a full explanation, this is still true today: research seldom prospers when ruled by bureaucracy. True, in the eighteenth century there was greater religious freedom in Prussia than in Britain or France. But intellectual circumstances have to be favourable too.

Scientific progress can be stifled if government permission is required for communication between one research worker or one laboratory and another. There were no such restrictions in eighteenth-century Britain. The country had had habeas corpus since 1673, parliamentary control of the executive and a Bill of Rights since 1689, and freedom of the press since the reign of George III (1760–1820), when John Wilkes and his *North Briton* had successfully defied attempts to silence them, as has been seen (p.293).

The United States were the first to follow Britain's libertarian example, and to improve upon it by separating Church and state.

France, even before the Revolution, had enjoyed a degree of religious tolerance; but until 1870 her history saw successive waves of liberty, terror, and despotism, with liberty gradually prevailing more and more. So Britain and France, each with a powerful 'intelligentsia', and each politically freer than other countries, had good reason to be centres of creativity, discovery, and invention.

The Swiss Confederation, Belgium (independent after 1830), Cavour's Italy, and the partially democratic Germany created by Bismarck, with universal suffrage for the Reichstag – all in turn joined the ranks of Europe's free societies.

Necessity: the mother of invention

Invention is also a function of *need*. When demand outstrips supply, it stimulates efforts to improve the means of production.

Edmund Cartwright, who invented the power-loom, was a clergyman and poet. He had never seen a loom or studied mechanical problems until the day when he heard Lancashire manufacturers complain that they urgently needed a power-loom but were unable to make one. The role of such amateurs became more and more important during the nineteenth century, although the average inventor was either a pure scientist or someone working in the industry. The engineer as such only gradually emerged. James Hargreaves, the inventor of the spinning jenny, was a weaver and carpenter, while Samuel Crompton, who produced the mule, was a weaver. Both were Lancashire-born.

EUROPE AT THE CENTRE OF WORLD PRODUCTION

Economic cycles

Scientific inventions, when applied to manufacturing industry, trade, and agriculture, should in theory lead to *constant growth* in production.

In so general a history it is difficult to evaluate qualitative growth. As for quantity, studies on the output of various products or services all point to the same conclusion: general progress. There are, however, upswings and down-turns. Some commentators, such as François Simiand or N. D. Kondratieff, have argued that there are economic or trade 'cycles', linked in particular to the available quantity of gold. When gold becomes scarce, its value increases, and the amount of gold needed to pay for the same quantity of goods accordingly falls. As a result, so does the price of those goods expressed in currencies based on gold, which 'deflation' in turn can cause problems for manufacturers. Then production falls, or grows less quickly. This is what Simiand called a 'B' phase. If on the other hand there is a glut of gold, its value falls and the price of goods rises – Simiand's 'A' phase. When, of course, currencies are no longer tied to gold (as from 1971 onwards), cycles of this kind should automatically cease.

Between 1750 and 1940, on Kondratieff's findings, 'A' and 'B' phases of greater or lesser intensity succeeded each other as follows: A: 1790–1815; B: 1815–1847; A: 1847–1873; B: 1873–1896; A: 1896–1920; and B: 1920–1940.

Huge discoveries of gold in California, the Klondyke, and Australia are said to explain the 'A' phase from 1847 to 1873, while that between 1896 and 1920 followed the opening of the new South African mines.

Economic expansion

Despite these economic cycles, there was clearly global progress.

Under the First Empire, France had practically no steam engines. In 1850 she had 5,322, with a total of 67,000 horsepower. By 1913 there were fifteen times as many, producing fifty-three times as much power.

Energy consumption over forty years increased steadily in Europe, but grew exponentially in the United States. Already by 1900, the USA – in a sense Europe's giant offspring – was in a position to become the world's leading economic power.

According to Lesourd, coal production in Europe increased greatly between 1810 and 1913: the United Kingdom's 10 million tonnes grew to 290; Germany's 0.3 grew to 277; France's 0.8 grew to 40.9; and Belgium's 1.5 grew to 22.9. The United States was already way ahead of Europe, having increased from 13.3 million tonnes in 1860 to 513 in 1913, on the way to its future economic preponderance.

France's total trade increased eightfold. That of Germany and the United States grew much more rapidly than Britain's. By 1913, German trade was 3.5 times its 1875 level, and American trade 4.7 times, while Britain's was only twice as great. In 1914, however, Britain was still the world's biggest trading power. Up to 1913, different countries' shares of world trade were changing, to the advantage of Germany and the United States but to the detriment of Britain and France.

Germany's national income quadrupled between 1871 and 1910, while that of the United States increased fivefold. For a similar increase in Britain, the baseline must be pushed back to 1851. British national income quadrupled between then and 1911.

Europe as a banking centre

The Industrial Revolution involved growing numbers of inventions in pure and applied science. It responded to growing needs and rising living standards. It both reflected and fostered psychological change. But it also required capital. This had been accumulating ever since Europeans had become rulers of the seas, colonizers, and large-scale traders. To enable such capital to be deployed in large quantities and with great flexibility was the role of the banks. It was a role that had never ceased to develop, from the medieval 'money-changers' onwards.

In the nineteenth century, 'the reign of the banks began,' as Jacques Laffitte remarked in 1830, shortly before he became Prime Minister of France. First, every state had its own national bank. Following the example of the Bank of England, founded in 1694, the Bank of France was set up in 1800, the Nederlandsche Bank in the Netherlands in 1814, the Banco de San Carlos in Spain, and the National Bank of Austria in 1817. Alongside them there were large numbers of private and family banks. In Germany they were owned by such families as the Mendelssohns, the Bleichröders, and the Rothschilds. Five Rothschild brothers, the 'Five Gentlemen of Frankfurt', opened a network of banks in different European countries – Solomon in Vienna, Karl in Naples, Nathan Mayer in London, James in Paris; the eldest brother, Anselm Mayer, remained in Frankfurt to carry on the house his father had founded there.

In London there were the Barings, the Lazards, the Schroeders, and the Hambros. In Paris, bankers were often Protestants or Jews, like the Lazards, the Hottinguers, the Foulds, the d'Eichtals, the Mallets (from Geneva), the Vernes, the Mirabauds, the de Neufflizes, and so on.

The new factor was the huge increase in the number of small depositors and users of banking services, discounting trade, managing investments, dealing in securities, etc. The great joint-stock or commercial banks, with numerous branches, appeared mostly after 1850, in contrast to the much older merchant banks. In France, the commercial banks include the Crédit Lyonnais and the Société Générale; in Germany the 'four Ds' (the Darmstadter Bank, the Diskonto-Gesellschaft, the Deutsche Bank, and the Dresdner Bank); and in Britain the 'big four' – Barclays, Lloyds, Midland, and National Westminster.

The merchant banks were and are involved in long-term investments and backing for large-scale enterprise – financial affairs. The commercial banks are more concerned with current operations – banking business.

Europe, banker to the world

The extraordinary growth of banking led Europe to become what Herbert Feis called, in the title of a celebrated book, 'the world's banker'.

With large financial resources derived from savings, various European countries (notably, in order of magnitude, Britain, France, and Germany) willingly invested abroad to enjoy higher interest than they could command at home. They did so in many different ways: by offering short-term credit; by financing loans floated by foreign governments or sometimes local authorities; by buying shares; by investing in foreign capital projects (railways, ports, lighthouses, public works, and every kind of factory); by setting up foreign subsidiaries of native firms; or by establishing foreign branches of their own.

The places which received the most capital from Britain, France and Germany were Russia, Italy, Eastern Europe, the United States (which was a net debtor before 1914 and became a creditor only after 1920), and Latin America. Other major recipients were certain colonies, and especially India. In 1914 the approximate figures for capital invested abroad were: by Britain, $20 billion; by France nearly $9 billion; by Germany, just over $6 billion. Each had her own favoured methods and recipients.

It is worth pointing out that the theory of 'economic imperialism' argued by the British economist J. A. Hobson in 1902 (in *Imperialism, a Study*), and by Lenin in 1916 (in *Imperialism, the Highest Stage of Capitalism*), is not confirmed by history. Lenin believed that imperialism, and especially Europe's conquest of its colonies, originated in the era of 'monopoly capitalism', when industrial capital was absorbed by the banks. These, and the state (which in Lenin's view was the representative of 'large-scale capital') were supposedly out to conquer territory in which to invest their excess wealth.

In reality, first, most European countries acquired their empires *before* they reached the stage of 'monopoly capitalism'. Secondly, although the British made some 50 per cent of their foreign investments in their colonial Empire, neither the French nor the Germans invested much in the colonies which belonged to them.

Where did most of Europe's investments go?

Britain invested abroad £4 billion, or about a quarter of her wealth. Some fifty British banks specialized in the business: they included the Imperial Bank of India and the Bank of Hong Kong. Only 25 per cent of these overseas investments went into foreign government loans; 94 per cent went outside Europe, and about half of them to the British Empire. Others financed a number of mines and railways, for example, in Latin America and the Middle East: the government advised bankers on the political importance of certain projects. In 1913, when Britain's national income was £2.2 billion, one tenth of this sum came from the interest on overseas investments.

France came far behind Britain, with £1.8 billion invested abroad. There were many other differences, too. France invested very little in her colonies. She also, after 1815, lent a great deal to foreign states, and the French government authorized or prohibited such loans according to its policy aims. This authorization was known as 'admission to quotation' (on the Stock Exchange). Thus, for example, from 1871 to 1914 no German stock could be quoted on the Paris Bourse. A further difference from Britain was that, while France did invest outside Europe (in Asia, the Ottoman Empire, and Latin America), most of its investments were within Europe – as, for instance, in the Bor mines in Serbia, the Agulas mines in Spain, or the Laurion mines in Greece. France also helped to finance much of Europe's railway network.

From 1887 onwards, the country most sought after by French investors was Russia. The interest was mutual. France wanted an ally against Germany, whose population now outnumbered hers; Russia needed capital to repair the damage done by her inept financial policy – a need which became all the greater after Russia's defeat by Japan in 1905. As time went on, moreover, French capital went less and less towards state loans and more towards private investment in industry, railways, mines, oil, textiles, metals, chemicals, and, of course, banks. French bankers and businessmen tended to call Russia 'France's Far West' – which understandably annoyed their Russian counterparts.

Germany invested a great deal in the Austro-Hungarian Empire with which it was in alliance; but German capital also went to Spain, Russia, Portugal, Romania, Africa, and Latin America. It financed a railway in the Ottoman Empire, the so-called 'Baghdad Bahn'. Germany also had interests in China, connected with her Kiao-Chau concession, in Shantung province. In Italy, she took advantage of the Italian 'economic war' with France to replace French influence and, through the Banca Commerciale Italiana, acquired a real and lasting hold on Italian business. German loans to foreign governments, moreover, were 'tied': a clause in the contract required the borrower to buy German goods. French lenders made no such stipulation unless compelled by the government to do so. The result was that several European countries used French money to buy arms from Krupp in Essen rather than from Schneider in Le Creusot. Germany, like Britain, was much more a trading power than France, which outstripped either of them in agricultural production.

Thus it came about that France was Russia's biggest creditor, while Germany was her biggest supplier and customer.

A BRIEF EXPERIMENT IN FREE TRADE

Napoleon III, Cobden, and Michel Chevalier

When Bonaparte's nephew Napoleon III came to power in France after the 1848 Revolution, he might perhaps have been expected to give a fresh shape to some of his uncle's European dreams. He did not. He contented himself with periodic vague declarations, expressing hopes rather than intentions. 'With all my heart,' he told the Senate on 21 November 1863, 'I long for the day when the great questions which divide governments may be resolved in peace by a European tribunal.' In 1867, he expressed his desire for a 'United States of Europe'. It is hard to see in this much more than rhetoric. Realists like the German statesman Otto von Bismarck had nothing but scorn for such vague sentiments. The next chapter will show how different Bismarck's Europe was from that of his hapless French rival.

However, while Napoleon III did little to create a political Europe, he did for a time build Europe in economic terms. During the 1860s, indeed, Europe became a real economic entity; and this was due to tenacious efforts by Napoleon III.

'In the mid-nineteenth century,' wrote the economic historians Charles Gide and Charles Rist, 'the doctrine of Adam Smith conquered Europe... Free trade was accepted as an unassailable dogma by economists everywhere. In Germany, Britain, France, or Russia, all scientific authorities were in agreement. The Socialists either ignored the subject or, when they looked at it, echoed the economists.' Still, between 'scientific authorities' and governmental authorities there was a great gulf. Britain was the first to cross it. Richard Cobden's Anti-Corn-Law League, which had been campaigning against the tariff on corn imports since 1838, finally triumphed when the Prime Minister, Sir Robert Peel, reversed his previous stand and carried the Bill repealing the Corn Laws in 1846. In the years that followed, Britain took further anti-protectionist measures and set a real example of international free trade.

In France, very probably, nine-tenths of the industrialists and businessmen were protectionist. The 'French Association for Free Trade', set up by a hopeful economist, Frédéric Bastiat, had no success before its founder's death in 1851. Bastiat believed that the completely free operation of 'market forces', with no state intervention, would lead to favourable results. His main work was entitled *Economic Harmonies*.

Although Bastiat did not live to see his theories triumph, he did convert to his militant cause a powerful personality: Michel Chevalier, Professor of Political Economy at the Collège de France. Chevalier had been a disciple of the Socialist Claude Henri de Rouvroy, Comte de Saint-Simon (1760–1825), and an assistant to the Saint-Simonian Barthélémy Prosper Enfantin. In 1832, Enfantin (who among other things advocated 'free love') was prosecuted and imprisoned for a year. Chevalier was imprisoned with him, but for six months only; and during their confinement at Sainte-Pélagie he broke with Enfantin and with Saint-Simonian theories. A realist, and something of a careerist, Chevalier realized that 'the Saint-Simonian religion' clouded his prospects. His views evolved further during a trip to the United States to study the railway system – he had been top of his year at the Ecole Polytechnique and was an Engineer in the Corps des Mines. He also visited Britain, and as a result of his travels proposed a large-scale railway network for Europe. As a former Saint-Simonian, he was naturally inclined towards free trade. Frédéric Bastiat completed his conversion, and Chevalier was soon its most effective and dynamic champion.

He was not, however, a liberal in political matters. This too was typical of the Saint-Simonian school. Chevalier actually welcomed the authoritarian Empire of Napoleon III, and enjoyed the favour of this new regime. He used his growing authority to promote free trade in France, on the model of the British example. His aims in this were not solely economic. While he certainly saw free trade as a way to develop industry and increase wealth, he was a sincere pacifist and – for his time – incredibly free from nationalism. By increasing trade he hoped to bind the nation-states so closely together that war would become impossible. In this he was at one with Richard Cobden, with whom he kept up a long correspondence on increasingly friendly terms.

Napoleon III, too, was attracted by free-trading ideas. On the one hand, he admired the Saint-Simonians and listened to their advice. They included not only Chevalier, now a professor and later a senator, but also bankers like the brothers Emile and Isaac Péreire, the Paulin Talabot family, or the d'Eichtals. On the other hand, one of Napoleon III's great ambitions was to make France as prosperous as Britain while maintaining good relations with London. He had lived in Britain after his escape from the French fortress of Ham, just at the time when the British were adopting free trade. His difficulties, however, came from the elected legislature, which remained largely protectionist.

The Cobden Treaty of 1860 between Britain and France

It was Michel Chevalier who suggested to the Emperor a legal way to overcome protectionist opposition. The 1852 constitution gave him the right to sign and ratify commercial treaties without submitting them to the legislature. Chevalier was accordingly instructed to negotiate with Cobden, in the utmost secrecy, a treaty which made drastic cuts in customs duties between Britain and France. French duties on coal and most manufactured goods were cut to a maximum of 30 per cent; the British reduced their duties on French wines and brandy. On 23 January 1860, the official French *Moniteur* published the Treaty, which had the force of law. French industrialists protested violently, but to no avail.

The Cobden Treaty was only a beginning. In the years that followed, France passed a number of liberal measures, in particular for the free importation of industrial raw materials, for the simplification of navigation laws, and for the extension to foreign firms in France of the same rights as those enjoyed by French firms. Various other European countries signed similar treaties with France: they included Belgium and Turkey in 1861, the Prussian *Zollverein* or customs union in 1862 just before Bismarck came to power, Italy in 1863, Sweden and the Netherlands in 1865, and Austria in 1866.

These countries also signed commercial treaties with each other. The result was not completely free trade, but it was not far off it. The American historian Rondo Cameron pointed out in *France and the Economic Development of Europe*, that because of the most-favoured-nation clause, and the conclusion of similar treaties by other nations, France became the cornerstone in a system which brought the world closer to full free trade than it had ever been. As the British historian David Thomson put it, France became 'the focus of a great European movement for the freeing of international trade'. Only Russia remained completely protectionist.

In this Europe of virtually free trade, there was also something like monetary union, at least on the continent. The gold franc was the currency of France, Switzerland, and, after 1830, Belgium. It was also used, under the name of the lira, in Piedmont, which extended it to the whole of Italy, and until 1867 in the Rhineland. The franc was furthermore the basis of the Greek, Spanish, Serbian, Romanian, and Finnish currencies – Finland having a certain autonomy in the Empire of the Tsars. In 1865, to counter the effects of the depreciation of gold, France, Belgium, Switzerland, and Italy formed a 'Latin Monetary Union' and invited other countries to join them. Hungary and Austria became associated with it in 1867, and Greece joined as a full member in the following year. But in Germany Bismarck was reluctant to commit himself; and despite pressure from commercial and financial quarters, he preferred to give Germany a new currency – the Mark.

Free trade no guarantee of peace

The free movement of goods, persons, and capital; monetary union; and even 'conventions on the right of establishment': all made the Europe of the 1860s a kind of economic entity. It was more of a 'free trade area' than a 'common market'. But at the time it involved the highest degree of economic integration ever achieved. Was its promise likely to last? Were Cobden and Chevalier right to see mutual trade as a factor for peace? Alas, no. They had taken too little account of nationalism and its irresistible strength. Commercial considerations were no match for patriotic glory, territorial ambition, or national prestige. Napoleon III himself pursued these dangerous goals; and Bismarck, having defeated France in the Franco-Prussian War of 1870, seized Alsace and Lorraine in the name of German unity, despite the unceasing protests of their inhabitants, who saw themselves as French. What was more, economic *rapprochement* had been encouraged by a period of prosperity and rising prices. When a serious economic depression began in 1873, the temptation was to abandon free trade, especially since the protectionist Louis Adolphe Thiers was in power in France from 1871 to 1873. But it was in Germany, in 1879, that the decision was taken, by Bismarck, to return to high customs tariffs. In 1881 France took counter-measures; and from 1887 to about 1897 there was a Franco-Italian 'tariff war'. In 1892, Félix Jules Méline raised the French tariff to forbidding heights. The dream of an economically united Europe, fleetingly made real, had been dispelled by the very first storms. From 1871 onwards, in letters to the Prussian former Minister von der Heydt, Michel Chevalier expressed his despair at the ruin of his hopes.

In fact, if Bismarck had put up with free trade between 1862 and 1871, it had been for practical reasons, not for the sake of Europe. As a Prussian nationalist, he had opposed German unity in 1848, but finally achieved it under the aegis of Prussia. Historians still debate whether Bismarck was converted to belief in German nationalism, or whether he cynically exploited it for the aggrandizement of Prussia. And when he was faced with the idea of changing his objective from German to European unity, it simply struck him as grotesque.

Europe for Bismarck was the traditional Europe of inter-state rivalry checked by the balance of power; after 1871 he was statesmanlike enough to seek no further conquests. Europe was not even, in his eyes, the Europe of law. He never declared 'Might is Right'. He simply regarded law as based on treaties, not morality or justice; and treaties, he well knew, were often the outcome of a trial of strength.

The triumph of protectionism

In economic affairs, Bismarck was not doctrinaire. But to justify the abandonment of free trade, he had just the doctrinaire for the job. In 1841, the German economist Friedrich List had published *The National System of Political Economy*. For List, traditional economic thought was too universalist: it seemed to see humanity as united in one great community purged of war. But List believed that the nation was essential in developing 'the forces of production'. 'Political or national economy' was 'that which, taking the idea of nationality as its point of departure, teaches how a given nation, in the present state of the world and its own particular circumstances, can maintain and improve its economic situation.' From this List concluded that a country seeking to industrialize itself must be protectionist to ward off competition from industrial countries that were further advanced. This, said List, was precisely the line taken by the United States, whose policies he had watched very closely.

In the great battle of ideas between liberal economics and the economic nationalism of Friedrich List, it was List who won decisively at the end of the nineteenth century. For Europe, this was a blow whose repercussions it would be impossible to overstate.

EUROPE AND GREATER LONGEVITY

Human beings have an immense appetite for life.

In prehistory, the expectation of life was for various reasons extremely short. There were natural disasters such as frost, flood, and drought; there was disease, with the mere rudiments of medicine; there were famine, violence, and war. Naturally, human beings struggled continually against all of them. Gradual progress in farming methods, irrigation, land clearance, reclamation and improvement, and the selection of plant and animal species, all helped to reduce famine. Trial-and-error medicine had some effects on disease. And efforts to prevent war, unavailing as they generally were, continually preoccupied those with political responsibility.

The scientific revolution

The Industrial Revolution, and the scientific revolution which caused it, achieved more in two centuries than in all the rest of human history. The results, however, were unevenly spread between Europe and the rest of the world. A prime indicator is life expectation at birth. From this point of view, both the annual birth rate and the annual death rate per thousand inhabitants need to be considered.

Their interplay is complex. Since calculations are all on a national basis, figures for birth and death rates in Europe as a whole are elusive.

In Britain in 1740, the birth rate was 39.2 per cent and the death rate 38.5 per cent. By 1800, the birth rate had fallen slightly, to 38.4 per cent, but the death rate had dropped to only 27.1 per cent.

France was the first country whose birth rate declined so steeply as to match, and in the 1830s fall below, the death rate: hence the characteristic ageing of her population, later followed in the whole of Europe.

In Spain, the population rose from 15,500,000 in 1857, the date of the first reliable census, to 21,300,000 in 1920. During that period, the birth rate fell from 36 per cent to 29.3 per cent and the death rate from 31 per cent to 23.2 per cent.

After 1715 there was no really widespread famine in Europe, despite isolated instances, including the terrible potato famine in Ireland in 1846–8.

The toll from disease was greatly reduced in the years after 1796, when the English physician Edward Jenner established the efficacy of vaccination against smallpox. Despite initial opposition, it was soon widely adopted. Previously, smallpox had accounted for 10 per cent of deaths, and 30 per cent of those among children from one to four years old. As Jacqueline Beaujeu-Garnier wrote in her *Géographie de la Population*:

The discovery of vaccination, and the researches of Louis Pasteur, saved many young lives. In 1888, the Pasteur Institute was founded ... In England, the number of deaths from typhoid fever fell from 5,800 in 1870 to 2,439 in 1906. In Italy, over the period between 1887–1892 and 1949, the death rate per million inhabitants fell from 2,061 to 492 for tuberculosis, from 567 to 2 for malaria, and from 3,696 to 383 for other infectious diseases.

At the same time, however, there was an increase in deaths from circulatory disease and cancer – afflictions essentially due to deterioration, which a greater average life-span could only increase.

A further marked fall in the death rate followed the great discovery of modern times, that of antibiotics. In France, the average expectation of life at birth rose from forty years in 1860 to fifty in 1913, fifty-six in 1938, and sixty-six in 1950.

All this medical progress would have been much less effective, much slower to spread, and perhaps in some cases totally academic, if there had not at the same time been great and widespread economic advance. Better education, transport, and trade arrangements all helped to extend and expand medical knowledge. In northern Italy, for example, between 1861 and 1881, illiteracy was reduced by 13 per cent. But the fundamental change was the rise in the standard of living.

If the health of the average European improved, it was largely because agricultural progress had preceded, accompanied, and made possible progress in other aspects of life.

All resulted in spectacular increases in life expectation at birth. Recent studies set it in context. In Ancient Egypt, at the time of the late Pharaohs, it was just under twenty-four years; in thirteenth-century Hungary, twenty-seven years. In Sweden, between 1751 and 1790, it was 33.72 years for men and 36.64 years for women; and between 1791 and 1815, 33.35 years for men and 38.44 years for women.

According to research by Jacqueline Beaujeu-Garnier, figures for the first half of the twentieth century run as follows: in France, men's life expectancy rose from 48.3 years in 1900 to 61.9 years in 1950. Women's life expectancy rose from 48.7 years to 67.4 years. In Norway, men's life expectancy rose from 54.8 years to 67.8 years, while women's rose from 57.7 years to 71.7 years. In England and Wales, men's life expectancy rose from 58.7 years in 1930 (no figures for 1900) to 66.5 years, and women's from 62.6 years in 1930 to 71.2 years. In

Italy, men's life expectancy rose from 44.2 years in 1900 to 53.7 in 1930 (no figures for 1950), and women's from 44.8 years to 56 years.

These figures for Europe, which reflect the benefits of the Industrial Revolution, may be compared with those for a number of non-European countries.

In Algeria, in 1955, the expectation of life at birth was 47 years – the figure for France in 1900. In Guinea, the former French colony, it was 30–31 years in the interior, and 35–36 in the towns. For Africa as a whole, the figure was 40 years. In Korea, between 1926 and 1930, the expectation of life at birth was 32.4 years for men and 34.9 for women. In industrialized Japan, it was 45 years in 1925–30, 50 years in 1948, and 68 in 1956 – 67.2 for men and 70.2 for women. In China, in 1938–40, it was 41.1 years for men and 45.7 years for women.

Population growth in Europe

What is striking is the overall growth of the population in Europe. In 1789, Europe outside Russia had 141 million inhabitants. By 1955, it had 396 million. In area, it represented 3.8 per cent of the Earth's surface on dry land: but it contained 16.2 per cent of the world's population.

From 1850 to 1900, the annual rate of growth of Europe's population was 9.6 per cent, compared with a world rate of about 6.5 per cent. From the beginning of the twentieth century, however, owing to a slower increase in the birth rate and despite a decrease in the death rate, Europe's population growth was less rapid, compared with the huge birth rates in the rest of the world. In around 1800, Europe's population was about a fifth of the world total; by 1950, it was only a sixth.

Emigration from Europe

One of the results of working-class poverty, as of nineteenth-century political strife, was mass emigration from Europe. Between 1815 and 1914, 50 million people went overseas, establishing vast European outposts. The biggest, clearly, was the United States, which took 32 million Europeans. Then came Canada, with 4.5 million, followed by Australia, New Zealand, and South Africa. Brazil took 4.6 million, and Argentina 6 million.

The sources of the emigrants were as follows: Great Britain and

Ireland 17 million; Germany 10 million; Italy 9.5 million; the Balkans and the Danube basin 4.5 million; Spain 4.4 million; Scandinavia 2 million; Portugal 1.6 million; and Belgium and the Netherlands 0.5 million.

Only France contributed little to emigration from Europe. Her sole emigrants went to Algeria, which also received Italians, Maltese, and most of all Spaniards – all of whom, once settled there, became French citizens.

THE OTHER SIDE OF THE COIN: THE PROLETARIAT

The Industrial Revolution began as a purely European phenomenon. It was still largely European in 1914, despite the rise of Europe's American offshoot in the United States, soon followed by Japan.

Altogether, the Industrial Revolution transformed the face of the world, bringing with it greater global wealth, longer expectation of life, and much improved comfort.

The labour movement

However, like all great human phenomena, it had ambivalent effects. On the one hand, it increased Europe's military, political, and economic advantage over the rest of the world – to the latter's cost. On the other, by transforming the conditions of manufacture, it caused a profound social change.

The upshot was the emergence of a new social class, the so-called 'proletariat', made up of those described by Karl Marx, more than a century ago, as having nothing but their labour to sell.

The nineteenth-century proletariat, living in appalling squalor, largely disappeared when workers received contractual or legislative guarantees against occupational disease, accidents, and unemployment, as well as minimum wages, maximum working hours, paid holidays, and old-age and invalidity pensions. To extend the word 'proletariat' to the mass of wage-earners now is to distort reality.

Most of these workers' guarantees were won by the creative efforts of working people themselves. 'Primitive capitalism' practised every kind of abuse: starvation wages, exhausting hours of work, child labour, no protection against accidents, and utter poverty for the old, the sick, the disabled, and the unemployed, all of whom could be helped only by private or public charity.

Against such conditions there arose, at first haphazardly, then more and more systematically, what became known as the labour movement. Alongside it, intellectuals and other influential figures, horrified by the new poverty and oppression, evolved new social and economic ideas. These were many-sided and sometimes contradictory: but they had in common what may legitimately be called socialist concerns. Their aim, that is, was to put some constraint on absolute *laissez-faire* liberalism, essentially in two ways. The first was collective action by the workforce, through 'friendly societies', 'co-operatives', and trade unions. The second was legislation – passing welfare laws which brought to bear on industry the machinery of the state. It intervened either to prevent violence, by making concessions as part of its duty to maintain public order, or to respond to pressure from workers' representatives or sympathizers in parliament, more and more of whom were elected from the second half of the nineteenth century onwards.

Socialism began – in about 1830 – as a utopian, romantic aspiration. Then, from about 1850 onwards, it became realistic, rational, and reformist, with people like Pierre Joseph Proudhon in France, Ferdinand Lassalle in Germany, and Robert Owen in Britain. Finally, there appeared revolutionary socialism, whose main element was Marxist.

The real success achieved by working people – too slowly, in their eyes – came after 1880, when the labour movement and socialism began to collaborate and even unite.

The socialists were mainly either reformists, who were predominant in Britain, or Marxists, who tended to prevail in Germany, where the Party called itself 'Social-Democratic'. The two tendencies were sometimes of comparable strength, as in France, where in 1905 the reformists led by Jean Jaurès merged with the group led by Jules Guesde, who proclaimed a simplified form of Marxism.

The emergence of the proletariat and the destruction of the guilds

This is not the place to discuss countries outside Europe. They, due to Europe's overwhelming armed power, were subjected to colonization, oftentimes of a very brutal kind.

The British Empire abolished slavery in 1833; the French colonies did so in 1848; and in the United States it was eliminated by the Civil War of 1861–5. But exploitation continued in other ways; and material progress in the colonies (roads, ports, medicine, schools) could not make up for the humiliation of foreign rule.

It was in Europe, however, as has been suggested, that the seamy side of material progress was most evident, insofar as the Industrial Revolution created the new social class, the industrial proletariat.

True, human labour had always been organized. Since the high Middle Ages there had been craft guilds, each with its own regulations, comprising masters, journeymen, and apprentices. Some crafts were more highly organized than others, being bound by oath. In many cases, they enjoyed a monopoly and the support of the state, or at least the commune, for their rules and privileges. In principle, a journeyman could become a master once he had proved his skill by making a 'masterpiece'.

The accumulation of capital, however, especially in the eighteenth century, made such promotion more and more difficult: the wealthy master came to be distant, socially, from his artisans. Meanwhile, although mergers were still rare in the eighteenth century, they began to lead to the creation of 'manufactures' or factories, and the further distancing of middle-class employers from working-class factory-hands.

Combination and strikes

The ideas of the revolutionary period, proclaimed by a triumphant bourgeoisie, led to the dissolution of the guilds in the name of 'freedom of labour'. According to the Declaration of the Rights of Man, individuals were 'free and equal before the law'. In reality, however, they were not. The dissolution of the guilds was accompanied by laws against all forms of 'combination', whether groups of employers seeking to impose prices or groups of workmen trying to defend their interests by means of strikes.

In France, the ban was imposed by the Constituent Assembly under the so-called 'Chapelier Law' of June 1791, which was incorporated in Articles 431, 432, and 433 of the Penal Code. In Britain, where guilds still existed (as witness the 'Statute of Artificers'), the Combination Acts of 1799–1800 forbade both cartels and associations of working people. In Prussia, the French system was adopted in the former Kingdom of Westphalia. The departure of the French led to the re-establishment of the guilds (*Zünfte* or *Körperschaften*) until about 1845–8. Not until 1890 was there free entry into all crafts.

Of course, an employers' association, formed by a small number of people, could easily operate in secret. An association of employees, sometimes involving many people, was more difficult to organize and conceal, and was more severely punished. The labour movement at first consisted essentially of dangerous strikes and efforts to organize strikes and associations.

In Britain, the Combination Acts were abolished in 1824–5. Strikes thus became legal, subject to a number of restrictions which the labour movement gradually managed to have lifted. In France, the right of association was not accorded to work-people until 1864, under a law inspired by Napoleon III.

Working people and 'primitive capitalism'

Before examining how trade unions organized collective action and strikes, it is worth looking back once again at how the industrial proletariat emerged.

When industry was developing at considerable and growing speed, the demand for labour was very great. Rather than live in semi-poverty in the countryside, a number of agricultural labourers, and even smallholders with too little land, hoped to find a better life in the towns. The growth of the population also favoured recruitment. But the workers were unorganized and unprotected; they were too many for the available jobs, and in some cases unable to return to the lives they had left. As a result, they were at the mercy of the employers, who bought their only possession, their labour, as cheaply as possible. The only lower limit was subsistence level, since labour was needed: but there was a large 'reserve army of the proletariat' – other potential workers ready to replace any who protested that wages were too low.

In Britain, then in France and Belgium, and later in northern Italy and Germany, there were appalling abuses: fifteen hours' work a day, child labour from age five onwards, no safety measures, no sickness or unemployment pay, and no pensions.

Around 1850, a working-class family in Britain is estimated to have spent 60 per cent of its income on food (much of it bread), 20 per cent on housing, 10 per cent on clothes, and 10 per cent on everything else.

There were no paid holidays, and only one rest day a week. Dwelling-places, often far away from the workplace, were slums (known as *courées* in northern France). Discipline was brutal. A worker could be sacked at his employer's whim. After that, there was nothing for it but public charity.

These conditions have been described so often and so fully that elaboration is unnecessary. But it was understandable that throughout Europe the misery of the labouring poor, and resentment against those who exploited them, often led to violence, and ended in a powerful organized movement.

The British trade unions

At first on a small scale and illegally, then with legal backing, working people began to band together.

Britain set the example. First came the Friendly Societies, with a million members in 1815, and 4 million by 1872. But the fighting organizations were the trade unions. A few existed before the abolition of the Combination Acts. Afterwards they developed openly, with some 100,000 members in 1845, although then including only skilled workers such as mechanics. In 1868, the British unions formed a joint body, the Trades Union Congress or TUC. By then, there were 118,000 unionists. Within two years, the figure rose to 735,000 before falling back. But from 1889 onwards, the trade union movement spread among the unskilled workers. Whereas the 'old unionists' – the skilled workers – had formed alliances with one or other of the two big middle-class political parties, the Conservatives or the Liberals, the 'new' unions fought methodically to obtain a minimum wage for an eight-hour day. 'Eight hours' work, eight hours' play, eight hours' sleep and eight bob a day' was their slogan.

With these 'new' unions, the number of trade unionists grew from 1,600,000 in 1891 to 4,000,000 in 1914. Only a minority, however, was revolutionary.

The *Chambres syndicales* in France

In France, working people were more prone to violence than in Britain. They were the mainspring of the 1830 revolution, of numerous revolts in the decade that followed, and of the revolution of February 1848.

One of the revolts, that of the so-called 'Canutes' or Lyon silk-weavers in November 1831, was not political, seeking democracy, but purely social, seeking better conditions. The same was true of the June 1848 rebellion, in which 4,000 people were killed, and above all of the insurrectionary Paris Commune in 1871, which had 17,000 victims.

Yet it was only from 1867 onwards that there appeared the workers' organizations known as the *Chambres syndicales*, literally 'syndical chambers'. In 1862, a delegation of 200 working men had been sent to the second great International Exhibition in London, the successor to that held in Crystal Palace in 1851. They returned full of admiration for the British trade unions, and petitioned the government to allow similar unions in France. On 31 March 1868, a Circular approved by the Emperor himself authorized the *Chambres syndicales* – eighty of which had already been formed in Paris.

Those in Paris merged in 1869, and 'national federations' were established for a growing number of trades. The leading militant of the period, Eugène Varlin, tried to set up a 'Federation of the Federations'; but he was killed during the Paris Commune in 1871, and his project died with him. In 1884, freedom to join a trade union was confirmed by law; but not until 1895 did the unions form a national federation, the Confédération Générale du Travail, or CGT; and it was 1919 before the Catholic Confédération des Travailleurs Chrétiens, or CFTC, was set up. Even in 1914, France had only 600,000 unionists out of a total workforce of 10 million people, half of them employed in industry.

German trade unionism

In Germany in 1907 there were about 15 million wage-earners, 8,640,000 of them working in industry. The great sociologist Werner Sombart estimated that 67–8 per cent of the population belonged to the proletariat: but this is true only on a very broad definition of the term, not on the strict interpretation given by Karl Marx.

The first German trade unions appeared in Saxony shortly after 1860. But the equivalent of Friendly Societies, known as *Knoppschaften*, had already become widespread; and socialist 'free trade unions', as well as Catholic and Protestant and other unions, were not slow to follow.

By 1890, despite Bismarck's efforts to curb the socialist trade unions, they had 300,000 members. They set up the 'General Confederation of German Unions', or ADGB, which by 1913 had 2.5 million members, more than either the Catholic trade unions, with 814,000, or the independent unions, with 765,000. Altogether, Germany had 4 million trade unionists – eight times as many as France.

The labour movement and socialism

The labour movement, of which trade unionism was the most concrete and effective manifestation, made a growing impact with its main weapon – strikes. These took many forms: long or short, large or small, quiet or with mass demonstrations, peaceful or violent, tolerated or savagely repressed. Their success or failure often hinged on whether the unions could afford strike pay, to tide over strikers and their families while their wages were stopped. Trade union action was essentially concerned with social questions of pay and conditions, negotiated either with individual firms or in a collective agreement with a whole industry.

But the political impact of the labour movement was not fully felt until it joined forces with another cause launched in Europe at about the same time – the campaign for socialism.

The word 'socialism' first appeared, in English, French, and German, at the beginning of the 1830s; and at about the same time the word *social* completely changed its meaning in French.

It was a period of revolutions in continental Europe – in France, Belgium, Poland, Germany, and Italy – and of great unrest in Britain, where the Reform Bill of 1832 helped to calm matters by an extension of the franchise. The British historian Alfred Cobban referred tellingly to the revolutions that never happened because of counter-measures taken in time.

In this turbulent atmosphere, and facing a new kind of urban and industrial poverty, many people searched their consciences. Appalled by the new problem, they looked for a radical solution. In France, they gave a new meaning to the word *social*, which had traditionally been applied to those defending society as it was. Now, it came to denote those seeking to reform society, to improve the lot of what Saint-Simon called 'the most numerous and the poorest class'. And the French word *socialiste,* which had broadly meant 'traditionalist' or 'Royalist', was now used to describe social reformers.

The word 'socialism' was used in Britain by the reformer Robert Owen in 1830–1, and *socialisme* in France by Pierre Leroux in 1831–2. In Germany, the word *Sozialismus* also made its appearance in 1831–2. Curiously, neither Saint-Simon, who died in 1825, nor Charles Fourier, who died in 1837, used the word 'socialism' to describe his social theories.

From 1840 onwards, however, it had passed into the vocabulary of politics. 'Social' now came to be used in contradistinction to 'political', as implying concern for living and working conditions. Sometimes egalitarian, sometimes collectivist, socialism became the *bête noire* of the industrial bourgeoisie, and even of many peasants, who in France denounced the socialists as 'claimants' or *partageux*.

Romantic or Utopian socialism

What has been called 'Romantic' Socialism was predominant until about 1850. It was rooted in compassion, and its advocates were highbrows, not members of the working class. Many of them believed that if, at some point on the globe, a social microcosm could be created in accordance with their views, the example would be so attractive that it would gradually transform the world. The pioneer of this type of thinking was the British manufacturer Robert Owen.

Because Britain led the Industrial Revolution, it was there that from the late eighteenth century onwards a number of writers first envisaged reforms to improve the lot of the poor, whether factory employees or workers on the land. The Napoleonic Wars held up practical progress. Then the industrialist Robert Owen, the owner of a large and prosperous factory at New Lanark in Scotland, undertook to reform society. As an atheist, he proposed abolishing religion, and he planned to establish colonies organized on communist lines. He went to the United States with his father and founded 'New Harmony' in Indiana. It was a total failure; but Owen returned to Europe with enhanced prestige. At a time when the small trade unions were developing, he tried to federate all British working people in one huge union, spanning every trade. But in 1834 this enterprise collapsed, together with the co-operative society he had associated with it. So Owen had more influence on socialist theories than on the labour movement itself.

Other Romantic and Utopian socialists in Britain formed a movement in which social questions were subordinated to politics. This was Chartism, led by moderates like William Lovett, but also by militants like the Methodist minister J. R. Stephens and the burly Irish mob orator Feargus O'Connor. For a time, it won large numbers of adherents; but it soon declined, and petered out in 1848.

In France, Charles Fourier believed that a series of his proposed 'phalansteries', made up of carefully chosen men and women passionately devoted to various trades, would form an ideal society. In three years, he thought, the whole world would be covered with phalansteries, even as far as Tibet. A great theorist of the 'passions' – passionate vocations – which he saw as the spiritual counterpart of the laws of attraction in physics, he believed that he had identified no fewer than 814. Needless to say, the rare attempts to establish phalansteries failed to develop according to Fourier's plans.

Etienne Cabet, a former deputy and former attorney-general of Corsica, was also a member of the republican secret society, the *Charbonnerie*, French counterpart of the Italian *Carbonari*. In 1834, he went into voluntary exile in Britain, where he met Robert Owen. In 1840, he published his *Voyage en Icarie* or *Voyage to Icaria*, in which he too proposed the establishment of a model colony. In 1848, he sent a group of 1,500 'Icarians' to Texas; but the experiment in communal property proved an utter failure. In 1849, Cabet followed them to America, and transferred them to Illinois, but his autocratic rule led to his banishment in 1856, the year of his death.

In 1840–50, there were about thirty such colonies and phalansteries in the United States. The mass of American opinion, however, remained indifferent to them.

On a more modest scale other socialist intellectuals were at work: Philippe-Joseph Benjamin Buchez, a Christian socialist physician and disciple of Saint-Simon; Pierre Leroux, a writer friend of the novelist George Sand; and the historian and journalist Louis Blanc. They produced doctrines; they formed associations, such as the 'Working People's Production Associations' or *Associations ouvrières de production* set up by Buchez; they even promoted legislation, including the right to work, which was proclaimed at the beginning of the Second French Republic in 1848.

In Germany, 'Romantic' socialism had less success than in Britain and France. Saint-Simon had some disciples there, thanks in particular to the writings of the poet Heinrich Heine, who settled in Paris from 1831 onwards. But with very little by way of a free press, the labour movement in Germany was weak – although in 1846 a weavers' strike in Silesia ended in bloodshed, commemorated by Heine in an indignant poem, *Die Schlesischen Weber*, with its sombre threat: 'Germany, we are weaving your shroud.' German refugees in France founded, first, 'The Federation of the Banished' and then 'The Federation of the Just'. One such refugee was Karl Marx, although he was expelled in 1845. But of all the German philosophers, only the group known as the 'Hegelian Left' developed the Romantic variety of socialism. One of its prominent spokesmen was Moses Hesse.

There were some prominent Italian socialists. An early example was Philippe Buonarroti, who in 1795–6 was a disciple of the French revolutionary communist François Noel ('Gracchus') Babeuf, guillotined in 1797 for attempting to overthrow the Directory. Buonarroti's main work was *The Conspiracy for Equality*, published in Brussels in 1828. As a campaigner for the liberation and unification of Italy, he was in touch with the *Carbonari* and with the 'Young Italy' movement of Giuseppe Mazzini, who himself was not only a political republican but also a Romantic socialist. Mazzini's disputes with Marx and Mikhail Bakunin were both significant and characteristic. Other Italian socialists included some disciples of Saint-Simon in Florence and Pisa; and the police uncovered a communist association in Ferrara. Meanwhile, in Spain, Flores Estrada published *The Social Question* in 1839.

All these were spokesmen for a compassionate, reformist, somewhat unrealistic socialism which played a part in the European revolutions of 1848, especially in France and in the German Rhineland. Elsewhere, similar movements were above all national and liberal.

Rational reformist socialism

Midway between the Romantic Utopians and the so-called 'scientific' socialism of Karl Marx and Friedrich Engels, there were more moderate and rational thinkers, inspired less by impetuous feelings than by the principles of political economy.

One such man, in France, was Pierre Joseph Proudhon (1809–65), still extremely significant for his continuing influence on non-Marxist socialists. Initially, he was a leading light for Karl Marx – who later attacked him violently. He was also one of the very few early socialists to attach importance to Europe, which he sought to unite in a federation. As early as March 1848 he wrote to a friend: 'As I was saying, the confederation of European states is in the making, and all that remains for us to deal with is the social question. That's quite enough.' Proudhon, an early French Socialist and a convinced European, opposed the existing property system, declaring 'Property is theft': but he was firmly opposed to Karl Marx and Communism.

Here, plainly, Proudhon was over-optimistic. But he could also be more prophetic. In 1853, in his *Philosophy of Progress*, he wrote: 'It is certain ... that Europe is a federation of states bound together by their interests, and that in this federation, made inevitable by the growth of trade and industry, the initiative and the ascendancy are with the West.' And if federation were not achieved? Then, 'the old Europe is heading for ruin ... We are likely to end up with five or six great powers bent on restoring divine right and exploiting the lowly plebs. Smaller states are doomed, as Poland once was. Then in Europe there will be no more laws or liberties or principles or morals. Then too will begin the Great War between the six great powers.' This last quotation comes from a letter Proudhon wrote in 1860, just fifty-four years before the Great War of 1914.

Proudhon had many disciples. But he was not the only influential reformist adherent of socialism. There was a similar reformist wing of Italian socialism, represented by the Party's founder there, Filippo Turati.

Marxist socialism

In considering reactions against the dark side of the Industrial Revolution, the importance of Marxism cannot be overstressed. In origin, it was the historical and economic philosophy evolved by two eminent German thinkers – Karl Marx (1818–83) and Friedrich Engels (1820–95). But their doctrine, unlike Proudhon's, in no way militated in favour of a united Europe. On the contrary, for 130 years it was one of the main obstacles to unity.

So much has been said and written about Marx and Engels that this account of them can be brief.

As a philosopher of history, Marx adopted the materialism of Ludwig Andreas Feuerbach and the dialectical ideas of Georg Wilhelm Friedrich Hegel, to present history as a vast movement whose driving force was class war. In his view, the bourgeoisie, helped by the proletariat, had broken the power of what he called the 'feudal' regime – more accurately, the aristocracy of the *ancien régime*, conquered in France by the 'bourgeois' revolution of 1789, completed in 1830. Then would come (and soon, thought Marx and Engels) the proletariat's victory over the bourgeoisie. Marx believed that the proletariat would grow ever larger by absorbing most of the middle and lower middle classes, through their constant 'pauperization'. When it had realized its own unity and strength, it would seize power by revolution, destroying such forces as the army and police, which were tools of the bourgeoisie. This whole dialectical movement, thought Marx, would be international.

The Communist Manifesto

In the *Communist Manifesto* of 1847, printed in 1848, Marx and Engels launched their famous slogan: 'The workers have nothing to lose but their chains. They have a world to gain. Workers of the world, unite!' For national divisions, in other words, Marx and Engels sought to substitute divisions of class.

Marx, who lived in Britain after the upheavals of 1848–50, helped to found the First International in London in 1864, with the backing of the British TUC, the French led by Eugène Varlin, and a large number of Germans. The First International did not survive the Paris Commune of 1871, in which its leaders, with many other revolutionaries, had taken part. A Second International, founded in 1889, the first centenary of the French Revolution, was active until 1914.

Das Kapital

Marx's philosophy of history was based on the economic theory which he expounded in the first volume of his main work, *Das Kapital* (*Capital*), in 1867.

Everything depended, he claimed, on the 'productive relationship'. The proletarians had nothing to sell but their labour. Yet instead of receiving the full profit from it, they were paid only a strict minimum:

the capitalist employer pocketed the 'surplus value'. This was sheer robbery. It made possible the accumulation and concentration of wealth, so that 'big business' grew richer and richer, and 'monopoly capitalists' fewer and fewer. Their resources enabled them to pay those who defended them, their 'lackeys'. What further helped the employers was the surplus of proletarians, a 'reserve labour force' which enabled wages to be cut. The true price of goods, thought Marx, should be determined by the quantity of labour that produced them, taking account of the long preparation by those who invented the machines and made them work. The revolution would enable the proletariat to seize power and so abolish profit from capital. At that point, the dialectical process of history would stop. The state would 'wither away'. It would also be the end of history, which was made up of conflicts, and the beginning of communism, based on the principle 'To each according to his needs' – which presupposed abundance.

Marx and Engels called their socialism 'scientific'. Naturally enough, the political parties inspired by their ideas used this term in their propaganda, claiming that they alone could explain history scientifically. In reality, their explanation rested on postulates or assumptions which only history itself could prove. After more than 150 years, there is still no sign of such proof. What they regarded as 'scientific' in their theory was the fact that they were not seeking to improve the condition of the working classes out of sentiment, pity, or guilt, but trying to discover inevitable 'laws' under which the lot of the proletariat would be transformed through the dialectical process described above.

The historical importance of Marxism

The historical importance of Marxism lies in the enormous influence it has had on world events: first, by its development within the socialist parties which were first established in European countries; secondly, through the conclusions drawn from it by another theorist, a politician of genius, Vladimir Ilich Ulyanov – better known as Lenin – who managed to seize power in his own country of Russia in November 1917; and thirdly, owing to the fact that the vast, multiform, and many-sided socialist movement, so great a factor in twentieth-century history, very soon split into two. One was a Marxist (or Marxist-Leninist, 'communist') tendency, more systematic, revolutionary, and violent: the other was a reformist tendency, which preferred to bring about reforms by means of legislation progressively improving the lot of the workers, rather than seeking dialectical revolution. The two forms of socialism are mutually incompatible. Of the two, only 'reformist' socialism can be 'European'.

In August 1915, in an article entitled 'The Formula of the United States of Europe,' Lenin wrote: 'In a capitalist regime, the United States of Europe are either impossible or reactionary ... One can imagine the United States of Europe as an agreement among European capitalists, but aiming at what? Merely at a common policy to crush socialism in Europe and to keep the colonies which were seized by brigandage.' Against this Lenin proposed 'the United States of the world' – a world previously conquered by the proletariat.

The beginnings of the socialist parties

When the labour movement and socialism came together, they transformed the political scene. By 1914, the trade unions were already a force in Europe. How did the socialist parties compare?

In Great Britain, the power of the TUC, which by tradition was overwhelmingly reformist, reduced Marxist influence to a minimum. The socialists – Labour – at first allied with the Liberals. A breakaway Socialist Party, the Independent Labour Party or ILP, was set up in 1893. But it was in 1900 that the socialist politicians and the trade unions established the 'Labour Representation Committee', which made it possible to form a new socialist party, the Labour Party. In 1906 it won twenty-nine seats in the House of Commons, in January 1910 forty-one, and forty-three in December 1910 – the last general election held before the Great War of 1914.

Marxist influence was stronger in France. From the 1880s onwards, small socialist parties had emerged, chief among them the 'French Worker Party' or *Parti Ouvrier Français* led by Jules Guesde, preaching his simplified Marxism. They united to fight the election of 1893, and won forty-three seats.

In 1905, after the International Socialist Congress in Amsterdam, the two French socialist parties then remaining decided to merge: they became the 'Unified Socialist Party' or *Parti Socialiste Unifié*, the French Section of the Workers' International *(Section Française de l'Internationale Ouvrière* or SFIO), with the Marxist Jules Guesde and the great orator Jean Jaurès, who believed in a synthesis between Marxism and the ideas of the eighteenth-century Enlightenment. The merger led the socialists to growing success: fifty-five deputies in 1906, seventy-four in 1910, and 104 in 1914, out of a total of some 600.

In Germany, the first socialist party was formed by Ferdinand Lassalle in 1863. He died, however, in the following year, and German 'Social Democracy' came more and more under Marxist influence. It was the strongest of all the socialist parties in Europe. In 1871 it had two representatives in the *Reichstag*, twelve in 1881, twenty-four in 1890, forty-four in 1893, fifty-six in 1898, seventy-nine in 1903, and 110 in 1912.

In Italy, where universal suffrage was delayed until 1912, the Marxist movement had a very remarkable theorist in Antonio Gramsci. The first socialist deputies were elected in 1895. By 1900, there were thirty-three of them, out of a total of 480. At that time, strikes were particularly violent. There was even a general strike in Rome in 1903. In the election of 1912, the socialists won 850,000 votes and fifty seats.

In the Netherlands a new socialist party, a section of the Workers' International, won seven seats in 1905 and eighteen in 1903, out of a total of ninety.

In Belgium, a Worker Party (*Parti Ouvrier*) was formed in 1895, subsequently joining the International. After the electoral reform of 1893, the so-called 'plural vote' reform, there were 1,350,000 new voters with 2,066,000 votes. The socialists promptly won twenty-nine out of a total of 152 seats. After a further electoral reform, they won thirty-three seats in 1899. In 1912 their gains were hard to quantify, since they put up joint lists with the Liberals.

In Switzerland, a Social Democrat Party on the German model was founded in 1880. In 1893 it won no seat on the National Council; but it won seven in 1902 and fifteen in 1911, out of a total of 182. The Party was strengthened by immigrant workers from Germany and Italy.

CONCLUSION

The Europeans were outdistanced in technology by the Chinese and the Arabs until the twelfth century, and they avidly took over the inventions made by these two great civilizations. In the fourteenth and especially the fifteenth century, they overtook their mentors, not only in pure science but also in navigation, armaments, medicine, and architecture.

The 'revolution' which began in the eighteenth century added to these advances an immense step forward in manufactures of all kinds, in transport, and in biology and medicine.

From invention, Europeans moved on to mass production, which in turn led to detailed improvements, as further inventions suceeded one another. Increased resources, combined with better food and better medicine, lowered the Europe death rate, before there was a fall in the birth rate.

But this huge expansion had its seamy side. The beginnings of large-scale capitalism were accompanied by poverty and oppression among the industrial working class, greater inequality between Europe and the rest of the world, and eagerness to conquer non-European peoples. At the same time, heavy emigration established 'outposts' of Europe in some Latin American countries, but above all in the United States, Canada, Australia, New Zealand, and to some extent South Africa.

Europe's success as an industrial producer is undeniable. Some writers have referred to a 'second industrial revolution' between 1870 and 1950, based on oil and electricity; others to a 'third industrial revolution' based on electronics, nuclear energy, and the exploration of space. There has even been talk of a 'fourth industrial revolution' based on industrial robots and computers.

But all this progress, far from encouraging Europeans to come together, sharing their inventions, too often provoked rivalry, envenomed by the nationalist crisis to be discussed in later chapters.

Finally, the period after 1914 saw what can be called 'the decline of Europe' – in relative terms, admittedly, but a decline nevertheless.

16

Europe, Romanticism, and the Nations

THE CONGRESS OF VIENNA (1814–15)

The twelve-year drama of the Napoleonic Wars was at an end. There would now be no united Europe ruled by France; and everyone was pleased – including many Frenchmen, who resented conscription, disliked Bonaparte, and were weary of conquest and endless war.

Who had won? Undoubtedly, the men of the old Europe: four 'legitimate' kings and their ministers, who imposed on France the fifth such monarch, the Bourbon Louis XVIII, brother of Louis XVI. Did this mean that they were anxious, and able, to restore the pre-1789 political status quo? No. There were too many impediments. Among other things, the long ordeal had left people divided, largely between partisans of the 'old Europe' and those of the new. The former included some who had 'learned nothing and forgotten nothing'; like many aristocrats throughout Europe, or those diehard *émigrés* who returned to France in Louis XVI wigs. An individual example in Prussia was the young Otto von Bismarck-Schönhausen, born in 1815, who learned from his family that the Prussian monarchy was supreme and that the French were the Prussians' principal enemy. Only after 1850 did Bismarck decide to adopt a more flexible policy.

The most intelligent advocates of the 'old Europe', in 1815, knew that they had to compromise, and that some of the achievements of the French Revolution, spread abroad by conquest, were irreversible – such as, for example, the nationalization of Church property. The great 'liberal' traditions which lived on had more complex roots, in the British and American spirit of freedom, or the principle of 'free study' of the Bible. Other liberties – freedom of the press, freedom to meet and form associations, trade union freedom and the right to strike – went on being debated for decades. The great symbol was the constitution (a written document except in Britain). Some countries had no constitution, and were therefore authoritarian; others had a constitution or 'charter' conceded to the people by their sovereign — a gesture on his part, not a right on theirs. But there were countries whose constitution emanated from the nation or the people and represented national or popular sovereignty, whether expressed by a constituent assembly or by a referendum.

The dividing-line between moderate partisans of the 'old Europe' and moderate partisans of the new lay fairly precisely between the charter accorded from on high and the constitution representing the sovereign nation.

Almost everywhere, both Catholic and Protestant clergy were partisans of the 'old Europe'. It was the so-called 'union of throne and altar'.

The partisans of the 'new Europe' were much more various. In Britain, the majority of influential people — aristocrats, bourgeois, and merchants — had not fought Napoleon because he stood for a 'new Europe'. They had no objection to that: their reason for opposing him was simply the national interest. This perhaps accounts for the extraordinary welcome Napoleon received as a prisoner at Torbay and Plymouth in 1815.

> Our arrival in England [he told Las Cases] produced an extraordinary effect. Seeing the Emperor aroused a curiosity verging on frenzy. It was the newspapers that told us this, while at the same time condemning it. All England flocked to Plymouth ... The sea was covered with a multitude of boats around us ... When the Emperor appeared, the noise, the movement, and the gesticulations of so many people made a strange spectacle. At the same time it was easy to see that there was no hostility ... One could even see that popular feeling was growing warmer. At first they had been content to look; then they had raised their hats, and some remained bare-headed while others actually cheered ... But all this did us no good in the eyes of the ministers and their followers.

Only in France and among a few rare foreign loyalists were there now any true 'Bonapartist' partisans of the Emperor. But the men of the 'new Europe' were very different one from another. A whole section of the bourgeoisie was 'liberal' — a word first used around 1818–19: in the countries conquered by Napoleon it was also 'national'. But among ordinary people in the towns — artisans, employees in the new factories, tradespeople, officers, petty-bourgeois, and students (such as the *Burschenschaft* or 'fraternities' in Germany) – there were some revolutionary republicans who believed that 'the blood of martyrs never flows in vain', and who were ready to mount against 'tyrants' attempts at revolt which were usually ill-prepared. There were also secret societies, the best known of which, the Italian *Carbonari*, had offshoots all over Western Europe, such as the *Charbonnerie* in France. Even in Russia there were similar, if fewer, extremists, notably among the young officers, like those who in December 1825 staged the abortive 'Dekabrist' or 'Decembrist' plot against Nicholas I.

The mass of Europe's peasantry, meanwhile, remained deeply pacifist and was often suspicious of these early republican movements. But the peasants continued their slow, stubborn efforts to abolish those feudal privileges that remained, as in Austria, to put an end to serfdom, as in Russia, and to assert their own property claims against the great estates.

So complex and rapidly changing was Europe's situation that no mere sketch of this kind can do it justice. Some such summary, however, may help to give the context of the Congress of Vienna, and of later events in Europe.

Three great Congresses marked the history of modern Europe: the Congress of Westphalia which ended the Thirty Years' War; the Congress of Vienna in 1815; and the Versailles Peace Conference of 1919. Each had its own style and nature. At the first, Europe's sovereigns were represented by negotiators, and sometimes by princes. At Vienna, with only two exceptions – George III and Louis XVIII – it was the sovereigns themselves, with ministers from their courts, who led the negotiation.

The presence in Vienna, from 3 October 1814 to 9 June 1815, of the crowned heads of Europe and their glittering entourage created an exceptionally festive atmosphere. Metternich, noting that the victorious campaign against Napoleon had already brought together the Tsar Alexander I, the King of Prussia Frederick-William III, the Austrian Emperor Francis II, the French representative Talleyrand, and the British Foreign Secretary Viscount Castlereagh, described the Congress as follows:

> Thanks to a combination of circumstances unique in the annals of the world, the main actors in the drama were all assembled in the same

place ... The representative of the British Cabinet was in almost constant contact with his colleagues from Austria, Prussia, and Russia ... Diplomatic niceties had to yield to necessity. The most difficult affairs, and the most complicated questions, were dealt with as it were from one room to the next: no couriers, no exchange of written notes, no intermediaries came between the Courts ... The most serious questions were always discussed and dealt with in informal talks among the three sovereigns and among the chief representatives of the Cabinets. Only when these questions had reached a certain degree of maturity were they remitted to the Ministers, who held formal conferences and drew up the documents.

Naturally, the smaller powers teemed around the great. The aim of the Congress was not to make peace with France – the 'First Treaty of Paris' had been signed on 30 May 1814 – but to share out the spoils she had abandoned. So every prince with any claim to legitimacy took good care to be present. The main losers were those who had remained loyal to Napoleon, and the former princes of the Church.

The detailed results of the Congress of Vienna were important for the individual countries concerned: but it also had a broader impact on Europe as a whole.

Talleyrand, legitimacy, and the balance of power

The most remarkable of the negotiators at Vienna was Charles-Maurice de Talleyrand-Périgord, Prince of Benevento (1754–1838). A former Bishop of Autun, Talleyrand had conducted Mass only three times in his life, and was notorious for his disregard of celibacy. He had become a revolutionary, but without being a member of the National Convention, and then had played a crucial role in the Directory and under Napoleon. There seems no doubt that his only concern was his own interest, for which he was ready to sell himself and betray others, as he had for Napoleon. In 1814–15, his interest was linked with that of the Bourbons, and he devoted to them his extraordinary intelligence and negotiating skill. France, although defeated, had somehow to remain among the great powers. The fault, said Talleyrand, had been Napoleon's, not that of the French people. Hence his disappointment in March 1815, when the ex-Emperor landed from Elba in the Golfe Juan, raised an army – but barely aroused the nation – and began his 'Hundred Days' escapade. The 'Second Treaty of Paris' (20 November 1815) was harsher than the first, so as to punish France for having welcomed Napoleon back.

Meanwhile, Talleyrand worked out his strategy, and even managed to divide the four victorious powers, by having France conclude an alliance with Britain and Austria against Prussia and Russia.

Talleyrand in fact supplied the intellectual underpinning for the new European system. It was based on two great principles: legitimacy and the balance of power. The primary task, in other words, was to restore all European lands to their legitimate sovereigns; and if there were no such claimants – as in the case of Church principalities, free cities, or former republics – then they could be distributed so as to maintain the balance of power.

Whether or not he was personally sincere, Talleyrand gave this system its most logical *raison d'être*: 'The balance of power will be nothing but an empty phrase if it ignores, not the ephemeral and deceptive strength produced by the passions, but the true moral strength which is virtue. And in relations between peoples the primary virtue is justice.' Justice, in Talleyrand's view, had nothing to do with peoples' rights: it was simply the justice of legitimacy. He railed against the idea

> that confiscation, condemned by the domestic laws of enlightened nations, should in the nineteenth century be sanctified by the general law of Europe; ... that sovereignty should be lost or won by the mere fact of conquest; that the nations of Europe are bound together by moral ties no greater than those which link them with the South Sea Islands, that they live together under nothing but the pure law of nature, and that what is known as the public law of Europe does not exist; ... that the customs established among the nations of Europe, which they have universally, constantly, and reciprocally observed for three centuries, are in no way a law for them; in a word, that might is right.

There could be no more vigorous assertion of the idea that there was such a thing as fundamental, European solidarity, and that this, based upon legitimacy and the balance of power, was the strongest guarantee of peace.

What Talleyrand envisaged was to activate the European balance of power. As it happened, Britain was concerned to see Russia expanding too much in Poland, while Austria was uneasy at Prussia's annexation of Saxony. Prussia and Russia, meanwhile, connived at each other's conquests.

Talleyrand succeeded in persuading Castlereagh, George III's representative in Vienna, and Metternich of Austria to sign a triple alliance treaty which obliged Russia and Prussia to come to terms. When he announced the good news to Louis XVIII in a letter on 4 January 1815, he omitted to mention that Britain, no less concerned with the balance of power against France, had obtained for Prussia, in exchange for part of Saxony (which remained independent), a sizeable area in the Rhineland and Westphalia. This made Prussia France's immediate neighbour, in charge of the 'Watch on the Rhine', celebrated twenty-five years later in the German patriotic song '*Wacht am Rhein*'. At the same time, the 'Kingdom of the Low Countries' – Belgium and the United Provinces – mounted the watch on the Meuse. Later events showed that all this had substantially changed the balance of power.

Metternich

Talleyrand's most helpful colleague was the Austrian Chancellor, Klemens von Metternich. More honest than Talleyrand, and less cynical, he was also more rigid – so much so that he was likened to a corner-post.

France had had good reason to promulgate some basic principles of European policy; but although she was the first to do so, she was by no means the last. Some had fewer illusions. In a memorandum of 12 February 1815, the German-born Austrian diplomatist Friedrich von Gentz pointed out that:

> Those who at the time of the Congress of Vienna had fully grasped its nature and objectives could hardly misjudge its operations, whatever they thought of its results. Fine phrases about 'reconstructing the social order', 'regenerating the political system of Europe', and 'a lasting peace based on a just distribution of power', etc., etc., were trotted out to tranquillize the people and give this solemn meeting an air of dignity and grandeur; but the real aim of the Congress was for the victors to share out the stolen or conquered spoils.

Although less cynical than Gentz, Metternich was more concerned with the balance of power than with legitimacy. In a note written on

10 December 1814, opposing Prussia's annexation of Saxony, he declared:

> We repeat: Austria is not jealous of Prussia. On the contrary, she regards her as one of the most useful counter-weights in the European balance of power ... Situated as they both are between the two great Empires of the East and the West, Prussia and Austria complement their respective defence systems; united, the two Monarchies form an impregnable barrier against the inroads of any conquering prince who some day, perhaps, might once more occupy the throne of France or Russia.

What Metternich intended was to profit from the disappearance of the Republic of Venice in order to recover the Illyrian Provinces, occupy Venetia, and re-establish Habsburg domination over Lombardy.

Alexander I of Russia

Tsar Alexander I considered himself Napoleon's chief conqueror; and as such he affected a desire to protect him. It took a very contrived Royalist demonstration in Paris, and much insistence by Talleyrand, to make him accept the return of Louis XVIII to the throne of France. Changeable, sometimes mystical, and ostensibly liberal, Alexander was anxious above all to rival the influence of Great Britain and – like his Soviet successors from 1960 onwards – to turn his country into a naval power.

The Napoleonic Wars had enabled Russia to make considerable inroads in Europe. The attractions of the West were still powerful, and contacts multiplied. Alexander himself felt essentially European. His political ambitions drew him towards Central Europe, and in particular towards the whole of the Warsaw Grand Duchy. When the Napoleonic eagle fell, Alexander was at least the ruler of Warsaw itself.

At one of their meetings in Vienna, the Tsar and Talleyrand had a strange conversation in which the cynical Talleyrand argued for principles while Alexander, the professed mystic, preached reasons of state:

'What I have I hold.'
'Your Majesty would surely wish to keep only what is held legitimately.'
'I am in agreement with the great powers.'

'Does Your Majesty consider France a great power?'
'Certainly, but if you object to everyone's finding what suits him, what are you asserting?'
'I put the law first, and what suits people afterwards.'
'What suits people, in Europe, constitutes the law.'
At which Talleyrand turned aside, exclaiming:
'Europe! Unhappy Europe!'

Britain

Once Napoleon had been deprived of the ability to do further harm, and placed under British control on a distant, inaccessible, and unhealthy island managed by a mean-minded governor, Britain pursued only two aims. In Europe, she had no territorial ambitions, but sought to maintain the balance of power, notably against the Tsar. Overseas, her aim was to retain most of the possessions she had captured from Holland and France, and to prevent Spain reconquering the American colonies that had thrown off Spanish rule. British trade with these areas was on the increase. Not only did Castlereagh foster the balance of power: he also used the expression 'the Commonwealth of Europe' to indicate the general solidarity among the great powers.

Saint-Simon, visionary

While the Congress of Vienna was a great European event, it was linked none the less to an extremely reactionary, backward-looking past, and those who took part in it were ill-fitted to understand the future.

This makes all the more significant the part played by Claude Henri de Rouvroy, Comte de Saint-Simon (1760–1825). Little-known at the time of the Congress, he had served under George Washington in the American War of Independence and been promoted to Colonel at the age of twenty-two. Thereafter he had led a wandering life, haunted by a vision in which he had been told that he would be 'a great regenerating philosopher'. He travelled widely in Europe, took an interest in German philosophy, knew Mme de Staël, and was greatly influenced by men like the historian Augustin Thierry and the philosopher Auguste Comte.

The Congress of Vienna in 1814 seemed to him the opportunity to make his ideas known. He sent every negotiator a brochure entitled *The Reorganization of European Society, or the Need and the Way to bring together the Peoples of Europe in a single Political Body, while preserving the Nationality of each*. How was this to be done? By assembling a great European Parliament, which would draw up a code of universal ethics. When the Congress of Vienna proved indifferent to Saint-Simon's proposal, he and his disciples drafted the code themselves. Underlying it was one important and fruitful idea: the realization that industrial expansion would have great and ever-growing international repercussions. Saint-Simon was not, however, much attracted to democracy. For the European and later universal government that he proposed, he envisaged a number of scientists, chaired by a mathematician. His preference for such people rather than courtiers, and for industrialists rather than the nobility, made him unpopular with the authorities. If France lost her men of talent, he wrote, she 'would become a body without a soul'.

Saint-Simon certainly became more of a universalist than a European. His last book, *New Christianity*, led his disciples for a time to embrace a strange religion. Yet, obscure as he then was, he showed to many people some of the things that Europe was going to achieve: railways, the Suez Canal, tunnels through the Alps, international banks, large-scale industry, and expanding free trade. All these featured in the visions that finally made Saint-Simon, through his disciples, the 'great regenerating philosopher' he had set out to be.

In the end, however, tradition triumphed at the Congress of Vienna. Its 'Final Act', signed on 9 June 1815, was 'Europe's Territorial Charter'.

THE 'CONCERT OF EUROPE'

Constitutional traditionalism

The aim was to crystallize the situation created by the treaties of 1814–15 while respecting the principle of legitimacy. Napoleon's 'Hundred Days' had seemed to threaten the new European system. Could the coalition that had defeated him not become a permanent body which would 'guarantee' the existing state of affairs?

And what did 'guarantee' mean? There could be a guarantee against France; it could go further and guarantee the frontiers of Europe in general, as they had now been set. There could even, in the last resort, be a guarantee of the regimes as well as of the frontiers.

Except for the new Swiss Confederation and for free cities in Germany, all the states in Europe were monarchies, some of which had constitutions 'granted' by their sovereigns. In Prussia, Austria, Russia, Denmark, Spain, Portugal, and all the Italian states, the sovereign's power was absolute. So to guarantee the regimes would be to uphold the principle of legitimacy not only against the Republicans, who were largely insignificant, but also against the 'liberals' – a word soon to be applied to all those who invoked the national or popular will and sought to limit royal power. The champion of resistance to such changes was Metternich.

The Holy Alliance

On 26 September 1815, on the initiative of Tsar Alexander I, the treaty known as 'the Holy Alliance' was signed, 'in the name of the most Holy and Indivisible Trinity', by the Russian Orthodox Tsar, the Catholic Emperor of Austria, Francis II, and the Lutheran King of Prussia, Frederick-William III. These three sovereigns agreed to 'remain united by the bonds of true and indissoluble brotherhood' and to give each other 'at all times and at all places help, assistance, and aid'.

Subsequently, to please the Tsar, the Kings of France and Spain joined the Holy Alliance; but in general it was regarded sceptically, and it never played any political role. The expression itself, however, came to denote absolutist policies, the suppression of liberal protest, and the dashing of national aspirations.

Castlereagh, for Britain, initiated more practical steps. His opportunity was the second Treaty of Paris, signed on 20 November 1815, which involved two important decisions.

The first was embodied in Article 6 of the Treaty, which sought to make such contacts permanent:

> To ensure and facilitate the execution of the present Treaty and consolidate the close ties which today unite the four Sovereigns for the good of the world, the High Contracting Parties have agreed to renew at fixed intervals, either under the auspices of the Sovereigns or in the

person of their respective Ministers, meetings devoted to their great common interests and to the examination of those measures which on each occasion may be judged the most salutary for the ease and prosperity of their peoples and for the maintenance of peace in Europe.

The second decision was the establishment in Paris of a Conference of Ambassadors to supervise the implementation of the Treaty of Paris, with particular regard for the payment of war reparations and the military occupation.

The Quadruple Alliance

As the European system took shape, France remained the great outsider, despite her support from the Tsar. It was only after solving the problem of the heavy war reparations fixed in 1815 that a Congress was held in Aix-la-Chapelle (Aachen) in 1818 to put an end to the occupation of French territory and proclaim France's admission into the 'concert of the Allies' – Austria, Britain, Prussia, and Russia. For fear of revolutionary movements or Bonapartist plots, a compromise was reached. France became a full member of the Alliance, but the other four powers secretly renewed the anti-republican and anti-Bonapartist provisions agreed upon in 1815. As a practical institution, the Quadruple Alliance soon lapsed.

The Congress of Aix-la-Chapelle

The Aix-la-Chapelle Congress had another result. It set the seal on the principle of the 'concert of nations', comprising all the great powers but only the great powers. There were no plenipotentiaries from smaller states, including Spain and the United States of America, which in any case preferred 'non-entanglement' in the affairs of Europe. The Duc de Richelieu, the French Prime Minister, had naturally bent every effort to ensure the inclusion of France.

Metternich and the Concert of Nations

Metternich identified three types of international assembly. The first was the Congress, at which entertainment took more time than negotiation as such; the second was the conference, usually among ambassadors, but on an official basis and producing 'protocols'; and the third was the meeting, where ambassadors held unofficial talks and no 'protocol' was signed.

The 'Concert of Europe' lasted until 1914: but there were few Congresses at the highest level save those of Paris in 1856 and Berlin in 1878.

The Congresses of 1820–3, however, deserve more attention. Those of Troppau in Silesia, at the end of 1820, and Laybach (Ljubliana) in Carniola, at the beginning of 1821, entrusted Austria with 'restoring order' (i.e. absolutism) in Naples and Piedmont. Still more serious was the decision of the Conference of Verona, in October–December 1822, regarding affairs in Spain.

Between 1819 and 1823, in fact, violent liberal revolts had broken out in Spain, Portugal, Naples, and Sardinia. They had at least one feature in common: all had been prepared and set off by officers in league with secret societies such as the *Carbonari* or the Freemasons. Their common aim was to establish or re-establish a constitution like that which the Spanish Cortes had produced to counter the French invasion in 1812. This had espoused the principles of the French Revolution, but had been much more realistic than the French Constitution of 1791. In this it remained a model. Spain was the first, in fact, to rise against Ferdinand VII, who had re-established absolutism. Portugal followed, and her King John VI had to accept a constitution similar to that of the 1812 Cortes. In Naples the revolt was led by officers loyal to Joachim Murat and by the *Carbonari*; in Piedmont-Sardinia, it was liberal and nationalist.

At Verona, the Allies decided that a French military expedition would restore King Ferdinand to absolute power in Spain. It was a fateful decision, and one largely responsible for the isolation in which Spain continued for more than a century, torn between the liberals and the absolutists (the nobility and much of the clergy). A savage repression was followed by a smouldering, intermittent civil war which took its most tragic form between 1936 and 1939. The situation was further clouded by the Carlist conflicts, which began with the dispute for the succession to King Ferdinand between his widow Christina of Naples and his brother Carlos. There were also incessant military coups or *Pronunciamentos*; and the 'Hohenzollern candidature' to the throne of Spain was the pretext if not the reason for the Franco-Prussian War of 1870.

Portugal was even more isolated than Spain. There too 'constitutionalists' confronted 'absolutists'; but British influence, since the Methuen Treaty of 1703, was the only real link with the rest of Europe.

Altogether, the Concert of Europe embodied an imperfect vision of vague European unity. In Spain and Portugal, its role was wholly destructive. Spain's exclusion from the system, indeed, was a further proof of its inadequacy.

NATIONALISM, 'HYDRA OF REVOLUTION'

The 'Hydra of Revolution' was an expression invented by Metternich, referring to the many-headed monster of Greek legend. He knew from experience that if a national, liberal, popular revolution were crushed in one place, another would spring up elsewhere. In his view, the danger came from nationalist movements among the conquered peoples; and, as has been seen, nationalism was a frontal challenge to the traditional 'legitimacy' endorsed by the Congress of Vienna, whose sole defence was the Concert of Europe. The latter served only the interests of the great powers, and their subsidiary interests at that. To solve major problems, the only recourse was to violence and war, which were clearly incompatible with any sense of community in Europe.

The general background

The various nationalist movements were all part of a general phenomenon affecting the whole of Europe in different ways. Everywhere, there was now an indissoluble link between political liberalism and the principle of nationality. Everywhere, there was incessant friction between the partisans of liberty and the defenders of absolute power.

In the first half of the nineteenth century there were three successive waves of revolutionary and national unrest: the first lasted from about 1818 to about 1825, mainly in Germany, Italy, and Spain; the second was from about 1830 to about 1834, mainly in Belgium, France, Poland, Italy, and Germany; and the third ran from 1848 to 1851, on a much larger scale, in all of Europe except Russia.

True, revolution was everywhere suppressed: but great changes were on the way. Liberalism and the nationality principle had acquired immense momentum; and a number of new states were formed by secession. They included Greece (1829), Serbia (1829), Belgium (1830), Romania (1856–9), Bulgaria (1878), and Norway (1905), as well as Thrace, Macedonia, and Albania, which left the Ottoman Empire as a result of the Balkan Wars.

Nationalism by secession

What were the reasons for this vast upheaval? Since 1945, historians in Eastern Europe, like Dimitrije Djordjević, have tried to explain it in terms of class war. There were indeed mass uprisings, often by peasants, against foreign owners of large estates, from British landlords in Ireland to German landowners in Bohemia, western Poland, and so on. But this explanation seems too simplistic. There were intellectual and emotional reasons which were sometimes more important still. Philologists and poets championed respect for national languages; historians probed the past for national origins and lost independence. Examples in Germany were the great nineteenth-century historiographers Barthold Georg Niebuhr, Theodor Mommsen, and Leopold von Ranke.

Greeks

In Greece, it was a Thessalian patriot, Rhigas Pheraios, who composed a national anthem modelled on the Marseillaise. He was executed by the Turks in 1798; but very soon there were associations of 'Philhellenes' all over Europe.

Southern Slavs or Yugoslavs

Among the southern Slavs, where only Serbia came close to independence between 1805 and 1829, three nationalist writers stood out. Vuk Stefanovic Karadžić, born in Herzegovina in 1787, restored the Serbian literary language and simplified its Cyrillic spelling to make it accessible to the nation rather than to an elite. He greatly influenced the Serbian nationalist poet Branko Radičević, and above all the Croatian writer and publicist Ljudevit Gaj, who introduced Serbo-Croat into polite society and transliterated it into the Latin alphabet, with diacritic signs as used in Czech. Gradually, the language won respect and admiration and ceased to be regarded as a mere dialect.

Bulgarians

In Bulgaria in 1762, a monk from Mount Athos, Païsios of Kapsokalÿvia, born in 1722, wrote a *Bulgarian Slavic History of the Bulgarian People, Kings, and Saints*. It was not published until 1844. In 1835, the first Bulgarian lay school was opened; but the Bulgarian Church played an important part in the nationalist movement. In 1870, it became in effect independent from the Greek Orthodox Church, with a 'Bulgarian Exarchate' rather bigger than present-day Bulgaria and in some sense a national ideal.

Alongside these new peoples, emerging from centuries of obscurity, there were also three ancient nations which had long been restive under foreign conquerors: the Kingdom of Poland, carved into three under Austrian, Prussian, and above all Russian domination; the Kingdom of Bohemia (the Czechs), destroyed in 1620 at the Battle of the White Mountain; and the Kingdom of St Stephen (Hungary), whose whole Eastern area had slowly been recaptured from the Turks.

Poland

Poland did not become independent again until 1919. Here, eighteenth-century cosmopolitanism had flourished most brilliantly. The Poles had welcomed French, British, Italian, and Slav culture 'on a foundation of Latin and Roman civilization'. Their much-travelled luminaries included the poet Adam Mickiewicz, born in 1798, the revolutionary leader Prince Adam George Czartoryski, the musician Frédéric Chopin, and Julian Ursin Niemcewicz, the statesman and translator of Voltaire.

British and French sympathizers took a keen interest in Poland through the National League for the Independence of Poland and the *Comité polonais*.

Northern Slavs: Czechs

In Bohemia, it was the great historian František Palackÿ (1798–1876), the author of a *History of the Czech Nation*, who played the leading role.

Not until the Great War of 1914–18, however, did such Czech leaders as Tomáš Masaryk and Edvard Beneš demand more than autonomy within the Austrian (later Austro-Hungarian) Empire.

Hungary

In Hungary, nationalism found its main support among those members of the nobility who were hostile to the Habsburgs and anxious to restore the 'Crown of St Stephen'. But there too a poet, Mihály Vörösmarty, inspired romantic nationalism with his epic *Zalán Futdsa* (1825), celebrating the Hungarians' conquest of their country. While some nationalist leaders, like Baron Jószef Eötvös or Ferencz Deák, were moderate, others, like Lajos Kossuth, took a more violent line, and a real war broke out, in which Austria was eventually defeated in 1866.

The following year saw a compromise or reconciliation, whereby Hungary won equal status with Austria in what came to be called Austro-Hungary or the Double Monarchy. Under the 1867 Constitution, the various nations which made up the Empire were given equal rights (*Gleichberechtigung*) on a number of points, but without establishing a federal system.

The old nations

National feelings were no less intense in some of the existing nations. Here and there they led to extremely violent disputes – in Spain over Gibraltar; in France over the policies of Napoleon III; in the British Isles, over Catholic emancipation in 1828 and Irish demands for 'Home Rule'. Norway, meanwhile, resented her dynastic union with Sweden, and in 1905 became fully independent. No less significant were developments in Belgium and Switzerland.

Belgium

The case of Belgium is of particular interest. Consisting as it did of the former Catholic Low Countries and the Bishopric of Liège, the country had been by turns Burgundian, Spanish, Austrian, French, and, finally – from 1815 to 1830 – united with the Dutch Protestants, whose King William I thus became King of the Low Countries, a buffer state to the north of France. The Belgian Catholics, who disliked the Protestant Orange dynasty, and the Belgian Liberals, who were anti-clerical but also opposed to the authoritarian regime, both felt oppressed and victimized. In 1828, they concluded a union between them. Then, on 25 August 1830, inspired by the 'July Revolution' in Paris, they staged a revolt. Setting up a provisional government, they declared Belgium independent, and a National Congress met to draw up a constitution.

Many French people believed, quite wrongly, that the Belgians wanted union with France. Only a minority had that aim. The French King Louis-Philippe and his London ambassador, Talleyrand, realized that Britain, who had fought for twenty years to prevent France's retaining Antwerp, would renew the war if she were to annexe Belgium. A five-power conference in London confirmed Belgian independence under a constitutional monarchy neither republican nor Orange; and the state thus established in 1830 was largely based on the Catholic–Liberal Union. About half of its inhabitants, including the most fervent Catholics, had the Flemish form of Dutch as their mother tongue, although it was looked down upon as a dialect by the French-speaking intellectual elite. The Belgium of 1830, in fact, seemed to be what the great Belgian historian Henri Pirenne later called 'a Frenchified bloc'.

This linguistic inequality led to the emergence around 1840 of a militant 'Flemish-speaking movement'. Until about 1860 it remained essentially linguistic and literary, adopting as its motto *'De taal is gansch het volk'* – 'The language is the whole people'. In 1856, Flemish and French were given equal status in the Flemish provinces, with official documents, laws, decrees, etc., translated into Flemish, while Flemish regiments were to be given Flemish orders and words of command. From that time onwards, Flemish won increasing legal recognition until between 1914 and 1930 there was what one of its spokesmen, Max Lamberty, called 'the Flemification of all Flemings' – *'la flamingantisation de tous les Flamands'*. Needless to say, this situation led to friction which sometimes threatened Belgian unity.

Switzerland

The case of Switzerland was quite the opposite. There, it could certainly not be said that 'the language was the whole people'. The historian Georges Andrey, in his *New History of Switzerland and the Swiss* (*Nouvelle Histoire de la Suisse et des Suisses*), entitled his chapter on the period 1798–1848 'The Quest for a National State'.

During that period, Switzerland was under French influence: but she threw it off, and during Napoleon's 'Hundred Days' Swiss troops joined the Allies. On 20 November 1815, by the Second Treaty of Paris, the five great powers – followed later by Portugal – gave 'formal and authentic recognition to the perpetual neutrality of Switzerland', and guaranteed 'the integrity and inviolability of her territory within the new frontiers'. The powers thereby recognized a principle that the Swiss had always proclaimed.

In 1823, the Director of the Helvetic Republic, Frédéric-César de La Harpe, wrote: 'We poor Swiss are no longer a Nation.' In 1832, the Mayor of Zurich, Jakob Hess, undertook to avoid any important reform 'until the People wishes to become a Nation'.

In fact, Switzerland became an especially vigorous nation. Patriotism, the prestige of neutrality, the multiplicity of national, federal, patriotic, and multilingual societies for education, singing, and literature – all played their part. So did the cult of the past, with great celebrations and much evocation of William Tell, and the influence of Giuseppe Mazzini, with 'Young Switzerland' inspired by his 'Young Italy'.

Within frontiers unchanged since 1816, where three main languages were spoken and cosmopolitanism was encouraged by the presence of 50,000 foreigners in an 1848 population of 2.4 million, any tension or clashes tended to be religious or economic rather than linguistic.

Only the Catholic Cantons were tempted by the idea of secession – which in 1847 gave rise to the *Sonderbund* War' or 'War of the Separate Alliance'. It lasted only from 4 November to 30 November, and claimed only some hundred deaths. The *Sonderbund* was easily defeated. A new constitution, a genuine 'charter for a modern federal state', was adopted in 1848.

Two mergers

Alongside Europe's ancient states and the new nation-states established by secession (accomplished peacefully only by Norway), two new great states were created by the merger of a number of the small states which in 1815 had still been separate. These were the Kingdom of Italy and the German Empire.

The Kingdom of Italy

Italy, in Metternich's view, was merely 'a geographical expression', made up of six states and one Austrian dependency, the 'Lombard-Venetian Kingdom', which included Milan and Venice. In 1815 there appeared the first signs of a movement for Italian national revival, soon known as the *Risorgimento*. After the defeat of the Kingdom of Piedmont-Sardinia by the Austrians in 1848 and 1849, its King Victor-Emmanuel II and his Prime Minister Camille Benso di Cavour realized that they needed the support of a great power with a strong army. Securing British neutrality and the backing of Napoleon III of France, they defeated Austria in the Italian War of 1859. In April 1861 the Kingdom of Italy was proclaimed. It annexed Venetia in 1866 and Rome in 1870; and it laid claim to Trentino and Trieste, although they remained in Austrian hands until 1918.

The German Empire

In 1815, the Congress of Vienna had endowed Germany with a fairly lax 'Germanic confederation' or *Bund*, in which the two largest Germanic states, Austria and Prussia, competed for influence. A Liberal attempt to set up an elected Assembly, the so-called 'Frankfurt Parliament' was foiled in 1849–50.

To achieve real unity, the brilliant diplomatist who became Minister-President of Prussia in September 1862, Otto von Bismarck-Schönhausen, had to fight three wars. In the first, the War of the Duchies in 1864, he seized Schleswig and Holstein from the Danes. In the second, the Austro-Prussian War of 1866, he defeated the Austrians at Sadowa (or Königgrätz) on 3 July, then dissolved the Germanic confederation, replacing it with a north German confederation from which Austria was excluded. The third, the Franco-Prussian War of 1870, enabled Bismarck to establish the 'German Empire' or *Reich*, with a Constitution which came into force on 1 January 1871. The Empire had a Parliament, the *Reichstag*, and the title of Emperor was offered to King William I of Prussia. The new *Reich* was consolidated by the annexation of Alsace and much of Lorraine as 'Imperial Territory', belonging collectively to all the states which made up the new unified Germany under the domination of Prussia. The Imperial Chancellor – which Bismarck remained until 1890 – was almost always Minister-President of Prussia at the same time; and in those fields where there was no Imperial Secretary of State, it was the appropriate Prussian Minister who held the essential power (e.g. the Prussian Minister of War).

ROMANTIC EUROPE

The Romantic Movement in literature, art, religion, and sensibility was certainly a phenomenon on a European scale. At a pinch, it could perhaps be considered as a 'Nordic' reaction against 'Mediterranean' classicism. This was the claim of James Macpherson (1736–96), author of one of the finest literary forgeries in history. In 1762 and 1763 he published *Fingal* and *Temora*, and in 1765 *The Works of Ossian*, all supposedly translations from the near-legendary third-century Gaelic bard and warrior Oisin, but in fact lengthy inventions with a tiny substructure of Irish Celtic source-material. But if Celts, Scandinavians, and Germans seemed the originators of Romanticism, Italians like Alessandro Manzoni and Giacomo Leopardi were very worthy representatives of the same movement – to say nothing of Victor Hugo, Alfred de Musset, and George Sand in France. Romanticism was essentially an attitude in which feelings and emotions could carry more weight than reason and calculation. In its most exalted state, it evoked a visionary Europe.

Europe and patriotism

Before the middle of the nineteenth century, and certainly until 1848, the nations of Europe were generally seen in an optimistic light. Two ideas were dominant: the mission incumbent upon every people when once it had become a nation, and the harmony which would result from this Europe of the nations.

Even before 1830 these ideas were widespread, although still imprecise, because the concepts of state and nation were frequently confused. The French poet Pierre-Jean de Béranger expressed them very clearly, if rather crudely, in his 'Holy Alliance of the Peoples' (*Sainte-Alliance des Peuples*) in 1818. In this, Peace addresses Humanity:

'Ah!' quoth She: 'Equals in valiance,
Ye Peoples of French, English, Belgian, Russian, or German lands,
Form together a Holy Alliance,
And, thus united, shake hands.'

The great German philosopher Georg W. F. Hegel applied his dialectic to the concepts of the state and of Europe. The state, in his view, was a true personality, the Absolute, the expression of the Spirit of the people. 'The State is the Idea of the Spirit in the external manifestation of the human Will and its Freedom.' But in the present phase of human development, the state was an expression of the Western spirit. 'Universal history goes from East to West, for Europe is absolutely the end of History, of which Asia is the beginning.' The development of history was thus a development of the spirit. Its culmination was Europe, whose essence was Germany. Hegel entitled the last part of his work 'The German World'. 'The German nations, under the influence of Christianity, were the first to become aware that humanity, as such, is free, and that its essence is the freedom of the spirit.'

Hegel was a theorist of the state, not of the nation. The French philosopher Théodore Simon Jouffroy, who like Hegel was spiritualistic and liberal, wrote in *The Present State of Humanity* (1826):

> Europe's civil wars are over. The rivalry of its peoples is receding into the distance, like that of the Greek cities under the rule of Alexander ... In the same way, Europe is beginning to be but one nation, now that there are an America, an Asia, and an Africa. It is with the unity of Europe against these masses that humanity should now concern itself, and with the balance of these masses among themselves.

Whereas for Hegel the essence of Europe was Germany, for Jouffroy, France was, as Denis de Rougemont put it, 'the advance-guard of Europe as a nation'. The French historian and statesman François Guizot later expressed similar ideas.

Both Hegel and Jouffroy combined the ideas of national missions and European unity. Many others combined the idea of mission with that of supremacy; in the years after 1830 this became a fervent creed. In 1831, in his *Introduction to Universal History*, Jules Michelet wrote: 'What is least simple, least natural, most artificial, least inevitable, most human and most free in all the world is Europe. What is most European is my country, France.' Twelve years later, the Italian priest, philosopher, and statesman Vincenzo Gioberti entitled his most important book *The Moral and Civil Primacy of the Italians* (*Il primato morale e civile degli Italiani*).

The Italian poet Giovanni Berchet, however, spoke of a 'state of suffering in which sorrow, Reason, and enlightened people are all in their different ways developing a sense of European nationality which is beginning to bring peoples together'.

The development of the European idea

The word 'European', at this time, appeared in the titles of a number of periodicals. There was the *Journal européen* published by Muhrard in Berne in 1817; there was the *Revue européenne*, predecessor of the *Correspondent*: it was this which provoked Vicomte François-René de Chateaubriand's famous 'Letter to the editors of the *Revue européenne*'. There was Philippe Buchez's *L'Européen*. There were studies of 'European civilization', like François Guizot's *Histoire générale de la civilisation en Europe* (1828), and of 'European literature': the first article by the very young Giuseppe Mazzini, in the *Conciliatore* in 1829, was entitled '*Di una letteratura europea*' – 'About a European Literature'.

From 1830 onwards, the idea of a Europe made up of a harmonious group of nations became more general and more popular. In his book *Le grand schisme de 1830: Romantisme et 'Jeune Europe'* (*The Great Schism of 1830: Romanticism and 'Young Europe'*), Fernand Baldensperger has clearly shown the split which developed at that time within the Romantic Movement. Some remained faithful to its purely literary ideal; but others, in ever growing numbers, espoused a political ideal that was radical and nationalist. As Pierre Renouvin wrote in his *Histoire des relations internationales, XIXe siècle* (*History of International Relations, 19th Century*): 'The desire for emancipation was henceforth dominant among Italian and Polish and some German Romantics, who sought to use literature to awaken national self-awareness.'

But the Romantic dream did not stop at the frontiers of the nation. It embraced Europe, which it believed could take harmonious shape – without, however, giving much thought to the legal structure this would need. In France, this line of thought derived essentially from Saint-Simon. In his opinion, reorganizing the European community was 'the only philosophic goal worthy of the attention of educated people'. The Saint-Simonian 'Church' founded after Saint-Simon's death, with its 'Father' Prosper Enfantin, paid little heed to such problems, drifting into pseudo-religious mysticism – which a few realists like Michel Chevalier, Gustave d'Eichtal, and the brothers Péreire curiously linked with industrial expansion and the construction of a vast European rail network. European rhetoric was used above all by dissident Saint-Simonians such as Auguste Comte and especially Philippe Buchez.

Buchez

Philippe Buchez was the founder of the French *Charbonnerie*, the counterpart of the Italian secret society, the *Carbonari*. A

Saint-Simonian who had become a Catholic convert, he was a great admirer of the 'Convention Montagnarde' – the extreme democratic party in the French Revolution, so called because they occupied the 'mountain', the highest benches in the National Convention. From about 1830 until his death in 1865, Buchez headed a school of Christian and socialist philosophers whose influence was at times considerable. From 5 May to 6 June 1848, he was the first President of the Constituent Assembly and therefore, for a month, the real Head of State in France.

Although his main concern was to improve the lot of the workers, he was also a fervent advocate of 'European Federation'. It would be achieved, he thought, only after 'a long and painful struggle', and when the 'equality and liberty proclaimed by Christian law had been established *de facto* and *de jure* as the bases of society'.

Buchez exerted undeniable influence, in particular on Henri Feugueray, who became one of the pioneer champions of the 'United States of Europe'. In the period before 1848, however, it was not in France but in Italy that the vision of a Europe of the nations was promoted most brilliantly. The brilliance was less the result of precise or vigorous thought than of the dazzling prestige of Giuseppe Mazzini.

Mazzini

Mazzini was without any doubt the supreme hero of nationalist and European Romanticism, however vague, mystical, and utopian his thought might seem. 'Rarely,' wrote Carlo Curcio, 'has any political writer used the word "Europe" as often as Mazzini.'

Once a member of the *Carbonari*, Mazzini left the society and founded *La Giovine Italia* (Young Italy) while staying in Marseille. His aim was then purely nationalist: to unite his country as a republic. In his periodical of the same name he discussed the role of Italy in a new Europe and pursued a theme close to Buchez's heart – the mission of each nation in Europe. From the idea of a people's mission it was only a short step to that of a union of European peoples; and this Mazzini began to advocate after the thwarting of his revolutionary efforts in Italy and Savoy. In exile in Berne, he and sixteen other militants (Italian, German, and Polish) signed on 15 April 1834 the Pact of 'Young Europe'. Its slogans included 'Liberty, Equality, Humanity', 'Fraternity of Peoples', and 'Continual Progress'. The signatories declared their conviction that every people had a particular mission which 'of necessity aids the accomplishment of the general mission of humanity'. Their fraternal pact linked the movement's different associations – German, Polish, Italian, Swiss, French, and Austrian – which were to meet as the *Congrega* or 'Assembly of Young Europe'. But Mazzini went further: he envisaged a sort of federation of European republics, of which he reckoned there were fourteen. Pierre Renouvin has pointed out that this 'redrawing of the map of Europe was more important than the plan for organizing international relations in the future, because Mazzini was convinced that a fraternal spirit would link these republics from the start.'

Both Buchez and Mazzini had a further ambition: Christian socialism, animated by faith.

The idea of moving from the nation to Europe attracted a large number of other Italian thinkers, including the philosopher and statesman Vincenzo Gioberti and the federalist Carlo Cattaneo. Cattaneo was one of those who in 1848 used the expression 'United States of Europe'.

The 'United States of Europe'

The ideas of the poet Heinrich Heine, as Denis de Rougemont pointed out, 'oscillated between Germanic nationalism and universal liberalism'. In one breath he could declare: 'All the peoples of Europe and the world must go through this agony so that life may arise out of death and Christian fraternity may replace pagan nationality' (*On Poland*). In another he could exclaim: 'Yes, the whole world will be German!' Between these two extremes, Heine would seem to have favoured what de Rougemont calls 'the nationalists' International' along Mazzinian lines.

For a very short time after 1848, there were attempts to go further than the harmonious Europe of the Nations and to prepare a 'United States of Europe'. The expression was used in a speech at Rouen on 25 December 1847, by a lawyer named Vésinet, then in the *Moniteur universel* on 28 December. On 28 March and 1 April 1848, it appeared in two articles in *The London Telegraph* by the Scottish journalist Charles MacKay; on 14 August 1848, it was used by Emile de Girardin in *La Presse*; and on 30 September 1848, it appeared in the *History of the Milan Insurrection* by Carlo Cattaneo.

In the *Revue nationale* of 23 March 1848, Buchez's disciple Henri

Feugueray emphasized the economic, spiritual, and political solidarity of Europe, and proposed a confederation of states – but with no suggestions for its legal rules. Emile de Girardin simply asked: 'Why should there not be a United States of Europe as there is a United States of America?' And Cattaneo repeated Mazzini's assertion: 'We shall have peace when we have the United States of Europe.'

Peace Congresses

Peace congresses were held in Brussels in September 1848, in Paris in August 1849, and in Frankfurt in 1850, largely on the initiative of the American pacifist and philanthropist Elihu Burritt, commonly known as 'the learned blacksmith'. The most interesting of the congresses was that which met in Paris under the chairmanship of Victor Hugo. He made a fine speech there, despite its lack of concrete detail:

> A day will come when you France, you Russia, you England, you Germany, you all, nations of the continent, without losing your distinctive qualities and your glorious individuality, will forge yourselves into a close and higher unity: you will form a European fraternity, just as Brittany, Burgundy, Lorraine, and Alsace are all united within France ... A day will come when these two great groupings that face each other, the United States of America and the United States of Europe, will join hands across the seas, exchanging their goods, their trade, their industry, their arts, and their genius, reclaiming the world, colonising the deserts, improving creation under the gaze of the Creator.

Later, in an article entitled 'The Future' in 1867, Victor Hugo added:

> In the twentieth century there will be an extraordinary nation. This nation will be large, which will not prevent its being free. It will be illustrious, rich, thoughtful, peaceful, friendly towards the rest of humanity ... This nation will have Paris as its capital, but it will not be called France: it will be called Europe. It will be called Europe in the twentieth century; and in the centuries that follow, transformed still more, it will be called Humanity.

Grand projects and fine prophecies: these were what the Romantics brought to the idea of Europe. In practical terms, in the transition from nationalism to Europeanism, they stopped short. The road from dreams to reality was long and hard.

DISTURBANCES AND WARS (1848–71)

Lord Hankey, the eminent negotiator at the Versailles Peace Conference in 1919, remarked in his book *Diplomacy by Conference* (1946) how strange it was that the 'Concert of Europe' or balance of power which developed after the fall of the Quadruple Alliance, should have been at all successful in preventing or in limiting wars. Hankey particularly stressed the period between the Treaty of Berlin in 1878 and the Italo-Turkish War of 1911, which he compared to the Antonine age of the Roman Empire.

But the problem is surely more complex. Was it the 'Concert of Europe' which prevented wars? Or did the absence of wars – itself due to quite other causes – make possible the so-called 'Concert'?

At all events, after thirty-one years of peace among the great powers, there followed twenty-three years of revolutions and four great wars – the Crimean War, war in Italy, the Austro-Prussian War, and the Franco-Prussian War. These twenty-three years marked a real break in the history of the nineteenth century.

Napoleon III

After the 'reaction' and *coup d'état* of 1850–1, which made Napoleon III first President and then Emperor of France, he seemed wholly to dominate the political scene. He was too imaginative not to have had some thoughts about European union; and in the economic field, as has been seen, he was a quasi-disciple of the Saint-Simonians, and certainly managed to establish a sort of 'free trade area' open to all Europeans except the Russians.

His political thinking can be gleaned from a brochure written in 1839 under the title *Napoleonic Ideas* (*Les idées napoléoniennes*). Its central theme was that there must be some kind of 'European association'. Its prerequisite was that national aspirations should be satisfied; and the 'European mission' of France was to ensure that this be achieved. The text of the brochure was in many respects close to the ideas of Buchez and Mazzini: but it also expressed the mystical and insatiable ambition of a man who believed in his destiny.

Once he had become Emperor in 1852, Napoleon III certainly tried to redraw the map of Europe to make it reflect better the 'natural frontiers' between nations. He played an essential role in the unification of Italy, and supported German unity, save in its final stage. He quarrelled with Russia in 1863 because he had proposed an international conference to decide on the demands of the Polish rebels; he protected the Romanians, the Serbs, and the Montenegrins. At the same time, however, he tried to obtain 'compensation' for France so that it could expand to its 'natural frontiers'. He annexed Nice and Savoy, and he coveted Belgium and the Rhineland. This earned him some enemies.

A great Congress in Paris

On 1 March 1856, the Congress of Paris met to put an end to the Crimean War, settle the problems of the Ottoman Empire, make the Black Sea neutral, and give autonomy to the Romanian principalities. Various points of international law were raised, and Cavour took the opportunity to bring up the question of a united Italy. From then onwards, Napoleon III became enamoured of congresses. 'The idea closest to his heart, which truly obsessed him from 1859 to 1863, was that of congresses and conferences.' Of all his projects, however, only one succeeded: this was the Paris Conference on the union of Moldavia and Wallachia, from 22 May to 15 August 1858.

Bismarck and Napoleon III

Bismarck, as has been seen, became Minister-President of Prussia in September 1862. He knew Napoleon III and had taken his measure.

All that counted for Bismarck was Prussia and its King; yet it was he who in 1866 and 1871 united all the Germanic lands save Austria. Two interpretations are possible. Either Bismarck was slowly converted from the views of a Prussian Junker to those of a German nationalist, or he used German nationalism as a means of increasing Prussian power.

Everything Bismarck did, in fact, increased the greatness of Prussia and profoundly harmed the cause of a united Europe. True, Napoleon III did no more to unite Europe, insofar as he encouraged the creation and development of nation-states: but he somewhat made up for that by his systematic use of congresses. Bismarck, on the contrary, fragmented Europe by trying to isolate those he wished to defeat: Austria, to keep her out of Germany, and France, to make her accept German unity, which she had avoided since the days of Cardinal Richelieu and the Thirty Years' War.

In 1863, for instance, Bismarck stirred up enmity between the Tsar and Napoleon III at the time of the Polish Revolution. He managed to isolate Austria a year later during the German 'War of the Duchies'. His skilful manoeuvres then left his hands free to deal with Austria, soundly defeated by the Prussian army at Sadowa on 3 July 1866. Before that war he had avoided the French proposal of a European Congress to prevent it; after the war, he declared it no longer relevant, and condemned what he called the 'policy of tips and gratuities' – meaning the 'compensation' sought by Napoleon III.

The War of 1870

It was in July 1870 that Bismarck drew France into war. Persuading the French Ambassador to present France's requests for 'compensation', he published an exaggerated summary of the Prussian King's rejection of them, in a telegram from Ems, so as to inflame public opinion on both sides. On 14 July the idea of a Congress was suggested, to which Napoleon III instantly agreed: but the belligerent mood, pressure from the Empress Eugénie, and the provocative actions of Bismarck, all combined to drag France into war.

The 'splendid isolation' of Victorian England

Britain was then at the height of its economic power, with a vast Empire, and undecided between imperialism and granting autonomy: Canada became a dominion in 1867. In Europe, she contributed no more to unity than did France or Germany. As a commercial power, having adopted free trade (between 1846 and 1850), as the world's warehouse for many raw materials, and as a world banking centre where gold and currency were freely convertible, Britain was more universal than European, looking out over the oceans rather than across the Channel to the continent. What did Britain seek in Europe?

First of all, the balance of power, enabling her discreetly to keep in check the main military power, which from 1856 to 1866 was certainly France. None of Britain's leading statesmen at that time looked for alliances. The essence of their European policy was to safeguard the Ottoman Empire, and to keep a firm grip on Gibraltar, Malta, Cyprus (after 1878), Egypt (after 1882) and Suez. They grudgingly accepted the various losses suffered by the Ottoman Empire owing to secession by Greek Orthodox Christians. All this made much more sense to Britain's leaders and her public opinion than any attempt to build a United States of Europe, which she would not dream of joining, and which, if formed without her, would be an intolerable threat.

CONCLUSION

Europe had thus reached a period in which France, Germany, and Britain in their different ways were all diminishing any chance of European unity, while the other powers had little interest in the subject. The tragic upshot was the bloodbath which began in 1914.

17
The Road To European Disaster: 1871–1914

On 11 May 1875, after a talk with the Italian Foreign Minister in Rome, the French Ambassador, the Marquis de Noailles, wrote: 'Signor Visconti Venosta agreed with me that one of the main reasons for our present dangers was the absence of what used to be called "a Europe".' Some years later, in *Tonkin and the Mother Country* (*Le Tonkin et la Mère-Patrie*), the French statesman Jules Ferry expressed a similar idea: 'People say that there is no longer a Europe: but can they not see that this is precisely why we are weak? It is in our interest to have a Europe once more, and to be present wherever it meets.'

No longer a Europe? What did that mean? There remained geographical Europe, perhaps including Russia. There remained some vestiges of the 'Concert of Europe' – not only the ambassadorial meetings at which certain problems were discussed, but also conferences at a higher level: the Congress of Berlin in 1878 at the end of the Russo-Turkish War, or the Colonial Conference, also held in Berlin, in 1884–5. Equally, Europe's diplomatists were still recruited in the same way from the same social classes, and they still shared the same conceptions, language, and methods, as throughout the nineteenth century.

THE ESCALATION OF NATIONALISM

There was nothing reprehensible about moderate nationalism, patriotic sentiment, and a rational attitude to the adjustment of frontiers. The Romantics, with their excess of optimism, even believed that satisfied nations would necessarily live in harmony, and that the United States of Europe would result. Kant and Mazzini were among those who shared this view.

A new ideal

Sadly, bitter memories of war, uncertainty about frontiers, and Romantic delirium produced a quite new hierarchy of values. The relative decline of religious idealism led many Europeans to exalt above all the ideal of the mother country – for which a patriot must be willing to die, to vanquish, to conquer, to dominate, and to destroy. The patriotic songs of the period are brimming with pride and blood.

This new ideal, strangely enough, came to be known by the name of a certain Nicholas Chauvin, an old soldier made famous by popular cartoons and plays for his absurdly exaggerated veneration for the victories of Napoleon. The word 'chauvinism' made its way into a great variety of languages: *chauvinisme* in French, *Chauvinismus* in German, *sciovinismo* in Italian, *szowinizm* in Polish. All too easily, chauvinism could engender fanaticism. Any supposed insult to the mother country could be a reason for going to war. The affair of the 'Ems telegram' already mentioned was a clear example.

Mistrust

Still more serious than chauvinism or even nationalist hysteria was the growth of mistrust. Given the structure of the nation-state system, there was no compulsory arbitration to deal with international disputes; and the cynical realism which became the keynote of European diplomacy led nations to mistrust one another in everything they did. There was mistrust even between allies and professed 'friends'. The only form of protection, therefore, was armed might.

Even if governments were more reasonable than some of their more extreme supporters, they dared not always resist nationalistic pressure, for fear of causing unrest or being accused of treason. A parliamentary government could be outvoted if it seemed to lack patriotic zeal; and even an autocratic regime could not afford to ignore the army, which in many cases shared the views of the most militant nationalists. Thus it was that in 1912 the German government accepted the Schlieffen Plan for the invasion of France through Belgium in the event of war. Chauvinist fervour could force a government to break a solemnly signed treaty if the military were powerful enough.

Contentiousness seemed to be general. There was Russian Pan-Slavism, at loggerheads with the revolutionary Pan-Slavist movement led by the egalitarian socialist and opponent of the Tsar, Mikhail Bakunin. There was the Pan-Germanism of the *Alldeutscher Verband* in Germany. There was imperialism and 'jingoism' in Britain. French nationalism, aiming at 'revenge', had its League of Patriots, its Boulangists (devoted to the highly political General Georges Boulanger), its League of the French Fatherland, and its *Action Française*, with Charles Maurras and his 'total nationalism'. Italian nationalism, in its extreme form, was irredentist, calling for the return to Italy of all Italian-speaking territories.

'Reasons of state' became for the nationalists an unquestionable ideal. At the time of the Dreyfus case, when the Jewish Captain Alfred Dreyfus was falsely accused of treason, some French nationalists argued that it was better to keep an innocent man in prison than to ruin the honour and prestige of the army.

Of the Pan-German party and its racist ideas, the American historian William Langer declared that there was nothing in the whole Bismarckian period which could be compared with its exaggerated national egotism and its burning passion for conquest.

BISMARCK, 'REALISM', AND 'ARMED PEACE'

Until 1890, foreign policy in Europe revolved around Germany, not only on account of Bismarck, but also because it was a country in full demographic and industrial expansion whose military victories in 1866 and 1871 had given it both power and prestige. Bismarck was a character, however, who in Pierre Renouvin's words towered above all others. Like it or not, Europe then was Bismarck's Europe.

Bismarckian Realpolitik

As has been seen, Bismarck was first and foremost a Prussian statesman. He was a patriotic German too, but on condition that Germany be dominated by Prussia. He disdained national sentiment and despised 'public opinion'. The state, not the nation, was all that mattered. He was therefore determined to preserve an 'historic' state like

Austria-Hungary; he made no attempt to annexe territory outside Germany simply because its inhabitants spoke German; and he thought it perfectly normal for Germany to include Polish, Danish, and even French minorities.

His attitude was well described by the characteristically Bismarckian expressions *Realpolitik* and *Interessenpolitik*. They signified in the first instance contempt for sentimentality. In a letter dated 2 May 1857, Bismarck wrote: 'I base my conduct with other governments solely on the good or the harm that I judge them able to do to Prussia.' The only healthy basis for a great state, he declared in a speech in December 1850, 'is egotism, not romanticism. It is unworthy of a great state to fight for anything which is not an element in its own interests.' He added: 'In my opinion, even the King has no right to subordinate the interests of the country to his own feelings of friendship or hatred towards foreigners.'

Bismarck had no belief, therefore, in international or European law. To an Austrian diplomatist who reminded him of the adage, *Pacta sunt servanda* ('Pacts should be observed'), he retorted: 'Austria and Prussia are states too big to be bound by the text of a treaty. They can be guided only by their own interest and convenience. If a treaty stands in the way, then it must be broken.'

Furthermore, Bismarck believed that only big states really had rights. In 1868 he told Prince Napoleon, cousin of Napoleon III: 'The importance of a state is measured by the number of its soldiers ... It is the destiny of the weak to be devoured by the strong.'

Bismarck against Europe

In these circumstances, 'Europe' was clearly destined to disappear. In 1876, the Russian statesman Prince Alexander Gorchakov sent a Note to Bismarck in which he declared: 'The problem is neither German nor Russian, but European.' In the margin Bismarck wrote: 'Anyone talking of Europe is wrong: geographical notion.' There is no better proof of how the traditional idea of Europe had declined since 1815. Bismarck further remarked: 'I have always heard the word "Europe" from the mouths of statesmen who wish to obtain from a foreign power something which they would not risk requesting for themselves.' Already in 1863, when Sir Andrew Buchanan, the British ambassador in Berlin, had said that Europe would not put up with

Poland being occupied by Prussia, Bismarck had replied: 'Who is Europe?' He always greatly feared any collective intervention by 'Europe', as for instance during his months of victory over France in 1870. 'My task,' he wrote in his *Reflections and Reminiscences*, 'was therefore to reach a settlement with France before the neutral powers could agree on the influence they should exert on the peace treaty.'

Bismarck's view was certainly not shared by the majority of other governments. But what could they do? Queen Victoria wrote to the King of Prussia:

> I have until now regarded Prussia as one of the great Powers which ... have been the guarantors of treaties, the guardians of civilisation, the defenders of law, and the veritable arbiters of Nations ... If you, dear Sir and Brother, abdicate from these obligations, you will also have abdicated from this position for Prussia. And if such an example were to find imitators, then the civilisation of Europe would be delivered to the hazards of the storm.

The German-born Max Müller, Oxford philologist and Professor of Philosophy, spoke in 1886 of 'the horrible and truly barbarous situation in which we live', adding: 'We live like beasts of prey in prehistoric times. What will become of Europe when no State feels secure unless it has more cannons than its neighbour?' This was also the opinion of the British statesman William Ewart Gladstone – 'Professor Gladstone', as Bismarck scornfully called him.

Bismarck's relative moderation

Yet there remained some vestiges of Europe in Bismarck's mind. What he acknowledged was the practical necessity for a European balance of power. In this, at least, he remained a great statesman. His aim was to make Prussia the supreme great power: but he never sought to make her the only one. There can be no comparison between Bismarck and Adolf Hitler. In Chapter XXVI of his *Reflections and Reminiscences*, Bismarck showed that in 1875 he had had no intention of waging preventive war against France, as the French had feared:

> A war of that kind could not, in my opinion, have earned lasting stability, but would have provoked an agreement among Russia, Austria, and

Britain, based on mistrust of ourselves, and probably leading to positive action against the new and unconsolidated Empire. We should thus have taken the road which brought the Second Empire in France to destruction, through a continual policy of aggrandizement and war. Europe would have regarded our actions as a misuse of our newly acquired power.

Significantly, Bismarck used the word 'Europe' here, but in the context of the balance of power. He continued:

> It was only the peaceful character of German policy after the astonishing demonstration of the Nation's military might, that led foreign powers and domestic enemies ... at least to tolerate the further development of the Nation's strength.

Bismarck also wrote, in Chapter XXIX of the same book:

> For Russia, there is a limit beyond which the power of France in Europe cannot be further reduced ... That limit was reached, I believe, in the Treaty of Frankfurt in 1871.

Discussing alliances, he also referred to 'the indispensable elements of the European political balance', and added: 'Without them, we should be in danger.'

Finally, Bismarck carried his respect for the balance of power as far as wanting to demonstrate in word and deed 'that German hegemony in Europe is more useful, less partisan, and also less dangerous for the freedom of others than hegemony by France, Russia, or Britain.' 'Respect for the interests of others,' he claimed, was more easily found in Germany than elsewhere, partly because of the 'German character' and partly because 'we do not seek to increase our own territory.' 'Once we had established our unity within workable frontiers, it was always my ideal aim to win the confidence, not only of the smaller European states, but also of the great powers, and to convince them that German policy would be just and peaceful, so long as the "injuries of the past" – the dismemberment of the nation – had been repaired.' Germany, he often said, was now 'saturated'. He even urged France into colonial ventures, not merely to create trouble for her with possible rivals, but to turn her away from 'the blue horizon of the Vosges' and give her some compensation for the loss of Alsace and Lorraine.

Nevertheless, the cynical realism of Bismarck's policy, and its utter disregard of 'sentiment', infected European diplomacy with germs which proved dangerous among lesser politicians. Three interrelated examples were Alsace-Lorraine, the alliances, and the arms race.

Alsace and Lorraine

When he annexed Alsace and part of Lorraine, Bismarck did not expect to encounter any lasting national hostility. His reasons had been largely military; and his view of nationality – if there were such a thing – had been shaped by the theories of Johann Gottfried von Herder. So, for Bismarck, Alsace and Lorraine were no more than German regions with a French veneer which would rapidly peel off. The fact that the deputies elected by the two provinces, in 1871 for the French National Assembly, and in 1874 and 1887 for the *Reichstag*, were every one of them 'protesters' merely irritated him. He was irritated, too, by the great wave of indignation that the annexation aroused throughout Europe, at a time when nationalism was at its height. 'I have an apprehension,' wrote Gladstone to his Foreign Secretary the Earl of Granville, 'that this violent laceration and transfer is to lead us from bad to worse, and to be the *beginning* of a new series of European complications.'

His prophecy was right. For more than forty years, France contested the annexation. While 'revenge' to recover the 'lost provinces' was never part of French policy, despite pressure from minority groups, and while Alsace and Lorraine were in no way the catalyst of war in 1914, their annexation was at least a source of lasting enmity between Germany and France.

Alliances in time of peace

Bismarck knew this very well. He even exaggerated France's desire for revenge, believing that she could not resist preparing for it. So he felt uneasy; and his whole policy, like that of his successors, was based on isolating France by forming alliances against her, and on acquiring more weapons: hence the arms race. He took the initiative in 1879 with the Dual Alliance between Prussia and Austro-Hungary, followed in 1882 by the less solid Triple Alliance which brought Italy in.

In 1892, France riposted by signing a Military Convention with

Russia; and on 8 April 1904, despite disagreements over the colonies, she signed with Britain the *Entente Cordiale* or 'Friendly Understanding'. On 31 August 1907, Britain formed a similar *entente* with Russia.

In this way, Europe was divided into two opposing camps: the Triple Alliance and the Triple Entente. Both were permanent, insofar as the Franco-Russian alliance was supposed to last 'as long as' the Triple Alliance, which in turn was renewed on account of the Franco-Russian alliance, and so on. Never in the history of Europe had permanent alliances been signed in times of uninterrupted peace: never had they been more than the product of shifting circumstances. Now, any European crisis, any conflict which in the past would have been minor, risked setting off a general explosion. As ill luck would have it, that explosion finally occurred.

Erich Eyck, the great biographer of Bismarck, had no hesitation in laying the fundamental blame on him. 'The annexations,' he wrote, 'made impossible a real and lasting peace between Germany and France. Bismarck's sleep was haunted by the nightmare of coalitions against Germany. The whole European continent became an armed camp. Germany's prime duty seemed to be to arm herself ever more powerfully. No one seemed more important than the soldier and the officer: militarism reigned supreme.' Other German historians, including Gerhard Ritter, have made the same point. In doing so, they in no way minimize the greatness of Bismarck, 'saturated' with conquests and a man of peace, having accomplished a prodigious achievement, the unification of Germany, so long prevented by the policy of France. But the same historians have shown that German unity could have been forged without annexing Alsace and Lorraine, and that the strategic considerations which guided Bismarck also blinded him to the irresistible force of national feelings.

'Armed peace' and crises

It would be unjust to blame Bismarck alone for creating a Europe of 'armed peace'. In 1924, when Friedrich Meinecke wrote his great book *The Doctrine of Raison d'Etat and its Place in Modern History* (*Die Idee der Staatsraison*), he was deeply affected by the French occupation of the Rhineland in 1923, which like many contemporaries he thought brutal and unjust. He barely mentioned Alsace and Lorraine, and with what seems undue warmth he saw in Bismarck 'the most sublime and successful synthesis between the old *raison d'état* of the chancelleries and the new strength of the people'. It also seems over-optimistic to declare that 'between 1871 and 1914 Europe was consolidated and pacified to a degree rarely attained in the course of modern history.' In fact, at the very beginning of the twentieth century, 'armed peace' had degenerated into a succession of serious crises. There was the first Moroccan Crisis (between France and Germany) in 1905; the Bosnia–Herzegovina Crisis (between Russia and Austria-Hungary) in 1908; the second Moroccan Crisis (between France and Germany again) in 1911; and the crisis of the Balkan Wars in 1913, involving Russia and Austria-Hungary. There was also the naval arms race crisis between Britain and Germany; and finally came the crisis of July 1914, when the great powers went to war because of what they believed to be mortal threats. The belief that war was inevitable sowed the seeds of war. It is hard, therefore, to admire the forty-four years of 'armed peace' which led to such massive slaughter. But could the war of 1914 have been avoided?

Raison d'état

Meinecke was right to point out that events were fundamentally affected by a 'mechanism' of deep and perhaps irresistible forces. One was the general adoption of military service, at first as a 'defensive idea', but turned by 'the nations' expansionist fervour' into 'an offensive weapon and a general threat to peace ... The result was that modern militarism, combining professional vocation with universal conscription, involved all Europe in the risk of war – a risk made all the greater by modern nationalism.'

Modern capitalism was a further determining force.

> It made Europe and its great powers able for the first time to reach a monstrous, unheard-of level of material wealth. Bursting with strength and energy, they fought each other, developing and using all conceivable tactics until they had totally ruined Europe as a whole. Militarism, nationalism, and capitalism – none of them by itself can be blamed for the disaster. It was their fatal conjunction which first enabled the great European Powers to attain great heights, then plunged them into depths which could have been fatal even to those that won.

EUROPE CONTINUES HER CONQUEST OF THE WORLD

The resumption of colonization

Many of Europe's great powers competed for colonies in the last twenty years of the nineteenth century. The end of virtual free trade, and the re-establishment of customs tariffs by countries with expanding industries – begun by Germany in 1879 – encouraged them to win new markets overseas by force of arms. Ambition for power, now that the emergence of new nations had reduced the scope for expansion in Europe, made them look for lands to conquer elsewhere. The development of steamships called for the establishment of refuelling bases. Larger armies needed more recruits, who were easy to find overseas. And the larger the colonial territory, the greater a country's wealth and prestige.

The sudden and hasty colonization of Africa, South-East Asia, and Oceania had a profound effect on the idea of Europe itself. At first sight, despite fierce rivalry among the colonial powers, it appeared to re-establish some harmony in Europe. Lands opened up by conquest were solemnly pronounced by lawyers to be *res nullius* (no one's property). When France was at war with China in 1885, Germany offered her good offices, in no way concealing the fact that she thought herself on the side of European powers. In 1900, when foreign legations were under siege in Peking during the Boxer rebellion, all the European powers – joined by the United States and Japan – came together to suppress the rising.

The 'civilizing mission'

Before the great rush for colonies, one might have thought that Europe would agree to make its 'civilizing mission' a collective task. That seemed – but only seemed – to be the aim of King Leopold II of the Belgians, when in September 1876 he convened in Brussels a conference of thirty-five geographers and explorers from Britain, Germany, France, Russia, Italy, Austria, and Belgium itself. 'The subject which brings us here today,' he said in his opening speech, 'is one which supremely deserves to occupy the heart and soul of humanity. To open to civilization the only part of the globe it has not yet reached, to pierce the darkness which envelops those populations – that, I make bold to declare, is a crusade worthy of this century of progress.' Joint action was needed to 'set the pace, combine our efforts ... and avoid wasteful reduplication.'

Out of the conference came an International African Association. But this achieved little, since the French and later the British grew suspicious of King Leopold's plans. In fact, the King's ambitions were strictly Belgian and even personal. He subsequently formed an International Congo Association, whose members were almost all Belgians.

The idea that civilized nations had a 'mission' among the 'natives' was indeed a screen for all kinds of ambition and appetite; and it quickly took on a purely national form. In France there was an eager response to the notion, launched by Albert de Mun, that 'superior races' had special rights and duties. 'The superior races,' Jules Ferry told the Chamber of Deputies on 28 July 1885, 'have a right because they have a duty. Their duty is to civilize the inferior races.' To which Georges Clemenceau riposted that the argument seemed weak: the Prussians had used it to explain why they had defeated France. In 1990, in the *Quinzaine coloniale* or *Colonial Fortnightly*, Charles Depincé alluded to the Declaration of the Rights of Man: 'Conquest ... has only one excuse: that the conquering nation improves the material and moral condition of the conquered race.' In 1910, the French Governor-General of Algeria, Merlin, put the point more strongly still. 'We went,' he said, 'by virtue of a civilized race's right ... to occupy land left fallow by peoples made backward by barbarism.' Similar sentiments were expressed in Britain, as witness Rudyard Kipling's poem 'The White Man's Burden'.

The European balance of power in Asia and Africa

The colonization of Africa affected the idea of Europe in another way too. It was as if the Europeans had decided to transpose to their distant possessions the machinery of the European balance of power.

This included the system of 'compensation', the maintenance of buffer states, and the Concert of Europe. As Harry Hinsley put it in *The Cambridge History of the British Empire*:

> European rivalries and anxieties, restrained as they were within the continent, were projected externally on to the wider canvas of the

outside undeveloped world ... From the beginning of the phase the policies of the governments, if not all elements in the States, were dominated by strategic rather than by economic and financial motives, by considerations of balance and relative position, in Europe no less than throughout the world.

It is not surprising, therefore, that the initiative came from France, with the conquest of Tunisia in 1881. For Jules Ferry,

> Merely to impress without acting, without intervening in the affairs of the world, to remain aloof from all European entanglements, and to see as a trap or an escapade any expansion towards Africa or [Asia] – to live like that, believe me, would be to abdicate and, in less time than you can imagine, to fall from the first rank to the third or fourth.

In the same speech, Ferry nevertheless defended himself for having negotiated 'compensation' by way of colonies for the loss of Alsace and Lorraine. Public opinion was very sore on this subject, readily echoing the reproach made by the League of Patriots' leader Paul Déroulède: 'You take my two children, and you give me twenty servants.'

Bismarck, although he had long claimed that he was not a colonialist, finally reasoned in just the same way. So did Francesco Crispi in Italy, and so did countless British Imperialists, with the 'Primrose League' founded in 1883 and the 'Imperial Federation League' formed in 1884.

Partition, compensation, and buffer states

Sometimes, instead of partition or reciprocal compensation, rival states established quasi-independent buffer states between them. Already practised in Europe, this system was extended overseas. It was the basis for the creation of the Independent State of the Congo under the Belgian sovereign. There was a similar series of agreements to maintain the independence of Siam, Iran, and Afghanistan – which even received, on its north-east corner, a long, narrow band of almost empty territory to ensure that India and Russian Central Asia had no common frontier. China, finally, escaped partition in 1900 when the Europeans endorsed the 'doctrine' of the 'Open Door' proposed by the United States.

Although most colonial questions were settled in bilateral negotiations, the Concert of Europe also played some part. Its main appearance was at the Colonial Conference held in Berlin in 1884-5, which laid down rules and conditions for annexation in Central Africa. The Concert intervened mainly in order to preserve some degree of freedom to trade in territory coveted by one of the great powers. Two conferences, in Madrid in 1880 and Algeciras in 1906, thus proclaimed the principle of equal commercial access to Morocco.

It is a moot point whether Europe's great colonial expansion between 1880 and 1914 promoted European unity or European rivalry. Although colonial conquests led to serious crises, it remains quite false to claim, as Lenin did, that 'the law of unequal development' made the partition of the world inevitable, and that this resulted in the war of 1914. In fact, however much the Europeans extended their mutual competition to other continents, they rarely saw these distant lands as part of their vital interests; and it was because certain powers' vital interests seemed to be threatened that the Great War broke out. What was more, all the great powers had settled their colonial differences bilaterally by 1914.

THE WEAKNESS OF 'EUROPEANISM'

In opposition to the complex forces which were driving the nations of Europe into ever more extreme positions, there were pacifist movements and the socialist doctrine of international working-class solidarity. Their influence was clearly somewhat exaggerated by their spokesmen, for in August 1914 socialists in every country, including France and Germany, marched off to war to defend their threatened motherlands. Yet, on an intellectual level, the opponents of nationalism were feverishly active. This was one reason why on 24 August 1898, Tsar Nicholas II proposed an international disarmament conference: he was responding to a wave of pacifism which remained powerful despite a certain decline in the 1870s and 1880s. Its most energetic champions included W. T. Stead, editor of the *Review of Reviews* in London, and the slightly less vigorous radical, Léon Bourgeois, in France.

Proletarian internationalism

Proletarian internationalism was certainly the main element in the forces seeking to combat the excesses of nationalism. Marx had declared: 'The proletariat has no country'; and the absolute denial of nationality certainly had its partisans. In France the best known of them was Gustave Hervé, a former teacher at the College of Sens. 'We detest our motherlands,' he declared: 'We are anti-patriots.' Orthodox socialists, although less extreme, were like Hervé in being anti-militarist, hostile to the 'military caste' and to standing armies. Jean Jaurès believed that war must be prevented by whatever means. But like many others he defended the idea of the mother country, and had no objection to war against 'the aggressor, the enemy of civilization, or the enemy of the proletariat' – i.e. any state refusing arbitration.

At the International Congress in Stuttgart in 1907, Lenin, Rosa Luxemburg, and the Menshevik Julius Martov had the following paragraph voted: 'If war should nevertheless break out, they are in duty bound to intervene to bring it rapidly to an end, and to do their utmost to ensure that the economic and political crisis caused by the war be used to arouse the masses and precipitate the fall of capitalist domination.' Between these two extremes of chauvinist nationalism and internationalist pacificism, there also remained an intellectual movement which may be called 'European'. Remarkably, some of the leading writers and thinkers of the period produced the most vigorous arguments on the need to transcend nationalism and discover Europe's underlying solidarity. They came from several European countries.

Ranke and Nietzsche

In Germany, the great historian Leopold von Ranke – perhaps the greatest of his century – was certainly no anti-patriot: he loved his country deeply. But he was alarmed by 'the ever greater importance attached to national sovereignty'. Europe was more than its constituent nations. Ranke saw 'the complex of Europe's Christian states ... as a whole, not unlike a state'. There was such a thing as an 'embryo of the West'.

While Ranke was a Christian and an optimist, Friedrich Nietzsche was anti-Christian and pessimistic. But he could not ignore a physiological phenomenon which seemed to him to be growing every day: the 'resemblance among Europeans'. In his view, despite 'the morbid estrangement which the lunacy of nationality has produced', despite 'the short-sighted and hasty-handed politicians' who pursue 'the politics of disintegration', 'the most unambiguous signs are now being overlooked, or arbitrarily and lyingly misinterpreted, which declare that *Europe wants to become one.*'

Other German writers also discussed European unity. One was Konstantin Frantz, who championed a federal 'Greater Germany', and was hostile to the hegemony of the Prussian state, although he was one of its officials. He was in fact a partisan of world federalism, and so laid little emphasis on a federal Europe, moving somewhat airily from Central Europe to universal concerns. Another was Julius Fröbel, whose book *Amerika, Europa and die politischen Gesichtspunkte der Gegenwart* (*America, Europe, and the Political Viewpoints of the Present Day*) was published in 1859.

Switzerland

Partisans of European unity were not lacking in Switzerland, where a practical example of federalism was plain to see. One of the most remarkable was Johann Kaspar Bluntschli, from Zürich. 'Switzerland,' he wrote, 'has produced and applied ideas and principles which are a source of growth and prosperity for European States as a whole, and which will one day ensure peace in Europe.' In an article entitled '*Die Organisation des europäischen Staatenverein*' ('The Organisation of the European Union of States'), published in the newspaper *Gegenwart* in 1878, he proposed a Union of eighteen sovereign European states run by a Federal Council representing the states and a Senate representing their peoples. But he held back from suggesting a supranational organization, because 'the European States consider themselves sovereign. One cannot therefore go beyond co-operation or collaboration.' In his book *Die Schweizerische Nationalität* (*The Swiss Nationality*), published in 1875, he added: 'Any European constitution establishing a new European state, within which hitherto sovereign states would be incorporated, is impossible to achieve.'

The famous historian Jakob Burckhardt, from Basle, believed that a kind of European unity already existed. 'There is something that we need not desire, because it is at our disposal (no matter whether we like it or not): that is, Europe as the home, at once old and new, of life in its myriad aspects, the land of so many contrasts which form a single whole.' But Burckhardt feared that states might evolve into 'military dictatorships claiming to be republican'. 'My vision of these, the "terrible simplifiers" that Europe will experience, is very far from agreeable.'

Italy

In Italy, the idea of a United States of Europe was championed by the successors and disciples of Carlo Cattaneo. Already in 1851, Angelo Brofferio declared the need for not only 'the United States of Italy' but also 'the United States of Europe'. The same views were expounded by Mauro Macchi at the Geneva Congress of Peace in 1868. In 1878 Alberto Mario, who also quoted Cattaneo, argued that only a war against the oppressors 'will lead us to the United States of Europe, that is to the League of Sovereign Peoples'. In 1905, Tullio Martello published a book proposing a Franco-Italian customs union and a United States of Europe; while in 1899 Stefano Jacini had written of 'the imperative need to establish a semi-federal body of states, capable of holding its own against the two colossal giants which are arising on the threshold of the new century: Russia, irresistible in Asia, and the United States of North America, each of which will have a hundred million inhabitants.'

Outside the Cattaneo tradition, other Italian writers tackled similar themes. They included Terenzio Mamiani, author of *D'un nuovo diritto europeo (Of a New European Law)*, published in 1859, and the young historian Guglielmo Ferrerò, who in the latter part of the nineteenth century visited a number of European countries and in 1896 published *L'Europa Giovane (Young Europe)*, followed in 1913 by *Tra i due mondi (Between Two Worlds)*.

Spain

After the stagnation and isolation that Spain had suffered for most of the nineteenth century, when she had lost almost all her American Empire, she faced a further disaster as the century ended. The war of 1898 against the United States, brought to an end by the Treaty of Paris on 10 December 1898, stripped her of Cuba, Puerto Rico, and the Philippines. It had also cost her dear in men and money. The 'generation of 1898', otherwise known as the 'generation of the disaster' sought to react against the past. For the most part they were military men, politicians, and intellectuals. They wanted to 'regenerate' Spain, and they shared the ultra-nationalism that was general in Europe. But for them regeneration meant modernization and contact with the rest of the world. Their purpose, wrote José Martinez Ruiz Azorin, was 'a violent reaction against a funereal Spain, taking its pleasure in spectacles of cruelty and death'.

Spain did indeed produce at that time a fine group of novelists and poets, as well as a number of philosophers interested in Europe. They included Miguel da Unamuno (1864–1936), Professor of Greek and Rector of the University of Salamanca, 'a Basque bewitched by Castile'; José Ortega y Gasset (1883–1955), author of *The Revolt of the Masses* (1930), who spent five years in Germany and left great influence there; and Salvador de Madariaga, who in 1929 published an article, 'United States of Europe: A Spaniard Objects', and a few months later referred in an American magazine to 'The Disunited States of Europe'. In 1952, however, he published *A Portrait of Europe*, exclaiming '*Eppur Europa si muove*' – 'And yet Europe is on the move.'

A brilliant disciple of Ortega y Gasset, Luis Diez del Corral, has clearly shown, in his book *El rapto de Europa* (*The Rape of Europe*), published in 1954, that the 1898 generation had always been torn between Europe and the nation. 'Our history,' he wrote, 'has been subject from the earliest times to the swing of the pendulum between isolation and universalism.' First, flowering in the Roman Empire, then shrinking inwards with the Goths. It was this alternation that the great historian Ménendez Pidal identified – a wave of nationalism, followed by a wave of Europeanism, the latter predominant under Alfonso VI, Alfonso X, Charles V, and Charles III.

And yet, while Spain's position on the Western edge of the continent made her peripheral to Europe, her varied geography made her, as Madariaga put it, a 'Europe in miniature'. Finally, she had an exceptionally rich inheritance from history: pre-Roman antiquities, medieval relics both Arab and Christian, Renaissance and baroque architecture, the most industrialized modern city, a Mediterranean coastline, and 'Americanized' urban development.

France

Many French writers discussed Europe, from the socialist and federalist Pierre Joseph Proudhon to the economist Frédéric Le Play, who called for a return to paternalist family rule which he thought would restore the glorious Middle Ages. Geographers like Vivien de Saint-Martin and Vidal de Lablache sought to define Europe as distinct from the rest of the world. Charles Lemonnier, an austere and somewhat contradictory humanitarian rationalist, began in 1872 to publish a review entitled *Les Etats-Unis d'Europe* (*The United States of Europe*) which had a surprisingly long life. Very much a theoretician, he believed that under pressure from the people, states might move peacefully from 'the rule of war' to 'the rule of law'.

Three names, however, stand out from the rest: Ernest Renan, Georges Sorel, and Romain Rolland.

Ernest Renan

In a letter written on 15 September 1871, soon after the end of the Franco-Prussian War, Renan declared:

> The European nations, as fashioned by history, are the peers in a great Senate whose every member is inviolable. Europe is a confederation of States united by the idea of civilization that they share. The individuality of each nation derives, to be sure, from its race, its language, its history, and its religion, but also from something much more tangible – the agreement and desire of its various provinces to live together.

In *Qu'est-ce qu'une nation?* (*What is a Nation?*), published in 1887, Renan meditated on the loss of Alsace and Lorraine and came to some profound conclusions on the subject of nationality. No one has more effectively stated the case for the 'French' or 'Classical' definition of the nation, founded on its citizens' will, as against the 'German' or 'Romantic' thesis that the nation is based on language. 'Language is an invitation to unite, not a compulsion ... There is something in human beings which is superior to language: that is their will. The will of Switzerland to be united, despite its multiplicity of languages, is a fact much more important than a linguistic uniformity, sometimes compulsorily imposed.' Renan likewise rejected nationality based on race, and the notion of 'strategic' or 'natural' frontiers. And he went further. Hegemony, he declared, must be destroyed.

Georges Sorel

Georges Sorel, writing at the beginning of the twentieth century, foresaw the coming catastrophe. 'Europe,' he said in October 1908, 'is above all the land of war and cataclysm. Pacifists are either imbeciles who know nothing of elementary laws, or scoundrels who play the demagogue and live by lies.' He went on:

> In America, they have made a federation of people who are all alike, living in similar states ... Bravo! But how do you propose to federate the Slavs, who are either religious or mystic revolutionaries; the sober Scandinavians; the ambitious Germans; the freedom-loving English; the greedy French; the Italians with their economic crisis; the Balkan poachers; and the belligerent Hungarians? How will you settle this basket of crabs which snap at each other all the livelong day? Miserable Europe! Why conceal what is in store for her? Within ten years, she will sink into war and anarchy as she has always done two or three times every 100 years.

And on 18 December 1912, Sorel declared: 'Europe, this cemetery, is filled with people who sang before killing each other. The French and the Germans will be singing soon.'

Romain Rolland

It is hard to imagine more bitter or more justified pessimism. But what is also significant is that Sorel was thinking in terms of Europe. The same was true of Romain Rolland, best known as the author of the ten-volume novel *Jean-Christophe*. He was the least nationalistic of people, so deeply aware of the international essence of culture that he protested indignantly against the results of patriotic frenzy. It took courage to publish, in September 1914, an article entitled 'Above the Battle' – '*Au-dessus de la mêlée*'. In it, Rolland spoke of the 'crime against Europe and civilization into which the peoples have been led by their governments, and by the bankruptcy of those forces whose duty it was to preserve the peace – socialism and Christianity.'

The crisis of 1914 carried all before it. The 'European War' destroyed not only millions of human lives, but all the battered remnants of the old Europe.

CONCLUSIONS

1815–1914: a hundred years of dazzling progress in science and industry, but also one of the most troubled centuries in Europe's political history. Europe faced many challenges: war, nationalism, the system of alliances, and even some forms of universalist pacifism or theories of class struggle, both incompatible with concentration on Europe.

For that whole century, national history was extraordinarily rich: but European history was reduced to a loose organization of great powers operating at the expense of the small – the so-called Concert of Europe. Its only hopeful sign was that it also involved some thinking about European unity.

A glance at some contemporary notions will suffice to show how far Europe was from enjoying the *belle époque*, which some have seen in the end of the nineteenth century.

The Nation?

The concept of the nation certainly came to birth. But under the pressure of Romanticism and the apocalyptic ideas born of revolution, nationalism ceased to be reasonable and became chauvinistic.

On the one hand, there grew up among the nations of Europe a rooted mutual mistrust which could only end in war; on the other, there arose the notion that 'since my nation is superior to the others, it has the right to persecute and even destroy them.'

The States?

Certainly, there was progress towards the autonomous 'nation-state', governed by itself: hence the gradual break-up of multinational states like the Ottoman Empire or Austria-Hungary. Hence also the gathering into one state of the different parts of Italy and Germany. But the state was a law unto itself. It had supreme power, including the power to declare war.

War?

The hundred years in question fall into four main phases:

1. From 1815 to 1854: apparently no great wars, but many 'expeditions', usually punitive, anti-liberal, or colonial.

2. From 1854 to 1871: five great European wars in sixteen years (the Crimean War, the Italian War of 1859, the War of the Duchies, the German-Austrian War, the Franco-Prussian War).
3. From 1871 to 1914: apparently a period of peace. This was true of the great European Powers: only Russia was defeated, by Japan, in 1904–5. But there was much disquiet, and there were many crises!
4. The last of these crises ended in a European war which became a World War, steeped in blood and creating no lasting peace.

The Alliances?

Their aim was security. But in 1879, for the very first time, alliances were formed at a time of uninterrupted peace. The result was to set two opposing forces against each other in ever-growing mutual hostility.

The Empires?

There was a race for colonies, especially after 1881.

When Europeans could no longer fight for territory in Europe that had become 'national', they transposed their territorial disputes to Africa, South-East Asia, and the Pacific.

18
Europe Destroys Itself: (1914–45)

'THE GREAT WAR' AND ITS WIDER EFFECTS

The First World War, known at the time as 'the Great War', was fought by two opposing camps whose respective societies had a great deal in common. On one side stood the 'Central Powers' (Germany, Austria-Hungary, then the Ottoman Empire, then Bulgaria); on the other, the 'Entente' or 'the Allies' (Russia, France, Britain and the Dominions), as well as Belgium, Serbia, Japan, then Italy, Romania, and Portugal, with the United States as an associate rather than an ally, followed by Greece and China and a number of Latin American States.

The main battlefields were in Europe: the Franco-Belgian Front, the north-east Italian Front, the Serbian Front (until 1915), the Salonica Front, the Romanian Front, and the Eastern Front, until Russia's capitulation in 1917.

Outside Europe, there was fighting in Syria, Arabia, Transcaucasia, Iran, the far east of Siberia, and in various regions of Africa. But the decisive battles were on the Franco-Belgian or Western Front.

There is no need to recapitulate here the diplomatic exchanges that preceded the War and the military campaigns that decided it. More to our purpose is to examine the underlying reasons for the War. In fact, it marked the disastrous collapse of an out-of-date system, the European balance of power; and it ended in victory for one of the two opposing sides only when a power from outside Europe, the United States of America, eventually intervened.

The immediate causes of the war

On 28 June 1914, the Austrian heir-apparent, Archduke Franz Ferdinand, was assassinated with his consort in the streets of Sarajevo, in Bosnia. The Austro-Hungarian government suspected that Serbia had had a hand in the crime and decided 'to have done with the Serbs'. They, since a *coup d'état* in 1903, had been pressing hard for a national Pan-Slav union of all the southern Slavs or Yugoslavs.

As an ancient Habsburg state anxious to preserve its own existence, Austria-Hungary naturally resisted these claims; and she had the full backing of Germany.

On 23 July the Austro-Hungarian government sent Serbia a 48-hour ultimatum, demanding among other things the suppression of all propaganda against Austria-Hungary. When on 24 July the other powers heard of the ultimatum and of its support by Germany, Europe was thrown into crisis. That day, the German Chancellor, Dr Theobald Theodore von Bethmann-Hollweg, sent them all a warning Note:

> The present case is something to be settled exclusively between Austria-Hungary and Serbia. We wish the dispute to be localized at once, because any intervention by another power, in view of the diversity of the obligations imposed by the alliances, would have incalculable consequences.

On 28 July Austria-Hungary declared war on Serbia. On 31 July, Russia announced general mobilization: the Russian government felt that it could not allow Serbia, a Slav state, to become an Austro-Hungarian satellite. On 1 August, following an ultimatum, Germany declared war on Russia; but because of the Schlieffen Plan, under which the first attack was to be on France via the invasion of neutral Belgium, Germany also declared war on France on 3 August and promptly crossed the Belgian frontier. On 4 August, Britain declared war on Germany, feeling morally obliged to intervene because the Anglo-French Naval Agreements of 1912 required her, and her alone, to defend the eastern end of the Channel.

Faced with these events, public opinion looked for individuals to blame. Kaiser Wilhelm II? Helmuth von Moltke and the German General Staff? The Austrian General Staff and Konrad von Hötzendorff? The French President, Raymond Poincaré? Baron Alexander

Isvolsky, the Russian ambassador in Paris? The whole question of war guilt continued to poison the atmosphere long after the War. As it was, both the French and the Germans – like the other powers – felt they had right on their side.

The fatal process

Today, after more than a hundred years and with access to most of the archives, it seems clear that the Great War, unlike Bismarck's wars, was not begun deliberately by either side, but was set in motion by a fatal process which the statesmen of the time were unable to halt. It operated as follows:

Given the deep-rooted mutual mistrust among European states, and the violence of nationalistic feeling, the governments had taken precautions and decisions arranged in advance to deal with fearful and uncertain future events. It was a policy of 'just in case'. Germany had decided to go to war just in case she risked being abandoned by her Austro-Hungarian ally. France had decided to go to war rather than break the Franco-Russian alliance; Russia had decided to go to war rather than let more Slavs in the Balkans (in this case the Serbs) fall under Austrian domination. Britain had decided (in 1793!) to go to war rather than allow any great power to take over Antwerp. Austria-Hungary, very different from the other countries because of its multinational nature, had decided to go to war rather than disintegrate under the pressure of a nationalist movement among its own Yugoslav people, supported by Serbia.

Everything was ready, in other words, for events which triggered off the fatal chain reaction – of governments actually doing what they had earlier decided 'just in case'. If they failed to act, they feared for their very existence.

When other countries entered the War later, it was no longer as part of this process, but deliberately and after careful thought. One Italian Minister called it 'sacred egoism' – a calculated risk in the hope of recovering territory.

The failure of the balance of power

The Great War demonstrated a remarkable phenomenon: that the traditional organization of European affairs, based on the Concert of Europe and the balance of power, could lead to catastrophic bloodshed.

This emerged not only in the fact of war, but in its actual strategy. At first, the War was expected to last only a short time: a long-drawn-out war, it was thought, would prove impossible to finance. Then it was found that, by spending capital and borrowing on future prospects, anything could be funded so long as the population agreed. By November 1914, everyone was resigned to a long and total war.

The Germans' Schlieffen Plan failed. France was not encircled, and neither side won the 'race to the sea' to turn the flank of the opposing armies. The result was the stalemate of the famous trenches, in which soldiers on both sides faced their enemies along a line in France running south as far as Soissons and then eastward to the Vosges. For months on end, despite furious attacks and counter-attacks, the line barely moved. Dug into the earth, it was the cruellest imaginable embodiment of the European balance of power, turned to death and destruction.

The Americans and the European stalemate

The Russian Revolution of October 1917 was followed in December by an armistice between Russia and Germany, and then, on 3 March 1918, by the Treaty of Brest-Litovsk which finally took Russia out of the War. This left the German General Erich von Ludendorff free to mount an offensive on the Western Front, which might have broken the stalemate.

In the end, however, it was broken by the intervention of the United States. By the time of the final Armistice on 11 November 1918, more than 2 million Americans were fighting in Europe. The history of how they came to be there shows very clearly that the United States, although in large part a nation of European immigrants, did not enter the War for Europe's sake. Far from it. After having announced that the Americans should remain neutral not only in their actions but in their hearts, President Woodrow Wilson first proposed a 'peace without victory' on 22 January 1917, on account of the Allies' naval strategy, which included the seizure of 'war contraband', and the Germans' submarine warfare, which in 1915 had already sunk the British liner *Lusitania* with the loss of 118 American lives.

At that time, President Wilson had warned Germany that the United States would treat any further such action as 'deliberately unfriendly'. This served as a deterrent: but on 1 February 1917, Germany once more declared 'unrestricted submarine warfare'.

It was a policy that Wilson could not accept: it threatened 'the freedom of the seas'. When the first American cargo ships were attacked, he gained the backing of Congress to declare war on 6 April 1917.

Detesting 'German militarism', the American President prepared to act as arbiter in the global conflict, and in January 1918 he drew up his peace aims, the famous 'Fourteen Points'. Although they formed the basis of his foreign policy and contained quite specific proposals, they omitted to mention the nationality principle.

Wilson put his peace plan first to the Germans (who on that basis asked for an armistice on 4 October 1918), and then to the Allies.

The Great War would not have ended as it did without the Americans. By themselves, the Allies were outnumbered and financially ruined. The United States brought them, more than anything, hope.

Wilson, however, was unfamiliar with Europe. He blamed the War on the balance of power and, as will be seen, he neglected its advantages when planning the post-war world.

The First World War 1914–1918

1914

28 June	Assassination of the Austrian heir-apparent Franz Ferdinand in Sarajevo
28 July	Austria-Hungary declares war on Serbia
1 August	Germany mobilizes and declares war on Russia
3 August	Germany declares war on France
3/4 August	German troops invade Belgium
4 August	Belgium and Great Britain declare war on Germany
23 August	Japan declares war on Germany
26–30 August	Russians defeated at Battle of Tannenberg (East Prussia)
5–12 September	Battle of the Marne
10 October to 10 November	'Race to the Sea': Franco-British forces fail to encircle German troops: static warfare begins
7 November	Japan captures Kiaochow and the German North Pacific islands (Mariana, the Carolines, the Solomon Islands, and the Marshall Islands)

1915

February	German offensive: winter battle in East Prussia
19 February onwards	Land and sea battles in the Dardanelles
23 May	Italy joins the Entente and declares war on Austria-Hungary
14 October	Bulgaria allies with Germany
5–8 September	Zimmerwald Conference in the Canton of Berne

1916

21 February	Battle of Verdun
31 May to 1 June	Battle of Jutland
24 June	Franco-British offensive; Battle of the Somme
24–30 August	European left-wing socialists meet at Kienthal in the Canton of Berne, Switzerland
27 August	Romania declares war on Germany and Austria-Hungary. Italy declares war on Germany
12 December	Germany sends Peace Note (rejected by the Allies)
26 December	General Joseph Joffre made Marshal of France and replaced as Commander-in-Chief of the French armies by General Georges Robert Nivelle

1917

22 January	US President Woodrow Wilson calls for 'Peace without victory'
1 February	Germany declares all-out U-boat war
12 March	Liberal Revolution in Russia; abdication of Tsar Nicholas II; Provisional government headed by Prince Lvov
6 April	United States declares war on the side of the Allies
16 April	With German assistance, Lenin returns to Petrograd from exile in Switzerland

2–20 May	Philippe Pétain replaces General Nivelle; mutinies in the French army
9 August	General strike in Spain
October	Italians defeated by the Austrians at Caporetto; they retreat beyond the river Piave
November	General strike in Switzerland
6–7 November	Bolshevik revolution in Russia
16 November	New French government under Georges Clemenceau
22 December	Peace negotiations between Russia and the Central Powers

1918

8 January	Woodrow Wilson proposes peace aims in his 'Fourteen Points'
9 February	'Peace of Bread' with the Ukraine concluded by Germany, Austria-Hungary, and Turkey (in exchange for grain)
3 March	Treaty of Brest-Litovsk: Russia gives up Livonia, Courland, Lithuania, Estonia, and Poland; Finland and the Ukraine recognized as independent States
21 March to 6 April	Decisive campaign on the Western Front; German offensive in Picardy
18 July	Allied counter-offensive under General Ferdinand Foch; German front driven back
8 August	Battle of Amiens ('the black day of the German Army')
3–4 October	German government offers armistice to Woodrow Wilson
3 November	Armistice between the Allies and Austria-Hungary
11 November	Armistice (at Compiègne) between the Allies and Germany

THE PEACE TREATIES AND THEIR FAULTS

'The miserable Europeans,' wrote Paul Valéry in 1931 in his *Regards sur le monde actuel* or *Glimpses of the Modern World*, 'preferred to play at being Armagnacs or Burgundians rather than take on that great role in the world which the Romans assumed and maintained for so many centuries.' Eight-and-a-half million dead: that was the human cost. In material terms, many areas – Britain and Germany for instance – escaped widespread destruction. But Central and Eastern Europe were plunged into famine, poverty, and chaos.

Wilson's world plans

The 1919 Peace Conference was just as important as the Congress of Vienna in 1815. But the differences were immense. Now, Europeans were discussing terms on the basis of an American plan; and the American President, who wanted to inaugurate what he called 'the new diplomacy', was actively involved in the task of arbitration. He found it hard to conceal his mistrust of his European colleagues, who in his eyes were dangerous imperialists. It was also his belief that he, even more than the United States, represented world opinion, and that therefore he could appeal directly to peoples rather than governments. A convinced universalist, he was disinclined to think in European terms. The cornerstone of his plans was the League of Nations, not a European but a world organization to be responsible for keeping the peace. 'The world,' he told Congress, 'must be made safe for democracy.' His 'new diplomacy' – 'open covenants of peace openly arrived at' – harked back to the *philosophes* of the eighteenth century and to Europe's nineteenth-century liberals. His achievement was to have given practical political inspiration to a great country.

The Europe of hatred

Among the incalculable evils of the Great War, one of the worst was the seemingly permanent hatred that it left behind. Both sides, victors and vanquished alike, believed that they had been the victims of their opponents' lust for war. President Wilson's attempt to distinguish between the 'German militarists' and the good, peaceable German people was ill-received on both sides. The Allies believed that the Germans were just as guilty as their leaders; the Germans were convinced of their own and their leaders' innocence.

Hatred gave rise to the idea of punishment, symbolized by the 'reparations' demanded of the defeated enemy. 'Germany will pay' was the slogan in France. 'To the last penny,' added the British. And during the 1918 general election campaign a British minister, Sir Eric Geddes, made the charming promise to squeeze Germany 'until the pips squeak'. Article 231 of the Versailles Treaty declared:

> The Allied and Associated Governments affirm and Germany accepts the responsibility of Germany and her allies for causing all the loss and damage to which the Allied and Associated Governments and their nationals have been subjected as a consequence of the war imposed upon them by the aggression of Germany and her allies.

Although the authors of the Treaty had not intended to introduce into it the idea of moral guilt, the Germans regarded this Article, which they had been forced to sign, as implying that they recognized such guilt.

Germany thought herself the victim of abominable injustice, and her hatred for the Allies only grew. The call for revenge poisoned public life. The main beneficiaries were the ultra-nationalist groups which now sprang up – in particular the 'National Socialist German Workers' Party' – the Nazi Party – which Adolf Hitler joined in 1919.

By then it was certainly true that Europe had crumbled. Could it be rebuilt?

The new Europe

How did the 'Europe of Versailles' compare with the 'Europe of Vienna' a century before?

Two great 'historic states' – the Ottoman Empire and Austria-Hungary – had disappeared. The Ottoman Empire had been waning throughout the century: the Great War had merely finished it off. For Austria-Hungary, in the autumn of 1918, the end had been sudden and brutal, the result of defeat. A jumble of small 'successor states' Balkanized Central Europe; and since on the nationality principle each of them was completely independent, they soon split into rival groups and factions, the 'satisfied' and the 'dissatisfied'. The former – Poland,

Czechoslovakia, Yugoslavia, and Romania – aligned themselves with France; the latter – Bulgaria and Hungary – with Italy. The break-up of the Austro-Hungarian Empire not only transformed the European balance of power: it also removed a barrier against Germany. Hitler turned it to good account.

The political map of the new Europe in 1919 corresponded much more closely to the map of its nationalities; but there remained some confusing and explosive situations, since most of the new states included sizeable foreign minorities. Their life was made no easier by economic problems: such small countries needed to work with their neighbours to be economically viable, but few were able to do so. The nationality principle, carried to excess, had led to an impasse.

Czechoslovakia was an entirely new state; Poland was a state re-established after 123 years' eclipse. In the Baltic, carved out of Russia, there now were Finland, Estonia, Latvia, and Lithuania. Europe, in effect, was fragmented. This was all the more dangerous in that the new states, strategically very vulnerable, were on the frontiers of two great powers – Soviet Russia and Germany. For the moment, both were weak, and Germany was weighed down by the Versailles Treaty. But in the long term both could become powerful enough to annihilate their neighbours.

The Versailles Treaty, moreover, had been imposed on Germany and negotiated in the absence of Soviet Russia. Very clearly, a treaty concluded without one great power and against another could not be a model of what Talleyrand had called 'European public law'.

And the League of Nations? It was crippled from the start when the US Senate refused to ratify the Treaties. Three of the world's seven great powers, then, were missing from among its founder members; the United States, the USSR, and Germany. The USSR was admitted in 1934; but although Germany joined in 1926, she resigned in 1933. Japan and Italy also left the League. What was more, it never dared to act effectively over *any* of the conflicts it had been established to prevent.

ARISTIDE BRIAND AND 'EUROPEAN UNION'

Sometimes as Prime Minister, sometimes as Foreign Minister, Aristide Briand was responsible for French foreign policy in 1921 and from

1925 to 1932. Able, supple, and conciliatory, he kept in touch with the development of public opinion, and initiated a policy of *rapprochement* and reconciliation with Germany which culminated in the Locarno Pact of 1925, followed by German membership of the League of Nations in 1926. He was far from doctrinaire, adapting quickly to altered circumstances and new ideas. He deeply regretted the absence of any European organization, especially now that the idea of greater unity was in the air. In July 1929, when still Foreign Minister, Briand announced that he was going to propose a form of European union; and in his Prime Ministerial speech soon afterwards he spoke of a 'United States of Europe'. Finally, on 7 September, he presented to the League of Nations what came to be known as 'the Briand Plan'.

Coudenhove-Kalergi and 'Pan-Europa'

Behind Briand's proposal, among other things, was the 'Open Letter to French Members of Parliament' that Count Richard Coudenhove-Kalergi had published in 1924. At that time, a general election had just caused the resignation of Raymond Poincaré, who had been Prime Minister since 1922, and in charge of enforcing the Versailles Treaty. He was replaced by the *Cartel des gauches*, a left-wing coalition, in favour of the League and more sympathetic towards Germany. Coudenhove-Kalergi, the son of an Austro-Hungarian diplomatist (and a Japanese mother), had since 1922 been publicizing his ideas about 'Pan-Europa' in the Austrian and German press; and in 1924 he produced a 'Pan-European Manifesto'. The question it put was: 'Can twenty-five states live together on the small peninsula that is Europe, in a state of international anarchy, without succumbing to the most appalling political, economic, and cultural catastrophe?'

In his Letter to the French Members of Parliament, Coudenhove-Kalergi argued that Europe should unite so as to match three great entities: the USSR, the British Empire, and the United States. While praising 'the greatness of the Russian people's soul', he declared: 'Every European must recognize the Russian danger; and Europe's independence can be assured in only one way, through the United States of Europe.' The 'British world', when it had been a 'mere state', had been 'a constituent part of Europe. Now it is no more than a neighbour ... Britain's entry into a Pan-European confederation would be possible only if the Dominions parted company with London.' Coudenhove-Kalergi's 'Pan-European Programme' included: 'A political, economic, and military Alliance; arbitration and guaranteed treaties among all the democratic States of our continent; understandings with Britain and America; peace with Russia and the Far East.' Among the many distinguished figures who backed this plan were Count Carlo Sforza, Thomas and Heinrich Mann, Selma Lagerlöf, Sigmund Freud, Paul Claudel, Paul Valéry, Jules Romains, Lucien Romier, Miguel da Unamuno, Ortega y Gasset, Salvador de Madariaga, and Albert Einstein.

The French statesman Edouard Herriot was another. On 25 January 1925, when he was Prime Minister, he expressed his hope of seeing 'a United States of Europe'. Except for Napoleon III, he was the first French head of government in office to propose such a thing.

In October 1926, the first 'Pan-European Congress' met in Vienna. Its members included Herriot, Paul Painlevé, Albert Thomas, Léon Blum, Edouard Daladier, and Paul Boncour; Philip Noel-Baker from Britain; Hjalmar Schacht and Josef Wirth from Germany; and Eleftherios Venizelos from Greece. Aristide Briand, who urged Coudenhove-Kalergi to 'Move fast!' (*Marchez vite, vite, vite!*), became the movement's sole Honorary President in 1927.

This was the background against which Briand made his speech to the League of Nations on 7 September 1929, with warm support from the German Foreign Minister Gustav Stresemann – who sadly died a few weeks later, on 3 October.

Briand's speech

Briand's proposal in fact formed part of a much longer speech. He came to it, he said, 'somewhat diffidently'. As he explained, 'I have been associated for the past few years with propaganda for an idea which people have been kind enough to call "generous", perhaps to avoid calling it "unwise".' Then came the nub of his proposal:

> I believe that among peoples who are geographically as close as those of Europe are, there should exist a sort of federal link. These peoples must have the opportunity at any moment to make contact with each other, discuss their common interests, take joint decisions, and establish bonds of solidarity which, when the time comes, will enable them to face any grave situations that may arise. It is these bonds I should like

to try to forge. Obviously, such an association will act first and foremost in the economic field, where matters are most urgent. But I am also sure that the federal link can be beneficial in political and social affairs, without affecting the sovereignty of any of the nations that might belong to such an association.

So there was nothing revolutionary – no assembly to be elected by the people or appointed by national parliaments, no representation of 'interest groups', no supranational 'High Authority'.

Following this speech, the twenty-seven European member states of the League of Nations met and asked Briand to draft a Memorandum. He submitted it on 1 May 1930, with a request for reasonably prompt reactions. It was an eloquent and prophetic document, and it caused a considerable stir in Europe. Meanwhile, however, the world had been rocked by the Wall Street stock market crash of October 1929 and the resultant economic crisis.

The Briand Plan

Economic crises sour public opinion and inflame nationalistic mistrust. In the Memorandum of 1 May, therefore, Briand and the French Foreign Office took every precaution. They stressed 'the very clear sense of collective responsibility in the face of the danger to peace in Europe, in the political as well as the economic and social fields'. They guaranteed that national sovereignty and equal rights would be fully maintained.

Already in 1930, however, the Memorandum referred to 'the European Community' and to a 'common market' involving 'the gradual liberation and methodical simplification of the movement of goods, capital, and persons'. It also discussed the question of whether economic or political steps should come first – a subject endlessly debated after the Second World War.

As regards institutions, the Memorandum proposed a small secretariat serving a 'European Conference' of national representatives, modelled on and operating within the League of Nations.

Rejection

The replies from France's twenty-six partners, which all arrived between 25 June and 4 August 1930, revealed all too clearly how remote government thinking still was from the idea of a European organization, let alone a European union.

With the exception of Yugoslavia, Bulgaria, and (with minor reservations) Norway, Greece, and Czechoslovakia, the general response was a polite refusal. Aristide Briand was well ahead of his time. The various criticisms of his Memorandum, moreover, proved that the fragmentation of Europe by the Versailles Treaty actually reflected the way people thought.

Criticism of the Briand Plan

The arguments of Briand's critics can be summarized under six main headings.

1. Insistence on absolute national sovereignty. Only the Netherlands, whose other comments were fairly critical, stressed the need to limit or transfer sovereignty.
2. Fear that a European organization would harm the League, and preference for a world organization. All the respondents backed the League: but a number of them refused the Briand Plan on account of it. They included the Netherlands, Italy, Denmark, Sweden, the United Kingdom, Switzerland, and Poland.
3. Desire for a less onerous institutional structure. Some governments believed that everything could be done by meetings of the League. These were Sweden, Switzerland, Ireland, and above all the United Kingdom.
4. Preference for economic over political action. This was expressed by the Netherlands, by Austria, by Romania, and by Germany. The German reply, influenced no doubt by the *Kohlensyndikat* coal cartel set up in 1926, declared: 'Direct agreement among certain economic sectors based on private enterprise remains a form of activity which should have an important place in the new organization of the European economy.' In Norway's view: 'It would be more natural to base European co-operation primarily on the solution of economic problems, since it seems easier to obtain results in this field, where the failings of the present system are most obvious.' Portugal, Hungary, Sweden, Luxembourg, and Albania argued

in similar vein. So did Belgium: 'Although neither is subordinate to the other, politics and economics, the two main motives for human activity, influence each other.' The British reply even managed to suggest that the Briand Memorandum meant the opposite of what it said: 'His Majesty's Government is also in agreement with the French Government in thinking that it is above all in the matter of economic relations that closer co-operation among the nations of Europe is urgently required.'

5. A concern to extend the association to European states outside the League (the USSR and Turkey). Italy pointed out 'the usefulness of proposing to the other governments concerned that the government of the Union of Soviet Socialist Republics and the government of the Turkish Republic be invited to take part in the procedure of working out the draft for European Federal Union'. Estonia wished 'all the peoples of Europe' to be included. Germany opposed the exclusion of Russia and Turkey; Hungary and Greece proposed Turkish participation; Lithuania, Luxembourg, and Bulgaria wanted to admit the greatest possible number of European countries, and preferably all.

6. Insistence on responsibilities outside Europe. This was a point made by Spain, thinking of her 'special relationship with Latin-American countries' and her position in Africa; by the Netherlands, which also had territory outside Europe; and by Germany and Denmark, which called attention to the political and tariff relationships between certain European states and non-European territories. Portugal argued likewise: but here once again it was the United Kingdom which expressed the strongest reservations.

The negative attitude of Germany, then led by the Catholic Chancellor Heinrich Brüning, is also worthy of note. Altogether, this first attempt in history to 'take the pulse' of Europe showed that in 1930, at least, it had a very feeble beat.

THE ECONOMIC CRISIS AND BEGGAR-MY-NEIGHBOUR POLICIES

The Great War had thrown into sharp relief the economic decline of Europe relative to the United States. Already in 1914 America had been the world's foremost economic power; and her advance continued. Setting the tone of the world economy, she spread prosperity between 1923 and 1929, and set off the great crisis of 1929–33. It was America, finally, which decided to remedy the crisis by her own methods rather than by international co-operation, thereby contributing more than any other country to the compartmentalization of the world economy which became the rule after 1933.

When the United States had entered the War on 6 April 1917, the Allies were financially drained. They had obtained private loans in America, but their credit was almost exhausted. A law voted by Congress in April 1917, however, enabled them to borrow from the American Treasury, and on a much larger scale.

Still more important was another phenomenon, in the investment field. In 1914, American investments abroad had amounted to $2,500 million, while European investments in the United States had totalled between $4,500 and $5,000 million. The huge volume of goods which America had supplied to the wartime Allies had enabled her to mop up much of the European capital invested in the United States, while her immense profits enabled her to invest more than $9,000 million abroad.

The growth of America's wealth during the Great War is confirmed by the rise in her national income, and in the demand for consumer goods. It was a real economic boom. The most spectacular increase was in consumer durables – cars, houses, refrigerators, and radio sets. The economy reached the stage of what Walt Rostow has called 'high mass consumption', with the result that Americans were from now on ahead of Europeans in their supply of all consumer goods. Admittedly, there were pockets of poverty – among the Black population, the 'poor whites' in the South, the unemployed, and the derelicts of the inner cities. Farmers, too, gained little from the industrial boom. Nevertheless, a new and more affluent society was emerging, and one which Europeans treated with a mixture of envy and irony.

Reparations

With their wealth and the influence it gave them, the Americans dominated the international money market until 1929. After 1929, they swamped it with the economic crisis and its after-effects. The follies that ensued for ten years thereafter had their origin in the huge international debts caused by the War. Some of these were the result of the German reparations imposed by the Treaty of Versailles. Others were debts owed by the Allies to each other (with Britain the main creditor), and above all to the United States Treasury (with Britain, in this case, the major debtor).

The amount of the reparations to be paid by Germany was not fixed until the spring of 1921, when the Allied Reparations Commission produced the figure of 132,000 million gold marks, to be increased later if Germany was thought capable of paying more. The British economist John Maynard Keynes condemned the scheme as morally detestable, politically foolish, and economically nonsensical. It was also arithmetically illusory. The total was divided into three different sets of liabilities, with interest, amortization, and moratorium arrangements which disguised the fact – especially abhorrent to the French, with their slogan 'Germany will pay' – that Germany would never in reality pay more than a fraction of the sum theoretically due.

The main claimants to German reparations were France, Britain, Italy, and Belgium, in that order. Others besides Keynes were convinced that the system was impracticable. Already on 22 December 1918, the French Deputy André Lebon had asked how 70 million Germans were going to be forced to work for fifty or sixty years 'in the knowledge that the only recompense for their toil, and all they earned by it, would go to pay off debts incurred by past generations?' Yet successive French governments left public opinion to its illusions. The British, heavily influenced by Keynes's masterly study, *The Economic Consequences of the Peace*, published in November 1919, were much quicker to drop their intransigence and be willing to revive the German economy, which offered good opportunities for British exports.

The Germans, although unanimously hostile to reparations, hesitated between two ways of reacting: refusal to pay (urged by the ultra-nationalists and by some big Ruhr industrialists, such as Hugo Stinnes); and the so-called *Erfüllungspolitik*, the 'policy of fulfilment', followed by Walther Rathenau in 1921 and 1922, and by Gustav Stresemann from October 1923 onwards. 'Fulfilment' meant meeting initial demands for reparations so as to restore Allied confidence, then negotiating for a reduction in the total amount.

In 1921, the Allies practised a policy of constraint, occupying three towns in the Ruhr in addition to the Rhineland (which, although remaining German, was due under the Versailles Treaty to be occupied by Allied troops for fifteen years). In January 1923, in protest at the suspension of reparations payments, French and Belgian troops, backed by the Italians but opposed by America and Britain, moved into the whole of the Ruhr. In the following year, the Dawes Plan (named after the American president of the committee which drafted it, Charles G. Dawes) provided not only for Germany to borrow abroad to finance reparations, but also for these to be scaled down. The new rate was fixed at 1 billion gold marks for the first year, rising annually to 2.5 billion marks after five years, and currency transfers were no longer to be made by Germany, but by a General Reparations Agent located in Berlin.

War debts

The Americans had practically renounced all claim to reparations for themselves. Regarding them as 'political debts', they thought it best to write them off. It was a wise policy: but that was where the Americans' wisdom stopped. It was out of the question, they thought, to write off the 'commercial debts' that were owing to them. Those were sacrosanct, and international morality, as they saw it, required that they should be paid, even if the result made very little difference to American prosperity.

Faced with American demands, the Europeans were obliged, one by one, to sign agreements to pay. The British were the first, on 18 June 1923, with the so-called Baldwin–Mellon agreement between Stanley Baldwin, the UK Prime Minister and Chancellor of the Exchequer, and Andrew Mellon, US Secretary of the Treasury. On 14 November 1925, Italy secured a rather more favourable deal.

France resisted longer. The franc crisis which coincided with the successive governments of the *Cartel des gauches*, from 1924 to 1926, made it urgent to secure American financial support but difficult to reach an agreement. In a mere two years, France had nine different Ministers of Finance. Not until 29 April 1926 did Henri Béranger sign the 'Mellon–Béranger' agreement: but the Chamber of Deputies refused to ratify it, and the result was a long dispute in the press and public opinion between France and the United States. But at least, since the Dawes Plan had begun to be applied in 1925, Germany had regularly paid her reparations. Was it a miracle? A proof of German ability to pay? In reality, Stresemann wrote to the German Crown Prince in 1925, the payment of reparations would be impossible from 1927 onwards. It was once more the United States that falsified this reasonable prediction.

American loans

Enjoying the height of prosperity, the United States had excess capital to invest abroad. But Herbert Hoover, the Secretary of Commerce, had convinced two of his key colleagues – Charles Evans Hughes, the Secretary of State, and Andrew Mellon, Secretary of the Treasury – that the export of private capital ought to be controlled. In the summer of 1921, all three secured an undertaking from John Pierpont Morgan, Jr, that neither his bank nor its colleagues would invest abroad without consulting the State Department. No loans would be made to governments or to citizens of countries which had not met their obligations to the United States. As a result, the Americans refused to lend to Japan, the USSR, and France. But Germany, which for obvious reasons had no war debts to repay to America, became the main target for American investors.

Thanks to the influx of American capital, Germany between 1923 and 1930 had plenty of currency with which to pay reparations. As Hjalmar Schacht, then President of the *Reichsbank*, wrote in his memoirs, the cost of reparations 'was finally borne by those foreigners who gave us credit'.

In this way, under the unbridled pressure of American business, with the Administration looking on unperturbed, money embarked on a ludicrous merry-go-round. The Americans lent it to Germany. Germany paid it in reparations to the Allies. The Allies returned it to America in settlement of their debts. 'When is this little game going to end?' asked one French politician. Heady with apparent success, the world failed to realize how fragile the whole mad system was.

Economic growth in Europe

Less boldly and dizzily than the United States – because facing more difficulties – the main European powers also enjoyed post-war economic growth. The only exception was the USSR.

In 1913, Britain's national income had been £2,021 million. By 1921 it had fallen to £1,804 million; but by 1929 it had risen again, to £2,319 million. The French national income (in 1938 francs) had been 328,000 million in 1913, and had dropped to 250,000 million in 1920, only to increase again to a peak of 453,000 million in 1929. Germany's national income, which in 1914 had been 45,700 million gold marks, reached 57,500 million in 1931.

The 1929 Crash

Until 1929, the world's economic system was based on the optimistic American model. There was no political curb on production, with the result that overproduction became more and more of a threat. To stimulate demand, customers were encouraged to buy on credit or to borrow from the banks, who made huge profits from interest rates. But as soon as there was a sudden credit squeeze for any reason, demand would fall, stocks would accumulate, and prices would collapse – a real catastrophe, given America's dominant role in the world. This in essence is what happened in 1929, triggered by an abrupt crisis of confidence at a time of excessive speculation. The fatal date was 'Black Thursday', 24 October, the day of the Wall Street Crash.

The crisis hits Europe

The first countries to be affected by the crisis in the United States were those which supplied her almost exclusively with raw materials. Latin America, already poor, became poorer still. The symbolic image was that of Brazilian coffee being burned as locomotive fuel. Argentina, Uruguay, and Australia went off the gold standard, devaluing their currencies in a vain attempt to promote their exports.

American capital lent abroad, especially on a short-term basis, seemed at first impervious to the crisis: between October 1929 and the spring of 1930, some further loans were made. By the end of that year, however, the flow of capital had virtually stopped, and it remained below $60 million a year compared with $200 million in 1929.

Direct investment continued, but at a low ebb in 1930 and 1931, and only to disappear altogether in 1932. In the opposite direction, to pay their own debts, Americans repatriated vast sums that they had placed overseas, while foreigners, on a smaller scale, withdrew funds from America.

The repatriation of American capital had the biggest effect on Germany, which had absorbed 40 per cent of it. Then came Austria, and then the United Kingdom. Between the end of May and the middle of July, 1931, the *Reichsbank* lost $2,000 million in currency and gold.

At the same time, it became much harder to export to the United States. Not only were Americans buying less; on 17 June 1930, they erected one of the most formidable tariff barriers of all time. The new Hawley-Smoot tariff averaged 50 per cent, compared with 26 per cent for the previous Fordney-McCumber tariff. Troubled and uneasy as it was in 1930, in 1931 the European economy collapsed.

The most resounding crash was that of the great Austrian bank, the *Kreditanstalt für Handel und Gewerbe*, in May 1931, followed by a number of German banks, including in particular the *Danatbank*. In June, July, and August, Britain began to be affected. France, Belgium, the Netherlands and Italy – countries on the gold standard, of which more later – seemed for a time less vulnerable, partly because the archaic structure of some elements in the French economy actually muffled the blows. But by the end of 1931 and the beginning of 1932 the situation had become catastrophic. Using the index 100 for industrial production in 1928, the figures in Germany were 100.1 in 1929, 87 in 1930, 70.1 in 1931, and 58 in 1932. In Britain, in 1933, the index stood at 86.5. In France, it was 109.9 in 1929 and 1930, 95 in 1931, and 81 in 1932.

The political effects of the crisis differed considerably from one country to another. In Germany, it certainly explained the huge advance of the Nazi party in the election of July 1932, when with 230 seats it became the biggest single group in the *Reichstag*, paving the way for Hitler's assumption of power and for expansionist totalitarian dictatorship. In Italy, where Benito Mussolini had already established dictatorship, the crisis prompted him to seek a colony where Italians might settle, and to impose his dreams of empire on Ethiopia. There were similar reactions in Japan.

In Britain, by contrast, the crisis had the curious effect of attracting the voters to the Conservative Party, under the auspices of a 'National' Government led, despite his Labour Party allegiance, by James Ramsay MacDonald.

In France, the crisis accentuated government weakness, ministerial instability, and divisions among the French. In the United States in 1932 it even seemed to threaten revolution: there were riots among unemployed workers and ex-servicemen, and strikes by farmers. In the event, the election of November 1932 saved the day. Herbert Hoover, who had become President in 1928, had seemed to represent prosperity and optimism, but had proved powerless to deal with the crisis. He was soundly beaten by his Democrat rival Franklin Delano Roosevelt, with 22,822,000 votes against 15,762,000.

Fighting the crisis: the international approach

Statesmen and financiers throughout the world were disconcerted by the crisis, and above all by its extent. What was to be done? And on what basis? Should each country try to solve its own problems separately, or could there be an international solution? Until 1933, hesitant efforts were made to find one; but in that year, at the London Conference, Franklin Delano Roosevelt deliberately brought them to a halt.

Once the crisis had reached Europe, the problem of international debt settlements had become virtually insoluble. The idea of writing off all reparations and war debts had again been mooted; and in view of the disaster which had struck Germany in May–June 1931, the then President Herbert Hoover, after a conversation with the US Ambassador in Germany, Frederick M. Sackett, had thought of proposing a year's moratorium on intergovernmental debts. An appeal from the German President Paul von Hindenburg made up Hoover's mind, and on 20 June 1931, he made public his moratorium plan, under which all governmental debt repayments would be suspended for a year. On 20 July a financial conference opened in London; and despite some resistance from France, not yet hit by the crisis, the moratorium was agreed on. It clearly covered both reparations and war debts. But Hoover, true to the traditional policy of the United States, intended to maintain a firm distinction between them.

When the moratorium expired in June 1932, the American Secretary of State Henry Stimson, who had been travelling in Europe, suggested that reparations and war debts should be written off. As a first step, to avoid upsetting American public opinion, could the moratorium not be prolonged for a further year? Hoover totally opposed the idea. 'He told me,' wrote Stimson in his diary on 11 July 1932, 'that he thought that the debts to us could and should be paid.'

The end of debts and reparations

The Europeans had meanwhile been meeting in Lausanne, and had decided – again despite French misgivings – to cancel German reparations. However, they came to a 'gentlemen's agreement' not to ratify the decision until the United States agreed to write off their war debts. It was a vain hope.

The vast majority of American public opinion, as well as the President and Congress, condemned the 'gentlemen's agreement' as 'a European conspiracy'. On principle, and in the absurd belief that annual repayments would help to ease the crisis, they demanded the impossible: that the European countries, already destitute, should continue to pay. The result was that the Europeans, except for 'brave little Finland', suspended payments unilaterally. This encouraged American isolationism, and an international solution to the crisis looked increasingly unlikely.

Before his defeat in the 1932 Presidential election, Herbert Hoover had agreed to a World Economic Conference to be held in London by the League of Nations in the spring of 1933. His Democrat successor, Franklin Delano Roosevelt, appointed as his Secretary of State Cordell Hull from Tennessee, a free-trader and champion of 'economic disarmament'. Hull headed the US delegation when the Conference opened on 12 June 1933. But at the beginning of July, Roosevelt sent the Conference a message declaring that it would be 'a catastrophe amounting to world tragedy' if it were diverted from its main purpose to deal with monetary exchanges. There was to be no 'international' solution. Finally, on 13 January 1934, the United States passed the 'Johnson Act' forbidding even private loans to countries which had not yet paid their war debts.

While the Europeans hesitated, then, the United States clearly forced everyone to seek national solutions to the crisis. The three main types of solution they found were deflation, devaluation, and exchange controls.

Deflation and the gold standard

The first of the three methods, attempted in Germany under Chancellor Heinrich Brüning in 1930-2, and in France until 1936, was deflation. There was no manipulation of the currency, whose value remained fixed against gold; but since that risked making the prices of exports too high for world markets, costs had to be brought down willy-nilly. This could be done by reducing state expenditure, and cutting back wages and salaries. But although apparently logical, it was bound to lead to social unrest. Brüning's 1930 decrees explain why 107 Nazis and 77 Communists won seats at the election of 14 September in that year. Pierre Laval's decrees explain why the Popular Front triumphed in France in 1936. Yet from 1931 to 1935 the gold standard was sustained, in Western Europe, by France, Belgium, Italy, the Netherlands, and Switzerland.

Devaluation

The second way was to manipulate the currency and practise devaluation. This was done successfully by Britain (in September 1931) and the United States (in April 1933), but unsuccessfully by the Popular Front in France (in September 1936). Its main aim was to stimulate exports by lowering their price on the world market. To succeed, it had to keep internal prices more or less stable; but since it made imported goods more expensive, there had to be either high tariffs to limit their inflow (the American system) or an advantageous source of cheap raw materials (the British system of Imperial Preference, applied to the Dominions by the Ottawa Agreement of 1932, and extended to the Crown Colonies in 1933).

Exchange controls

The third option, unlike the other two, involved isolation from the world market. This was achieved by exchange controls, adopted by pre-Hitlerite Germany in June 1932, by most of Central Europe and the Balkans, and by some countries in Latin America. In all such cases, the state controlled the import and export of currency. If a foreign producer sold to a purchaser in Germany, say, a certain quantity of goods, the sum he received for them could not leave Germany, thus discouraging imports. The vendor then had a choice. Either he could spend in Germany the money he was owed there, or he could try to reach a 'clearing agreement', whereby he would be paid in his own country by German exporters to it, while they were paid (from his earnings) in Germany.

This system certainly hampered foreign trade. It implied, at least initially, a refusal to settle foreign debts, owing to the impossibility of converting the national currency into foreign exchange. Its attraction was that it enabled a big country like Germany to establish an economic hold over states (in Central Europe and the Balkans) which needed to sell it their products – Romanian oil, Hungarian wheat, Greek tobacco, etc. To repatriate their earnings, these countries had only one expedient: they had to buy German goods. As will be seen, exchange controls could either be used as a temporary expedient, an isolation ward in which to cure a sick economy (Hjalmar Schacht's method), or as a definitive solution intended to secure autarky (Hermann Goering's and Hitler's plan).

DEMOCRACY, BOLSHEVISM, AND FASCISM

Just when Woodrow Wilson was declaring that 'The world must be made safe for democracy', there appeared in Europe or on its frontiers two great political, economic, social, and ideological systems which challenged that very idea. One was Bolshevism, embodied in the Bolshevik party which had emerged in 1933 under Vladimir Ilich Lenin, disciple of Karl Marx and champion of the class struggle. The other was Fascism, founded by the Italian journalist and former socialist Benito Mussolini. The Bolsheviks seized power in Petrograd (now Saint Petersburg) in November 1917. Mussolini took office after the so-called 'March on Rome' (in his case an overnight train-ride) in October 1922. No less significant was the legal assumption of power in Germany, Europe's leading industrial power, by a visionary ex-serviceman, mob orator, and demagogue of genius, Adolf Hitler, on 30 January 1933.

Totalitarianism

Totalitarianism involves sacrificing everything – life, liberty, individual rights – to one supreme ideal. The 'cause' justifies anything: treachery, lies, cruelty, massacre, genocide. There is a single, obligatory doctrine, the ideology of the state. In democracy, by contrast, the end cannot justify the means. The only true cause is the human being – every human being. Its best symbol is the doctrine of human rights.

Everyone has the right to do as he or she wishes, provided there be no harm to others. As compared with a totalitarian state, where only *raison d'état* rules and there are no human rights, everyone in a democracy can choose his or her own ideology.

The honeyed promise of Bolshevism was the victory of the proletariat throughout the world. But the nation-state reappeared on the scene as soon as Russia became the 'fatherland of the proletariat'. Fascism, under Mussolini, was less cruel than Nazism under Hitler. Nazi doctrine was a form of ultra-nationalist racism, alleging the superiority of tall blond Aryans (the Indo-Europeans), supposedly better preserved in Germany than elsewhere. The Bolshevik leader Josef Stalin, in the name of the class struggle, organized the massacre of millions of his opponents (in particular the kulaks or prosperous peasants). Adolf Hitler, in the name of racial purity, organized the massacre of millions of Jews. Both Stalin and Hitler established hideous concentration camps where obedient executioners did their best to destroy their prisoners' human dignity, as well as their lives.

The three main groupings in Europe between the wars – Bolsheviks, Fascists, and democracies – exploited their different advantages; but the democracies were less bold, rapid, and efficient than the others. During the 1930s, there was some *rapprochement* between the democracies and the Bolsheviks; but then, suddenly, in 1939, the Bolsheviks and the Nazis made the Nazi-Soviet Pact.

The roots of the Spanish Civil War

One of the most dramatic results of this tripartite division – until the Second World War itself – was the Spanish Civil War. It was very long, lasting nearly three years, and very bloody: a million died, out of a population of 25 million.

To begin with, the Civil War was an internal, Spanish affair. Since 1824, the country had been constantly torn between progressive, democratic, liberal forces, and the forces of ultra-conservatism. No government had permanently healed the breach. This was all the more regrettable in that Spain was anxious to end her isolation. The hopes of the generation of 1898 were still alive. First-rate writers, outstanding composers like Manuel de Falla or Pablo Casals, and some great painters including above all Pablo Picasso, won world reputations; but very often they lived outside Spain, in a less febrile atmosphere better suited to their work.

Moreover, despite remarkable mineral resources and some wholly competitive industrial centres, the Spanish economy was backward. In Spain, the great world crisis took a revolutionary turn. In 1931, the monarchy was overthrown, and there ensued five years of turmoil. In February 1936, the Popular Front came to power as the leading group in terms of votes cast as well as seats won: but if the centre and right had added their votes together they would have had a small majority. This explains why a new *Pronunciamento* was prepared by a number of generals, including Francisco Franco, by many officers, and by the Falange, a political party set up in 1933 and led by José Primo de Rivera, the son of the 1920s dictator. Insurrection broke out on 17 July 1936, four days after the murder of a Royalist politician, José Calvo Sotelo. It was not successful everywhere: hence the war.

Among other things, the Spanish Civil War revealed how deeply Europe was divided. Fascist Italy sent volunteers to assist Franco's insurrection: so did Nazi Germany, whose air force also intervened. Hitler used Spain as a testing-ground for his weapons. On the other side, Spain's Republican government was backed, in theory at least, by France and Britain, because it was democratically elected. But the British government was Conservative, and Léon Blum feared a civil war in France. It was the Soviet Union that gave the Spanish Republicans massive aid. There was thus a confrontation of Fascists, democracies, and Bolsheviks, of which the Fascists were the most determined. Stalin cynically bided his time, waiting for the moment when *rapprochement* with Hitler would enable him to recover the territory lost in March 1918 by the Treaty of Brest-Litovsk. The least that can be said is that the weakness shown by the democracies gave him no incentive for a *rapprochement* with them. Nor should it be forgotten that before 1934 the Soviets regarded the socialists as communism's worst enemies.

The fall of Barcelona in January 1939, followed by that of Madrid in March, put an end to the Spanish Civil War and inaugurated the rule of General Franco – a dictator, but not a thoroughgoing Fascist. He did his best to calm the two Fascist powers that had helped him. The country he had seized was steeped in blood, covered in ruins, and torn by hatred, with hundreds of thousands of refugees received in the direst conditions in France. Franco took every precaution to ensure that Spain was not embroiled in the Second World War.

THE AGE OF ANXIETY

The 1920s and the 1930s produced nothing comparable, in the intellectual sphere, to the immense influence of Adam Smith or the French *philosophes* in the eighteenth century.

Countless writers, of course, published hundreds of books and thousands of articles; and several great names stand out. The German philosopher of history Oswald Spengler produced *Der Untergang des Abendlandes* (*The Decline of the West*) in Germany in 1918, and its English translation in 1926–8 made it an international best-seller. In 1919, Paul Valéry wrote: 'We civilizations know now that we are mortal.' In 1930, the great Spanish philosopher José Ortega y Gasset published *La rebelión de las masas* (*The Revolt of the Masses*). The Russian refugee Nicholas Berdyaev entitled his most famous book *The New Middle Ages*. From 1918 onwards, the Italian economist and future President of the Republic Luigi Einaudi published his 'Political Letters' in the Milan newspaper *Il Corriere della Sera*, analysing the reasons for Europe's decline. His compatriot Guglielmo Ferrerò, a historian and essayist, wrote *La Vecchia Europa e la Nuova* (*The Old Europe and the New*); the German physician and philosopher Karl Jaspers wrote *The European Spirit*, followed in 1931 by *The Spiritual Condition of Our Time*. In 1920 the French geographer Albert Demangeon published *The Decline of Europe*; in 1927 Julien Benda published *La trahison des clercs* (*The Treason of the Intellectuals*) and Henri Massis his *Défense de l'Occident* (*Defence of the West*). In 1937 the English Catholic writer Hilaire Belloc published *The Crisis of Our Civilization*. *The Crisis of Civilization* had also been the title of a book published in 1928 by the Dutch historian Johan Huizinga. The same year saw the publication of *The Crisis of the Modern World*, by René Guenon, and *Le jeune Européen* (*The Young European*) by the novelist Pierre Drieu la Rochelle. In 1931, the poet and dramatist Jules Romains published an essay entitled '*Pour que l'Europe soit*' ('That Europe May Live'), and Edouard Herriot wrote *Europe*.

Even this summary list of works by fairly well-known authors shows that in Germany, France, Spain, Austria, Holland, and Italy, people were convinced that they were living through a dramatic crisis. The comparative rarity of such works in Britain reflected the fact that as yet the British were less conscious of their relative decline, and less accustomed to think in European terms. Curiously, it was two Catholic writers, Hilaire Belloc and G. K. Chesterton, who in Britain seemed most aware of the problem. For them, there was an ideal solution: 'In this crisis, only one choice remains: to cure our ills by restoring the Catholic faith.' The French Catholic writer Jacques Maritain was more realistic. All he asked for was 'a modicum of moral agreement'.

Such intellectual turmoil had little effect on the mass of the people. They, however, were stirred by more fundamental phenomena, and in particular by communism. It sprang, of course, from the words and deeds of outstanding thinkers – Karl Marx, Friedrich Engels, Vladimir Ilich Lenin: but after Lenin's death in 1924, and throughout Josef Stalin's lifetime, it was not its intellectual ingenuity or philosophical finesse that made it attractive. It won recruits because it promised the poor a clear solution and a new order to replace disorder and contradictions.

Nor was it philosophy that made Fascism seductive. Mussolini was no doctrinaire: he was a journalist avid for sensation who encouraged all the excesses of chauvinist nationalism.

Nazism, by contrast, was a doctrine. Hitler expounded it in his autobiography *Mein Kampf* (*My Struggle*), published in 1925 and 1926; his henchman Alfred Rosenberg discussed its racial and cultural theories in *Der Mythus des 20. Jahrhunderts* (*The Myth of the Twentieth Century*). But it was a shabby doctrine, based on the false premise of racial inequality, and exacerbating the worst instincts of the supposedly 'superior' race – domination, brutality, the love of war and mass murder.

Facing economic crisis, the voters – especially in Germany – flocked to the extremist parties, Nazi and Communist, and abandoned the various moderates who represented, however feebly, the old and increasingly neglected European traditions.

Pessimism

A large number of writers at this time both detected and shared a deep psychological malaise.

Paul Valéry, for example, in his *Regards sur le monde actuel* (*Glimpses of the Modern World*, 1931), saw three great influences as having shaped European civilization. One was Rome, which 'gave majesty to institutions and laws'; the second was Christianity, which 'gradually probed the depths of consciousness' and made human beings equal before God; the third was Greece, which made humanity the measure of all things, 'the reference system to which everything must be able to be subjected'. This meant the development of both body and mind. 'As for the mind, it will curb its own excesses, its reveries, and its vague and purely illusory outpourings, by carefully analysing its own judgments, rationally employing its different abilities, and respecting orderly form.' Or so it should. But vast numbers of Europeans were now abandoning the intellectual discipline which once protected them.

The rule of law ceased as soon as war – i.e. force and pillage – replaced 'European order', an element of 'European public law', however imperfect it might be. The absolute national egoism preached by the Fascists, the implacable hatred of the socialist state for its bourgeois neighbours, and its wish to destroy them, made any move towards a *pax romana* impossible. Christianity, more and more threatened by secularism, was no longer a safeguard against the appetites of self-declared supermen. And on Greek humanism Thomas Mann gave his verdict in *Achtung Europa!* (*Warning Europe*, 1938):

> All humanism has an element of weakness, owing to its hatred of fanaticism, its tolerance, and its fondness for indulgent scepticism – in other words, its natural goodness ... What we need today is militant humanism, affirming its virility, and convinced that the principle of liberty, of tolerance, and of free study has no right to let itself be exploited by its enemies' shameless fanaticism. Has European humanism become incapable of resurrection?

General pessimism was the dominant characteristic of European thought between the two World Wars. 'For the moment,' wrote Carl J. Burckhardt, 'it nevertheless seems that the world will be destroyed before one of the great nations of Europe gives up its demand for supremacy ... If we have another fratricidal European war, we shall reach the point where we can only contaminate the rest of the world with our poisons.'

Pessimism was justified: the 'fratricidal war' actually took place. But pessimism sometimes engendered a certain optimism. 'Is it as sure as we are told,' asked Ortega y Gasset, 'that Europe has become decadent and undisciplined, and in a word is abdicating? May its apparent decadence not be a salutary crisis which could enable Europe to become truly European? Is the obvious decadence of European *nations* not *a priori* necessary, so that the United States of Europe should one day be possible, and plurality be replaced by real European unity?' Perhaps: but the historian looking back has to admit that any such birth implied appalling labour pains. Julien Benda admitted as much when he wrote in 1946:

> Spiritually as well as politically, the twentieth century may once again, perhaps, see the making of Europe: but it began with the cruellest and most deliberate affirmation of anti-Europeanism that the world has ever seen ... Today, when the idea of the nation seems to have run its course and become noxious to Europeans, the idea of Europe has emerged. But let us not deceive ourselves. Let us not imagine that this idea will triumph naturally. Let us realize that the idea of the nation, which it seeks to dethrone, will put up strong opposition, prolonged resistance, and very serious obstacles.

It remains all the more moving to see how stubbornly, even in the 1930s, some intellectuals and activists were already campaigning for the United States of Europe.

The optimists

One such was Count Richard Coudenhove-Kalergi, who in 1924 had published 'The Pan-European Manifesto'. In 1939 he published *United Europe*, noting the fact that Americans, Russians, Africans, Asians, and Australians were all familiar with the concepts of 'Europe' and 'European': 'The only people in the world who know nothing of Europe, and do not regard either themselves or their neighbours as Europeans, are the Europeans themselves.' Compared with the 'order' reigning in the United States of America, there was only 'anarchy' among the 'Disunited States of Europe' – 'thirty-four states among which there is no law, no organization, no constitution, no tribunal, no police force, and not even the vaguest form of solidarity in any field whatever ... Here, might is right ... It recalls the darkest days of the Middle Ages, when towns and castles destroyed each other in constant wars.' Europe, despite what the racists wanted, should not be united by force. That would lead to an arms race. But 'the fragmentation of the European market into twenty-eight separate economic areas' led to dumping – 'to the detriment of the working classes ...

Only a great European market of 400 million consumers would offer a way out of the impasse.'

Clearly, 'Pan-Europe' was impossible so long as large parts of Europe were in the hands of dictators. But Coudenhove-Kalergi did not lose hope. He believed that public opinion would eventually realize how absurd and needlessly costly it was for Europe to be fragmented. He saw Switzerland as a working scale model of 'Pan-Europe'. The Pan-Europe Movement strongly emphasized economic affairs: it held a Pan-European Agrarian Conference in Vienna in 1936.

Another activist writer who was less well known but very imaginative was Gaston Riou, the author of several books, including *S'unir ou mourir* (*Unite or Die*), 1929, and *Europe ma patrie* (*Europe my Motherland*). Riou suggested that 'the great man of tomorrow' should persuade all the states to elect a Constituent Assembly, which in turn would set up a 'super-state with its own financial, juridical, diplomatic, and military weapons . . . a real state, united in tariffs, currency, law, diplomacy, and military and naval affairs'. Riou was not content with writing: he also organized a large-scale 'Conference of European Youth' in 1937.

Riou and Coudenhove-Kalergi were not alone. The review *Etats-Unis d'Europe* (*The United States of Europe*) continued to appear; so did many books and pamphlets on the same theme. One of the most celebrated was *The Builders of Europe* (1931), by Count Carlo Sforza, past and future Italian Foreign Minister, who was then in exile from Mussolini's Fascist regime. Towards the end of the decade, too, a group of young militants in Britain founded the Federal Union.

But this whole wave of militancy was a mere trickle compared with the tidal wave of racist nationalism that Adolf Hitler unleashed in Europe.

ADOLF HITLER'S NIGHTMARE EUROPE

Hitler's foreign policy was based on his simplistic dogma of racial inequality. Tall, blond, long-headed 'Aryans', better represented in Germany than elsewhere, were in his view a master race. Only they were truly creative; only they were destined to dominate Europe and later the world. This dogma was spiced with a neo-Darwinian belief in natural selection, according to which only the strong survived.

Since these were the tall, blond, long-headed Aryans – i.e. the Germans – they had the right to dominate others and to exterminate those who threatened the purity of the race.

Since, as we know from specialist studies, the 'races' of Europe have been intermingled since Neolithic times, Hitler's racial theory, the work of an over-confident autodidact, was ludicrously crude. But he had come to power in a well-organized nation-state which in other respects was among the leaders of world civilization. He therefore had immense scope to put his absurd theories into practice. The power of a simplistic and fanatical doctrinaire can end in appalling disaster.

Britain faces Hitler

Hitler's undoubted diplomatic skill contributed largely to his success, which continued until 1941. Until 1942, his method was not at all that of 'total war'. Hitler and his generals adapted the plans for each stage of their conquests to the local situation. The process of territorial acquisition had begun in 1938, and it continued until the last quarter of 1942 – which could be described as the great turning point in the War.

For a year, from the French armistice in June 1940 to the Nazi attack on the Soviet Union on 22 June 1941, Britain stood practically alone against Germany and Italy. She had lost all of the continent except Gibraltar; but the Royal Air Force had prevented an invasion of her own soil. She thereby acquired unique prestige. Moreover, despite enemy jamming, the occupied countries could hear broadcasts from the BBC. True, Britain alone could not win the War: but she seemed 'the saviour of Europe'.

Continental Europe was in the hands of Hitler, from the Russian Front in the East to the Pyrenees in the south-west. Only Sweden and Switzerland were completely neutral, and even they traded with Germany. The Europe of 1942 was both the 'Fortress Europe' that Hitler declared to be impregnable and the 'New Europe' he claimed to be able to establish for a thousand years to come. Two neutral countries governed by dictators, Franco's Spain and the Portugal of Antonio de Oliveira Salazar, played a special role. Neither went to war as Hitler's ally: they even made some concessions to the French Resistance and to escaping Allied pilots; and in June 1943 Britain secured Portuguese permission to establish an air base in the Azores.

Adolf Hitler's 'New Europe'

In the centre lay 'Greater Germany', with some 100 million inhabitants. It stretched from Alsace-Lorraine and Luxembourg in the West to Nemel in the East, and from Schleswig in the North to Slovenia in the South – later, in fact, as far as Trieste on the Adriatic. Hitler had annexed to Germany only those places where German was spoken, but with the curious exception of the Slovenes, whom he regarded as a Germanic people which had lost its language owing to the misfortunes of history.

Directly under the German Reich were the 'protectorates'. The first was Bohemia–Moravia; then came the 'Government-general of Poland', the 'Government-general of the Eastern Territories', and the 'Government-general of the Ukraine' – the embryo of the extra *Lebensraum* or 'living space' that Hitler sought. The protectorates were entrusted to high-ranking Nazis who ruled them with pitiless brutality, especially in Russia under Alfred Rosenberg.

Also directly under the Reich, but governed by military authorities, were the 'occupied territories': Norway, Denmark, the Netherlands, Belgium, the Occupied Zone of France, and Yugoslavia and Greece, except for their 'Italian' parts. In each of these territories, the supreme authority was the *Militärbefehlshaber* or military commandant. In Denmark, the former civil government continued in office, but dealt as little as possible with the occupying power. In Norway, where the legal government had taken refuge in London, and in Greece, where it had gone to Cairo, the Nazis imposed their own puppet governments: the leader of that in Norway, Vidkun Quisling, gave his surname to ordinary usage as the synonym for the traitor he was. In Belgium and the Netherlands there were no real collaborator governments. In France, the government was headed by the aged hero of the First World War, Marshal Philippe Pétain; and the country was divided into different areas. Alsace and Lorraine were annexed, *de facto*, by Germany. The North and the Pas-de-Calais remained until February 1943 under the military commandant in Belgium. But above all, France was cut in two – the Occupied and the Non-occupied Zones. In the former, the French administration remained, but closely controlled by the *Militärbefehlshaber*. In the Non-occupied Zone, the government (established in the spa town of Vichy) was theoretically free, but in fact subject to very heavy German pressure. Relations between France and Germany were in principle dealt with by a German Armistice Commission stationed in Wiesbaden in Germany, some 130 kilometres from the nearest French frontier. But various German authorities were keen to be represented in Paris. The German Foreign Minister, Joachim von Ribbentrop, appointed an ambassador there; Josef Goebbels set up a propaganda section; and the Gestapo was present too.

The Second World War 1939–1945

1939

23 August	Nazi-Soviet Non-aggression Pact
1 September	Nazi attack on Poland
3 September	Britain and France declare war on Nazi Germany; 'Phoney War' in the West
17 September	Russia invades eastern Poland
27 September	Poland capitulates
26 October	Establishment of '*Generalgouvernement*' in Poland under Hans Frank

1940

9 April	Hitler conquers Denmark and Norway
10 May	Winston Churchill becomes British Prime Minister; Nazi attack on the Netherlands, Belgium, and France
10 June	Italy enters the war in alliance with Hitler
13 June	The Nazis reach Paris
16 June	Vichy regime in France under Marshal Philippe Pétain
18 June	General de Gaulle broadcasts appeal to the French from London
25 June	French armistice
June–July	The USSR annexes the Baltic countries (Latvia, Lithuania, Estonia)
July–September	Japan occupies northern Indochina
27 September	German-Italian-Japanese Three-Power Pact

1941

April	German-Italian offensive in North Africa under General Erwin Rommel
6 April	The Nazis occupy Yugoslavia and Greece
13 April	Soviet-Japanese Non-Aggression Pact
22 June	Nazi attack on the USSR
14 August	Franklin Roosevelt and Winston Churchill issue 'Atlantic Charter'
7 December	Japanese attack on Pearl Harbor; beginning of war against the USA
11 December	Nazi Germany and Italy declare war on the USA
25 December	The Japanese take Hong Kong

1942

1 January	Washington Pact: declaration by the Allied 'United Nations' that none would make a separate peace
15 February	Japan conquers Singapore
8 March	The Japanese occupy the Dutch East Indies
2 May	The Japanese conquer Burma
26 May	Anglo-Soviet Alliance
3–7 June	US fleet wins the Battle of Midway
28 June	Second Nazi offensive in Russia
8 November	Allies invade French North Africa
11 November	The Nazis occupy the whole of France

1943

14–24 January	Casablanca Conference (Roosevelt and Churchill)
2 February	Nazi Sixth Army capitulates at Stalingrad
5–13 July	Third Nazi offensive in Russia; Battle of Kursk; Soviet counter-offensive
7 July	Fall of Mussolini
10 July–17 August	Allies capture Sicily
14–24 August	Quebec Conference

8 September	Italy capitulates
12 September	Mussolini freed by the Nazis; Repubblica Sociale Italiana founded (the Republic of Salò)
19–30 October	Allied Foreign Ministers' Conference in Moscow
28 November–2 December	Teheran Conference (Roosevelt, Stalin, and Churchill)

1944

4 June	Allies enter Rome
6 June	Allies invade Normandy
July	'Polish National Liberation Committee' (Lublin Committee) founded
15 August	Allies invade the South of France
25 August	General de Gaulle enters Paris; Liberation of Paris and France
9–18 October	Churchill, Stalin and Eden meet in Moscow
22–25 October	Naval battle of the Philippines
10 December	France and the USSR sign pact of alliance and mutual aid

1945

12 January	Major Soviet offensive on Nazi Eastern Front
4–11 February	Conference of 'Big Three' (Stalin, Roosevelt, and Churchill) at Yalta
26 March	The Americans capture the island of Iwo Jima
12 April	Death of Roosevelt; Harry S. Truman becomes President of the USA
25 April	American and Soviet troops meet at Torgau on the Elbe
28 April	Mussolini killed
30 April	Hitler commits suicide in Berlin; Admiral Dönitz succeeds him as 'Reich President'
2 May	Capitulation of Berlin

7–9 May	Capitulation of Germany in Rheims and Berlin-Karlshorst
23 May	Dönitz's government dissolved by the Allies
5 June	Berlin Four-Power Declaration
21 June	Americans occupy Okinawa
6 August	First atomic bomb dropped, on Hiroshima
8 August	USSR declares war on Japan
9 August	Second atomic bomb dropped, on Nagasaki
21 August	Japanese capitulate to the Red Army in Manchuria
2 September	Japan capitulates
8 September	Americans officially enter Tokyo under General Douglas MacArthur

The last group of countries dominated by Hitler comprised Germany's 'allies', all of which in fact became 'satellites'. The 'alliance' was formed by joining the Tripartite Pact of 27 September 1940, signed by Germany, Italy, and Japan, which proposed to establish a 'New Order in Europe'. The countries that joined were Hungary, Slovakia, and Romania (in 1940), and Bulgaria and Croatia (in 1941). Spain merely promised to join.

Italy, Slovakia, Finland, Hungary, and Romania all declared war on the USSR. Spain sent a 'blue legion' of volunteers to fight there. The satellite status of Germany's allies was made obvious in several ways: the presence of German troops, the autonomous existence of Nazi parties for German minorities such as the 60,000 Germans in Hungary, the complete or partial seizure of power by Fascist parties (the 'Iron Guard' in Romania, the 'Ustase' in Croatia, the 'Arrow Cross' in Hungary), and much anti-semitic legislation.

Hitler's economic Europe

In parallel with this political hierarchy, Hitler's 'New Europe' also formed a vast economic grouping run by Germany for its own ends.

To add to her own farm and factory production, she devised various methods of appropriating from others. To begin with, the exchange rate was rigged in favour of the occupying forces: in France, for example, the rate of 20 francs to the mark was twice the latter's real value. Furthermore, Germany imported much more than she exported, but since she imposed exchange controls, her debts were only partially cleared. Thus by August 1944 France had 163,327 million francs on deposit in Berlin. The French State – as Pétain's government called the erstwhile Republic – had had to advance the money to pay its own exporters. Now, with no way of using it, all this had to be written off. A third means of extortion was the 'Occupation Indemnity'. In the case of France, this amounted to 400 million francs a day, then 300 million, then (in November 1942) 500 million, and even (in June 1944) 700 million. In all, France paid 681,866 million francs – whereas the real cost of the Occupation has been estimated at 74,000 million, a mere eighth of that sum. One French representative estimated that the country had paid 'enough to keep an army of 18 million men'. Fourthly, under various pretexts, Germany seized gold, stocks, and shareholdings, some of them in French or other factories (including press concerns), others shares in foreign firms held by nationals of the occupied power. In this way, France had to give up her shares in the Bor mines in Yugoslavia, in Romanian oil, and in Hungarian banks. Finally, a fifth way of exploiting the situation of wartime restrictions was to authorize various German groups to make large-scale 'black market' deals.

Altogether it was systematic pillage; and Hermann Goering, Hitler's Planning Commissioner, made no bones about it. On 6 August 1942, he told the Commissioners for Occupied Territories: 'In the past, it was called pillage. Today, we are much less frank. Never mind. I intend to pillage, and to pillage thoroughly.'

In December 1944, Dr Hans-Richard Hemmen, head of the economic section of the Military Command in France, admitted that: 'More and more of France's economic strength was drained away to meet Germany's needs. So that the French economy, including its production of raw materials and munitions, was finally used almost exclusively for German ends.'

Naturally, such pillage was much more ruthless in the countries of Eastern Europe, where the Nazi leaders made no secret of their indifference to the fate of millions of Poles or Russians starving to death.

Nazi Germany's 'allies' were not spared either, especially towards the end of the War. Hungary, for instance, already an important supplier of food, was controlled from 1943 onwards so as to ensure, as the German Armaments Minister Albert Speer said in March 1944, 'the best possible exploitation of Hungarian industrial capacity, in line with German needs'. Hungary, like France, was also obliged to pay occupation expenses and in effect write off German debts. During the first nine months of 1944, 692,000 of her 760,000 tons of bauxite production went to Germany, as did 641,000 of the 825,000 tons of oil she produced.

Foreign workers

Another form of economic exploitation was the conscription of foreign labour to work either locally on fortifications built by the 'Todt Organization', or in Germany itself.

This became settled policy only in 1942. Before then, the Nazis had let two million Soviet prisoners die of hunger rather than use them as labourers. Even as late as March 1943, the Nazi Governor of the Ukraine, Erich Koch, declared: 'We are a master race, which must remember that the lowliest German worker is racially and biologically a thousand times more valuable than the population here.' In fact, German workers were often put into uniform to fill the gaps at the front, and they had to be replaced. In February 1942 the able young architect Albert Speer was appointed Minister of Armaments and Munitions, and a *Gauleiter*, Fritz Sauckel, who was a former sailor and had been a member of the Nazi party since 1921, was given the title 'Plenipotentiary General for Labour Mobilization'. With the utmost brutality, Sauckel recruited a veritable army of civilian foreign workers to add to the prisoners of war and the political and racial prisoners from the concentration camps. In the case of the Jews, women, children, and old men were exterminated, while men were worked until they dropped.

Altogether, Hitler's 'New Europe' can be reckoned an economic success for Germany – but for her alone. Despite Allied bombing, production increased in 1943. For Germans, the standard of living remained acceptable at a time when the occupied countries were reduced to destitution and even famine, especially in Greece and occupied Russia.

Psychologically, the Nazis and their Minister of Propaganda Dr Josef Goebbels did their best to cement unity in 'the New Europe'. But the task was difficult when the future being promised was domination by the Master Race. Goebbels therefore sought short-term remedies. The whole of the press was strictly controlled if not actually owned by the occupying power, which lavishly rewarded those journalists who agreed to act as its spokesmen.

However, after the Battle of Stalingrad and the Allied landings in North Africa, the public in the occupied countries knew how to read between the lines.

The Anti-Bolshevik Crusade

In search of a common cause, the Nazis hit on the notion of an 'Anti-Bolshevik Crusade'.

'I want Germany to win,' said Pierre Laval, the French Vichy Minister, 'because, without her, Bolshevism would triumph everywhere.' The slogan had some effect on part of the population, but only extreme right-wing militants acted on their anti-communist ideas. In France, a 'League of French Volunteers Against Bolshevism' recruited some 3,000 or 4,000 soldiers who wore German uniforms. A smaller 'Tricolour Legion' was formed and sent to fight on the Russian Front, this time in French uniforms. Similar efforts were made in the other occupied countries. Everywhere, an active propaganda campaign vaunted the exploits of the *Waffen SS*, and sought to recruit stalwart Aryan types thought worthy to join it. All Resistance movements were dismissed as 'communist'. The United States and Britain were described as decrepit countries: America, especially, was said to be corrupted by Blacks and Jews. Old international grievances were resuscitated – Waterloo, Fashoda, even Joan of Arc. The Jews were accused of every evil, echoing medieval anti-semitism. The press and the radio jeered at democracy as a Jewish invention. Human rights were abolished, and especially individual liberty: anyone could be arrested at any moment and shot as a 'hostage'. But the greatest horror of the Hitlerite system was its use of genocide.

The concentration camps and the massacre of the Jews

Unable to attract supporters for their 'New Europe', the Nazis opted for repression. In retrospect, this can be seen as the keystone of their system.

Hitler had first established 'concentration camps' to intern German political leaders and militants, and especially communists. Later, with the help of Heinrich Himmler and the SS, he extended them to all the countries under his control. They in fact became a Nazi trademark. From Estonia to the Vosges, the death camps created a 'concentration universe'. Its refinements are too notorious to need labouring here.

Given that six million Jews were exterminated by the Nazis (2,500,000 in the gas chambers, 2,000,000 in the Ukraine, 400,000 in the Warsaw ghetto, and so on), Hitler's 'New Europe' was clearly the negation of all humanity, on a scale unprecedented in the history of the world. 'I should like,' said Hitler in his *Table Talk* (*Hitlers Tischgespräche im Führerhauptquartier*, 1941–2), 'to see no one suffer, and to do no harm to anyone. But when I see that the human race is in danger, my feelings are replaced by icy reason.' To massacre six million Jews, and millions of others, on the basis of a pseudo-scientific doctrine: that was how Adolf Hitler used his 'icy reason'.

True, he really wanted to build a 'New Europe' of *Lebensraum* and economic autarky. 'Later generations,' he declared, 'will certainly accept, without the slightest demur, the unification of Europe that we are on the point of achieving, just as the majority of our contemporaries see Bismarck's founding of the German Empire as no more than a simple episode in history. People will soon forget the enormous labours involved in merging Northern, Western, Central, and Eastern Europe into a single entity.' Such a Europe, he added, would not be built 'by the efforts of a number of politicians devoted to the cause of unity, but created by force of arms'.

There was great rejoicing when the force of other arms put paid to such a monstrosity.

European reactions

In the face of the occupying forces, people tended to react in one of three main ways: 'collaboration', 'wait and see', or 'resistance'.

Except in a few of Germany's 'allies', collaborators were always a minority of the population; or else they tried, as in Finland (which saw the USSR as the enemy and needed German aid), to maintain a democratic organization. In almost every case, collaborators were recruited either in extreme right-wing circles, ideologically converted to Fascism and terrified of Bolshevism, or from among those who believed in German victory and thought it best to flatter the conquerors. Others were simply prepared to sell themselves to the highest bidder. In most of the occupied countries, the mass of people preferred to 'wait and see'. To begin with, they were aghast, then perhaps reassured for the moment by the disciplined, 'correct' appearance of German soldiers. Very soon, they began to detest their conquerors. But for various reasons they avoided serious conflict, and often pretended to ignore the occupying power.

Daily life, moreover, was hard enough to take up all the time and attention of ordinary men and women. Ever more severe rationing was imposed, not only because there were no more tropical products such as coffee, chocolate, tea, bananas, peanuts, etc., but above all on account of German requisitioning. A normal adult diet amounts to 2,400 calories a day. Below 1,600, death is likely in a matter of months. No wonder that in a country like France, where the official ration provided barely 1,200 calories in the towns, people were obsessed by food. France suffered no severe famine as in Greece – where the streets were littered with corpses no one was strong enough to bury – or Holland, where in the winter of 1944–5 people ate tulip bulbs. But many old, poor, ill, and lonely people starved to death. In countries with mixed farming, country-dwellers fared best.

A minority of the occupied peoples, finally, refused to wait passively for the war to end, and threw themselves into active resistance. Many of the first were idealists, nationalists resenting defeat and oppression, and anti-Fascists determined to destroy totalitarian regimes. After Hitler's attack on Russia on 22 June 1941, the various Communist Parties swung into organized resistance. Some individual communists had already taken the plunge. But truly mass resistance, throughout Europe, began only in 1943. Many Soviet historians ascribe this to the Battle of Stalingrad – which is certainly true for the USSR and for parts of Eastern Europe. Elsewhere, however, mass resistance was sparked off mainly by Gauleiter Sauckel's conscription of forced labour. Rather than go to work in Germany, hundreds of thousands of workmen and young people went into hiding and a clandestine way of life. How could they live without ration cards? The existing resistance circuits, with their own secret resources, now had an unprecedented supply of recruits. Guerrilla warfare very much needed 'outlaws'.

Resistance took various forms: guerrilla attacks were only its culmination. Geography influenced its methods as much as politics. The more mountainous and wooded the terrain, the fewer the roads, and the more isolated the farms, the easier it was to conceal partisan groups (known in France as the *maquis* from the French word for 'heathland' or 'scrub'). In Italy, for example, armed resistance developed more in the Alps and the Appenines than in the Po Valley; while in France it focused more on Brittany and the south than on the plains of the north. Yugoslavia, with its mountains, was ideal for partisan warfare: so were Greece and Slovakia; so were the vast forests of Russia and Byelorussia.

The risk to be faced was death, or at the very least a concentration camp, in both cases after appalling torture. Nor was the ordinary population spared. Increasingly, the Nazis exacted collective reprisals, as in the case of Oradour-sur-Glane, where the population was massacred by the German *Das Reich* division, which had suffered at the hands of the partisans. The result was the emergence of grim, hard leaders, impatient of weakness and obliged to punish without mercy. In some cases, when their countries were liberated, they wreaked terrible revenge. But these shadows in no way disguise the admirable role of those who dared to fight for freedom against Hitler's 'New Europe'. Their courage had symbolic as well as practical importance.

After the War, thanks to the writings of Mao Zedong and to much recent history, the strategic importance of guerrilla warfare came to be more widely understood.

The Liberation

In the face of 'Fortress Europe', firmly held by the Nazis, the Western Allies – the United States and the United Kingdom – had a choice of several strategies. But unless they were to allow the Russians to bear the full brunt of the War, with all the political and psychological consequences which that would involve, they had sooner or later to contemplate opening a Second Front. Moreover, at their first Atlantic meeting, off Newfoundland on 9–12 August 1941, the Americans and the British had agreed to give priority to the struggle against Nazi Germany. The Americans did so because like Clausewitz they believed in attacking the strongest enemy at his strongest point; the British because only some thirty kilometres of the Channel lay between them and Hitler's 'New Europe'.

In fact, Europe was liberated from outside.

In the East, the Red Army, at a cost of some 20 million Soviet lives both civilian and military, 'broke the back' of the German army, as Winston Churchill put it. After defeating the Wehrmacht's massive assault on Kursk in July 1943, the Russian army advanced westwards. It reached the Vistula in the summer of 1944, the Oder in January 1943, and Berlin in April 1945. On 30 April, Adolf Hitler killed himself in his Berlin *Blockhaus* near the Brandenburg Gate.

In the West, the countries of Europe were liberated after Anglo-American landings in Sicily (July 1943), southern Italy (September 1943), Normandy (6 June 1944), and Provence (15 August 1944).

Far worse than Napoleon's Europe, Hitler's Europe had proved unendurable.

CONCLUSION

The world's leading continent, richer, more powerful, and more advanced scientifically than any other, Europe virtually destroyed itself in the thirty-year period between 1914 and 1945. The First World War of 1914–18 was followed from 1918 to 1939 by the illusion of peace, and from 1939 to 1945 by a Second World War. Some, like Winston Churchill and General Charles de Gaulle, called this whole period a 'thirty years' war'.

That thirty-year period is perhaps one of the saddest in European history. Writers and thinkers from all over Europe realized and lamented the fact. All the great political and economic forces seemed to conspire against any sense of community. As we have seen, the US President Woodrow Wilson, who helped to resolve the First World War in favour of the Allies, was an advocate of 'world' solutions, and opposed the European balance of power, which he thought had caused the War. Russia, which became 'Bolshevik' and in 1922 became the USSR, was ideologically opposed to all other governments, including and especially socialist regimes. 'Socialism in one country' amounted to a new and vigorous form of nationalism. Soviet policy, which until 1939 was isolationist, did not rule out a tactical *rapprochement* with Nazi Germany. Although in the 1930s the USSR had attacked Hitler and acted as a champion of the League of Nations, Stalin – whose dictatorship and reign of terror were comparable to Hitler's – suddenly signed a pact with him on 23 August 1939, and remained his ally for nearly two years, until Hitler declared war on Russia on 22 June 1941. In the face of democracies that were dispirited (France), in favour of 'appeasement' (Britain), or isolationist (the United States), there arose efficient and brutal new regimes. Fascism in Italy was led by the anti-democratic, ultra-nationalist dictator Benito Mussolini, who seized power after the so-called 'March on Rome' in October 1922. In Germany, later, came Nazism, led by Adolf Hitler, who took power legally on 30 January 1933, and within a few weeks turned the country into a dictatorship and added racism to a basically Fascist creed. Both Fascism and Nazism favoured paramilitary formations: the Italian Blackshirts, the brown-shirted SA or *Sturmabteilung* of the Nazis, and finally the SS or *Schutzstaffel*.

Between 1933 and 1943, Hitler's policy of blackmail and force nullified those clauses of the Versailles Treaty which imposed burdens on Germany; brought all Germans together in a 'Greater Germany'; in 1940 destroyed the power of France, the 'hereditary enemy'; and began to acquire *Lebensraum* or living space.

It was when Hitler attacked the USSR on 22 June 1941, that he entered the road that led him to ruin. His 'New Europe', founded on racism and massacre, would have reduced its countries to slavery.

19

Europe's Recovery and Resurgent Hopes

IN THE WAKE OF DISASTER: THE PROPOSALS OF JULY 1948

The partitioning of Europe

The sight of ruins can sometimes strengthen people's resolve. From the War and the Resistance onwards, but above all after the Nazi capitulation, many Europeans felt that the sheer scale of Europe's devastation obliged them to start afresh. What they must do was heal past wounds and mend rifts – bring about, in fact, a profound and historic reform by uniting, in whatever fashion, the different European states.

Europe in 1945 was already partitioned. Not, as is too often alleged, by the Conference held at Yalta on 4–11 February 1945, but by the advance of the Red Army and the agreements reached in December 1944 on the zones of occupation in Germany. It might even be said that what remained of the 'spirit of Yalta' – that last flicker of friendship between the Eastern and Western Allies who had fought for a common cause – actually delayed the attempt to unite Europe. One of the principles of Soviet foreign policy at that time would seem to have been to prevent in every way the formation of blocs among Russia's neighbours, and to instil this idea into not only the French and Italian Communist Parties, but also those of the Middle East. Until the end of 1947, while private groups and associations, movements and committees and articles in the press never stopped promoting the grand design of European union, those countries where the communists were powerful, notably France and Italy, affected a stance of neutrality or arbitration between the Soviet Union and the United States.

Under General de Gaulle until January 1946 and Georges Bidault until July 1947, France claimed to be pursuing a policy of 'balance' between East and West. Negatively, this led the French to keep their occupation zone in Germany out of the Anglo-American 'bizone' proposed in Stuttgart on 6 September 1946, by the US Secretary of State James Byrnes. On the positive side, the only 'major' success was the adoption of the 'French line' when fixing the Yugoslav frontier in the region of Trieste – though the choice was less a triumph of French diplomacy than a compromise between the American line, further East, and the Soviet line, further to the West. How could France be a mediator when she had lost her prewar status?

The communists, who were hostile *a priori* to any idea of a 'Western bloc', sabotaged all attempts at unification where they had members in the government, as in France and Italy in the first years after the War. The French Constitution of October 1946, passed by a very small majority, little more than a third of those eligible to vote, contained a promising sentence in its Preamble: 'Provided that there is reciprocity, France agrees to those limitations of sovereignty that are necessary to the organization and defence of peace.' But this referred rather to the United Nations Organization, on a world scale, than to any European organization that might later be formed.

Italy, where a referendum had replaced the monarchy with a republic, played a full part in the Western community after the general election of April 1948, which saw the collapse of the pro-Soviet or at least neutralist 'Popular Democratic Front'.

Public opinion and Europe

Attentive to political events, but preoccupied by austerity and crises, much of public opinion ignored the communists' systematic efforts and began to place some of its hopes in a possible European union. So European countries were no longer 'great powers'? How then could they restore their greatness? By closer links with their colonies? In 1948 this hardly seemed likely, at least for France, Britain, Italy, and the Netherlands. But could they not recover their influence (or just the independence to which they were accustomed) by transcending their own narrow frontiers and forming a larger European entity? It could take any of countless different forms. Some, from among the French Resistance and the Dutch and Belgian socialists, wanted a federal Europe. In June 1944, a 'European Parliamentary Committee' was founded in Lyon. From Algiers came proposals made by General de Gaulle, inspired in particular by Jean Monnet and by the future Prime Minister René Mayer. As the War ended, other movements were formed, like the 'European Union of Federalists' set up in December 1946 and comprising some fifty different groups. In the words of the French historian Pierre Gerbet, their Congress in Montreux, in August 1947, 'was the first European demonstration in the post-War years'.

On the left, some argued that Europe and socialism must be achieved together. The Christian Democrats, meanwhile, formed the *Nouvelles équipes internationales* (literally, New International Teams) in March 1947. The Liberals wanted to go no further than a confederation or 'Commonwealth'. Winston Churchill, by then in opposition in Britain, advocated 'a kind of United States of Europe'; but he saw it as confined to the continent, and sought a more independent role for Britain herself. In France, the advocates of less demanding forms of unity included Raoul Dautry, André Siegfried, Paul Bastid, Paul Ramadier, Paul Reynaud, and Pierre-Henri Teitgen, all members of the 'French Committee for Europe'.

The Hague Congress

All these strands of opinion – federalists and centralizers, free-traders and *dirigistes*, left and right – were represented at the great Congress of Europe held in The Hague on 7–10 May 1948. It was a unique occasion, and one unlikely to be repeated on such a scale. For a time, anything and everything seemed possible. The Congress was chaired by Winston Churchill, and it brought together some 800 eminent people from all over Western Europe: Members of Parliament, ministers, former ministers, trade union leaders, writers, journalists, university teachers. Among them, leading a fifty-strong delegation, was the President of the German Christian Democrats, Konrad Adenauer. The Congress's cultural commission was headed by the Spanish writer Salvador de Madariaga, with the Swiss Denis de Rougemont as its *rapporteur*. In its final resolutions, the Congress called for the merging of certain national sovereign powers, in preparation for economic and political union, the establishment of a European Assembly, and the creation of a European Court of Human Rights.

To pursue these ends, the Congress set up a liaison committee which on 25 October 1948 officially became the 'European Movement'. This had four Honorary Presidents: Winston Churchill (whose son-in-law Duncan Sandys was extremely active in the movement), Léon Blum from France (later replaced by Robert Schuman), Alcide De Gasperi from Italy, and Paul-Henri Spaak from Belgium. There was a national Council of the European Movement in each of the member countries.

Georges Bidault's statement

The Congress of Europe in The Hague was a private venture; but it brought about official action by the public authorities, the governments. Now was the time, even in Italy, when the policy of 'balance' and 'third-force' neutrality began to be replaced by that of Western alliances. The decisive step was taken on 20 July 1948. At a meeting in The Hague of the five governments which in March of that year had signed the Brussels Pact (France, Britain, the Netherlands, Belgium, and Luxembourg), the French Foreign Minister Georges Bidault declared: 'This is a moment, perhaps unique in history, when Europe can begin to be built. So the governments must support this movement and fulfil the aspirations it represents.' He then made two proposals. One was for the five nations to form a customs and economic union open to all European countries that wished to join. The other was to establish a European Assembly, 'representing not only our parliaments but also those of the other states that wish to take part in this great and noble endeavour'.

This was in fact a turning point in European history – or a point of departure. For the first time, a government was making an official proposal with a view to uniting Europe. And while the notion of supranationality was not explicitly mentioned, Bidault's plan by no means ruled it out. Before 1914, the idea of Europe had always implied the 'balance of power'. Now, the objective was some form of unity; and in this Bidault was speaking for a current of opinion strongly backed, in particular, by the Christian Democrat movements which had become influential in a number of countries, including Austria, Belgium, France, Germany, Italy, and Luxembourg.

The political results were considerable; but before examining them it may be worthwhile to look at the circumstances which led to this new departure, limited as it was to Western Europe.

The Iron Curtain

It was Winston Churchill who declared, on 5 March 1946, at Fulton, Missouri, that 'an iron curtain has descended across the continent'. The advance of the Soviet Red Army, and the decisions taken over the demarcation lines, had the unexpected effect of cutting Europe in two, with an almost impregnable frontier between its Eastern and Western halves. The 'Prague coup' of 24 February 1948, which completed the tally of communist governments in Eastern Europe, left no doubt possible. From that moment on, Western Europe found itself isolated from Central and Eastern Europe, with the partial exceptions of Finland and of Greece, which was still suffering from a communist-inspired civil war. A quite new type of threat now loomed over the West.

Europe impoverished

The main economic problem facing West Europeans after 1945 was that of the 'dollar gap'. Hungry and impoverished, with their capital equipment half-destroyed, all the nations of Western Europe urgently needed both machinery and food. The only country whose economy the War had not damaged, but developed, was the United States of America. How could Europeans buy foodstuffs and machine tools from America if they had virtually no foreign currency or gold? And how could they earn foreign currency if their industries could not export because they had not been revived?

Haunted by the idea of 'full employment', the Americans thought it right to supply dollars to the Europeans by artificial means. At first they gave ad hoc aid, case by case. This ruled out any overall planning of Europe's recovery; but at least it kept the patient alive, with the help of various loans, cut-price supplies of US army surplus products, and so on.

Then, in the face of growing dangers and of Britain's withdrawal from the Eastern Mediterranean, the Americans proposed an organized system of aid spread over several years, consisting mainly of gifts. President Harry S. Truman announced the 'Truman Doctrine' on 12 March 1947, with a programme of economic and military aid for Greece and Turkey; and on 5 June 1947 General George Marshall unveiled the 'Marshall Plan' of aid to the whole of Europe, including – if she had accepted it – the USSR.

The Marshall Plan, or European Recovery Program, as it was officially called, was not approved by the US Congress until April 1948. Meanwhile, however, a really serious crisis had broken out in the autumn of 1947. In France and Italy, in particular, the communists had been excluded from the government, and the response had been a series of paralysing strikes.

Faced with new economic difficulties and a growing pre-revolutionary mood, the Europeans saw their financial reserves draining away. For Georges Bidault, the critical period began on 15 October 1947. In response to urgent requests for 'interim aid', General Marshall persuaded President Truman to call a special session of Congress. This voted enough money to tide France and Italy over until Marshall Aid arrived, and prevented either of them swinging over to the communist camp. It was one reason, no doubt, for the Christian Democrat victory in the Italian election of April 1948.

The preponderance of the United States

The United States was convinced that a united Europe would be better able to stand up to the communist threat than a scatter of small countries. The Americans also remembered their own history and the federation of the thirteen colonies. So they pressed for federation in Europe. They rather minimized the difficulties – Europeans' long history, lingering bitterness caused by pitiless wars, and the multiplicity of languages. The pressure came less from the administration than from Congress, which tried to make its aid depend upon the Europeans achieving unity. The Americans' insistence that the Europeans get together to share out Marshall Aid was in part a result of this Congressional pressure, which sometimes embarrassed the administration. Economically, the Marshall Plan was very important to Europe's recovery: but its institutions – the Organization for European Economic Cooperation (OEEC) and the European Payments Union (EPU) – made little political impact. The Americans always had a grandiose and simplified vision: they tended to underestimate the difference between Europe's situation and that of the thirteen colonies in 1776; but they did understand the need to go beyond narrow national frontiers.

The Marshall Plan, moreover, paved the way for just such further progress. The young and brilliant technocrats of the Economic Cooperation Administration, which ran the Marshall Plan, were in constant contact with the French Planning Commissioner, Jean Monnet; and many of them formed extremely close links with him. Monnet's American admirers, during the Fourth Republic and under de Gaulle's Presidency, facilitated the immense influence he had on some US Presidents, and especially on J. F. Kennedy. But that, of course, was not yet evident in 1948.

The Soviet threat

It was in 1947 that the 'Cold War' became a fact of life. The two great Allies of the Second World War had become potential enemies; and when the Prague coup took place the risk of a Third World War seemed greater than ever before. Western defence experts estimated that a Soviet offensive could reach Brest in a fortnight. General Clay, the US Military Governor in Germany, sent a telegram to the head of the intelligence service saying that he thought that 'war could break out with dramatic suddenness'.

On 30 March 1948, Marshal V. D. Sokolovsky, head of the Soviet occupation forces in Germany, imposed restrictions on rail traffic coming into Berlin from the West (the 'little blockade'); and on 24 June he halted such traffic. Soon, the ban was extended to canal and road transport, and by 4 August 1948, the city was under siege (the 'big blockade'). Its only supplies of food, fuel, men, and mail from the West had to be flown in by the fifteen-month 'airlift' of 200,000 flights carrying 1.5 million tons of supplies.

Not surprisingly, the events of which this was a climax led the West to think in terms of alliance. On 17 March 1948 came the Brussels Pact – planned long before the Prague coup; and in April Ernest Bevin, the British Foreign Secretary, proposed expanding it to develop a plan for security on an Atlantic basis. On 11 June, the US Senate voted a Resolution from Senator Arthur H. Vandenberg calling for regional arrangements and 'mutual aid'; and it was with this backing that US officials began to prepare what became the North Atlantic Treaty. Such was the background – of crisis but also of hope for strengthening the West – against which Georges Bidault made his European proposal of 20 July 1948.

The division of Germany

Up to and including the time of the Yalta Conference in February 1945, all the wartime Allies had said that they wanted Germany dismembered. When Josef Stalin, in a celebrated speech on 9 May 1945, announced that Germany would one day be reunified, the British and Americans realized at once that Germany had become a stake in East–West relations. As a result, they reasoned, they could not afford to lose German sympathy by continuing to insist on dividing or sharing out German territory. Only France disagreed with their conclusion. Like Marshal Foch before him, General de Gaulle called for Germany to part with the Rhineland.

When de Gaulle resigned as Prime Minister on 20 January 1946, Georges Bidault continued his policy, first as President and later as Foreign Minister, until the end of 1947. On 1 January that year, following a speech in Stuttgart on 6 September 1946 by the US Secretary of State James Byrnes, Britain and the United States merged their occupation zones of Germany into a 'bizone'; but France refused. In March 1947, however, at a meeting of the four Foreign Ministers, Bidault noted that the British and the Americans were willing to accept dismemberment on a small scale, by allowing the Saar to be attached economically to France, subject to its status being reviewed when there was a peace treaty. The USSR was totally opposed to the arrangement; but, combined with the Soviet military threat, it triggered off a profound change in French foreign policy. On 5 December 1947, at the subsequent London meeting of the four powers, Bidault announced that he was prepared to treat Germany as a single economic entity, provided that the Saar be attached economically to France. From 15 December onwards, the 'bizone' began to be the 'trizone'.

This led eventually to the establishment of West Germany, the Federal Republic, given the Soviet refusal to respect previous arrangements. The key meeting was the London Conference in the following spring: the London agreements of June 1948 set in motion the procedure whereby the constitution of a future West German State was to be drawn up by the representatives of the *Länder* and submitted for approval to the three Military Governors. When Georges Bidault made his proposal on 20 July, therefore, he was aware that a German state might well re-emerge. The German problem, as will be seen, had a key role in the development of Community Europe.

THIRTY YEARS OF EUROPEAN PROSPERITY

European economic growth

Before looking at the successive political decisions involved in the 'building of Europe', it is as well to consider the context in which they were reached. Numerous issues could be studied – in particular the East–West conflict, and its internal corollary, the influence of West European Communist Parties, which were anti-European on principle. But it may be best to concentrate on two major developments which until 1974–75 – i.e. for some thirty years – were generally helpful to the European idea. One was Western Europe's formidable economic growth. The other was the cessation of colonial rivalry owing to the end of Empire.

Thirty years of prosperity: the French economist and sociologist Jean Fourastié has nicknamed them 'Thirty Glorious Years', *les trentes glorieuses*. The allusion in English is to the 'Sixty Glorious Years' of Victorian prosperity. In French, the comparison is with a famous episode in the history of France. The revolution of 1830, which overthrew the elder branch of the Bourbon dynasty, succeeded in three days, 26, 27 and 28 July. Those three days have been called *les trois glorieuses*, 'the glorious three'. Just over a century later, the number was thirty, not three, and the units were years, not days. However, even a long period of quantitative growth could not guarantee universal happiness; it blinded some to the seamy side of growth; and it concealed some extremes of inequality.

Furthermore, economists have detected in this thirty-year period an alternation between phases of startling prosperity and those which, while hardly crises, can be called recessions. Nor was the pace of growth identical in all countries, although taken as a whole the results were much the same. Only one country lagged behind. That was Britain.

In twenty-three years, British industrial production only doubled. That of Germany multiplied by five, that of France by four. This has been called 'an accentuation of backwardness'. There was talk of a 'British sickness', sometimes said to be the result of achieving the 'welfare state' too rapidly, assisting and protecting people to the point of instilling a 'welfare mentality' and sapping their initiative. At the beginning of the century, Britain had been the world's biggest trading power. By 1973, she had dropped to fifth place, behind the United States, Federal Germany, Japan, and France – though in 1976 she overtook France once again.

The American economist Charles P. Kindleberger, in his book *Economic Growth in France and Britain 1851–1950*, estimates that France developed at the same pace during those hundred years, and that from 1945 onwards a new form of 'Saint-Simonism' gave France a will to expand and grow that promised a very bright future. After the oil crisis of 1974–5, this turn of speed was checked. Renewed growth in Britain caused an eminent French economic historian, François Crouzet, to entitle a book in 1985: *De la supériorité de l'Angleterre sur la France: L'économique et l'imaginaire, XVIIe–XXe siècles* (*On the Supremacy of Britain over France: The Economic and the Imaginary from the Seventeenth to the Twentieth Century*).

One of the most interesting cases is that of Spain. After a period of economic stagnation in the first half of the nineteenth century, she rapidly developed her mining industries in the second. The Civil War, and the 'quarantine' into which Franco's Spain was banished, kept the country economically weak. Then a number of factors combined to bring about what might be called 'the great mutation of 1958–65'. They included American and Argentine aid, the opening of frontiers, and the growth of tourism. Spain then followed the Western model, joining the International Monetary Fund and the Organization for Economic Co-operation and Development (OECD), the broader successor to OEEC. Closer links were forged with the United States and her Harvard-trained economists, and also with the relatively authoritarian France of General de Gaulle, who sent the economist Jacques Rueff to advise on the Spanish economy. A substantial reform of the banking system, the adoption of an indicative development plan, and an injection of foreign capital, all helped to stimulate growth. In the decades following 1960, Spain had an annual average industrial growth rate of 9 per cent – a figure surpassed only by Japan and South Korea. The results were especially striking in iron and steel, shipbuilding, car manufacture, and electrical equipment. Spain was called 'the world's tenth economic power'. This partly explains her entry into the European Community in 1985.

The decline of European creativity

During these optimistic years, the growth of science and technology, coupled with the rapid rise in purchasing power, which in Western Europe doubled between 1955 and 1973, transformed human life, putting past 'golden ages' in more sober perspective. Yet it has to be recognized that if Europe had a monopoly of inventions in the nineteenth century, she was outclassed in the second half of the twentieth. The Soviet Union was the first to launch a satellite, the 'Sputnik', around the Earth, followed by the first manned spacecraft; the United States was the first to put a man on the moon. Western Europe's scientific research certainly surpassed that of Eastern Europe, which was hampered by undue secrecy and control, especially in the USSR; but in developing and exploiting inventions, Western Europe lagged far behind the United States and Japan.

It would be impossible to list here all the inventions which, at an ever faster pace, have revolutionized the way people live. They cover every field: the proliferation of synthetic materials and products, developments in electronics, telecommunications and television, miniaturization, and successive generations of computers, robots, and automated machine-tools.

One of the most fundamental discoveries, made shortly before the Second World War, was that of how to split the atom. The first applications, from 1945 onwards, were military, and they overshadowed the world with a terrible threat. Then, between 1950 and 1960, nuclear power stations began to be built. The oil crisis of 1973 onwards contributed to their success: but it was a qualified success, because the deliberate or accidental destruction of a nuclear reactor could be a very large-scale catastrophe. Great strides were also made in aeronautics, in jet engines, and in medicine and biology, both of which considerably increased the normal span of human life. At the same time, the study of genetics opened the way to possible human mutations which could in the last resort have terrifying consequences.

The human problems arising from rapid technological progress are too complex to allow simple generalizations. Suffice it to say that, in the past, the slow pace of change gave people the time to acquire new habits.

THIRTY YEARS OF DECOLONIZATION

Rapid retreat

The collapse of the colonial Empires after 1945 was sudden and spectacular. The only exception was the Russian Empire, which had been conquered by land, not sea. Although covering a vast area, it formed a single bloc. There was Siberia, extending as far as Kamchatka and, to the south-east of the Sea of Okhotsk, the 'Maritime Province' which the Russians had seized from China in 1858–60, and where they had founded Vladivostok, 'the Pearl of the Orient'. There was Central Asia, stretching to the frontiers of Iran and Afghanistan – prolonged eastwards to the Chinese border to avoid any contact between Russian territory and British India. There was Transcaucasia between the Caspian Sea and the Black Sea, consisting of Azerbaijan, Georgia, and Armenia. But this huge geographical mass is outside our immediate concern.

The rest of the world had been colonized, directly or indirectly, by Europeans: the exceptions were China and Japan, as well as the relatively small areas held by Japan and the United States. Decolonization, which at first concerned only the vanquished, very soon affected the victors. Germany had lost her colonies in 1919; Italy lost hers *de facto* in 1943 and *de jure* in 1949. France lost control of her mandated territories, protectorates, and colonies between 1945 and 1962, leaving only a few tiny remnants such as Djibouti and the Comoro Islands. In the case of Britain, the years 1945–57 saw independence achieved by all her territories in South-East Asia – India, Pakistan, Burma, Ceylon, and finally Malaya. In 1949 the Netherlands had to accept the independence of Indonesia. From 1957 onwards, Africa began to be independent: Britain, Spain, Belgium, and Portugal all had to bow to what Harold Macmillan, the British Prime Minister, called 'the wind of change'.

Thus, by the end of thirty years, the 'dependent territories' were no more than a scattering of islands or tiny areas destined either to secure a form of independence which remained purely theoretical because they had only a few thousand inhabitants, or to be assimilated by the 'mother country' – Hawaii by the United States; Martinique, Guadeloupe and French Guiana in America, and the island of Réunion in the Indian Ocean, all absorbed by France.

Europe and the end of colonial rivalry

The repercussions were considerable. For European unity, decolonization was a blessing. For four and a half centuries, Europe's military superiority had enabled her to dominate other peoples of the world. Perhaps it was inevitable that she should. Weak, ill-protected areas attract powerful invaders, who tell themselves that someone else will march in if they do not. Cecil Rhodes, Jules Ferry, Francesco Crispi, Leopold II of Belgium, and many others used this argument for colonial conquest.

The race for colonies was in fact an extreme instance of what might be called 'anti-Europeanism'. Overseas conquest might have been a common effort on the part of countries that thought themselves the most 'civilized': they did after all regard African territory as legally *res nullius*, i.e. belonging to no one. But neighbours in Europe who had more or less settled their disputed frontiers soon found fresh outlets for their fierce rivalry overseas. Between Spain and Portugal, the Netherlands and Britain, Britain and France, the colonies were the subject of ferocious, pitiless wars until 1815.

After that date, colonial rivalry led to many crises, but very few wars. The exceptions were the Crimean War (1854–6), whereby the British sought to protect the trade route to India against the Russians; the Spanish–American War of 1898, over Cuba, Puerto Rico, and the Philippines; and the Russo–Japanese War of 1904–5, over Manchuria. In his pamphlet *Imperialism the Highest State of Capitalism* (1916), Lenin argued that the 'redistribution' of possessions among countries industrializing at different speeds was one of the causes of the Great War: but he was certainly wrong. All the major colonial powers had made bilateral agreements among themselves which all found more or less satisfactory (see Chapter 17). But Germany's loss of her colonies in 1919, and Italy's failure to secure colonies at that time, led the Fascist dictators of both countries to issue demands. Mussolini, in particular, more or less squeezed out of Central Europe by Hitler, sought to conquer Ethiopia, and threatened not only Egypt but also Tunisia and Chad. Even between countries which in principle were friends or allies, colonial questions caused disputes. One example was Franco-British rivalry in the Arab Middle East: this continued until 1945, when a British ultimatum forced the French to give up what was left of their mandates in Syria and Lebanon.

Then, suddenly, the colonist's enemy was no longer a fellow-colonist, but a group within the colony itself. Its elites discovered that the principle of self-determination, which they had learned in European universities, applied also to them and to their fellow-citizens. When Winston Churchill, with Franklin D. Roosevelt, signed the Atlantic Charter in August 1941, he had not seen the principle that peoples should choose their own forms of government as applying *a priori* to the British colonies. Yet in fact the British had long since envisaged decolonization, and had begun the process with the Dominions. Churchill's Labour successors in government could look back to the prediction made by William Ewart Gladstone in the 1860s, to the effect that sooner or later the colonies would become independent. All that Labour was doing was to move faster. In France there was no such tradition, and the original intention was to let nothing go. The Brazzaville Conference organized in 1944 by *la France combattante* (Fighting France) expressly excluded from its post-war plans for the French Empire any idea of independence, secession, or autonomy. This ultra-conservative attitude was the reason why for seventeen years, from 1945 to 1962, France's only response to nationalist rebellion was repression and war. As well as facing unrest in the Levant, Madagascar, Tunisia, and Morocco, the French fought two colonial wars, each of which lasted eight years: in Indochina from 1946 to 1954, and in Algeria from 1954 to 1962.

Post-war experience, then, obliged the colonizing powers – now called 'colonialists' – to recognize that independence for the colonies was becoming inevitable. This required statesmanlike realism; and those who practised it were violently attacked by some sections of the public. The example of General de Gaulle was instructive. Only his great prestige – in the face of threats and assassination attempts – made it possible to solve the problem of Algeria, where 10 per cent of the population was of European origin, through the referendum of April 1962, in which 90 per cent of the French voted for Algerian independence. In Southern Rhodesia, the only British colony where European colonists made up 10 per cent of the population, the United Kingdom in 1962 refused to recognize the 'independence' proclaimed by a white government led by Ian Smith.

Decolonization was perhaps encouraged by good intentions on the part of some Europeans; but it was also a matter of necessity. Among other things, the two post-war superpowers, the United States and the Soviet Union, were both anti-colonialist – the former by tradition and in memory of its own War of Independence, the latter on doctrinal grounds. The Europeans also discovered that the possession of colonies, far from being a source of power as in the past, had become a liability if large numbers of troops had to be sent to quell uprisings, and if interminable wars had to be fought, alienating world opinion.

Europe and the economic results of decolonization

The European states had seen in their colonies a number of advantages: an area for development, economic benefits, a strategic hinterland in wartime (very valuable for France from 1940 to 1944), and a reservoir of manpower for the armed forces. Decolonization deprived them of all that. They therefore had to redeploy their efforts in a quite different direction.

Some countries, like Switzerland, had always had their 'backs to the wall' in this way, depending for survival on their own resources alone. Japan, which had conquered territories by force of arms, found herself in the same situation when the war ended. As a defeated nation, she had to rely for survival on effort and ingenuity, not physical power. The results turned out to be spectacular.

The former colonial powers now found that many of their reasons for quarrelling had finally disappeared. The old links between the colonies and their 'mother countries' began to be replaced by links among the Europeans themselves. There remained, of course, cultural ties with the former colonies, and some common economic interests. But direct unilateral aid from the mother country to the former colonies began to be supplemented and in part supplanted by multilateral assistance, such as that supplied by the European Community, first mainly to African ex-colonies, and then to the so-called ACP countries in Africa, the Caribbean, and the Pacific. The fading of colonial rivalry and the growth of multilateral organizations both favoured the unity of Europe.

THE MAKERS OF EUROPE

The Council of Europe

The proposal made by Georges Bidault in July 1948 was immediately backed by the Belgian Foreign Minister, Paul-Henri Spaak, the Dutch Foreign Minister, Dirk Stikker, and the Luxembourg Foreign Minister, Joseph Bech. Robert Schuman, who succeeded Bidault at the French

Foreign Ministry on 26 July 1948, proposed with the support of the French Cabinet that negotiations take place 'with a view to forming a European Assembly composed of representatives of the Parliaments'. But this proposal met opposition from Britain's Foreign Secretary, Ernest Bevin. He was not against associations with continental Europe, but he feared an assembly from which an 'Executive' might emerge. So he made a counter-proposal: periodic meetings of a simple 'Committee of Ministers' appointed by governments. As a Labour politician, Bevin also feared that if Conservatives were elected to the European Assembly they might try to thwart his own policies. In the end, on 29 January 1949, a compromise was reached. It was agreed to set up a Council of Europe with two institutions: (1) the Committee of Ministers, whose meetings would be held in private, and (2) the Consultative Assembly, meeting in public. Each country was to appoint its own representatives. The powers of the Assembly were to be very limited, and its agenda was to be drawn up by the Committee of Ministers. So the Council of Europe, as it took shape, was closer to the minimalist position of the British than to the supranational hopes of the other four powers. It was understandable that Britain, one of the three great victors in the Second World War, should at that stage have preferred a traditional policy looking towards the Commonwealth. The English language, moreover, profiting from the immense growth of American power, seemed to favour 'Atlantic', Anglo-American ties rather than links with the continent.

The Statute of the Council of Europe was signed on 5 May 1949. Denmark, Ireland, Italy, Norway, and Sweden had already been invited by the other five powers to join the negotiating conference; it was agreed that the Council would be open to all seventeen members of the OEEC. At the opening session of the Assembly in Strasbourg on 8 August 1949, there were thus ten members: Britain, France, and Italy with eighteen seats each; Belgium, the Netherlands, and Sweden with six seats each; Denmark, Ireland, and Norway with four seats each; and Luxembourg with three. Greece and Turkey joined in 1949, and Iceland in 1950.

The political reappearance of Germany

But in the meantime a much more important problem had arisen. In September 1949, after a long process of separate consolidation in the Eastern and Western zones of Germany, agreement among the three

Western occupying powers ended in the establishment of the Federal Republic of Germany, with the Mayor of Cologne, Konrad Adenauer, at once elected as its Chancellor. This led on the Soviet side to the creation of another Germany, the communist-led German Democratic Republic – not recognized by the Federal Republic, which claimed to be sole legitimate successor to the former German state, dissolved in 1945. The years 1948 and 1949 had seen a deepening of the crisis between East and West, with Stalinist purges in Eastern Europe, the Berlin Blockade of March 1948 to June 1949, and the signature on 4 April 1949 of the North Atlantic Treaty by the United States, Canada, and ten West European countries. All these events primarily concerned Europe: but they also strengthened 'Atlantic' cohesion, economically and militarily.

The reappearance of Germany as an active force in international politics did not make the building of Europe any easier. An example of this was the Saar affair. The first national reaction on the part of the German Federal Republic was to protest against France's attempt to detach the Saar from Germany, economically and perhaps even politically. If Germany agreed to that, she might be agreeing in principle to the loss of Eastern Germany and the territory east of the Oder–Neisse Line.

The Council of Europe suffered as a result of this dispute. Its powers proved so limited that the press and public opinion, which had passionately followed its debates in 1949, soon lost interest.

Jean Monnet

It was during this discouraging phase of the building of Europe that there came on the scene a small number of remarkable men. First and foremost was Jean Monnet. Born in Cognac in 1888, he had had no university education, but had come to know Britain and America as a salesman for his father's brandy firm. During the First World War, at his own request, he had co-ordinated Franco-British supplies as representative in London of the French Ministry of Trade, and had had an influential role there, especially from 1916 onwards. After the War, he had become Deputy Secretary-General of the League of Nations, and then an international banker. In 1939, again at his own suggestion, France and Britain had established a joint organization for their wartime supplies, with Monnet as the Chairman of its London-based

Co-ordinating Committee. After the fall of France, he did not join de Gaulle, but preferred to serve the Allied cause with the British Purchasing Commission in the United States, where he was a friend of President Roosevelt and of his adviser Harry Hopkins.

Sent to Algiers in 1943 after the Anglo-American 'Torch' landings, he successfully helped to set up and take part in a 'French Committee of National Liberation' with Generals Henri Giraud and Charles de Gaulle – who very soon outshone Giraud. In 1945, Monnet proposed to de Gaulle the establishment of a French Modernization Plan. De Gaulle appointed him as its Commissioner. He stayed there until 1950. The 'Monnet Plan' became the symbol as well as the instrument of France's economic rebirth. Together with the 'Marshall Plan', it brought about very close Franco-American co-operation, and a new network of friends for Jean Monnet.

Monnet's wholly original historic role depended upon two in particular of his extraordinary gifts: that of making friends, especially in high places, and that of finding for many problems highly original solutions, gradually worked out with his small group of colleagues and assistants, and then launched with energy and vigour.

The Schuman Plan

In 1949 and 1950, Monnet was worried by a whole series of problems. There was the dispute over the Saar, a mining and metalworking area of great importance, which stood in the way of Franco-German reconciliation: Germany was protesting forcefully against the new Franco-Saar Conventions. There was a shortage of coal for West European industry. There was the slowness of progress towards a united Europe, with the Council of Europe semi-paralysed.

With a small group of advisers, including the legal expert Paul Reuter and the economists Etienne Hirsch and Pierre Uri, Monnet worked out an ambitious and highly original plan. He put it first to Georges Bidault, who was then Prime Minister; but failing action from that quarter, he showed it to Robert Schuman, the French Foreign Minister from July 1948 to December 1952, who was instantly won over. Instead of institutional or political integration in Europe, Monnet proposed 'concrete achievements which first create *de facto* solidarity'. How was this to be done? By placing 'the whole of Franco-German coal and steel output under a common High Authority, in an organization open to participation by the other countries of Europe'.

Owing to this supranational High Authority, overseeing coal and steel production and trade, any Franco-German war would become impossible. The fact that coal and steel accounted for the greater part of the Saar's economy would in the long run enable that political problem to be solved. Reconciliation – European authority: two birds to be killed with one stone. On 9 May 1950, Robert Schuman persuaded the French government to back Jean Monnet's plan. It has gone down in history as the 'Schuman Plan'; and although Schuman was not its author, it has to be said that only his energy made it possible to overcome some very powerful opponents. They included the communists, but also the French steel employers' organization, the *Comité des Forges*, a number of French nationalists, and also the British government. The Schuman Treaty was signed on 18 April 1951, by six founder-members: Belgium, France, Germany, Italy, Luxembourg, and the Netherlands – France also signing on behalf of the Saar.

Why did Britain not join at the start? Partly because, remembering the negotiations for the Council of Europe, where Britain had blocked any possibility of establishing a supranational authority, Schuman and Monnet insisted that any country wanting to take part in the negotiations must first accept the supranational principle. Both the British Conservative party and the Labour government, in full agreement for once, rejected this precondition. A Labour party pamphlet entitled *European Unity*, published on 12 June 1950, categorically rejected the abandonment of even one iota of national sovereignty.

Thus was formed the embryo of the 'Europe of the Six'. It retained that number, in successive guises, until 1971–2. The European Coal and Steel Community, the ECSC, was its first organization. This comprised:

1. A High Authority of nine members appointed for six years. Eight of them were chosen by common accord of the member states, with no more than two members of the same nationality. The eight then co-opted the ninth.
2. A Council of Ministers in which each government was represented by one of its own members. Its task was to co-ordinate the policy of the High Authority and that of the governments.

3. A Common Assembly, chosen by and from the national parliaments, with eighteen members each from France, Germany, and Italy, ten each from Belgium and the Netherlands, and four from Luxembourg. The Assembly was empowered to overthrow the High Authority by a two-thirds vote of no confidence.
4. A Court of Justice with seven judges appointed by common accord for six years.

The Schuman Treaty obtained a majority of 377 votes against 233 in the ratification debate in France, and 232 against 143 in the German Bundestag.

Schuman, Adenauer, De Gasperi

It was a spectacular achievement. Jean Monnet and Robert Schuman had realized the need to think big and act fast. The Americans, for the most part, had been enthusiastic. But the plan had also been fortunate in having the support of other convinced Europeans, including Konrad Adenauer in Germany and Alcide De Gasperi in Italy.

Schuman, Adenauer, and De Gasperi were all staunch Christian Democrats. They all came from frontier regions: Adenauer from Cologne, Schuman from Lorraine, and De Gasperi (1881–1954) from Trentino, where he had been born a citizen of Austria, and in the days before Fascism was a Deputy in the Austrian Parliament. When Fascism was overthrown in Italy, De Gasperi was a member of the government led by Ivanoe Bonomi from June 1944 to June 1945, subsequently becoming Prime Minister himself. He made a great contribution to the building of Europe, which at times was largely dependent on his support.

Adenauer, born in 1876, had been the Chairman of the *Zentrum* or Centre Party, which between 1871 and 1933 was the main political organization for German Catholic voters. Having suffered under the Nazi regime, he was protected by the Americans in 1945 and returned to his old post as Mayor of Cologne. A co-founder of the German Christian Democrat party, the CDU, he took part as a member of the Parliamentary Council in drafting the Federal German constitution. His watchword was reconciliation. As a European, he preferred to see a revived and modernized Germany join a united Europe rather than seek German reunification in the name of discredited nationalism.

The European Defence Community proposal

The very success of Jean Monnet's ideas contributed to a crisis in the building of Europe. Since the Community of the Six seemed to meet a real need, might it not be used to solve other problems which appeared insoluble? The Korean War, which broke out six weeks after the launching of the Schuman Plan, when communist North Korea attacked South Korea on 25 June 1950, could hardly fail to remind Europeans of another country divided in two: Germany. The Western occupying powers had committed themselves to keeping Germany disarmed; but their commitments paled before the thought that, if East Germany launched a Korea-like attack, West Germany must help to defend herself. Of all twelve members of the Atlantic Alliance, only France opposed West German rearmament. This led to sharp tension among the Allies. So the French Prime Minister René Pleven, strongly encouraged by Jean Monnet, proposed to use the framework of the Six to rearm the Germans without re-establishing a German army, by recruiting them and troops of the other nations into a European army. The Americans, at first, opposed this novel idea: but they warmed to it when General Dwight D. Eisenhower, former Allied Commander-in-Chief, agreed to take command of the integrated force of the Atlantic Alliance, SHAPE, or Supreme Headquarters, Allied Powers, Europe. Under Monnet's persuasive power, Eisenhower became a keen supporter of the European army. When he was elected US President in November 1952, he and his Secretary of State John Foster Dulles were its enthusiastic partisans.

The negotiations to establish a European Defence Community (EDC) in parallel to the ECSC were very long-drawn-out. Originally, it was proposed to incorporate national troops at battalion level (about a thousand men); later, more realistically, it was agreed to do so at divisional level. Not until 27 January 1952 was the Treaty signed, in Paris. At the same time, provided the Treaty was ratified, it was agreed that Federal Germany would recover its full status as a nation. All this was complicated by the perennial question of the Saar, to which the French public was rather indifferent, while Germany remained highly indignant – a proof of how persistent national feelings still were.

The failure of EDC

From then on, the task was to ratify EDC. Its proposed institutions were not particularly supranational, and its proposed army, some forty small national divisions comprising 13,000 men in a European uniform, would come under SHAPE and hence be subordinate to an American general. Nevertheless, the ratification debates were successfully concluded in Germany (spring 1953), the Netherlands (July 1953), Belgium (November 1953), and Luxembourg (April 1954). In France, the opponents of EDC included the communists and some socialists, who were against any rearmament of Germany, even in this European form. Also hostile were traditional and moderate nationalists like the President of the Republic, Vincent Auriol, Edouard Herriot, and, above all, General de Gaulle.

The critics of EDC used a number of arguments against its convinced 'European' supporters. Some feared that, to prevent the revival of a German army, the French army would be destroyed. Some said that the European army, under American command, would not even be European. Others argued that France needed to use a large part of its military resources in the colonial war in Indochina, while further similar wars were threatening to break out in Morocco, Tunisia, and Algeria. Finally, it was pointed out that Britain, the only other West European country comparable in size to France, had been careful to avoid any involvement in the European army.

The French National Assembly rejected EDC, by a procedural vote, on 30 August 1954. Those against included the Communists, the Gaullists, half of the Radicals, and half the Socialists.

When Jean Monnet was asked about this setback, some years later, his answer was that EDC had failed because it was not a good plan: 'We needed time,' he said, 'to build more solidly.' The building of Europe, he considered, was not the intellectual pursuit of a vision but the adaptation of the vision to reality. Whereas a 'High Authority' could take decisions about *things*, such as coal and steel, the same system could not be applied to armies, which are groups of *men*. One could not denationalize a military organization without overcoming the national feeling that so many people had for their own army. In 1954, without a doubt, the attempt was premature.

The 'alternative' to EDC

The defeat of EDC had two sequels: the 'alternative solution', and the 'relaunching of Europe'. The former need not detain us long.

John Foster Dulles had claimed that there was no alternative to EDC: but one was found in a matter of two months by the French Premier, Pierre Mendès-France, with the help of Anthony Eden, the British Foreign Secretary, and Konrad Adenauer. It was decided to strengthen the Brussels Pact of 1948 by establishing a Western European Union, made up of the Brussels Pact signatories plus Italy and Federal Germany. At the same time, at intensive negotiations in London (28 September to 3 October 1954) and Paris (20–23 October 1954), Mendès-France and Adenauer agreed to give the Federal Republic what she sought: a national army – to which French public opinion turned out to be far less opposed than the governments had thought; equality, and the end of the occupation statute; and, finally, full and equal membership of the North Atlantic Treaty Organization (NATO), which Greece and Turkey had joined in 1950, making its total number fifteen.

Meanwhile, an agreement on the Saar was laboriously hammered out. There was to be a first referendum or plebiscite to see whether the inhabitants would accept the 'Europeanization' of the Saar, whereby it could become the site of a federal capital of the United States of Europe on the model of Washington, DC – a plan put forward by the Dutch statesman Marinus Van der Goes Van Naters. If and when (and it was a big 'if', given the Soviet attitude) a 'German peace treaty' was signed, there would be a second plebiscite. In the event, the first referendum was held in October 1955; and pro-German parties were authorized to campaign. The result was only 201,000 votes for Europeanization, and 423,000 against. The French government at once drew the logical if not legal conclusion, and decided to allow the Saar to return to Germany. This removed the last political grievance between France and Germany, since that of Alsace and Lorraine had been settled when the two main German political parties, the SDP and the CDU, had declared that, in line with their peoples' will, both provinces should remain French.

The 'relaunching of Europe'

More important in the present context was the 'relaunching of Europe'. Here, too, Jean Monnet – who well deserved his nickname 'the Father of Europe' – played an essential role. Since 1952 he had been the first President of the High Authority of the ECSC in Luxembourg: but a new initiative was needed after the defeat of the EDC. In 1955, Monnet left the High Authority to establish, on a private basis, the 'Action Committee for the United States of Europe'. This consisted of all the non-Communist and non-Gaullist political parties and trade unions of the six Community countries, represented at top level; and its aim was to launch and further ambitious ideas. Monnet and his colleagues proposed: (1) to 'Europeanize' the peaceful uses of atomic energy, which was then seen as a key to the future; (2) to 'Europeanize' all other sectors of the economy outside the field of coal and steel; (3) no longer to stress the supranational character of future institutions, but instead of the High Authority of the ECSC to set up a Commission and leave the main authority to the Council of Ministers.

Somewhere similar ideas had already been mooted in Europe, where on 1 July 1953, the European Organization for Nuclear Research (CERN) had been established in Geneva. Even before setting up his Action Committee, Monnet put his proposals, through intermediaries, to the Messina Conference in June 1955. This was a conference of the Foreign Ministers of the six Community countries, invited to Sicily by Gaetano Martino, who had been Italian Foreign Minister since October 1954, and who was also Rector of Messina University. The meeting was chaired by Joseph Bech, from Luxembourg; the others present were Antoine Pinay from France, Walter Hallstein from Germany, Paul-Henri Spaak from Belgium, and Johan Willem Beyen from the Netherlands. The ministers appointed the French statesman René Mayer to replace Jean Monnet as President of the ECSC High Authority. Then they decided that the time had come 'to pass to a new stage in the building of Europe'.

The 'Messina Resolution' declared that the six governments 'consider it necessary to work for the establishment of a united Europe by the development of common institutions, the progressive fusion of national economies, the creation of a common market and the progressive harmonisation of their social policies'. The 'common market' was to be 'established by stages' and 'free from all customs duties and all quantitative restrictions'.

The Resolution also called for a series of studies – of transport, energy, and nuclear power. The preparatory work was to be done by a committee, which met at Val Duchesse on the outskirts of Brussels, and was chaired by Paul-Henri Spaak. Others involved in its work included Dirk Spirenburg, Dutch member of the High Authority; Félix Gaillard, Jean-François Deniau, Pierre Uri, and Paul Delouvrier from France (and in the last two cases from the staff of the High Authority); Hans von der Groeben from Germany; and Albert Huppertts, a diplomat from Belgium. The French were mainly interested in nuclear energy, to be dealt with by 'Euratom'; the others pressed hardest for the 'Common Market'.

In reality, the enormous influence of the United States helped to limit the role of Euratom from the start. To establish more than a mainly research organization for the peaceful uses of atomic energy, the Europeans would have had to unite and build a joint isotope separation plant, to produce enriched uranium for use in nuclear power stations. But the Americans had a virtual monopoly on isotope separation in the West; and they had a very simple means of outflanking any European rival. All they had to do was greatly to reduce the price of Uranium 235 – which is what President Eisenhower proposed on 20 February 1956. After that, to build a European isotope separation plant would clearly have been absurd. Euratom went on to be established. But what really counted in the 'relaunching of Europe' was the Common Market.

The Treaties of Rome: the Common Market and Euratom

On 25 March 1957, after difficult negotiations, the Treaties of Rome were signed. Their basis had been the 'Spaak Report' from the Committee at Val Duchesse. Once signed, the Treaties were ratified without difficulty in all six Community countries.

The two Community organizations they established – the European Economic Community (EEC) and the European Atomic Energy Community (Euratom) – shared with the ECSC the same Court of Justice and the same parliamentary Assembly, enlarged from 78 to 142 members. The Executive, as has been seen, was not a further High Authority: the decision-making body was the Council of National

Ministers, with two independent Commissions to make proposals, safeguard the Treaties, and act as honest brokers – one of nine members for the Common Market, one of five for Euratom. (Later, the Commissions and the High Authority were merged, with the respective powers of each maintained intact.) There was no agreement, however, on a single site for the three Community organizations. Brussels was chosen as the 'provisional' location for the EEC and 'Euratom'; but the ECSC and the Court remained in Luxembourg.

The new Community institutions took office on 1 January 1958, with Walter Hallstein as President of the EEC Commission and Louis Armand from France as President of the Euratom Commission (whose nickname he had invented). From that date began the successive stages in the reduction of customs duties between the member states.

Would the new venture succeed? The British, uneasy about their trade relations with the Community, proposed establishing with it a large European Free Trade Area. And on 1 June 1958, after a *coup d'état* in Algeria, General de Gaulle came to power in France. He was an ardent champion of the nation against internationalism and supranationality.

THE BUILDING OF EUROPE IN THE FACE OF GAULLISM

Charles de Gaulle in France

Having been the symbol of French independence during the Second World War after his appeal of 18 June 1940, and through his action as the leader of 'Free France', later renamed 'Fighting France', de Gaulle had abruptly resigned as head of the French Provisional Government on 19 January 1946. Perhaps he believed that the French people, weary of continual government crises and party squabbles, would beg him to come back. They did nothing of the kind. He had to wait until 13 May 1958, the date of the Algiers coup. Then, he insisted that a new constitution be devised by himself and submitted for approval by referendum. Once this had been promised, he became the last Prime Minister of the Fourth Republic on 1 June 1958. On 20 September, with the approval of some 80 per cent of the voters, the Constitution of the new Fifth Republic was adopted, establishing a stronger and more stable executive power.

Adenauer and de Gaulle

De Gaulle's return to power had a deep and complex effect on the history of Europe. His first act, in agreement with the German Chancellor Konrad Adenauer, was to rescue the Common Market from the danger of drowning in the wider Free Trade Area proposed by the British. French and German negotiators energetically opposed a system which would have given Britain a position uniquely privileged: continued preferential access to Commonwealth markets, denied to her European partners; free access to all European markets for her industrial goods; cheap food from Commonwealth and world markets, while her own (higher-cost) farmers were supported by 'deficiency payments' from the Exchequer; and a home agricultural market virtually closed to (equally higher-cost) produce from other European countries, including Germany and France.

But what would de Gaulle make of the Community institutions? He was known to be opposed to 'supranationality' and he had helped substantially to destroy the EDC. To the relief of Europeans, after a very cordial meeting with Adenauer in September 1958, the General seemed reconciled to the Common Market. After the rejection of the large Free Trade Area project, Britain and six other countries (Austria, Denmark, Norway, Portugal, Sweden and Switzerland), joined later by Finland, established a smaller free trade area, the European Free Trade Association (EFTA), around but outside the Common Market. Europe was now, as was said at the time, 'at sixes and sevens'. The Americans, after much hesitation, decided to support the Six of the Community rather than the EFTA Seven: and in April 1961, while not pressing Britain to seek membership of the Community, President Kennedy told the British Prime Minister Harold Macmillan that America would regard this as a positive step. On 10 August, Macmillan took it, and formally applied to join all three European Communities.

France's partners against the Fouchet Plan

General de Gaulle's Europe was by no means that of Jean Monnet or the other great founding fathers. Unlike Monnet (and especially

Hallstein), de Gaulle did not believe that economic union would necessarily lead to political union. He could accept an economic Common Market, but not a European government. His Europe was a Europe of the states. It might become a confederation, but every member would retain national sovereignty. It was also a 'European Europe' – built to resist the power of the Soviet Union, but also that of the United States.

De Gaulle believed that such a confederation should have a harmonized foreign policy. In October 1961, a committee of representatives of the Community's member governments, chaired by the Gaullist Christian Fouchet, presented a draft Treaty, which became known as the Fouchet Plan. What it proposed was a mere 'Union of the States', not a 'United States of Europe'. The draft was adopted as a basis of discussion by Germany, Italy, and Luxembourg. Paul-Henri Spaak for Belgium, and Joseph Luns for the Netherlands, opposed the plan. They wanted Britain to join the Community, and they refused to discuss political union without her. They also feared that the policy of 'European defence' suggested by de Gaulle might weaken the Atlantic Alliance. It was at this point that, on 13 August 1961, the Soviets found a brutal solution to the Berlin Crisis they had set off in November 1958: by building a breeze-block wall across the city, they made it almost impossible for East Berliners to escape to the West.

The division of opinion between de Gaulle and Monnet was fundamental. What divided them were two conflicting conceptions of Europe and of her relations with the United States. President Kennedy was a friend of Monnet's; and it was Monnet's view that he shared and backed.

President Kennedy's 'Grand Design'

In 1962, General de Gaulle at last freed himself from the Algerian War, and determined to play his part in world politics. Also in 1962, strongly inspired and encouraged by Jean Monnet, President Kennedy proposed his 'Grand Design'. In his speech on Independence Day, 4 July 1962, he proposed that the United States of America and the future United States of Europe (including Britain) should form what he called an Atlantic 'partnership', with total equality between them – politically, socially, intellectually, and, as will be seen, economically. Only on one point did the Americans not propose equality: nuclear and thermonuclear weapons. Why should the Europeans make pointless efforts to build such weapons when their loyal transatlantic ally already possessed a full armoury?

In the economic field, Kennedy presented to Congress – which for once was in agreement with him – the Trade Expansion Act, passed in October 1962. This formally empowered the President to negotiate the US tariff down to zero on goods in which the Community and the US did 80 per cent of world trade, as well as on some tropical products, and down to half the previous level on most other goods. It was so designed as to be more liberal if Britain joined the Community. However, the American tariff was calculated as a percentage of the American selling price, not that paid by the importer. This, like other technicalities, promised tough negotiation in the ensuing 'Kennedy Round' of tariff negotiations; but at long last tariffs were largely cut by a third and in some cases a half.

Trade disputes, however, were not General de Gaulle's main concern. It was in the nuclear field that he was most inclined to react. France exploded its first atomic bomb at Reggane in the Sahara in January 1960. Its technology was essentially French. But the Americans, when they had decided to support the Common Market rather than EFTA, had wanted to compensate the British by offering them a 'transfer of technology' in nuclear weapons. How did the British see this? Were they henceforth tied hand and foot to the United States? Or would they, under their Prime Minister Harold Macmillan, agree to the French plan for a 'European Europe'? The Cuban Missile Crisis of October 1962, when the US had detected Soviet missiles on the island, had led Kennedy to take a calculated risk in pursuing deterrence. He had won, and in his enthusiasm he had said that now more than ever the Americans should exercise their 'leadership' in the West. It was a word much used in France – but in the sense of 'command', whereas Kennedy certainly saw a 'leader' rather as a 'model' or a 'guide'.

De Gaulle rejects the 'Grand Design'

General de Gaulle was host to Macmillan at Rambouillet on 15–16 December 1962; and on that occasion he believed that the British Prime Minister agreed with his European views. He was therefore furious when, on 18–21 December 1962, this same Harold Macmillan, meeting President Kennedy at Nassau in the Bahamas, accepted the American proposal of US Polaris missiles for Royal Naval submarines under NATO command. This, de Gaulle thought, would swallow up Britain's small nuclear arsenal within the enormous American deterrent system. To add insult to injury, a similar arrangement was offered to France.

General de Gaulle gave his response to the whole 'Grand Design' in a press conference on 14 January 1963. He turned it down flat. In the first place, he formally rejected Britain's bid to join the Common Market. She was not yet ready to be linked with the continent. Equally, de Gaulle rejected any idea that France's future nuclear force should ever be integrated into the American force or the Atlantic command. 'I repeat, as I have often said in the past, that France intends to have her national defence in her own right.'

Gaullist anti-Americanism

This notorious press conference provoked very sharp reactions among France's European partners, as well as in Britain and the United States. The Germans expressed their mistrust openly. A Franco-German Treaty, signed on 22 January 1963, to put an end to centuries of hostility, was ratified by the German parliament only after the addition of a careful, restrictive preamble. Jean Monnet's Action Committee for the United States of Europe also, after a long period of reflection, spelled out a policy opposed to that of de Gaulle.

Thus began five strange and difficult years. The atmosphere of the debate in Europe was now totally transformed. The enthusiasm and goodwill that had marked the 'relaunching' of Europe gave way to bitter arguments where national interests took pride of place. Was it, as de Gaulle's opponents claimed, entirely his fault? Or did the very fact that economic union was now developing lead to tension and rivalry? An underlying factor was certainly the General's marked anti-American policy. Not content with rejecting Kennedy's Grand Design, he went further. In January 1964 he officially recognized the People's Republic of China without consulting the United States in advance. On 7 March 1966, he announced that France was leaving the military component of NATO, while remaining in the Alliance – hence the subsequent transfer of the integrated command from Paris to Brussels; at the same time, he asked the Americans to withdraw their bases and depots from France before April 1967. For a number of years, he attacked the world monetary system, whose gold exchange standard favoured the US dollar. From 20 June to 1 July 1966, he paid a friendly visit to the USSR. On 1 September 1966 he made a speech in Phnom Penh, Cambodia, accusing the Americans of sole responsibility for the Vietnam War, and reiterating his view that Indo-China be neutralized. In June 1967, during the 'Six-Day War' between Israel and the Arabs, he placed an embargo on the export of aircraft that Israel had ordered from France – and paid for. And on 24 July 1967 he made a speech in Montreal in which he appeared to side with the French-speaking Quebec separatists by repeating their rallying cry 'Long live Free Quebec!' – '*Vive le Québec libre!*'

These various episodes have one common characteristic. General de Gaulle rejected American propositions and preferences. But in those rather rare instances where he made clear proposals of his own, they were not adopted.

The progress and limits of the EEC

The first step towards opening the Common Market was taken on 1 January 1959. A primary aspect of the European Economic Community was the liberalization of trade across its internal frontiers and the gradual removal of all barriers to the movement of goods, money and people, whether quotas, embargos or customs tariffs. Fiscal frontiers, however, remained – a sign that national interests would not be easily overcome. Largely on French insistence, the Community adopted a Common Agricultural Policy, but with enormous difficulties. France insisted that the ever more rapid liberalization of trade in industrial goods be accompanied by increased outlets for its farm products. In this highly complex and technical area, the Ministers concerned held long (sometimes nightlong) meetings. Prominent among such 'agricultural marathons' were those of December 1961 to January 1962 and December 1963 to January 1964.

In 1965, the EEC's executive body, the European Commission, proposed a package deal involving a large increase in the Community budget, more powers for itself and the European Parliament, and some financial advantage for France – all this to coincide with a new phase laid down by the EEC Treaty in which some decisions previously taken by unanimous agreement in the Council of Ministers would now be taken by qualified majority vote (QMV). All this spelt supranationality, and General de Gaulle reacted with furious energy. On 1 July 1965, the French Cabinet decided that France would no longer take part in Community meetings in Brussels. Not until after the French presidential election in 1965 – in which de Gaulle was re-elected, but in a run-off partly caused by a pro-European rival – was a solution to the Brussels 'empty chair' crisis found. On 28–30 January 1966, a *modus vivendi* was adopted to enable France to return to the Council of Ministers: the 'Luxembourg Compromise', which was in effect a 'gentlemen's disagreement' and an extremely subtle one. The principle of majority voting was maintained, but where 'very important interests' were involved 'the discussion should continue until unanimous agreement was reached'. Clearly, and in line with the General's wishes, this largely nullified the supranational procedure laid down by the Treaty; and it certainly affected the Community's development. The political progress envisaged by the Commission had suffered a severe setback.

In November 1967, France rejected a second British application for membership of the Common Market, made this time by the Labour Prime Minister, Harold Wilson. Yet, despite the blockage of political or institutional progress, the Common Market achieved remarkable economic results. Trade within the Community increased sixfold from 1958 to 1970. The proportion of intra-Community trade in the total foreign trade of the Six rose from 30 per cent in 1958 to 52 per cent in 1972. This was not to say that all problems were solved. The serious unrest which disrupted universities in a large number of countries, complicated in France by a general strike, showed that a new form of discontent had emerged. In April 1969 this in effect cost General de Gaulle his tenure of power. His departure reduced French ambition to more modest and suitable proportions, and thereby helped make possible further progress in the building of Europe.

CHANGE IN EUROPE AFTER DE GAULLE

The wartime sacrifices made by the Soviet Union, and its heroic victories, as well as the role of many communists in the Resistance, helped to create in post-war Europe a social and intellectual climate very favourable to Marxism. A number of Europeans seemed to be convinced that the Soviet regime was preferable to American 'capitalism' and 'imperialism'. In 1968 and 1969, when turmoil in the universities was at its height, this tendency appeared to be triumphant. It was intensified by the Vietnam War between communist North Vietnam and the United States.

Decline of communism as a 'dominant ideology'

As the post-war years proceeded, however, communism began to decline as a 'dominant ideology', largely on account of lack of freedom in the USSR and its 'satellites'. The 'Prague Spring' of April 1968, when Czechoslovakia had tried to establish a liberal form of communism, had been followed in August by Soviet military intervention and finally, in February 1969, by the extinction of the last traces of 'communism with a human face'. The West had also discovered what the exiled Russian writer Aleksandr Solzhenitsyn unforgettably called the 'Gulag archipelago' of vast Soviet concentration camps. Other Soviet dissidents, the best known of whom was the late Andrei Sakharov, the academic and atomic physicist, made known in the West the true conditions of life in the Soviet Union – including not only political restrictions and the abuse of police power, but also the unsatisfactory standard of living. Economic progress was falling behind that of the West; scientific invention was much less advanced than in the United States, Japan, or Western Europe. For many Westerners, perhaps especially in France, a great illusion was destroyed. The invasion of Afghanistan by the Red Army in 1980, and the Moscow-inspired attack on the Solidarity trade union movement in Poland, whose success contradicted Leninist doctrines: these were further blows to the orthodoxy of the communist or fellow-travelling left. If the principles of that ideology were disproved by history, what remained except a formidable military power?

The illusion of 'Euro-communism'

For a brief period in 1975 and 1976, it looked as if Western Europe might produce a new kind of communism known as 'Euro-communism'. The Italian Communist Party, which in June 1975 had won a record

34.7 per cent of the votes, followed by its Spanish counterpart and, much more timidly, by some of the French, seemed for a time to favour a more liberal policy, less dependent on the USSR. The idea was soon rejected by the French communist leadership; and in the case of the Italian Party, the US State Department published a note in January 1978, condemning in advance any idea that communists should enter the government. In France, the socialist majority which ruled from June 1981 to March 1986 decided to appoint three communist ministers (among some forty ministers and secretaries of state). But political disagreements between them and the socialists, which ran deep, led to their leaving the government and returning to opposition in July 1984, when there was a change of government and the communists could not persuade it to meet their demands.

The widening of democracy in Western Europe

The waning of communist influence in the West may have augured well for closer European integration, since the USSR and the communist parties had always firmly opposed it. But other events of equal importance also favoured the building of Europe, at least in the longer term: the return to democratic government in Greece, and above all in Portugal and Spain.

In Greece, it was rivalry with Turkey over the future of independent Cyprus which helped put an end to the so-called 'Colonels' regime'. Hoping to conceal their internal difficulties by a success abroad, the Colonels staged a *coup d'état* against the President of Cyprus, Archbishop Mikhail Makarios, in July 1974. The result was a disastrous defeat: the Turks landed and occupied 40 per cent of the island in the North. In August 1974, the Colonels' regime in Greece collapsed, and democracy was restored. The monarchy, which in the eyes of public opinion had been in league with the Colonels, was replaced by a Republic, which in a referendum won 70 per cent of the votes.

Portugal had been a dictatorship since 1926, first under Dr Antonio de Oliveira Salazar, then from 1968 under Marcello Caetano. In April 1974, a group of officers who thought it both pointless and dangerous to fight nationalism in the colonies seized power under Generals Antonio de Spínola and Francisco da Costa Gomes. They were backed by the 'Armed Forces Movement' of junior and middle-ranking officers; and they officially recognized the Communist Party, led by a young Stalinist, Alvaro Cunhal. Two communists were even recruited into the Provisional Government – an exceptional case in Western Europe. For eighteen months, the atmosphere was revolutionary. General Spínola was ousted; in March 1975 there was a right-wing coup, but it failed. In April 1975 there was an election in which the Socialist Party, led by Mario Soares, won 58 per cent of the votes, compared with 13 per cent for the communists. In November 1975, there was another unsuccessful attempt at a *coup d'état*, this time mounted by the left. It was followed by a return to order, long overdue in view of the state of the economy. In June 1976 the election as President of General Antonio dos Santos Ramalho Eanes marked the triumph of Western-style democracy.

In Spain, to many people's surprise, the return to democracy took place without major disorder. Since the outbreak of the Civil War in July 1936, Spain had been outside the mainstream of European events. Backed in his domestic struggle by Hitler and Mussolini, General Francisco Franco had had great difficulty in resisting their pressure to renounce his quasi-neutrality during the Second World War. He did indeed send an *Azul* or blue division to fight alongside the Germans in the USSR; and although his authoritarian regime was not strictly comparable to those of the Fascist dictators, after the War it seemed to the European left to be the only remnant of the Axis still surviving in Europe. The French government, in particular, with General de Gaulle at its head and Georges Bidault as its Foreign Minister, tried to bring about Franco's downfall, by closing the frontier and seeking – unsuccessfully – United Nations economic sanctions against Spain. Not until 1959, in fact, was Spain admitted to OEEC. She was not a member of the European Free Trade Association or the Common Market, although she signed a preferential agreement with the latter in 1970. Only in 1977 did she join the Council of Europe.

Meanwhile, however, General Franco had died, on 20 November 1975. Everything had been prepared for the re-establishment of the Bourbon monarchy, and the Pretender Juan Carlos now became King of Spain. In the first election, the Communist Party was authorized to stand; but although it was led by an anti-Stalinist, Santiago Carrillo, it won only 11 per cent of the votes. At the International Communist Congress in Berlin in June 1976, the Spanish Party firmly opposed the idea of Soviet primacy in the international movement, and called for the withdrawal of the Red Army from Czechoslovakia.

The democratization of all of Western Europe was a landmark in its history as a community of nations, matched only by subsequent events in the East. Countries with different languages, rich and various cultures, proud and ancient histories, and often rival economic interests, can hardly come together in a thorough-going association – 'an ever closer union', to quote the Treaty of Rome – without a general consensus that only time and patience can achieve. All the countries of Europe, now, seem to oscillate between two main political tendencies. One, which is socialist or social-democratic but less and less Marxist, believes that the state must play a major role, and seeks to increase the influence of the trade unions. The other, conservative but concerned with welfare, emphasizes private enterprise and initiative. But their disagreements are very far from the dialectic extremism of the class war which was once supposed to determine the future. Socialism prizes liberty; conservatism respects the need for social security. Since the pendulum swings continually between these tendencies, at least in the West, any table purporting to show the strength of either would rapidly become out of date.

From Six to Nine in the European Community

Against this wider background, the building of Europe proceeded at its moderate pace. It was more successful in enlarging the Community of the Six than in making it more supranational.

The resignation of General de Gaulle as President of France on 27 April 1969 made possible the first enlargement of the Community. De Gaulle's successor, Georges Pompidou, more committed to uniting Europe, decided to lift the veto that the General had placed on British membership. On 10 July 1969, he declared that he had 'no objection in principle to the possible entry of Great Britain or any other country'. The French government accordingly proposed a summit meeting of heads of state and government. This took place in The Hague in December 1969, shortly after the election in Germany, which had brought to power the Social Democrat leader Willy Brandt, in alliance with the Liberals. His election marked the beginning of a systematic policy of *détente* in relations with the East, the so-called *Ostpolitik*, which led to a *modus vivendi* between the two Germanies and the signature of the far-reaching Helsinki Agreement between East and West in 1975.

At the Hague Summit, in which the Belgian President of the

Commission, Jean Rey, also took part, Willy Brandt showed himself the most decided champion of European unity. It was agreed to set in place by 1 January 1970 the definitive regulations that would complete the common market in agriculture. Less progress was possible on common monetary and nuclear policies; and the rule of unanimity was maintained. 'Supranationality' seemed further off than ever. But the main decision concerned the enlargement of the Community.

Britain, Denmark, Ireland, and Norway were welcomed to negotiations, and on 22 January 1972, they all signed treaties of accession. On 10 May 1972, a referendum in Ireland, in which 70 per cent of those eligible voted, produced an 83 per cent majority in favour of Community membership. In Denmark, the referendum was held on 2 October: there was 89.4 per cent participation, and a 'yes' vote of 56.7 per cent. In Norway, however, a referendum on 24 and 25 September 1972, with a large turnout, produced a 'no' vote of 54 per cent. Nationalists, small farmers, fishermen, artisans, and traditionalists had joined the neutralists and the communists to block Norwegian membership.

There remained the United Kingdom. The Labour government led by Harold Wilson, which had applied to join, intended to negotiate very hard for a number of amendments reducing Britain's contribution to the Community budget and for various transitional arrangements. On 18 June 1970, however, the Conservative Party won a general election, and the pro-European Edward Heath became Prime Minister. Even so, the negotiations were long and very technical. As has been seen, they culminated in the treaty signed on 22 January 1972. It provided for a transition period of five years. The House of Commons duly approved the treaty. On 28 February 1974, however, Harold Wilson and the Labour Party returned to power and asked to 'renegotiate' the terms of accession. The renegotiation lasted until March 1975, and a referendum was held on 5 June. Of those eligible, 65.5 per cent voted: the 'yes' vote was 67.2 per cent against 32 per cent voting 'no'. Like Gaullist France, Britain was opposed to any political 'European union', and she stressed the importance of her links with the Commonwealth and the United States.

In France too, President Pompidou decided to hold a referendum – although more as a domestic political move intended to divide the two partners in the 'Union of the Left', the socialists being for Europe and the communists against. The attempt failed. The communists voted 'no', but the socialists abstained, with the result that barely 60 per cent of those eligible voted at all. There was, however, a large majority in favour.

From 1973 onwards, the Europe of the Nine thus replaced the Europe of the Six. And at that very moment, a new type of economic crisis threatened the world, and especially Europe. Its main origin was the decision taken by the Organization of Petroleum Exporting Countries (OPEC) to force a large and sudden rise in the price of crude oil, in support of the Arabs in their struggle against Israel after the 'Yom Kippur War' of October 1973.

It was in May 1975, finally, that Jean Monnet decided to wind up his Action Committee for the United States of Europe. The great champion of a united Europe had decided to spend his remaining years writing his memoirs, 'which I hope,' he told the Committee's members, 'will help to explain what we have achieved – the philosophy behind the idea which has been ours all along – and the profound reasons which have persuaded our countries to unite'.

European Council and European Parliament

In respect of the institutions of European integration, two great reforms were achieved in the 1970s. First, the 'European summits' convened by Georges Pompidou – with six participants in The Hague and nine in Paris in October 1972 – were replaced by a new high-level formation, mainly inspired by Jean Monnet, but backed by Pompidou, Heath and Brandt. This was the European Council, formally established after Pompidou's death, under the French Presidency of Valéry Giscard d'Estaing (from 19 May 1974 to 21 May 1981) and the German Chancellorship of Helmut Schmidt (from 14 May 1974 to 1 October 1982). The Belgian Prime Minister, Leo Tindemans, greatly encouraged Giscard to agree to the European Council, which was finally set up in December 1974. It consisted of regular meetings of the heads of state and government of the Community countries to guide its 'political co-operation', in effect foreign policy, and other major initiatives. At a time when the Council of Ministers (which could be Ministers of Agriculture, Economics and Finance, etc.) was submerged in highly technical problems, the European Council was able to reassert a broader, strategic view. At the very least, it could cut through Gordian knots and give stronger leadership to the system. The establishment of the European Monetary System (EMS) in 1979 was one of its early achievements.

The other institutional reform was perhaps still more important.

This was the agreement that the (pre-existing) European Parliament should be directly elected by universal suffrage simultaneously throughout the Community. The decision was taken, in fact, by the European Council on 15 July 1976. There were to be 410 Members of the European Parliament, elected for five years: eighty-one each for Britain, France, Germany, and Italy; twenty-five for the Netherlands; twenty-four for Belgium (twelve Flemings and twelve Walloons); sixteen for Denmark; fifteen for Ireland; and six for Luxembourg. The national voting system in each country would remain the same. This reform was popular, according to the opinion polls. The first two European elections – held in June 1979 and June 1984 – produced centre-right majorities, but, perhaps more importantly, increased the political impetus towards stronger common policies, notably to deepen Europe's internal (or 'single') market and develop a single currency.

From Nine to Ten to Twelve

The second enlargement of the Community was an opening to the South. Greece, which had been a candidate since 1961, renewed her bid for membership in June 1975, and finally joined in 1981.

Spain applied for membership on 27 July 1977, when Mario Soares was Prime Minister. Portugal had preceded it by applying on 28 March. In both cases, the applications signalled a powerful move towards Europe by two countries that had at last recovered democratic freedom. Portugal had joined the Council of Europe in 1976, and Spain in 1977. Problems arose from the fact that both Italy and southern France produced wine, fruit, and vegetables which would face direct competition from Spain and Portugal who they feared might undersell them. So the negotiations were slow – less on account of the applicants than because of the existing member states. They finally succeeded, however, and Spain and Portugal joined the Community on 1 January 1986.

Although the European Community of the Twelve has many shortcomings – no real supranational authority, no common security system, no single currency, and is still too narrowly limited to the West – it is, and must be, an increasing pole of attraction for the countries of Eastern Europe, which are recovering control of their future as the Soviet grip on them is relaxed. Not even the Economic Community – and until 1992, not even its common market – can be regarded as complete. The pressure for progress continues.

ENVOI

The aim of this book has been to enquire whether a united Europe – whatever form it might take – would be an artificial creation *ex nihilo*, or the culmination of a long historical evolution which has given it a unique personality of its own, distinct from the other great regions of the world.

The forty years that have elapsed since the end of the Second World War have been unlike previous centuries and even millennia. For the first time in history, the governments of a number of European countries officially embarked on a 'process of unification' by mutual agreement, and not by hegemony or force.

One could look at this period from the viewpoint of ideologists, and argue that the great characteristic of the post-war years was the 'East–West conflict' – psychological, doctrinal, economic, political, and military. One might equally consider the 'right of peoples to self-determination', and note that in thirty years all the territorial Empires – except, until recent signs of fragmentation, the Soviet Empire – have crumbled. From that point of view, the essential post-war phenomenon has been decolonization, the achievement of independence by peoples hitherto unfree.

One may, finally, see this phase of history in a European light, and observe how many objective factors have combined with creative acts of will to make possible the first step towards a united Europe. Naturally, this third preoccupation has concerned us most, although it cannot be isolated completely from the other two.

The text of Jean-Baptiste Duroselle's Europe: A History of its Peoples *was completed in spring 1989 and published in November 1990. Some sections have been slightly re-edited to take account of developments at and since that time, and to dovetail the text with the Afterword which follows.*

Afterword

The Making and Breaking of Post-Wall Europe, 1985 to 2023

Anthony Teasdale

The story that Jean-Baptiste Duroselle tells in the original edition of *Europe: A History of its Peoples* ends in 1989. It is a moment when literally one chapter of European history closes and another opens. The division of Europe after the Second World War into two rival blocs of capitalism in the west and communism in the east, defined at Yalta and Potsdam and sustained by a Cold-War stand-off over forty-five years, is finally overcome. A spectacular 'reverse domino effect' takes hold, in a new 'post-Wall' setting, as one country after another moves from autocracy and central planning to free elections and a form of market economy. The prospect of a more united, democratic Europe beckons – a 'Europe whole and free', in a phrase popularized by the then US President, George H. W. Bush – raising huge hopes on both sides of the former Iron Curtain. The triumph of Western liberal values – heralded in Francis Fukuyama's idea of the 'end of history', itself echoing the 'end of ideology' announced by American sociologist Daniel Bell thirty years before – seemed not only possible, but almost inevitable.

FROM SCLEROSIS TO RELAUNCH: THE NEW EUROPE OF JACQUES DELORS, 1985–89

Delors' continental vision

The second half of the 1980s saw history accelerate spectacularly on several fronts. For Europe, these years were a period of rebirth, just as for the United States, they were marked by growing economic success and rising global power. The 'Euro-sclerosis', economic stagnation and pervasive pessimism of the early 1980s were superseded by a new belief in the potential of economic integration to relaunch the European Community. The vision and ambition of Jacques Delors, who became President of the European Commission in January 1985, helped to align political leaders throughout the Community behind a detailed programme to complete (or more accurately to create) a single market in Europe by 1992. Delors identified a collective 'public good' that was both missing and achievable by practical action at European level. This was the economic dividend that could flow from removing the remaining non-tariff barriers to trade in Europe – based on the free movement of goods, services, capital and people – with common standards and a single regulatory system across the continent. A complex technical exercise was converted into a political initiative of huge potential. The Brussels-based Commission calculated the likely boost to European GDP as being in the order of 5 per cent – and indeed, in the twenty years from 1987 to 2007, just before the economic and financial crisis struck, the advent of the single market was to add almost exactly that amount to the size of the European economy.

In the mid-1980s, a barrier-free Europe was an idea whose time had come. In France, President François Mitterrand was looking for ways to move beyond the contradictions and disappointments of his early experiment with 'socialism in one country', by playing a new leadership role in Europe. As Mitterrand's finance minister from 1981 to 1984, Delors, an ascetic figure hailing from the political centre, rather than traditional left, had already forced France to prioritize monetary discipline over domestic expansion. Now he helped reconcile the country to Europe-led, supply-side reform. At the same time, in Britain, Prime Minister Margaret Thatcher, at the height of her political dominance, quickly embraced the single market in the hope of shifting European priorities towards economic liberalism – as well as building a wider market for her own fast-reviving economy and presenting Britain as the venue of choice for inward investment into Europe. In Germany, Chancellor Helmut Kohl welcomed both France's return to the European mainstream and the potential opportunities for his own domestic manufacturing sector offered by a growing single market – not least in the context of the impending enlargement of the Community to include the new democracies (and fast-emerging economies) of Spain and Portugal in 1986.

AFTERWORD

Spillover effects

The dynamic of completing the single market in Europe unexpectedly proved to be a powerful political force in its own right. Delors had hoped, right from the start, that once the single-market programme (comprising over 300 individual pieces of legislation) was underway, he might be able to make the case for other ambitious European reforms that had seemed impossible when he took office. He soon argued successfully for some limited reform of the Community's institutions, with greater use of qualified majority voting (QMV) to make it easier to adopt single-market measures in the Council of Ministers, where unanimity had previously been the norm. The 1986 Single European Act, the first significant revision of the 1957 Rome Treaties, was the result. As well as broadening the writ of QMV, the Act set down the completion of the single market by 1992 as a legal goal. With active British support, it also codified Europe's hesitant joint activity in foreign policy as 'European political co-operation', the genesis of the more systematic common foreign and security policy (CFSP) of today.

The impact of the Single European Act in turn proved much greater than Delors or others expected, mainly because the process of widening the scope of QMV in the Council of Ministers undermined the legitimacy of invoking the Luxembourg Compromise – the convention whereby decision-making would normally be frozen, even in areas where QMV applied, if any member state asserted that a 'vital national interest' was at stake. Forced on the Community by French President Charles de Gaulle in January 1966 – after the 'empty chair crisis' in which Paris boycotted the work of the Council for six months – this convention had fostered a 'veto culture' among governments, matched by a mood of generalized pessimism about decision-making at European level that had frustrated progress on many fronts over the next twenty years. Now the unexpected demise of the Luxembourg Compromise freed up the Community institutions to deliver policy outcomes much more easily. As Joseph Weiler has written, agreement in the Council was henceforth to be reached not 'under the shadow of the veto', but 'under the shadow of the vote' – with an even longer shadow, the one cast by the General over the path to European unity, finally lifting.

The growing success of the single market programme, speeded by the Single Act, generated a new logic in favour of European integration. The years of stasis in Europe since the 1960s had seemed to discredit those political scientists – such as Ernst Haas and Leon Lindberg, the so-called 'neo-functionalists' – who had predicted that integration in one policy sector would quietly but remorselessly build pressure for integration in other areas too. They had argued that, driven by business, consumer, labour or governmental interests which could benefit from simpler, common rules across national boundaries, joint action in one area was likely to 'spill over' progressively from sector to sector, on a modular basis, generating pro-European momentum. Led by Delors, this is exactly what started to happen in the mid- to late-1980s, with the transformation of the continental economy revitalizing the whole European-level political system.

Delors argued that to balance the liberalizing impact of the single market – the take-off of which was proving much more successful than he had expected – it was desirable to develop a 'social Europe' that would extend common minimum employment rights to workers across the Community. A social action plan and a Social Charter followed. Likewise, common environmental and consumer protection standards would dovetail neatly with the Europe-wide technical standards being adopted through the far-reaching 1992 programme. The distributional impact of the single market on peripheral areas in turn justified a doubling of central Community funding for transport infrastructure, regional development and other 'cohesion' projects designed to modernize the economies of Greece, Spain and Portugal, in particular. Germany and Britain successfully insisted that this new spending should be matched by tighter financial discipline, multi-annual budgeting and reform of the Common Agricultural Policy (CAP). The share of farm spending in the Community budget began to fall by about 1 per cent a year and continued to do so for the next three decades.

Most importantly, Delors relaunched the debate, dormant since the mid-1970s, about the possibility of developing a single currency for Europe. He saw very quickly that synergies between the single market and a single currency could help realize economies of scale, facilitating trade, increasing competition and boosting growth among participating countries. In June 1988, Delors manoeuvred his own appointment to chair a committee of the Community's national central bank governors, with a mandate to look at the possible route to economic and monetary union (EMU). Driven by both the determination of its chair and the analysis of its chief adviser, Tommaso Padoa-Schioppa, the Delors Committee reported nine months later, proposing a three-stage move to full EMU, based on a common monetary policy and a single currency.

For Delors, Mitterrand and Kohl, the idea of moving to a single currency in Europe – agreed over a year before the fall of the Berlin Wall, and not after that event, as is often assumed – was a crucial turning point. It represented less of a Franco-German compromise than a strategic choice by Kohl in favour of dissolving the most potent symbol of post-war German economic success, the Deutschmark, into a wider European framework, based on a new, common monetary sovereignty to be established at European level. It was Kohl's key European choice, with huge consequences that are still being felt. The Bundesbank President, Karl Otto Pöhl, initially reassured an increasingly vexed Thatcher that the EMU process could and would be resisted or contained, as indeed much of the German financial establishment hoped, only to be overridden by his Chancellor.

Thatcherite contradictions

From the summer of 1988 onwards, Thatcher moved decisively against the European project, which she now feared had started to run out of control. The success of the single market, which she had strongly promoted as a projection of her own domestic reform agenda on a continental scale, had ironically set off a process of supranational integration of the kind she most feared. She vowed to try to halt any move towards EMU – if necessary, standing alone – setting herself against her most senior, but more pragmatic, ministerial colleagues, her Chancellor of the Exchequer, Nigel Lawson, and her Foreign Secretary and later deputy prime minister, Geoffrey Howe. The successive resignations of these two previously loyal standard-bearers of the 'Thatcher revolution', in the autumns of 1989 and 1990, symbolized the destructive potential of Europe within British Conservative politics, an issue that was henceforth to haunt the party whenever it was in power.

Conservatism had been hugely successful as a political force in the United Kingdom, over many decades, not least because it had managed to combine and embody the twin imperatives of the 'nation' and the 'state' – of representing and celebrating national institutions and patriotism, on the one hand, and of exercising the will to power and addressing the need to make hard choices in government, on the other. Thatcher's own success in the 1980s was a testimony to her ability to ride these two horses at once, much as Ronald Reagan's was across the Atlantic. Now Europe was beginning to prise those two components apart in Britain and to pit them against each other, revealing tensions, indeed contradictions, at the heart of Thatcherism.

Market freedom and open international economics were decisively eroding the substance of sovereignty, as frontiers fell and economic interdependence thrived in what the Japanese management consultant, Kenichi Ohmae, dubbed (in 1989) the 'borderless world'. The notion of national parliamentary control – which was really national executive control – so dear to Thatcher's heart, was being gradually dissolved by the very economic freedom that she had done so much to pioneer. Ironically, Delors and other advocates of the pooling of sovereignty saw this as a way to retain or regain some measure of that control – by exercising it collectively at European level. And Britain's national strategy of acting as a gateway to Europe for inward investment – and as a transatlantic bridge for Europe to America in defence and security – was ultimately becoming dependent on the success of Europe as a more cohesive political and economic entity, and on Britain staying close to the centre of gravity of any new European power.

'EUROPE WHOLE AND FREE': THE END OF COMMUNISM AND REUNIFICATION OF GERMANY, 1989–90

Gorbachev's 'new thinking'

Just as 1985 represented a turning point in Western Europe, relaunching the process of European integration, that year also saw a decisive change in the Soviet Union and Central and Eastern Europe. Mikhail Gorbachev became secretary-general of the Soviet Communist party in March 1985 and set in train an internal reform process – captured in the words *perestroika* (restructuring) and *glasnost* (openness), and the general concept of 'new thinking' – that led within six years to the fall of the Berlin Wall, the collapse of communism across the Soviet bloc, the reunification of Germany and finally the disintegration of the Soviet Union itself. Gorbachev's intention was not the destruction of the system over which he presided, but rather its radical modernization to ensure its own survival. His will to reform was emboldened by the sluggish and evasive official response to the first major crisis he faced in office, the meltdown at the Chernobyl nuclear power-plant in April 1986 that required the evacuation of 130,000 people and contaminated an area of over 150,000 square kilometres in northern Ukraine. But in the spirit of Alexis de Tocqueville's celebrated observation in *L'Ancien régime et la révolution* that 'the most dangerous moment for any bad government is when it seeks to reform its ways', the new Soviet leader found that attempting to transform a centrally planned economy and blocked society into a less rigid system and encouraging it to engage more openly with the West would set off a range of forces that Moscow could not easily steer or control.

Gorbachev allowed limited democratic elections in the Soviet Union in March 1989, with official party candidates being beaten for the first time in any communist state. However, the movement for democratic change accelerated most rapidly in the Soviet satellites, notably in Poland and Hungary, where Moscow increasingly chose to turn a blind eye to popular pressures for greater freedom. A critical staging-post in legitimizing this process was Gorbachev's own landmark speech to the UN General Assembly in December 1988, in which he suggested that all countries in Europe, east and west, should enjoy 'freedom of choice' over which political and economic model they followed. This in effect renounced the hated 'Brezhnev doctrine' and marked the end of the Kremlin's professed right unilaterally to suppress any move in any 'socialist country towards capitalism'. As Archie Brown has written, this 'new tolerance in Moscow provided the decisive stimulus to change in Eastern Europe' and 'once it began, it was contagious'.

From contagion to collapse

In Poland, the Solidarity trade-union movement, encouraged by Pope Jean-Paul II, had fought a long and very visible campaign for reform, capturing the imagination of the world. Its leader, the Gdańsk shipyard worker, Lech Wałęsa, organized in effect an alternative, underground government and played an important role in bringing the despised regime of General Jaruzelski to the negotiating table. In April 1989, not only was Solidarity made legal and the status of the Catholic Church recognized, but a pathway was established to the free election in June that year of half of the country's parliament. In parallel, the communist leadership in Hungary agreed to institute a multi-party system and free elections, with the country adopting a new, post-communist constitution in October 1989 and preparing for free elections the following May. In the Soviet Union itself, sporadic discontent began to emerge, less at the centre in Moscow — except ironically among agitated party hardliners resistant to Gorbachev's reform drive — than in some of its component republics, notably the three Baltic States and Georgia, which saw the prospect of greater democracy as potentially synonymous with national independence.

The growing 'contagion' in Central and Eastern Europe acted as a warning to the Chinese Communist Party, which was also under pressure to concede serious political reforms. Gorbachev visited Beijing in mid-May 1989 on a trip that was meant to herald a new era of friendship among communist rulers, but he spent much of his time trying to avoid fuelling student protests on the streets. Poignantly, on the same day that Chinese demonstrators were being crushed in Tiananmen Square, 4 June, the Polish people elected their first free parliament in over forty years, a contest which saw the governing party suffer a devastating defeat. When Gorbachev visited West Germany later the same month, there was an outpouring of 'Gorbymania', which this time he did nothing to suppress. The world's two major communist systems were beginning to move on radically diverging paths.

Although the authorities in East Berlin and Prague initially tried to hold the line, with some recidivists even hinting at a possible 'Chinese solution', they were disabled by inertia in Moscow and then soon overwhelmed by people power. East Germans began to escape to the West through Hungary, where the border with Austria had first been breached in a 'European picnic' during the summer, while popular demonstrations in the major cities of the German Democratic Republic (GDR) built up during the autumn — forcing the retirement of the country's veteran leader, Erich Honecker, in mid-October — until suddenly, almost in a fit of panic by the authorities, the Berlin Wall was opened on the night of 9 November 1989.

As East Berliners flocked towards the Wall to see if the news on West German television was actually true — namely that the communist regime had announced its intention to liberalize travel restrictions 'immediately, without delay' (words that were seemingly a mistake on the part of the official spokesman who uttered them) — startled border guards froze in the face of the sheer number of people who were gathering in front of them and the logic of the crowd took control. That night, thousands of individuals who separately went to see if history might be made ironically became the very people who were making history itself. One piece of graffiti painted on the Wall in the following days, when two million East Berliners crossed over to visit West Berlin, captured the mood: 'Only today is the war really over'.

Why the Fall?

The dramatic collapse of communism confirmed and justified the highly controversial stance that Thatcher and Reagan had taken from the early 1980s, with Chancellor Kohl in close support, of building up NATO defences against the Soviet Union – including deploying intermediate-range nuclear weapons on West German soil to counter Soviet missiles of the same kind – and then, from a position of growing strength, pursuing a strategy of détente with Gorbachev, a man with whom Thatcher famously declared she could 'do business'. Washington shrewdly calculated that Moscow could not sustain the arms race on which both sides had now embarked, and that the internal strains of the economic system across the Eastern bloc would gradually move towards breaking point.

To objective economics was added the changing mood of the people. The younger generation in Warsaw Pact countries, in particular, felt increasing discontent with their inability to share in Western economic, cultural and political freedoms, real or imagined. The partial opening of the border for limited tourism or family visits to the West during the 1980s – a reform from which Polish, Hungarian, Czech and East German citizens increasingly benefited – seems only to have whetted people's appetites and made the problem worse. Visitors saw a Western Europe that was preparing confidently for the opportunities of a huge single market in which all internal barriers would soon be removed – as Timothy Garton Ash has put it succinctly, '1992 was a cause of 1989'. The contrast was perhaps most striking with Romania, where not only was food severely rationed in a country with strong agricultural potential, but individual typewriters had to be registered and duplicators and photocopiers were banned. By the late 1980s, the growing culture of individual empowerment in Western societies, driven by consumer freedom, was invading the consciousness of citizens on the other side of the Iron Curtain. As Victor Hugo remarked of an earlier revolutionary period, while 'one can resist the invasion of armies, one cannot resist the invasion of ideas'.

There was, however, no inevitability about the fall of the Berlin Wall, nor indeed the collapse of communism more widely, coming exactly when it did. Indeed, it was scarcely foretold by any respected commentator or diplomat. When Reagan appealed to the Soviet leader at the Brandenburg Gate in June 1987, with the words 'Mr Gorbachev, open this gate; Mr Gorbachev, tear down this wall', few believed that any such prospect was imminent. There was certainly a growing debate among foreign-policy experts about the potential for convergence between east and west, based on military de-escalation and gradual liberalization in the east, but few expected a sudden acceleration towards the collapse of the communist system itself.

During Gorbachev's visit to the Federal Republic in June 1989, the Soviet leader ambiguously suggested that the Berlin Wall 'could disappear once the conditions that generated the need for it had disappeared', but any timescale was difficult to fathom. The *Economist*, in a special feature on West Germany published just twelve days before the Wall was breached, speculated about a possible reunification at some point in coming decades, inviting readers not to 'dismiss as wild fantasy' the idea of a united Germany by the end of the century. It cited an opinion poll showing that while 80 per cent of West Germans hoped for reunification someday, only 3 per cent thought it would come about 'within a foreseeable time-span'.

Grand bargain

The fall of the Berlin Wall was quickly to interact with the process of European integration in a very dynamic way. It greatly strengthened the advocates of both monetary union and wider political integration in Europe. Whether the single currency would ever have happened – or at least have happened so quickly – without the collapse of communism and reunification of Germany is one of the most interesting counter-factual questions of recent European political history. Even though Chancellor Kohl had already agreed in principle to abandon the Deutschmark by early 1988, the rise in German power implicit in reunification now effectively locked the process in, guaranteeing it in practice – despite considerable scepticism among German public opinion, and indeed the Frankfurt financial community, about the merits of adopting a single European currency.

The grand bargain, eventually crystallized in the Maastricht Treaty, agreed in late 1991, was very simple: a stronger Germany would disperse its greater power in a stronger European Community, to be redubbed the European Union. Monetary union would be a crucial part of that, as would be a greater role for the European-level institutions in many other policy fields – notably stronger collective action in foreign and security policy, and in justice and home affairs. These changes would be underpinned by acceptance that law-making in conventional Community fields would use more qualified majority voting in the Council of Ministers, allowing countries to be outvoted, and involve greater legislative power-sharing between the Council and the European Parliament ('co-decision'). These various features – together with respect for the principle of subsidiarity (decision-making at the lowest practical level of government) and introduction of the concept of European citizenship, as a parallel to existing national citizenship – were ambitiously styled 'political union'. The new European Union displayed more pronounced federal features than the previous Community, but it still maintained strong intergovernmental components and fell far short of anything approaching free-standing statehood.

Hence the irony that, while the fall of the Wall should have been Margaret Thatcher's moment of greatest vindication, it disoriented her politically, weakened her both at home and abroad, and exposed the limitations of her vision for the future of the West. She feared its potential to promote what she dismissively termed a 'European superstate', to be controlled in effect by Germany. For her, post-war European unity was less a 'peace project', designed to promote Franco-German reconciliation and make war impossible through economic interdependence, than it was a 'Cold War project' to hold Western Europe together in the face of Soviet power, provocation and potential aggression.

The sudden removal of the communist threat from the east meant that Thatcher saw no need to step up European integration, whether through monetary or political union, whereas many of her fellow leaders drew the opposite conclusion. They considered such moves necessary, if not imperative, to stave off the risk of disintegration and of moving backwards into divisive nationalism. Kohl had told an audience in Oxford, as far back as in May 1984, with Thatcher in the audience, that 'our passionate advocacy of European unification' flowed from an 'awareness that a positive settlement of the German question is only conceivable within a greater European framework'. He said that West Germany's leaders would never give up on the idea of reuniting Germany and that the best structure for that would be 'the political union of Europe, without ifs and buts'. But the message had seemed largely rhetorical or theoretical in Whitehall at the time it was delivered and was essentially ignored.

Thatcher was not alone in her worries about future German power. The Italian and Dutch prime ministers, Giulio Andreotti and Ruud Lubbers, both expressed strong concerns behind the scenes, while President Mitterrand allegedly told her that, through reunification, 'the Germans will get in peace what Hitler could not get in war' and that 'Europe would have to bear the consequences'. Mitterrand visited East Berlin in December 1989, reassuring the collapsing regime that it could 'count on France's solidarity with the GDR' and implying that he preferred an independent, democratic, neutral, socialist state in the east to a single, united Germany, based on the existing Federal Republic and rooted in the Atlantic Alliance.

But Mitterrand was a more subtle and agile figure than Thatcher on the European stage and was careful to conceal the depth of his misgivings in public. Once he had concluded that his preferred position of maintaining two Germanys was politically impossible, especially in the face of strong US support for reunification, he focused instead on using this unique moment to extract concessions from Bonn in building a European framework that would contain future German power, both on EMU and more widely. He told Thatcher that he had now concluded 'there was no force in Europe that could stop [reunification] happening' and proceeded accordingly. He floated, but then dropped, the idea of anchoring a reunited Germany in a wider configuration than the European Community – in some kind of new, grand 'European confederation' encompassing both Western and Eastern Europe – and then limited himself to pluralizing and mutualizing the exercise of German power through what was to become the European Union. Since Kohl himself professed such a move to be the natural corollary of German reunification – 'There will be no Fourth Reich; this united Germany will be part of a peaceful Europe' – it made sense for Paris to take full advantage of Bonn's unilateral willingness to 'compromise' while the opportunity lasted.

AFTERWORD
Forms of German unity

There was no inevitability about the precise form that German reunification would take either. By taking risks and asserting his will, Chancellor Kohl succeeded in imposing the basic formula that he wanted – the complete ending of the East German state and its incorporation as five individual Länder into an enlarged Federal Republic, as allowed by Article 23 of the latter's constitution – and he did so in the face of scepticism, if not active resistance, from several quarters. Kohl overcame pressures not only that East Germany should continue as a separate country or that a unified Germany should be a confederation of two parallel states – as advocated, for example, by West Germany's leading novelist, Günter Grass – but also that a united Germany should be a neutral state, perched uneasily between East and West, or that only the former West Germany should stay within the Atlantic alliance.

The all-German neutrality option was favoured by Hans Modrow, the last prime minister of the GDR, while differential membership of NATO was countenanced by Hans-Dietrich Genscher, the Federal Republic's veteran foreign minister and leader of Kohl's coalition partner, the liberal FDP. The Chancellor's position was greatly strengthened by the dramatic success of the 'Alliance for Germany' – in effect a mirror party to his own CDU – winning 48 per cent of the vote in the first democratic elections in the GDR, held in March 1990. In the event, there would be no new German constitution and no change in the relationship with NATO or the United States – only a commitment that a unified Germany would pay the cost of Soviet troop withdrawals from the east, would not possess nuclear or chemical weapons in the future, and would limit the size of its own armed forces to a maximum of 375,000 personnel.

Critical to this outcome was the consistent support given to the German Chancellor by policy-makers in Washington. Backed by a formidable team of foreign-policy advisers – including Brent Scowcroft, Condoleezza Rice and Robert Zoellick – President Bush and his Secretary of State, James Baker, endorsed all of Kohl's key choices before and during the 'Two plus Four' talks that brought together the Federal Republic, the GDR and the four victorious allies from 1945 – the United States, Soviet Union, United Kingdom and France. In effect, the Bush–Kohl double-act ensured that the Chancellor got the most important thing that he wanted – the merger of East Germany into the existing Federal Republic – and the US President secured his most critical need – the anchoring of the whole of the unified Germany firmly within the NATO system. Bush's personal respect for Kohl – and for the latter's historic commitment, like that of Adenauer before him, simultaneously to both European and transatlantic unity – was captured in his later description of the 'unity Chancellor' as 'the greatest European leader of the second half of the twentieth century'.

Meanwhile in Moscow, Mikhail Gorbachev was taking considerable political risks to align on broadly the same approach. As he commented laconically to journalists, 'history has started working in an unexpectedly rapid way'. He beat back hardliners who wanted to invade East Germany militarily in a repeat of the Soviet occupation of Czechoslovakia in 1968. After some hesitation, he accepted the logic of German reunification and gave up attempts to try to trade unity for neutrality, negotiating instead on the terms of Soviet retreat. Critically, he agreed that the new Germany could choose to stay within NATO, if it wished. In a landmark statement, the Soviet leader declared that a 'united Germany will get back its full sovereignty – and, as a sovereign country, decide on its own whether it will join an alliance, and which one'. However good Gorbachev was at capturing world attention with phrases like 'new thinking' and a 'common European home', he was much less successful in shaping the concrete terms of German reunification – which was ironic given the huge part he played in triggering the process – just as he was never to get to the stage of successfully reinventing communism, his original hope.

Peaceful revolutions and 'price of victory'

The collapse of communism in Poland, Hungary and East Germany was followed in quick succession by the toppling of the established order in Czechoslovakia and Bulgaria (in November 1989) and Romania (the following month). It was not long before the situation began to be replicated in the Soviet Union itself, where the three Baltic States gained independence between November 1989 and June 1990. Gorbachev's hold on power was badly buffeted by the sudden resignation in December 1990 of his reform-minded foreign minister, Eduard Shevardnadze, who feared the revenge of the hardliners, declaring 'dictatorship is coming'. Leading members of Gorbachev's government and the military did attempt to seize power in an aborted coup the following August, with the Soviet leader kept under house arrest for three days at his presidential dacha in Crimea. The beneficiary of these events was the charismatic and volatile head of the newly devolved jurisdiction of Russia, Boris Yeltsin, who had been elected in a popular vote only two months before, against Gorbachev's preferred candidate. Yeltsin effectively fended off the coup in Moscow, famously appearing in front of the parliament building to lead the public resistance, in the process both restoring Gorbachev to power and positioning himself as his de facto successor.

The Soviet Union as a system was unable to withstand the dramatic events of August 1991, with the Communist Party collapsing soon after and more and more individual republics declaring independence during the autumn. In a quiet coup of his own, Yeltsin transferred authority over the Russian economy and military to his own jurisdiction, even if he had no legal right to do so. The USSR finally broke up in December 1991, with Gorbachev relinquishing office and Russia becoming one of fifteen separate states, each with its own currency. A loose and pointedly named 'Commonwealth of Independent States' was founded by ten of the successor countries, led in effect by Russia. In parallel, the Warsaw Pact was dissolved in July 1991. 'Mrs Thatcher was vindicated in her fear that Gorbachev would lose power as a result of the rapidity of developments in Central and Eastern Europe,' commented her foreign policy adviser, Charles Powell, 'but not quite in the way she expected.'

Except in Romania, the various transitions of 1989–91 occurred largely peacefully, with relatively little violence – indeed the one in Prague was dubbed a 'velvet revolution' – and the successor regimes were generally committed to the development of constitutional democracy. Only where the communist government forcibly resisted change, in Bucharest, was there a violent uprising, involving the loss of a thousand lives and culminating in the execution by firing squad of the country's dictator, Nicolae Ceaușescu, who had been in power since 1965. As Philipp Ther has noted, the 'essential difference between 1989 and 1789, 1848 and 1917 was its predominant lack of violence and wilful destruction', with no 'mass terror', making the events of 1989 more like 1776 in the United States than previous European revolutions. One reason may be that the central force driving the remarkable changes of 1989–91 was not the utopian idea of building a completely new society, but rather a pragmatic desire to share in a prosperous and peaceful 'normality' that was widely seen to prevail in the West. Indeed, François Furet, historian of the French Revolution, remarked that 'not a single new idea [came] out of Eastern Europe in 1989', while Jürgen Habermas styled the events of that time 'catch-up' or 'rectifying' revolutions.

In the stirring rush of events that marked the end of the Cold War, the boundary of Western freedom moved in effect one thousand kilometres to the east, decisively changing the geopolitics of the European continent. There was, however, a 'price of victory' for the Western leaders in the way they conceived and handled the challenges of the moment, and one largely unappreciated at the time. In one year, Russia lost all the territories that it had first acquired in its westward imperial expansion between 1667 and 1795. This sudden reversal of fortune generated a sense of loss and wounded pride deep within the Russian psyche, something which was to re-emerge as a potent political force in later decades, leading to a time-lagged instability of a different kind in 'post-Wall' Europe.

EUROPE IN THE UNIPOLAR DECADE, 1990–2000

Benign outlook

The disappearance of the Soviet Union as a political force ended the superpower confrontation that had defined the whole post-war era and left the United States as the only significant strategic player, both in Europe and on the wider international stage. This 'unipolar moment', as Charles Krauthammer immediately dubbed it, stretched out to become a unipolar decade, and it was to prove to be a largely benign, if uninspiring, one for the new Europe. Under President Bush and his Democratic successor, Bill Clinton, America's new global hegemony was used to positive effect for Europe in the 1990s – not only to facilitate the reunification of Germany and bind the new, stronger Germany in a tighter European embrace, but to support democratization and economic reform across Central and Eastern Europe, and to extend the NATO system to include former Soviet satellite states. This process was underpinned by firm support in Washington, as well as in many European capitals, for open markets, free trade and the increasing economic and political interdependence that was soon to become known as 'globalization'.

The 1990s can now be seen as the apogee of the Bretton Woods system of international institutions founded after the Second World War – a high watermark for the 'global rules-based order', reflecting essentially Western interests and operating under Western guidance, even as it expanded to embrace newly industrializing states in Asia. The successful conclusion of the Uruguay Round of negotiations to liberalize world trade in April 1994 reflected the reigning orthodoxy, leading to the admission of China to the new World Trade Organization in 2001. Whatever domestic crises or economic difficulties individual countries might confront, the new Europe could feel comfortable in a setting where unipolarity and multilateralism seemed to thrive in tandem – and where the promise was of a global future in which other jurisdictions and peoples would become 'more like us'. In effect, a freer and more united Europe was being sponsored and protected by the United States, without any great American fear that the resulting continent would become either a rival or a constraint. The traditional ambivalence of US policy identified by Henry Kissinger back in 1969 – that Washington consistently 'urged European unity while recoiling before its probable consequences' – was to be much less acute in the decade after the fall of the Berlin Wall.

Brutal transition

The transition to market economics in Central and Eastern Europe proved, however, a much bumpier and more brutal experience than many predicted. A lack of preparation for an abrupt change in economic regime in most of the east coincided with a general cyclical downturn across the continent as a whole. GDP among the new democracies fell sharply at the beginning of the decade – contracting in Poland, for example, by 7 per cent in both 1990 and 1991 – even if it then stabilized and gradually recovered from 1993 onwards, so that incomes were higher in real terms by the end of the decade than at the start. However, lost jobs, supply shortages and high inflation in some countries were not easily endured or forgotten, and the new economic settlement was marked by growing inequality and insecurity, especially for older workers and the retired.

Economic growth was disappointing in much of Western Europe too, falling from an average of 4 per cent a year in 1988 to zero in 1993, and then stagnating, before returning again to almost 4 per cent by 2000. After growing spectacularly, at around 5 per cent in 1990 and 1991, Germany – now Europe's largest economy by far, but beginning to bear a heavy financial burden for reunification – faced a period of stagnation. The shock of unity, which put three million East Germans out of work within a year and forced 80 per cent of workers to change jobs within a decade, was compounded by Kohl's insistence on an immediate intra-German currency union, with the Ostmark substituted by the Deutschmark at a strict one-for-one parity. Soon after reunification, the West German taxpayer began to cross-subsidize the new Eastern Länder by over 100 billion euro a year – building up to a total of two trillion euro over the subsequent thirty years – with per-capita East German incomes rising gradually from 37 per cent of the West German average in 1989 to 73 per cent thirty years later.

East Germany was in a uniquely privileged position in being absorbed into a successful Western capitalist economy. There was, however, no comparable financial transfer or cushioning by Western Europe for the other new democracies in the east, where some political remnants from the Soviet era were to survive on the back of nostalgia, especially among older voters. Ideas of launching a post-1989 Marshall Plan for Central and Eastern Europe came to nothing, with only a modest multilateral lending facility, the European Bank for Reconstruction and Development (EBRD), being put in place, initially under Mitterrand's former foreign policy adviser, Jacques Attali. The increasingly divergent economic paths of the two halves of Czechoslovakia played a role in the country's (largely amicable) decision to split into separate states in January 1993. The political agility of Václav Havel, the Czech writer who had moved from dissident leader to national president in December 1989, helped ensure that Slovak separatism could be realized without leaving a strong legacy of mutual recrimination.

Political and economic turbulence

Just as the economic crises of the early 1990s helped disillusion the populations of Central and Eastern Europe about the sudden move to capitalism, so the downturn in Western Europe did little to make the macro-political settlement embodied in the new European Union very popular either. This turned out to be particularly significant because, for the first time, the pooling of sovereignty at supranational level provided for in the Maastricht Treaty was sufficiently obvious that it was subject to popular votes by referendum in certain EU member states. The ratification of the treaty, initially assumed to be a formality, proved a much more dangerous political process than expected. Not only did it become enmeshed with the public's discontent about the recession and its (perhaps surprising) indifference to the largely successful handling of the end of the Cold War by their various leaders – as President Bush was to discover painfully when he failed to secure re-election in November 1992 – it also sparked an incipient 'sovereigntist' revolt, notably on the right, against the growing centralization of power implicit in the prospect of a single currency for Europe.

In June 1992, the Danish people unexpectedly voted to reject the Maastricht text, setting off a year-long ratification crisis in several other member states. The French public only narrowly accepted the treaty in September 1992 (by 51 to 49 per cent) and the British parliament almost rejected the text, with the opposition Labour party voting against it on the disingenuous grounds that it was insufficiently pro-European. The Danes themselves finally approved the treaty in a second vote (in May 1993), after receiving a permanent opt-out from EMU (like Britain), as well as special assurances on European citizenship and defence.

The countdown to the French referendum on 20 September 1992 – the holding of which was itself a major, unforced political error by President Mitterrand – proved unusually fraught, with Britain and Italy being blown out of the exchange-rate mechanism (ERM) of the European Monetary System (EMS) on 'Black Wednesday', four days before the French vote. Britain's ejection from the ERM was a humiliating political blow to John Major, Thatcher's successor as prime minister (from November 1990), who had staked considerable political capital on putting the country 'where it belongs, at the very heart of Europe'.

Exchange-rate parities across Europe had been under considerable strain as a result of German reunification, with the Bundesbank insisting on higher domestic interest rates to offset rising public borrowing – the German budget deficit quickly rose to over 5 per cent of GDP – so pushing up the value of the Deutschmark. Traders shorted currencies which they considered overvalued in their own right (notably sterling) and/or those whose value would be sure to fall (such as the Italian lire and Spanish peseta) if the Maastricht Treaty were to be rejected and the EMU project either seriously dented or abandoned. One hedge-funder, George Soros, allegedly made one billion pounds on Black Wednesday, in what he correctly calculated to be a one-way bet against sterling.

In the event, despite exchange-rate turbulence that exploded again in the summer of 1993 – when the permitted margin of currency fluctuation within the ERM had to be widened from 2.25 to 15.0 per cent – the Maastricht Treaty finally entered into force in November that year, with Germany ironically the last country to ratify it, as a result of a legal challenge in its constitutional court. While the strong consensus in Italy was to seek to re-join the ERM as soon as it could, which it eventually achieved in November 1996, there was no political will to do so in Britain, where the power of pro-European forces had been permanently damaged. Indeed, the Maastricht ratification crisis and Black Wednesday propelled the rise of 'Euroscepticism' – intellectual objection and resistance to the process of European integration as a matter of principle – first and most spectacularly in Britain, and then, over time, more widely.

NATO's uncertain role

Although Mitterrand and Delors remained in office until 1995, and Kohl until 1998, in each case their historical achievement was to be measured in their handling of the fast-moving events of 1988 to 1992, four 'hinge' years which radically reshaped the European order. The mid- to late-1990s in Europe were, by contrast, a period of relative stability in Europe, underpinned by the gradually improving economy. At the end of Delors' ten-year tenure as Commission President in Brussels, the European Union expanded to include Austria, Finland and Sweden in 1995, raising the number of member states from twelve to fifteen, in perhaps the least disruptive enlargement in its history. NATO was widened too, to embrace Poland, Hungary and the Czech Republic from 1999. The Washington NATO summit of that year set nine more former Soviet bloc countries on the path to joining the alliance over the ensuing decade, even if Gorbachev later claimed that in 1990 there had been a clear understanding that NATO 'would not move an inch to the east' after the end of the Cold War. Whether this latter assurance was extended is a matter of intense dispute, but even if it was given, it would contradict Gorbachev's own assertion in 1988 that all European countries should be free to choose which kind of political and economic system they wished to adopt, including by implication their own arrangements for security and defence.

The greatly reduced threat of armed conflict on European soil was underpinned by the successful 'de-nuclearization' of the non-Russian parts of the former Soviet Union, specifically Belarus, Kazakhstan and Ukraine. Ukraine alone would have been the world's third largest nuclear power if it had retained the ballistic arsenal (of almost 2,000 warheads) that it inherited from Moscow. The voluntary disarmament of these successor states was matched by a commitment – signed by the US, UK and Russian governments in Budapest in December 1994 – to respect the new countries' independence, sovereignty and borders, and to 'refrain from the threat or use of force' against their territorial integrity, political independence or economic well-being. Heralded at the time as a triumph for arms control and non-proliferation, the assurances contained in the 'Budapest memorandum' were already seen by some as of uncertain value in the absence of more concrete Western security guarantees.

The move to 'unipolarity' in international politics left many national capitals uncertain about the future role of NATO and the place of defence in a post-Cold War world. Many European governments (as well as the US and Canada) sought to release a 'peace dividend' by significantly reducing defence spending – which fell on average from 2.5 to 1.8 per cent of GDP in NATO countries during the 1990s, and which continued to decline to 1.4 per cent over the following twenty years. At the same time, NATO itself suffered a growing identity crisis as it sought to transition from a purely defensive alliance – whose forces had never actually been deployed, except on practice missions – to a series of new, more amorphous and ambiguous 'out of area' roles, such as peace-keeping, peace-making and humanitarian aid. When, in 1990–91, Washington put together a coalition to reverse Iraq's invasion of Kuwait, there was no suggestion that the resulting Gulf War should be conducted under the aegis of NATO, even though Operation Desert Storm involved twelve of NATO's then sixteen member countries.

Crisis in the Balkans

The limitations of European defence (and arguably of European values) were soon to be powerfully exposed in the Western Balkans, where a spectacular after-shock of the collapse of communism was the break-up of Yugoslavia – essentially an artificial federation of six states established as a Socialist republic in 1945 – and the descent into war within and between its component parts. As Kristina Spohr has put it, 'if the Soviet Union disintegrated peacefully, Yugoslavia imploded violently'. A complex web of armed conflicts saw the previously dominant Serbs attempt to forestall the independence of secessionist states, matched by internal struggles within individual states. This brutal multi-dimensional civil war led to over a million people losing their homes and left more than 130,000 dead. The events in the Balkans also offered early evidence that some of the ethnic and ideological divisions of the pre-communist era had a more powerful potential to reassert themselves than was widely assumed by commentators at the time.

Declarations of independence in June 1991 by two of the components of the Yugoslav federal republic, Slovenia and Croatia, sparked war with the central government of Slobodan Milosevic in Belgrade. The recognition of these moves, first by Germany (despite French and US doubts) and then by the European Union as a whole, proved controversial. Then, in April 1992, the conflict spread to Bosnia-Herzegovina, which also broke away from Yugoslavia, following a local referendum. Here, (Orthodox) Serbs were in a minority compared with the 'Bosniac' Muslims and (Catholic) Croats – who both supported independence – but were determined to retain control. Led by Radovan Karadzic and supported by Milosevic in Belgrade, the Bosnian Serbs engaged in ethnic cleansing and laid siege to the state capital, Sarajevo, for four years. Macedonia also left the federal republic in 1992, while Montenegro sought to stay aloof from the conflict, as the only remaining part of the now much-truncated Yugoslav republic alongside Serbia.

The reaction of the international community to the increasingly intractable Balkans crisis was inert and half-hearted. A UN peace-keeping mission was launched in February 1992, but it was under-resourced, enjoyed only a limited mandate and proved largely ineffective on the ground. NATO air-power was made available to the UN from the following June, but was subject to a 'dual-key' system of control that involved complicated lines of command, generating tensions between and within both the UN and NATO, as well as among the European states. As the crisis deepened, the United States under Bill Clinton (President from January 1993) preferred to keep its distance from a potential quagmire: 'Their enmities go back five hundred years, some would say almost a thousand years', he pointedly remarked. In a comment that he later came to regret, the British Foreign Secretary, Douglas Hurd, said that intervention would simply create a 'level killing field' among warring factions.

Srebrenica and US intervention

The slaughter and destruction on the ground reached an agonizing climax in July 1995, when over 7,000 Bosnian Muslims were murdered by Serbian forces under Ratko Mladic at Srebrenica, a Muslim enclave in a Serbian dominated part of Bosnia-Herzegovina. The Srebrenica massacre, which saw the biggest single loss of life in any one event in Europe since the Second World War, finally prompted an international outcry and generated a much greater sense of urgency, notably in Washington. (The retirement of President Mitterrand, who was highly cautious on the issue, in May 1995, also played a role.) NATO was mandated by the UN to intervene militarily to end the conflict. When it came, the deployment of US airpower proved decisive and overwhelming. During Operation Deliberate Force in August–September, the US flew 20,000 sorties, whereas Britain and France flew 800. (Italy contributed just one airfield, even though the war was virtually on its doorstep, 500 kilometres away, and Spain made available six aircraft.)

With Serbia facing defeat in the field, the United States successfully brokered a peace agreement, signed in Dayton, Ohio, in November 1995. The Dayton accords divided Bosnia-Herzegovina into two sub-states, whose boundaries broadly reflected the situation on the ground at the end of the war – a Bosnian Serb entity, known as the Republika Srpska, and a Muslim-Croat entity, known somewhat confusingly as Federation of Bosnia and Herzegovina. NATO land forces were deployed in the country until 2004, when they were replaced by those of the EU's Operation Althea. In a coda to the Balkans conflict, ethnic Albanians in the Kosovo province of Serbia fought a final, brutal war for independence in 1999. Ethnic cleansing of Albanians by the federal army led to a second NATO military operation against the Serbs that summer, with Kosovo subsequently placed under UN administration, guaranteed by NATO troops.

The handling and outcome of the Balkans crisis revealed both the continuing dependence of Europe on the United States for its own peace and security, and the contrasting attitudes to power on either side of the Atlantic. Jacques Poos, the Luxembourg foreign minister occupying the six-month rotating presidency of the EU Council of Ministers, had confidently asserted, at the start of the crisis in June 1991: 'This is the hour of Europe, not the hour of the Americans. If one problem can be solved by the Europeans, it is the Yugoslav problem.' The clear implication was that European leadership and a European solution to the crisis would be forthcoming, based on at least equal burden-sharing with the Americans. But as Henry Kissinger had observed back in 1968, 'countries do not assume burdens because it is fair, only because it is necessary', and the willingness of any country to act in foreign policy depends not only on it having the resources to do so, but also critically on that country having 'a certain view of its own destiny' as a player in world affairs. In practice, the Balkans crisis suggested that, in the 1990s at least, Europe had neither the means nor the will to fulfil such a destiny, at least when the use of armed force might be involved.

Third-way politics

Although there was some soul-searching in Europe about the implications of the Balkans war and about the broader reality of US global dominance – with French foreign minister Hubert Védrine dubbing America the new 'hyper-power' – the debate was largely confined to foreign policy experts. In the United States itself, the public was distracted by landmark events of a very different kind, heralding a new era of media-driven celebrity, notably the O. J. Simpson trial (1995) and the Monica Lewinsky affair (1998). For many, not just in the US, there was also a growing sense of personal freedom and opportunity during the 1990s, making it what Douglas Coupland, author of the novel *Generation X* (1991), has dubbed 'the good decade'. Hillary Clinton, First Lady to her husband, Bill, in the White House, later joked when challenged about the legacy of those years: 'Which part of peace and prosperity didn't you like?'

In Europe, national politics proceeded on a fairly orthodox course, with power shifting between political camps depending essentially on whether the centre-right or centre-left had been longer in government in any particular country. The harsh and divisive ideological battles that had often characterized political debate in the 1970s and 1980s were softened by the end of the Cold War, with traditional parties of the left in particular increasingly moving to the centre and accepting the logic of market economics. A British sociologist, Anthony Giddens, captured the mood with an influential tract on the future of progressive politics, *The Third Way*, which spoke of the 'death of socialism', invited the left to 'get comfortable with markets [and] the role of business in the creation of wealth', and argued that the key issue was now 'how far, and in what ways, capitalism should be governed and regulated'. The Giddens approach had strong echoes of the 'middle way' advocated by Harold Macmillan in Britain in the 1930s and the 'social market economy' pioneered by Konrad Adenauer and Ludwig Erhard in West Germany after the Second World War.

After eighteen years of Conservative rule in Britain, John Major's moderate centre-right administration gave way, in May 1997, to an equally moderate 'New Labour' government under the charismatic modernizer, Tony Blair, who emerged as the global standard-bearer for 'third way' politics and was elected by the largest landslide in Britain since the Second World War. Despite the economy performing better than at any time since the 1950s, Major and his popular Chancellor of the Exchequer, Kenneth Clarke, received little credit for their achievement: the Tories never recovered from a general loss of credibility delivered by Black Wednesday in 1992 and they then became mired in a long series of minor scandals.

Once in power, Blair showed early skill in his handling of the death of the hugely popular Diana, Princess of Wales, killed in a car crash in Paris in August 1997. He spoke for the nation when he called her the 'people's princess' and successfully steered Queen Elizabeth away from her initially distant reaction to the death not just of a member of the Royal Family, but of a global celebrity and icon. He then secured a major political triumph with the 'Good Friday' peace agreement in Ireland the following April. This ended almost thirty years of violent sectarian conflict in Northern Ireland, the so-called 'Troubles', in which over 3,500 people had been killed. It also removed the shadow of Republican terrorism from mainland Britain and provided a new, more positive foundation for Anglo-Irish relations generally. The Irish settlement helped delegitimize the use of violence in political disputes more widely. For example, in Spain, even if ETA continued its armed struggle for Basque separatism until 2010, it became increasingly divided, conceding several aborted ceasefires, in the face of increasing outrage at each remaining terrorist operation it undertook.

AFTERWORD

In Germany, after sixteen years in office, Chancellor Kohl's governing centre-right CDU-CSU-FDP coalition finally ran out of steam and was replaced, in September 1998, by an SPD-Green coalition under Gerhard Schröder – the nearest continental equivalent to a centrist modernizer in the Blair–Clinton mould. Indeed, Blair and Schröder issued a joint manifesto – entitled predictably The Third Way/*Die Neue Mitte* – in which they set out their common philosophy and vision (before their personal relations turned sour). Meanwhile, in France, after fourteen years in the Élysée, Mitterrand was succeeded as French President by the veteran post-Gaullist leader and Mayor of Paris, Jacques Chirac, who also attempted to reinvent himself as a centrist reformer. Elected in May 1995, he casually lost his parliamentary majority two years later to the left, when he unnecessarily dissolved parliament, and then had to 'co-habit' with a Socialist premier, Lionel Jospin, ironically the man he had defeated for the presidency in the first place.

Even in Italy, the process of 'modernization' appeared finally to be taking off, as the ossified confrontation between Christian Democrats and Communists suddenly gave way to a new bipolar struggle between Silvio Berlusconi's Forza Italia and an 'Olive Tree' alliance of moderate centre-left forces. Although the 1992, 1994 and 1996 general elections in Italy each led to a different result and the country had eight prime ministers in nine years (from 1992 to 2000), they mostly pointed towards the centre and some resulted in modest reforms. Romano Prodi, a former Christian Democrat minister who became leader of the centre-left, headed up the most successful of these short-lived administrations in 1996–98, before becoming President of the European Commission in 1999. His trajectory underlines the wider point: despite changes of parties in power, the political outcome across Europe was marked less by any decisive break with the recent past than by a period of broad continuity in policy and a general blurring of ideological lines.

Millennium's end

At EU level, on the road to a single currency, the irrevocable fixing of exchange rates between eleven national currencies – including those of all six founding member states of the European Community – and the adoption of a common monetary policy, administered by the new

European Central Bank (ECB), were achieved with surprising ease in January 1999. This launch of the third and final phase of the EMU process was, by any standard, an astonishing historical achievement, especially coming only a decade after the initial commitment by Kohl and Mitterrand to move to a single currency. However, its significance went largely unremarked at the time, not least because the euro would exist only as a virtual currency for the next three years, until euro-denominated notes and coins finally entered circulation in January 2002 (itself a major technical accomplishment).

The political decision, taken by the European Council in May 1998, to allow countries to move to this final stage which did not strictly meet the Maastricht convergence criteria – notably Italy with public debt of over 100 per cent of GDP – seemed economically justifiable at the time. However, this made it more imperative to address certain EMU design issues left open in the Maastricht settlement – notably the need for more powerful macro-economic stabilizers between countries and more ambitious domestic supply-side reform within them – but instead these questions were avoided. The unusual ideological convergence that marked European politics in the mid- to late-1990s might have allowed a stronger EMU to have been constructed from the start, but instead potential problems were side-stepped and left for another day.

As Europe prepared to celebrate the passage from one millennium to another, the mood across the continent was mostly one of benign complacency. The advance of information technology was creating what became known as the 'new economy' – with an early form of digitization reducing costs and widening consumer choice, on the back of the multiple opportunities opening up through Europe's single market. Some of the less attractive features of this process, such as widening inequality and greater financial instability, shortly to become apparent in the 'dot-com bubble' in the United States, had yet to significantly impact Europe. As the economy continued to grow at over 1 per cent per quarter, there was still little awareness of the potential of the digital revolution to destroy jobs, as well as to make the economy more efficient, or to impinge on citizens' privacy as data increasingly became commoditized.

In fact, by December 1999, most of the continent's citizens had never been richer or healthier or safer or freer, or more empowered as individuals. GDP per capita and life expectancy – at $30,000 per year and 77 years respectively – were on rising curves and the highest in history. After the turbulence of the early- to mid-1990s, the Western and Eastern European economic experiences were slowly but steadily converging. And all of this was happening in what was still a strikingly positive geopolitical setting. For the first and only time in the twentieth century, Europe no longer faced any obvious external military threat or risk of inter-state warfare, and the logic of multilateralism, in which European leaders and institutions naturally felt comfortable, was widely accepted as the way forward, at least among advanced economies worldwide.

THE FRAYING OF EUROPE'S POLITICAL CONSENSUS, 2001–08

September 11

The real twenty-first century began, in Europe as in America, twenty-one months into the new millennium, on 11 September 2001. Simultaneous suicide attacks by the Islamic terrorist group al-Qaeda, using three hijacked commercial airliners, destroyed the twin towers of the World Trade Center in New York and seriously damaged the Pentagon building in Washington, killing nearly 3,000 people (including citizens from eighty countries, not just the United States). A fourth aircraft crashed in Pennsylvania when its passengers heroically overcame the hijackers before they could reach their intended target in Washington, thought to be either the Capitol Building or the White House.

The immediate effect of '9/11', as it instantly became known, was to unite Europe in support of an injured United States, with emotional expressions of solidarity in the face of a new, spectacularly brutal, form of terrorism. The mutual defence clause of the NATO Treaty, Article Five, was deployed for the first time – ironically, with European countries committing to support an America under threat, rather than the other way round, as its drafters had assumed. But the perpetrators of 9/11 almost certainly calculated that they could, by blindsiding the United States and provoking it into an aggressive reaction, divide and confuse the West – and if so, their strategy was in time to prove effective.

The stock of personal goodwill in Europe towards the recently elected US President, George W. Bush – the eldest son of the previous President but one, George H. W. Bush, who had handled the end of the Cold War so adroitly – was not very great. Not only did the son lack the charm, experience or sensitivity of his father, he had also been elected (in November 2000) with fewer popular votes than his opponent, the outgoing Democratic Vice-President, Al Gore, in a highly contentious and divisive contest that was ultimately settled in the Supreme Court. Addressing the US Congress nine days after September 11, with British Prime Minister Tony Blair sitting in the gallery, the new US President announced the launch of a global 'war on terror'. This war was to be focused initially on al-Qaeda – which purveyed 'a fringe form of Islamic extremism', with the goal of 'remaking the world and imposing its radical beliefs on people everywhere' – and then potentially it would be pursued more widely.

The US decision in November 2001 to depose the Taliban government in Afghanistan, which harboured al-Qaeda, was greeted with relative equanimity among the European nations that had so recently invoked Article Five. However, the identification of a wider 'axis of evil' by President Bush the following January, in his 2002 State of the Union speech to Congress, received less acclaim. A grouping of Iran, Iraq and North Korea was deemed to comprise state sponsors of terrorism or developers of weapons of mass destruction that threatened Western interests and security. Although there was no proof of any direct link between (the pro-Sunni Muslim) al-Qaeda and the (anti-Shia) regime of Saddam Hussein, the two became increasingly intertwined in the minds of many American 'neo-conservative' thinkers, including in the White House, who were looking for a convenient pretext to broaden the global war on terror beyond Afghanistan, to include Iraq.

Iraq war

The US invasion of Iraq, starting in March 2003, was to divide European opinion as starkly as the Vietnam War had done a generation earlier, but with the difference that this time Europeans (essentially 45,000 British troops) were directly engaged in the conflict. Not only were Bush and his entourage seen by many to embody a trigger-happy militarism that was alien to post-war European values; there was also more substantive scepticism about whether, however disagreeable the Iraqi regime might be, it really posed any meaningful threat to

European or US security – and specifically whether it either possessed chemical weapons or was in the process of acquiring nuclear ones, as Washington claimed.

In the event, although as many, if not more, European governments backed the US-led 'coalition of the willing' to topple Saddam as opposed it, the balance of public opinion in most countries was slanted very strongly against the war. In every single European country, a majority of those polled was hostile to intervention in Iraq – certainly without a mandate from the United Nations – by a margin of between 40 per cent in Britain and 70 per cent in Germany. The divergence between the positions of various European governments highlighted emerging fault-lines about the legitimacy of American power. The US defence secretary, Donald Rumsfeld, famously divided the continent into a hesitant or hostile 'old Europe' – embodied by France and Germany at the heart of the classic European Community – and a less inhibited 'new Europe', made up of both some stalwart NATO allies, notably Britain (and somewhat less obviously, Italy and Spain) and many of the new democracies of Central and Eastern Europe (the so-called 'Vilnius ten'). Even if the latter had yet to be admitted to the Union, the continent's 'centre of gravity', Rumsfeld claimed, was already 'shifting to the east'.

Rumsfeld's distinction concealed divisions even among the 'old Europe' governments opposed to the Iraq war, not least after France moved on to the offensive in the UN Security Council, aligning itself with Russia and China against the US, and acutely exposing divisions among the leading Western nations. The position of Chirac's foreign minister, Dominique de Villepin, was far from identical to that of his German counterpart, Joschka Fischer, or of the broader policy community in Berlin, many of whom feared the consequences of growing anti-Americanism in Europe. As one diplomat observed drily at the time, 'Germany does not share France's muscular view of Europe as a future counter-weight to US hegemony on international security issues.'

Twin legacies of distrust

Compounding such differences between and within the competing blocs of governments, the Iraq war also left twin legacies of distrust on the part of public opinion. The first was a specific distrust towards the United States in its self-professed role as global policeman and enforcer of common Western values, generating a marked antipathy to future foreign entanglements under American leadership. The second was a wider distrust of political elites, at home and abroad, who were thought to be increasingly out of touch with the instincts and priorities of 'ordinary' citizens. This 'disconnect' between the governing and the governed was to become an increasingly prominent theme in European politics over coming years.

The Iraq war proved hugely problematic for many of its advocates. Not only did it spark some of the largest demonstrations ever held on the streets of European cities – one in Rome in February 2003 allegedly attracted three million people – but several leading political figures or governing parties (of all persuasions) were to lose power directly or indirectly as a result of supporting the war. For example, José María Aznar, the Spanish conservative prime minister, sensibly announced his retirement in advance of the March 2004 general election in which his Partido Popular suffered a bad defeat. The scale of that defeat was increased by the government rushing to attribute a series of deadly terrorist attacks at Madrid railway stations – which killed almost 200 people, three days before polling day – to domestic terrorists (the Basque separatist ETA), rather than (ironically) to al-Qaeda. Soon after the election, the new socialist government of José Luis Rodriguez Zapatero withdrew Spanish troops from Iraq. Likewise, in Portugal, the opposition socialists won the general election in February 2005 – the centre-right premier, José Manuel Barroso, having adroitly catapulted himself into the role of President of the European Commission (replacing Prodi, who wished to return to domestic politics). In Italy, in May 2006, Silvio Berlusconi duly saw his centre-right coalition break up and relinquish power to the centre-left (now led once again by Prodi).

Even in Britain, where Tony Blair's 'New Labour' was re-elected (for a second time) in 2005, he secured only 35 per cent of the vote and was forced to retire as prime minister two years later, after a decade in Number Ten. Blair's reputation suffered especially badly from the Iraq link, with a widespread view that he had lied to the public and parliament over the threat posed by Saddam Hussein. His spokesman, Alastair Campbell, had memorably claimed that Iraq's weapons of mass destruction could be deployed within forty-five minutes against Britain, when the evidence to support this claim was scant and unconvincing.

Ironic malaise

There was an ironic malaise at the heart of European politics in the mid-2000s: while the economy continued to expand and personal opportunities to widen, the result was not a confident continent at ease with itself or its place in the world, but a restless Europe that seemed increasingly disillusioned, fractious and introverted. The principal political leaders who had resisted the Iraq war, President Chirac and Chancellor Schröder, failed to reap much political dividend or to inspire the public, let alone match the stature of their predecessors, Mitterrand and Kohl. Paradoxically, it was the social democrat (Schröder) who managed to carry through some significant labour market and social security reforms to modernize the German economy – the so-called 'Hartz concept' of 2002–05 – while the conservative (Chirac) proved unable to overcome entrenched opposition from vested interests against, or to energize his supporters behind, even a modest updating of the French employment or pensions regimes.

The pattern of economic reform varied greatly between Northern and Southern Europe. It proved easier to achieve in countries where the public accepted change as necessary in order to embrace, or at least manage, the implications of globalization – as in Britain and Germany respectively – than in countries where the instinct was to contain or resist globalization, as in Italy or France. In Italy, at least, appeal to, and the mobilization of pride around, the 'imperative of Europe' still had some political traction. Indeed, historically, as Vivien Schmidt has observed, 'in no other country has the discourse of European integration played such a central and sustained role in promoting acceptance of change', and in the 2000s this helped justify efforts in Rome to correct the country's public finances under EMU. While Prodi and Barroso as Commission Presidents talked positively of Europe 'mastering' and 'harnessing' the forces of globalization, the reaction in many quarters was more sluggish and sceptical.

The generally unsettled political mood was powerfully illustrated in the aborted attempt to develop and enact a 'Constitution for Europe' in the first half of the decade. While the new Convention on the Future of Europe – convened by EU heads of government in early 2002 and headed by the former French President, Valéry Giscard d'Estaing – brought together many of the best and brightest of Europe's political class and produced a consistent (if rather lengthy) set of proposals to make the EU a more coherent and integrated political system, its conclusions failed to generate any great public enthusiasm or traction. The outcome was then rejected in the French and Dutch referenda of May and June 2005.

Whatever its strengths or weaknesses, the proposed European Constitution was a high-profile victim of growing popular alienation from the assumptions of what many voters increasingly saw as a freestanding political elite, matched by a growing view that European solutions were the instinctive recourse of that elite. Ironically, Giscard's successor but one as French President, Jacques Chirac, only called his referendum after Blair, wounded by the Iraq war, had promised one in Britain. There may also have been an element of misplaced hubris, with Chirac hoping that he could use the vote to reassert French leadership in Europe and divide his domestic opponents on the left, with whom he was co-habiting in government. If so, this proved to be an unfortunate miscalculation. There was quiet satisfaction in London that France would be held responsible for the failure of a political initiative for which Britain had little enthusiasm but had to profess support. Giscard later remarked wearily that, in rejecting the text, the French people had made a 'mistake which will have to be corrected'.

Tryptic societies

Some of the dividing lines revealed by the French referendum – with richer, better educated, more liberal and more urban voters generally supporting the European Constitution, and poorer, less educated, more conservative and more rural ones opposing it – were a signal of wider fissures developing in Western societies. Despite the ostensible economic progress of the early- to mid-2000s, there was a growing sense that the fruits of prosperity were being shared much less widely or evenly than in the past, with a larger slice going to a smaller group of highly educated or versatile individuals – to the 'exam-passing classes', as Vernon Bogdanor has called them – who were best equipped to meet the complex challenges of digitization and technical change. The post-war assumption that 'meritocracy' was inherently a good thing was being increasingly challenged.

Societies were beginning to fracture into three distinct groups. First, a successful elite group saw its personal living standards continue to rise and felt broadly comfortable with globalization and interdependence, including with the process of European integration, which can be seen as a kind of miniature (but deeper) form of globalization in one continent. Second, a new 'squeezed middle' – to use a phrase coined by Bill Clinton – was experiencing fewer opportunities for personal advancement as traditional jobs disappeared and real incomes stagnated or fell. This very substantial group of lower middle-class and working-class citizens was becoming increasingly disillusioned with the promises of politics and politicians – including at the European level, which seemed particularly remote from popular concerns. A third group comprised an expanding under-class of marginal, disconnected individuals, often immigrants, who subsisted largely outside the traditional social and political systems, and for whom Europe seemed simply irrelevant.

The political implications of this 'tryptic' society were potentially serious, especially as the second group, the 'squeezed middle', started to shear away from traditional political parties of centre-right and centre-left, shrinking the centre ground on which governing majorities were traditionally built. This group started to express its resentments by experimenting with nationalist or populist alternatives, first in European Parliament elections, and then in general elections, as well as by voting against Europe in the growing number of referenda held on EU treaty changes or the euro. The 17 per cent scored by Jean-Marie Le Pen on the first ballot of the French presidential election in April 2002 – which catapulted the leader of the Front National into the second ballot against incumbent President Chirac and knocked the socialist candidate, prime minister Lionel Jospin, out of the contest – was a harbinger of things to come, as a 'missing centre' started to complicate electoral contests and make them less predictable.

The rise of the Front National in France focused attention on the issue of immigration, in particular, which was becoming increasingly intertwined with questions of radicalization and counter-terrorism. One of the side-effects of 9/11 and the Iraq war was to 'politicize' Islam as a phenomenon in contemporary European society, with a popular reflex of assuming that a very small minority of religious fundamentalists somehow represented an entire community. Although the overall rise in the Muslim population in Europe was relatively modest and gradual – at about 0.2 per cent a year across the EU as a whole, with less than half of that increase due to migration – the increase was largely concentrated in major cities in Northern Europe, notably in France, Germany and Britain, where it began to acquire greater political salience.

Some of these cities were also subject to terrorist attacks launched by al-Qaeda in the mid-2000s: the Madrid train bombings of 2004 were followed in July 2005 by a similar series of explosions, known as the '7/7 attacks', which killed over fifty people travelling on public transport in central London. Later the same month, eight people were murdered in an Algerian Islamist attack on the Paris metro, followed by a similar explosion, killing four, in December 2006. In addition to posing an immediate security threat, such atrocities pointed to a bigger, longer-term challenge for policy-makers: how to defuse pockets of radicalization while (and through) better integrating the Muslim minority – expected to rise to between 10 and 14 per cent of Europe's population by 2050 – as full and equal members of society.

Catch-up in the east

One area of marked progress during the 2000s lay in the economic catch-up finally being experienced in Central and Eastern Europe. In May 2004, almost fifteen years after the collapse of communism, the European Union expanded to include eight countries from the former Soviet bloc – Poland, Hungary, the Czech Republic, Slovakia, Estonia, Latvia, Lithuania and Slovenia – as well as Cyprus and Malta. This 'big bang' enlargement, the largest by far in the Union's history, was followed by the accession of Romania and Bulgaria three years later, in January 2007, and of Croatia in July 2013. The mood among the accession states mixed euphoria with a sense of relief that a long journey was ending. Lech Wałęsa declared: 'I fought for our country to recover everything it lost under communism and the Soviets ... and now my struggle is over. My ship has come to port.'

The years of painful transition in the east were finally rewarded with the advantages and opportunities of EU membership. These included not only access to the single market, but receipt of very substantial transfer payments from the Union budget. The latter have averaged over 3 per cent of GDP per year for the Visegrád Four and the Baltic states ever since, with around half of all public investment coming from EU funding. GDP per capita started to rise: in the fifteen years from 2004 to 2019, income per head in Poland, for example, increased from 50 to 75 per cent of the EU average, meaning that incomes there are now three times as high in real terms as when communism ended. A similar pattern has been evident, to a somewhat lesser degree, in the other accession states. The enlargement experience stands in marked contrast to the trajectory of ex-Soviet states outside the Union, which failed to take off from the mid-1990s onwards. For example, while Poland and Ukraine had broadly similar living standards back in 1990, thirty years later, the former was more than twice as prosperous as the latter.

These very different experiences inevitably led to a growing desire among some of the ex-Soviet states in the remaining (or 'new') Eastern Europe, notably Ukraine and Georgia, to envisage their own eventual EU membership – or to enjoy what became known euphemistically as a 'European perspective' – much to the growing irritation of Russia. Vladimir Putin, the ex-KGB operative who became President of Russia in May 2000, after initially echoing the pro-Western language of his predecessor, Boris Yeltsin, moved firmly to forestall the further loosening of ties within the country's remaining zone of influence. Putin's experience as a Soviet intelligence officer in Dresden in 1989–90, as the GDR and communist system collapsed, appears to have permanently marked his attitude to power. Exuberant talk in the 1990s – by President Clinton, John Major and some other Western leaders, as well as by Yeltsin himself – about Russia eventually becoming a member state of the EU (matched presumably by the countries geographically in between) was to be superseded by a harder-edged language in Moscow of national independence and patriotic prowess.

Putin's 'historical injustice'

The change in Moscow took some time to become apparent. In his early months in power, Putin seemed open to continuing the process of rapprochement with the West, building on the 'Partnership for Peace' between NATO and Russia, as well as Russia's inclusion in the 'Group of Seven' (G7), which became the G8, that had defined the Clinton–Yeltsin era. During their brief cross-over in power in 2000, for example, Putin is even reported to have discussed with Clinton the possibility of Russia joining NATO, with the Russian leader allegedly expressing 'no objection' in principle to the idea. However, over the coming years, the tone gradually hardened, just as Russia reverted from being a putative multi-party democracy to an increasingly authoritarian regime.

AFTERWORD

The turning point in Putin's foreign policy appears to have been induced by the 'Orange revolution' in Ukraine in autumn 2004. When a tightly contested presidential election in October–November of that year resulted in the pro-Russian Prime Minister, Viktor Yanukovych, being declared the winner, street protests exploded in Kyiv against alleged ballot-rigging, leading to the outcome being overturned by the Ukrainian supreme court and the election re-run at Christmas. The second election was narrowly won by Yanukovych's pro-Western rival, Viktor Yushchenko, who favoured NATO and EU membership, with the subsequent Ukrainian government seeking to negotiate an association agreement with the Union. The election of Mikheil Saakashvili as President of Georgia earlier in 2004, on a broadly similar platform, suggested an emerging pattern that threatened Putin's hope that these two states (as well as perhaps Belarus and Moldova) would remain dependent on Russia or, at worst, where there was geographic contiguity, become a kind of non-aligned buffer zone between Russian and NATO/EU spheres of influence.

Speaking to the Russian parliament in 2005, Putin described the collapse of the Soviet Union as 'a major geopolitical catastrophe', leaving 'tens of millions of our co-citizens and compatriots . . . outside Russian territory'. His words were designed to appeal to the wounded pride of many Russians in losing an empire and also to play on resentments about an economic transition in the 1990s that had proved especially harsh, with the country's GDP contracting more or less continuously, while suffering high inflation, throughout the decade that Yeltsin had been in power. Russians did not even have the satisfaction (of their Central and Eastern European neighbours) of knowing that, after the fall of the Wall, they had been liberated from foreign rule or that anti-communists had replaced communists in power. The 'strangeness' of the Russian story from Yeltsin through Putin was that, as Ivan Krastev and Stephen Holmes observe, it involved 'the victory of one group of ex-communists over another'.

At the softer end of Putin's strategy to correct Russia's perceived 'historical injustice', as he put it, was the development of the country's 'civilizing mission in Eurasia'. This involved developing a Russian-led single market, stretching from the Belarus border with Poland in the west to Vladivostok in the east, backed by other forms of practical cooperation with potential client states. Initially launched as the Eurasian Economic Community in October 2000, this arrangement has been known as the Eurasian Economic Union since 2014. More problematically, however, Putin was preparing to counter the westward drift of Georgia and Ukraine by more aggressive means. The decision of the two countries formally to apply for NATO membership – a goal confirmed by the NATO summit in Bucharest in April 2008 – seems to have been decisive in prompting his shift towards the potential use of force.

In August 2008, when President Saakashvili sought to suppress separatist discontent in the Georgian province of South Ossetia (itself allegedly fermented by the Kremlin), Russian troops suddenly invaded the province and began to move towards the country's capital, Tbilisi. Putin would have been looking closely at the response in Western capitals. The European reaction was divided, with some countries (Poland, the Baltic States and Britain) favouring sanctions, and others, especially if they were dependent on Russian oil (France, Germany and Italy), firmly opposed. In the end, international mediation led to a ceasefire and Russian withdrawal, but the eight-day war cost 800 people their lives and left Putin with the clear impression of likely foreign inertia or disarray in the face of any future armed assertiveness by Moscow in its immediate vicinity.

First mover and Polish plumber

The impact of the EU enlargement process was not without risk for 'old Europe' in other ways too. The most notable uncertainty lay in the potential or actual effect of the free movement of people – one of the core rights of European citizenship and ideally a factor in promoting a stronger sense of common European identity – in adding to the emerging resentments and dividing lines among voters in Western Europe. Confronted with potential disruption of their labour markets, the existing EU member states cautiously gave themselves the option of preventing the (over 100 million) new European citizens from coming to live and work in their countries for up to seven years after accession. Most of the EU-15 activated this one-off derogation – reflected in popular fears in France and Germany, for example, about the impact of the 'Polish plumber' – while Britain, Ireland and Sweden saw opportunity, rather than risk, in allowing free movement immediately. The Blair government, in particular, used this as a chance to gain 'first mover' advantage in attracting some of the best and brightest potential migrants in the years 2004–11, while significantly under-estimating the likely numbers involved.

In the event, some 550,000 Poles came to the UK during the seven-year transitional period (and 270,000 subsequently). More widely, the number of citizens from all other EU states living in the UK rose from 1.5 million in 2004 to 2.6 million in 2011 (and to 3.5 million by 2016). This turned out to be the most rapid and substantial influx of foreign citizens into the country in its history. Even if the overall economic impact was clearly positive – because those coming to the UK tended to be younger, better educated, more productive and less reliant on state support than the British population as a whole – the speed and intensity of the change were to build political pressures that proved problematic in the longer run.

Advent of Mrs Merkel

In November 2005, Angela Merkel replaced Gerhard Schröder as Chancellor of Germany, the first former GDR citizen to hold that post. Although there were initially fears within the 'Rhineland' wing of the centre-right CDU that Merkel might not prioritize Europe to the same degree as Helmut Kohl or Konrad Adenauer, she devoted her country's rotating presidency of the EU Council of Ministers in the first half of 2007 to reasserting German leadership on the issue. After a couple of years in which the European Constitution had looked politically dead, Merkel used her rising political capital to gently revive the text. She overcame the initial caution of José Manuel Barroso – whose own presidency of the European Commission (starting in November 2004) had been badly winded by the failed French and Dutch referenda on the Constitution – to launch careful negotiations designed to dilute some of the more explicitly federal features of that document. The word 'constitution' was itself dropped and the unwieldy structure of the existing treaties retained; recognition of state-like 'symbols of the Union', such as its flag and anthem, was removed; acknowledgement of the supremacy of Union law was deliberately blurred; and the upgraded post of High Representative for foreign and security policy was no longer to be dubbed 'Union Minister for Foreign Affairs'.

Rebranded the Lisbon Treaty, the successor text to the European Constitution was able to gain broad support, including in Paris and The Hague, where the French and Dutch parliaments agreed to ratify it without recourse to further popular votes. The awkward and unexpected hiccup of rejection of the new treaty in June 2008, in the one country that did legally require a referendum, Ireland, was reversed by a second referendum sixteenth months later. To secure that outcome, all member states were assured that they would be allowed to keep their individual European Commissioners and Ireland was guaranteed that nothing in the text could affect its neutrality. The Irish experience was part of a broader pattern: the decade running up to this second Irish vote had seen ten referenda held in EU member states on Europe – whether on treaty change or euro membership – and in six of those ten votes, the pro-European stance of the government had been rejected by the public. After the Lisbon Treaty came into effect in November 2009, there was to be little appetite for further EU institutional reform, still less for further referenda – other than among Eurosceptics in Britain.

Path of economic virtue?

The rather formless politics of the early to mid-2000s in Europe also characterized its economics. An unexpected and fairly brief recession on both sides of the Atlantic in 2001–02, driven by the twin impacts of 9/11 and the bursting of the US 'dot-com bubble', was followed by a period of recovery between 2003 and 2007, with low interest rates and growth that returned to around 3 per cent a year. While the high ambition for the European economy expressed by EU leaders at the Lisbon summit in March 2000 – that the Union should become 'the most competitive and dynamic knowledge-based economy in the world' by the end of the decade – showed little sign of being realized, public finances gradually improved and the single currency was considered to be progressing well. Although the budgetary disciplines set down in the Maastricht Treaty were infamously (if briefly) flouted by both Germany and France in 2002, a new culture of fiscal restraint appeared in fact finally to be taking hold within the eurozone and across the Union more widely.

By early 2008, the average budget deficit among EU member states had fallen to less than 1 per cent of GDP (with many countries running a primary surplus) and average national debt was finally dropping below the 60 per cent ceiling stipulated by the Maastricht Treaty, even if (importantly) certain member states still stood out from this trend. Yields on sovereign debt, which had diverged markedly among the Euro-11 before 1999, now largely converged around the value of German bonds and it was assumed that this process would become permanent. Germany itself was becoming the exemplar of economic success, as it benefited from wage costs growing consistently less rapidly than productivity. This in turn reflected the combined effects of Hartz labour-market reforms, a developing shift to decentralized collective bargaining, the growth of new markets to the east and the offshoring of some production to those markets. A sustained upward appreciation in the value of the euro – by 30 per cent between 2002 and 2007 – suggested that much of Europe might be locking on to a German-style path of economic virtue, accepting pressures to improve efficiency, rather than prioritize short-term growth. Sadly, however, such hopes were quickly to prove premature.

AGE OF ANXIETY: THE ECONOMIC CRISIS OF 2008 AND ITS AFTER-SHOCKS

Inverted pyramid of debt

Beneath the surface, the European economy was, in fact, in a much more brittle and unstable state than many assumed when, starting in the autumn of 2008, it was suddenly hit by the most serious financial crisis since the end of the Second World War. The underlying problem, as in most such crises during the last century, was an accumulation of debt – with the triggering events taking place on the other side of the Atlantic. 'A vast, global, inverted pyramid of bank, business and personal debt', Robert Skidelsky has written, 'was built on a narrow base of underlying assets – American real estate. When the base tottered, the pyramid fell.' A powerful cocktail of low capital requirements, excessive lending and financial ingenuity beyond the control of regulators had left the US banks and other lenders increasingly exposed. By 2008, gross private debt as a share of US GDP had trebled over the previous thirty years, to almost 300 per cent, while financial sector debt had risen six-fold, to 120 per cent.

The US financial crisis developed as the country's domestic housing market crashed, many homeowners fell into negative equity, and a large volume of mortgage-backed securities and other collateralized debt became unsellable. With bad loans and other 'toxic assets' accumulating rapidly, over-leveraged banks became increasingly unable to service their costs. What was first thought to be a containable 'sub-prime mortgage' crisis spiralled into a much broader, systemic crisis that required a massive government response. The federal government initially bailed out the state-based mortgage lenders, Fannie Mae and Freddie Mac, as well as investment bank Bear Stearns. But it refused to intervene to save Lehman Brothers, whose bankruptcy on 15 September 2008, the largest collapse in US corporate history, set off two weeks of financial panic around the world. In response, the Federal Reserve reduced interest rates to zero, while (after initial resistance) the US Congress authorized a $440-billion bank bail-out package and an $840-billion fiscal stimulus (representing respectively 3.0 and 5.7 per cent of US GDP). As Martin Wolf remarked wryly, individuals who thought they had been borrowing discovered that they were actually engaged in public spending.

The knock-on effect in Europe was immediate and severe, as stock markets tumbled and the balance sheets of many European banks were revealed to be highly fragile. As in the US, the easy availability of credit and the poor pricing of risk had built a similar 'inverted pyramid of debt' that now threatened the entire system. Starting in October 2008, national governments were confronted with a sudden downturn in their economies, with average GDP growth in the Union falling from 3 per cent in 2007 to minus 4 per cent in 2009. At the end of 2008, the European economy was contracting at a rate of more than 3 per cent a quarter. Yield rates on government bonds started to diverge significantly between countries, making it difficult for the worst-hit economies to finance their existing debt, let alone new debt. Italian bond yields moved from 2.0 to 7.8 per cent in eighteen months, while those in Spain rose from 2.0 to 6.1 per cent. During the two years after the crisis first hit, public authorities ended up providing 1.5 trillion euro in rescue support to the financial sector (or about 5 per cent of EU GDP per year) – in liquidity, recapitalization or guarantees – saving over a hundred major banks from collapse.

Eurozone debt crisis

With government finances suddenly under acute pressure, any country in Europe that had failed to reduce its deficit and debt levels earlier in the decade now found itself highly exposed, especially if the immediate option of depreciating its national currency had been removed by adoption of the single currency. The problem was even worse where growth itself was being built on the one-off effect of lower interest rates (from the advent of EMU) in reducing the costs of servicing public and private debt. In the most extreme case, Greece, the budget deficit and national debt had been allowed to rise significantly during the 2000s – developments deliberately under-reported by the national authorities – and across much of Southern Europe, governments had largely failed to raise productivity through supply-side reform. In effect, many of the potential benefits of moving to a single currency and common monetary policy had been squandered in short-term state or personal spending. In Northern Europe, Ireland was facing a distinctive variant of the debt problem: while its public finances had been corrected (and national government was spending only 25 per cent of GDP), excessive private-sector borrowing was generating a massive asset bubble, with personal, corporate and banking sector debt rising to over 450 per cent of GDP.

The origins of what became known as the 'eurozone debt crisis' of 2009–12 lie in the 'asymmetric' impact on different countries of the financial and economic crisis unleashed in autumn 2008. While the German economy contracted by 5.7 per cent in 2009, it recovered to its previous level within two years, growing slowly thereafter. Much of Northern Europe saw a similar pattern of sharp downturn, followed by a clear rebound, even if this was somewhat slower than Germany's. The Greek economy, by contrast, shrank by 20 per cent over two years and struggled to gain any traction thereafter. The public finances of certain highly exposed states became unsustainable, requiring emergency action to avoid default. Starting in May 2010, Greece, Ireland and Portugal were successively bailed out by the European Union, while both Italy and Spain found themselves frequently on the verge of needing urgent financial support.

Working at high speed and in conjunction with the IMF – ironically on the sixtieth anniversary to the day of the Schuman Declaration of 9 May 1950 – EU finance ministers and the European Commission invented new intergovernmental and supranational financing facilities on a scale never previously envisaged. These were later consolidated in a single European Stability Mechanism (ESM), funded to a joint total of 750 billion euro. As the then French finance minister, Christine Lagarde, put it, 'The only thing the markets understand is money. We had to get real, which meant, get big.' In return, severe public sector retrenchment and/or tough programmes to promote structural reform were imposed on the three bail-out states, with Ireland rebounding most quickly. This adjustment process was monitored by a joint 'Troika' of the Commission, IMF and European Central Bank, a bureaucratic combination that often proved unpopular on the ground, especially in Greece.

Germany was quickly revealed as the dominant force in determining the contours of the immediate response to the eurozone debt crisis, just as it had been critical in shaping the terms of EMU itself in the first place. The crisis also revived the debate, which Kohl had largely succeeded in closing down in the early 1990s, about whether the unequivocal pooling of monetary sovereignty (in the design adopted in Maastricht) should have been matched by a much more ambitious and 'genuine' economic union, along the lines originally hinted at in the Delors Report. In reality, however, any tentative moves towards a greater degree of 'European economic governance' – through a co-ordinated European macro-economic policy, a loosening of the Stability and Growth Pact and/or an active external exchange-rate policy for the euro – were rejected by policy-makers in Berlin. The 'governance' idea remained basically a French concept with German content, while the Merkel government's dogged refusal to countenance any mutualization of eurozone debt, through eurobonds, or the development of pan-European budgetary stabilizers, fuelled resentments which were to linger across Southern Europe for some years to come.

After-shocks

The economic shocks of 2008–12 had other lasting impacts too. Not only was personal hardship experienced by a larger proportion of the population for a longer period than in any previous post-war downturn, there was also a widespread feeling that this was a different kind of crisis. The damage to the economy was perceived to originate not in an external shock or inherent fluctuation of the economic cycle – as say in the oil crisis in the mid-1970s or the 'boom and bust' of the early 1990s – but rather in the irresponsible, if not illegal, behaviour of a small minority of people who had managed to enjoy disproportional rewards while in effect 'crashing the system', and who were able to do so with seeming impunity from accountability, let alone possible prosecution.

AFTERWORD

The popular groundswell against brokers and 'banksters' reinforced an existing, slow-burn discontent about the way that even pre-crisis economic growth had often been concealing under-employment and rising inequality, leaving many people struggling at the margin – with less opportunity for advancement for the many and the fruits of prosperity concentrated in fewer hands. During and after what has now become known as the 'great recession', there was a much wider questioning of the operation and values of the modern market economy and even the democratic structures that underpinned it. Those in power were scrutinized and judged more harshly than before, both for their personal behaviour – illustrated in the damaging 'expenses scandal' which suddenly rocked the British House of Commons in 2009 – and for poor judgement on a wide range of policies, present and past. The public mood was increasingly one of resentment and disappointment, and sometimes anger, with after-effects that are still apparent today.

The immediate political consequence of the economic crisis was that governing parties in the countries under greatest pressure found it increasingly difficult to retain power, regardless of their ideological persuasion. The government in Greece rotated rapidly between rival political forces as three general elections were held between 2009 and 2012 – with the governing majority moving from the centre-right to the socialists, to a coalition between the two, and then back again to the centre-right. In 2011, the centre-right replaced the left in power in Portugal, while Fine Gael replaced Fianna Fáil in Ireland, again in elections provoked by the crisis. During the same year, the centre-right coalition of Silvio Berlusconi collapsed (again) in Italy, to be replaced by a technocratic government, led by Mario Monti, a former European Commissioner, and sponsored in effect by the country's international creditors; while in Spain, the socialist government of José Luis Rodriguez Zapatero prompted its own demise by holding an election that it knew it would lose to the opposition Partido Popular, rather than persist in its efforts to address the crisis. Meanwhile, in France, Chirac's successor as President, a fellow post-Gaullist, Nicolas Sarkozy, failed to gain re-election in 2012, losing out to a colourless socialist party functionary, François Hollande. In all these countries, the various shifts were still mainly between mainstream forces of the centre, centre-right and centre-left, rotating in power. However, a more fundamental political change, which had been brewing slowly for some time, was to be greatly accelerated by the economic crisis: the rise of 'populism'.

POPULISM IN EUROPE IN THE 2010s

The party's over

The traditional party system in Europe had already been under strain for several decades. Starting in the 1980s, political scientists began to observe that, as in the United States, turnout at elections across Europe was falling (at a rate of about a third of 1 per cent each year), that the electorate's identification with established political parties was eroding, and that the swings between parties were becoming bigger and less predictable over time. The old, inherited allegiances to party, usually based on class or religion, that had given stability to democratic systems in Western Europe after the Second World War, were gradually loosening, as societies became more individualistic and traditional identities broke down. As Ingrid von Biezen has shown, in the three decades after 1980, party membership declined in most Western European democracies by between a third and two-thirds. The only countries where it increased were Greece, Spain and Portugal, all of which had recently thrown off military dictatorships.

In fact, wider changes in society and culture had been redefining the relationship between citizens and politics in a way that reduced public interest and confidence in the classic political process. As Anthony Giddens pointed out in 2003, until perhaps the 1980s, 'conventional politics was seen to belong to the citizen' and to be something in which he or she could and often did 'easily participate', through party and interest group activity, as well as by the act of voting. But slowly politics was becoming 'part of an external world which people view from outside', with the role of parties and political leaders seen as 'separate from the world of the citizenry'. Conversely, the new world of media and celebrity entertainment was moving in the opposite direction: 'Previously television was something which reflected an external world which people then watched. Now television is much more a medium in which you can participate.'

The scene was set for televisual politics to become more and more a branch of entertainment, with a dumbing-down and trivialization of public life. Respect for politicians declined, political memories and attention spans shortened – speeded by the introduction of twenty-four-hour rolling news channels in the late 1990s – and arguments about the tough choices of governing became more difficult to conduct. Critically, office holders were increasingly seen to be part of a self-referential political elite, enjoying a lifestyle choice made possible by public patronage but detached from the real-world experience or concerns of ordinary citizens.

The subsequent explosion of online social media took this process to a new level, transforming the way that news was disseminated and political debate conducted. Starting in the mid-2000s and accelerating rapidly throughout the 2010s, the advent of new platforms such as Facebook and Twitter meant that the previous de facto monopoly of party politicians and classic print and television journalists in defining the political agenda was broken. User-generated content became more and more common, while people's choices about which news sources to follow online – as well as deliberate search-engine prompting – led them increasingly to inhabit 'filter bubbles' of the like-minded. The so-called 'splinternet' tended both to screen out competing perspectives, dividing society into sub-groups with more exclusive world views, and to sharpen the tone and coarsen the texture of political discussion. Traditional parties became much less relevant to defining public choices and shaping public debate, especially as citizens enjoyed burgeoning opportunities to express their views electronically on any subject in real time.

New political forces

Politics as a profession was shifting gradually from an 'apprenticeship' system, in which aspirants worked their way up a party hierarchy, to more of an 'entrepreneurial' system, in which strong and distinctive individuals sought to take existing parties by storm, to create new rival parties, or to work outside party structures altogether. An early example of the first was Blair's success in the 1990s in relaunching the Labour party as 'New Labour', a centrist modernizing force set on creating a 'New Britain'. An example of the second was Berlusconi's reconfiguration of the Italian centre-right, using his own media empire as a springboard (and sounding-board) for his views: Forza Italia in effect absorbed and replaced the Christian Democrats as a mainstream conservative party for a more individualist and consumerist age. As a harbinger of things to come more widely, Berlusconi leveraged his lack of political experience (he first ran for office at the age of 58) by presenting himself as an outsider whose real-world experience meant that he was more closely in touch with 'the people' than his political opponents, even if the prospect of parliamentary immunity from prosecution for previous business misdemeanours may also have appealed. More recently, the sudden emergence of a youthful establishment figure, Emmanuel Macron, as the dominant player in French politics – winning election to the presidency in May 2017 (and then re-election five years later in April 2022) at the head of a party specifically invented for this purpose, La République en Marche, since rebranded as Renaissance – has shown that new parties of the centre can still be born and win power, even in an era of cynicism and disillusionment with conventional politics.

However, the distinctive theme of European politics in the 2010s was not one of mainstream renewal, but rather of the electoral success of forces that consciously defined themselves *against* the party system, as agents of radical change. This was not, of course, an entirely new phenomenon. As early as the mid-1980s, European politics had already seen the arrival, on a more modest scale, of new types of party that challenged the established forces that monopolized power – such as the Greens in Germany and the far-right Front National in France – and they presented themselves as less interested in holding office than in disrupting a cosy system. This was followed by a broader range of mainly right-wing protest parties in the 1990s and early 2000s, notably in Austria (the Freedom Party), Denmark (People's Party), the Netherlands (List Pim Fortuyn followed by Freedom Party), and the Flemish region of Belgium (Vlaams Blok, later renamed Vlaams Belang). Now, in the years after the 2008–12 economic crisis, there was a further and very marked upsurge in new 'populist' forces across Europe, especially on the right – a process which continued even as the effects of the 'great recession' gradually wore off.

In France, for example, the Front National scored 18 and 21 per cent on the first ballots of the 2012 and 2017 presidential elections; most strikingly, however, in the second ballot of the 2017 contest, Marine Le Pen put on a further 13 per cent of the vote (to 34 per cent) and three million votes (to 10.6 million), whereas her father in 2002 had only increased his share of the vote by 1 per cent between the two ballots.

The shadow hanging over Macron's electoral success was thus one of increasing polarization between two very different visions of France. In Germany, a new populist party, Alternativ für Deutschland, won just under 5 per cent of the vote in 2013 – something seen at the time as shocking – rising to 13 per cent four years later. In Italy, Matteo Salvini rebranded the Northern League, a regionalist conservative party, as simply 'the League', projected it as a national party of the populist right – occupying the space left by the implosion of Forza Italia once Berlusconi had been convicted and debarred from office – and saw its vote rise from 4 per cent in 2013 to 37 per cent five years later.

Anatomy of populism

Since the word is more often used as a term of abuse, rather than of analysis, it is useful to try to identify what populism is and how it differs from traditional politics. As Heather Grabbe defines it, drawing on the work of Cas Mudde, populism is primarily a 'view of the world and of the structure of society, with a central claim that society and indeed politics are divided into a corrupt elite and a pure people'. The populist leader presents himself – occasionally herself – as the 'representative of the pure people', someone who is 'directly in touch with the will of that people and who does not therefore need the checks and balances of democratic institutions and the rule of law'.

Right-wing populists generally define 'the pure people' in some kind of ethno-nationalist or 'nativist' way. They hold that their traditional national community, whatever that might be, is under active or potential threat – externally, from immigration and free trade, and internally, from an unrepresentative and detached elite group driven by 'liberal internationalist' values – and that such threats can best be resisted by exclusionary policies that protect citizens at home and abroad. These views diverge considerably from post-war centre-right politics in Europe, with both Christian Democracy and conservatism having favoured, in varying degrees, open societies and market economies, based on international cooperation and interdependence. Logically, the process of European integration represents the antithesis of right-wing populist politics – as an internationalist project, operating above the level of the nation state, driven by transnational economics and administered by (what is presented as) a remote, disconnected, technocratic elite.

Left-wing populism is less xenophobic and less hostile to liberal internationalism, and more trusting of the potential role of the state, but among its central beliefs is the view that society is divided into '99 versus 1 per cent' and that an unrepresentative elite group often betrays the masses through pursuit of its own self-interest, propositions it basically shares with the right. Left-wing populism crystallized in the 'Occupy' movement in 2011–12, when young protesters engaged in sit-ins, starting in Wall Street and then spreading throughout the democratic world. Both right- and left-wing populists think less in terms of classic political programmes or of party structures than of redefining the relationship between the governing and the governed. Populist forces thus represent a systemic challenge to the classic notion of politics as a left–right electoral competition for swing votes in the centre, driven by traditional socio-economic issues and interests, and leading to an alternation of centre-right and centre-left parties or coalitions in power – the pattern seen in most democratic political systems in Europe since 1945.

Economics in the 'two thousand and tense'

Economics was one important driving force in the rise of populism during the 2010s. Although the European economy was finally emerging from the 'great recession', many of the scars inflicted by the recent downturn remained very painful for those who had lost income, jobs or business. There was a pattern of gradual, if unspectacular, recovery as the decade progressed, helped by an unexpectedly loose monetary policy from the European Central Bank, whose President, Mario Draghi, famously declared in July 2012 that he was 'ready to do whatever it takes to preserve the euro' by stabilizing the European economy. His predecessor, Jean-Claude Trichet, had prioritized financial orthodoxy, the hallmark of the ECB during its first decade, until he left office in October 2011. Between 2015 and 2018, the ECB bought up 2.6 trillion euro of sovereign debt, worth 7,600 euro for every person living in the eurozone. Although the EU growth rate averaged 2 per cent between 2014 and 2019, leaving the continent's economy overall 9 per cent bigger than before the onset of the economic and financial crisis, this upward drift was insufficient to pull many who had suffered badly after 2008 into better times, while the benefits of recovery were far from evenly spread, whether socially or geographically.

While the percentage of adults employed in the Union rose from 68 to 73 per cent during the 2010s – with the number of people in work in the EU rising from 217 to 240 million – unemployment continued to drift up in large swathes of Southern Europe, matched by a rise in the number of 'working poor'. By the end of 2019, Italy's economy had yet to regain its size in mid-2008, whereas Germany's was 13 per cent bigger. Such differences were mirrored in the trajectory of public finances: whereas Italy's debt to GDP ratio rose from 120 to 135 per cent of GDP over the decade, Germany's fell from 80 to 60 per cent. Many countries in between struggled to bring down their debt ratios despite modest growth – and especially, but not only, in the weaker states, citizens dependent on the state suffered as continuing austerity in government spending took its toll. For many, economically and in other ways, the decade was to prove the 'two thousand and tense'.

Paradox on the left

The modest and uneven economic recovery of the 2010s took place against the backdrop of the longer-term impact of the economic and financial crisis in corroding assumptions about the efficiency and fairness of the financial system in particular, and the incentivizing role of markets more generally. The climate of ideas turned against the 'neoliberal' assumptions that had largely dominated Western thought since the intellectual triumph of Reaganism and Thatcherism in the 1980s. The emphasis was now less on enterprise and opportunity, and more on the contradictions of capitalism and the enabling role of the state.

This shift in mood had in fact started even before the crisis, as the heady confidence of books like John Kay's *The Truth about Markets* (2003) or Martin Wolf's *Why Globalization Works* (2004) gradually gave way to a more troubled view that the true spirit of capitalism was (ironically) being subverted by individual and collective greed, an argument voiced, for example, in Kenneth and William Hopper's *The Puritan Gift* (2007). After the crisis, the tone sharpened markedly. Mariana Mazzucato's *The Entrepreneurial State* (2011) argued that distinctions between the public and private sectors were largely meaningless, while Thomas Piketty's *Capital in the Twenty-First Century* (2013) claimed that, with the value of labour declining, the driver of Western economies in the future would be return on capital, marked by rising inequality and low growth.

The centre of gravity on the centre-left in European politics – that is, of traditional socialist and social democratic parties – mirrored this move from the Blair–Schröder–Monti politics of economic reform in an era of expansion, where diverging class interests seemed to have become irrelevant, to a renewed stress on equality and redistribution in straitened times. Yet, paradoxically, the political parties of the centre-left, which might otherwise have been expected to benefit from continuing economic hardship and discontent in many countries, were to fare particularly badly during the 2010s. While the rise of populism logically involved a shrinking of both the centre-right and centre-left in European electoral politics, the retreat of the centre-left was to prove particularly striking, and indeed in some cases near fatal. For example, the Democratic party's share of the vote declined from 33 per cent in 2008 to 19 per cent in 2018, and that of the German SPD fell from 34 per cent in 2005 to 20 per cent in 2017. While the French Parti Socialiste had received 26 per cent of the first-ballot vote in the 2007 presidential election, it secured only 6 per cent ten years later.

It seems that, across much of the continent, not only had the centre-left's traditional core support among the working class been evaporating over time – as manual labour declined and society became more atomized and individualistic – but that part of this support base also drew a different conclusion from the economic and financial crisis to the one that most commentators expected. With the notable exception of Greece – where the rise of Alexis Tsipras's Syriza party was fuelled by a sense of national humiliation generated by the eurozone debt crisis – the primary response was not to boost calls for redistributive economics, or to promote a more interventionist state, but rather to revive and strengthen 'identity politics', as many working-class and lower middle-class voters turned inward and became more parochial. The outward-looking liberal internationalism of earlier decades was giving way to a new form of 'illiberal nationalism', with the mainstream centre-left especially challenged by events that it initially assumed would play to its advantage. The shift in political mood in Europe was more akin to the reaction to the inter-war depression than to, say, the oil crisis of the 1970s.

Maidan, Russia and Ukraine

A series of other developments, at home and abroad, accentuated the underlying mood of tension and anxiety in Europe, in the early- to mid-2010s especially, and they indirectly made more potent the protective appeal of populist forces, especially on the right. The first was a general deterioration in the security situation in Europe's neighbourhood. Starting in 2011, long civil wars emerged in Syria and Libya, which disoriented strategists on both sides of the Atlantic – exposing limitations to the roles which Western capitals could play in stabilizing the Middle East and North Africa, while opening up a major opportunity for Russia to assert itself as a regional player. This was enhanced when the UK's planned involvement in Syria was aborted after it was unexpectedly rejected by the House of Commons in August 2013, reflecting the hesitancy of public opinion post-Iraq, and resulting in a parallel failure of nerve by President Obama in Washington. In September 2015, Putin began a process of direct Russian intervention in the Syrian civil war, fighting on the side of President Bashar al-Assad.

Russia's increasingly confident foreign policy was also evident in Ukraine, where Viktor Yanukovych had won the country's presidency on his second attempt in 2010. Putin now pressurized the government in Kyiv to abandon ratification of the association and free-trade agreement that it had negotiated with the European Union in 2013, and to focus on the Eurasian Economic Union instead. Echoing the Orange Revolution of 2004, massive pro-European street protests broke out to stop the country's emerging 'European vocation' from being abandoned. Centred on and named after the capital's Independence Square, the 'Euromaidan' uprising of autumn 2013 and the 'Maidan Revolution' of February 2014 ended with President Yanukovych being expelled from office by parliamentary vote. The emerging choice of 'national futures' for Ukraine, highlighted by these events, was something that decision-makers in many Western capitals preferred to obfuscate or avoid, while the 100 plus demonstrators who were killed on Independence Square, some of whom certainly saw themselves as martyrs for the European cause, were a source of silent embarrassment in Brussels.

Later in the same month, February 2014, Putin exacted his revenge. He invaded and annexed Crimea, a region of Ukraine where the majority population is ethnically Russian, and he opened up a proxy war in the Donbass region of eastern Ukraine, promoting separatist feeling in an area where a significant minority are also ethnically Russian. The new situation in Crimea was 'legitimized' by holding a referendum on absorption into Russia the following month. The US and European reactions mixed incredulity with virtual inaction. While the US Secretary of State, John Kerry, declared that in the twenty-first century, 'you just don't behave in a nineteenth-century fashion by invading another country on a completely trumped-up pretext', only a modest set of sanctions was imposed by Western countries, limited essentially to Russian leaders and their assets, while Russia's voting rights in the Council of Europe and its participation in Group of Eight (G8) summits of world leaders were suspended. John McCain chided his former Senate colleague and other Western leaders for their weak response. In refusing even to share intelligence with Kyiv, let alone supply Ukraine with the defensive weapons 'they were begging for', Europe and America were building up an even bigger problem for the future, he argued. 'There is nothing that provokes Vladimir Putin more than weakness.'

In parallel to territorial expansion, the Kremlin intensified a wider 'soft power' propaganda war that it had begun to conduct through state-sponsored outlets, such as its *Russia Today* television channel and Sputnik news agency. An active strategy of disinformation was developed to destabilize and polarize opinion in Western democracies. The intention was, as Neil MacFarquhar put it, to 'undermine the official version of events – even the very idea that there is a true version of events – and foster a kind of policy paralysis'. Since the mid-2010s, there has been a lively debate about how far, and to what effect, Russia has involved itself surreptitiously in foreign elections and referenda, especially in the United States and United Kingdom, using what Fiona Hill has called 'a creative mix of old-style propaganda techniques and new cyber-tools', notably through the manipulation of social media. Any benefit of the doubt that the Russian authorities might have enjoyed was removed by the attempted assassination of Sergei Skripal, a former Russian military officer and double agent for UK intelligence, using the Novichok nerve agent, in Salisbury in March 2018. The attack echoed the mysterious death twelve years earlier of Alexander Litvinenko, a Russian intelligence officer who had defected to Britain and was killed by radioactive polonium after lunching at a sushi bar in central London.

Terror attacks across Europe

A second unhappy development was the dramatic re-emergence, after a decade of relative quiescence, of Islamic terrorism in Europe. The mid-2010s saw a series of brutal attacks that captured the attention of the world. In January 2015, armed gunmen shot dead a dozen journalists and cartoonists at the Paris offices of the veteran satirical weekly, *Charlie Hebdo*, which had once ridiculed Charles de Gaulle and now lampooned the Prophet Muhammad. The atrocity prompted demonstrations on all continents, with over three million people marching in France and the phrase '*Je suis Charlie*' becoming an international statement of solidarity with the plight of France and of sympathy for the victims of terrorism everywhere. A second attack across northern Paris – involving a co-ordinated series of three bombings and six shootings at different locations – saw 130 people murdered, notably inside the Bataclan theatre, in November the same year.

Other cities were to follow. Four months after the Bataclan massacre, 32 people were killed in explosions at Brussels airport and on an underground train at the Maelbeek metro station near the EU institutions in the Belgian capital. Then, on 14 July 2016, in Nice, a truck driver deliberately ploughed his vehicle into crowds celebrating French National Day on the Promenade des Anglais, killing 86 people. A similar van attack on tourists walking along Las Ramblas in Barcelona in August 2017 killed 14 people of eight nationalities. Al-Qaeda claimed responsibility for the Paris attacks and Islamic State for the Brussels and Nice ones; the Barcelona murders were also attributed to Islamic State. Meanwhile, in Britain, a series of attacks by 'home-grown' or 'lone-wolf' Muslim extremists killed 12 people (between March and June 2017) on or near Westminster and London Bridges, and murdered another 22 people after a pop concert at the Manchester Arena.

Migrant odyssey

The most potent vector for a right-wing populist advance, however, was the sudden and unexpected upsurge in migration to Europe in 2015. The deteriorating security situations in Syria, Afghanistan and Iraq led to the largest population exodus in or around Europe since the Second World War, with some 650,000 people from those three countries seeking refuge in the Union and almost as many again arriving from a variety of other countries during that year. Most sought entry by travelling, often in inflatable boats or dinghies, across the Mediterranean from Turkey or North Africa – putting immense pressure on Greece and Italy, in particular. Many of the people entering Greece then took a land route through the Western Balkans on to Hungary, Austria and finally Germany or other northern states. (The Western Balkans itself was also a source of asylum seekers, with around 170,000 people coming from Kosovo and Albania.) Some 4,000 people died in failed sea crossings and the image of a young Syrian boy washed up dead on the beach at Bodrum in Turkey in September 2015 touched hearts around the world. While the EU had established free movement between member states in the 1980s, the management of the Union's external frontier had not been effectively co-ordinated or adequately reinforced. Although those seeking asylum were supposed to be held in the country of arrival and purely economic migrants turned back, in practice these rules quickly collapsed into chaos.

Germany found itself in the eye of the storm, which was a major psychological shock to a country which, despite a combination of rising economic success and slow demographic decline, had attracted relatively few immigrants in recent years. In August 2015, in an act of 'national duty' which came back to haunt her politically, Chancellor Merkel agreed that Germany should open its doors to those who were trying to get into the country, accepting almost 900,000 asylum seekers in the course of a few months. The atmosphere in Hungary and Austria was less relaxed and they started to build border fences to stem the flow.

The initial enthusiasm of the German public – captured in Merkel's confident assertion that '*Wir schaffen das*' ('we can do it') – gradually waned as the autumn wore on. Soon the Berlin government was tightening entry restrictions, pushing for EU deals both on burden-sharing among member states and with Turkey to hold back potential new flows into the Union, and encouraging a refusal by Balkan states to allow continued passage from Greece. The European Commission came forward with a plan for burden-sharing, but even its modest proposal that 120,000 people should be distributed among member states failed to get airborne, although an EU–Turkey joint action plan (eased by six billion euro of EU funding) proved surprisingly effective. A number of security incidents involving failed asylum seekers in Germany, culminating in a terrorist attack on the Christmas market in Berlin in December 2016, killing twelve people, soured the domestic atmosphere there still further.

One country in which the 2015 migration crisis had a particularly strong political impact was the United Kingdom, even if paradoxically it was relatively marginally affected – ranking only seventeenth in terms of asylum applications to EU member states that year. Images of thousands of people sailing across the Mediterranean and then walking northwards through Europe in search of better lives played into an existing populist agenda, spearheaded by the UK Independence Party (UKIP), under Nigel Farage, that sought to link the issues of Europe and immigration in what proved to be a potent mix. The way that free movement of labour within the EU had already boosted the UK population by nearly two million over the previous decade was fomenting a neuralgic issue which Farage was adroitly able to exploit. Even before scenes of the migrant odyssey became ubiquitous, UKIP had already put in unexpectedly strong performances in the 2014 European Parliament elections and 2015 general election in Britain – winning respectively 26.6 and 12.6 per cent of the vote – disproportionately at the expense of the Conservatives, whose political confidence they had winded. Now the experiences of Germany and Greece, in particular, corroded public confidence in the Union and fuelled fears about the future, adding to a pessimistic narrative, already widespread during the eurozone debt crisis, that Britain should keep its distance from deeper European commitments.

Contrasting European values

A parallel, but slightly different, phenomenon was also to be seen in some of the new democracies of Central and Eastern Europe, where populist forces were already on the rise. Although EU membership was, and generally remains, popular in the enlargement states – reflecting the new opportunities brought by market opening, free movement and transfer payments from the European budget – these countries have struggled to assert themselves politically within the EU institutions, where they often suffer a feeling of second-class status, compared with their longer-established and more self-confident neighbours in the West. In return, they have been accused of having too transactional an attitude towards European integration and of not fully sharing 'European' values.

Even though it became fashionable in the 2010s to argue that Europe was united less by common interests, institutions or law, than by a set of common values, it was becoming clear that the notion of a 'Europe of values' can mean different things to different people. The issue has taken two main forms. The first is that many Central and Eastern Europeans have a more conservative value system than the citizens of the pre-2004 Union. Surveys show that for people living in the former communist countries, religion in particular remains a significant factor in their own individual and collective identities, and more so than before the end of the Cold War. By contrast, in Western Europe, there has been an ongoing process of secularization that shows little sign of abating. There are also marked divergences in attitudes towards multiculturalism – a 2018 survey showed, for example, that 88 per cent of Dutch people would be willing to accept a Muslim into their own family, compared with only 12 per cent of Czechs – as well as on issues of personal morality and sexual orientation, such as abortion and same-sex marriage. In short, there appear, if anything, to be two contrasting sets of 'common' values in Europe, defined largely by geography, which co-exist rather uneasily alongside one another.

This divide in attitudes has been enhanced by population shifts, with more liberally minded young people in the enlargement states being the most likely to use their free-movement rights to live and work abroad. Combined with low birth rates, this means that the population has been shrinking and ageing in much of Central and Eastern Europe, often quite rapidly. Romania's population is now almost 10 per cent lower than when it entered the Union in 2004, and that of the Baltic States has contracted by 17 per cent. Croatia's population has been falling by 0.75 per cent a year since it joined in 2013, prompting its Prime Minister to talk of a looming 'existential crisis'. In several countries, demographic change has also led to a deeper urban–rural divide, both culturally and politically, while the remaining populations have become more conservative overall.

The second dimension of the values issue relates to the political process. In many former communist states, attitudes to the exercise of democratic power are much less settled than in Western Europe and are still suffused with a lack of mutual trust between parties, which often fear the consequences of alternation in government. While almost everyone professes to subscribe to democracy and the rule of law, what exactly these terms signify is frequently contested. The oft-heard complaint of non-socialist forces in the 2000s that an entrenched post-communist nomenklatura was still running the state apparatus in many countries has now transitioned into a much more muscular desire by conservative parties, once they acquire and occupy power, to try to entrench their position by recasting society in their own image, rather than simply accepting that social values would 'modernize' through internationalization and growth.

AFTERWORD
Politics of loss and threat

This helps explain how and why the 'populist' experience in Central and Eastern Europe – where a harder-edged form of nationalist conservatism has been developing, especially (but not only) in rural areas, even in the absence of large-scale immigration or recession – is different to that in Western Europe. Both strands of populism are driven by a kind of identity politics that resists globalization and the erosion of borders – whether through markets or European integration. Western European populism, however, is primarily about expressing a sense of loss – through economic failure, immigration, declining social status and a feeling of being alienated from and ignored by the political system. By contrast, Central and Eastern European populism is more about the perception of a potential threat to traditional values – essentially to notions of nation and society – often among people who ironically have never been as affluent as they are today, and who generally believe that their political system can and will protect them against future changes that they fear.

This distinction appears to have been compounded by a specific legacy of Marxism-Leninism in Central and Eastern Europe. In many communist countries, the regime had sought to legitimize its hold on power by promoting a strong sense of patriotic unity – seeking to fuse two universalist concepts, communism and nationalism, in an attempt to mirror the historic relationship between liberalism and nationalism in much of the West. As Cheng Chen has argued, 'Paradoxically, the more successful this Leninist nation-building was, the more difficult it would be for post-Leninist elites to define a liberal variant of nationalism, given how deeply Leninist principles became embedded or fused with the nation's self-image'. The result has been a tendency of successor leaderships in those countries to project themselves as protagonists of national identity and pride, matched by a corresponding difficulty for liberal values to embed themselves in the fabric of political culture. Soon after the collapse of communism, the philosopher Isaiah Berlin expressed a fear that 'After years of oppression and humiliation, there is liable to occur a violent counter-reaction, an outburst of national pride, often aggressive self-assertion, by liberated nations and their leaders'.

These various patterns may help explain why so many Western European populists present themselves as 'outsiders' who want to tear down the existing institutional order – and are often contemptuous of establishment bodies such as conventional political parties, the judiciary, civil service, church or public-service broadcasting – whereas the reflex of Central and Eastern European populists is usually rather different – to take over, occupy and/or leverage such traditional institutions, to assert themselves firmly as 'insiders' who can then defend and entrench their own world-view from within the system. This is reflected in the fact that leading populist figures in post-communist countries often played a mainstream role in the politics of the 1990s, before moving to a more radical stance, whereas comparable figures in Western Europe rarely had any background in conventional party politics.

The great moving right show

In Poland, the Kaczyński twins, who founded the Law and Justice party in 2001, were both former Christian Democrats who had served in government before re-emerging as 'born-again' champions of patriotism and family values. Their success as a political force coincided with the country's entry into the EU and the start of a sustained period of economic growth, years before the factors driving populism in Western Europe became acute. In September 2005, Law and Justice emerged as the largest party in the Sejm, and the following month, Lech Kaczyński was elected President of the country. His brother, Jarosław, became Prime Minister nine months later. Poland had only a negligible foreign-born population and it managed to grow its way through the 2008 economic and financial crisis, never even entering recession.

Although the Civic Platform party of the moderate centre-right governed from 2007 to 2015, Law and Justice secured absolute majorities in the Sejm in the 2015 and 2019 general elections. During the intervening period, Law and Justice moved markedly to the right on a range of issues, including on Europe – a process fuelled by the political impact of the death of Lech Kaczyński, whose presidential aircraft crashed in Russia in April 2010, on the seventieth anniversary of the Katyn massacre. Whereas in 2006, Lech Kaczyński was proposing a European army, so long as it was tied to NATO, by 2016 his brother, Jarosław, was declaring 'we have the right to rule on our own here and decide ... the shape of Poland', and the country's second

(Law and Justice) President, Andrzej Duda, has since described the EU as an 'illusory community' with 'few benefits for us'.

In Hungary, the pattern was broadly similar. The initially mainstream Fidesz party, founded by Viktor Orbán and other ex-students at the time of the 1989 revolution, started to shift to the right in the late 2000s, drawing in part on the experience of Law and Justice in Poland. Orbán himself evolved from being essentially a Christian Democrat to advocating the 'building [of] an illiberal new state on national foundations', as he put it strikingly in 2014. His party has won super-majorities (big enough to change the domestic constitution) at successive general elections since 2010.

The governments in Poland and Hungary have used state power to build and maintain support among working-class and lower middle-class voters in particular, with rising prosperity enabling them to channel public spending in politically effective directions. A subsidy of 500 złoty (about 110 euro) per child per month in Poland, for example, has proved popular with the working poor (and more widely) and is designed to help to fend off population decline and promote family values. (The government has promised to increase the subsidy to 800 złoty (about 177 euro) in 2024.) Cultural homogeneity enables leaders to play on fears that migration would dilute national identity and destabilize society. As Aleks Szczerbiak has noted, the fact that, 'unlike in many Western European cities, there have been no Islamist terrorist attacks in Poland increased Poles' sense that they lived in a relatively safe country and that this was threatened by alleged EU-imposed multi-culturalism'.

Institutionally, the Polish and Hungarian governments have been accused not only of colonizing public appointments with political sympathizers, but of seeking to undermine democratic institutions and the rule of law. In the words of Anna Grzymala-Busse, they have 'followed the same template: target the highest courts and the judiciary, then restrict the independence of the media and civil society, and finally transform the constitutional framework and electoral laws in ways that enshrine their hold on power'. Criticisms of the two countries led the European Commission and European Parliament to launch 'Article 7' proceedings (under the EU Treaties) against Poland and Hungary in (respectively) December 2017 and September 2018. This process may be activated when a country's behaviour suggests 'a clear risk of a serious breach' of the fundamental values on which the Union is based, and it can lead ultimately to suspension of its voting rights in the Council of Ministers. Interestingly, other Central and Eastern European governments have generally been cautious in speaking out against Poland or Hungary, while the domestic political embarrassment seems to have been limited, with both the Law and Justice and Fidesz parties still securing re-election by decisive margins at subsequent general elections.

BREXIT: THE DYNAMICS OF BRITISH EXCEPTIONALISM

Clashing political cultures

The biggest political victory for populism in the 2010s was not to be measured in the performance of political parties in elections anywhere in Europe, but in the outcome of one referendum, held on 23 June 2016, when the electorate of the United Kingdom voted, by 52 to 48 per cent, to leave the European Union. Arguably the most important single political event to take place in Europe during the first two decades of the twenty-first century, the 'Brexit' vote had, of course, multiple origins. However, perhaps critically, the acceleration of European integration from the mid-1980s onwards posed particularly acute problems for Britain, where the political system has long been based on the concept of sovereignty residing, not in the people, or in a constitution, or in a supreme court interpreting that constitution, but in its own national parliament.

The notion of 'parliamentary sovereignty' lying at the heart of the political system is unique to Britain among European countries. It derives from the unusual continuity of the kingdom's central institutions from an era before written constitutions had developed. This was made possible in turn by the enforced submission of the monarchy to parliament in the seventeenth century – which was the outcome of a civil war in which the king was executed – and by the happy absence of invasion, occupation or defeat in foreign war since that time. As the historian David Cannadine has written, for all its many faults, the Westminster legislature is 'a uniquely enduring institution of political authority, government legitimacy, popular sovereignty and national identity' in ways unmatched in perhaps any other democratic state.

AFTERWORD

The practical form that parliamentary sovereignty takes in Britain means that there are few constitutional safeguards against transient majorities in the lower chamber legislating as they wish. This is matched by the idea that policy outcomes can be reversed at subsequent general elections. The use of a majoritarian electoral system, rather than proportional representation, to elect the House of Commons has ensured a 'winner-take-all' political culture, dominated by two main parties, alternating in the exclusive exercise of power – with coalition governments and power-sharing rare, other than in times of war. The proposition that 'Europe operates according to pre-established rules: incoming governments must respect the word of those who preceded them', as Jean-Claude Juncker has put it, or that 'new majorities cannot unpick' existing European rules, to quote Angela Merkel, is not one that would find ready favour in Britain.

Equally difficult to digest in the British political system is the more fundamental idea that national sovereignty should or could be pooled or combined systematically with the sovereignty of others, at a higher, supranational level, as part of what the founding Six called 'a destiny shared in common'. The stark reality of EU membership – where states agree to bind themselves permanently into common policies, backed by superior European law, adopted by a European legislature and interpreted by a European court – was something that successive British governments avoided discussing directly, claiming instead that the country somehow remained an 'independent sovereign state'. This was technically true only in that Britain could always renounce its membership of the European Union, as indeed it would eventually choose to do.

Unlike the experience of many continental countries, membership of the Union failed to 'Europeanize' British domestic political parties, elites or debates – with an understanding or acceptance of the new power structure confined largely to those parts of the civil service, civil society, business and academia that interacted with the EU institutions as part of their daily working lives. Instead, much of the British political system and the media insisted on maintaining the 'otherness' of Europe – seeing the Union as some kind of unidentified political object that had mysteriously descended on London SW1 – while the country more widely struggled awkwardly, in the words of Hugo Young, 'to reconcile the past she could not forget with the future she could not avoid'.

AFTERWORD
Britain's European problem

The fateful decision of David Cameron, who became British Prime Minister in May 2010, to seek 'renewed consent' for UK membership through a referendum followed a long period when successive prime ministers had grappled with a major conundrum at the heart of British politics and foreign policy. This was the question of how to stay a central player in a Union based on the pooling of sovereignty, when many in the UK, especially (but not only) in its political elite, felt highly uncomfortable with the notion of such power-sharing and refused to see Europe as the central prism through which Britain's political future would be refracted.

The classic Whitehall response was to stress the practical advantages of EU membership in concrete ways that benefited businesses and citizens, as if the Union was simply an international organization like any other, downplaying the political dimension of the process, with use of phrases such as 'sovereignty sharing' or 'European integration' kept to a minimum. The irony was that to outsiders, the UK was often seen as disproportionally influential in guiding the general direction of the Union – for example, the former Swedish prime minister, Carl Bildt, wrote in 2017: 'For all its public ambivalence, there is little doubt that on the inside, Britain has been very powerful in shaping the evolution of the EU. It has been in the vanguard of the single market, free trade, competitiveness and enlargement drives [of recent] decades. It has given weight to the efforts to build a common EU foreign policy.' To the puzzlement and disappointment of many foreign observers, these successes had little, if any, recognition or cut-through in domestic British politics.

The one major policy area where Britain had proved unable to set European priorities was to render the country's membership of the Union increasingly problematic. The landmark commitment to build a full economic and monetary union (EMU) in Europe sharpened the difficulties and contradictions faced in London, especially from the turn of the century onwards, very much as Margaret Thatcher's pro-European critics had predicted a decade before. Geoffrey Howe, for example, had warned in his resignation speech in 1990 that the implications for British power of detachment from EMU could be 'incalculable and very hard ever to correct'. The reality of the single currency gradually reinforced the centrality of Berlin and Paris in the European policy process – even if their views often did not easily coincide on either economics or international power – while highlighting the growing awkwardness for London in any attempt, as Howe put it, to 'hold and retain a position of influence in this vital debate'.

Wishful thinking about alternative models for Europe during the early Blair years – whether in the form of a 'new intergovernmentalism', a 'new bilateralism' or even a Franco-German-British 'triple alliance' at the heart of Europe – could not get round the inevitable, long-term consequences of the UK's own choice to distance itself from the euro. As Zbigniew Brzezinski wrote in 1997, the UK's reluctance to participate in the single currency 'reflects the country's unwillingness to identify British destiny with that of Europe' and corresponded to a recurrent pattern of declining to maximize its influence in or through a European Union created by others. Brzezinski characterized these as the attitudes of an increasingly 'retired geostrategic player' that was 'disengaged from the great European adventure in which France and Germany are the principal actors'.

Defensive manoeuvres

It was precisely to address this issue that Tony Blair, the only seriously committed 'European' to occupy Number Ten since Edward Heath in the early 1970s, wanted Britain to join the single currency, a move which could have finally and decisively wedded the country to a European destiny of the kind Brzezinski talked about. Although Blair spoke confidently of Britain 'leading in Europe' and 'never being isolated in Europe', on the most important issue, namely EMU, he lacked the courage of his ostensibly pro-euro convictions. He was frustrated by stubborn resistance from his Chancellor (and successor from June 2007), Gordon Brown, who in turn was much closer to domestic public opinion, which consistently split about two-to-one against the idea of giving up sterling. Blair's critical concession that a referendum would need to be held before any adoption of the single currency – mirroring a similar commitment made by his Conservative predecessor, John Major, before the May 1997 general election – effectively rendered EMU entry very difficult, if not impossible. It also ironically paved the way for the possibility of a much broader and more dangerous referendum on the question of Britain's EU membership itself.

During the early years of the new century, Blair, Brown and Cameron found that being outside the single currency made successful

British membership of the Union increasingly complicated, as more and more countries adopted the euro – rising from 11 member states in 1999 to 19 by 2015 – and the interests of the eurozone states gradually became synonymous with those of the Union as a whole. In parallel, national capitals which had already conceded a long string of opt-outs to London in the past – on EMU itself, employment policy (subsequently rescinded), justice and home affairs, Schengen (complete free movement) and the Charter of Fundamental Rights – became increasingly tired of the seemingly inexhaustible demands and needs of British exceptionalism.

The successive Amsterdam, Nice and Lisbon Treaties, all concluded while Blair and Brown were in power, echoed the Maastricht Treaty in exempting the UK from specific Union policies, and the appetite for further concessions was dwindling. The idea that 'Britain merely wanted not to be excluded, without being willing to participate', as Perry Anderson has put it, began seriously to grate. It was rather like a driver determined to proceed as slowly as possible in the fast lane of a motorway, with others behind starting to flash their lights in protest. The delicate balancing act that successive UK governments had attempted, of minimizing the country's obligations in Europe while retaining its influence as a major member state, was becoming less and less easy to sustain.

Two-speed Europe

Traditionally, the United Kingdom fought hard to avoid the perception that a two-speed Europe was developing, refusing the image of Britain relegated to the outer tier or rearguard, but under Cameron that changed. Whereas Blair as Prime Minister had made it clear that London would 'not accept a two-speed Europe' and his predecessor, Major, had talked of a 'real danger' of such a division – advocating instead a 'mix and match' Europe, based on opt-outs – Cameron was less shy about the concept and more willing to allow it to evolve in practice. While Brown fought tenaciously to secure a place for Britain at eurozone summits, Cameron chose to stay away from such meetings. The Whitehall line shifted to the proposition that while the eurozone might well need to deepen, and the UK would not stand in its way, any 'deeper European integration was for the eurozone only'.

This distinction was bound to be exposed as incoherent over time, as nearly every legislative act adopted by the Union would in some way deepen the degree of integration, whether or not it related to EMU. However, the new strategy ran out of road very quickly, in December 2011, when Cameron felt obliged to veto a set of fast-track EU treaty changes, which were designed to tighten the budgetary rules within EMU, rather than submit them to Westminster for approval (and even though they would not apply to Britain). Much to their irritation, the UK veto forced the eurozone states to adopt a more cumbersome and less binding intergovernmental treaty of their own. Cameron assumed that he would not be alone in his stand and could forge and lead a coalition of the euro 'outs', but in practice eight of the ten non-eurozone countries, firmly encouraged by Merkel and Barroso to see themselves as 'pre-ins', quickly signed up to the new 'fiscal compact' treaty anyway. Three years later, in June 2014, Cameron sought to prevent the choice of the long-standing and recently retired Luxembourg Prime Minister, Jean-Claude Juncker, as Barroso's successor as Commission President. Whereas the hostility of Cameron's predecessors to 'federalist' Belgian prime ministers holding the job had won the day – Major opposed Jean-Luc Dehaene in 1995 and Blair resisted Guy Verhofstadt in 2004 – this time, Cameron's preference for a less integrationist candidate was simply ignored.

Fateful referendum

When Cameron unexpectedly won an absolute majority for his Conservative party in the May 2015 general election, and was thus no longer constrained by his earlier coalition with the pro-European Liberal Democrats, he found that he had no choice but to deliver on his commitment to hold a referendum. With the European migration crisis in full flow, the wider political context was hardly ideal, but instead of playing for time, Cameron promptly set about trying to renegotiate the terms of UK membership – as he had (unnecessarily and rashly) promised to do, without any idea of where exactly those negotiations might land – and then submitted the result to a national vote on whether to remain in or leave the Union. In bringing matters to a head in this way – to 'lance the boil' of the issue once and for all, as he put it – Cameron may have been emboldened by his success in defeating advocates of Scottish independence in a (Scotland-only) referendum on that subject in September 2014. However, this time, he was quickly trapped by the logic of his own initiative, reverting to the default position of successive prime ministers in refusing to discuss the true nature of European integration with the British public, but now with much more serious potential consequences.

So, rather than setting out a confident case, from first principles, for why Britain's national interest might lie in staying in the European Union and defending the degree of sovereignty-sharing it necessarily involved – regardless of the outcome of any renegotiation, which he could not control – Cameron presented the choice facing the country as a purely transactional exercise, initially proclaiming himself to be 'relaxed' about either outcome. When he secured only a relatively modest series of rather arcane institutional concessions in his so-called 'new settlement' – slightly increasing the (marginal) role of national parliaments in EU law-making and exempting Britain from the symbolic goal of 'ever closer union' – he found himself unable decisively to shift public opinion in favour of remaining in the Union. By contrast, the Eurosceptics' simple proposition that they were fighting a sovereignty war about who governed Britain, and that the public should 'take back control' of the nation's affairs, appealed to many (especially older voters) who had never warmed to the ambiguities and realities of EU membership and who hoped to return to a largely mythical past in which the country could avoid 'continental entanglements'.

The outcome of the June 2016 referendum blindsided the political establishment in Britain. To the extent that successive governments since 1979 had pursued any consistent national strategy to speak of, it was one of the country being 'open for business' as an outward-looking trading nation, embracing economic interdependence with others, seeking to become a major centre for inward investment, accepting a high degree of inward migration, and using EU membership as a vehicle to promote British competitiveness in and through the single market. Politically, for even longer, Britain had also sought to maximize its credibility in Washington by being a key player in Europe, while in turn enhancing its power in Brussels by building and boasting a special relationship with the United States. This was the essential insight that Harold Macmillan had offered back in the early 1960s, when Britain first sought to join the European Community, and it had guided the foreign policies of the Thatcher and Blair years in particular. This whole approach to national prosperity and power was now thrown into question by the unexpected referendum result.

AFTERWORD

Scrambled alignments and hardening attitudes

The June 2016 vote also scrambled political alignments within the United Kingdom itself. It established (or revealed) a strong new fault-line between younger, better educated, richer, more urban, more mobile and more internationalist 'Remain' voters, and their mirror-opposites on the 'Leave' side, cutting across traditional left-right party divisions and with the potential to supersede them. This division was very similar to the one evident in the French referenda of 1992 and 2005, but it was politically much more potent. The outcome also revealed strong majorities for continued EU membership in both Scotland and Northern Ireland, complicating the question of their own positions within the United Kingdom and in effect strengthening the long-term position of advocates of Scottish independence and a united Ireland.

Paradoxically, even as the domestic debate about 'Britain in Europe' became much better informed after the referendum than it had been before the vote, most opinion polls initially suggested a continued hardening of attitudes on each side, rather than any serious shift between positions. Most voters soon began to say that their view on the European question was stronger than their allegiance to any political party. The debate and division proved more neuralgic, precisely perhaps because the margin between victory and defeat had been so narrow. The 'Remain' camp questioned the legitimacy of so big a change being decided by so few votes, without a minimum threshold – those voting for Brexit represented only 37.4 per cent of the registered electorate – fuelling demands for a second referendum.

Among the parties, the Conservatives were the most seriously disoriented by the result. Cameron immediately resigned as prime minister and his successor, Theresa May, a centre-right figure within the party, embarked on an elaborate political exercise that tried, unsuccessfully, to reconcile the many competing pressures that she faced. While a majority of her own MPs (and most of British business) had supported continued British membership – and a large overall majority in the Commons still wanted the country to stay in the Union – an even bigger majority of her own party supporters in the country had voted to leave, with the latter's strength of feeling growing all the time. May chose to eschew the option of seeking to build a cross-party majority in parliament for a 'soft' Brexit – perhaps based on modular participation in some specific EU policy areas, with continued sovereignty-sharing, along the lines of the European Economic Area (EEA). Instead, she decided to triangulate between the forces within her own party, in the hope of finding a position that was acceptable to most Conservatives while somehow also being marketable to the remaining 27 EU member states, represented by the European Commission in Brussels.

In the ensuing exit negotiations, May sought to retain or replicate many of the benefits of EU membership – such as 'frictionless' access to the single market and de facto membership of the customs union – without wanting to accept the formal obligations which they implied, notably respect for EU law. Her notion of 'Brexit means Brexit' involved 'taking control of our borders, laws and money' while 'achieving the same outcomes' – in terms of the free movement of goods, services and capital at least – as if Britain were still a member state. Now that Britain was leaving, it ironically seemed to want to be 'in, without being in', having previously wanted to be 'out, without being out', as Martin Westlake has amusingly put it.

Into the Brexit vortex

As the complexities and contradictions of the UK position intensified, Theresa May found herself in the unusual and unenviable position of pursuing a central policy – departure from the European Union – that was at least passively opposed by her own parliament. The irony was, as Vernon Bogdanor acutely spotted, that even if Brexit had been predicated on the principle of the 'sovereignty of parliament', the effect of the referendum result was in fact to create a new, alternative, higher 'sovereignty of the people', from which neither government nor parliament could easily escape. The Prime Minister's awkward balancing act satisfied few other members of her own government or party, still less the wider political community or general public. She decided to try to break the stalemate by dissolving the House of Commons in a general election that she was expected decisively to win. The result of the June 2017 election was, however, almost as surprising as that of the referendum a year before. The Conservatives lost thirteen seats, failed to secure an absolute majority, and in order to stay in power, were left dependent on Unionists from Northern Ireland – a situation which Edward Heath had refused on principle to countenance in the comparable circumstances of an early general election that went wrong, in February–March 1974.

AFTERWORD

The Irish dimension of the Brexit negotiations proved particularly intractable, as departure from the EU's single market and customs union raised the prospect of the need to reinstate a 'hard' border between North and South, putting at risk both a central achievement of the Irish peace process and a key practical underpinning of Northern Irish prosperity. The exit deal which May eventually struck in November 2018 sought to solve this problem by accepting that the whole of the UK might need to stay in the customs union, if no 'alternative arrangements' could be devised, through the operation of a so-called 'back-stop', which could apply for a potentially indefinite period. To minimize trade disruption between Britain and the Union, it also envisaged a 'common rulebook' – with the UK in effect choosing to align on EU technical standards, even if it was no longer part of the single market, backed by a formal commitment not to undercut the Union on environmental, labour or consumer protection standards. These concessions proved unacceptable both to Unionists and to many Conservative backbenchers, who repeatedly voted against the deal when the government brought it before the Commons for ratification.

Right-wing opponents of May's withdrawal agreement were joined by the opposition Labour party, led by a closet Brexiteer, Jeremy Corbyn, whose lacklustre endorsement of the Remain side in the 2016 referendum was seen as one of several factors that had tipped the balance towards departure. The Labour front bench sought opportunistically to maximize Tory discomfort and division – just as they had done twenty-eight years before over the Maastricht Treaty – ostensibly in the hope (at various times) of securing a better exit deal (while remaining elusive about its exact content), forcing another general election, and/or holding a second referendum on continued EU membership. The government's withdrawal agreement was rejected in three successive Commons votes in the first quarter of 2019, even if the majority against it fell from 230 to 149 to 58.

Against her natural instinct, May finally decided to open talks with Labour, in the hope of getting the Brexit deal across the line, but to no avail. Corbyn (and his Europe spokesman, Keir Starmer) insisted that the government sign up to a second referendum as the price of any agreement, something she was unwilling to concede because she feared it would fatally divide her party. Eventually, in June, exhausted and facing a revolt among Conservative MPs against her continued leadership, May chose to resign, rather than hold and lose a fourth vote. Having already destroyed, in different ways, Thatcher, Major and Cameron, the European issue in British politics now consumed its fourth Conservative Prime Minister in a row.

Breaking the stalemate

Boris Johnson, the flamboyant Brexiteer who replaced May in July 2019, faced an increasingly truculent Commons that, somewhat bizarrely, was determined to block any departure from the EU without a deal, while also being unable to coalesce around any positive alternative. While a majority in the Commons managed to wrest the initiative from the executive to pass specific legislation to make 'no deal' unlawful, it then failed to support every concrete option put before it, including staying in the EU customs union or single market. After trying to suspend the parliamentary session for several weeks in the early autumn to disable his opponents – only to find this move overturned by the Supreme Court – Johnson struck a deal with the EU-27 in late October 2019 that was very similar to May's agreement of eleven months before, except in two key respects.

First, Northern Ireland (but not the whole of the UK) would remain subject to the EU customs code, so requiring checks on exports from Great Britain to Northern Ireland, creating in effect an administrative border in the Irish Sea. Second, the idea of a common UK–EU 'rulebook' was abandoned, along with any formal UK commitment to keep to at least the same standards as the EU on environmental, employment and consumer policy. However, Northern Ireland would still be subject to EU single-market rules for goods, as well as the jurisdiction of the European Court of Justice, even if this situation could be rescinded by the Northern Ireland Assembly in the future.

With the Conservative party largely united behind him, Johnson jettisoned the Unionists (who accused him of a 'great betrayal') and decided to call the bluff of Labour and the Liberal Democrats, who were now both demanding an immediate general election, seemingly against their own political interests. In December 2019, Britain went to the polls for the third time in fifty-five months, with Johnson campaigning to 'get Brexit done'. Winning eighty more seats than all other parties combined – each of which was opposed to his deal for differing reasons – the Prime Minister obtained the pro-Brexit majority that had eluded his predecessor. Johnson's withdrawal agreement was duly ratified in January 2020 and Britain finally left the European Union at the end of that month.

United European front

Throughout the Brexit negotiations, the twenty-seven other EU member states proved consistently united behind a common position brokered by the European Commission's chief negotiator, Michel Barnier. This prioritized maintaining the integrity of the single market and the Irish peace process over the shifting imperatives of British domestic politics. Recurrent internal EU tensions on other issues – notably foreign policy, future financing and the reform of EMU – led many in the British government to expect that the EU-27 would splinter in the face of losing the Union's second largest national economy and (arguably then still) its most important political player on the world stage. Instead, London found – just as it had experienced on entry in the early 1970s, even if nobody remembered – that once certain common policies and laws have been agreed at European level (which is rarely an easy process), the individual interests of member states gradually converge around the compromises struck, melding them together to form a new set of common interests. The Commission is then able to act as a tough negotiator for, and strong defender of, this new status quo. The claim that Britain would have 'all the cards to play' in any negotiation, which would be 'one of the easiest in human history', as leading Eurosceptics casually claimed before and after the referendum, began to look seriously ironic, if not comic.

Now the same well-informed, clear-sighted (and often very effective) external negotiating tactics that the Commission had deployed for many years on Britain's behalf, as one of the Union's member states, were to be used at Britain's expense, as it chose to leave and become a 'third country'. These last two words particularly rankled in Whitehall and Westminster, which expected some measure of sympathetic or special treatment after more than four decades inside the club. Instead, London was told that 'cherry picking' was impossible and non-membership had, by definition, to be more disadvantageous than membership, as Michel Barnier repeatedly stressed. So, even after the withdrawal agreement came into effect, a further round of negotiations on Britain's longer-term economic relationship with the Union – including the terms of over 700 billion euro worth of trade each year – proved tortuous and fractious, even if it eventually resulted in a deal on Christmas Eve 2020, just a week before the transition period expired. Only time will tell whether the clash of official worldviews apparent in the successive negotiations will leave such a legacy of bitterness and distrust that Brussels and London drift decisively away from each other in the years ahead. In the short term, however, simply navigating the post-Brexit environment promises to be, at the very least, a complicated and unhappy process.

FROM POLY-CRISIS TO CORONAVIRUS

Donald Trump and the decay of the West

In June 2016, just before the Brexit referendum, the then President of the European Commission, Jean-Claude Juncker, referred to Europe as facing a 'poly-crisis'. The European Union and national governments were confronting a series of immediate challenges – slow growth, the refugee crisis, and security threats from the south and the east – which had in turn been grafted on to a deeper, slow-burn public disillusionment with politics and government, with the whole combination fuelling populist responses across the continent. The seeming inability of Western governments to make progress on further trade liberalization and the looming shadow of climate change also added to a growing feeling of unease. The poly-crisis then spectacularly deepened, not only with the outcome of the Brexit vote, but with the equally unexpected election, five months later, of Donald Trump as President of the United States. Just as events in America in 2001 and 2008 had already done much to shape Europe's experience in the new millennium, so the continent was now, once again, buffeted by a dramatic development across the Atlantic over which it had no control.

The new US President's populist policies and aggressive style of governing challenged a deep assumption in most European capitals – as indeed within the Washington establishment – that post-war economic and political interdependence and common action between America and Europe served a strong mutual interest. Not only was Trump highly allergic to free trade and contemptuous of the institutions of global governance – abandoning transatlantic trade talks, withdrawing from the Paris accord on climate change and abrogating the Iranian nuclear deal – he even seemed to question the continuation of the Atlantic Alliance as the cornerstone of Western security. The growing unreliability of the US as an ally and the potential loss of the wider sense of a 'Euro-Atlantic community' was profoundly unsettling for political leaders in Europe and it set off something of a slow-motion political earthquake across the continent. As one German politician is alleged to have said, without irony, on realizing that the US had in effect unilaterally ended negotiations on a Transatlantic Trade and Investment Partnership (TTIP), 'Hang on a minute, I thought that we were the ones who got the right to say no.'

Peak populism?

The combination of Brexit and Trump generated fears that the rising populist wave in Western democracies would soon engulf conventional political parties and not only halt, but reverse, the process of European integration. The prospect that the UK vote might set off a chain reaction of departures from the Union provides an additional explanation as to why the EU-27 held together so effectively in the Brexit negotiations towards the end of the 2010s. Ironically, the populist advance was gradually broken as the complexities of those negotiations – and a growing awareness of what the UK would lose from life outside the EU – together with the vagaries of Trump's behaviour in the White House, gradually discredited the simple assertions of anti-system figures. Surveys showed positive feeling among European citizens towards the Union rise from 34 per cent in spring 2016 to 42 per cent in autumn 2019, with hostility falling back from 27 to 20 per cent. This mood change had spill-over effects in other parts of political systems too: for example, in the two main regions where separatist movements were gaining traction during this period – in Scotland and in Catalonia, where campaigners for independence from Spain won a regional referendum in October 2017, setting off a major constitutional crisis – the advocates of independence were increasingly keen to present themselves as unambiguously pro-European.

Rather than register further gains, as most media commentators expected, the May 2019 European Parliament elections left populist parties no stronger than five years before, suggesting that electorally 'peak populism' might have been reached. A distinct rise in turn-out at the elections (from 43 to 51 per cent) made it difficult to argue that the legitimacy of the EU system was under ever greater strain, while many of the Western European populist parties themselves, meeting in Milan during the Euro-election campaign, committed to working 'towards a common-sense Europe' from within the structures of the Union. The departure of Britain from the EU soon afterwards also ended the highly visible role of Nigel Farage (with his successive UKIP and Brexit parties) as a kind of continent-wide standard-bearer for Euroscepticism, further weakening their collective impact.

In the few cases where populist parties had entered government in Western Europe, their experience of power usually failed to confer any political advantage. Both the Austrian Freedom Party and Matteo Salvini's League in Italy entered office in 2017 only to exit from government two years later. In Vienna, the Freedom Party's leader, Heinz-Christian Strache, was exposed as soliciting illicit Russian funding for his party, resulting in the collapse of his coalition with the mainstream centre-right People's Party. In Rome, Salvini proactively walked out on his coalition partners (and catch-all rivals), the Five Star Movement, in an attempt to force an early general election which he hoped to win. This manoeuvre backfired when Five Stars linked up with the centre-left Democrats in September 2019, to form an (equally opportunistic) alternative government, pushing the election further away. In short, anti-system parties found it difficult to manage or transform the system from within, in Western Euopre at least, and they rarely seemed to benefit electorally from the experience of being in power.

Interests and values

If the Brexit–Trump experience delivered a form of 'shock therapy' to European public opinion, it also focused minds at elite level about a possible 'existential' threat to European interests and values in the years ahead. The prospect was not only of the European Union finding its open, multilateralist world-view challenged by others, but of an unprotected continent being surrounded, if not besieged, by sources of instability and/or threat on multiple fronts. Fears about the potential loss of Britain and America as reliable allies and of Anglo-Saxon culture as an integral part of Europe's evolving identity cut deep in many countries. This in turn opened up a more urgent debate about whether the EU needed to move beyond projecting itself primarily as a 'union of values', reliant on the appeal of soft power, to become much more tough-minded and self-confident in defining its own interests and in developing the capabilities to defend and advance those interests at home and abroad.

This shift reflected a wider reappraisal in European capitals of the dynamics of the changing international environment, where the outlook seemed to be becoming decidedly less benign. Instead of globalization and digital technology leading to the future triumph of liberal internationalism and democratic choice, driven by a new global middle class of empowered individuals who would be 'more like us' – as many had assumed at the start of the 2010s – digitization was now strengthening the power of states as much as individuals, with a new form of authoritarian market economy, epitomized by China under President Xi Jinping, developing to rival the Western model. The Schumpeterian proposition that free markets would automatically foster and sustain free societies came under increasing strain, just as the notion that a multipolar world would necessarily be a multilateral one looked less and less obvious, especially if the United States were to abdicate its remaining leadership role.

Soon after his first election as French President in May 2017, Emmanuel Macron began to talk about the need to develop a greater degree of 'European sovereignty' in various policy areas. At the time, Macron's view was still seen as an outlier in the debate, even if his concept was well received in the EU institutions in Brussels. However, after two more years of capricious decision-making in the White House, matched by the exhausting drama of the Brexit negotiations, the mood crystallized around the need for Europe to possess greater 'strategic autonomy' or 'strategic sovereignty', so as to reduce (or diversify) its dependence on others – whether in defence and security, digital policy, energy supply, ownership of strategic economic sectors or access to critical raw materials – and generally to enjoy more freedom to choose its own path and to act alone, when it wished.

Autonomy and interdependence

After a series of major, unexpected disruptions during the first two decades of this century – from September 11, via the Iraq war, economic and financial crisis, eurozone debt crisis and migration crisis, through to the rise of populism and advent of Brexit – there was a growing desire in Europe to try to get ahead of events and gain a greater measure of control over future developments. So whereas Jean-Claude Juncker declared, on entering office in 2014, that he would lead a 'political' Commission — a phrase which referred largely to an inter-institutional power-play in Brussels — his successor five years later, Ursula von der Leyen, caught the mood when she asserted (in July 2019) that hers would be a 'geopolitical' Commission.

This linguistic evolution was more than just a play on words, as von der Leyen and her new Commissioner colleagues quickly made it clear that they intended to take the 'global lead on the major challenges of our times', seeking to shape the terms of international debate on certain major policy issues, notably climate change and digital regulation. They would 'work for a just globalization' and 'make change happen by design, not by disaster or by diktat from others'. The ambitious proposals since tabled by the Commission and already largely enacted by the EU legislative process — notably for a European Green Deal, designed to make Europe the first carbon-neutral continent by 2050, and the regulation of digital services, digital markets and artificial intelligence (AI) — add up to what Heather Grabbe has called a 'normative and transformative' agenda with the potential to impact not just Europe but multiple jurisdictions for decades to come.

Although the concepts of strategic autonomy and multilateralism ostensibly point in differing directions — the one based on independence, the other on interdependence — the hope was, and is, that these could be combined in such a way that a more hard-headed Europe would be able to work with others as its first preference, but still enjoy the capacity to act alone when necessary, based on a higher degree of collective self-sufficiency. However, developing European capabilities — and the greater internal resilience that follows — would necessarily depend on many factors, some of them difficult to achieve. These include a greater willingness or preparedness (than so far) to think politically about Europe's future place in the world, to countenance the use of sanctions and of force in a strategic way, to mobilize significantly more financial resources to fund European initiatives, to identify weaknesses in existing policies and fill the gaps that persist, to confront national or commercial vested interests threatened by such action, and to override resistance by individual member-state capitals on issues they consider highly sensitive. These were not new issues, but they were now suddenly becoming more acute.

In the past, it has always proved 'easiest' to build common European policies in fields where two conditions were met: first, where

joint action could obviously achieve more than any individual country acting on its own; and second, where such action could be taken without visibly challenging the political authority of national governments, individually or collectively. The Union had thus been well suited to the integration and collective management of policy areas that were the classic preserve of technical experts or independent bodies, such as agriculture, competition policy, customs tariffs or non-tariff barriers to trade, and more recently, the operation of monetary or criminal justice policy. It had always proved more difficult to generate common action in areas requiring the explicit pooling of sovereignty over issues that were highly divisive, especially along left-right lines, in member-state parliaments – such as macro-economic policy, taxation, labour market reform, migration or foreign policy.

The same problem has applied wherever major new public spending commitments were required, with the potential to generate bitter distributional struggles between contributor and recipient member states. As a result, the EU budget has remained very modest – hovering around 1 per cent of collective GDP for the thirty-year period between 1990 and 2020. Many EU spending programmes have been seen in member-state capitals as less like a classic national budget 'writ large' than as a series of convenient 'special-purpose vehicles' adopted to meet tightly defined, ad-hoc goals, such as managing the countryside, preserving fishing stocks or promoting major infrastructure development.

Constrained in this way, the Union had progressively become, by the start of the current decade, a kind of 'regulatory state', founded on the completion of the single market and flanking policies (notably the environment), and also increasingly an emerging 'regulatory superstate', based on the market-driven or policy-led export of many of its single-market norms worldwide, what Anu Bradford has called the 'Brussels effect'. But the EU had not managed to impinge meaningfully upon taxing, spending, health, education, welfare, defence, or many other core responsibilities of modern government. Conversely, in those fields where it did apply, the process of 'integration through law' had already built a high degree of mutual interlocking or *engrenage* between the participating states, further deepening their interdependence and common interests over time. Cumulatively, this process meant that many parts of the EU system were, and are, in fact much more resilient to shocks than often assumed. This underlying strength can often be camouflaged by recurrent images of division and deadlock at high-profile meetings of European leaders, giving the impression of a continent staggering from one bruising political show-down to another. The EU system's practical ability to keep delivering policy outcomes in many fields, whatever is happening at the summit, is too often lost from sight.

Competing narratives

In recent years, the default setting among commentators about the future of Europe, at least in English-speaking circles, has been largely one of pervasive pessimism. Since the mid-2000s, there has been a lively 'declinist' literature confidently predicting Europe's demise as a political and economic force – much as there was before 1985, on the eve of Europe's unexpected relaunch. Books with titles such as *Europe's Decline and Fall*, *The Strange Death of Europe* and *Euro-Tragedy* abound. In continental capitals, the climate is more benign, with a general assumption, especially among smaller states, that European integration offers them what Hugh Thomas once called 'a fine ride in the forest of politics whence they can at last command a view of their own futures'. This reflects less a romantic or idealistic notion of Europe than a cool assessment that the continent's combined scale and weight offer them the best available means of exercising influence in an increasingly forbidding world. These competing European narratives – the one of internal contradictions and failed promise; the other of collective strength and potential power – vary in their intensity or currency at any given time, and neither ever seems to enjoy a decisive intellectual victory. Writing and discussion about Europe usually polarizes around two alternative versions of reality – and implicitly two different visions of the future – with the actuality of Europe stuck stubbornly somewhere in between.

One way of reconciling these views is to look at the European Union's development since the 1950s as part of a process of saving and empowering the nation-state, as much as threatening or submerging it – what Alan Milward once called the 'European rescue of the nation-state'. In other words, whatever the theoretical arguments about sovereignty and accountability, the practical effect of common policies has often been, as Milward suggests, 'not to supersede, but to reinforce' national political systems by enhancing their day-to-day ability to deliver policy solutions for their electorates. The possibility of generating new collective public goods at supranational level is one of the most important distinguishing features of the EU system. Sometimes this process occurs through a rational assessment of the potential 'added value' of joint action – as it did with decisions in the second half of the 1980s to complete the single market and create a single currency – and sometimes it happens because pressing and often unexpected events necessitate the sudden invention of new common solutions that can 'change the context', as Jean Monnet put it, in a way that national action on its own cannot offer.

Building Europe through crisis?

Sudden rushes to common action help account for the oft-remarked tendency of the Union to 'progress' through crisis – with its policies and institutions frequently (although not always) emerging strengthened, rather than weakened, from otherwise traumatic events that initially seem to reveal its shortcomings. Looking at crises so far this century, the reflex is apparent, for example, in new common policies in justice and home affairs at European level after 9/11, with much stronger EU action to counter terrorism and cross-border crime. We also see the same reflex during and after the 2008–12 economic, financial and eurozone debt crises, with the introduction of much tighter EU regulation of financial services and parallel moves to develop a 'banking union' (of common supervision, resolution and deposit insurance) to prevent sovereign and non-sovereign debt markets from infecting one another in the future. This was matched by the creation of a permanent bail-out mechanism for use in future crises and a much more activist role for the European Central Bank. Similarly, the migration crisis of 2016 resulted in more serious efforts to strengthen the outer border of the Union, both to protect the Union externally and to safeguard the survival of free movement internally.

In the eurozone and migration crises, the situation was complicated by the crises themselves being consequences, in part, of the 'incompleteness' of existing or new European policies – a monetary union without an economic or banking union, and the free movement of people within a Union that lacked common migration and asylum policies. The crises have led to moves to 'complete' the policies, a process amusingly dubbed 'failing forward' by Erik Jones and other political scientists, as failure leads to new attempts at more ambitious versions of the existing policies – or as Jones puts it, 'a sequential cycle of piecemeal reform, followed by policy failure, followed by further reform'. The policies in question were, of course, incomplete for a reason, namely that each compromise represented a lowest common denominator between the states and more coherent solutions usually involved deeper sovereignty-sharing than certain major national capitals were willing to concede at the time. So even when crises have pointed to the need for EU policies to be completed, the strengthening of those policies is itself often partial and ambiguous, and frequently takes, at least initially, an intergovernmental form. Now that significant treaty change is difficult to envisage without referenda in many countries, crisis-driven arrangements are more likely to stay intergovernmental for longer than in the past.

The ambiguity inherent in this process has usually proved sufficient to reassure any sceptical ministers or parliamentarians in (most) EU member states, as their domestic political systems have become increasingly interlinked with the European system over time. However, not all states have found it equally easy to manage the fluidity of this interface. Large countries with a strong tradition of state unity, democratic culture and external power – in effect, France and the United Kingdom – have grappled with the challenge more anxiously than others. However, as Vivien Schmidt has written, 'whereas French notions of political rights are justified philosophically by reference to the universal rights of man as declared at the time of the French revolution, the British notion of political rights as embodied in parliamentary sovereignty is justified by history and the traditional liberties of Englishmen'. As a result, while 'European integration for the French can represent an enhancement of their universally established rights, for the British it is more likely to be seen as a threat to their nationally, historically established rights.' In this context, Brexit can perhaps be understood as an extreme reaction to the injection of a new, alternative power-centre into a country that was almost genetically incapable of tolerating the degree of power-sharing that a common political future for Europe would imply.

2020: Year of living dangerously

Until 2020, the history of Europe since the Second World War seemed to divide naturally into two parts: a 'post-war' period from 1945 to

1989, and a continuing 'post-Wall' period comprising the three decades since the end of the Cold War. The post-war years seem in retrospect a long period of relative stability, even if at the time the feeling was one of consistent uncertainty and ideological tension. The post-Wall years opened with great optimism that gradually turned into a mixture of disappointment and complacency, followed by a series of shifts, shocks and 'big surprises' that were to make the first two decades of Europe's twenty-first century an almost permanent period of crisis. The critical year connecting the two periods, 1989, has a claim to be regarded, in the words of Timothy Garton Ash, as 'a year of wonders' and perhaps 'the best year in European history'.

Then, as it entered the 2020s, Europe was suddenly hit by the biggest surprise of all – and one which brought many of the assumptions of the post-Wall era to a juddering halt. On the very last day of 2019, the World Health Organization was notified of an outbreak in Wuhan, China of a new strain of coronavirus, Covid-19. The virus first surfaced in Europe in late January 2020, driven by tourists returning from China, and by mid-March, it was spreading rapidly – in Italy, Spain, France and Britain, and then more widely. With infections at one point more than doubling each week, health services rapidly came under strain and a growing sense of public panic ensued.

As national governments reacted one by one, often invoking states of emergency, the personal freedoms that Europeans took for granted were dramatically curtailed. To minimize contact, lockdowns were imposed across much of the continent – with most factories, shops, bars, restaurants and hotels closed – and citizens were forced to stay at home, forbidden to meet friends and family, and forced to work from home where they could, often for many weeks. Free movement between countries was severely limited, border controls were reinstated, and the dwindling number of international travellers had to quarantine on arrival at their destination. After a promising respite over the summer of 2020, a second wave of the pandemic surged during the autumn and winter, with a further round of lockdowns imposed, including in Germany, which had survived the first wave largely unscathed. Striking the right balance between opening up and closing down – especially in the education, retail, hospitality and leisure sectors – was to prove a very difficult conundrum for policy-makers, with sudden switch-backs and many mistakes.

AFTERWORD

Costs of the pandemic

Even though accurate figures can never be available, in 2020 at least 27 million people across Europe (including Russia) were infected by the coronavirus (out of 87 million worldwide) and at least 615,000 people died from the disease (out of 1.8 million worldwide). The comparable figures for 2021 were even higher – at 76 million infections (out of 213 million worldwide) and 1.1 million deaths (out of 3.5 million worldwide) – but at the time, the 2021 figures seemed less shocking because the progressive roll-out of state-purchased anti-Covid vaccines throughout the year eased people's fears about the consequences of becoming infected.

The elderly proved particularly vulnerable to the virus, with nine-tenths of deaths occurring among those over sixty-five. The psychological effects of enforced isolation and 'social distancing' were serious – with family members and work colleagues often only in contact through endless video-calls, and many grandparents never seeing their families physically for many months. The celebration of Christmas 2020 was in effect abandoned and that of 2021 was much curtailed. To avoid living dangerously, people quickly learned how to live digitally, changing patterns of social interaction permanently. The crisis also revealed what Stephen Holmes has called the unequal 'distribution of danger' in society and how it did not correspond to financial reward, with many low-paid and immigrant workers forced to continue to go to work to sustain essential public services, shops and delivery networks, while the middle class could largely stay at home, in relative safety. In some rural areas, there was particular resentment towards some affluent city-dwellers who were able to escape to second homes in the country, bringing with them the risk of contagion.

The economic impact of the crisis was severe: the European economy contracted very sharply, by 12 per cent in the second quarter of 2020, and it shrank by 6 per cent in 2020 overall, the biggest downturn since before the Second World War. (The contraction varied between 4 per cent in Poland and 13 per cent in Spain.) Public finances deteriorated rapidly, as governments lost tax revenue, deferred other receipts, spent more on unemployment and social security, and in some cases (like Britain) chose to sustain the incomes of those who would have lost their jobs, had they not been 'furloughed'. The overall effect of governments' counter-cyclical taxing and spending policies was to cushion the contraction significantly – by 16 per cent in Germany, 14 per cent in France and 10 per cent in the UK. The European economy then bounced back in 2021, growing by 5.4 per cent, helped by the growing roll-out of state-purchased anti-Covid vaccines throughout the year. However, the 'scarring' to the supply side of the economy was serious – with many businesses unable to re-open or to function fully, and international supply chains left disrupted – while the projected path of public debt among European states was expected to rise over time by between 15 and 30 per cent of GDP.

Coronavirus and Europe

The coronavirus crisis exposed both the limitations and potential of the European Union. The chaotic initial scramble by countries to purchase personal protective equipment for their healthcare workers (and to ban their export) highlighted a striking lack of co-ordination among European countries. This was partly a consequence of the Union's limited legal 'competence' in this policy field – where it can support or supplement action by the member states, but not determine it – but it was also the product of a strong political preference over many years that health should remain firmly in the hands of national capitals. The closure of intra-EU borders revealed the ease with which free movement could be halted or reversed – for example, for several months it was illegal for ordinary French or German citizens to cross the Rhine, except for work – while disruption to the single market showed how reliant on integrated supply chains and just-in-time delivery the modern European economy had become. In addition, key aspects of both EU competition policy rules (against state subsidies and cartels) and the Stability and Growth Pact (on national budget deficits and debt within the eurozone) were formally suspended. Governments faced acute pressures to support failing companies and sectors, to stave off bankruptcy, at the same time as public finances were under unprecedented strain.

A more positive view would be that, after a faltering start, the European Commission successfully intervened to stop export bans on personal protective equipment (as in Germany), launched the collective procurement of such items, secured agreement on joint EU purchasing of vaccines, organized the simultaneous roll-out of the first vaccine across the Union (starting in December 2020) and launched a global fund for research into vaccines and testing, raising 10 billion euro. The Commission also quickly developed a plan for a proactive 'European health union' that could declare continent-wide health emergencies, harmonize national preparedness plans, and stockpile medical supplies for future emergencies. The perception that Europe had 'failed' gradually shifted during 2020 to a view that common European action could enhance the credibility and resilience of member states – 'not to supersede, but to reinforce' those states, as Milward would have put it.

The coronavirus crisis also induced a sizeable macro-economic response at European level, one which ended the real-terms freeze on EU spending of the previous thirty years. In reaction to Italian and Spanish claims that their sinking economies had been 'abandoned by Europe', President Macron and Chancellor Merkel overcame Franco-German differences in May 2020 to propose a 500-billion euro 'recovery fund' to finance counter-cyclical grants to regions worst affected by the crisis, notably in Southern Europe. The Commission quickly reformatted this initiative as a wider 'Next Generation EU' (NGEU) fund, by adding on a 250-billion euro loan facility. The 750-billion euro package was eventually agreed by EU leaders at a five-day summit in July, against resistance from a new coalition of Austria, Denmark, the Netherlands and Sweden, dubbed the 'frugal four', who had previously sheltered behind the more powerful Germans and British on budgetary issues. The biggest change the four secured was to shift the balance between grants and loans in favour of the latter – with grants to comprise 390 billion of the total and loans 'only' 360 billion.

The NGEU recovery fund has in effect doubled EU spending from 1 to 2 per cent of GDP, with the fund itself to be financed by a mixture of borrowing by the Commission and new EU own resources. On each count, this represents a significant shift of position by Berlin, in particular, which has traditionally opposed higher spending, deficit financing and new sources of revenue for the Union. And this comes on top of a renewed willingness by the European Central Bank to resume asset purchases on a huge scale – of up to 1.8 trillion euro in total from 2000 to 2022, under its 'pandemic emergency purchasing programme' – a process with influential detractors in Germany, in particular.

Had Berlin's six-month rotating presidency of the Council of Ministers not fallen in the second half of 2020, it is difficult to know whether Merkel would have proved quite so responsive to French and Southern European insistence on an EU financing initiative of major scale. Just as Germany's previous presidencies of the Council of Ministers in 1988 (under Kohl) and 2007 (Merkel's first) had seen important initiatives of a pro-European kind, so the same pattern of German leadership was repeated this time, with the relatively new President of the European Council, former Belgian Prime Minister Charles Michel, relegated to a more marginal role than Herman van Rompuy in the eurozone crisis a decade before.

Reversion to the state

The immediate political effects of the coronavirus pandemic were very different to those that characterized the economic and migration crises of a few years before. Governing parties generally saw their public support hold up surprisingly well, especially at the start of the crisis, and even where they declined, the principal beneficiary tended to be the mainstream opposition party, rather than newer parties of the extremes, as in the 2010s. In Germany, for example, Merkel's CDU/CSU initially jumped around 13 points in the opinion polls, and when that immediate effect wore off, it was her partner in power, the centre-left SPD, that gained most. The latter's victory in Germany's September 2021 general election – when Merkel's finance minister in the 'grand coalition', the SPD leader, Olaf Scholz, replaced her as Chancellor – was marked by continuity, with Scholz presenting himself as her natural successor. In Britain, Boris Johnson's Conservatives retained an opinion poll lead throughout the crisis until late 2021, while in France, President Macron's approval rating gradually drifted up, from 32 to 40 per cent, between early 2020 and the end of the following year.

This pattern seemed to be linked to the effect of the pandemic in restoring confidence in the role of government. The sudden use of emergency measures reassured the public about the protective potential of the state, with citizens looking for responsible leadership, rather than theatrics, from those in office. (By contrast, the 'great recession' had not led to calls for a stronger state, but rather increased alienation from it.) As Ivan Krastev wrote at the height of the pandemic, people had no choice but to 'rely on the government to organize their collective public health and depend on governmental institutions to save economies that are in free-fall.' In return for significant limitations on their personal freedom, the reflex of citizens was to expect decisive state action, with citizens often prepared to give incumbent leaders the benefit of the doubt as they struggled to confront a fast-changing situation. This was perhaps less surprising in countries, such as Germany, Denmark and Finland, where there was already what Fareed Zakaria calls a generally 'competent, well-functioning, trusted state' and which were seen to handle the crisis well, but it also applied in countries whose state performance was traditionally less impressive, such as Italy, Spain, Britain and Belgium.

Conversely, Europe's populists generally had a bad coronavirus crisis. As Michael Leigh observed at the end of 2020, 'Migration, their core issue, has lost its edge, for now, as arrivals have fallen because of the epidemic. The eurozone and Schengen rules, to which populists object, have been suspended,' while the tendency of some populists to oppose coronavirus restrictions on libertarian grounds enjoyed only limited public support. The risk remained, however, as Krastev predicted, that once the 'fear factor' associated with the pandemic began to recede, an amorphous anti-system anxiety would re-emerge, especially if there were a sustained economic downturn or simply a period of prolonged stagnation, matched by falling living standards and widening social divisions.

In the event, the onset of a major 'cost of living crisis' in many European countries – with inflation across Europe rising from 2.9 per cent in 2021 to 9.2 in 2022 and peaking at 10 per cent in January 2023 – seems to have helped drive a populist recovery. Marine Le Pen won 41 per cent of the vote on the second ballot of the French presidential election in April 2022. In the parliamentary elections that followed, President Macron lost his majority, with Le Pen's Rassemblement National winning eighty-nine seats as the third-largest party (up from eight in the previous National Assembly). Five months later, the far-right Sweden Democrats emerged as the second-largest party in the Riksdag, with 20 per cent of the vote. They agreed to support a new centre-right government, without taking any ministerial posts. The same month, September 2022, saw Giorgia Meloni's Fratelli d'Italia break through to displace Matteo Salvini's League as the new standard-bearer of the right in Italian politics. Heading a coalition that won 44 per cent of the vote and 59 per cent of the seats – a parliamentary majority generated by an electoral system that now automatically rewards winning coalitions – Meloni, who is Italy's first female prime minister, has promised to end the political instability that generated seven different governments, under six prime ministers, over the previous eleven years. Only time will tell if her experience in power proves happier than that of other populist leaders, whether in Italy or the rest of Western Europe.

Transatlantic hopes and fears

Across the Atlantic, the defeat of Donald Trump in his bid for re-election as US President in November 2020 was an important precondition for, and possible staging-post towards, any return to global 'normalcy'. Europe initially breathed a huge and palpable sigh of relief when Joe Biden's victory was confirmed, although the mood of optimism was quickly dampened when, on 6 January 2021, Trump supporters, egged on by the outgoing President, stormed the Capitol Building in Washington in an unsuccessful attempt to prevent the formal proclamation of the election result. If successive events had exposed the United States as a divided and increasingly broken society – and left many Europeans fearful for the prospects of American democracy itself – Trump's departure from the White House at least provided some precious breathing space and halted the wilful dismantling of the multilateralism that Ursula von der Leyen says 'is in Europe's DNA'. Even if European capitals were shaken by Biden's sudden and chaotic withdrawal of US troops from Afghanistan in August 2021, they equally knew that Biden's presidency offered both Europe and America the best hope of working together once again to defend Western values, interests and structures, and that this opportunity should not be squandered.

During the Trump years of 2016–20, the United States had perhaps learned that it had fewer friends than it imagined and that others, especially the Chinese and Russian governments, were working actively to undermine its authority and exploit its weaknesses. For its part, Europe had begun to see that many of its soft-power assumptions about the modern world were rooted in an earlier, happier age – essentially in the immediate post-Wall, post-Maastricht era of the 1990s – when US influence was still predominant and Washington believed in using that influence to build a more stable international order. Many European and American policy-makers emerged from the Trump experience less naïve and more realistic about their diminished options on the international stage, and this awareness offered them the potential to build a more mature and balanced partnership for the future.

Brexit realities and Reaganomics revived

The years after 2016 were also to offer something of a 'sentimental education' to the United Kingdom. Whereas the advocates of Brexit had promised that a UK–US free trade agreement would quickly fall into place, President Obama's prophesy – much criticized as hyperbole at the time of the referendum – that Britain would find itself at 'the back of the queue' if it left the EU, proved much closer to the mark. There was little desire by either the Trump or Biden Administrations, still less the US Congress, to open negotiations or to offer any special economic favours to London as part of the 'special relationship'.

The 'hard Brexit' chosen by the May and Johnson governments made the transition more difficult for the British economy, as new trade barriers and broken supply chains increased costs and reduced returns on capital. The country witnessed lower inward investment, slower growth and higher inflation than any projection of what a 'dummy' UK would have achieved if it had stayed inside the EU. The Centre for European Reform's calculation of the 'cost of Brexit' suggests that by the summer of 2022, the British economy was already over 5 per cent smaller than it would otherwise have been. If so, there has been a loss of just under 1 per cent of national income each year since 2016, and this figure is of course cumulative.

Buoyed by his substantial victory in the December 2019 general election, Boris Johnson developed an increasingly casual style of government that eventually led, in July 2022, to fifty members of his front bench resigning, forcing him from office. A series of scandals, involving parties at Number Ten during the pandemic lockdowns, and several other embarrassing episodes led to a growing view that he was simply unfit to govern. Johnson's successor as prime minister, his Foreign Secretary, Liz Truss – chosen in September by 57 per cent of the 142,000 members of the Conservative party who voted in the leadership contest – herself lasted only 49 days in power. Whereas Johnson was thought unable to distinguish between truth and untruth in politics, her weakness lay in a confusion between fantasy and reality in economics. A major financial crisis was induced by her sudden attempt to reflate the economy through £105 billion of unfunded tax cuts and spending increases, at a time when borrowing was already very high. In response to this attempt at a British version of Reaganomics, the bond market froze and sterling fell sharply. In an attempt to save herself, Truss sacked her Chancellor of the Exchequer and closest ally, Kwasi Kwarteng, a move which was followed by her own resignation five days later.

The impact of the financial and political crisis of September–October 2022 on Britain's international economic standing was considerable. Meanwhile, at home, the coincidence of the Truss premiership with the death of the world's longest reigning monarch, Queen Elizabeth II, who had been on the throne for seventy years, led to a mood of sobriety and realism. The contrast between the quiet and respected service of the queen and the lack of substance of recent Conservative leaders seemed overwhelming. Irritated by the self-indulgence and incompetence of Conservative politics, the public turned decisively away from the party, with Labour's lead in the opinion polls jumping from 8 per cent to 37 per cent in one month.

The spectacular failure of 'Kwasinomics' discredited free-market liberal economics in Britain, even if those Conservatives who could remember the 1980s recalled wryly that it had taken Margaret Thatcher's government seven years before it could reduce the tax burden, and that Geoffrey Howe's famous 1981 budget had done the exact opposite of what Truss and Kwarteng had rashly attempted to do. They understood that unless you were an economy of the scale and versatility of the United States, and boasted the world's largest reserve currency, Reaganomics was not an option. Truss's successor as prime minister, Rishi Sunak, whom she had defeated only two months earlier, adopted a low-key approach to governing, avoiding exorbitant claims and emphasizing delivery, in the hope of reviving the party's fortunes before a general election to be called by the end of 2024.

Putin's invasion of Ukraine

One important change in Washington when Donald Trump left the White House in January 2021 was that the new Biden Administration adopted a much more critical attitude towards Russia and encouraged European capitals to do likewise. Initially, there was a marked reluctance in Brussels, Paris and Berlin to be drawn in this direction, reflecting not only an awareness of Europe's (especially Germany's) heavy dependence on Russian energy, but a genuine desire to avoid the process of worsening relations becoming a self-fulfilling prophecy, and of driving President Putin into a narrower and narrower corner. However, during 2011 and early 2012, the rhetoric in Moscow on the country's plight and place in the world hardened decisively. Putin's historical revisionism now went beyond simply attacking the West for denying Russia its satellite states at the end of the Cold War and started to condemn successive Soviet leaders, from Lenin onwards, for succumbing to 'odious and utopian fantasies inspired by the [1917] Revolution' and allowing too much independence to individual Soviet republics, rather than building a completely centralized state. The practical focus of this analysis was (once again) Ukraine, which Putin said was 'not just a neighbouring country for us, but an inalienable part of our own history, culture and spiritual space'.

When the EU High Representative for foreign and security policy, Josep Borrell, visited Moscow in February 2021, he was in effect humiliated by his opposite number, veteran Russian foreign minister Sergey Lavrov. Borrell predicted that relations would drift apart as Russia was 'progressively disconnecting itself from Europe'. The Commission President, Ursula von der Leyen, had wanted to go to Moscow instead of Borrell, but had been persuaded by her advisers not to do so. Soon thereafter, Russia started to amass military equipment and personnel in Crimea and on its border with Ukraine, arousing fears of a possible invasion. Although many troops were withdrawn in June, much infrastructure was left, ready for potential reactivation at any time. The Russian build-up was resumed in October 2021, leading to a growing sense of crisis. Troop numbers reached over 100,000 by early in the new year and eventually around 150,000. In December, Moscow asked for treaty guarantees that Ukraine would never join NATO and that troop numbers in Central and Eastern Europe should be wound down, with an implicit threat of military action if these demands were not met.

Even though Washington shared intelligence with European capitals that offered clear evidence of a planned Russian invasion of Ukraine, there was a marked reluctance to accept that prospect, with the implication that it could lead to a complete breakdown of relations with Russia and the first war between states in Europe since 1945. On 19 February 2022, G7 finance ministers threatened that any military aggression against Ukraine would have 'massive consequences, including financial and economic sanctions on a wide array of sectoral and individual targets', imposing 'severe and unprecedented costs on the Russian economy'. Two days later, Moscow unilaterally recognized the Donetsk and Luhansk regions in eastern Ukraine as independent states and deployed troops to the Donbass. On 24 February, Putin launched a full-scale invasion of Ukraine, which he disingenuously styled a 'special military operation' to ensure the 'demilitarization and denazification' of that country.

THE END OF POST-WALL EUROPE: UKRAINE AND THE FUTURE

Harsh new reality

The Russian invasion of Ukraine in February 2022 marked the end of the post-Wall era in Europe. An arc of events that began with the fall of the Berlin Wall and collapse of Communism in 1989–90 was coming to a juddering and unhappy close. The intervening third of a century had started in a mood of optimism and confidence, with individual freedom, economic liberalism and global interdependence becoming the lodestars of a new world order. After the relatively benign decade of the 1990s, a long series of political and economic shocks, starting in 2001, exposed the weaknesses and contradictions of that new order. With the invasion of Ukraine, there was both a sense of disbelief and a growing fear of the future. Few in Europe were able to understand a turn of events that they considered not only immoral and antediluvian, but also irrational and contrary to Russia's own interests. Several commentators dubbed the invasion 'Europe's 9/11', a sudden and unexpected development that shook and shocked a whole continent into awareness that a harsh new reality was dawning.

Although it was clear that the implications of a ground war in Europe would be serious and far-reaching, nobody could be sure exactly what they would be. If anything, there was a general assumption that, despite the confident words of G7 finance ministers before Putin acted, both European unity and transatlantic cooperation would be put under major strain, and perhaps sorely tested, with the potential for divergent reactions on multiple fronts. Even if meaningful economic sanctions were to be imposed, the concern was that, as in the past, decisive Russian action would allow Moscow to establish 'facts on the ground' and, in the process, highlight EU and US unwillingness to confront Putin politically in the face of (even gross) provocation.

In the event, predictions that Russia would make rapid and widespread advances into Ukraine were quickly confounded by different kinds of facts on the ground. As General David Petraeus put it on only the second day of the offensive: 'This is not going the way that Moscow intended or many commentators assumed.' Poor Russian planning and coordination, inadequate military equipment and stronger than expected Ukrainian resistance all combined to blunt Moscow's attack. Although the Russian army managed to capture 120,000 square kilometres of territory in the first few days of the war – to add to the 42,000 square kilometres Russia already occupied (so giving it about a quarter of Ukraine in total) – its attempt to advance on Kyiv quickly stalled and had to be abandoned. Over the ensuing months, Ukrainian forces then managed to claw back Kharkiv and Kherson, two of the most important cities in the invaded territory, while Russian missile and drone attacks on Ukrainian cities failed to break the nerve of their inhabitants.

In Moscow, Putin found himself increasingly bogged down in a 'stalemate war', whose battlelines shifted painfully slowly in a way that exposed the inadequacies of his military, damaged his economy and opened him to accusations of being a war criminal. By contrast, the relatively new Ukrainian President, Volodymyr Zelensky, a former comedian and actor, emerged rapidly as a brilliant global communicator, offering strong leadership to his own people while endearing himself to public opinion throughout the West. Zelensky became a frequent visitor to foreign parliaments and international summits, as he persuaded his new allies to supply ammunition, tanks, aircraft, missiles and air-defence systems – to ensure that, as he put it to the US Congress, Ukraine secures 'absolute victory' over Russia, or, in the more cautious words of his US opposite number, Joe Biden, 'Ukraine will never be a victory for Russia.'

Europe's response to the war

The European response to the Ukraine war was much more coherent and substantive than many had feared. By early summer 2023, ten packages of economic and other sanctions – including asset freezes, travel bans, the severing of transport links and the halting of trade in many goods and services, including oil, steel, coal and banking – had been adopted, usually unanimously, by the twenty-seven EU member states, and then applied more or less successfully. Viktor Orbán's Hungary, the most sympathetic government to Russia within the EU, was usually brought around, after some resistance. Close alignment in the sanctions process was maintained with both Washington and London, to ensure a strong, common EU–US–UK approach.

The EU has also emerged, for the first time, as a serious military power in its own right. It made available over €5 billion for arms purchases for Ukraine in the first fifteen months of the conflict – out of a total of €72 billion in all forms of support to the country so far – activating the new €7 billion European Peace Facility (EPF) to fund arms supplies, and engaging in innovative joint procurement of arms (first of ammunition and now missiles). Although there was no 'European army' to deploy as such, the Ukrainian army has emerged in effect as a kind of surrogate European army in a way that nobody could have foreseen. The relationship between the EU and NATO has also been significantly strengthened, with their potential complementarity underlined by the wide range of fronts on which common action was needed in an era of the 'weaponization of everything' in war. The decision by two neutral EU states, Finland and Sweden, to join NATO, together with discussion about whether Ireland might also renounce its neutrality, has pointed to a closer crossover in membership of the two organizations, which, although both based in Brussels, have sometimes looked as if – as a US ambassador to NATO joked in the 1990s – they were 'living in the same city, but on different planets'.

The pattern of rising defence expenditure in Europe, already apparent during the Trump years, has been decisively accelerated by the Ukraine war. In 2022, total European defence spending was already 30 per cent higher in real terms than a decade before, and this trajectory is set to continue. In one year, Finland increased its defence spending by 36 per cent, Lithuania by 27 per cent, Sweden by 12 per cent and Poland by 11 per cent. The new SPD-FDP-Green government of Olaf Scholz in Germany has used the war as an opportunity to announce a *Zeitenwende* ('sea-change') in Berlin's foreign and security policy, with defence spending planned to rise from 1.5 to at least 2 per cent of GDP, driven by a €100 billion special fund for military purchases.

Chancellor Scholz's unexpected break with the policies of the Merkel years has also involved a major realignment of German energy policy, to free the country of dependence on Russian gas. Driven by Green and FDP ministers within the coalition government, this has included the abandonment of the new Nord Stream 2 gas pipeline through the Baltic Sea, so strongly supported by former SPD Chancellor Gerhard Schröder. Parts of the underwater pipeline were subsequently blown up by unidentified agents in September 2022, creating the largest gas leak in human history. The shift in German energy policy has been framed in a wider EU determination to promote greater self-reliance in this field, both for reasons of 'strategic autonomy' and to reduce the economic impact of the Ukraine war. Under its 'RePower EU' initiative, the Union managed to reduce Russia's share of its gas imports from 41 to 8 per cent in only eighteen months, based in part on joint gas purchasing by member states for the first time.

Classic and emergency European Unions

Coming on the heels of joint vaccine purchasing during the coronavirus pandemic, and taken alongside joint arms purchases for Ukraine, the move to joint gas purchasing marks a further deepening of common EU action in response to the successive crises that have hit Europe in recent years. New forms of intergovernmental cooperation have been developing at European level, which – even if they usually use the European Commission as their service provider – often do not follow the classic 'Community method' of decision-making and are routinely funded outside the normal EU budget. The difficulty of engaging in treaty reform, now that member states fear holding referenda, means that there is no obvious transmission mechanism for these new areas of policy, frequently in areas of high sensitivity to member-state governments and parliaments, to be gradually brought within the ambit of the conventional EU system. Apart from the codification of the European Stability Mechanism (ESM) by the eurozone states in 2012, there has been no treaty change since the Lisbon Treaty came into force in 2009, the longest period of 'treaty inertia' in EU history.

As a result, the relative simplicity and coherence of the EU institutional settlement, finally defined at Lisbon, is being eroded over time. In effect, two distinct European political systems are now emerging. The first is the 'classic' EU system, in which free-standing

European-level institutions adopt supranational law and are empowered to act under it. That law is proposed by the European Commission and usually adopted through co-decision between the Council of Ministers and the European Parliament, with the Council mostly acting by qualified majority voting (QMV). The policies adopted under this law are then funded through the EU budget. Any disputes about those institutions, laws, policies or budget are adjudicated by the Union's supreme court, the European Court of Justice.

This 'classic' EU comprises the vast majority of existing EU policy areas – from the single market and external trade to environment and transport – with a few areas (notably taxation) where unanimity still applies in the Council, and some others (notably energy, employment, health, education, research and development) where there is an intricate division of responsibilities between the EU and member states. Only in the field of common foreign and security policy (CFSP) can there be said to be any serious ambiguity about where power and responsibility lie, and that is effectively concealed by the continuing need for unanimity in the Council.

Now, in parallel, we are seeing the emergence of a second 'emergency' or 'crisis' EU system that blurs many of these features in a series of ad-hoc initiatives that mix EU and national responsibility and money. Justified as necessary responses to immediate crises, they constitute a new sphere of policy that political scientists Stefan Auer and Nicole Scicluna have dubbed 'emergency Europe'. The 'instruments' used are sometimes adopted outside the Treaties, and even when they operate within the Treaties, they usually rely on elastic provisions (such as the Article 122 'solidarity' clause) that minimize accountability and reporting requirements, and allow an intermingling of European and national cash. In these areas, such as joint purchasing, we are witnessing a significant expansion of executive discretion, with a corresponding lack of parliamentary oversight, at either European or national level, so generating a new form of 'democratic deficit'.

Without the prospect of treaty change, there is a corresponding 'impossibility of constitutionalizing emergency Europe', as Auer and Scicluna put it, matched by an ironic situation where member states may be unwilling to transfer enough responsibility to European level for effective supranational action, but obviously lacking the weight or resources to tackle these challenges properly on their own. If so, the risk is that these new policy areas will be condemned to repeat the 'failing forward' experience already seen in EMU and migration policy in the past, with Europe staggering from one crisis to another and coming up, at best, with incomplete solutions at each stage.

Machiavellian and Hamiltonian moments?

Today, just as in the mid-1980s, when this chapter began, nobody can know how Europe will fare in the uncertain times ahead – whether it can turn events to its advantage and engage in a process of renewal, or whether it will be frustrated, perhaps overwhelmed, by forces that it cannot guide or control. However, there is agreement that the stakes have been rising and the choices ahead are bigger and potentially more definitive than before. The growing divergence between the continent's desire for influence and its shrinking political and economic weight in the world – its share of the global economy has fallen from 25 to 15 per cent since 1985 – is becoming too wide to ignore. The recent shocks of Brexit, Trump, coronavirus and now Ukraine have all helped to concentrate minds, not least by raising the possibility that the European Union may not be immortal and could be confronting forces that will deliberately or inadvertently destroy it. Such a realization creates the potential for what Luuk van Middelaar, invoking the historian of ideas, J. G. A. Pocock, has called a 'Machiavellian moment'. This is the moment when a polity decides to take control of its own destiny by summoning the will to become 'a sovereign player in historical time'.

Some thought that coronavirus might bring matters to a head. Now there is the potential that war in Ukraine will do so, forcing Europe to make a clear choice between alternative futures, to avoid seeing that choice made for it by others. If this happens, it would almost certainly be not just a Machiavellian moment, but a 'Hamiltonian moment' too – in that, if Europe really wants to master its destiny, it would have to envisage a step-change in the degree and intensity of its own integration.

At such a moment, Europe's peoples and leaders would finally address two difficult but consequential questions, the clarity of which they have been trying to avoid for some time. First, should the European political system become an activist federal state – with new common policies and resources, and deeper sovereignty-sharing in many fields – in the way that the United States became such a state in the 1930s and 1940s, between the launch of the New Deal and the end of the Second World War? And second, will Europe not only aspire to be a serious global actor, but take the tough decisions necessary to become one – stepping up to the responsibilities of power, with all the burdens, as well as opportunities, that this role would bring – as America did during and after the Second World War?

Europe's coming choices

The first choice would be an act of internal consolidation to build European strength and resilience against potential threats, now and in the future. The second would be an act of external projection, reflecting a desire to shape or reshape the world which Europe inhabits. The two choices are clearly linked, and both require an exceptional measure of political will. To paraphrase Bernie Cornfield, the issue can perhaps best be captured in a single question to Europe: 'Do you sincerely want to be powerful?' If the answer is 'yes', then many of the challenges that America faced in the middle third of the twentieth century will have to be confronted and resolved in Europe, a process potentially made easier by Britain's decision to take a different path by leaving the Union. If the answer is 'no', then the Brussels institutions and national capitals will almost certainly try to sustain, as far as possible in its current form, the unique balancing-act that has characterized the EU system for the last thirty years – seeking to continue to tread a delicate path between unity and diversity, between technocracy and legitimacy, between economics and politics, and between supranational and national power.

What may settle the question one way or the other is, however, the reality that, in political life as in all human affairs, things cannot and do not stay still forever. In a world where the future of US leadership is highly uncertain, where Russia has re-emerged as a serious threat to stability on the European continent, and where the rise of China creates a new geopolitical rivalry between Washington and Beijing – in which Europe will find it impossible to avoid taking sides – the default settings of the past may not be available for very long. The Union is likely to find that 'becoming a serious global actor' is no longer just a theoretical act involving the 'external projection' of power for its own sake, but increasingly a defensive act aimed at trying to preserve and maintain all that is best and most enlightened in the European way of life, under challenge from abroad and possibly from within. The process of becoming 'a sovereign player in historical time' may be less a matter of free choice, designed to realize the fullest potential of Europe, than a practical necessity to ensure that what it has already achieved is not lost.

Destinies old and new

The political will to leap into a new European destiny has been generated in the relatively recent past – even if it is largely taken for granted today – when ministers from the founding Six came together for their first joint meeting, in Paris in April 1951, and declared that henceforth theirs would be 'a destiny shared in common'. Profoundly shaken by the experience of the Second World War – and guided by the institutional ingenuity of Jean Monnet, the true 'architect of interdependence' in post-war Europe – they gave meaning to their words by signing the first European Community treaty, creating supranational powers above those of the classical state. This radical move was designed to make a further Franco-German war materially impossible, by pooling Europe's coal and steel sectors under independent control beyond the writ of any single country.

This was not simply an idealistic act, still less a utopian one. It represented a concrete solution to a growing problem facing decision-makers in Europe and America at the time. This was the conundrum of how to move beyond the failing, initial post-war policy of containing Germany's economic and political might – which was based on quantitative restrictions on German industrial production, notably of coal and steel, and refusing to allow the country to rearm – given both the strong hostility of French public and parliamentary opinion to any such change, and the growing inability of the United States to carry the burden of the post-war reconstruction of Europe on its own.

Monnet's special insight was to understand that by merging the two countries' coal and steel industries under joint European control, the French fear of German dominance could be assuaged and the opportunity created of rationalizing and modernizing production in a way that national pressures would not allow. Such a 'coal and steel pool' could help create the conditions for German reindustrialization and rearmament, and so resolve simultaneously a range of problems in Paris, Bonn and Washington. This solution was radical not only in invoking supranational power, but also in breaking completely, as

F. Roy Willis has written, with classic French foreign policy, which 'since Richelieu's time had been based on the axiom that the weakness of Germany is the strength of France', and thus 'made possible an entirely new approach' to a whole series of problems and disputes.

The unique experiment launched in Paris in 1951 was deepened in Rome six years later, as the ambition of the 'founding fathers' widened to that of integrating the whole European economy through a common market, a customs union and several other joint policies. Their approach allowed the emergence of a different kind of Europe during the second half of the twentieth century, bringing new freedoms and helping to generate a level of prosperity for many that was unthinkable before that time. The willingness of Monnet and his colleagues to look beyond the confines of existing national borders and political systems – as well as their ability to see the positive potential of common action through pooled sovereignty – marked them out decisively from many of their contemporaries, whose perspective was still trapped in the logic of the classic nation-state.

Over seventy years later, can today's leaders of Europe summon up the same kind of imagination and courage to repeat what the founding fathers did, so unexpectedly but successfully, in seeking to define a new future for their countries? Can they think beyond the confines of orthodoxy and vested interest to 'change the context' with bold initiatives, as the shapers of a new Europe did in the 1950s? Can they step up to and exploit the Machiavellian or Hamiltonian moments that seem to be fast arising in the twenty-first century? The more complicated world emerging from the coronavirus crisis and Russia's invasion of Ukraine will be full of risks and dangers, but such challenges may also bring huge opportunities for Europe's renewal and rebirth.

London
1 June 2023

Acknowledgements

Anthony Teasdale would like to thank Vernon Bogdanor, Juan Carrizosa, Frédéric Delouche, David Levy, Jacqueline Philips, Roger Liddle and Martin Westlake for their helpful comments on an early draft of his Afterword. Any errors of fact or judgement which remain are the author's alone. He would also like to thank Kristina Spohr, who has popularized the phrase 'post-Wall Europe', for kindly agreeing to its use in the title of the Afterword.

The authors

Jean-Baptiste Duroselle (1917–94) was one of France's leading twentieth-century historians. Educated at the École Normale Supérieure, he was Professor of Contemporary History at the Sorbonne from 1964 to 1983 and President of the Académie des Sciences Morales et Politiques of the Institut de France from 1985 to 1986. In addition to *The Idea of Europe in History* (1965) and *Europe: A History of its Peoples* (1990), he published books on the history of migration, Western ideas, France before and during the First World War, both French and US foreign policy, and Franco–American relations.

Anthony Teasdale is Visiting Professor in Practice at the European Institute of the London School of Economics (LSE) and Adjunct Professor in International and Public Affairs at Columbia University, New York. From 2013 to 2022, he was Director General of the European Parliamentary Research Service (EPRS) in Brussels, having previously served as Special Adviser at the Foreign Office and HM Treasury in London. He is co-author of *The Penguin Companion to European Union*.